Improbable Excellence

Improbable Excellence: The Saga of UMBC

George R. La Noue

George R. La Noue
1/6/2017

To Sally,
Your helpfulness, good cheer and information about our program has often saved me from mistakes and made working here a joy.
George

Carolina Academic Press
Durham, North Carolina

ISBN 978-1-61163-938-4 hardback
ISBN 978-1-5310-0277-0 paperback
LCCN 2016935641

Carolina Academic Press, LLC
700 Kent Street
Durham, North Carolina 27701
Telephone (919) 489-7486
Fax (919) 493-5668
www.cap-press.com

Printed in the United States of America

Contents

List of Figures

Preface

In UMBC's spring 2012 commencement program, President Freeman Hrabowski wrote:

> "Ours is a special community—committed to nurturing people, ideas, and the values that support excellence and service. It is a community that cherishes a common past and looks forward to an exciting future."

To a casual campus visitor, UMBC might seem an unlikely candidate to be considered a community, let alone one "that cherishes a common past." A visitor's skepticism would be wrong about UMBC's sense of community. In an amazing, utterly unpredictable way, UMBC has become a community flourishing in good times and persevering in bad. In the way of rapidly growing new institutions, however, it has not always remembered its common past, let alone cherished it.

This book is an attempt to create a record so current, past, and future members of the UMBC community can understand the building of the University. It will also serve as a reminder to the Baltimore region, the state of Maryland, and wider academic circles, just how uncertain, complex, and remarkable is the creation of a great university. As the University approaches its Fiftieth Anniversary in 2016, the time is propitious for such a history. Intellectual historian, Richard Wolin, has written: "It is generally accepted that after a period of 40 years, generational memory begins to fade. At this point, 'collective memory' cedes to 'cultural memory' as a type of imaginative reinvention of tradition."[1] This book seeks to be as accurate and well-documented as possible. Many of the events recorded here will soon slip into oblivion from living memories.

On the morning of July 22, 1965, if you had been observing the bulldozers taking their first bites of farm earth to prepare the site for the University of Maryland, Baltimore County, what predictions would you have made for the success of this new institution? After a bruising fight over whether the campus should be located in the exciting new harbor redevelopment in Baltimore City or in the growing Baltimore County northern suburbs, would the chosen site between Catonsville and Arbutus seem like an exile into irrelevancy? Since UMBC was five miles from the University of Maryland professional schools in downtown Baltimore, thus preventing development of the array of professional schools typical of major state universities, what would that reality auger for its future? Would the fact that the Baltimore region al-

1. Richard Wolin, *Chronicle of Higher Education,* April 19, 2013, B10.

ready had four, and soon to be five, other public higher education institutions with established reputations and political connections, as well as several fine private institutions, mean that there would be little room for a new campus to achieve excellence? Would the close proximity of those other campuses, creating constant conflicts over program development, suggestions of mergers, and even the threat of campus closure, undermine emergence of a strong UMBC institutional identity?

Then, there was the problem of the name: the University of Maryland, Baltimore County, the only four-year school in the country to have "County" in its title which everywhere else indicates a community college. Even the University of Maryland designation was problematic. When the University System of Maryland was created in 1988, there were eleven campuses in the system, but to many people in and out of state only the University of Maryland, College Park was the "University of Maryland." If UMBC had been a stock in 1965, would you have wanted to invest by choosing it over the approximately 3,000 United States higher education institutions then existing?

Now fast forward to 2012 as this book was finished. Could you have imagined a campus of nearly 13,700 students with a budget of $355 million attracting about $86 million in research and training dollars? Could anyone have forecast that in 1998 *Newsweek* would call UMBC a "powerhouse in Baltimore offering a topnotch, rigorous education to scholars who don't want to pay Ivy League prices"?[2] Or in that same year, *Kiplinger's Magazine* would include UMBC in its list of "State Universities to Cheer About."[3] By 2003, *Newsweek* was touting UMBC as one of twelve schools on its national "America's Hot Schools" list.[4] In 2008, *The Princeton Review* found UMBC's suburban campus to be the second most diverse of all universities in the United States.[5] The 2009 *Princeton Review/USA Today* study ranked UMBC as one of the top one hundred "best value institutions" in the country, along with Harvard, Yale, Princeton, Stanford, Virginia, and Georgia Tech.[6] Also in 2009, *U.S. News and World Report* listed UMBC among its top five most innovative national universities. In that magazine's rankings, UMBC was also a breathtaking number one among "up and coming" universities in the United States. That number one ranking was repeated in 2010, 2011, and 2012. Perhaps more significantly, in the category of commitment to undergraduate teaching, UMBC was the number one public university nationally and fourth ranked (tied with Stanford one year and

2. "How to Get into College: Five Schools with a Mission," *Newsweek,* August 8, 1998, 22.

3. "State Universities to cheer about." *Kiplinger's Personal Finance Magazine,* Issue 9, 52 September 1998.

4. Kaplan/Newsweek, *How to get into college* (2003 Edition) (New York: Stanley H. Kaplan Educational Center, 2002).

5. The Princeton Review, *The Best 368 Colleges,* (2009 Edition) (New York: Princeton Review, 2008).

6. In 2008 and 2011, the *Review* named UMBC as one of the fifty best value public institutions. http://www.usatoday.com/news/education/best-value-colleges.html (accessed June 27, 2009).

Yale the next year) among all universities.[7] UMBC was additionally included in that magazine's unranked list of twenty universities providing the best research opportunities for undergraduates. Perhaps even more important is the Carnegie Foundation's classification of UMBC in its High Research Activity tier of doctoral/research universities. There is evidence that UMBC's growing reputation has received global recognition. In its 2012 ranking of universities in the world founded in the last fifty years, the *London Times* included UMBC, ranking it eighth among United States' institutions.[8]

Recognition for UMBC's achievements and his leadership on and off campus has come to Freeman Hrabowski. In 2010, *Time* magazine named President Hrabowski one of the top ten university presidents in the United States[9] and in that year Harvard awarded him an honorary degree. The next year, TIAA-CREF awarded UMBC's President the Theodore M. Hesburgh Award for Leadership Excellence. The Carnegie Foundation and the Heinz Family Foundation recognized Hrabowski with their national educational leadership awards in 2011 and 2012. Also in 2012, *Time* added to his previous honors by including Hrabowski on its list of the one hundred most influential people in the world. It is a breathtaking set of honors for the president of an institution too often the subject of hostile or indifferent Maryland political attitudes.

As it turned out, UMBC would have been a very good stock pick in 1965, but how did this University overcome its multiple challenges to become such a well-recognized, even admired, institution? It takes a book to answer that question and hopefully this book will achieve that goal.

This book has a different structure than is common among campus histories. Universities are exceptionally complex institutions. From the outside, campus organization may appear conventionally hierarchical. In fact, the activities creating excellence on a daily basis are quite decentralized, taking place in hundreds of classrooms, laboratories, library facilities, conference rooms, offices, artistic and athletic performance sites, as well as in cyberspace. Bursts of energy, creativity, discovery, and success can occur anywhere, anytime. Capturing the context, evolution, and significance of these activities is challenging. While each chapter in this book is largely chronological, the chapters are topical. Readers interested in UMBC's founding, politics, campus development, finances, administration, faculty, research, students, arts, athletics, and service activities can read those chapters. Wherever possible, relevant statistics are reported in figures or appendices, so that the book's generalizations are data-based rather than conjecture.

Historian Joe Tatarewicz once pointed out to me that producing a university history is like writing a family history writ large, very large. Both such histories can gen-

---

7. In 2012, UMBC was on *US News and World* report list again in the category of commitment to undergraduate teaching tied for eighth nationally with Duke University, University of Chicago, University of Notre Dame, and the University of California-Berkeley.

8. www.timeshighereducation.co.uk.

9. *Time*, "Dean's List: The Ten Best College Presidents in America," November 23, 2009, 51.

erate a cadre of critics who are often very knowledgeable and very nearby. Every historian, indeed every social scientist, must use a lens or a theory to construct a coherent narrative out of the welter of events and personalities that influence sizable institutions. Otherwise the result would be an encyclopedic compilation.

This book focuses on the external actors (politicians, governing boards, Regents, system leaders, accrediting bodies, competition referees, and benefactors) who have shaped UMBC. It also describes the campus figures who influenced and responded to external supports and challenges to create the contemporary University. Necessarily some persons and events are omitted, resulting in some difficult choices. For example, there is a chapter on the Performing Arts at UMBC because their very existence was often in jeopardy, while the treatment of the social sciences is more scattered because the basic social science disciplines were in place at the University's founding and have not been threatened.

There are a number of alternative lenses that could have been selected to interpret the events and personalities in UMBC's history. I have chosen to use a political lens to focus on the external forces that shaped the University and the internal reaction to those forces. Those who would prefer a more cultural, curriculum, or departmental based history will need to wait for what I hope will be many subsequent explorations of UMBC's story. Perhaps they will find this book which covers events that occurred until the end of 2012, a useful context as they create their narratives.

This book is not an official history. Although many have read and commented on the chapters as they have been developed or asked questions at public presentations, the structure of the book and judgments in it are my responsibility. The mistakes are mine as well. It is a tribute to the deep commitment to academic freedom at UMBC that I was given this liberty and I am appreciative.

Certainly, I have relied on a large group of knowledgeable caring persons about UMBC who have contributed enormously to the completion of this book. I regret I cannot list them all. I am deeply grateful to John Jeffries, Dean of the College of Arts, Humanities and Social Sciences, distinguished twentieth century historian and forty year UMBC veteran, who provided key administrative support and wise counsel throughout a four-year process. Provosts Arthur Johnson, Elliot Hirshman, and Philip Rous were generous with their time and backing. In its earliest stages President Freeman Hrabowski, mathematician and polymath, understood the value of telling the UMBC story and gave me unconditional encouragement. My chairs, Devin Hagerty and Jeffrey Davis (Political Science) and Don Norris (Public Policy) were always cheerful, I think, about the distractions the book created in my departmental duties.

Providing the book with valuable historical resources were a set of in-depth audio and video interviews with past and present UMBC leaders conducted by Professors Joseph Tatarewicz, Edward Orser, and Barry Lanman. In addition, I conducted about a dozen formal interviews and countless journalistic inquiries (is this fact, date, hypothesis, or insight right?) with persons who have made major contributions to the campus and knew details not available in the written record. References to many of these interviews embellish the chapters and my thanks go to those who participated in, organized, and transcribed them. Most of these transcripts can be found in the Special Collection area of the campus library. As this book began, not many people were aware the University even had archives. It was immensely fortuitous that UMBC hired archivist Lindsey Loeper in 2007. With her help and that of Tom Beck, Chief Curator of the Albin O. Kuhn Library Gallery and Special Collections, and Larry Wilt, Library Director, access to older records and the ability to document key events were greatly enhanced. Two colleagues, Hugh Davis Graham and George Keller, who added greatly to my knowledge about higher education policies, unfortunately passed away before this manuscript was completed. The undergraduate "UMBC History Team" (David Bennett, Nimit Bhatt, Bridget Flynn, Grant Foerhkolb, Amanda Hickey, Yasmin Karimian, Matthew McNey, and Amber Spry) provided valuable research into several dimensions of the University (see photograph). Their reports can be found in the Albin O. Kuhn library archives and are referenced in many of this book's chapters. Special thanks are due to Mike Bowler, long-time education reporter of the *Baltimore Sun,* who read much of the draft manuscript. A lot of the grubby day-to-day archival work was done by two Public Policy research assistants, Arayh Fradkin and Alexia Van Orden, as well as history graduate student, Jeremy Spahr, who were also good company in the writing. Theresa Donnelly labored editorially to help me follow the vagaries of the Chicago Manual of Style. Jim Lord designed the admirable cover. Richard Byrne had to navigate the many delays in getting this manuscript into print by a University system that does not have its own press.

My closest companion was, of course, my wife Patricia La Noue, long-time Director of UMBC's Interdisciplinary Studies Program. She has lived UMBC's history for forty- three years with me and her insights, editorial talent, and critical skills have been invaluable.

In 1972, when I was being interviewed for a position as Professor of Political Science at UMBC with the mandate to help develop a graduate public policy program, I called Patricia to consult about the possible move. Leaving Columbia University, where I directed the Politics and Education Ph.D. program, to move to a six-year-old institution was not an obvious choice. Looking out at the new campus with few buildings and no graduate programs, I told her that it was not what UMBC was then that should attract us, but what it might become. This book is dedicated to the literally thousands of students, administrators, faculty, staff, and benefactors who have contributed to what UMBC has become.

George R. La Noue
Professor of Political Science and Professor of Public Policy
December, 2013

Improbable Excellence

CHAPTER I

The Founding

A. The Land's Story

Looking out in 1964 at the land on which the new campus was to be built, some of its history could be seen, but there was much that was not apparent. Certainly the archaeological evidence, later discovered on campus grounds, suggesting human habitation dating back to 8000–5500 BCE, the early archaic and late woodland periods, was not visible.[1] In the seventeenth century, the Piscataway tribe, once a population of 2500, lived in thirty villages, including some near Catonsville. The tribe eventually was decimated by contact with European diseases, by harassment from warlike Susquehannocks to the north, and occasional slave raiders from the south.[2] Yet as late as the first decade of the eighteenth century, local white residents claimed bounties on wolves killed for them by friendly Indians.[3] The Piscataway and their carnivorous prey have long since vanished, but a few of their arrowheads have been found on the campus and the progeny of the gentle deer they once hunted may still inhabit the campus woodlands.

Until 1632, when King Charles I first granted a charter to George Calvert, the first Baron Baltimore, campus land was a part of the Virginia colony. As commerce eventually developed, the road immediately to the south of the campus land came to be called Rolling Road because it was used to roll hogsheads of tobacco down to ships at Elkridge Landing.[4] In the eighteenth century, most of the land near Catonsville

1. The site was discovered first by UMBC Professor of Biology Austin Platt and later excavated by several UMBC professors and students. Several "projectile points," pottery fragments, and "worked stone implements" or hammer stones were found on the campus at a location that has been undisclosed to avoid intruders. Karen Vitelli, editor, "U.M.B.C, 18-BA-71," Miscellaneous Papers No. 10, Archaeological Society of Maryland, June 1975. See also, R. Christopher Goodwin & Associates, Inc. "Phase I and II Archeological Investigations for the UMBC Research Park and Playfield, Baltimore County, Maryland, Final Report," November 15, 1999. UMBC's Albin O. Kuhn library sponsored an exhibition of the artifacts in 2003 which are now housed in the Archeology Laboratory in St. Mary's City. "UMBC Campus Life: A Tale of Two Histories—8,000 years of Prehistory and 37 years of Archaeology."

2. http://www.catonsvilleweb.com/history.html.

3. A helpful history of the campus land and its environs can be found in Bayly Ellen Marks, *Hilton Heritage* (Catonsville: Catonsville Community College Press, 1972), 2.

4. There are two useful histories of Catonsville. See George C. Keidel, *Colonial History of Catonsville* (Catonsville: The American Centennial Committee of Catonsville 1976), 100–101 and by two UMBC professors, Edward Orser (American Studies) and Joseph Arnold (History), *Catonsville: 1880–1940* (Norfolk, VA: Donning Company, 1989).

was owned by Charles Carroll who gave much of it to his son Charles Carroll of Carrollton, a signer of the Declaration of Independence and at one time reputedly the richest man in America.

In the nineteenth century, campus lands for a time were part of a tract called Owing's Adventure. By 1964, only the ruined foundation remained of the Sulphur Spring Inn that existed on the campus grounds from 1790 until the Civil War. No sulphur has been found, although its "medicinal waters" once attracted Daniel Webster and Henry Clay to the Inn.

A specimen white oak tree and a tulip poplar which predate the Revolutionary War could certainly be seen on what is now called Giffen Hill.[5] A "Bleak House" Victorian style administration and dormitory building (circa 1860) of the Manual Labor School for Indigent Boys (1839–1922) was also located near Giffen Hill, until it burned down in 1916.[6] The school used most of the land to teach "respectable but indigent boys" farming and other skills. Two of the school's out-buildings, the Stone House, a farm house preceding the school, and the Grey House (circa 1885), however, would have been visible.[7]

A visitor could also see the result of the demise of the Manual Labor School. The school transferred the land to the Stabler family for farming and that family later sold a parcel to a state hospital. In 1964, some Stabler farm buildings could still be viewed, although the farm's existence had been terminated by the state's invocation of eminent domain to acquire the campus land. The farm's grain silo which now rises to greet visitors to the campus south entrance and Pig Pen pond which now borders UMBC's research park are the only remaining visual evidence of the land's agricultural past. The main campus of the Spring Grove Hospital Center, formally called the Maryland Hospital for the Insane,[8] is now about half a mile from UMBC. A once elegant Georgian-style hospital out-building (circa 1921) called Hillcrest was torn down by the University in 2007.

The most important thing the observer's eyes would not have seen was the national movement in higher education that led to the establishment of UMBC and

5. http://www.umbc.edu/inds/findyourplace/history.html.

6. There is now a large commemorative plaque below Giffen Hill which contains this quote from a 1903 news article, "Just outside the pretty little village of Arbutus, about seven miles from Baltimore, there is a farm whose principal product for sixty years has been men." Coalition for the Preservation of Southwest Baltimore County. See also Joe Arnold's article on the school. "Baltimore Manual Labor School for Indigent Boys (Farm School) 1839–1922, in *History of the Arbutus Area*, Baltimore County Public Library, www.bcpl.info/community /history-arbutus-farm-school.

7. The Stone House was later razed by UMBC, while the Grey House, UMBC's first administration building, burned down in 1972. *The Catonsville Times,* April 19, 1973, 3A.

8. Hillcrest was "historically significant because it was the first building constructed for the care and treatment for mentally ill prisoners to be built as a state psychiatric hospital anywhere in the United States." The Spring Grove Hospital Center website contains a fascinating history of the hospital. (w.w.w.springgrove.com.)

other similar universities and the great controversy about creating this particular campus and placing it at this specific location. These stories need to be told first.

B. New Wave Urban Universities

The sprawling diversity of American higher education often seems created without a systematic intent. As the nation spread across the continent, mismatches developed between the location of educational opportunities and the growth of the country. With about the same population, there are more than three times as many public universities in Maryland as in Arizona. There are many more great private research universities in the 400 mile Boston-Washington corridor than in the 1,000 mile Seattle-San Diego corridor. There are more liberal arts colleges in Ohio than in the whole Mountain States region. This maldistribution of educational resources was not without any planning. There were, in fact, hundreds of plans, each spawned by the aspirations of religious groups or local boosters, but there was little coordination.

Until the 1960s, the idea that the distribution of higher education resources should be rationally planned was rarely taken seriously. Despite the many charming college towns scattered around the country, where the academy dominated economic and cultural life, a new paradigm was needed. As the nation became more urban, it became less tolerable that important metropolitan regions were left without public research universities. After civil rights groups pointed out educational inequalities, no longer was higher education accepted mainly as a privilege for white upper and middle class eighteen- to twenty-two year olds. Commuting, part-time, first-generation, immigrant, and minority students in some areas had little or no access to public research universities. The pattern was common in many states. Neither the Indiana University Bloomington campus nor the Purdue West Lafayette campus could easily serve Indianapolis students, unless they could afford the time and money to take up residence. The University of Illinois Champaign-Urbana campus is 138 miles from Chicago; the University of Massachusetts Amherst campus is 92 miles from Boston and so forth. Institutions might carry state-wide names, such as the University of Texas, but the Austin campus, however large it grew, could not fully meet the needs of burgeoning populations in Dallas, Houston or San Antonio.

About the same time, there was increased recognition of the benefits research universities might bring to their regions as economic engines. Land-grant colleges had played that role for agriculture, mining, and other rural and small town businesses for a century. Now the new high-tech and biomedical industries might benefit from urban synergies and university research. Universities had also long been a source of state-wide pride and of cultural and athletic entertainment. Surely they could play these roles for urban centers as well. Politicians began to see the need for "their" metropolitan region to have its "own" university. As educational theorist Ernest A. Lynton wrote: "A new breed of American universities, the metropolitan university is an institutional model committed to be responsive to the knowledge needs of its surrounding region and dedicated to creating active links between campus, community, and commerce."[9]

So in a twenty-year period from the mid-1950s to the mid-1970s, a new wave of public urban research universities was created in major metropolitan areas, which were not well served by "flagship" universities founded in the eighteenth or nineteenth centuries when state populations were very different. In addition to UMBC (1966), among the most prominent universities in this category are: University of South Alabama (Mobile) (1963); University of Alabama, Birmingham (1969); University of Arkansas at Little Rock (1969); University of California, San Diego (1960); University of California, Irvine (1965); University of Colorado, Colorado Springs (1965); University of South Florida (Tampa) (1956); Florida Atlantic University (Fort Lauderdale) (1961); University of Central Florida (Orlando) (1963); Florida International University (Miami) (1965); University of North Florida (Jacksonville) (1972); University of Louisville (1970); University of Illinois at Chicago Circle (1965); Indiana University-Purdue University Fort Wayne (1964); Indiana University-Purdue University Indianapolis (IUPUI) (1969); University of New Orleans (1956); University of Southern Maine (Portland) (1970); University of Massachusetts Boston (1964); University of Missouri-Kansas City (1963); University of Missouri-St. Louis (1963); University of Nevada Las Vegas (1968); SUNY at Buffalo (1962); University of North Carolina at Greensboro (1964); University of North Carolina at Charlotte (1965); Cleveland State University (1964); Wright State University (Dayton) (1967); University of Texas at Dallas (1969); University of Texas, San Antonio (1969); Old Dominion University (Norfolk) (1962); Virginia Commonwealth University (Richmond) (1968); and the University of Wisconsin-Milwaukee (1956).[10]

The new urban universities were often seen as threats to the older "flagship" universities which cherished their statewide titles and the status and funding that accompanied them.[11] The formidable academic senate of the University of California system opposed the creation of a new university in San Diego because of the probable diversion of funds from UC's existing Berkeley and Los Angeles campuses. To assuage their fears, Roger Revelle, one of the San Diego founders, suggested the new campus should focus on research with only 1,000 undergraduates and that, if it ever should

---

9. Ernest A. Lynton, "What is a Metropolitan University?" in *Metropolitan Universities: An Emerging Model in American Higher Education*, ed. by Daniel M. Johnson and David A. Bell (Denton, TX: University of North Texas Press, 1995).

10. Some of these universities had earlier origins as private or limited purpose institutions. The dates given here are when they joined the state systems, became branches of flagship campuses or were given charters as new campuses.

11. "The newer campuses of the research university systems with their vision of a UCLA—like future represented a threat to established institutions." Hugh D. Graham and Nancy Diamond, in *The Rise of the American Research University: Elites and Challengers in the Postwar Era* (Baltimore, MD: The Johns Hopkins University Press, 1997), 164.

foolishly create a football team, he hoped it would never win a game.[12] In 1965–1966 the Penn State flagship campus at State College, inaccessible to most in the state, except on football weekends, had to concede that the formerly private University of Pittsburgh and Temple University (Philadelphia) would become state-related urban universities. But Penn State's principal strategy was to sprinkle branch campuses (at last count twenty-eight of them) around the state with enough control to be certain they would never rival their mother campus. In other states, there were different forms of accommodations between old and new campuses. Indiana University and Purdue University could not agree on who should control the Indianapolis turf, but they could agree they did not want a new independent public campus in the capitol city. So their 1969 compromise was the ungainly named IUPUI, jointly controlled by the older institutions.

In most states, however, the compromises were not so clear-cut and the new campuses were created with some purposeful ambiguities about the extent of their mission and autonomy. These are not small issues for new institutions, since they could be decisive in determining future enrollment growth, the balance of faculty teaching and research responsibilities, programs and curriculum and, of course, funding. Flagship campuses have insatiable appetites for money and status as they engage in perpetual national and international competition. Being a branch campus, when all the power is located in the flagship, is not a platform for greatness. On the other hand, the dispersal of resources among multiple campuses can be a recipe for across-the-board mediocrity. In many states, these rivalries are fought out in court houses, legislative committees, trustee boardrooms, foundation meetings, and even on playing fields. Sometimes these struggles take place beneath the public view like the thrashing about of great sea creatures. Sometimes they flare up in displays of anger that everyone in higher education publicly deplores, while preparing for the next round.

In Maryland, many of these factors were in play. The University of Maryland, College Park (UMCP) was founded in 1856 as the Maryland Agricultural College on a former plantation, but over the next century that land became a densely populated suburb of Washington, D.C.[13] By 1960, however, about 55 percent of the state's population was in Baltimore City and its four surrounding counties. There was and is almost no public transportation from the Baltimore area to College Park. If I-95, which opened in 1964, and the Washington I-495 Beltway were free-flowing, and, then assuming a campus parking space could be found, UMCP was at least an hour's commute by car from the Baltimore area.

---

12. Nancy Scott Anderson, *An Improbable Venture: A History of the University of California, San Diego* (La Jolla, CA: The UCSD Press, 1993), 44. In 2010, UCSD had about 24,000 undergraduates, but no football team.

13. George A. Callcott, *A History of the University of Maryland* (Baltimore: Maryland Historical Society, 1966). This essential book traces the history of the University from the founding of the Medical College in Baltimore in 1807 and the creation of the College Park campus in 1856 to 1966 when the book was published.

Yet by some reckonings, unlike metropolitan centers in other parts of the country,[14] Baltimore City and County already had a plentiful supply of higher educational institutions in the 1960s.[15] The premier private university Johns Hopkins was one of the nation's elite and it had from its founding in 1876 a strong research mission. Entering the twenty-first century, it would become the City's largest employer and the recipient of the largest amount of federal research dollars in the country. Its undergraduate enrollment, however, was and is small, about 4,700 in 2010 with very competitive admissions policies, not targeted to Baltimore region students.[16] In the 1960s, there were also three private liberal arts colleges in Baltimore, Loyola (1852), a Catholic men's college, Notre Dame (1873), a Catholic women's college, and Goucher (1885) a non-sectarian women's college. Each of them expanded their enrollment (Loyola admitting women in 1971 and Goucher men in 1986) and their missions, but in the 1960s they served a limited part of the spectrum of the Baltimore region's students.

In the Baltimore area public college sector, there was an unusual array of five institutions, each with a distinct history and mission. The oldest, the University of Maryland at Baltimore (UMB), was founded as a medical school in 1807, and had since developed other professional schools: law (1823), dentistry (1840), pharmacy (1841), nursing (1889), and social work (1961). Somewhat overshadowed for many years by the Johns Hopkins medical complex, which is often seen as the best in the world, UMB emerged in the late 1980s and early 1990s, as a research and economic power in its own right.[17] While some other flagships, such as the University of California, Berkeley or the University of Alabama have their medical schools in nearby urban centers, the more typical pattern is to cluster all the professional schools around the "main" campus. The University of Maryland, however, has always been bifurcated into a professional schools campus in Baltimore and liberal arts and sciences undergraduate and graduate school campus in College Park. The University of

14. Only New York has more public campuses (nine) than Baltimore, but those campuses are part of a single system (City University of New York) with a single graduate school. Chicago has only three public campuses and Philadelphia and Boston one each.

15. These institutions were small, however. According to the Curlett report, in 1961 full-time enrolled undergraduates numbered at Morgan (2,255), Towson (1,708) Johns Hopkins (1,441), University of Baltimore (1,103), Loyola (845), Goucher (734), Notre Dame (617), and Coppin (351). Commission for the Expansion of Public Higher Education in Maryland, *Public Higher Education in Maryland 1961–1975*, Baltimore. 1962. See Tables 3, 6 and 7 on pages 25, 31, and 35.

16. A very useful description and analysis of Baltimore higher education can be found in Ernest M. Kahn, "Universities and Urban Affairs: Case Studies of the Colleges and Universities in the Baltimore Area in the 1960's," Ph.D. dissertation, University of Maryland Graduate School, 1972. Kahn's focus was on what Baltimore institutions were doing to respond to the "urban crisis." Kahn wrote about JHU that a persistent problem was whether Hopkins was "in the city but not of it." (68). While other Hopkins leaders have addressed this issue, President Ronald J. Daniels inaugurated in 2009, has made working on Baltimore's problems a major priority. Dale Keiger, "The Accidental Academe," *Johns Hopkins Magazine*, December 2, 2009, 3.

17. UMAB or UMB, as it is now called, has no comprehensive history, so this estimate of its emergence comes from interviews with its current top officials.

Baltimore (1925), formerly a private school, was added to the state system in 1975, but its undergraduate offerings were originally limited to a few majors for upper level students. It had its own law school, located about twenty blocks from the University of Maryland School of Law, and a few other professional schools. Morgan State University also began as a private institution.[18] Founded in 1867 by the Methodist Episcopal Church, it became a public institution in 1939. While Maryland had been a divided border state during the Civil War, it had adopted a southern segregated pattern of education that it maintained after Emancipation. Morgan's transformation into a public institution was due in part to the state's effort to provide education for blacks separate from public white campuses. Morgan which now offers some doctoral and graduate professional programs is still very much identified as a historically black institution. Another reflection of Maryland's segregated past was the creation of two teacher training institutions. Towson University (1866), located in the county seat of Baltimore County, originally focused on training white teachers. It has since greatly expanded its mission and now enrolls more than 20,000 students of all races in many academic areas. Coppin State University was born in 1900 when the Baltimore City School Board created a one-year training course for preparing African-American elementary school teachers. In 1938, the institution became a four-year normal school for teacher training. In 1950, it joined the state system as pressure to desegregate higher education was growing, but did not award its first Bachelor of Arts degree until 1967.

C. A Controversial Birth[19]

Given the diversity of well-established public and private Baltimore regional institutions in the early 1960s, it was not immediately obvious that Baltimore needed a new university. Of all the new wave urban universities established nationally during that period, no other campus faced such formidable local competition with such a tenuous hold on the support of local politicians and other elites than did the University of Maryland, Baltimore County.

So why was UMBC created amidst the nine other higher education campuses in the City and the County? There were several factors.

Maryland experienced substantial population growth after World War II. As the state's only comprehensive campus, though racially segregated until 1951, College Park experienced dramatic enrollment increases. In 1953–54, College Park's enrollment was 9,003 in all of its schools, but by 1965–66 the student body had grown to

---

18. Edward N. Wilson, *The History of Morgan State College: A Century of Purpose in Action: 1867–1967* (New York: Vantage, 1975).

19. A comprehensive collection of newspaper clippings about the contentiousness regarding UMBC's creation is in Albin O. Kuhn's Family "scrapbook," Collection 127. Special Collections, University of Maryland, Baltimore County Library.

26,265.[20] As University of Maryland historian George Callcott noted, "While enrollments over the country grew at the rate of 4 percent each year after 1954, the students at Maryland grew at the rate of 8 percent annually."

But those dramatic numbers understate what was actually happening. The University had created a University College division (UMUC) in 1947, first to serve Maryland students who needed part-time, mostly evening courses or remedial work, and later to serve American military overseas.[21] By 1965–66 UMUC enrolled 12,667 "stateside" students. Many of those students took their courses in the evening on the College Park campus.

Further higher education growth seemed imminent, since demographers were predicting that total college enrollment in Maryland would double in the 1960s and more than triple in the 1970s. The problem demanded serious consideration.

In 1955, Governor Theodore McKeldin and the legislature created the Maryland Commission to Study the Needs of Higher Education, also known as the Pullen Commission. While the Commission was named after its chair, Superintendent of [Public] Schools Thomas G. Pullen, Jr., seven of the nine members were college presidents or their designees. Almost all the Baltimore area campuses were represented. The Commission recognized that increased college enrollment would occur soon, but opted for a response that protected existing institutions. Regarding four-year education, the Commission estimated existing independent colleges could "accommodate at least 1,500 [additional] students." Specifically, the Commission recommended that there was:

> no need for the extension of or the establishment of branches of any existing institution in another part of the State. In the Baltimore metropolitan area, for example, it is believed that existing institutions of higher education, public and private, along with the community junior colleges that should be established, can for the foreseeable future absorb the expected influx of added students.[22]

Consequently, the Commission advocated expanding the five existing community colleges and creating several new ones. Substantial new state funding was made available for this purpose. Between 1955 and 1965, ten new community college campuses were established across the state and enrollment in that sector quadrupled.[23]

Following the Pullen Commission report, University of Maryland President Wilson Elkins appointed a faculty committee from College Park to consider a UM re-

---

20. These enrollment statistics are from Callcott, *A History of the University of Maryland*, 396–397.

21. Ibid. The story of the creation and progress of University College is told by Callcott, *A History of the University of Maryland*, 347–349.

22. The Report of the Commission on the Needs of Higher Education in Maryland, appointed by Governor Theodore R. McKeldin Recommendation 2, 100. (1955) UMBC historic documents collection, Special Collections, University of Maryland, Baltimore County.

23. The Advisory Committee on Higher Education in the State of Maryland Report as described in, Callcott, *A History of the University of Maryland*, 398.

sponse. The committee suggested establishing a Baltimore undergraduate UM campus with a limited mission serving full-time freshmen and sophomore students who would then transfer to College Park to finish their baccalaureate degrees. The faculty of the new campus would be appointed and supervised by College Park faculty.[24]

But it was not enough. There was still a growing demand for four-year education and with the increasing number of institutions, there needed to be a better system of regulation and coordination. Consequently, in 1959, Governor J. Millard Tawes created a Commission to study the "Problem of Expansion of the University of Maryland," or the Warfield Commission after its chair, Edwin Warfield III, a publisher and grandson of a former governor.[25] According to Albin O. Kuhn, UMBC's first Chancellor, "Teddy Warfield chaired the Warfield Commission like he flew his fighter plane in World War II. He really took charge and.... he had a good commission appointed by the Governor, and they set forth a pretty sound plan for expanding the University of Maryland."[26]

Reporting a year later, the Commission took an unusually aggressive position and called for converting the three largest and, not coincidentally, the three white state teachers colleges (Frostburg, Salisbury, and Towson) into regional centers of the University of Maryland.[27] Their governance would be shifted from the State Board of Education to the University's Board of Regents. In return, these colleges would add a liberal arts curriculum and their students could transfer to College Park for special courses.[28] To the teachers college supporters and, particularly to the State Board governing them, the Warfield recommendations looked like a power grab by the University that would diminish the essential role of teacher training. Kuhn acknowledged,

---

24. Rudy Storch, "UMBC: The Early Planning," a report to Albin O. Kuhn UMBC Chancellor, August 31, 1970, UMBC Founders Oral History Project, Interviewer Briefing Book, UMBC historic documents collection, collection 55, Special Collections, University of Maryland, Baltimore County, 2.

25. Commission to Study the Problem of Expansion of the University of Maryland, February 1960. (Hereafter referred to as the Warfield Commission) (Available in the UM Law School library).

26. Albin O. Kuhn, interview by Joseph Tatarewicz, August, 14, 2001.7. This interview and other interviews in the bibliography can be found in Special Collections, University of Maryland, Baltimore County.

27. The Warfield Commission also recommended that when the three former teachers colleges had been established as regional centers of the University of Maryland, three additional centers should be established (Washington/Frederick Counties, central Eastern Shore and southern Maryland). "A Plan for Expanding the University of Maryland." (Hereafter referred to as the Warfield Commission). The existence of the four historically black colleges in Maryland was essentially ignored in this report.

28. The Warfield Commission additionally recommended that a Central Region center of the University of Maryland should be established north of Baltimore City because students in the City and the southern and southwestern parts of the metropolitan area could be served by College Park, presumably as commuters. Consequently, the Commission concluded "that it would be in the best interest of all concerned to convert the State Teachers College at Towson to a branch of the University of Maryland." 16.

"University of Maryland was feared a bit. It was not welcomed in Baltimore.... [the] President of the State College at Towson could preach a real sermon on why the University of Maryland should stay in College Park, and it wasn't needed in Baltimore."[29] After Governor Tawes waffled about supporting the report, the legislature tabled consideration of it and ordered a third study.

In 1962, the Commission for the Expansion of Public Higher Education in Maryland, or Curlett Commission, after its chair John N. Curlett, President of the McCormick Spice Company and President of the Baltimore Board of School Commissioners, was created.[30] This Commission viewed the much-lauded California plan as a model. That plan created three tiers of institutions with different missions, funding, and status: (1) community colleges; (2) four-year state colleges and universities with relatively open admissions, focused on undergraduate teaching with limited research and graduate programs; and (3) the University of California (UC) campuses with very competitive admissions and world-class undergraduate, professional, and graduate research programs. The UC Berkeley and UC Los Angeles campuses were the pride of American public higher education.

In the Curlett Commission's Maryland version, community colleges were to be organized as one system under the State Board of Education. The five former teachers colleges were to expand their missions to include liberal arts primarily for undergraduates and would be directed by a new board, while the University of Maryland would continue under its own Board of Regents and would have primary responsibility for graduate and professional teaching and research.[31] Given the value of cooperation and the probability of boundary disputes, the Commission recommended the establishment of a new coordinating body, the Advisory Council on Higher Education, made up of representatives of all Maryland public higher educational institutions.[32]

The legislature welcomed the Curlett report and enacted many of its proposals into law in April 1963. The basic higher education structure created in this law functioned until 1988 when the University of Maryland System (UMS) was established.[33] The new governance structure, however, did not in itself expand access to the University of Maryland or reduce overcrowding at College Park, so the legislature au-

29. Albin O. Kuhn, interview by Joseph Tatarewicz, August 14, 2001. 9.

30. Commission for the Expansion of Public Higher Education in Maryland, *Public Higher Education in Maryland 1961–1975* (Baltimore, 1962).

31. Ibid., 46 and 62–63. The Curlett Commission recommended a new Board of Trustees of the State Colleges which was to include Morgan in its governance. Martin D. Jenkins, Morgan's President and a member of the Commission, objected to Morgan being asked to join the new system and he prevailed. He was not successful, however, in his insistence that Bowie and Coppin not add liberal arts instruction, but instead be restricted to educating elementary school teachers.

32. The successor to the Advisory Council was the State Board for Higher Education (SBHE). Currently the coordinating body for both public and private institutions is called the Maryland Higher Education Commission (MHEC).

33. In 1997, the University Maryland System (UMS) nomenclature was changed by statute to the University System of Maryland (USM). These names will be used as chronologically appropriate.

thorized the University to establish four additional campuses. Bearing the hallmarks of political compromise and not very careful planning, the four new campuses were to be in Baltimore County, western Maryland, southern Maryland, and on the Eastern Shore.[34] As it turned out, no campuses were built in southern[35] or western Maryland,[36] and the name of the University's existing historically black Princess Anne college campus was not changed to the University of Maryland Eastern Shore (UMES) until 1970.[37]

Championed by Baltimore County State Senator James A. Pine, however, the Act's main focus was on a new Baltimore County campus because:

> About one-third of the current undergraduates now attending the College Park campus come from the Baltimore Metropolitan area and the greatest number of these students come from Baltimore County.... If a branch were established in Baltimore County, it would not only provide relief which is so necessary for the ever-increasing number of qualified students but would also serve as a nucleus for scientific research and development in this area.... Baltimore County is blessed with a number of science-based industries which are currently engaged in highly specialized research and development work and a graduate branch of the University would undoubtedly be of great assistance to these industries and would attract new industry into the metropolitan region.[38]

Given future controversies, this language was important because it clearly established legislative intent that the new campus would be located in the County, not the City, would enroll students qualified to attend the University of Maryland,[39] and that it would have a graduate and research mission, particularly in the sciences.

---

34. This recommendation goes back to the Warfield Commission report, but the reference to a university center in Central Maryland then meant the expansion of the Towson campus at the undergraduate level and the Baltimore campus for professional and graduate school students.

35. St Mary Seminary Junior College became a four-year institution in 1966.

36. In 2005, a regional center was opened by USM in a former Hagerstown's department store where five units of the System now offer twelve undergraduate majors and seven master's programs to western Maryland residents.

37. UMES began its life in 1886 as the Delaware Conference Academy, established by Methodist Episcopal Church. It was acquired by the University of Maryland from the then Morgan College in 1935, but was meagerly supported. As the University's only Negro branch, President Curley Byrd sought to increase its funding by arguing, "If we don't do something about Princess Anne, we're going to have to accept Negroes at College Park, where our girls are." Quoted by Callcott, A *History of the University of Maryland*, 351.

38. Chapter 537, Laws of Maryland, (page 785).

39. George H. Callcott in *The University of Maryland at College Park, A History* (Baltimore: Noble House, 2005) 100–101 stated "The University's first initiative in controlling enrollment was the creation of a branch campus, awkwardly called UMBC, the University of Maryland, Baltimore County. UMBC's establishment, however, permitted College Park to cap enrollment and in 1969 UMCP turned away from admitting any high school graduate to require such to be in the top half of their class."

From UM's first formal consideration of expansion in 1956, in response to the Pullen Commission's opposition of any new campuses, it took a decade to open the new Baltimore County campus. Although this campus was not intended to duplicate existing Baltimore area campuses, any new campus has an effect on its neighboring institutions. As Albin O. Kuhn, UMBC's first Chancellor, recorded in his family memoirs, "The ability of the U of M to attract students made both the public and the private institutions in the Baltimore area fearful."[40]

D. Locating the New Campus

Choosing a site for a Baltimore area campus soon became quite controversial.[41] Part of the conflict was caused by the tension between the new state Advisory Council on Higher Education and the UM Board of Regents as each tested its authority in the new governance system. The UM campuses felt out-numbered and threatened by the smaller, former state teachers colleges now represented in the Council and that anxiety was reciprocated by those schools concerned about the political clout of the older, larger UM campuses. Locating the new Baltimore campus would be a challenging political problem, since Towson already had a suburban County campus and Morgan and Coppin were in the City.

The Board of Regents Advanced Planning Committee began to explore various sites in the spring of 1963 and eventually considered thirty-four locations and inspected nineteen.[42] Site selection was a complex activity. According to *Maryland Magazine*, "Countless details were involved in selecting a site. Tax maps had to be checked, price of land acquisitions considered, engineering feasibility studies made, access to available utilities checked, test borings made, terrain and drainage considered." As the magazine summarized, the final campus site was "the fusion of thousands of ideas and details."[43]

Most of all, difficult political issues had to be settled. A new campus was attractive to both City and County politicians. Various interest groups weighed in and, as always in Maryland higher education, racial politics began to play a role.[44]

---

40. Albin O.Kuhn family "scrapbook."

41. *Baltimore Evening Sun* published editorials on September 5, 10,16, 17 and 20 urging caution in site selection and opposing the right of the UM Regents to make the decision unilaterally.

42. Storch, "UMBC: The Early Planning," 6.

43. John Blitz, "A Campus is Born," *Maryland Magazine*, (Fall, 1966) 11. The four-page article written by a UMBC public relations officer features six pictures of the new campus.

44. For a view of the tumultuous racial politics of the 1960s and 1970s that engulfed both Baltimore City and County, see Antero Pietilla, *Not in My Neighborhood: How Bigotry Shaped a Great American City* (Chicago: Ivan R. Dee, 2010). The founding of UMBC is not mentioned.

Expanding Morgan State College to make it "the" major Baltimore public university might have been an option.[45] Howard P. Rawlings, then president of Maryland Black Coalition of Higher Education and who later served 24 years in the House of Delegates, expressed a common view in his community. He wanted to establish a "coordinated university built around Morgan and headed by a black chancellor," but also said the Black Coalition would "fight any proposal that does not result in Morgan becoming an urban university with greater autonomy over its institutional destiny."[46]

The Curlett Commission never publicly considered that idea, and in its tripartite division of academic responsibilities, Morgan was assigned to the second tier along with the former state teachers colleges. Given the lack of a written record, the motivations of the Commission and other political actors almost a half-century ago are not clear. A self-described radical organization called the New University Conference of the University of Maryland, Baltimore County (NUC) was sure that race was the reason for that campus's suburban location and the decision not to make Morgan "the" Baltimore university.[47] But it may have been that the UM Regents were looking to create a new stand-alone UM campus to strengthen the tripartite system with UM at the top and did not want to enhance the fiercely independent Morgan as a potential rival.[48]

Whatever the Regent's motivations, sociologists Christopher Jencks and David Riesman wrote about the missed integration opportunity:

45. This was the ambition of Morgan's President Martin D. Jenkins who wrote in his January, 1968 annual report (two years after UMBC opened), "Morgan State should be the public university serving Baltimore City." Morgan State College, Annual Report of the President for the year 1966–67" (January, 1968). According to Kahn, Jenkins' report "outlined plans for a greatly increased racial integration on all levels of the college and expansion of academic work leading to [Morgan's] university status as the Baltimore State University." "Universities and Urban Affairs," 113.

46. Sue Miller, "Proposed Metro University Held Sabotage Attempt, *Baltimore Evening Sun*, October 14, 1974.

47. New University Conference of the University of Maryland, Baltimore County, "Racism in Maryland Higher Education with Special Reference to UMBC." Baltimore, April,1970. Special Collections, University of Maryland, Baltimore County. NUC stated that it is "a national organization of radicals who work in, around, and in spite of institutions of higher education. We are committed to struggle politically to create a new, American form of socialism and to replace an educational and social system that is an instrument of class, sexual, and racial oppression with one that belongs to the people." According to long-time UMBC Professor of Sociology and a member of the local NUC chapter, Fred Pincus, the chapter and the campus Black Caucus of Faculty and Staff of UMBC paid for the pamphlet critiquing the decision to locate UMBC in a suburb and sponsored a state-wide conference "Racism in Maryland Higher Education" attended by 150–200 people in the spring of 1970. Fred Pincus, email message to the author, May 14, 2013.

48. David Simon quotes Morgan President Andrew Billingsley as declaring, "I think it is safe to say that if anyone forwards a plan for higher education that threatens Morgan's independent governance or historical role, then we would have to react strongly." David Simon, "Missing: Baltimore's Great Urban University," *Baltimore Magazine*, September 1982, 102.

> Morgan State was for many years the only public institution in Baltimore. When whites began to demand a public commuter campus in the Baltimore area, the legislature never seriously considered developing Morgan for this purpose. Instead, a new University of Maryland campus was begun in the Baltimore suburbs, ensuring a large measure of defacto segregation in the foreseeable future.[49]

Jencks and Riesman are serious scholars, but they may not have been familiar with the details of higher education in the Baltimore area. Morgan did not become a public institution until 1939, while the University of Maryland Baltimore began in 1807; Towson in 1866 and Coppin entered the state system in 1950. They cannot be faulted, however, that their "foreseeable future" did not predict that UMBC would become one of the most ethnically and racially diverse campuses in the country.

So if the new campus was to be a new UM institution, there were basically three choices for its location (Baltimore City, northern Baltimore County, or southern Baltimore County). Mayor Theodore Roosevelt McKeldin had lobbied hard for a City location in the Inner Harbor area. He argued that the campus could revitalize downtown Baltimore; that a number of cities had successful downtown branches; that the Pratt Library and the other cultural resources could enhance the campus; and that the City would assemble the land and sell it to the University.[50]

McKeldin, though a Republican in a predominantly Democratic city and state, was a major political force.[51] Mayor of Baltimore from 1943–1947 and 1963–1967 and also Governor of Maryland from 1951–1959, he usually spoke with a powerful effect, but he was not even given the opportunity to testify before the Curlett Commission. According to his aide, McKeldin "was a voice in the wilderness and was unable to stimulate support for his position until confronted with a definite University decision."[52]

On January 25, 1965, virtually as the shovels were to go into the ground in Catonsville, the Baltimore City Planning Commission issued a report arguing for yet

---

49. Christopher Jencks and David Riesman, *The Academic Revolution* (Garden City, N.Y.: Doubleday & Company, 1968), 470.

50. Storch, "UMBC: The Early Planning."5. Also lining up against the Catonsville location for the new campus were the Greater Baltimore Committee and the Baltimore chapter of the American Institute of Architects. *Baltimore Sun,* November 21, 1963. Two month later the Baltimore Teachers Union weighed in against a suburban location saying: "Great campuses located in the heart of cities have much to do with upgrading the intellectual and cultural climate of their urban surroundings." *Baltimore Sun*, January 14, 1964.

51. Buildings are named after McKeldin on the Bowie, College Park, and Morgan campuses. McKeldin eventually reconciled himself with UMBC and was the speaker at the 1969 Founding Day celebration and donated some books to the library. Letter from Albin O. Kuhn, September 8, 1969. Origins box, UMBC historic documents collection, Special Collections, University of Maryland, Baltimore County.

52. Interview with Stanley Mazur, March 1970 as quoted by Kahn, "Universities and Urban Affairs" 16. During the site location debate, Mazur surfaced publicly for the first time the racial implications of a suburban location. Stephen E. Nordlinger, "U.M. Branch Site Linked to Bias. McKeldin Aide Sees Effort to Limit Negro Attendance," *Baltimore Sun,* January 31, 1964.

another UM campus, this time in downtown Baltimore.[53] Replete with maps showing how long it would take to get to UMBC by bus from various metropolitan locations, the report was too little, too late to have any influence. Of more concern were threats by Baltimore City state legislators who argued against the Catonsville location. Senator J. Joseph Curran predicted that there were not enough votes in the State Assembly to pass the $2,000,000 needed for start-up costs. Delegate Julian L. Lapides made a more personal attack charging that UM President Elkins was trying to "build an empire" and that proposed new branches were "a means of preventing the State colleges from developing in their own right."[54]

County politicians also were interested in the new campus. Baltimore County, then the second-most populous of the Maryland counties, has a land mass of 599 square miles. It forms a sort of closed horseshoe surrounding Baltimore City, stretching to the Pennsylvania border in the north, but extending beyond City limits only a few miles to the south. The Science Industry Development Council of the Baltimore Association of Commerce and some Baltimore County legislators hoped for an "industrial-educational complex" in the Towson area.[55] The logical place for a new Baltimore County campus might have been in the fast-growing northern suburbs ringing the City.[56] That site would also serve those Baltimore area students who otherwise would have the longest commute to College Park. There was only one problem with this logic. Towson State College, having recently expanded its liberal arts activities, was vigorously opposed to having a UM competitor near its campus and received support from its former teachers college peers. In fact, Towson did not want any new four-year public campus anywhere in Baltimore County. Noting the existence of Catonsville Community College, Towson President Earle T. Hawkins and his ally, Public School Superintendent Thomas Pullen urged that the new campus enroll only junior and senior students.[57] UM President Kirwan responded that idea was "wholly impractical, and that "having both institutions would have a tendency to better serve the community."[58]

53. Baltimore Department of Planning, "A Third Campus, A Statement of Need For An Undergraduate Branch of the University of Maryland Based on New Enrollment Projections," January 26, 1965. A decade later, the Community College of Baltimore was given a few acres for an Inner Harbor campus and the first building went up in 1977. It turned out not to be a good decision for the College or the City, and, under urging by the City it later leased one if its buildings to Best Buy and Filene's for retail space and has considered moving to a new location for the rest of its operations. Brent Jones, "BCCC Set to Move on Renewal Plan," *Baltimore Sun*, July 8, 2008.

54. Nordlinger, "U. M. Branch," January 31, 1964.

55. Kahn, "Universities and Urban Affairs,"118.

56. Governor Tawes and other state officials made a considerable effort to find a site in northern Baltimore County, examining over seventy-five locations. County Executive Spiro T. Agnew, in the early stages, was very eager to place the new campus in one of these sites. When asked about the impact on Towson State, his planning director, George Gavelis replied, "The two institutions should complement each other, rather than compete." Stephen E. Nordlinger, "3 possible U.M. Sites Inspected," *Baltimore Sun*, September 6, 1963.

57. Gerald W. Clark, "U.M. Site Review is Rejected," *Baltimore Sun*, November 27, 1963.

58. Stephen E. Nordlinger, "Catonsville U.M. Campus is Backed by State Board," *Baltimore Sun*, November 13, 1963.

Having lost his argument with the Regents, McKeldin then asserted that the issue should be decided by the new Advisory Council on Higher Education. Attempts to "forum shop" between the Regents and various statewide coordinating boards are a constant theme in Maryland higher education politics. At first, the Council, led by Superintendent Pullen, asserted that even though the legislature had approved the new UM campus, "No legislature can bind its successors and the purpose in establishing the advisory council is to review in the acts of all previous legislatures respecting higher education in Maryland."[59] A few months later, the Council discovered the site location issues were a political hornet's nest and reversed itself, denying it had authority on this subject.[60]

McKeldin did not give up. As the 1964 legislative session began, Governor Millard Tawes showed reluctance to fund start-up campus costs, McKeldin and city allies again tried to have the branch campus built in the City. One of McKeldin's aides insinuated publicly that the County location was chosen to limit the attendance of black students, but the Mayor disavowed that claim.[61] Nevertheless, the City pressed on. On February 13, 1964, McKeldin put an open letter on the desk of each state legislator asking for reconsideration of the proposed site and City legislators introduced a bill calling on the Governor to appoint a committee of "specialists" to study the location issue, thus circumventing both the Regents and the Advisory Council. But the votes were not there and a week later, the City recognized the inevitable and withdrew its objection. On March 3, 1964, the House rejected by a vote of 107–23 a motion to strike initial funding for the Baltimore County branch.[62]

In the end, the Regents decided on their own to locate the new campus at the southern end of Baltimore County as far away from Towson State University as possible.[63] In its survey of various sites, at the urging of Maryland Comptroller Louis L. Goldstein, UM officials began to focus on Spring Grove State Hospital land in Catonsville. It had the advantage of being owned by the state and thus available im-

59. Gerald W. Clark, "County Branch of U.M. Due Study," *Baltimore Sun*, October 30, 1963.

60. Prominent politicians lined up on each side. Baltimore County Executive, Spiro T. Agnew, perhaps reflecting Towson's opposition to a County site or anticipating his run for the Governorship, reversed his earlier position and supported a City location. On the other hand, Baltimore County legislators and perhaps most important, the Governor supported a County site. Storch, "UMBC: The Early Planning" 5. See also three articles in the *Sun*, by Gerald W. Clark, "New Agency is Divided on U.M. Site," September 21, 1963; and "U.M. Site Review is Rejected," November 27, 1963 and "Door is Closed to McKeldin Bid," December 15,1963;. As an example of the passions this debate engendered, the Council Chair, James P. Casbarian, was quoted in the last Clark article, as saying that he took, "violent exception" to the Mayor's request to speak in favor of a city branch because "I am unalterably opposed to studying the site.... It's finished. The Board of Regents has made its decision and it's been ratified by the Governor and the Board of Public Works."

61. Storch, "UMBC: The Early Planning" 7.

62. Ibid.

63. The Regents recommended its Spring Grove choice to the Board of Public Works on November 12, 1963. See also Regents' Minutes March 12, May 14, and June 11, 1965. See also *Baltimore Sun*, January 26, 1964 and June 18, 1965.

mediately. Commissioner of Mental Health Dr. Isadore Tuerke agreed to give up the land in part because changes in therapeutic practices rendered the farmland less functional for the hospital. At an estimated value of $7,000 per acre in 1963, the "free" land was important to the Comptroller. Goldstein also recalled that early one morning as he and Governor Tawes were looking over the tract, the Governor was excited about its potential and said, "This is beautiful. This is the place."[64]

Still, at first impression the site, distant from both the political and commercial centers of City and County and accessible by very little public transportation, might have seemed a poor compromise. In hindsight, however, as attractive as a Baltimore waterfront location might have been aesthetically, it would not have been a good choice for either the City or the University. Whereas in the 1960s, inner harbor land was marred by derelict warehouses and rotting piers, the creation of Harbor Place and other developments after 1980 made it the most valuable property in the state. In retrospect, the City could have ill-afforded to have this prime location for tourists and businesses used for a tax-exempt campus. Furthermore, as that campus inevitably needed to expand, it would have been subject to perpetual political struggles over land use, taxes, and the ambitions of other institutions.

Though the State already owned most of the campus land, the Spring Grove site had some disadvantages. It had no natural political significance that would consistently lead to powerful legislative representation for its educational needs. The political center of Baltimore County is Towson, which has its own university. Anne Arundel, Baltimore, and Howard Counties have their own community colleges. Just twenty-seven miles from College Park, UMBC also could seem too close to that campus's gravitational pull

The old hospital site, however, also has some important advantages. It is spacious, roughly 530 acres,[65] permitting the development of a campus not impeded by intruding roads, housing developments or businesses. The campus is walkable, safe, and green. Further, it is at the corner of the Baltimore Beltway (I-695) and I-95, the great, if sometimes infuriating, national north-south super highway, so the campus is fairly accessible by auto from many neighborhoods in the metropolitan area. From UMBC, it is usually only one stoplight and about twenty minutes to downtown Baltimore and even less time to BWI-Thurgood Marshall airport and commuter trains. As the 1976 Middle States report commented: "This site enables UMBC to draw on the vast public resources of Baltimore and the counties, while at the same time offering its students a well built campus which can give them the leisure and concentration of withdrawal without the isolation of exile."[66]

On balance, UMBC's location is now seen as a plus.

---

64. Leslie Rice, "Pioneer Spirit is recalled," *Catonsville Times*, September 25, 1991.

65. The original site was 425 acres, but additional land was soon purchased.

66. An Evaluation Team Representing the Commission on Higher Education of the Middles States Association, "Report to the Faculty, Administration, Trustees, Students of the University of Maryland Baltimore County," Collection 50, President's Office Records, Box 37, Folder 1, March 21–24,1976. 3 (hereafter Middle States 1976 report).

E. Does an Institution's Name Matter?

How an institution is named can have a considerable influence on its branding and status. One expects the University of California, San Diego or the University of North Carolina at Charlotte to be substantial institutions. Examining the names of the new wave urban universities, two patterns are apparent. Most of these new institutions were given the name of the city in which they were located (Boston, Cleveland, St Louis, etc.), while a few others were given regional names (Central Florida, South Alabama) or names that tied them to particular state traditions (Old Dominion, Virginia Commonwealth). The logical name for UMBC would have been the University of Maryland, Baltimore or even the University of Baltimore, but both were taken. The University of Central Maryland didn't seem right and Old Line University doesn't have the claim on Marylanders that Old Dominion may have on Virginians. In many states (Michigan, Iowa, Oklahoma, Colorado, etc.), there is the "University of...," which is the arts and science campus, and "State University," which is more often the land grant agricultural and engineering campus. But in Maryland, College Park offered almost every undergraduate and graduate arts and science discipline and had specialized land-grant university programs as well. Furthermore, when the state took over the Princess Anne campus from the Methodist Episcopal Church in 1948, that institution was called Maryland State College, so the "State" name was already taken.

The UMBC campus was located between two unincorporated suburban towns and there was a Maryland tradition of naming state teachers colleges after small towns or cities (Bowie, Frostburg, Salisbury, and Towson). Arbutus, a Latin term for a wild strawberry tree, has an attractive sylvan ring to it, but the blue-collar town with a struggling business district did not quite resemble Chapel Hill or Ann Arbor. Catonsville was more upscale, but it was already home to Catonsville Community College. The campus was located on land owned by Spring Grove hospital, and that name has a pleasant lilt to it, but close association with the former Maryland Hospital for the Insane had some down sides. Some have alleged that the failure to include Catonsville in the University name was because of the notoriety of the Catonsville Nine incident, where Catholic activists led by Father Phillip Berrigan napalmed draft board records in the village. This symbolic act caused great national interest during the Vietnam War,[67] but it occurred in 1968, two years after the University was founded.

Initially there was uncertainty about what to name the campus. New "UM unit," as some articles, referred to the prospective campus did not have much appeal. An article on the dedication of the campus in the *Baltimore News American* was titled

67. Daniel Berrigan, Robin Andersen and James Marsh, *The Trial of the Catonsville Nine*, (Boston: Beacon Press, 1970) and a 1972 film of the same name by Gordon Davidson II, director and Gregory Peck, producer.

"'Cat Campus' Sprouting Rapidly."[68] A similar article in the *Baltimore Sun* referred to the new campus as "Cate State." Fortunately, those monikers disappeared quickly.[69]

As it turned out, calling the new campus the University of Maryland, Baltimore County was almost an afterthought. According to its first Chancellor Albin O. Kuhn, the person most likely to know these things, because the founding legislation had called for a campus in Baltimore County, UMBC became the name without much debate.[70] Kuhn later conceded, "Some people chaff a little about a university with a county name, but I always thought we were distinctive in that."[71]

Although there were solid reasons for choosing the name University of Maryland, Baltimore County, it was and is an uncomfortable fit for a research university. UMBC is the only four-year higher education institution in the country with the name County in its title.[72] Wayne State is not Wayne County University, nor is the University of California, Irvine the University of California, Orange County, though county titles would be quite accurate in both cases. In Maryland and indeed across America, a county name (Anne Arundel, Frederick, Howard, Montgomery, and Prince George, etc.) attached to a higher educational institution means a junior or community college. UMBC could shout that its name should indicate research university, but America did not always listen. For many years, UMBC was like a low-watt radio station whose signal and identification faded with a little distance.

In most branding situations, if you have to explain a name, it is not a good name. Several things happened because of this ambiguous name. UMBC faculty publications or other achievements would get attributed to the University of Maryland which to most people meant College Park. In the extremely status-conscious world of higher education, UMBC faculty suspected that some invitations might not be forthcoming when the choice to invite was a close call. When the invitations did come, the institutional name on the program selected by the host might simply be the Uni-

68. October 28, 1966. That name was apparently used first by a staffer of the UMCP *Diamondback*. Lowell Sunderland, "Catonsville Campus Opened," *Baltimore Sun*, September 19, 1966.

69. Ann Groer, "UM to Open New Unit:750 New Frosh Expected," *Baltimore Evening Sun*, September 1966. The writer predicted "... football fans may someday see a great rivalry between 'Cate State' and the Maryland Terrapins."

70. Whether Kuhn ever had cause to ponder connecting the campus name to Baltimore County's reputation in this era for white flight and resistance to desegregation and its tradition of political corruption is unknown. In 1973, former County Executive, Spiro T. Agnew resigned the Vice-Presidency for accepting kickbacks, and a year later his successor Dale Anderson as County Executive was sent to prison for extorting bribes. Pietila, "Not in My Neighborhood," 211–235.

71. Albin O. Kuhn, interview by Ed Orser, February 2, 1994, 10.

72. Linda Leggett Meyers, "What's In A Name? UMBC Review, 9. no.2 (Spring 1991). Chancellor Hooker raised the name issue in 1991 and asked for a faculty survey of the issue. Although there was a majority in favor of a name change, in the end Hooker asked the State to take the matter off the table because "we might conserve our momentum during this period of budgetary constriction." 3.

versity of Maryland. Some alumni, asked one too many times about the fate of the Terrapins, might finally give up and just become UM alums. No one knows for sure how the name affected student applicants, but it might have been a factor in UMBC's perennially low out-of-state enrollment. Towson (1997) and Salisbury (2001) dropped State from their names to appeal to more non-Maryland students. Coppin (2004) and Loyola (2009) changed from colleges to become universities. More dramatic name changers in Maryland's private sector were Western Maryland College to McDaniel College in 2002 and Villa Julie College to Stevenson University in 2008.

The issue of reconsidering the campus name was apparently first formally raised in 1974, when the Barton-Gillet Company, a consulting firm, produced a report on campus public relations for new UMBC Chancellor Calvin Lee. The report concluded bluntly that "UMBC is still an idea for which there are few labels" and that the campus "should give serious consideration to a new expression of its own identity."[73] The firm suggested half-heartedly that UMBC: Maryland's University in Baltimore County or UMBC: Maryland Public Liberal Arts University in Baltimore be considered as a name change. Perhaps not the most euphonious of public relations products, those titles died a quick death.

USM Chancellor Donald Langenberg, after coming to Maryland in 1990 from leading the University of Illinois at Chicago Circle, which he wryly noted was the only university named after a traffic crossroads except Oxford and Cambridge, thought UMBC should change its name.[74] But the campus was not prepared to take that momentous step. Some thought Baltimore County officials might be annoyed, though the County provided no regular funding for UMBC. Moreover, since Towson is the seat of county government, many of its political leaders think of that namesake university as the County's own. There would be some expense in changing signs, stationery and some advertising, but surely that was manageable.[75] More important was the reality that as a new rapidly expanding university, UMBC was constantly making demands on state government and its top administrators were reluctant to use their blue chips for a name change.

So UMBC tinkered. In 1996, it changed its address from 5401 Wilkens Avenue, Catonsville, Maryland to 1000 Hilltop Circle, Baltimore, Maryland. It decided to use its initials (a la UCLA) whenever possible rather than its full name. Sophomore humorists snickered that UMBC stood for "U Made a Bad Choice," "U Must Be Crazy," "U Must Be Chinese" or other unflattering sobriquets. Administration efforts to suggest that UMBC stood for the "University of Maryland's Best Campus" were not entirely persuasive.

73. The Barton-Gillett Report, 1974, UMBC historic documents collection, Special Collections, University of Maryland, Baltimore County, 12 and 15.

74. Donald Langenberg interview by the author, July 4, 2009. UICC became the University of Illinois, Chicago in 1982.

75. Loyola officials estimated those costs at about $250,000 in connection with their 2009 name change. Childs Walker, "Advance Degree: Loyola College Officially Celebrates its Change to a University Friday," *Baltimore Sun*, September 24, 2009. 3.

In 1995, North Charles Street Design Organization, (NCSDO), a consulting company, was brought in to consider rebranding.[76] NCSDO thought UMBC had a "murky identity," but then said somewhat mysteriously, "With reluctance, we must concur that there is no opportunity on the horizon for UMBC to change its name." Whether the lack of a name change "opportunity" was because of the opposition of a powerful person or group or some other factor was not clarified. Consequently, NCSDO recommended that the institution use its initials for identification wherever feasible and attach the phrase "An Honors University in Maryland" to UMBC.

NCSDO thought this would:

- Attract the attention of the kinds of students UMBC wants most to enroll, and will be particularly effective out-of-state where there is virtually no awareness of the university.
- Create a platform enabling UMBC to present and explain the opportunities it makes available to able students.
- Tend to influence administrative decision-making within UMBC in the direction of enhancing the academic experience across the university.
- Inform and provide direction for decisions related to marketing and image building.
- Be expected to produce a halo effect beneficial to the marketing of quality programs across-the-board.
- Creates a platform on which UMBC can build an effective case for financial support.

There were some mixed reactions to this change. St. Mary's College, often thought of as a sectarian private liberal arts college, had its own name problem.[77] It won legislative approval to be called a Public Honors College and was not pleased by UMBC's self-designated new title. UMBC academic and athletic recruiters were uncertain whether the honors designation was an asset or a liability in attracting non-honors student prospects. Faculty who had close encounters with undergraduates who did not always fit the honors mode were sometimes skeptical. Journalists, guidance counselors, other academics, indeed any non-UMBC constituency, could not be expected to attach the Honors tag line when discussing UMBC.

Under the direction of Provost Arthur Johnson, a nineteen-member faculty, staff, and student task force was convened to make the Honors University nomenclature meaningful. Chaired by Angela Moorjani, Professor of Modern Languages and Linguistics, the task force took as its charge: "We aspire to continue to our development as an honors university which seeks to combine the traditions of the liberal arts acad-

---

76. North Charles Street Design Organization, "UMBC Marketing Communications Plan," May 1995. NCSDO's methodology was generally interviews and focus groups, but no details were provided.

77. The school's origins go back to 1840 when it was St. Mary's Female Seminary. It became St. Mary's Junior College Seminary in 1926 and then converted to a four year school in 1966.

emy, the creative intensity of the research university, and the social responsibility of the public university."[78] The group recommended the establishment of an honors code, growth of study abroad programs, more undergraduate research opportunities, improved learning assessment outcomes, increased cross-cultural inquiry, and restructuring the curriculum to stress critical and analytical thinking, intensive in-course writing in the disciplines, and the integration of new information technologies. Almost all of these recommendations were implemented within the always present budgetary restraints.

Except for some occasional grumbling in faculty meetings, one might have imagined that the name change issue was dead. Then in April 2010, the *Sun* ran an editorial that commended UMBC for its many achievements and concluded: "If the University of Maryland College Park is the flagship of the state university, UMBC is certainly one of its crown jewels." The paper wondered, however, why UMBC didn't have the cachet it deserved and suggested that the "provincial reference to Baltimore County" in the University name might be holding it back.[79] In the internet era, it didn't take long for a response. By the next day a remarkable 172 student messages were posted on a blog. Some were frivolous, but many were genuinely concerned that "County" would disadvantage them after graduation. During a subsequent meeting of chairs and top administrators, President Freeman Hrabowski was asked about a name change. He responded that it would cost millions of dollars and there was no consensus alternative name, but that his Presidential successor might consider it.

Although the County name still inflicts a sort of status drag on university activities, as UMBC has become more successful in gaining research grants, better-prepared students, more alumni and, finally, some external recognition, a name change has become more difficult and less necessary. There is still some interest in a Maryland State University or University of Maryland Chesapeake or a Chesapeake University name or if Bill Gates should want a university named after him, well....

78. Report of the Honors University Task Force, UMBC, June 15, 2000.

79. "UMBC Chess Champs Need a School Name Worthy of the World-Class Institution They Attend," *Baltimore Sun*, April 12, 2010.

CHAPTER II

Forever Politics

A. Introduction

This chapter tells the story of the most important political trials, tribulations, and triumphs in the building of UMBC, so it is useful here to outline the structure and the players in the political arena.

The 1962 Curlett Commission's mandate to expand access to the University of Maryland, led it to endorse a new Baltimore campus for a limited purpose:

> To help meet its obligation for undergraduate education, the University [of Maryland] has long proposed the establishment of an additional campus in the Baltimore metropolitan area. This campus would be primarily designed to serve prospective students from Baltimore and adjacent areas. At the present time more than one-third of the Maryland undergraduates enrolled at College Park are from the Baltimore Metropolitan region. Total undergraduate enrollment at the University is expected to climb from 12,120 to 25,300 by 1975. The University believes that the establishment of an undergraduate campus in Baltimore would bring its facilities much closer to the large portion of the undergraduate body which resides in this densely populated area, while avoiding any over-crowding of facilities at College Park in the years to come.[1]

This recommendation became Maryland law in 1963, but what was the new Baltimore campus to become? Would it be a major autonomous university in its own right or merely a branch campus of College Park, serving the surplus of undergraduate students the older campus no longer wanted, and condemned to second rate status? Charles P. McCormick, Chairman of the UM Board of Regents was quoted as saying, "We think this [campus] will relieve some of the pressure at the main university where attendance is now getting close to almost full capacity. It will also enable a great many Baltimore youths to attend college locally instead of traveling all the way to College Park."[2] If some thought UMBC's principal role was to serve under-

1. Commission for the Expansion of Public Higher Education in Maryland, *Public Higher Education in Maryland 1961–1975*, Baltimore. 1962. (Curlett Commission), 34.

2. Charles P. McCormick, "Board Chairman Nods Approval of UMBC Faculty, Facilities," *UMBC News*, 1, no.4 (October 30, 1966),5.

graduates who could not be accommodated at College Park, what graduate and research responsibilities and opportunities would the Catonsville campus undertake?

As public universities expanded in the 1960s, both autonomous and branch campus patterns were followed. In Callcott's history of the University of Maryland, completed just as the first UMBC buildings were being constructed, there was little information about academic goals for the new campus and, perhaps, not much interest either. Callcott noted that "At first officials predicted 3,000 students by 1975, then they said 10,000 and then talked of the not-distant day when the branch would have more undergraduates than College Park."[3] Perhaps that expansive talk was a device to speed along needed state appropriations. Callcott's book included a striking pair of 1965 photographs showing an overhead view of the beautiful Georgian architecture of the 26,215 undergraduate and graduate student College Park campus coupled with a view literally of the holes in the ground that would become the new Catonsville campus.[4] (See photo section.) Aside from robust enrollment predictions, what was the academic future of the new university or branch campus? That outcome would be determined by politics, a difficult arena for any new institution, but one in which UMBC was particularly disadvantaged.

All major universities are creatures of politics determined by both internal and external forces. In 1650, Harvard's charter, granted by the Great and General Court of the Massachusetts Bay Colony, designated the first seven members of the Harvard Corporation and outlined the powers of the Board of Overseers to "conduce to the education of the English and Indian youth of this country, in knowledge and Godliness."[5] For about the first 150 years in this country, governments established and subsidized universities with no clear lines between the authority of public and private officials. Those arrangements came to an abrupt end in *Trustees of Dartmouth College v. Woodward* (1819).[6] In that case, the United States Supreme Court surprised the New Hampshire legislature by ruling it had no power to alter the powers of private trustees by naming new public trustees to make the College accountable to government authorities. The Court held that the College's 1769 charter granted by King George III, and by extension all such charters, was a form of contract. Under Article I, Section 10 of the federal constitution, states could not abridge such contracts. The case turned out to be the birth mother of public higher education in the United States, since it was now clear that private colleges were beyond the control of public authorities. "Private" institutions still remain most prominent in New England, but in other regions where higher education developed later, public institutions predominate.

---

3. George A. Callcott, *A History of the University of Maryland*, (Baltimore, Maryland Historical Society. 1966), 400.

4. Ibid., 343.

5. http://library.harvard.edu/university-archives/using-the-collections/online-resources/charter-of-1650.

6. 17 U.S. 518 (1819).

B. Governing Maryland Higher Education

The characteristics of academic governance and institutional missions varies by state, since, unlike other countries, there is no central or federal government role in these issues. Sometimes there is a single public flagship campus (e.g., Minnesota, Vermont, and West Virginia) reducing all other institutions to second tier and often second rate status. Sometimes two campuses share roughly equal status. That is most common where there is one major public liberal arts campus and one major public land-grant campus. The latter, frequently, is called "State" (as in Michigan and Michigan State or Oklahoma and Oklahoma State etc.), but Alabama and Auburn and Indiana and Purdue also follow that pattern. California is the example of a multi-campus three-tiered system where the nine University of California (UC) campuses share equal research university status, if not equal prestige. At least, they support each other when the ambitions of the much larger California State University system threaten UC prerogatives.

Maryland's higher education structure does not fit exactly any of the three models. There are now eleven universities and two research and service components in the University System of Maryland (USM). Within USM, the four campuses that bear the University of Maryland name are quite dissimilar. The College Park and Baltimore professional schools campuses have very strong research programs and many nationally ranked programs. Research and teaching prominence for the Baltimore County campus has been more recently recognized. The University of Eastern Shore (UMES) campus is a system anomaly, since its admission standards and research productivity are not comparable to other UM campuses.[7]

There are five institutions (Bowie, Coppin, Frostburg, Salisbury and Towson) that at one time focused mainly on teacher preparation and had limited missions and financial support. They still have higher teaching loads for their faculty and less state financial aid per student than other Maryland public institutions. Consequently, faculty scholarly productivity and student admission test scores tend to lag behind the "research" campuses. Towson and Salisbury have dropped State from their names and made the most concerted efforts to change their status. Coppin State, woefully neglected for decades compared to its state peers, including Morgan, has embarked on a $400 million building effort, but it still has a lot of catching up to do.[8] Three

7. According to the 1968 Master Plan, that institution has long had a remedial role. The Plan, while urging the upgrade of that College, noted ".... Maryland State [now UMES] makes a special effort to accept into its student body those whose academic credentials may not be acceptable to other institutions." In 2012, the combined average freshman SAT scores at UMES were 850 and the six-year graduation rate was 36 percent. Maryland Higher Education Commission, "University of Maryland Eastern Shore Profile and FY2014 Budget," Vol. 3, R30B25.00. 172.

8. Yvonne Wenger, "Coppin State president addresses 'no confidence' vote at forum," *Baltimore Sun,* March 7, 2012. See also the report of the Special Review Committee on Coppin State

current public institutions (UMES, University of Baltimore, and Morgan State University) began as private schools and still have some traditions and a few alumni from those years. The University of Baltimore, until 2006, confined to the last two years of undergraduate education as a condition for becoming a state institution, also has limited graduate and professional offerings. Two public institutions have remained independent of the USM Regents and have their own Boards of Trustees. St. Mary's College looks like and functions similarly to a private liberal arts college. Morgan State University, with its loyal and politically powerful alumni, has sought frequently to expand its mission, while restricting the program offerings of other institutions. One of the most complicated dimensions of higher educational policy is that Maryland has four public historically black institutions, Bowie, Coppin, Morgan and UMES, among the highest numbers for any state.

Maryland higher education, then, does not have the neat symmetry of the three-tier California system, or a dual flagship arrangement of liberal arts and land-grant campuses, nor even a flagship and branch campus pattern. Maryland's public higher education is unique and many would say the diversity of its institutional offerings is a distinct plus. Maryland is a rich state, but also a small state (seven of the eleven public campuses are within forty miles of each other). The complexity of its higher education governance structure and the fluidity of campus missions guarantee constant political battles.

For Maryland public universities, the most significant arena is state government and the most significant player is the governor.[9] In Maryland, budgets must be balanced annually and only the governor can propose the state budget. The legislature can cut the budget, but cannot add to it. While overall the percentage of state funds granted to public universities nationally has been dropping steadily, all undergraduate Maryland public institutions depend on state funding. Therefore, the total dollars and the allocations for specific purposes awarded an institution in the governor's budget can be decisive, if a "good" budget can be protected in the legislative process. Decisions about capital projects are made differently. These expenditures must be approved by the Board of Public Works, comprised of the Governor, Treasurer, and Comptroller. Institutional ambitions most often collide and the fiercest lobbying takes place about new building decisions. The "if," "when," "size," and "amenities" of a new building are subject often to intense negotiations and tradeoffs.

Typically, the resources public universities bring to these conflicts are regional support from political and business elites and representation of alumni and other friends in decision-making bodies. As a new university in the crowded Baltimore higher education arena, UMBC had none of these political advantages. Instead, the young campus would have to make its case by demonstrating need, which it could do easily;

University, January 15, 2013. The Committee was chaired by UMBC President Freeman Hrabowski III.

9. Robert O. Berdahl, "Strong Governors and Higher Education: A Survey and Analysis," Recommended Readings. State Higher Education Executive Officers Association Archives, June 2004, http://archive.sheeo.org/govern/strongprecent20governors.pdf (accessed July 12, 2013).

by demonstrating that it was a good investment, which it could do generally; and by demonstrating effective and charismatic leadership, which it could do sometimes.

In 1988, Maryland enacted the Maryland Charter for Higher Education reorganizing its higher education governance to create the University System of Maryland (USM), with its own reconstituted Board of Regents, and the Maryland Higher Education Commission (MHEC) as the new coordinating body.[10] Theoretically at the apex of this arrangement is MHEC; in reality its powers are important, but limited. Maryland has 58 colleges and universities and more than 170 private career schools, and MHEC's task is to referee mission boundary and curriculum issues among them.[11] The key to MHEC's power is its ability to grant or withhold program approval when institutions seek additions.

Whereas Morgan and St. Mary's have their own Boards, the USM Board of Regents is responsible for thirteen institutions enrolling about 152,000 students and with combined budgets of almost $4.4 billion, including research awards of about $1.37 billion.[12] Sixteen of the seventeen USM Regents are appointed by governors for five-year terms.[13] While the University of Maryland does not have the constitutional status afforded some public universities in a few other states, the Autonomy Act of 1952 granted the Regents "all the powers, rights and privileges that go with the responsibility of management," without interference of other state agencies.[14] As a full body, the Regents usually meet about six times a year for three to four hours, though committees and task forces may meet much more frequently. Although the Autonomy Act speaks of Regents' "management" of the University, in practice that function is delegated to administrators and sometimes faculty, and the Regents' supervision of individual campuses is limited. The Regents have formal authority to make general USM policies and specifically to appoint the system chancellor, campus presidents, approve missions, budgets, and new programs. In theory, they also approve degree awards and tenure decisions, but, in fact, Regents almost always have full-time jobs that restrict their attention to these matters.

The public face, and in many respects, the real power in the USM is the Chancellor and his staff. Maryland has been blessed with three energetic and politically astute

---

10. A useful overview of this development can be found in "Historical Perspectives on the Governance Structure of the University System of Maryland," (1988). http://mlis.state.md.us/199rs/Taskforce/Historical_Perspective_Structure. The political controversy over this governance change and its perceived threat to UMBC is described on pages 31–35.

11. MHEC's predecessor, the Maryland Council for Higher Education (MCHE), first asserted coordinating and program approval powers in its 1968 Master Plan for Higher Education, Phase One," (November 1968) See pages 4 and 19–22.

12. Chancellor William E. Kirwan, "University System of Maryland FY 2011 Annual Report," (June 17, 2011).

13. Regents may serve two five-year terms, though one position is reserved for a student representative for a one-year term. There are minutes of all regular Board meeting and since 1998 an audiotape of these meetings in the Office of the Board of Regents. The minutes are mostly used to record announcements and decisions. They ordinarily do not reflect debates or split votes, if any.

14. Curlett, "*Public Higher Education in Maryland 1961–1975*," 45.

Chancellors since the System was founded (John Toll, 1988–89, Donald Langenberg, 1990–2002, and William R. "Brit" Kirwan, 2002–).[15] The Chancellors and their staffs are involved in all of the negotiations and recommendations that come to the Regents, who with a few notable exceptions have approved them.

Individual campuses have their own Boards of Visitors composed of luminaries and donors, but they are rarely decision makers, though their advice and political support is valuable. Presidents occupy a complicated, and yet essential, position in the governance structure. On one hand, they must be university leaders, which sometimes mean they must follow strongly held campus views. On the other hand, they are required to carry out USM and state policies. So they must advocate strongly for campus interests, without alienating either system or state officials who need, after all, to balance the interests of all the institutions. Presidents constantly face both internal and external demands constantly, while always under scrutiny.

Governance structures have enormous implications for the mission, financial support, and recognition afforded an institution. The structures also create and contain the vigorous competition that drives American public education. To the public, that competition's most visible form may be on the gridiron or the hardwood floor, but it's most important settings are in board, conference, and hearing rooms where dollars and programs are allocated.

Every budget year and every building decision creates tension between objective need and political clout.[16] There were several points in UMBC's history where its long-term fate was determined by political decisions by the State's governance structure where the campus had little influence. This chapter describes major political controversies under the categories of mission politics, proposed campus closure, the politics of institutional competition, and campus merger controversies.

C. Mission Politics

Institutional mission statements in the profit and non-profit sectors are often just collections of feel-good aphorisms, but they may articulate clear goals, which in times of turmoil can provide guidance for difficult decisions. In Maryland's tumultuous higher education politics, the language of mission statements has often been a weapon in settling disputes.

The 1963 enabling legislation for UMBC clearly stated the campus was to be a part of the UM system with a graduate and research mission. If one sought any other specifications about UMBC's future, however, the answers would not be found in the 1968 Master Plan for Higher Education. Though there are discussions about the

---

15. Prior to the 1988 reorganization, the top university post carried the title President and the campus leaders were Chancellors. After 1988, the titles were reversed and this book will reflect the titles in place at the time they were in effect.

16. Campus development will be described in Chapter III and budgets in Chapter VI.

mission and governance of every other state public institution, nothing was said about the new Catonsville campus. Whether that was an oversight or a reflection of some controversy about UMBC's future within the Maryland Council for Higher Education is uncertain.

In 1974, however, MCHE returned to the questions of institutional roles and UMBC did not fare well. The Council appointed a committee headed by Phillip Pear, a Bethesda attorney, to review higher education in the Baltimore Metropolitan areas.[17] In its report, the Pear Committee found that: "In view of the substantial black population in the city of Baltimore and the white concentration in suburban Baltimore, there has been created a dichotomy preventing the ultimate integration and coordination of higher education in the metropolitan area."[18] The Committee also believed that enrollment was leveling off in the state and that competition was creating a zero sum game among institutions. Consequently, it recommended full-time enrollment targets for each Baltimore campus, which in UMBC's case would have been 6,000 students. The Committee concluded that, if UMBC expanded beyond its target, "... there would be fewer full-time students available to the other institutions in the area resulting in some of them having excess space."[19] The Committee, consequently, recommended that UMBC not receive a proposed $22,000,000 for new building additions. In the Committee's view, UMBC was an institution designed only to serve local students with no distinction in its role from other local public four-year campuses.[20]

The Pear Committee also proposed that no new academic program duplication be permitted in the Baltimore region. While that might be a reasonable concept, if the campuses had similar histories, purposes, and student bodies, a rigid "no duplication" policy would have placed a heavy hobble on a new campus then only eight years old. UMBC had a very small program inventory and its eventual goal to reach students who would benefit from a more rigorous undergraduate education in a research setting could not have been realized without program expansion. To UMBC, the clearest threat from the Pear Committee was its conclusion that no doctoral programs should be approved in the Baltimore area, except one at Morgan in Urban Studies. The Committee also flirted with the concept of forming a State University of Metropolitan Baltimore Area (SUMBA) and a single governing structure for all

17. A year earlier, Pear chaired the committee that laid the foundation for state funding for private colleges in what is now called the Joseph A. Sellinger State Aid Program, named after the former Jesuit priest who was President of Loyola College for thirty years.

18. Report transmission letter from Phillip Pear to William P. Chaffinch, Chairman MCHE, November 2, 1974. The letter and the report can be found in UMBC historic documents collection, Special Collections, University of Maryland, Baltimore County.

19. Ibid., 23.

20. R. Lee Hornbake, Vice President for Academic Affairs, memorandum to President Wilson Elkins, December 23, 1974. "The direct casualty of the [Pear] report as I see it is the UMBC campus. Further capital improvements in the immediate future are seriously threatened by the 6000 enrollment ceiling." Unlike most such reports which are subject to compromise and thus eventually endorsed unanimously, there were five negative committee votes on the Pear Report.

four-year Baltimore institutions. Eventually the Committee backed away from that concept, finding no support on any of the campuses for SUMBA. It did recommend, however, a common academic catalogue for all Baltimore area schools.

Finally, the Pear Committee launched a new salvo in what had became a long, and often bitter, struggle between the advocates of a single statewide governing board representing all public and private higher education institutions and the UM Board of Regents which viewed itself as guardian of the University's graduate and research campuses. The Committee advocated a "strong central coordinating authority" with almost complete authority over every aspect of higher education. In particular, the report urged eliminating "segment boards," including the UM Board of Regents, because they:

> create an additional layer of coordination creating organizational problems and additional staffing which duplicate efforts at the Statewide level and do not contribute in the most effective way to a unified endeavor for the orderly growth and development of higher education in the state.[21]

In place of segment boards, the Pear Committee recommended that each of the fourteen public campuses have an individual board with limited authority. That would have broken the power of the Regents who were not even mentioned by name in the Pear report.

Since UMBC's main political and educational asset in those days was that it was a UM campus, the Committee's leveling recommendations were a serious threat to its future. The new Catonsville campus would have been disadvantaged in the scramble by state institutions for desirable new board members. It would have been impossible for UMBC to recruit the faculty and administrators it sought and develop the programs it needed, if the Committee's plans had been fully implemented.

UMBC responded sharply to the Pear report. Chancellor Lee wrote that, since the report's recommendation of individual campus boards was incompatible with the existing tripartite structure. "my basic question is whether the dismemberment of the University system is intended by the committee's report."[22] Lee also asked, since MCHE's 1971 enrollment model projected UMBC to grow to 12,500, why the MCHE's Pear committee was now recommending an enrollment limit of 6,000. The

---

21. Tom D. Day, Vice Chancellor to Acting Chancellor John W. Dorsey, memorandum, December 19, 1974. Dr. Day commented on the above quote that "A more stinging (and wrongheaded) slap at our Board of Regents would be hard to compose.... certainly today was a very bad day for the University of Maryland System."

22. UMBC Memorandum to Philip Pear, December 13, 1974. Other UM criticisms of the Pear report can be found in a November 25, 1974 letter to Harry Phillips, Executive Director, Commission on the Structure and Governance of Education in Maryland from Wilson H. Elkins, President of the University of Maryland citing a recent Board of Regents resolution defending UMBC's role in Maryland higher education. See also a December 13, 1974 memorandum to Philip Pear from R. Lee Hornbake challenging the proposed 6,000 enrollment limit for UMBC and pointing out that UMBC growth has been "restricted by the simple but direct turndown of proposed academic programs."

conflict over the role of various governing boards in Maryland higher education, however, would not be "settled" until 1988, and in many eyes, it has not yet been fully resolved.

In 1977, the State Board for Higher Education (SBHE), successor to the Maryland Council for Higher Education, again nearly ended UMBC's and several other institutions' aspirations to engage in doctoral work.[23] SBHE had the authority to "To approve or disapprove proposals for new academic programs at collegiate institutions based on state need, campus mission, their potential for quality, and affordability." That necessarily brought the Board into conflict with various institutional aspirations, particularly with what one SBHE staffer called "the huge educational empire of five university campuses" in the University of Maryland family. More generally that same staffer thought SBHE's ability to limit campus missions was no more welcome to colleges than air emissions standards are to automobile manufactures."[24]

A SBHE planning committee recommended that doctoral programs be limited to Johns Hopkins, University of Maryland College Park, University of Maryland at Baltimore, and Morgan State on the grounds that graduate enrollments were declining, doctoral programs were expensive, and that Morgan should be developed "into something that resembles a complete university that grants doctoral degrees." When Loyola College proposed creating a practitioner's doctoral program focused on school administrators working in the Baltimore area, the Board rejected it by a vote of 7 to 1.[25] Morgan was working on a similar proposal, but Loyola's was completed first. Towson State's President James Fisher, perhaps more concerned about competition from Loyola than Morgan, said: "We're committed to being the best [primarily undergraduate] institution in our state. If we are going to maintain an advanced degree institution, it should be at Morgan." President Fisher did not mention UMBC, but the State Board's restriction on offering doctoral work in the Baltimore area would have an obvious negative impact on UMBC. The *Baltimore Evening Sun* reported: "It would dim the hopes of many faculty members at the 11-year old University of Maryland Baltimore County who have been uneasy about that school's failure to develop into a major institution."[26]

---

23. The history of SBHE and a description of its principal staff members can be found in David Sumler, "Life Cycle: History of the State Board for Higher Education," an unpublished and unofficial 135 page manuscript written before Sumler's death in May 2012. Sumler was an academic analyst for MHEC for over 30 year, retiring in 2007 as Assistant Secretary for Planning and Academic Affairs. UMBC historic documents collection. Special Collections, University of Maryland, Baltimore County.

24. Ibid., 17.

25. Sister Mary Magdala Thompson, Dean of Graduate Studies at Loyola, had argued that its charter gave it "the unequivocal power to grant degrees equal to the highest offered anywhere in the state." Michael J. Himowitz, "Loyola Ruling on Doctoral Program Due," *Baltimore Evening Sun*, June 3, 1977. Loyola backed down, however, and did not finally receive permission to offer a similar doctoral program until 2009, when it also changed its name from Loyola College to Loyola University.

26. *Baltimore Evening Sun*, June 3, 1977.

In American higher education, whether an institution offers doctoral degrees is a matter of considerable consequence. There is an important status distinction between doctoral and non-doctoral universities, although those categories are now a little blurred around the edges because many institutions have been given permission to offer boutique or very specialized doctorates. Further, almost every institution with more than 2,000 students now calls itself a university. Still, when a university offers a wide range of doctoral programs, it means it should have a faculty typically recruited from elite graduate schools who have the ability to win competitive research grants, to do original research themselves, to publish that research, and to train the next generation of researchers. Possessing research skills differentiate faculty who create new knowledge from those who just communicate existing knowledge. In a world in which new problems constantly demand attention of our brightest minds and in which innovation is the key to global competitiveness, research is ever more important to the public good.

For UMBC, preserving doctoral ambitions was crucial to its identity, even to its existence. Doctoral programs were a necessary component of UMBC's participation in the top-tier of the California-like tripartite structure for Maryland higher education that the Curlett Commission adopted in 1962. If UMBC had lost its opportunity to offer doctoral degrees in a number of fields, it would have negatively affected funding, teaching responsibilities, and prestige. Slowly, but surely, many of its most distinguished faculty, so carefully recruited, would have accepted job offers elsewhere. The ability to build doctoral programs was a promissory note to its faculty that UMBC and the UM system had to redeem.

A week after the State Board's decision turning down Loyola's education doctorate, Hugh Graham, then UMBC Dean of the Division of Social Sciences, wrote a widely circulated memorandum about what he saw as a crisis. He began:

> Our future as a university campus will hinge on whether, in the coming year, the State Board for Higher Education is allowed to produce a master plan that will endow Morgan State University with exclusionary jurisdiction over doctoral programs in the Baltimore metropolitan area's public sector of higher education.... it portends ... the destruction of UMBC as the university we have envisioned and worked so hard to build. Our strongest resource is a vigorous young faculty, recruited in a buyer's graduate market from the finest training institutions and hence largely free of the accumulation of tenured dead wood that is too characteristic of older institutions. If the SBHE's master plan a year hence reflects the current thrust of racial politics in Maryland, our best faculty members will leave us and the remainder will atrophy.[27]

Graham thought that the SBHE had failed to use any systematic data in considering doctoral development, so in his memorandum he compared the UMBC and

27. Hugh D. Graham, memorandum, "UMBC and Morgan State," June 15, 1977. UMBC historic documents collection, Special Collections, University of Maryland, Baltimore County.

Morgan faculty which were then about the same total size. There was, however, a striking difference in the credentials and productivity of the two faculties. By looking at Morgan's catalogue, Graham noted that 72 percent of its full-time faculty members had not attained the doctorate themselves and thus according to academic convention would not be able to train doctoral students. Even among those who did possess the doctorate, Graham found UMBC had by far more faculty members who had been trained at nationally ranked graduate programs. Finally, Graham compared the citations for UMBC faculty and Morgan faculty, using the Science and Social Science indices, for biology, chemistry, and psychology. Almost none of the Morgan faculty had such citations, while the UMBC faculty in those departments had 577.

Graham concluded:

> And I know full well that such comparisons are crude and will strike the public as elitist or racist. We must make them forcefully nonetheless, but within a constructive context that supports SBHE's commitment to control the proliferation of doctoral programs, bearing in mind that our intention has always been to press quite selectively for only those doctoral programs where our strengths coincide with unmet metropolitan and regional needs.[28]

To this remarkable memorandum, Louis D. Kaplan, UMBC's Interim Chancellor, replied:

> I am grateful to you for the very careful analysis you prepared of the Morgan State University faculty ... It is a very useful collection of facts and supports my contention that the decision of the State Board for Higher Education must be fought with every instrumentality at our command.
>
> I have written a letter to Dr. Elkins [UM chancellor] recently expressing my chagrin and anger at this [SBHE] announcement and urging that we take all necessary steps to oppose this decision. On the more positive side, and being realistic, I am suggesting that College Park should be required by the Board of Regents to cooperate fully with UMBC in developing, where possible, joint graduate programs.[29]

In the end, UM was able to preserve enough flexibility so that UMBC could continue to grow a very selective doctoral portfolio, even if there were struggles about almost every program.

Perhaps threatened by perceived external ignorance or even hostility about UMBC's intended role in Maryland education, in the fall of 1979 the campus community engaged in an examination of the institution's mission. The key mission sentence developed was:

> The University of Maryland Baltimore County views its mission within the University of Maryland system as fulfilling the need of the Greater Baltimore

28. Ibid.

29. Louis L. Kaplan, letter to Professor Hugh Graham, June 23, 1977. UMBC historic documents collection, Special Collections, University of Maryland, Baltimore County.

> area for a public research university constructed around a solid core of Liberal Arts, fully comparable in the quality of its instruction, research and public service to the most prestigious public and private universities.[30]

This rather assertive view of UMBC's mission would not have been written by the Pear Committee or agreed to by other Baltimore campuses or by the SBHE. Indeed, since in 1979 UMBC enrolled only full-time equivalent (FTE) 4,551 undergraduates and 118 graduate students, the mission statement was more a statement of aspiration than reality. At that time, its combined undergraduate SAT scores were 822 or more than 100 points below the national average. By that measure and several others, UMBC had a long way to go before "prestigious" or even "comparable in quality" could be attached to its name. Nevertheless, stretching to meet goals, almost regardless of the limited resources at hand or a favorable political environment, has always been a UMBC tradition.

Getting to an appropriate mission and accompanying program development were challenging goals. After the 1988 higher education reorganization, MHEC set about "sharpening" campus mission statements, meaning that for some campuses, whole curricular areas could be ruled as not tenable in the future or even in the present. Programs were on the chopping block. Chancellor Donald Langenberg and the USM Regents echoed the need for institutional focus. The UMS plan was called "Vision II."[31] In their view, faculty qualifications and initiative should defer to master planning in determining what programs campuses could offer the student market.

For two years, in 1992 and 1993, the Regents' announcements set off a furious political response from every campus and program to be affected.[32] Most campus administrators conceded in principle that some programs growing like barnacles on a ship should be pried loose, but just not the ones at their institutions. While it is useful to have periodic reviews of programs, it is difficult on campus to cut anything. Though the Regents' initiative could have created a useful review, there was deep suspicion that the selection of particular hit-list programs was motivated more by politics than rational decision making.[33]

All of the campuses, except College Park because it was the "flagship"[34] and University College because it was largely self-supporting, were scheduled to lose core lib-

---

30. UMBC, "Periodic Review Report to the Middle States Commission on Higher Education," October 1981, 13.

31. Board of Regents, University of Maryland System, "Achieving the Vision in Hard Times: II An Action Plan for Reinvesting the System's Resources," December 16, 1992.

32. The story of the fight over program elimination is from Thomas W. Waldron, "UM Regents agree on $9.4 million cuts: Pressure saves academic programs." *Baltimore Sun,* April 9, 1993.

33. See opinion piece by William G. Rothstein, UMBC Sociology Professor, "Regents at Play: Carving up Campuses," *Baltimore Sun,* January 3, 1993.

34. The Regents plan did call for some UMCP program cuts mostly in specialized graduate programs, not because they were duplicative, but because they had low productivity or were not very academically rigorous. Regents, "Achieving the Vision," December 11, 1992.

eral arts programs. In theory, programs with few graduates or that were superfluous to a campus mission were targeted. Ultimately, the Regents approved the elimination or revamping of about sixty programs in the System. Six history and chemistry majors at various UMS campuses were to be scrapped. Though a land grant university, UMES was slated to lose majors in Agriculture, Biology, and Environmental Science. At former teacher training institutions, at Coppin, early childhood education was to be cut, while at Bowie and Frostburg, art and music education were scheduled to be eliminated.

The Regents insisted the UMBC campus find $1,678,000 in budget savings or "re-deployment.[35] Consequently Vision II resulted in the elimination of Aerospace Engineering and Chemical Physics which were at the time inactive and an African-American Studies MA program enrolling only four to seven students. More painful was the elimination of the Accounting certificate program, which was thought to intrude upon the turf of other institutions. Its loss cost UMBC about 4000 credit hours of enrollment with the accompanying tuition dollars.[36] Also lost was the RN-BSN nursing program which enrolled about 273 students. It was consolidated and offered only at UMAB in 1996.[37]

There were four other threatened UMBC programs, including Theatre, Ethnomusicology, Ancient Studies, and Social Work.[38] The overarching concept was that the Towson campus should house the distinctive arts and humanities programs in the Baltimore region. UMBC's Theatre, despite very limited facilities, had developed a national reputation for innovation and excellence. That it could be considered for elimination was shocking to its supporters and its survival was a close call.[39] The smaller Ancient Studies program called on the Baltimore Greek-American community and its own alumni for support.

In considering the campus appeals, Chancellor Langenberg spared Theatre, Ancient Studies and Social Work at UMBC.[40] But the Ethnomusicology program, which had begun to offer its distinctive doctoral degrees, was terminated and it took a

---

35. Ibid. 26.

36. UMBC, "Institutional Performance and Accountability MHEC Report," October 18, 1996.

37. Report of the Enrollment Management Task Force, January 28, 2013,7. UMBC later responded by creating a Pre-Nursing program teaching 64 credit hours of Nursing prerequisites. http//www.umbc.edu/advising/Allied Health /nursing_path.html.

38. The UMBC social work program had 393 majors compared to Coppin's 88. The pass rate for UMBC students on the State of Maryland Licensing Examination was 95% compared to 59% pass rate for other in-state programs. See also Gust Mitchell, Chair of Social Work to UMBC Community," Social Work fact sheet," memorandum, December 28, 1992. There was some muttering about whether the UMBC students or faculty would be willing to transfer to Coppin and in the end there seemed little efficiency in such an experiment.

39. By 1991, the UMBC theatre had been invited four times to the American College Theater Festival at the Kennedy Center. The story of the development of UMBC Theatre is told in Chapter IX.

40. Freeman Hrabowski to the UMBC Community, Chancellor's Recommendations on UMBC's Program Appeals," April 8, 1993.

decade or more for music at UMBC to recover.[41] By 1993, the new UMBC mission statement was approved by both the Regents and MHEC and another round of campus competition was over.[42]

By the time of the 1996 UMBC Middle States Self-Study report, these conflicts between UMBC's aspirations and the constraints other political forces wished to place on the campus had been formally resolved, though of course the underlying tensions remained. UMBC's mission statement had evolved to encompass an aspiration "to be one of the best public research universities of its size in the country, to be a major center for intellectual activity in the metropolitan Baltimore region, and to create a campus community that finds enrichment in cultural and ethnic diversity."[43] UMBC could now say accurately that it was "a medium-sized public research university offering bachelors, masters and doctoral programs in the sciences and engineering, arts and humanities, and the social and behavioral sciences."[44] Two decades after the Pear Committee sought to restrict UMBC's academic programs, the campus encompassing twenty-seven departments offered twenty-six masters and nineteen doctoral degrees, reflected the range of curricular offerings of a full-fledged university. The 1996 Middle States Association's final evaluation gave UMBC an unconditional accreditation declaring that the campus "has achieved truly remarkable progress in becoming an excellent center of undergraduate education and is poised to become a center of graduate education and research of the first rank."[45]

D. Campus Closure

While the 1974 Pear Committee and the 1977 SBHE restrictions on doctoral programs would have permitted the campus to survive in a severely truncated manner, an attempt to convert the campus to other uses entirely, obviously, would have killed the University. In 1981, Sheldon Knorr, MHEC's Executive Director, floated a trial balloon, suggesting the campus should be closed and turned into an industrial park

---

41. President Hrabowski was confident that a possible merger between UMBC's distinctive music program and UMCP's more traditional Musicology program would preserve some of UMBC's initiatives in this area, but that was not to be. Ibid. Hrabowski's overall assessment of the "Vision II decision making process can be found in his May 20, 1993 Memorandum to the UMBC Community.

42. Kelley Slagel, "Hrabowski hopeful that programs can be saved," *The Retriever,* February 2, 1993. Over the years, the name of the campus newspaper has changed. From its first issue in 1967 to April 1972 and again from September 1975 to April 1977 it was simply "*The Retriever.*" From September 1972 to May 1975 and April 1977 to August 2002, it was "*The UMBC Retriever*" and from August 2002 to the present it has been "*The Retriever Weekly.*"

43. UMBC, "Middle States Self-Study Report, January 1996. 2.

44. Ibid.

45. Timeline-History of UMBC. Special Collections. University of Maryland Baltimore County. http://lib.guides.umbc.edu/content.php?pid=417297&sid=3411009.

and its funds split between College Park and Morgan State.[46] After the story was repeated in Baltimore and Washington newspapers, the UMBC community was in an uproar. According to the UMBC *Retriever*, one thousand students "packed into the quad ... chanting slogans and cheering speakers in the largest mass meeting in UMBC's recent history." (See photo section.) Student Government Association (SGA) President Scott Rifkin challenged the crowd, "Somebody is serious about this proposal, and, if we are not, we could be at the University of Baltimore next year."[47]

UM President John Toll came to the campus and called the story irresponsible. But he also acknowledged that the incident was "maximally damaging to UMBC, coming as it did in the middle of our recruitment season for faculty and students and on the morning of our defense of the university budget before the legislature."[48] Later, UMBC Chancellor John Dorsey held a large open meeting in the biggest campus dining room. Dorsey, not known as a fiery speaker, scorned Knorr's suggestion and then, in his best Churchillian rhetoric, dared industrial park proponents to try to implement their ridiculous idea because "we will fight them on the Beltway, we will fight them on Wilkens Avenue, we will fight them on the Loop Road...."[49]

The focus on closing UMBC created an opportunity to tout the campus' achievements to audiences that previously had paid little attention. Regent Samuel H. Hoover wrote a *Baltimore Sun* opinion piece pointing out UMBC's rising enrollment and SAT scores, increasing research grants, and improving record of graduate and professional school admissions.[50] Politically, Toll and the UM Regents were more than a match for Knorr and MHEC. Finally, cooler heads prevailed and the industrial park threat dissipated under even minimal examination.

Economic theory suggests that regulatory bodies often function to restrict new entrants into a market.[51] Certainly the residual resentment that statewide coordinating boards and their supporters held toward UMBC has never quite disappeared. The fact that UMBC had been created and usually protected and promoted by the Regents over coordinating board objections was not fully forgiven. In 2010, Joseph Popovich, former MHEC Director of Planning and Research (1976–1990) and later Morgan State Vice President for Planning and Information Technology, (1990–2009), wrote that "the tendency of campuses to resist coordination that acts in the public interest is clearly on display during the period of the UMBC decision." Popovich continued that:

---

46. Robert Benjamin, "Knorr preparing new plans for consolidating state's colleges," *Baltimore Sun*, February 24, 1981.

47. Sherri Conyers, "One thousand jam quad to defend campus, protest closing proposal," *The UMBC Retriever*, March 4, 1981. 1.

48. Mara Gormley, "Toll refutes stories of proposed closing," *The UMBC Retriever*, March 4, 1981. Knorr later insisted that he had adopted no proposal and that closing UMBC was only one of several alternatives to be examined.

49. Jim Milani remembered once obscure Baltimore reporter, Oprah Winfrey, covered the rally for WJZ TV. Email to the author, April 19, 2013.

50. Samuel H. Hoover, "UMBC Provides Excellent Quality," *Baltimore Sun*, January 5, 1980.

51. George J. Stigler, "The Theory of Economic Regulation," *The Bell Journal of Economics and Management Science*, 2, no. 1 (Spring 1971), 3–21.

> The creation of UMBC was to a large extent the result of (1) University [of Maryland's] ambition to be the dominant institution offering college-level work throughout the state, (2) its strong reluctance to coordinate with or be constrained by other agencies, and (3) its ability to build a coalition of legislators and others from jurisdictions that were potential sites for University campuses.... it became readily apparent during the UMBC debate that there was a critical need for improving planning and coordination at the state level.[52]

The implication from this veteran of MHEC and Morgan's politics was that the creation and/ or development of UMBC could have been stopped by an effective coordinating board. This viewpoint was reflected in decades of controversy between the Regents and various coordinating boards over UMBC plans.

Nevertheless, UMBC had survived attempts to limit its enrollment, restrict doctoral development, prune its undergraduate programs, and even to close it altogether. Sometimes it seemed UMBC was living up to Nietzschean adage "That which does not kill us makes us stronger." But near-death experiences are not good recruiting tools.

E. Desegregation politics[53]

In America, states are generally the masters of determining the mission, curriculum, and budgets of their public universities, with one exception. If one of the ten states that had previously segregated its campuses were involved, then the United States Department of Education's Office for Civil Rights (OCR), under the authority of Title VI of the Civil Rights Act of 1964, maintains oversight and can intervene in any decision OCR determines is not consistent with desegregation.

Maryland had been firmly rooted in the Old South tradition of segregation, while allocating vastly inferior resources to the institutions serving black undergraduates.[54] For black graduate and professional students, the state sometimes paid tuition to out-of-state schools. In 1934, the University of Maryland Law School was sued by Donald Murray who sought admission and was successfully represented by a young

---

52. Joseph Popovich, "Higher Education Development in the Absence of Statewide Planning: A Case Study of the Creation of the University of Maryland Baltimore County," unpublished paper, (Revised February 2, 2010), 4, now Pop. Ex 11, in the *Coalition for Equity and Excellence in Maryland Higher Education, Inc. v. Maryland Higher Education Commission, Civil no.MJG-06-2773,* case discussed in Chapter XII. Many Maryland observers would be puzzled at Popovich's assertion that coordinating board decisions are objective and rational, while other actors are political and would note the irony that a top Morgan administrator would so earnestly advocate coordinating boards when Morgan has so consistently prized its independence.

53. I am greatly indebted in this section to the research in Alexia Van Orden's UMBC Public Policy Ph.D. dissertation, "Desegregation of Higher Education in Maryland," forthcoming.

54. Callcott, *A History of the University of Maryland.* 306

Thurgood Marshall. Two decades later after Marshall won the landmark *Brown v. Board of Education*[55] decision 1954 decision, the Regents declared every campus of the university must be open to all Maryland residents without regard to race.

That formal policy change was achieved with admirable speed and clarity, but what did it mean practically for the Bowie, Coppin, Morgan and Maryland State (later UMES) campuses? After *Brown* declared racially segregated schools inherently unequal, what was to be the role of what became categorized as Historically Black Colleges and Universities (HBCUs)? All were then underfunded and unlikely to attract a sufficient number of non-African-American students to become less racially identifiable. While the federal courts had clarified the legal rules for the desegregation of K-12 schools in the three decades after *Brown*, the rules and even the goals in higher education desegregation were anything but clear. The remedies that sometimes integrated public schools, such as redrawing district lines, reassigning teachers and administrators, and busing students, were not as a practical matter available in higher education. Moreover, unlike K-12 where black elites, at least in the early years after *Brown*, supported vigorous measures to integrate schools, there was a split in their opinion regarding the best course of action in higher education. While the NAACP favored ending the racial identifiability of all educational institutions, many members of the black professional class had been educated in HBCUs or worked there and were understandably wary of what integration might mean for the missions and traditions of those schools.

The federal government responded by requiring all states with previously segregated higher education systems to produce an integration plan. But what should the specific policies be? In 1971, a group called the Black Coalition of the University of Maryland Campuses met with top officials of the U. S. Department of Health, Education and Welfare (HEW) to urge the Office of Civil Rights to reject the state's higher education integration plan and to intervene more vigorously to integrate the University's institutions.[56] Among the Coalition's recommendations were that the federal government insure and underwrite the mechanisms that will guarantee every high school graduate in this nation, who so desires, an undergraduate education. More specific to Maryland, the Coalition commended UMES for having a 26 percent white student body and 42 percent white faculty, but argued that integration efforts on the Eastern Shore campus be halted until the racial composition of students, faculty and administrators at the other UM campuses "be brought in line" with UMES. The

55. 347 U.S. 483 (1954).

56. The Coalition's UMBC representatives were Howard P. Rawlings (who chaired the group), Norman V. A. Reeves, and Reginald Lawrence. The seven person HEW team included Sydney Marland, Commissioner of Education and Stanley Pottinger, Director of the Office of Civil Rights. See Black Coalition of the University of Maryland Campuses, "Position Paper," May 6, 1971. UMBC historic documents collection, Special Collections, University of Maryland, Baltimore County. Rawlings later became a politician of considerable stature, serving from 1979 to 2003 in the Maryland House of Delegates and being named before his death from cancer in that year "National Policy Leader of the Year" by the National Association of the State School Boards. His daughter Stephanie Rawlings-Blake became the mayor of Baltimore in 2010.

Coalition also demanded that Wilson Elkins, university president and Charles P. McCormick, chairman of the Board of Regents "show cause" why they should not be removed and that three blacks be added to that Board.[57] The Coalition also thought that Chancellor Albin Kuhn should give up leading UMBC to focus on the downtown UM campus.[58] Finally, the Coalition urged that the federal government should "greatly increase financial aid for Black colleges and universities." The Coalition left the meeting feeling optimistic that "shortly the Federal Government will initiate selective withholding of federal funds—from a total of over $30,000,000—from the University of Maryland until a substantive desegregation plan is proposed."[59]

Such withholding of funds was not to be and instead OCR and the State and UM engaged in four decades of litigation and rhetorical exchanges that as Chapter XII describes is not over yet and has sometimes created collateral damage for UMBC.

Frustrated by the slow progress toward integration and the inferior status of HBCUs in the State, the NAACP sued the federal government to require more enforcement. In an early attempt to end this confusion, Maryland counter-sued the federal government in *Mandel v. United States Department of Health, Education and Welfare*.[60] The State was granted an injunction against further enforcement activity until OCR provided clearer definition about what was expected of states. That ruling forced OCR to issue its 1978 "Revised Criteria Specifying the Ingredients of Acceptable Plans to Desegregate State Systems of Higher Education," a document which created a long term adversarial relationship between the federal government and Maryland.[61]

Seven years after this legal confrontation, the State and the OCR entered into a "Partnership Agreement."[62] This plan required Maryland's traditionally white institutions (TWIs) to continue integration efforts by creating non-white enrollment goals as well as recruitment measures, retention efforts, and affirmative action plans. The State also agreed to enhance HBCUs so that they would be "comparable and competitive" to TWIs in terms of capital facilities, operating budgets, and new academic programs. UMBC was the only public institution in the state that had not been a part of the segregation era, but the Partnership still created problems for the new campus because of its emphasis on financial and program preferences for HBCUs. Whether such plans met constitutional requirements was not addressed by the Supreme Court until 1992.

---

57. "Negroes Demand Place on University Board," *Baltimore News American*, March 17, 1970.

58. The UMBC Black Caucus pointed out to the search committee seeking a successor to Kuhn that "in spite of its proximity to the urban area and its pronouncements of being an urban institution, the fact remains that UMBC serves a predominantly middle class white suburban population."

59. "Position Paper and outcomes," 2.

60. 411 F. Supp. 542 (D. MD. 1976).

61. U.S. Department of Education, Office for Civil Rights, 43 FR 6658. (February 12, 1978).

62. http://mhecmarylandgov/highered/ocrplan/index.asp#marylandreport.

In *United States v. Fordice,* the Court ended seven years of litigation in Mississippi by outlining the responsibility of state higher education officials in complying with the Equal Protection Clause.[63] During the evolution of the case, the black plaintiffs moved from an integration agenda to focusing on enhanced resources without requiring much institutional change for HBCUs. In a complex and somewhat ambiguous decision, the Court, while sympathetic to the plaintiffs' claim of past discriminatory treatment of HBCUs by Mississippi, recognized the State had now abandoned *de jure* segregation. The problem was what steps to take next. The Court affirmed the continuing goal of integration by stating two principles. First, the Court criticized the concept that the Fourteenth Amendment would be satisfied by turning HBCUs into "publicly financed, exclusively Black enclaves by private choice." Second, the Court said that to eliminate vestiges of discrimination, the state needed to consider closing or merging institutions, consider creating uniform admission standards, and consider eliminating duplication of similar programs in HBCUs and TWIs.[64]

Those policy alternatives proved no easier to implement in Mississippi[65] than they have been in Maryland. In 1997, Maryland formulated a new post-*Fordice* plan, *Access and Success: A Plan for Maryland's Historically Black Institutions.* The plan paid lip service to the theory that enhancing HBCUs would integrate them by creating attractive programs for non-black students. In fact, however, Maryland began to adopt what was a *de facto* separate, but more equal posture, toward its four historically black schools. Additional financial resources, buildings, and programs were made available to the HBCUs. Between FY 2002 and FY 2006, HBCUs received a 7 percent funding increase, while the total growth in the higher education budget was 1.4 percent. Although HBCUs enrolled fewer than 20 percent of the students among Maryland's four-year higher education institutions, they received 35 percent of all the capital expenditures during those years. Maryland General Funds appropriations per HBCU student in the 2006–2007 school year averaged $8,939, while TWIs averaged $6,177 per student.[66] In some cases the enhancement of the HBCUs may have been long overdue, but a decade later it was not evident that the "enhancement will lead to integration" theory was working. Enrollment at the four HBCUs was 86 percent African-American in 1997 and 87 percent in 2007.

---

63. 505 U.S. 717 (1992).

64. Twenty four years before the Supreme Court's *Fordice* decision, the Maryland Council for Higher Education declared, "The achievement of racial integration is an extraordinary problem and its solution will require the taking of extraordinary measures." The Council recommended that white and Negro colleges should recruit members of the opposite race as administrators, faculty, and students and that "The process of racial integration could be accelerated if some special programs, not duplicated in the white colleges, are developed in predominantly Negro institutions." Master Plan for Higher Education in the State of Maryland, Phase One.(Hereafter 1968 Master Plan November, 1968. Pages 3–27 (available UMBC library).

65. See *Ayers v. Musgrove,* 2002 U.S. Dist. Lexis 1973 (N.D. Miss. 2002).

66. Defense exhibit 25, from the *The Coalition for Equity and Excellence in Maryland Higher Education, Inc. et.al., v Maryland Higher Education Commission, Civil no.MSJ-06-2773.* January 3, 2012.

In Baltimore, where two historically black public institutions were a few miles from three historically white institutions and from UMBC which was created after the segregation era, there was bound to be conflict over budgets and program expansion. UMBC and Morgan found themselves pitted against each other several times in competition for History, Modern Languages, and Engineering programs.[67] Morgan successfully objected to a UMBC master's program in history, an education doctoral program at Towson and a graduate business program at UB.[68] In 2005, Towson and the University of Baltimore reached an agreement to extend UB's MBA program to the Towson campus. Morgan again objected, since its MBA enrollment had dropped from 263 students (including 54 whites) in 1975 to 28 students (no whites) in 2004.[69] MHEC approved the new joint program, but the legislative Black Caucus succeeded in getting a bill through the legislature that would have forced MHEC to reconsider and permitted public colleges to sue one another over programmatic conflicts. Governor Ehrlich vetoed that bill, but the State gave Morgan $800,000 to strengthen its MBA program.[70] Nevertheless, a private coalition of Morgan supporters filed a lawsuit that seemed interminably mired in a Baltimore federal court.[71] In 2009, Morgan opposed the creation of a UMUC on-line Ph.D. program for aspiring community college administrators, and the Maryland Higher Education Commission blocked UMUC from offering its program in-state.[72] It will not be the last such conflict.

Whatever the educational merits of the outcome of these conflicts, the State's decisions about program allocations illustrated once again Maryland's overall difficulty in working out a rational civil rights policy and the inconsistency of OCR's goals.

As SBHEs Sheldon Knorr pointed out, OCR proposed requiring an annual black enrollment increase in predominantly white schools, but:

> if more [black students] go to white schools the weaker the black schools become. Consequently, just a 1 percent increase at College Park would mean

67. A more detailed description of these program conflicts is told in Chapter VII.

68. Jason Song, "Morgan's President again fights building competitor: Opponent of Towson MBA has squelched 4 programs." *Baltimore Sun*, June 13, 2005.

69. Ibid.

70. Gail Dechter, "Opponents face off in MBA war: Bill aims to dismantle Towson's program in favor of Morgan State's," *Baltimore Sun*, March 27, 2007.

71. "Unfortunate Competition," *Baltimore Sun*, March 30, 2007. See also *The Coalition for Equity and Excellence in Maryland Higher Education, Inc. v. Maryland Higher Educational Commission*, Civil No. MJG-06-2773 discussed in Chapter XII. Ironically, one of the defendants in the lawsuit was MHEC executive Calvin W. Burnett, former Coppin President, who argued Maryland had fulfilled it civil rights obligation and observed sarcastically, though not originally: "One of the great things about this country is that you can file a suit against a ham sandwich...." Gail Dechter, "Suit Seeks to toss out joint program at UB, Towson," *Baltimore Sun*, October 14, 2006.

72. Jonathan Pitts and Childs Walker, "Morgan wins fight with UMUC over online program," *Baltimore Sun*, October 22, 2009.

> an additional 300 black students a year which is more than the entering class at three of the four black colleges. Our best guess is that their (OCR) formula would kill the black colleges.

From the SBHE's viewpoint, enrollment was a zero-sum game and increased integration at TWIs was a danger to HBCUs.[73] One solution would be to decrease the racial identifiability of all schools. But Andrew Billingsley, Morgan's president, was skeptical of that approach, preferring that his school remain identifiably black. He argued: "The test of desegregation is that every student be free to attend any school for which he qualifies—even if some schools are mostly white or mostly black.... The Constitution does not require salt and pepper, but open access."[74]

Maryland's four historically black institutions face a difficult dilemma sixty years after *Brown*. If they retain a race-based image, they may lessen their attraction to students and faculty of other races. Recruiting from a more limited pool, they may not be able to close the achievement gaps that now exist between them and their peers which have worked harder to shed racial identities and which generally now vigorously recruit the most talented African-American students, athletes, faculty, and administrators. Or HBCUs could take affirmative steps to become institutions where racial identity is a defining part of their history, but not a part of their present, and compete equally with other public institutions for the best available talent of all races. That course might risk alienating intensely loyal alumni and other supporters and distancing themselves from a precious tradition.[75] Nationally, it is a dilemma few HBCUs have solved.[76]

---

73. The SBHE wrote in 1981, "Historically black institutions could face a precarious future. They are facing increasingly intense competition from predominantly white institutions in recruiting black students. The enhancement of historically black colleges is an important step in maintaining and strengthening these institutions." There was no discussion about the ultimate educational goal these institutions would play in a desegregated era. SBHE," Recommendations Concerning the Future Governance of Public Higher Education in Maryland." (October, 1981)7.

74. The Knorr and Billingsley quotes are from, William Raspberry, "Engineering Desegregation," *Washington Post*, January 9, 1984. There is a different view of the constitutional obligation to desegregate. In 1968, the Supreme Court in *Green v. County School Board* (391 U.S.430, 1968) found that "freedom of choice" plans permitting students to enroll where they wished would not lead to integration. Consequently the Court approved desegregation plans which sought to abolish the racial identifiability of schools. In 1992, eight years after Billingsley spoke, the Supreme Court in *Fordice* first confronted the failure to desegregate higher education and it seemed to frown on policies aimed at preserving the racial identifiability of any institution.

75. Thomas W. Waldron, "Integration Case Raise Doubts about Future of Black Colleges," *Baltimore Sun*, April 25, 1993. The author quoted long time Maryland State Senator and Morgan graduate, Clarence Blount, reflecting on the *Fordice* case," It appears to me that this whole push for integration is wrong."

76. Speaking at national symposium on the future of HBCU's, North Carolina Central University, Chancellor Charlie Nelms of the host institution, declared: "If we're going to be around as a group of institutions 25 years from now, we have to change our narrative and our approach and be strategic." Eric Kelderman, "Black Colleges See a Need to Improve Their Image," *The Chronicle of Higher Education*," July 2, 2010. A18.

F. Merger Politics

As in other areas of non-profit and for-profit institutional life, the possibility of mergers to provide more services, increase visibility, and strengthen competitive advantages is sometimes considered in higher education. Such mergers are more difficult in academia, where there are often stronger institutional loyalties, more of a tradition of shared governance, and tenured faculty who can resist top-down mandates. Further defining measurable advantages may be more complex in educational mergers. In a dated, but still the only comprehensive examination of higher education mergers, John D. Millett concluded:

> The process of merger is not a simple procedure. The advantages of a merger must be clearly articulated and, even then, these advantages cannot be expected to be acceptable to all faculty members, to all students, to all alumni, to all staff. The limitations of merger are seldom expressed by advocates, and tend to be overstated by opponents.[77]

Nevertheless, there are some examples of successful higher education mergers creating major universities. Carnegie Mellon (1967) in Pittsburgh and Case Western Reserve (1967) in Cleveland are exemplary mergers among private universities. The closest role model for an attractive Baltimore merger was the 1982 merger of the arts and sciences campus University of Illinois at Chicago Circle with the University of Illinois Medical Center, 1.6 miles away, to form a new University of Illinois at Chicago (UIC). Five years after the merger, commenting on UIC's selection by the Carnegie Foundation as one of the nation's seventy "Research I" universities, the *Chicago Tribune* said: "Dismissed by many Chicagoans as a lowly commuter college for the sons and daughters of the urban proletariat, the University of Illinois Chicago has elbowed its way into the academic big-time."[78]

Interest in a merger of Baltimore universities had several motivations. By the 1980s, the decline of Baltimore City as the population, political, and economic hub of the state was apparent. Although the metropolitan area was growing, the City had seen a precipitous thirty year reduction of residents from 949,708 in 1950 to 786,775 in 1980. Political power had shifted to the suburban counties and Baltimore's manufacturing base had eroded substantially. In an enormous blow to civic pride, Mayflower moving vans carried away the beloved Colts to Indianapolis in 1984.

---

77. John D. Millett, *Mergers in Higher Education: An Analysis of Ten Case Studies*, (Washington, D.C: Academy for Educational Development, 1976), 58–59.

78. John Camper, "In academic circles, UIC is a big-league player," *Chicago Tribune,* August 30, 1987. Kim Glasscock, "UI-Chicago panelists give advice on merger pitfalls," https://www.cu.edu/sg/messages/3482.html. "The merger was opposed by the Champaign-Urbana faculty, opposed by the medical [faculty] senate, and generally supported by the faculty on the Circle campus.... [The new] UIC enjoys a far stronger political position with the state legislature which enables it to obtain a bigger piece of the state funding pie for higher education, and has also a stronger position within the UI system."

As Baltimore elites came together to reconstruct a new future for the City, they focused on a resource that could not be moved: its higher education institutions. All over the country new or enlarged public universities were seen as vehicles for economic development and civic pride. The Baltimore area certainly had its share of public campuses (Morgan, Towson, Coppin, University of Baltimore, UMAB, and UMBC), but all had either limited purposes and/or limited visibility. None seemed likely to secure the regional political support necessary to obtain the resources to grow to be Baltimore's academic candidate for national prominence.[79]

UMBC's leaders, of course, could dream that it could become Baltimore's university. In the early 1980s, the University made a very tentative gesture. Walter S. (Wally) Orlinsky, rising political star and then President of the City Council, was invited to the campus to be entertained at UMBC's best effort at imitating a state dinner.[80] After the requisite exchange of pleasantries and flatteries and the plates cleared, Orlinsky was asked directly what UMBC could do to help the City. Orlinsky tipped his chair back and grumbled: "Move! As long as you are in the suburbs, we are not interested."

Not deterred, UMBC's Policy Sciences Graduate Program reached an agreement with Mayor William Donald Schaefer to attend his cabinet meetings with the idea that such observation could lead to providing the city with internships and research opportunities for UMBC. After about a year of watching the fascinating, if stormy, Schaefer cabinet meetings, the collaboration amicably disintegrated. The City had no money for and not much interest in academic research, and the Policy Sciences program did not have the manpower or financial resources to sustain the effort.

The lesson learned was that, if UMBC wanted to play an expanded role in the region, it might need partners from other campuses. Academic mergers were not unknown in Maryland. The University of Maryland itself was the result of the loose confederation in 1920 of the City campus's professional schools and the College Park campus. Loyola acquired Mount Saint Agnes College in 1971, when the latter encountered financial problems. The modern University of Baltimore is the result of a merger of Eastern College and the Mount Vernon School of Law in 1970 with the addition of the Baltimore College of Commerce in 1973. Under strong pressure from the Governor William Donald Schaefer, the governance systems of the five UM campuses and the six state college campuses were merged in 1988 to form a single University of Maryland System, then the twelfth largest University system in the country.[81]

---

79. During this period, the College Park campus was becoming a nationally recognized university, but to many Baltimoreans UMCP was really a Washington area institution and pinning Baltimore's aspirations on that campus was like asking them to transfer their affection to the Redskins. "Not gonna happen, Hon!"

80. The author attended the dinner. Orlinsky served as City Council President from 1971 to 1982. He resigned that post in a bribery scandal and was eventually pardoned by President Bill Clinton. *New York Times*, obituary, February 25, 2002.

81. Sharon Hudgins, *Never an Ivory Tower: University of Maryland University College, the First 50 Years* (Adelphi: University College, 2000), 7.

Still Baltimore's thirst to have its own great public university was not quenched. In 1969, Morgan President Martin D. Jenkins nominated his campus to play the *great university* role as a step toward rejuvenating the City because Morgan "is doing more than any other college or university in meeting urban needs."[82] This proposal was formally submitted in January 1969 to both the Board of Trustees of the State Colleges and the Maryland Council on Higher Education. An ad hoc MCHE committee urged that Morgan "be developed as a racially integrated, urban oriented university," but it rejected Morgan's specific plan and called instead for the creation of a State University of Metropolitan Baltimore (SUMBA) including Morgan, Coppin, Towson and UMBC.[83] The Council report also recommended eliminating the tripartite structure and moving toward a two state university system with dual flagships such as in Michigan or Iowa.[84] Since the tripartite system had just become a part of the state higher education master plan eight months earlier, the ad hoc committee's criticism may be regarded as a last-ditch rearguard action. When the Council held a hearing on its SUMBA proposal, twenty-four of the twenty-six speakers were opposed, including delegations of African-American students, administrators, and community organizations, as well as UM officials. Chancellor Albin O. Kuhn, at that time Chancellor of both UM's Baltimore campuses, argued that the tripartite system was just beginning to show its effectiveness and that a second university system would be costly and lead to unnecessary duplication and inefficiencies. He concluded that the growth of UMBC clearly showed that UM "is and will be increasingly associated with metropolitan Baltimore."[85]

As Chancellor Kuhn's statement reflects, UMBC's leadership at that time was content to accept its privileged status as a UM campus under the protection of the tripartite system. Gradually, however, some began to see that arrangement as more stifling than protective because there was little likelihood that the Baltimore County campus would ever have equal status and, more important, equal funding with the powerful College Park and Baltimore City campuses. Moreover, there was a continuing feeling in many quarters that Baltimore was not well served by the fragmentation and lack of coordination of higher education institutions in the region.

---

82. Morgan State College, *The President's Newsletter*, No.8 (May 1969)1. The urban focus was defined as recruiting more disadvantaged student, an adequate compensatory [remedial] program, increased services to the inner city, research on urban problems and enriching cultural activities.

83. The Council did not explain its decision, but in the 1969–70 academic year, only 86 (34 percent) of the 250 full-time Morgan faculty had doctorates. Kahn, "Universities and Urban Affairs,"126. A decade later, that figure had risen to 46 percent, but it was still the third lowest in the state. In comparison, 91 percent of UMBC's faculty had earned doctorate while at UB it was 63 percent and Towson 58 percent. So there may have been doubts in the Council about Morgan's readiness to assume the role of "the" Baltimore university. SBHE Consolidated budget FY 1982, Moos, *The Post Land Grant University: the University of Maryland Report.* 180.

84. Kahn, "Universities and Urban Affairs,"115–116.

85. Statement by Dr. Albin O. Kuhn, Chancellor of the Baltimore Campuses, August 1, 1969.

A year after John Sampson Toll became President in 1978 of what was then a four-campus UM system, he received a $190,000 grant from the Carnegie Corporation of New York to create a strategic planning project for the University. Malcolm Moos, former professor of political science at Johns Hopkins and later President of the University of Minnesota, directed the project. It was an extensive and unprecedented multi-task force effort for Maryland[86] and resulted in the publication of a 295 page book, *The Post Land Grant University: the University of Maryland Report.* In a chapter, called "The Curious Case of Baltimore," the author began with a powerful indictment of the lack of educational achievement among City residents. According to Moos, among seven comparable cities, despite all of the available local institutions, Baltimore had the lowest percentage of traditional college age (20–24) students attending college and the second lowest percentage of those completing college.[87] The report concluded, that "Maryland's greatest city has never had a high quality [public] undergraduate institution in its midst,"[88] and there was a particular shortage of public graduate school opportunities and a science and technology gap overall in educational offerings. Given that assessment, not surprisingly, the report recommended that "the University of Maryland should create a university center similar to that in College Park for the Baltimore area."[89] To achieve that goal, the report urged that UMBC, UMAB, and the University of Baltimore be merged or confederated to form a new University of Maryland, Baltimore. The report pointed to a parallel institutional arrangement at Johns Hopkins, where the Homewood campus is a few miles from the medical school-hospital complex, its School of Advanced International Studies is in Washington, and its huge Applied Physics Laboratory is in suburban Howard County.

At UMBC, the Moos report received substantial interest. It was, after all, the product of the University's own planning process. The governance details were unclear, but UMBC's role as the major source of undergraduate students as well as arts and science graduate programs in the Baltimore area was assured in the proposed merged institution. It certainly would be attractive to be a cornerstone of "a first-rate public research university in the Baltimore area"[90] on par with College Park at the other end of the Baltimore-Washington corridor, as the report recommended.

The merger proposal was only one of the sixty-four recommendations in the Moos report. Not surprisingly, most were never implemented, but there was considerable attention paid to the merger concept. Governor Harry Hughes and the legislature

86. UMBC faculty Gilbert Austin (education) and Hugh Graham (history) played prominent roles in the task forces.

87. Malcolm Moos, *The Post Land Grant University: the University of Maryland Report,* 1981, 143.

88. Ibid., 146. The report acknowledged that Johns Hopkins was the exception in terms of quality, but noted that the school was small and enrolled numerous out-of-state students.

89. Ibid., 148.

90. Ibid., 159.

each appointed a commission to examine four scenarios: (1) retention of the status quo; (2) elevation of UMBC to become the major Baltimore research university; (3) creation of a single governing authority for all Baltimore-area public institutions that would coordinate programs and emerge as an eventual rival to College Park; and (4) creation of a single governing board for the UM campuses and state colleges. After intense negotiations, one educator was willing to say anonymously, "The potential for a cohesive university system has never been so great. We might not only create a great university in Baltimore, we might do it with a minimum of bloodshed."[91] Governor Hughes, however, did not see it that way and reflecting on what he called "a complete absence of consensus," opted for the status quo.[92]

The dream of a great Baltimore university would not go away. In 1982, *Baltimore Magazine* published an extensive article titled "Missing: Baltimore's Great University."[93] Its clever graphic introduction showed the mascots of College Park, Towson, University of Baltimore, Morgan, and UMBC in adversarial poses behind a conference table. The piece began by quoting Toll's belief that UMBC could become Baltimore's great university and then continued with the objections of other area campuses asserting that alternative would short-change their potential. The article was replete with phrases such as "snarled in controversy," "turf wars, "duplication of ambition," and "fostering waste" to describe higher education in Baltimore. Despite providing a very insightful account of the conflict, the author, David Simon, then a senior at College Park, offered no solutions.[94]

The *Baltimore Sun's* diagnosis of the problem was much the same, calling the status quo "a feudal system of competing educational ambitions" or "the Higher Education mess."[95] Beginning in 1978, the *Sun* ran an eight-part editorial series repeatedly highlighting the issue.

One of its fusillades declared:

> What should burn the conscience of Governor-elect Hughes and the Commissioner of Higher Education, is that the Baltimore region has four public universities and a State college dedicated to undergraduate education, but there is not a the equivalent of one first class urban university among them. Metropolitan Baltimore, the urban heart of Maryland, needs, deserves, and must have at least the Baltimore equivalent of College Park, centrally located and offering a full range of unified educational services. The State Board

---

91. The politics surrounding this issue are well described in David Simon's article, "Missing: Baltimore's Great University," *Baltimore Magazine*, September 1982, 101 ff.

92. Ibid. After his election, Hughes had seemed committed to acting on restructuring Baltimore higher education.

93. Ibid.

94. Mr. Simon continued his gritty analysis of Baltimore's problems by becoming the writer and producer of the much praised TV series "The Wire," and "Homicide," which focus on crime, drugs, and corruption in Charm City.

95. *Baltimore Sun*, "Higher Education Mess (cont.)," February 15, 1978.

> should be given money and marching orders to close down, merge, pair, or do whatever else is necessary to give Baltimore a comprehensive quality university system.[96]

State Commissioner of Higher Education Sheldon Knorr, responded by making several recommendations to the SBHE, among them merging UMBC, the University of Baltimore and Morgan State University. The blowback was ferocious. In a hearing on February 13, 1980 in a downtown Baltimore hotel, over 900 people showed up and sixty testified in the day-long proceedings. There was little support and Morgan protectors of that University's autonomy were particularly vociferous in their objections. After that experience, SBHE board member felt "mistreated, misunderstood, physically threatened and angry."[97] That merger proposal was dead.

Almost a decade later, the *Sun* adopted the findings of a 1985 Goldseker Foundation report by Peter L. Szanton called "Baltimore 2000: A Choice of Futures." He found that not only was Baltimore a net exporter of talented youth, black and white, but that it lacked high technology programs to attract new industry and had no high-powered business school. Szanton's assessment was harsh claiming that Baltimore higher education was an "overbuilt and under ambitious conglomeration of public colleges and universities that lack distinction." He concluded soberly:

> The incentive to go on as before will be strong. Business and professional leaders will need to press the case that in the economy of the future wealth will be based on knowledge and new wealth on new knowledge. The governor ... will have to be willing to set a politically difficult course—strengthen the region's stronger institutions, especially in Baltimore and allowing weak or redundant schools to close.[98]

Szanton did not mention it, but in 1985 the UM Regents had taken a tentative step toward creating a major university in Baltimore by adopting the "two principal centers" model (College Park and Baltimore) and by merging the graduate and research functions of the two UM Baltimore campuses.[99] The *Sun* applauded the move declaring, "What may emerge is a major public, research-oriented graduate program

---

96. As quoted by Sumler. "Life Cycle," 41–42. Sumler's view of the problem was titled, "Baltimore: The Mother of All Higher Education Headaches." 39.

97. A description of this hearing can be found in Sumler, 44–45.

98. Peter L. Szanton, "Baltimore 2000: A Choice of Futures," (Goldseker Foundation, 1985). 33. Szanton, the founding President of the New York City RAND Institute, also focused on failures in the City's public schools (K-12) asking whether that system should be "blown up." The report expressed the anxiety of Baltimore's leadership for the city's future. While Szanton noted the development of the Inner Harbor and some other neighborhoods and the possibility of future successes, he also warned that by 2000 the City may "have been gutted—industry gone to Korea and Brazil, port traffic to Norfolk, and white collar jobs to the counties in Delaware and the Washington suburbs," Szanton, iii.

99. John W. Jeffries, President, Faculty Senate to John W. Dorsey Chancellor, "Report of the Principal Centers Task Force on the Consolidation of the UMAB and UMBC Graduate Schools, December 23, 1983. President's Office records, University Archives, Special Collections, University of Maryland, Baltimore County.

that will rival UM's dominant College Park campus at the other end of the Baltimore-Washington corridor."[100]

The two-principal centers model and the University of Maryland Graduate School Baltimore (UMGSB) graduate school merger were important steps for UMBC. The model signified that the Regents, at least, had increased their commitment to Baltimore and recognized that UMBC was an important partner in this activity. The merger strengthened the then small graduate enterprise at UMBC, as well as the graduate programs at UMAB which were overshadowed by the powerful professional schools, each of which had its own very autonomous Dean. On paper, the new UMGSB had 700 faculty, 85 graduate degree programs (including 38 at the Ph.D. level) and a research and training budget of over $40 million, all connected by a single Vice Chancellor and a seventeen-minute shuttle bus ride.[101] President John Toll wrote:

> One of the most successful developments in our educational system in the past 10 years was the merger in 1983 of our graduate schools at the Baltimore and Baltimore County campuses. That union has produced exactly the types of joint programs and faculty exchanges that we hope will become common as faculty throughout the new Maryland system begin working together to explore matters of mutual interest.[102]

There were actual cooperative programs (Center for Drugs and Public Policy, Master of Policy Sciences/J.D. program with the Maryland Law School, etc.), but each campus retained its own Chancellor and the graduate programs on neither campus were the center of gravity. UMGSB was essentially an administrative structure intended to facilitate some current and future cooperation, but it did not command deep loyalties, have much visibility or give Baltimore the major university it coveted.[103]

Under Governor Hughes, the Commission for Excellence in Higher Education (the Hoblitzell Commission named after its chairman Alan P. Hoblitzell, a Baltimore banker) issued an extensive report with forty-two recommendations in January 1987.[104] In this report UMBC was barely mentioned, UMGSB, not at all, and Balti-

---

100. "A Step toward Consolidation," *Baltimore Sun*, March 23, 1984.

101. Statistics are from Hugh Davis Graham and George R. La Noue, "The case for a 3-campus merger in the Baltimore area," *Baltimore Sun*, July 26, 1987. To make the UMGSB merger work, Graham gave up his UMBC Graduate School Deanship so that Barbara Hansen from UMAB could be the first UMGSB Vice Chancellor of Graduate Studies and Research.

102. John S. Toll, "President's Report 1987–88. UMBC historic documents collection, Special Collections, University of Maryland, Baltimore County. 3.

103. Nor did UMGSB mitigate the continuing rivalry between the Baltimore campuses and College Park. Reviewing a plan by the USM administration to improve graduate education in Baltimore, Regent Albert N. Whiting called the plan "amorphous" and "I don't see doctorates that are different from doctorates offered at College Park." Regent Margaret Alton, advised the University's Baltimore doctoral plans to be narrow. "Pick two," she urged. *Baltimore Sun,* December 1, 1989.

104. William Douglas, "Big changes urged for college system," *Baltimore Evening Sun*, January 7, 1987. A detailed view of an SBHE official on the politics of this era of governance change can be found in Sumler, "Life Cycle," 103–129. He summarized his opinion by stating, "After two years of constant turmoil over re-organization, the Maryland higher education community

more's higher education problems were discussed in the vaguest terms. The report focused on "enhancing" the College Park campus. It called that campus the flagship or keystone of Maryland higher education and offered it new funding, on the condition that it would cut its undergraduate enrollment by twenty percent to create greater selectivity.

There was, however, an important governance trade-off. The report urged creating a more powerful new coordinating agency, the Maryland Higher Education Commission (MHEC) to replace the State Board for Higher Education (SBHE).[105] According to the Hoblitzell recommendations, MHEC would have the power to transfer, modify or abolish existing academic programs, to create accountability guidelines, campus admissions requirements, to approve campus budgets, and to take over campus government of an institution "which fails to meet its mission."[106] That proposed authority, of course, threatened all existing governing bodies and campus stakeholders. For the UM Regents, it was a direct assault on their authority and the two-principal centers model, but the carrots being offered College Park were designed to make the plan difficult to oppose. The report was issued just as Governor Hughes left office.

The *Sun* and City leaders kept up a drum beat demanding state government give Baltimore a great public research university. After a decade of editorial writing, in 1987, the *Sun* called on newly-elected Governor William Donald Schaefer to take charge and make the necessary changes.[107] "Do it now Don" did seem likely to act, and there were two major options considered: (1) a Baltimore merger and/or (2) a consolidation of the governance of all state campuses under a single governance board as the Hoblitzell Commission had urged. Hedging their bets, all the public campus heads signed a letter supporting a draft plan similar to the Commission recommendations, while increasing behind-the-scenes lobbying to protect their divergent interests.

A group of 200 members of the American Association of University Professors, including faculty from Towson, University of Baltimore, Coppin, Frostburg, and Salisbury complained that the governance proposal would undermine academic freedom in the form of faculty participation in campus governance and that enhancing College Park would be at the expense of other campuses.[108] Morgan, speaking through retired Congressmen Parren J. Mitchell, declared: "For 30 years, there have been repeated attempts to rob Morgan of its autonomy.... We must start mobilizing and make sure

---

woke on July 1, 1988, with a new higher education system that was not one that anyone had desired." 129

105. For a discussion of state attempts to coordinate higher education, see Hugh Davis Graham, "Structure and Governance in Higher Education: Historical and Comparative Analysis in State Policy," *Journal of Policy History*, 1 (Winter 1989), 80–107.

106. Commission for Excellence in Higher Education, January 1986, page.v. UMBC historic documents collection. Special Collections. University of Maryland, Baltimore County.

107. *Sun*, "Higher Education Mess (cont.)," February 15, 1987.

108. Amy Goldstein, "Reforms jeopardizes state colleges, professors charge," *Baltimore Sun*, May 22, 1987.

we save Morgan again."[109] St. Mary's also objected, saying it had attracted high quality people to its Board and it didn't want to share their attention with twelve other institutions.[110] UM President John Toll favored a consolidated board, but nevertheless wrote his Board of Regents voicing concerns about leveling down the UM campuses.[111] Later, despite the financial inducements being offered their campus, thirteen College Park Deans signed a memo (probably leaked to the press) to their campus Chancellor John Slaughter, stating "We remain un-convinced that a consolidated board would better serve the interests of the College Park campus."[112]

For UMBC the political situation was dire. Its campus administrators could not oppose enhancing College Park. They could not oppose President Toll and the UM Regents who favored a new superboard, if they could control it. Nobody wanted to oppose Governor Schaefer who was determined to do something. But the prospect of being one of thirteen campuses under an all-powerful Board of uncertain friendliness was daunting. UMBC needed program growth. If that expansion could be blunted within the superboard by College Park at one end of the central Maryland region or other Baltimore colleges at the other end, the Catonsville campus might never reach its potential.

In response, UMBC faculty began to organize to protect their interests and to express ideas its administrators could not. It was one of those unusual moments when the security to take risky positions protected by faculty tenure clearly improved the public debate. For example, Hugh Davis Graham, UMBC's distinguished historian of educational and civil rights policy and former graduate dean, wrote a long opinion piece in the *Sun* criticizing the idea of a superboard. He argued it represented a misplaced belief that "a strong central board and its executive will enforce efficiency and economy though a kind of corporate model of specializations like Ford and IBM."[113]

As momentum toward the superboard slowed, Lt. Governor Melvin Steinberg resuscitated the Moos proposal for a three-campus (UMAB, UMBC and UB) merger, proclaiming that such a consolidation "would give Baltimore a strong hub of re-

---

109. Amy Goldstein, "Blacks insist on autonomy for Morgan," *Baltimore Sun*, September, 19, 1987. See also "Position Paper of the Task Force on Reform of Higher Education in Maryland," adopted by the Executive Committee of the Baltimore Branch of the NAACP. October 19, 1987, opposing the superboard and stating, "Graduates of the historically black institutions will not stand by idly and allow the destruction of their fore parents." UMBC historic documents, Special Collections, University of Maryland, Baltimore County.

110. Ibid.

111. Joan Jacobson, "Heads of Maryland's public colleges urge 'superboard," *Baltimore Evening Sun*, July 7, 1987.

112. Joan Jacobson, "13 UM Deans rap centralized system," *Baltimore Evening Sun*, October 30, 1987.

113. Hugh Davis Graham, "Be wary, Maryland officials, of the North Carolina 'model." *Baltimore Evening Sun*, July 23, 1987. See also Graham, "We Don't Need Superboards: It's Competition that has made U.S. Higher Education Great," *The Chronicle of Higher Education,* November 4, 1987.

search, graduate education and economic-development activity."[114] It would also eliminate duplicate programs, and he suggested combining the Maryland and Baltimore law schools, located about twenty blocks apart. The *Sun* quickly provided support with an editorial, "Three-Campus Powerhouse."[115] The newspaper said that concept would "give the city for the first time in its history a quality comprehensive public university." The editorial praised UMBC for its "nationally recognized research in biological sciences" and urged that it expand engineering to meet the needs of local firms. The paper agreed that the two law schools should be merged and surprisingly proposed that College Park's School of Architecture be moved to UMBC. While this desk chair journalistic over reaching created new enemies for the proposal, the *Sun* glowed:

> A tri-campus University of Maryland Baltimore would energize the local education scene. It would give this city's citizens the kind of prestigious degree-granting public university that they deserve. It would serve to muster the kind of statewide support for higher education that has long been missing, to the detriment of all institutions, including College Park. Maryland only ranks 37th among the states in education aid relative to per capita wealth.[116]

Four days later, the *Sun* published a 1,000 word article by UMBC faculty Hugh Graham and George La Noue analyzing and extolling the virtues of the three-campus merger. They pointed out that according to a number of higher education measures Maryland was behind other states. For example, in doctoral programs offered at public universities, Maryland ranked thirty-fifth. The merged university would have about 18,000 students (36 percent graduate and professional) taught by over 1100 faculty. It would possess a number of amenities currently missing at UMAB and UB, including student housing, Division I athletics, a symphony orchestra, and an award-winning theatrical program. Most promising were the academic synergies that could be achieved in the merged university's 66 academic programs in schools of arts and sciences, business, dentistry, engineering, law, medicine, nursing, pharmacy and social work and community planning. The professors concluded:

> Given the past characterized by too many under-financed public campuses jostling inconclusively for advantage, and a probable future of more of the

---

114. Amy Goldstein, "Steinberg seeks Baltimore-area college merger," *Baltimore Sun*, July 21, 1987. Steinberg was a Baltimore native and UB graduate. He served twenty years in the state Senate and twice as Lt. Governor under Schaefer. He ran for Governor himself in 1994, only to lose to Parris Glendening, who had been a College Park professor. Steinberg and Schaefer had some substantive disagreement about statewide consolidation, until the Governor reminded the Lt. Governor who was in charge. Joan Jacobson, "Schaefer at odds with Steinberg over higher education plan." *The Baltimore Evening Sun*, December 24, 1987. Two weeks later, the two had worked out their differences and Steinberg steered the restructuring though the legislature with a promise of $50 million more funding for higher education. Joan Jacobson and Thomas W. Waldron, "Compromise quietly worked out on college 'superboard,'" *Baltimore Evening Sun*, January 8, 1988.

115. *Baltimore Sun*, July 22, 1987.

116. Ibid.

same, the Baltimore region has a rare but difficult shot at creating a truly excellent research university its future demands.[117]

In September, 1987, Blair Lee IV, chief lobbyist for Montgomery County in Annapolis, put in hyperbolic print what many calmer heads in the Washington area thought privately about a three-campus Baltimore merger. His *Washington Post* opinion piece titled, "The College Park Campus is Under Siege: They want to move it to Baltimore," began by stating:

> The issue is economic development, jobs, and money. Research universities are the hottest new item in everyone's economic development strategy. They generate the ideas, intellectual energy, and talented workers that spawn the companies of the future. Baltimore's city fathers want a major research campus, like College Park's, to stimulate the city's growth. But how can the university serve Baltimore if it is sitting in College Park? The solution is simple: move it.[118]

Lee accused Governor Schaefer of having "his heart and home remain in the city. His appointments and programs primarily benefit Baltimore." The *Sun's* proposed relocation of the College Park's architecture school to UMBC (which UMBC never advocated) drew Lee's special scorn. He proclaimed:

> Ironically, Baltimore already has an architectural school at Morgan State University. But Baltimore's "Raiders of the Lost Arch" would rather hijack College Park's school than help build a program at a predominantly black local university.[119]

Lee concluded:

> Schaefer and Steinberg, Baltimore's fast talking tin men, are peddling their university "reform" as harmless and cost-effective. "We will not jeopardize

117. Graham and La Noue, "The Case for a 3-Campus Merger in the Baltimore Area." *Baltimore Sun*, July 26, 1987. The UMBC faculty authors prudently did not comment on the implications of the three-campus merger for Morgan State, but Maryland Delegate, Lawrence A. LaMotte, who had connections to UMBC, wrote that public research universities need certain ingredients to be successful competitors for talent and grant competition. These characteristics included faculty recruited from leading universities and laboratories, teaching loads that encourage faculty to take on new research and the risks accompanying it, and students with the preparation and career goals to make a research university education appropriate for them. Delegate LaMotte, concluded, "Despite its splendid traditions, Morgan State meets none of those criteria.... to tie the economic development of the Baltimore region to Morgan would be an unwise choice for either black or white citizens. We can't wait 25 years. We need to be as competitive as possible." LaMotte, "The college combination that would work in Baltimore," *Baltimore Evening Sun*, January 7, 1988, A21.

118. *Washington Post*, September 13, 1987. See also UMBC's provost, Adam Yarmolinsky response letter titled "Crying Wolf Over College Park." He rebutted specific points and concluded: "Let me assure Blair Lee that the College Park Terrapins and the UMBC Retrievers can and do peacefully coexist, even when some outsiders are crying wolf." *Washington Post*, September 27, 1987. See also, Hugh Graham's opinion piece "Educational monopolies are not the only way to excellence for universities," *Baltimore Sun*, October 11, 1987.

119. Actually Morgan's Institute of Architecture and Planning did not become a School until 2008, though the program had been accredited before then.

> any campus in this state. It will be a win, win situation." But D.C. area leaders smell a rat.

Baltimore versus Washington, a newspaper war, accusations of regional favoritism, political rivalries, and a little race baiting thrown in were not quite the right ingredients for a creating a rational educational outcome.

When the UMBC Faculty Senate reconvened in the fall of 1987, Chancellor Michael Hooker announced that the Governor had endorsed the consolidated board, but that, while Schaefer thought a Baltimore merger a "good idea," it would be too much to expect such a dramatic change in the same year as the enactment of the new board. Not coincidentally, the Governor had acknowledged that Maryland higher education was underfunded and said a twenty percent a year increase for five years was "reasonable." Money is the great lubricant of politics and the projected doubling of institutional funding assuaged a lot of wounds and undermined opposition.

At the UMBC Senate meeting, the faculty Ad Hoc Committee on the Reorganization of Higher Education reported that it had received a grant from the Abell Foundation[120] to sponsor a series of public forums on the question of a future Baltimore merger.[121] The Senate then reaffirmed its commitment to the two principal centers concept by an almost unanimous vote.[122]

With Abell money and the editorial approval of the *Sun*,[123] a faculty committee composed of three members from UB, UMB, and UMBC met to plan merger discussions and to invite speakers to a series of public forums on the issue. Then on September 27, 1987, Lieutenant Governor Steinberg dramatically announced that he

---

120. The Foundation, started with funding proceeds when the *Sun* was sold to the Times-Mirror Corporation, was solidly committed to the idea merging Baltimore campuses. Robert C Embry, Jr., its president, co-authored an article with prominent attorney Russell T. Baker, Jr. in the *Sun's* Maryland High-Tech-VIII series titled: "An Outstanding Public University," *Baltimore Sun*, December 20, 1987. The authors stated, "The goal should be a Baltimore-based university that would be in the Carnegie Foundation's 'Research I' class of elite universities that receive substantial federal research and development grants and award at least 50 Ph.D. degrees.... A great public university of this nature is essential not just to Baltimore city's future—it is critical to the entire area from Hunt Valley to Glen Burnie, from Columbia to Dundalk. It would securely anchor the northern end of the Baltimore-Washington region's great high tech growth. Fifteen years later, on its own UMBC received $60 million dollars in federal funding and awarded 50 Ph.D.s, but as the Carnegie Foundation had raised the bar, the top research designation has eluded the campus.

121. The first of those public forums featured George Keller, who had served as *de facto* chief of staff for President Johnny Toll, and was a principal researcher on the Moos report. Mr. Keller was blunt calling Baltimore higher education "sublime mediocrity," and blasting the superboard proposal as a superficial fix. "The latest report," Keller opined, "deals with the controlling boards as if Baltimore could be reformed by repositioning docks and wharves. The wharves belong to another era." Keller favored merging UB, UMAB, and UMBC and merging Coppin with Morgan as well, noting that Morgan's SAT scores were then lower than Coppin. Joan Jacobson, "'Sublime mediocrity' rules here, educators told," *Baltimore Evening Sun*, October 30, 1987.

122. UMBC Faculty Senate minutes, September 15, 1987. UMBC historic documents, Special Collections, University of Maryland, Baltimore County.

123. "Higher Educational Reform," *Baltimore Sun*, September 21, 1987.

was against the proposed consolidated board.[124] Two weeks later, President Toll came to UMBC to meet with its faculty committee on statewide reorganization, and in a follow up letter he affirmed the idea of a single consolidated graduate school built on the UMGSB framework, but including faculty from other Baltimore campuses. He also restated that the University would have two principal centers in College Park and in Baltimore.[125] UMBC faculty tried to reach out to their peers at College Park, arguing that a strong research university in Baltimore would increase funding for both campuses,[126] but UMCP's Chancellor John Slaughter testified before the Steinberg committee that Maryland did not need another research university besides College Park.[127]

In the meantime, Chancellor Michael Hooker and UMBC faculty leaders tried to fashion a strategy to secure campus interests. In a February 9, 1988 Faculty Senate meeting, the Chancellor confessed his personal dilemma:

> Obviously you want higher education to be as free from politics as is possible ... Clearly it is an issue for me right now because I am being expected to do something that by disposition I would just as soon not do. Obviously, I am between a rock and a hard place. I'm obligated to do what I am told to by my boss. My boss is the Governor. After that, the Board of Regents, and the President [John S. Toll]. And so I will do what I'm told to do.[128]

A UMBC faculty member commented:

> That is the first time I've heard him (Hooker) express that the chief administrator of this university works directly for the Governor [who] may tell him what to testify about. It raises a question about the confidence the public can place in what is being said.... if the governor not only writes the legislation, but can dictate the testimony of the educational experts.[129]

---

124. Amy Goldstein, "Steinberg opposes 1 board for colleges," *Baltimore Sun*, September 27, 1987.

125. Letter from John S. Toll to UMBC Faculty Committee on Statewide Reorganization, October 8, 1987. (UMBC historic documents, Special Collections) Committee members were William T. Brown (theater), Robert P. Burchard, (biology) Hugh D. Graham,* (history) George R. La Noue,*(political science and policy sciences), Angela Moorjani (French), and Philip G. Sokolove* (biology). * indicates also a member of the Baltimore Intercampus Committee. The UMAB representatives to the intercampus committee were Robert B. Bennett (dentistry), Angela M. Brodie (medicine) and William J. Reynolds (law). The UB representatives were Steven Davison, (law), Deborah Ann Ford (business) and Larry Thomas (liberal arts).

126. H.D. Graham and G.R. La Noue, "Let's form a Washington-Baltimore UM faculty consensus," *Faculty Voice* (Independent College Park Faculty Publication), 2, no. 3 (November 1987), 3.

127. Joan Jacobson, "College plan still a cauldron of controversy," *Baltimore Evening Sun*, November 23, 1987.

128. Joan Jacobson, "Doubts about Schaefer's college plan surface," *Baltimore Evening Sun*, February 24, 1988. This quote and the two that follow came from the meeting tape which was requested by the newspaper under the state's public information law. The article features a somber picture of Hooker above the caption, "Do what I am told to do."

129. Ibid.

Another professor noted that the Presidents of Morgan State University and St Mary's College were successful "in standing up to the system" and keeping their institutions out of the proposed consolidated board. Hooker replied that they have constituencies and "UMBC doesn't. They have a black caucus and they have the whole southern delegation."[130]

The Regents (all gubernatorial appointments) had made a brave show of trying to secure more funding in exchange for consolidation support. Board Chairman Allen L. Schwait met with Steinberg to ask for $310 million in discretionary funds over the next six years. But on February 9, Lieutenant Governor Steinberg responded that the administration would not agree because: "The governor and I have to balance the needs of transportation, mental health, primary and secondary education, health care, social services, the environment." Five days later, the Regents issued a four-page press release stating their full support for the Governor's consolidation proposal, even though it would abolish their current positions and promised no new funds. Schwait refused to discuss with a *Sun* reporter any details about the Regent's debate, but he did make the revealing comment that the Board wanted to work with this governor and lieutenant governor for the next three or seven years and that he hoped some of the current members of the Board would be appointed to the new more powerful Board.[131]

At the consolidation legislative hearings in late February, Hooker's earlier admission that he was testifying against his best judgment, caused a little flurry of questions. Toll, who would become the temporary leader of the new system,[132] accompanied by the five chancellors of existing UM campuses, denied that any of them had been compelled to support the bill, and none of the legislators directed questions to Hooker on that issue. There were opponents of the administration's 146-page bill. What the *Evening Sun* called "an unusual coalition of faculty members from the rival campuses of College Park, UMBC and University of Maryland at Baltimore"

---

130. Ibid. George N. Buntin, Jr., executive secretary of the NAACP's Baltimore Chapter declared, "We will fight the governor in any way possible to [preserve] Morgan's autonomy."Amy Goldstein, "Blacks insist on autonomy for Morgan," *Baltimore Sun*, September, 19, 1987.

David E. Sumler, who served both SBHE and then MHEC agreed privately with Hooker's assessment about the benefits of Morgan's and St. Mary's autonomy in political conflicts. Sumler wrote: "Morgan was the embodiment of the dreams of the African-American community, especially in the Baltimore region, for upward mobility and for cultural eminence for people of color. The Black caucus in the State Legislature was on call for Morgan's President. As the caucus grew in numbers during the 1980s, and as members matured into legislative leadership positions, so grew the ability of Morgan State University to compete for State resources.

St Mary's College of Maryland was a small college, but it represented the pride of the entire region of the State—Southern Maryland, which encompassed three rapidly growing and prosperous counties. Having its own governing board, the College could develop its influence by astute appointments to the board." "Life Cycle." 19.

131. Ibid.

132. In a little more than a year, the newly expanded Board of Regents forced Toll, who was seen as too polarizing and too partisan on behalf of the older UM campuses, to resign. Amy Goldstein, "MD Regents Get Some Help From Schaefer," *Washington Post*, July 7, 1989. 4.

criticized the restructuring and asked for more funding, autonomy, and an emphasis on graduate programs at the County and City campuses.[133] There were other critics, but opposition to a determined governor whose party controls the legislature is usually futile in Maryland. So even without a commitment of more money, the old UM organization and its Regents passed away. Some of the old faces and friends would remain in the new system, but UMBC was faced now with a new eleven-campus governing structure in which its interests could be easily overlooked or overwhelmed. One state college president testifying in favor of consolidation stated that the reason for the bill was not to end program duplication, but to control institutional ambitions, and identified UMBC as the overly ambitious institution.[134]

Early drafts of what became an Act concerning "Administration Action Plan for Higher Education-1988" said little about the role of the UM Baltimore campuses. Later language referring to those campuses as UM's "second principal center" was in the Act's preamble, but that phrase was replaced in the final version by two carefully worded sentences:

> The University of Maryland system shall maintain and enhance a coordinated higher education center for research and graduate and professional study in the Baltimore area. Based on their joint graduate and research programs, the University of Maryland at Baltimore and the University of Maryland Baltimore County shall be considered a single research institution for the purposes of determining peer institutions [for funding purposes].[135]

This artful ambiguity did not clearly acknowledge or abolish the statewide "two principal centers" concept, but left room for the two Baltimore UM campuses to work out their future relationship.

The politics of creating the consolidated eleven-campus USM board diverted the momentum for a Baltimore merger, but did not kill it. In later years, other merger proposals were made.[136] When the reconstituted Board of Regents finally released its

---

133. Joan Jacobson, "Senators skeptical of college reorganization," *Baltimore Evening Sun*, February 26, 1988.

134. Memorandum from the UMBC Senate Committee on Statewide Reorganization to the UMBC Faculty Senate and Departmental Chairs, February 29, 1988. UMBC historic documents. Special Collections. University of Maryland, Baltimore County. The memo urged a letter writing campaign to politicians and newspapers. But it was too little and too late.

135. Maryland Annotated Code, Education Article. Sec.10-209 (GO Laws of Maryland, 1988, 2386.

136. In 1981, SBHE suggested that Morgan State and Coppin State be governed by a single Board of Regents. "Recommendations Concerning the Future Governance of Public Higher Education in Maryland," October 1981. 8. A decade later, Shaila Aery, then Maryland Secretary of Higher Education and head of MHEC, recommended that it study the merger of Morgan and Coppin, the two historically black institutions about six miles from each other in Baltimore City. Calvin Burnett, Coppin's President opposed the merger, ostensibly because his College had primarily a teaching function, while Morgan did some research. Nothing came of this proposal. Calvin W. Burnett, "Why Coppin and Morgan Shouldn't Merge," *Baltimore Sun*, July 16, 1991.

In November 1977 a Task Force of the State Board for Higher Education rejected a possible merger between Salisbury State and UMES declaring that such a merger "means swallowing up

41-page plan for the new UMS, it called for a study of a possible merger of UMBC and the University of Baltimore.[137] There was some logic to this idea. Such a merger would give UMBC a downtown campus with a business and law school and a new name. UB students would have access to a much broader curriculum as well as the panoply of activities residential campuses offer.

In 1989, the Regents commissioned Peat, Marwick, Main & Co., a national management consulting firm, to do a $100,000 study of a potential UMBC and UB merger. Their resulting eighty-page report was negative about a merger prospect. While the report contained a lot of data, it was not clear who provided the anonymous interpretations of those facts.[138] What was clear was the theoretical framework with which the consultants approached their task. The report began by discussing the general difficulties of academic mergers and concluded that achieving a "critical mass" might be a handicap, not a benefit. It stated: "In fact, the larger an organization, the slower it is inherently in responding to changing demands."[139] The report noted that a UMBC-UB merger would probably be opposed by other Baltimore academic institutions, "the black community," and by College Park.[140] Further, while it conceded the two faculties were similar in qualifications and compensation, the report said that the UB faculty culture was focused on teaching and serving a non-traditional student body, while UMBC faculty was more research-oriented and served a more traditional student body.[141] Apparently the consultants thought that to be an irreconcilable difference, though campus faculty organizations were not asked for their opinion.

On December 20, 1989, the Regents, after a thirty-five minute discussion with little debate, voted against a UMBC-UB merger. As the *Washington Post* noted:

---

of a small black institution in a large white institution, which is intolerable to blacks and is probably politically impossible." The UM system also fought vigorously against the merger, promising many new resources to UMES. For a history of SBHE's consideration of changes in Eastern Shore higher education, see Sumler, "Life Cycle," 32–39. The SBHE Task Force instead recommended transferring programs, including agriculture, from UMCP to UMES. "Designs on College Park, *Baltimore Sun* editorial, November 1977. See also Michael Stewart, "Task Force Rejects UMES-Salisbury Merger" *The UMBC Retriever*, October 31, 1977. But four years later, the above mentioned 1981 SBHE report urged placing both institutions under a single newly created governing board. (see page 7 of that report). It did not happen, though the two universities currently have a number of cooperative programs. "Tricia Bishop and Nayana Davis, "Unusual collaboration at UMES, Salisbury benefits both schools." *Baltimore Sun*, October 11, 2013.

137. Amy Goldstein, "Regents approve change in direction for U-Md., Bowie State," *Washington Post*, August 8, 1989, B5. In this document, the Regents explicitly exempted the UM downtown professional schools from any future merger speculation about that campus because that possibility had caused its new Chancellor to resign in July.

138. UMBC Provost Adam Yarmolinsky, who had served as an advisor to Presidents Kennedy, Johnson and Carter, used to define consultants as persons who borrow your watch and then charge you to tell you what time it is.

139. KPMG Peat Marwick, "Study of the Proposed Merger Between the University of Baltimore and the University of Maryland, Baltimore County: Final Report." President's Office Records, Special Collections, University of Maryland, Baltimore County, December 13, 1989.

140. Ibid. 20.

141. Ibid., 30.

> The possibility of a Baltimore merger has created anxiety in College Park where professors and administrators have feared they could lose money and prestige.... The Board of Regent's vote now leaves the University's College Park campus as the undisputed hub of research and graduate training among the 13 public campuses.

Board Chairman George McGowan, however, said that, while killing the merger, the Regents still wanted more cooperation among Baltimore campuses: "Everything is not okay as far as Baltimore is concerned. We have a lot of work to do."[142]

What emerged was a proposal to create a loose consortium of all the public graduate schools in the Baltimore areas as a substitute for an actual merger of UB, UMAB, and UMBC.[143] As a practical matter, then and now with proper approvals, students can take courses at any USM campus to earn their degrees. So the proposal was mostly symbolic. Without the central administrative power to make budgets and appointments, approve tenure and courses, such a consortium would have created few synergies and have little quality control. UMBC faculty were opposed, fearing it would undermine the two principal centers concept and dilute the quality of the graduate programs they were building. There was not much support on other campuses either.

Still the logic of merging UMBC and the UMAB professional schools seemed compelling to some, and the new USM Chancellor Donald Langenberg had come from a background of a similar merger at the University of Illinois at Chicago.[144] By November 1991, a merger agreement had been worked out between UMBC President Michael Hooker and UMAB President Errol Reese with support of Chancellor Langenberg. These leaders argued that the merged institution would be more efficient and that competition would be good for College Park. Whether a Baltimore merger would have created a useful competition in the state was debatable, but the Greater Baltimore Committee (GBC) and the *Sun* continued to argue the Baltimore region needed this new entity. According to Tim Baker, a *Sun* political commentator, while College Park is only thirty miles from Harborplace, "It is simply, inevitably and inherently oriented toward Washington, not Baltimore." Baker pointed out that per-student appropriations in the state's 1990 budget were $8,400 for College Park and $6,000 for UMBC and the disparity was likely to rise. Instead, the GBC urged that

142. Amy Goldstein, "U-Md. Regents Reject Baltimore Campus Merger: Business Community had Sought Major Research Center to Bolster City Economy," *Washington Post*, December 12, 1989. B1.

143. This proposal was a variation of a recommendation by SBHE in 1981for a consortium to provide "a vehicle of cooperation among institutions.... A consortium will permit institutions to engage in a substantial amount of graduate activity *without* requiring large amounts of new resources ...' " (emphasis added) SBHE "Recommendations Concerning the Future Governance of Public Higher Education in Maryland." October 1981.

144. Langenberg had previously been invited by the Baltimore Intercampus Committee to report on the Chicago merger.

UMBC's budget be doubled to $100 million to create two nationally competitive public universities in the state.[145]

The UMBC/UMAB merger proposal was passed unanimously by the Regents, but it immediately triggered opposition by politicians identified with the College Park campus. Prince George's Delegate Timothy F. Maloney said "I don't believe it when they say it's not going to cost more. The flagship aspirations of the College Park campus have not been realized. We have got to examine the impacts of this on all the other institutions."[146] Nevertheless the House of Delegates approved the merger proposal 94–17. More significant was the opposition of Mike Miller, long time Maryland Senate President and prominent College Park alumnus,[147] who stated, "The proposed merger is not so much a merger of need as it is a merger of greed. It's a move promoted by business executives in Baltimore City." Miller continued that Maryland has "a shrinking pie of resources" and a consolidated Baltimore campus "would create a larger advocacy group to take a larger chunk from the pie than two individual campuses would be able to take."[148]

Both sides probably calculated the future state funding implications of a merger as a zero sum outcome. But the Baltimore merger proponents saw the competitive pie more in terms of federal funding, where in national competition having two strong institutions would help Maryland. Governor Schaefer agreed with the proponent's view, as did Dennis Rasmussen, Baltimore County Executive and Chair of the Baltimore Regional Planning Council.[149] Even Parris N. Glendening, who was a Professor of Government at College Park, wrote an opinion piece in the *Sun* praising the merger proposal, but then he was preparing to run for governor.[150]

The UMAB-UMBC merger proposal, which began with a burst of support among academics, businesses, the *Sun* papers, and many politicians (including an over-

145. Tim Baker, "Questions While Waiting for the Regents: Why Not Two Top Universities?" *Baltimore Sun*, May 15, 1989.

146. Fern Shen, "U-MD Approves Wedding Baltimore Branches," *Washington Post*, December 11, 1991. D1.

147. Miller became the Maryland Senate President in 1975 and has received several awards from the College Park campus, including the Tyser Medallion, bestowed by the University of Maryland Alumni Association 1999, and election to the University of Maryland Alumni Hall of Fame 2005.

148. Charles Babington, "Plan to Merge Md. Campuses Hits Snag: Senate President Says He will Kill Proposal," *Washington Post*, March 3, 1992. Miller wrote an opinion piece in the *Sun* titled, "The Case Against a UMAB-UMBC Merger," June 18, 1992. In this piece, he argued, somewhat ironically in the light of his 2012 campaign to merge UMB and College Park, "If national research universities could be manufactured by paper mergers and not additional tax resources, I would be leading the fight for them in every region in the state.... UMAB/BC merger will lead to additional confusion, more duplication, less cooperation and higher costs...."

149. Dennis F. Rasmussen, "Our Region's Missing Ingredient," UMBC historic documents collection, Special Collections, University of Maryland, Baltimore County.

150. See Charles Babbington, "Plan to Merge Md. Campuses Hit Snag," *Baltimore Sun*, March 23, 1992.

whelming House of Delegates vote), ended with a whimper when Mike Miller stifled even a committee vote in the Senate.[151] UMAB President Reese commented bitterly, "My reading is that there are 3 million people for it [the merger] and one person against it."[152]

A few months after the merger proposal was killed, Michael Hooker left UMBC to become the Chancellor of the University of Massachusetts's system.[153] Hooker had agreed in an effort to advance the merger not to seek the presidency of the combined institution and, as a result, entered the job market. He recalled:

> When the merger was first proposed six years ago, we met enormous resistance from the medical school faculty and the school's president. I was accused of trying to get control of their budget, and of trying to shift all the money to the arts and sciences. It was clear that I had become the issue ... The only way to move the merger forward was to get myself out of the picture.[154]

Although Errol Reese and Interim President Freeman Hrabowski[155] continued to voice support for a merger, Mike Miller wasn't going anywhere and he wasn't going to change his mind. The policy window had closed. The 1999 failure of the proposal to merge UMBC and UMAB was the last gasp of the era of serious Baltimore merger proposals.[156] From then on the six independent public campuses in Baltimore were left to their individual destinies. In particular, UMBC would have to fulfill its aspirations on its own. National visibility at that time did not seem a likely achievement.

G. Conclusions

Maryland higher education politics have historically revolved around conflicts between private and public institutions, historically black and white institutions, the UM campuses and former state teachers colleges, among UM campuses, and most

---

151. Thomas Waldron, "Battle to Merge UMAB, UMBC still being fought," *Baltimore Sun*, May 11, 1992.

152. Ibid. Shaila Aery, then Maryland Secretary for Higher Education and a strong merger supporter, tried to put a good face on the defeat saying to the *Sun*, "We can move forward with some things on our own. That makes our case stronger. Some bills take more than one year to pass."

153. Thomas Waldron, "College chief's legacy: Hooker's vision enhances UMBC," *Baltimore Sun*, July 2, 1999.

154. Paul Lipowitz, "Merger Would End Hooker's Tenure," *Catonsville Times*, October 30, 1991. See also Barry Rascovar, "Futures of UMBC, UMAB caught in state politics," *Cambridge Daily Banner*, June 18, 1992.

155. In his September 1992 letter to the UMBC community as Interim President Hrabowski avoided the word merger, but called for continuing work toward "unification" of the two campuses with a single mission statement.

156. See Chapter XII for a discussion of the 2011–2012 proposal to merge UMB and UMCP.

of all between the advocates of the UM Regents and the various statewide coordinating boards.[157]

UMBC was founded long after these rivalries had developed, but the new campus was inevitably caught up in them whether it was the centerpiece of a new battle or an afterthought. A more negative outcome to any of the political conflicts described in this chapter would have dramatically changed the current UMBC. The downside for UMBC that might have emerged from most of these conflicts is obvious. Had UMBC been restricted in the non-science curriculum it could offer as in the 1974 SUMBA proposal, or had it been forbidden to offer more doctoral programs as in the 1977 SBHE plan, or had it been confined in engineering and other subjects to those areas Morgan and other schools did not want, the University would have had limited potential. Becoming a site for an industrial park might not have been so farfetched.

The likely consequences of other proposed changes are more ambiguous. The statewide higher education reorganization and Baltimore merger conflicts in the 1980s and 1990s were extraordinary events. Never before had the purpose and structures of Maryland higher education received so much attention. Politicians, foundations, newspapers, presidents, chancellors, deans, and faculty all were active participants. The debate was at least vigorous and sometimes ugly and paranoid. UMBC faculty were perhaps the most visible statewide faculty group because of the dangers of board consolidation that might make their UM status meaningless. Such a status loss through consolidation would directly affect their research opportunities, amount of teaching required, and salary levels. UMBC faculty also were active in exploring the various Baltimore merger proposals, speaking openly when campus administrators needed to be wary of offending their bosses, the UM President and the Governor, and worrying about what the legislature might do about next year's budget.

It is probably fair to say that the USM superboard has neither been as harmful as opponents feared nor as successful as proponents hoped. UM Regents' Board Chairman Allen Schwait was concerned about the leveling effect of the new board and said "Each campus could come out of this four feet tall."[158] That has not happened. On the other hand, the enlarged Board of Regents, plus the retention of MHEC as a coordinating body, has not simplified higher education politics in the state. Within the system campuses there has been a more orderly mechanism for settling program-

157. These conflicts are long-standing. The 1924 Janney Commission recommended that the state depend on private institutions to meet expanded enrollment and objected to expanding the mission of the University of Maryland beyond its role as an agricultural college. The 1931 Shriver Commission took the opposite position and recommended phasing out state support for private colleges in favor of giving additional support to the College Park campus to expand its mission. The 1937 Sopher report recommended the state acquire Morgan College from the Methodist Episcopal Church and upgrade Coppin and Bowie from two year "normal" schools to four year institutions, but also suggested UM's Princess Anne Academy (the future UMES) be closed. "Historical Perspectives on the Governance Structure of the University System of Maryland," 1988. http://mlis.state.md.us/199rs/Taskforce/Historical_Perspective_Structure.

158. Joan Jacobson, "State superboard is proposed," *Baltimore Evening Sun*, June 1987.

matic disputes, but in the Baltimore area, since Morgan is not a USM member and can play the "civil rights" card to veto new program approvals, program development is not always education-driven or rational.

In 1987 the *Sun*, predicted that, "The merger of the UMBC-UMAB graduate school, will lead almost inevitably, to a full-fledged merger of the two schools."[159] "Inevitably" somehow got lost along the way. When UMBC graduate students receive their diplomas, it still says University of Maryland Graduate School Baltimore (UMGSB) on them, an echo of the combined UMBC/UMAB graduate schools. That entity has had limited functional significance and cooperation between the two institutions did not become much closer as each has found separate paths to success.[160] In research universities, the great motivators of individual academic ambition—promotion, tenure, merit salaries, publication, and research grants—are not much influenced by top down administrative structures without budgetary control. Cooperative activities and joint programs flower for awhile, but unless watered by money, their progenitors move on to other positions and other interests and only husks remain of former aspirations. After being threatened with a proposed UMCP/UMB merger in 2012 as will be described in Chapter XII, however, UMB and UMBC began to reassess and strengthen their ties again.

Even in hindsight, however, evaluating the potential of a Baltimore merger is difficult. A UMBC merger with UMAB would have converted Maryland into the two flagship model. UMBC would have become the essential undergraduate and graduate arts and sciences component of a powerful Baltimore university that could have eventually equaled College Park in budget and political prowess. The merged institution would have become an instant national player, but it would also have created some problems. By 2010, the UM Medical School budget alone was five times larger than the UMBC budget, and such schools are not modest in making their needs known within university structures. The energy that has so dramatically advanced UMBC might have been dissipated in a new Baltimore mega-university. There is no alternative history to evaluate that question.

In retrospect, all of Baltimore's public higher education institutions are stronger than they were two decades ago, so a case can be made that their diversity creates more benefits than any structural changes aimed at creating a more visible, powerful consolidation. But we cannot know for sure.

---

159. "Merge Baltimore Campuses," *Baltimore Sun* editorial, June 1987.

160. See the videotaped reflections of the difficulties in making UMGSB work by Kevin Eckert, interviewed by Joseph Tatarewicz, May 7, 2013.

CHAPTER III

Developing a Campus

In 1965, the seed that became UMBC was first planted; a decade after the Pullen Commission declared that for the "foreseeable future" there was no need for a new campus in the Baltimore area because existing institutions could expand. Dr. Albin O. Kuhn, splitting his time between his duties serving as Chancellor for the downtown Baltimore professional schools campus and creating UMBC, set up his administrative office for the new university in an old two-story farmhouse. Filing cabinets on the porch and a tiny sign, "University of Maryland, Baltimore County," were at first the only indications of the eventual transformations of the land. One of his first tasks was to hire a librarian, John Haskell, Jr., a registrar, Robert H. Turner, and a dean of the faculty, Homer Schamp.[1]

Kuhn chaired the facilities planning group which included the new UMBC hires and George Weber from UMCP and George Marston from UMAB.[2] As he recalled:

> Taking a campus from a fruit and vegetable farm ... was a real challenge.... The first darn thing you had to do, and it was fun really, was start listening ... I had the good fortune to travel a lot ... particularly in California, where there had been the greatest, most rapid expansion.... and also to try to profit from the mistakes of a campus like College Park. That's why, for example, we [UMBC] have this underground distribution system for utilities, because at College Park they were always digging up wires and a couple of people were electrocuted actually. And that's why the [UMBC] campus is more concentrated.[3]

The critical decision to create building density on the campus rather than to spread out over the more than 450 available acres came to Kuhn almost as a vision:

> I was sitting in a really boring meeting in Chicago, an education meeting of some kind, and doodling.... [I was thinking] Why not do what Baltimore does? Have a beltway around the [academic] heart of the campus ... and then parking outside, athletics outside, stuff like that?.... I wish I had saved the yellow pad that I doodled on....[4]

---

1. "UMBC strives for excellence," *Diamondback*, December 10, 1965.
2. Albin O. Kuhn, interview by Edward Orser, February 4, 1994, 13.
3. Ibid., 14. Kuhn conceded that his tunnel system cost a few hundred thousand more per building.
4. Ibid., 15.

The architects then took that concept as a key component of the campus plan.[5]

There were some political constraints. Originally there was no discussion about residential facilities because at that time the State paid for dormitories and, as college enrollments were booming, it had concluded such buildings were too expensive. Kuhn admitted:

> So this [being a commuter campus] was a big selling point, and if we had decided initially to sell a residential campus, I think it would have been much harder. We had enough problems getting UMBC approved by everybody without that one. A few years later, we could bring it up as an issue.[6]

As campus planners approached their task, they found the Spring Grove site had a number of advantages. Kuhn remembered that, "The University was anxious to get a large initial site, one that wouldn't disrupt the community around it and one with easy access to the Beltway."[7] There was very little bed-rock underneath the rolling terrain, thus reducing construction costs. Except for removing a few farm remnants, there were no other impediments to building. No industries, roads or housing developments existed to slow construction. A 1970 survey of the non-human inhabitants of the campus area found bullheads, carp, shiners, and sunfish in the ponds and on the land seventy-six species of birds and seventeen species of wild animals.[8] None of these species was endangered and many still exist in the wooded areas the University preserved. For an urban area, the UMBC site was a remarkable blank slate on which to build a new university.

A. UMBC Campus Concepts and Design

The all-important choice of an architectural firm culminated in the selection of Rogers, Taliaferro, Kostritsky and Lamb or RTKL as it is popularly known. RTKL was a relatively new firm, created in 1946 in Annapolis in one of the partner's grandmother's basement. While UMBC was one of the firm's first large projects, it is today a global business with 800 employees in ten offices in five countries, though still headquartered in Baltimore. When it has the right client and a plentiful budget, RTKL's work can be spectacular; witness the Shanghai Science and Technology Mu-

---

5. Kuhn's granddaughter remembers that as the concept of a campus beltway, or Loop Road as it was called, became accepted, Dr. Kuhn hopped on a tractor and marked out its path. Julie Kuhn, interview with the author, February 4, 2013.

6. Albin O. Kuhn, interview by Edward Orser, February 4, 1994, 15–16. The *Sun* quoted Kuhn as saying, "Under present plans, it will be a commuter campus for ten years. But I cannot say it will always be that way." Stephen E. Nordlinger, "Catonsville U. of M. is Backed by the State Board," *Baltimore Sun*, November 1, 1958.

7. John Blitz, "A Campus is Born," *Maryland Magazine,* Fall 1966, 11.

8. UMBC site 18-BA-71.5. UMBC Historic documents collection, Special Collections, University of Maryland, Baltimore County.

seum, the Chinese Museum of Film in Beijing, or the Principi Pio in Madrid. The firm does not list UMBC as among its most eminent achievements.

Since the campus was projected by some estimates to grow to 20,000 students over a twenty-year period,[9] the planning task was complex. RTKL's first master plan began, "UMBC was initially conceived as a commuter campus and should be designed for a majority of students arriving by car. Facilities for a maximum of 13,300 cars must be anticipated." Then, somewhat as an afterthought, the plan noted that public transportation was to be encouraged and that a proposed rapid transit system on the right-of-way owned by the Pennsylvania Railroad "will make the campus convenient to many parts of the Baltimore area."[10] Nevertheless, the master plan included spaces for fifty seven different campus parking lots![11]

Focusing on the buildings, RTKL asserted:

> An attractive campus is basic to all phases of the facilities planned. An architectural style distinctive to the campus is desired. Ideally the architectural style should reflect the character and achievements of the University of Maryland while expressing some identity with the region of the State in which the new campus is located.[12]

What did those lofty abstractions mean? In practice, there was concern that "the design and material of the building should produce a low average annual maintenance cost," which meant "reinforced concrete, exterior brick, minimal exposed glass, and minimal roof slopes are the subjects suggested by the University for consideration of materials and standards for construction."[13] Reading these words fifty years later, the lack of emphasis on aesthetics, decor, or comfort of the students and employees make the standards adopted seem more appropriate for a warehouse district than a university campus. The first UMBC construction, unlike some later efforts, did not produce any attractive or memorable buildings.

To be fair, however, with no endowment or private donors, UMBC could not afford to duplicate College Park's Georgian architecture. Collegiate Gothic was never considered. Furthermore, being modern was very much in the spirit of the new cam-

---

9. RTKL, Inc. "Master Plan for the University of Maryland Baltimore County, 1964." UPUBF3-009. University Publications, Digital Collections, University of Maryland, Baltimore County. (Hereafter "plan")There was no real basis for the 20,000 student enrollment figure projection to be achieved by 1985. (page 19) The number was frequently repeated, however, and when enrollment fell far short of that figure, the estimate became somewhat of a political albatross for the new campus. Kuhn believed that the campus might grow to be 25,000 to 30,000 students. Albin O. Kuhn, interview by Edward Orser, February 4, 1994. 2.

10. Plan, 2. Amtrak and MARC trains now run about four miles from the campus, though only the latter stops in Halethorpe. There is now shuttle bus transportation from the train stop to the campus, but rail has not developed into a very important element of UMBC commuting patterns.

11. Ibid., 30.

12. Ibid., 21.

13. Ibid.

pus. Dr. Kuhn reported, "The majority of those working on the Capital Improvements Committee felt that the College Park campus had attained a certain beauty because of its reasonably consistent architecture. But it was the unanimous opinion that the new campus should have its own distinctive style."[14]

As much as anything, the building style at UMBC reflected modernism, the dominant architectural style for corporate and institutional buildings in the late twentieth century.[15] Influenced by the availability of modern technology and building materials, modernist buildings are characterized by simplification of form and lack of adornment. Only in the last decade has that pattern at UMBC been altered. The addition of the esthetic library tower, the provocatively designed The Commons, and the Performing Arts and Humanities Building, together with more landscaping and mature trees, softened the impact of row upon row of predictable brick buildings.

At least UMBC's first architectural style was not as eclectic or mismatched as some other Maryland campuses. Perhaps that is damning with faint praise. Historian John Jeffries had what was a typical view of the new campus and expressed some of the architectural shock new faculty in the 1970s experienced:

> The schools I had been at from 1959 to 1973 were Harvard, Yale, Princeton, schools with fairly imposing architecture, images and so forth. Here is UMBC, a bunch of brick buildings [with] very small trees.... It was physically a stark place, but a place where some ... had, I thought, ambitions to make the department and the University first rate in terms of scholarship.[16]

Others admired the campus architecture or at least made very good rationalizations for it. Joe Arnold, another faculty historian, asserted:

> The library's architectural style, like the rest of our campus is stridently modern. Not a Gothic arch, a Georgian facade to be seen anywhere. This is as it should be. It is symbolic of the fact UMBC is the only one of Maryland's public universities which is a product of the post-World War era. It carries none of Maryland's long history as an aristocratic, conservative, racially segregated state.[17]

---

14. Blitz, "A Campus is Born," 12.

15. Ralph T. Jackson, the architect designer of the library tower, described the existing campus buildings as "designed to eschew symbolism. They were an architecture of the "Brutalist" variant of form follows function...." Ralph T. Jackson, interview by Aviva Karpe, March 15, 2011. Another view of a future campus plan complete with a bell tower in front of the library can be found in Danielle Dubas, "Field of Dreams: Our Blueprint for the Future," *UMBC Review*, 9, no. 3, (Spring 1991). The UMBC 2009–2019 Facilities Master Plan updated in 2010 describes the original campus plan in these terms: "The practical and systematic approach to planning predominated over the desire for consistency of architectural language, the creation of formal open spaces or the richness of landscape elements that define older campuses. UMBC historic documents collection, Special Collections, University of Maryland, Baltimore County. 3.

16. John Jeffries, interview by Joseph Tatarewicz, July 18, 2006, 43.

17. Joe Arnold, "A Signature Building—the Heart and Soul of the Campus," *UMBC Magazine*, Summer 1995. Actually the library tower interior is art deco.

The campus plan called for construction in phases, initially a lecture hall, a multipurpose cafeteria, a gymnasium, and an academic building, to be followed by a library, and then in the third phase, a physical science building, another classroom building, a lecture hall and a large central heating plant. Just listing these projected buildings suggests what an enormous task planning and building a new campus was and how much early students, faculty and staff had to "make do" as they began their work.

One of the most important planning decisions was to create the Loop Road (now more elegantly named Hilltop Circle) and to concentrate academic buildings within its circumference. Kuhn acknowledged that "The big idea RTKL brought to the planning was that the buildings should be clustered together and that you should have avenues, as in cities."[18] Nevertheless, it was largely a pragmatic decision rather than one motivated by any aesthetic concerns. The planners thought that, if buildings were too far apart, a ten-minute break between classes would not be sufficient. So they designed four-story buildings that were two to three times the size of typical higher education buildings at the time and lined them up in a row.[19] Further, as Guy Chisholm, long time UMBC Physical Plant Director, noted the Loop on this "chiefly commuter campus" would "help keep traffic at a minimum in the academic central portion of the campus."[20] As UMBC has grown and become more residential, the Loop Road concept has continued to be effective, making the interior of the campus very walkable and fostering a sense of community.

Another master plan objective proved not to be so durable. It envisioned five lakes to dot the campus. In addition to their aesthetic appeal, the lakes would serve to catch runoff water during heavy rains.[21] Except for the pond by the library, which waterfowl insisted on inhabiting to the dismay of groundskeepers, the "lakes" have not survived campus expansion.

There was not much controversy over campus design. The normal stakeholders—students, faculty, administrative staff or alumni—did not yet exist. There was little local political attention to or interference with the campus concept in this remote corner of Baltimore County, but there was some debate about who should actually control construction. As Kuhn remembered:

> Just before [Governor] Byrd left, he got legislation giving the Regents the responsibility for managing UM, so it now had personnel and contracting power. But the State Budget Director opposed, so he had the law amended to give his office control of any new campus. So in the first year, we had to get that law changed to put UMBC under the UM system, rather than the state budget office. But the first year we were under the state system and that complicated things.[22]

18. Albin O. Kuhn, interview by Edward Orser, February 4, 1994. 21.
19. Ibid., 20.
20. Blitz, "A Campus is Born," 12.
21. Lowell F. Sunderland, "Catonsville Campus Opened," *Baltimore Sun*, September 19, 1966.
22. Albin O. Kuhn, interview by Edward Orser, February 4, 1994.

The major ally became Governor Millard Tawes.[23] Kuhn recalled, "He [Tawes] told everybody, 'We want this job done, we want it done now, and don't get in the way.' And a Governor of Maryland has a lot of power."[24]

Kuhn's personal relationship with Tawes, both "country boys,"[25] was a major advantage to the new campus. In his fiscal 1966 budget request, the Governor, although generally a fiscal conservative who only had some trade schooling background, expressed his passionate commitment to higher education:

> I think we all recognize that one of the thorniest problems we face—and in all probability will face for years to come—is that of providing for adequate college and university facilities.... It is a twin problem in that it invested a tremendous expansion of plant to accommodate the population growth ... a continuing upgrading of the quality of education to meet the educational standards of our modern age ... it is significant that 73% of the capital budget I am recommending for next year is earmarked for improving the plants of the University of Maryland and the state colleges.[26]

The Governor then, as politicians will, mentioned new money for each Maryland campus, but he singled out UMBC and said, "Provision is made in both the operating budget and the capital budget, of course, for building, equipping, and staffing the vitally needed Baltimore County campus of the University....[27] Kuhn recalled: "He was just marvelous in helping us get things done for developing the campus ... The day we had our formal dedication and a couple of three thousand people were there, I can still see the tears come down the Governor's face when he was recognized."[28]

B. Building Histories

In a state system, such as Maryland's, every major building project reflects a specific set of architectural and political decisions. However practical, durable, functional, and economically prudent the early UMBC architectural style, it was not graceful or elegant in any way. Few loved it, in the way many campuses have build-

23. J. Millard Tawes had a remarkable political career, the only Marylander to be Governor, Treasurer, and Comptroller.

24. Albin O. Kuhn, interview by Joseph Tatarewicz, August 21, 2001, 19.

25. Tawes' hometown of Crisfield is still the site of "the must attend" for politicians, the annual J. Millard Tawes Crab and Clam Bake.

26. Executive Records, Maryland State Archives, Governor J. Millard Tawes, 1959–1967, Volume 81, 34–35.

27. Ibid.

28. Albin O. Kuhn, interview by Joseph Tatarewicz, August 14, 2001, 23. Tawes, governor from 1959–1967, was an advocate of higher education throughout the state. He has had buildings named after him on campuses at Coppin State, Frostburg, UMES, UMCP and Washington College, Since UMBC has never named a building after a politician, he is not so commemorated on the Catonsville campus.

ings or sites that alumni or families can't wait to return to see or show off to friends.[29] So there was always a question of how often to repeat the early building style, particularly after that style was no longer in architectural fashion.

Most of all there was the issue of whether any new building could get through the Maryland political maze and be constructed at all. As a new campus, UMBC naturally needed a larger share of the state's construction budget than its enrollment, reputation, or political support would ordinarily justify. The other Baltimore campuses, or indeed those in any part of the state, were not pleased to have their building projects put on hold, so that construction could begin in Catonsville or where-ever that campus was actually located. Nor did these decisions get any easier in later years, as UMBC needed to add new buildings and confronted the aspirations of other institutions with far greater political resources. Although often invisible to the outside world, and even to those on campus until after the fact, the greatest achievements of UMBC leaders were often in cajoling, nudging, and leaning on the political process that made critical construction decisions.

In Maryland, state-financed public construction must be approved by the Board of Public Works composed of the Governor, the Treasurer, and the Comptroller. Although these office holders are usually Democrats, they may have different agendas and political aspirations. The powers of this Board established by the Maryland Constitution of 1864 are unique in the United State and shape the lobbying for public buildings.

Early Buildings

At the opening of the campus, an investment of $2.2 million had produced three buildings (an academic building, a multi-purpose building which included a gym, student lounge, kitchen, and cafeteria, and a 196 seat lecture hall). A $1.6 million dollar library was being constructed, though the campus only owned 30,000 books.[30] Establishing a functioning library from scratch created a particular challenge. UMBC used a book list from the University of California, a state where many new campuses had been created, and then bought its first collection of 20,000 volumes which came pre-catalogued and ready for shelving.[31]

The other existing building on campus was Hillcrest which was erected in 1921. Most UMBC building stories are about design and construction; but in the case of Hillcrest, it is a tale of redesign and eventual demolition.[32] Hillcrest claimed to be the

29. A 1992 report by LDR International, "Design Guidelines: UMBC," stated: "Every campus has landmarks which serve to orient the visitor and give organization to the campus. At present, UMBC's landmarks are both unstated and unsophisticated." UMBC historic documents collection, Special Collections, University of Maryland, Baltimore County.11.

30. "Cat Campus's Sprouting Rapidly," *Baltimore News American*, September, 1966.

31. "Library Construction Work to Begin," *UMBC News*, October 3, 1966 (origins box).

32. G. Stewart Seiple, "A History of Hillcrest," February 2, 2002. A student paper done under the supervision of Professor Joseph Tatarewicz. (UMBC archives).

first psychiatric hospital building in the United States constructed specifically for the care and treatment of mentally ill prisoners. Despite its austere purpose, the building outside was an attractive Tidewater design with an expansive side porch overlooking what would become campus lands.

After UMBC opened, Hillcrest served as the Administration Building for a time and then was the site for the Residential Life Office and some student organization offices. Albin Kuhn recalled, "from time to time there were remarks about the appropriateness of the building that was constructed to house insane criminals becoming the location of the administration."[33] Hilltop's basement that once contained steel-barred isolation cells, after a time, was converted to a popular student social club called "The Rattskeller." Whether the student parties chased out the many ghosts alleged to live there is uncertain. What is clear is that by 2000 Hillcrest was vacant. As with many older buildings, there was sentiment to save it,[34] but remodeling needed to meet contemporary building codes would have been too expensive and the land was needed for student housing.

After the founding buildings, UMBC's earliest construction projects were investments in the scientific work on the campus. The biology building was completed in 1967, math/psychology in 1969, and chemistry in 1971 (now named the Meyerhoff Chemistry Building).

The tallest building on the campus is the ten-story Administration Building built in 1973. It is a slender structure characterized by exceedingly small windows. Albin Kuhn was asked whether it was an urban legend or true that "UMBC's architecture is siege architecture ... sometimes students were taking over buildings, and some of the buildings do have a monumental aspect and are hard to scale from the outside." Kuhn denied it, saying, "We were small enough that everyone knew everybody. And the planning actually went on before that stage of confrontation really began."[35] He did concede that he once favored the idea of putting up a tall fence down the middle of loop road so we could control who came on the campus. Schamp "told me I was crazy and you don't do that on a college campus...."[36]

During 1973, construction cranes were much in evidence on the campus and the Fine Arts and Social Sciences (now Sondheim) buildings were also completed.

Residential Living

Although Kuhn, for political reasons, was prudently vague about whether UMBC would ever have dormitories, faculty and others began to put pressure on the admin-

33. Albin O. Kuhn, "University of Maryland Baltimore County—Its Early Years of Development and Operation," unpublished manuscript, no date, Collection #107, UMBC historic documents collection, Special Collections, University of Maryland, Baltimore County.

34. Marcia Adams, "On UMBC campus, student urges preservation," *The Jeffersonian*, June 2, 2005; Jennifer Jones, "Hillcrest's rich history going to waste," *The Retriever*, December 12, 2006.

35. Albin O. Kuhn, interview by Joseph Tatarewicz, August 14, 2001.21

36. Ibid., 20.

istration to build residential facilities. An urban campus with city amenities can work well without on-campus housing, if it has good public transportation. UMBC, however, was built on former farmland without any shopping or dining in walking distance and no direct public transportation. Just before the campus opened, a reporter wrote, "Students planning to commute by bus to the new University of Maryland Catonsville campus this fall face an uphill, thirteen-minute walk from the nearest bus stop to class."[37]

Like so many other developments at UMBC, there was external political opposition to making the campus more residential. In 1968, UMBC proposed hiring an architect to design a three-hundred-bed dormitory. When the plans were presented to the State Board of Public Works, its members "expressed surprise that the facility in Catonsville will cater to residential as well as commuting students" and criticized the proposal as "a change of purpose for the campus."[38] Since the dorms would be paid for by bonds based on student rental fees rather than by state funds, the issue before the Board was really a turf battle. Governor Agnew's staff suggested that, if UMBC's proposal was approved the state would question whether Towson State and Catonsville Community College might be overbuilding their facilities. UM officials responded by urging the State to think in future terms when UMBC would have 7,500 to 10,000 students in 1975 (Elkins) or eventually 20,000 (Kuhn). There was a political price to be paid later when those overly optimistic enrollment targets were not met. To some, that signaled a failure on UMBC's part, but the barrier against making UMBC more residential was surmounted and the approval to begin residential construction was given.

The University built Susquehanna (309 beds) in 1970, Chesapeake Hall (309 beds) in 1971, and Patapsco (304 beds) in 1973.[39] On March 15, 1970, 118 students began to move in to Susquehanna and establish a residential presence,[40] though for many years after UMBC had the reputation of being a purely commuter campus. A dining hall, now called True Grits, a play on the name of the Retriever mascot, True Grit, was opened in 1971 to serve residents. Then, for a nearly a decade residential construction stopped, until the West Hill Apartments (284 beds) were built in 1981 and the Terrace Apartments (309 beds) were constructed a year later. Again, there was a considerable hiatus and it wasn't until 1992 that Potomac Hall (350 beds) was opened.

Without state funding for student housing, a new model was needed. Erickson Living, the largest builder and manager of senior citizen housing in the nation, had its corporate headquarters in a large retirement complex less than a mile from campus. Since Erickson had construction capabilities, a concept was developed that the

---

37. George Rodgers, "Bus Service Not Close," *Catonsville Times*, August 17, 1966.

38. Staff writer, "U. of Md. Buildup Blocked," *Washington Post*, January 12, 1968.

39. UMBC Facilities Master Plan Update, 2009–2019, "Size and Age of Existing Buildings on Campus," Table 3.1.

40. "UMBC opens its first resident halls, draws end to 3½ commuter years," *Retriever*, April 7, 1970.

company's foundation would lease the land, build the dorms at a cost of $14 million, and then collect the rents over an eight to twelve year period to pay off the loan.[41] That arrangement led to the opening of Erickson Hall (447 beds) in 2000, Harbor Hall (511 beds) in 2001, and finally to the Walker Avenue Apartments I (236 beds) and II–III (342 beds) in 2003–04.[42] The demand for on campus housing continued to grow and a 189-bed addition to Patapsco was built in 2011.

An urgent problem on the campus was a place for commuter and non-commuter students to congregate and to house student organizations. Although need for such student-centered buildings had been evident for some time, the State of Maryland has a policy that buildings for students, such as those used for eating, meeting, socializing, sleeping and playing, must be paid for by student fees.[43] That arrangement often means that there is a substantial time gap between the identification of a need and the accumulation of fees to pay for a new building, unless financed with a bond. Buildings such as The Commons, the Retriever Athletic Center, and residence halls were usually financed by state bonds which are eventually paid for by student fees. A partial remedy, the University Center, was constructed in 1982. The Commons, a more spacious, 144,000 square-feet, and architecturally interesting building, was completed in 2002. It contains extensive dining facilities for students, faculty and staff, a bookstore, bank, pub, and meeting rooms.

AOK Library & Gallery

The largest and most prominent building on the campus is fittingly the Albin O. Kuhn Library & Gallery. The current structure was built in three stages, the first in 1968, the second in 1974, and the third in 1994. Now seven stories high, it sits on a small hill with vistas that look out to downtown Baltimore. Conversely, drivers on the Beltway can catch glimpses of the library and residents of downtown apartments and condos can see the outline of the building. Otherwise, campus structures are generally obscure to passersby.

The first phase or west wing of the library which cost $1.7 million was in the original budget, but not completed until after the campus had been opened for two years. It was intended to have a distinctive appearance, unlike the brick facades that dominate the rest of the campus. From the ground level, it appeared to be one story, though the basement housed offices that could be viewed from the library pond, as

41. Todd Karpovich, "Erickson Foundation to Build UMBC Dorms," *Baltimore Business Journal*, November 23, 1998.

42. The Walker Avenue apartments contain some graduate student housing and an experiment in gender neutral housing. The latter concept includes "LGBT students, allies, straight couples, couples and best friends" who must apply and be screened by a residential life committee for access to several four bedroom apartments. Elizabeth Silberholz, "Gender-neutral housing being tested," *The Pretriever*, August 8, 2008. This is part of a national trend. Mary Beth Marklein, "Gender-Neutral comes to campus," *USA Today*, June 21, 2004.

43. Md. Code Ann. Educ. Title 19-Auxiliary and Academic Facilities Bond Authority Section 19–101 (2010).

well as an extensive underground storage and workroom area that few campus dwellers have ever seen. The textured limestone trim, some thought, gave the building a warm and inviting appearance.[44] The second phase or east wing was completed in a matching architectural style, though composed of precast concrete.

In 1982, the building was renamed after UMBC's first Chancellor. The ceremony to make that announcement coincided with Kuhn's retirement from the University of Maryland and UMBC's Chancellor John Dorsey decided to have a little fun at the otherwise decorous event. He presented Kuhn with a picture of the silo that sits by the south campus entrance and announced henceforth that it would be called the "The Albin O. Kuhn Silo." Kuhn may have been taken in by the ruse because he was, after all, a farm boy and later said that he thought the silo was just being preserved because it cost too much to take down. As things turned out, the AOK Library sounds just about right.

As the campus grew, the first two stages of the library were overwhelmed by the need for space for users and for storage space for books, journals, and electronic media. By 1981, Library Director Billy Wilkinson, was initiating discussions for Phase III. As UMBC graduate programs began to grow, the need for library space increased dramatically.[45] In 1986, a consultant's report declared:

> The University of Maryland Baltimore County (UMBC) has begun to fulfill the promise envisioned by its founders. Enrollments are growing in direct response to the strengthening and expansion of academic programs, despite predicted decline.... The overall enrollment increases have begun to tax the limits of existing facilities. This condition is most apparent with academic support facilities, such as the library.[46]

Some university authorities hoped for a ten-story tower that would match the number of stories of the Administration building.[47] But UMBC's twin towers were not to be. When Governor William Donald Schaefer announced on June 17, 1992 (eleven years after the need was first identified) that the Board of Public Works had approved Phase III of the library construction, the $19 million dollars authorized was only enough for a tower of seven stories. Even then, another $3 million had to be appropriated to finish and furnish the building.

The choice of the lead architectural firm, however, was auspicious. Shepley, Bulfinch, Richardson & Abott of Boston was one of the leading architects of academic buildings in the country. Its predecessor firm had designed the inner quadrangle of Stanford University in 1891 and the Harvard Medical School in 1906. In

---

44. Guy Chisholm, interview by Edward Orser, 1993.

45. Billy R. Wilkinson to Joan Pardo, February 16 and March 16, 1981 (memos UMBC archives).

46. Ingraham Planning Associates, Inc. "Addition and Renovation to the Albin O. Kuhn Library and Gallery," August 1, 1986.

47. "Administration: Ten Year Plan," University Relations, Folder 1 of 2. 1972–1974. President's Office records, Box 10, Folder 9. 25.

more recent times, the firm completed libraries for Colgate, Duke, Princeton, Rice, and Yale among others.[48] Its local architectural partner, a political and practical necessity, was Cho, Wilks and Benn.[49]

The design of the library tower posed a considerable challenge. It had to be built or imposed behind the squat limestone base of the existing library.[50] Ralph T. Jackson, the architect, described the problem and the challenge. The existing library was:

> functionally driven, understated on the skyline, although at the center of the campus.... we needed a sense of identity, heart and civic presence ... We used a form that was classical, a cube and a drum which resembled an abstracted renaissance urban form.... The architectural elements of the library were about order and civility rather than pragmatism.[51]

The tower floor plans needed to be wide enough to accommodate about 100,000 books per floor as well as study spaces. The design placed the bookshelves on the interior of the floors, so that students could use natural light as they were studying. Remodeling of the lower floor of the library had to accommodate space for the new technologies as well as a café site to welcome and nourish students. Later, a well-used 24 hour staffed Retriever Study Center was added. It was not obvious that all these functions could be achieved with any degree of harmony with the older structure or within budget.

Clearly the building would not look like any other on the campus nor imitate any traditional style. Library Director Larry Wilt described the library tower as, "light, open, current, and medium tech." The colors he thought were "southwest" with finishes influenced by "art deco/Japanese design."[52] Though not exactly in the Tidewater Maryland architectural vernacular, the building works well at a number of levels. For the exterior, the decision was made to use precast concrete in a color mixed to match the limestone on the first stage. The framework was then adorned with aluminum trimming that the architect intended to be "referential to aged copper."[53]

Given the explosion in print and digital media that was occurring even as the library expansion was being completed, an obvious concern was whether the three "lost" tower floors would someday be necessary. In 2006, the library reached one million books in its collection, but Wilt does not believe a new expansion will be neces-

---

48. http://www:shepleybulfinch.com/. Don Farmer was the project manager.

49. The firm, now Cho, Benn, Holbrook and Associates, is one of the oldest minority owned architectural firms in the state. Among other important projects, the firm was chosen for the design of the club level and private suites in M&T Bank stadium.

50. Nancy Quantock, manager of capital projects, said "We felt that in order to create a centerpiece showcase building, we needed to build a tower. The hardest part architecturally was integrating it with existing buildings."

51. Ralph T. Jackson, Principal Architect, Shepley Bulfinch, interview by Aviva Karpe, March 15, 2011. Ms. Karpe, then a UMBC undergraduate majoring in sociology, made substantial contributions to this section.

52. Larry Wilt, interview by Aviva Karpe, March 3, 2011.

53. Ralph T. Jackson, interview by Aviva Karpe, March 15, 2011.

sary. Some rearranging of shelving space is possible. More important, because of improved online access and electronic archiving, the number of print journals can be reduced. An increasing number of books will be digitalized.[54]

If there is expansion, it probably will be in the Special Collections section of the library which holds rare books, print archives, including biological sciences societies' archives, Maryland history, science fiction classics, and photographic prints and negatives. The last component is a special feature of the AOK library. It is not unusual for older, richer universities to maintain collections of old masters paintings, archaeological treasures, and zoological specimens, but those were not options for UMBC. There was a niche, however, where UMBC could make a substantial cultural contribution within its budget—photographs. By 2011, Special Collections owned 1.9 million images, many of them recording the social history of the state and the region. The Library Gallery presents three or four exhibitions a year and the Gallery and Library seventh floor are prime spaces for major campus lectures and special events.[55]

Cam Construction faced no particular problems in the two year building process and the building was ready for a "preview" ceremony on December 12, 1994. A large crowd of dignitaries and all the former UMBC Presidents and Chancellors were there to celebrate. Albin Kuhn told the crowd, "I must admit I feel very much at home in this new tower, because I am, in fact, standing on the very site of my former house—the house where my family and I lived while we were building UMBC."[56] The grand occasion went off without a hitch, but there was one concern. The limestone, steel and aluminum building was quite stable and the fireproof windows were tested to withstand a hurricane, but the architect became concerned about the potential effects of the celebration fireworks. After the event was over, neither the political hot air nor the fireworks had done any discernible damage.

Performing Arts and Humanities Building (PAHB)

This building is the result of aspirations that have existed for at least two decades. The Fine Arts building (circa 1973) had long been outdated, and its basic design was not well-loved by those who worked, performed, and studied there. As the campus grew, the major investments in academic buildings were for engineering

54. This is a national trend. "Most college library directors would order print books removed from their library if there was a robust and trustworthy way to provide access to electronic versions, according to a new study released today." Matthew P. Long and Roger C. Schonfeld, "Ithaka S+R Library Survey 2010: Insights form U. S. Academic Library Directors." See also Tom McGhee, "Libraries replacing hard-cover books with digital technology," *Denver Post,* October 20, 2010.

55. A list of Gallery exhibitions until 1984 can be found in Ingraham Planning Associates, Inc. "Additions and Renovations to the Albin O. Kuhn Library and Gallery, 12. For 1998 to the present see, http://aok.lib.umbc.edu/gallery/gallerypast.php.

56. Library Tower Preview, Program Agenda, December 12, 1994. For description of the jubilation caused by completion of the library tower, see "View from the Tower," *UMBC Magazine,* Summer 1995.

(1993), physics (1999), renovating biology (2000), information technology (2003), public policy (2003), and renovating chemistry (2003). It was time to do something for the humanities and performing arts. The obvious problem was that in the building competitions within the USM and, particularly in tight economic times, obtaining the political support to acquire the money for that purpose was exceedingly difficult.

UMBC followed a strategy that might seem counterintuitive. Instead of asking for a series of small, relatively inexpensive arts buildings which would have prolonged the political fight for a decade or more, the University requested a single 267,642 square-foot structure with an estimated cost of $168 million (2009 dollars). President Freeman Hrabowski then set about with enormous energy and unflagging tenacity to sell the State on the need for the building. In 2006, he scored his first success by obtaining a commitment for planning money for the PAHB.[57] Once that sort of commitment for a building is made, the issue is usually not "if," but "when." But in this instance, "when" was very uncertain. As the economy worsened, it became clear the building would have to be built in two stages. Even as the steel girders were rising for Stage I, there was uncertainty about whether the State would follow through on Stage II any time soon. In the difficult environment of the 2011 legislative budget process, UMBC was successful in having Stage II funding advanced from FY 2015 to FY 2013.[58]

When completed, the PAHB will contain the Departments of Ancient Studies, English, Philosophy, Dance, Music, and Theatre. It will also house a 275-seat main theatre, a 100-seat black box theatre, a 100-seat dance studio, a 350-seat concert hall, an instrument ensemble room, a recording studio, an archeology laboratory, and classrooms.[59] The building, which combines a distinctive cylindrical stainless steel clad concert hall with a more traditional rectangular brick structure, was designed by Grimm & Parker and William Rawm Associates.

Long-time UMBC Professor of Dance and arts advocate Carol Hess-Vait explained the significance of the PAHB in terms of its multiple constituencies.[60] She believes it will improve the work spaces for faculty, assist in recruiting top students, create venues for visiting artists, and attractively display the performances and research of the University faculty and students to the larger community. Catonsville, in particular, is really a college town; it just has not yet fully recognized it. The PAHB may be the magnet that finally brings the University and the community together.

---

57. Maryland Department of Budget and Management, FY 2007–2011, Capital Improvement Plan, USM. 141.

58. Hrabowski credited Governor O'Malley and House Speaker Pro Tem Adrienne Jones (UMBC'76) for their support. "Budget Update," April 12, 2011.

59. UMBC Facilities Master Plan Update, 2009–2011, Executive Summary. 14–15.

60. Carol Hess-Vait, interview by the author, May 18, 2011.

2009–2019 Master Plan

Periodically, the campus looks ahead to create a new master plan for facilities. The 2009–2019 plan updated the 2003 plan[61] and had the ambitious goal to:

> anticipate facilities needs to aid in realizing UMBC's aspirations: to become one of the nation's best research universities; to contribute to the intellectual, economic and cultural richness of the greater Baltimore area; and to engender pride among faculty, staff, students, alumni and the citizens of the state.[62]

This planning exercise involved over 120 members of the campus community and was presented to various on-campus forums and to representatives of adjoining communities. The ten year proposal was to add 938,000 gross square-feet and 592 residential beds at a cost of $874,000,000 (2009 dollars) to the campus.

The new plan projects several different types of construction for academic, student services, athletics and, of course, parking. The then projected Performing Arts and Humanities Building and the addition to the Patapsco residence hall and creation of a True Grits plaza were already underway by 2011. Other buildings were much farther from completion and at least one seemed to have an uncertain future. The next in line is most likely the Interdisciplinary Life Sciences Building which will replace the one-story student services and theater building in the center of the campus. Farther out chronologically will be a multidisciplinary building to be constructed where a parking lot behind the Physics building is now located. A new student life building will face The Commons and several buildings will be renovated. What might have seemed to be the most speculative building, because some of the projected $80 million funding would have to be private, was the UMBC Events Center to be built near Giffen Hill on the south side of Hilltop Circle. The Center would be used to house convocations, graduations, athletic events, and other performances.[63] The main space was projected to seat about 5,000. UMBC also wants to continue to house on campus about 75 percent of its freshmen and 40 percent of its total undergraduate student body, so there may be additions to existing dormitories, as well as additional construction along Walker Avenue. All buildings will be planned to meet or exceed LEED silver environmental rating required by the State. The University is aggressively trying to reduce demand for on-campus parking to preserve space for other purposes and to decrease its carbon footprint,[64] so some of the projected building in the next decade will be constructed on existing parking lots. Nevertheless, several high rise parking garages are also contemplated.[65]

---

61. LDR International, *1990 Facilities Master Plan*, UMBC. UMBC historic documents collection, Special Collections, University of Maryland, Baltimore County.

62. UMBC Facilities Master Plan, Update 2009–2019, March 25, 2010. 1-1.

63. Cannon Designs, B&D Venues, Barton Malow, "Campus Events Center Study," Final Report, July, 2013.Whitman Requardt &Associates, "The UMBC Events Center," December 16, 2013.

64. UMBC Facilities Master Plan, Update 2009–2019, 21–22.

65. Ibid. 21. The campus in 2012 had 7,091 parking spaces in 17 lots.

C. Research Park[66]

In 1989, Tim Baker wrote that "Until this year Baltimore was the only major metropolitan area in America without a university-affiliated high-tech incubator."[67] UMBC quickly set about to change that assessment and in that year opened the Technology Research Center in a 70,000 square-foot former juvenile detention facility.[68] The building was first repurposed to support the burgeoning graduate engineering programs approved in 1984. Their activities attracted such corporations as Martin Marietta and Westinghouse as collaborators to work with UMBC faculty and students on projects with immediate real world applications.

The University also wanted to foster the work of start-up businesses and so created The Technology Enterprise Center in a nearby modular 8,000 square-foot building to commercialize and market products and technologies developed by start-up private companies in UMBC laboratories. Santo Grillo, the first tenant and President of a three-person start-up Biotrax, Inc., expressed his gratitude for being able to move his business from his basement to the campus saying, "UMBC is sort of the University of Maryland's biotechnology and molecular biology flagship campus. That is a definite attraction.... For a biotech company UMBC makes sense."[69]

The incubator concept helps companies share resources and staff to lower overhead costs before products can earn income and to create supportive environments to spur innovative thinking. Nationally, completion of a business incubator program has increased the likelihood of start-up survival by 87 percent.[70] Typically, however, the expectation is that firms will not remain in the incubator stage for more than two years and during their transitions some fail to compete in the economy.

Consequently some administrators began to think that the next step should be the creation of a full-scale research park to permanently house the University's research partners and to give UMBC a bigger footprint in corporate and political circles. The decision to turn campus land over to a private corporation to create and manage a research park was controversial on and off campus.

---

66. Much of the research for this section was completed in 2010–11 by Grant Foehrkolb, then a UMBC undergraduate political science major and member of the UMBC History team in a paper "The Research Park at UMBC," now in the UMBC archives.

67. Tim Baker, "Incubating Success," *Baltimore Sun*, June 6, 1989.

68. The history of this building is recounted in James Milani to George La Noue email, April 17, 2013. The aggressive courting of business partnerships in this era, under the leadership of Craig Weidemann, is described in Lisa Libowitz, "When Business Speaks UMBC Listens. Can we talk?" *UMBC Magazine*, Fall 1994.

69. David Rosenthal, "Business incubator produces offspring at UMBC," *Baltimore Sun*, February 8, 1989. Bill McConnell, "Incubator Brewing Big Plans" Director Expects 20 Firms, Research Park," *Daily Record*, May 30, 1990. See also Alan Kline, "Biotech company hatches from UMBC incubator," *Baltimore Business Journal*, May 20, 1994.

70. University of Michigan, NBIA, Ohio University and Southern Technology Council, *Business Incubation Works* (Athens, OH: National Business Incubation Association, 1997).

In 1988, serious discussion began about what to do with land outside the Loop Road in the southern-most part of the campus.[71] These former orchards and farmlands were now speckled with scrub trees and bushes and populated by small wild animals. At a University with few financial assets, some saw these acres as a potential source of income. Others feared that, if UMBC could not find a use for them, the State might reclaim the land. There was also support for keeping it in an undeveloped condition as a recreation area and an ecological laboratory.

Under new President Michael Hooker, interest increased in finding the potential best purposes for the currently unused campus land. Hooker had been seeking to convince Baltimore's economic and political elites that the region's future should be knowledge-driven. "Research universities have an increasingly significant role to play," he urged, "The knowledge discovered and created in universities will be the fuel rods powering the economy of the 21st Century."[72] It was an attractive message for Baltimore City where the manufacturing base was eroding and its port's future uncertain. His proposal also was received favorably in Baltimore County, home to a number of defense-related industries. The end of the Cold War and an economic recession led to a cut-back in military contracts. Between 1989 and 1991 in Baltimore County alone, Westinghouse laid off 2,600 employees; Bethlehem Steel, 1,200; Allied Signal, 1,176; Martin Marietta, 796; and AAI, Inc. (formerly Aircraft Armaments, Inc.), 623.

Though the concept of harnessing university resources to build an economy was hardly a new concept nationally, Hooker's assertion that UMBC, with its recently developed science, engineering, and high tech programs, should be at the center of a Baltimore initiative seemed startling, if not naive, to some listeners.

A land use committee of faculty and administrators was formed in 1988 to consider various proposals for the ninety-four acres, then empty, south of the Loop Road. One of the earliest concepts was to build a small campus-focused shopping center, a hotel or campus inn, or even a sound stage for shooting movies.[73] No commercial interest developed for those enterprises and the idea died. Anyway those proposed uses were something short of "fuel rods" for "the 21st Century."

Much more serious was a proposal to build on this campus land a stadium for the return of professional football to Baltimore after the Colts left. Some thought the location ideal and others imagined that a pro stadium on the campus would put UMBC "on the map" with much favorable publicity. A planning meeting was eventually held with HOK staff, the country's foremost stadium architectural firm which had built Orioles Park at Camden Yards, among other projects. To spice up its campus presentation, HOK brought along Bart Starr, former Green Bay Packer quarterback and a member of the Pro Football Hall of Fame. Mr. Starr actually said very little, but his two massive Super Bowl rings had their own sort of eloquence. Initially,

71. Susan Thornton, "UMBC, Spring Grove sites eyed: Research park plans progress," *Catonsville Times*, April 20, 1988.

72. Michael Hooker's Vision," *Baltimore Sun*, May 31, 1992.

73. Ginny Cook, "Research Park Being Planned at UMBC," *The Daily Record*, June 28, 1989.

there seemed to be considerable enthusiasm for the stadium project among the UMBC representatives. Then someone asked about parking. The HOK consultant replied that there was a formula requiring so many acres for parking for each 1000 fans in the proposed 70,000 seat stadium. Someone quickly did the math and the meeting grew silent as it became clear that approving the stadium meant paving over a huge part of the campus. Cordial goodbyes were expressed; Mr. Starr's rings were admired; and the stadium idea was never raised again.[74]

The site also attracted the attention of another athletic entrepreneur, Ed Hale, who owned the Baltimore Blast indoor professional soccer franchise as well as several shipping companies. Hale mentioned the UMBC site at a news conference saying he wanted a "complex to attract big-name entertainers and conventions in addition to serving as a home for the Blast." With a proposed seating capacity of 22,000, Hale surely envisioned a potential National Basketball Association or National Hockey League franchise. UMBC responded coolly, saying that most of the land would be used for research, but that "UMBC will ultimately need space for graduations ... and a Division I basketball program."[75]

After those misguided efforts, attention increasingly focused on developing a research park.[76] Such parks connected to universities had become more common and, while not all were successful, some had made enormous contributions to their sponsoring campuses. A report on the Stanford Research Park summarized its development this way:

> Just after World War II, Stanford University was struggling financially. It was land-rich, but cash-poor, so its leaders had an idea: How about we create a new income source by using some of the land for industry?
>
> The Stanford Research Park, as it is now known, was the first of its kind in America. Today, the 700-acre spread has 10 million square feet of commercial real estate that generates millions of dollars for the university each year. It's home to such iconic brands as Hewlett-Packard, one of its first tenants, and the banks, consultants, restaurants, and law firms that serve them.... It's the epicenter of Silicon Valley.[77]

Nationally, about half of the research parks generated earnings that went to their sponsors or back into the park's budgets, but the amounts were generally small.[78] The

---

74. The author, as a member of the land use committee, attended this meeting.

75. Pete Kerzel, "Blast owner's UMBC arena plans 'premature,'" *Catonsville Times*, April 18, 1990.

76. Michael Luger and Harvey A. Goldstein, *Technology in the Garden: Research Parks and Regional Economic Development* (Chapel Hill: University of North Carolina Press, 1991). The Association of University Research Parks has about 170 members in North America.

77. Jeff Chu, "Stanford's Unique Economic Engine," *Fast Company.com*, October 1, 2010.

78. Battelle Institute, "Characteristics and Trends in North American Research Parks: 21st Century Directions," October, 2008.10.

University System of Maryland attempted to create a research park on 466 acres in Bowie, not adjacent to any campus. By 1991, that park was viewed as a failure, attracting only one tenant and creating a debt for the University of Maryland Foundation.[79]

In 1989, UMBC hired Bernard Berkowitz, former President of the Baltimore Economic Development Corporation, to be senior advisor for economic initiatives at UMBC. He promptly began to develop a master plan for a research park. Other than the general attractiveness of the location, at the intersection of highways I-195 and I-95 and just five miles from the Baltimore-Washington International Airport, there was not much to work with. Important questions about the necessary infrastructure and who would pay for it, whether the park would cover all ninety-four acres, what kind of businesses would be welcome, and what the actual benefits to the University would be were yet to be answered.

One early possibility for a tenant illustrated the problem of moving in an ad hoc manner. Berkowitz and Mark Behm, Vice President for Administrative Affairs, became interested in acquiring the Maryland Bioprocessing Facility, a project supported by the State and UMS, for the park.[80] Johns Hopkins University also wanted the Facility, so competition began to secure it for the UMBC park. As the Land Use Committee began to evaluate the proposal, however, the Facility's image of an innovative research enterprise with possible close ties with UMBC's scientists proved instead to be more of a light manufacturing operation for small bio-tech firms which needed to produce batches of pharmaceuticals to meet FDA testing and clinical trial requirements. This is a socially useful activity, of course, but the jobs involved were mainly unskilled labor with no research activity. UMBC retracted its interest and the project went to the Hopkins Bayview campus.[81]

A more promising project was a proposed Center for Toxics, Waste Management, and Bioremediation (CTWMB). The Center's purpose was to create an interdisciplinary program to develop technological solutions for the use and disposal of these substances and to examine the social, legal, and ethical problems that would be created. This was a project that could engage many scholars at UMBC, but it never went beyond a concept.[82]

Perhaps the most grandiose idea for a park tenant was an attempt to convince the U.S Food and Drug Administration (FDA) to move some or all of its 4000 employees scattered throughout Montgomery County to Catonsville. Partnering with

79. Pat Meisol, "UMBC presses controversial research park," *Baltimore Sun*, January 28, 1991.

80. Maryland Department of Economic and Employment Development, Joint Chairman's Report, Maryland Bioprocessing Facility, Skullney, Box 6. UMBC historic documents collection, Special Collections, University of Maryland, Baltimore County.

81. Liz Bowie, "Hopkins' Bayview campus picked as 'incubator' site," *Baltimore Sun*, February 14, 1992.

82. Joint Chairman's Report, Bioprocessing Facility, Skullney, Box 6, UMBC historic documents collection, Special Collections, University of Maryland, Baltimore County.

Baltimore County, UMBC had eighty acres rezoned and set about courting the FDA.[83] Connie Beims, assistant to Chancellor Hooker, said, "UMBC provides the world with most of its molecular technologists and has developed strong specialties in biochemical engineering which could become a source of specialists for agency like the FDA."[84] From the agency's perspective, there was an attraction to consolidating its resources adjacent to a university. Montgomery County, which had no such university, was, of course, not amused by UMBC's overtures to lure one of its major employers. A spokesperson for the Montgomery County Office of Economic Development said "It is an unwritten rule ... that officials shouldn't try to entice a company away from a neighboring jurisdiction."[85] Since a FDA move from county to county was projected to cost $400 to $500 million, it found little support among state or federal officials.

After these abortive attempts to jump-start a research park, resistance to the basic concept began to form. A faculty subcommittee of the Provost's Committee on the Campus Environment opposed the creation of a research park. Their manifesto read:

> 1. There is no compelling logic to justify the establishment of a research park on campus.
>
> 2. Using the land for the research park will sharply limit our ability to develop and strengthen environmental education and research.
>
> 3. Becoming deeply involved with and dependent on private economic interests could threaten our independence as a research university.[86]

As UMBC began to occupy more space within the Loop Road and the extensive research park was projected to occupy the land beyond it, a number of UMBC faculty and staff began to be concerned about how to reconcile University expansion with concern for the environment. By late 1994, the Committee on University Priorities created a subcommittee on the campus environment co-chaired by Robert Burchard, Professor of Biological Sciences and Patricia La Noue, Director of Interdisciplinary Studies. The campus environmentalists had some success. The Maryland Department of Natural Resources donated scores of trees that now grace the Loop Road. La Noue and her students planned and created the mile-long Herbert Run Greenway linking together various wooded and ecologically-significant campus areas. When the athletic department wanted to bulldoze into a wooded knoll to expand the RAC,

---

83. Lynda Robinson, "Catonsville envisioned as high-tech: UMBC, state seek extensive rezoning," *Baltimore Sun,* November 12, 1987.

84. Robert A. Erlandson, "UMBC hopes to attract FDA to rezoned property," *Baltimore Sun*, January 16, 1989.

85. "UMBC breaks 'unwritten rule,' courts FDA," *Montgomery County Journal*, January 18, 1989.

86. Working Group on Curriculum Priorities, "Statement of Opposition to Research Park," May 1996. UMBC historic documents collection, Special Collections, University of Maryland, Baltimore County.

there was a successful opposition to that plan led by campus environmentalists, and the administration agreed to relocate the expansion.

Other faculty wondered in the dawning internet era, when communications around the globe were becoming instantaneous and when research partners were frequently in many different locations, whether the purported advantages of proximity for cutting-edge research between the campus scientists and the park tenants were exaggerated.

The greatest opposition to the proposed park, however, came from the neighborhoods surrounding the campus. Word about possible bioprocessing facilities and toxic waste disposal set off alarm bells in Catonsville, Arbutus, and Relay. Previously neither the University nor nearby residents had paid much attention to each other. Mostly UMBC dealt with state officials. When the University needed local political support or approval for anything, it went to Baltimore County's offices twenty miles away in Towson and ordinarily did not ask adjoining neighborhood what they thought. Nor did campus neighbors see much of concern or interest in the development of the University. Contained within the Loop Road, UMBC appeared to create few problems, business opportunities or even much publicity of any sort. Even today, with a current University of a much larger magnitude, many residents don't think of Catonsville or Arbutus as college towns.

Neighborhood opponents formed the somewhat grandly named Coalition for the Preservation of Southwest Baltimore County. Their strategy was to raise a number of issues about the use of land: traffic and pollution concerns, destruction of historical sites, development on wetlands, and the treatment of biotechnology hazards. They succeeded in gaining the support of Berchie Manley, the Baltimore County Councilwoman from Catonsville, and challenged park development at every procedural step. There turned out to be a lot of procedural steps.[87]

In November 1989, the Maryland Historical Trust, under Coalition prodding, recommended that an "identification survey" of archeological sites be conducted, so there would be no "future construction delays" and mentioned that one historic and two prehistoric sites were known to be on campus lands.[88] The phrase "construction de-

87. The political struggle over creation of the Research Park is described at length in Grant Foehrkolb's paper, "The Research Park at UMBC," January, 2011, UMBC historic documents collection, Special Collections, University of Maryland, Baltimore County.

See also, "Community Concerns, UMBC Research and Development Park," prepared by the Southwest Coalition, Skullney, Box 5; UMBC historic documents collection, Special Collections, University of Maryland, Baltimore County. Paul Lipkowitz, "Opposition to Project Mounts," *Catonsville Times*, January 2, 1991; Leslie Rice, "BIG RETURN: Early returns show major opposition to research park," *Arbutus Times*, February 20, 1991; James Michael Brodie, "Anti-research Park forces on offensive," *Catonsville Times*, November 17, 1993.

88. Letter from William Pencek, Office of Preservation Services to Hans Meyer, Maryland Economic Development Corporation, November 20, 1989. Robert Erlandson, "Traces of 19th-century high society spa are found in wooded area near UMBC," *Baltimore Sun*, December, 15, 1991.

lays" was a bit of a euphemism. If a site with enough archeological significance had been found, "delay" might have meant "never." So there were some anxious moments for park planners, until it was proven that "yes" there were prehistoric dwellers on the land, but "no" they hadn't left any permanent sites that needed to be preserved.

The Coalition also objected at various project funding stages. When UMBC sought a loan from the Maryland Industrial Redevelopment Fund to begin park infrastructure, the Coalition pointed out that this use of tax dollars required evidence of community support for projects. President Hooker commissioned a local group to do the required survey and it turned up a positive result, though a Coalition sponsored survey turned up a negative response. More importantly, the Coalition pointed out that the Fund had a stipulation preventing construction for public educational facilities.

By April 1991, UMBC had won key endorsements for its proposed research park from Governor William Donald Schaefer and Baltimore County Executive Roger Hayden, but the local opposition was not daunted. Consequently, UMBC felt it had to confront the Southwest Coalition. President Hooker declared that "the park would be part of the solution to America's lagging competition with Japan and other industrialized nations for control of manufacturing technology and markets." He also threatened "that if the university had to drop the research park, it would have to expand in some other way, probably as a teachers college. That would mean doubling the student population to 20,000 which would create far worse traffic problems than the research park."[89]

The Baltimore County Council also had to approve a zoning change for the park, which the Coalition vigorously opposed, though only Catonsville Councilwoman Manley voted against the rezoning.[90] Even with County zoning approval, there were still other fights ahead. UMBC's plans called for twelve buildings on ninety-four acres, but when Michael Hooker left UMBC in 1992 to become President of the University of Massachusetts, there were only two trailers designed as incubators sitting forlornly on the land intended for the park.

Funding needed to be found to pay for infrastructure and UMBC did not have that money. After a lot of political activity, by 1992, the park had secured a pledge from Baltimore County for $450,000 and a $1.45 million dollar loan from the Maryland Economic Development Corporation.[91] It wasn't enough. The University wanted

89. Jay Merwin, "Politicians are undecided on a UMBC research park," *Baltimore Evening Sun*, May 1,1991.

90. Karen Saverino, "Zoning won't block research park," *Catonsville Times*, May 13, 1992.9; Patrick Gilbert, "Manley irks council by refusing to budge on rezoning issue. UMBC proposal leaves her isolated," *Baltimore Sun*, October 7, 1992; Karen Saverino, "UMBC won't be downsized: Manley lone dissenter," *Catonsville Times*, October 21, 1992; Councilman, now Congressman, Dutch Ruppersberger explained why the normal "courtesy" honoring a veto of projects in a local district of a Council member did not apply because the research park "could be a very positive thing for Baltimore County and the region."

91. Paul Lipkowitz and Pete Kerzel, "Panel OK's loan for research facility," *Arbutus Times*, January 20, 1992.

to get federal Economic Development Administration (EDA) money for the infrastructure expenses, so it had to meet various federal regulations. Why a research park on campus lands should be selected rather than 13 other sites identified in Baltimore County had to be justified. Acknowledging that the park was controversial locally and that ninety letters mostly in opposition had been submitted, UMBC responded to the eighteen separate issues raised. Perhaps, the most salient for the park's future was the opposition's objection to using tax dollars to "increase the profits of selected businesses," ignoring the fact that this is a common practice in Maryland and elsewhere. In response, UMBC pledged:

> The purpose of the research park is to encourage increased research collaboration between faculty, students and private companies. The occupants of the research park would be selected on the basis of benefits to the University. Market rents would be charged for the sites with net revenues from land rents going to the University.[92]

EDA also wanted the University to formally agree to certain restrictions on the use of the land, so in 1994 UMBC developed a Declaration of Covenants and Easements. There were prohibitions on manufacturing and assembly, warehousing and distribution, any sales, headquarters or general offices, hotels, or various forms of biological research that had Biosafety level 4 ratings, unless approved by the UMBC President and faculty senate.

In order to take the next step to obtain Phase I construction funding, it was decided that a major change in organizational structure had to be made. A UMBC Research Park Corporation was formed in 1994 and a long term ninety-eight year lease agreement for campus land was reached with the new entity. Berkowitz became the president of the Corporation and a nine-member Board was chaired by David R. Frederick, executive vice president of Colliers Pinkard, a commercial real estate firm.

On the surface it looked as though nothing much had changed. In several respects, however, there was a major shift. UMBC would no longer control the land for almost a century and would receive no income from it. The argument was made that, particularly since there needed to be a substantial government investment in infrastructure, UMBC was not entitled to profit from the Park and that state appropriations might be reduced if the Park resulted in income to the University. Less vocally, some wondered if UMBC had the expertise to run a research park or whether the many stakeholders in the University's shared governance model would be able to find the consensus to act quickly enough to seize entrepreneurial opportunities. So the Park's advocates began to tout the possibility/probability that the Park's benefits would be the research synergy between the Park tenants and UMBC faculty and employment for UMBC students. Those arguments quieted the on-campus debate and attention shifted to obtaining infrastructure money and defending against continued Southwest Coalition attacks.

---

92. These points are summarized in EDA Environmental Assessment written by Edward Hummel, December 20, 1993.

In October 1994, Governor Schaefer announced that the Board of Public Works had approved the lease of state lands to the Corporation and an additional $650,000 state loan saying, "This project is an important part of the infrastructure envisioned in the state's economic development strategy."[93] Phase I Park construction costs were estimated at $2,455,000, with total construction costs at $30 million. The majority of the money came from grants from various state and local sources,[94] but federal funding required that the Park have a viable business model and an understanding that tenants would finance their own buildings. That set off a search for an anchor tenant that would provide credibility to the Park and a rationale for quickly installing the infrastructure. In 1993, the Park thought Westinghouse would play that role, but cuts in the defense budget caused that Corporation to defer and the Park's first building's future remained uncertain. After Phase I funding was secured in the fall of 1995, Atlantic Pharmaceutical Corporation, a subsidiary of the Danish-owned NiroInc. agreed to become the first anchor tenant. This plant, a custom processor of "solid dose pharmaceuticals and biotechnology products," was supposed to employ twenty-nine people and produce about $160,000 in tax revenues a year.[95] In return, the building it intended to occupy would be financed with $5.45 million tax exempt bond and a $430,000 guarantee by Baltimore County.[96] But UMBC was still enmeshed in zoning conflicts spurred by Coalition objections, so Atlantic withdrew its proposal.[97]

With this setback, the momentum for UMBC to create a major initiative in working with businesses seemed stymied. Then the University got a major break. In late 1996, the merger of defense industry giants Lockheed Corporation and Martin Marietta created a surplus 170,000 square-foot building almost at the corner of I-95 and I-195 just off Gun Road.[98] MEDCO agreed to buy the facility for $10.8 million and lease it to UMBC for 30 years. Built to industry standards with an auditorium, meeting rooms, and its own cafeteria, the facility proved to be a superior space for the University's incubator activities. Its acquisition also permitted consideration that maybe the Research Park would not need all the land originally sought.

A year earlier, Ellen Hemmerly had replaced Berkowitz as Executive Director of the UMBC Research Park Corporation and she helped engineer a compromise that

93. Governor's Press Office, October 5, 1994.

94. The Economic Development Administration, Baltimore Corporation EDA grant was for $1.345 million, Baltimore County contributed $450,000 and the Abell Foundation $150,000. Memo by Adam Wasserman, Deputy Director Baltimore County Office of Economic Development to Baltimore County Council, February 13, 1995.

95. Ross Hetrick, "Drug Firm to locate at UMBC park," *Baltimore Sun*, February 1, 1995.

96. Wasserman memo. 2.

97. Jim Joyner, "NIRO bows out of UMBC Research Park," *Catonsville Times*, August 9, 1995. L. Atwood, "Tired of Zoning Battle, only tenant for UMBC Research Park departs," *Baltimore Sun*, August 10, 1995.

98. Richard Byrne, "The Best of Both Worlds," *UMBC Magazine,* Fall 2009. It is understood at the end of the lease that the building will revert fully to the University. It is managed by UMBC's techcenter department and has changed its name from UMBC's South Campus to bwtech@UMBC south. Email from Ellen Hemmerly to George La Noue, January, 13, 2011.

eventually mollified both the on-campus and neighborhood Park opponents.[99] The Park's footprint was reduced from the proposed 94 acres and twelve building to 20 acres and five buildings.[100] The 1995 UMBC Mission Statement contained an environmental plank. Andrew Miller and Sandy Parker, professors in the current Geography and Environmental Systems Department, saw an opportunity to take the campus lands not used by the Park and turn them into a natural laboratory for the study of different types of forest, riparian, and wetland environments. Consequently, most of the remaining land was designated the Conservation and Environmental Research Areas (CERA).[101] Though there were still some battles ahead, Manley was defeated for re-election to the County Council in 1994 and her replacement Sam Moxley was a Park supporter. The reduced Park size and some efforts by Hemmerly and the University to mend fences finally dissipated the fiercest opposition.

In 1997 Phase I of the infrastructure was completed. In the fall of 1999, RWD Technologies, Inc, an internet and technology company from Howard County, committed to be the Parks' first tenant by contracting to build a 40,000 square-foot laboratory. Now, the Park had an appropriate tenant, though moving a company from Columbia to Catonsville did not improve the State's tax yield.

By 1999, University authorities had to concede that finding appropriate tenants for the Park was going to be harder than anticipated. UMBC had hoped to require a written collaboration agreement that the Park's developer would enforce with prospective tenants. But Scott Bass, Vice Provost for Research and Dean of the Graduate School, wrote a campus-wide memo that stated:

> We have discovered ... that a written collaboration agreement interfered with the developer's ability to negotiate directly with tenants and expeditiously close on a lease. This posed an increased financial risk to the developers and their lenders and ... as the agreement now stands, the building would not be built.[102]

So UMBC agreed to give up its written cooperation mandate in favor of encouraging tenants to seek relationships with the campus. The existing shared governance committee that was charged with pre-lease negotiations cooperative agreements was disbanded in favor of an advisory body that would work with tenants.

In the end, the Southwest Coalition succeeded in delaying the opening of the Park by nine years and substantially reducing its size. After this prolonged, rocky start,

---

99. Hemmerly, a graduate of the Johnson Business School at Cornell University, had been vice president of the Baltimore Development Corporation before coming to UMBC. In 2003, she was named President of the Association of University Research Parks. In a sign that peace had returned to town and gown, she was awarded the "2007 Business Person of the Year Award" by the Greater Catonsville Chamber of Commerce, *UMBC Insights*, October 8, 2007.

100. Patrice Dirican, "UMBC, opponents eye pact," *Catonsville Times*, February 23, 2000; Liz Atwood and Dan Thanh Dang, "UMBC scales back plans for technology park," *Baltimore Sun*, March 31, 2000.

101. http://www.umbc.edu/cera/. A few acres were given over for athletic purposes to compensate for fields the Park needed.

102. "Research Park Cooperation to be Encouraged, Not Required," *Insights*, 13, no7, April 1999.

the Park, currently called bwtech@UMBC, is now generally regarded as a success, so much so that there is some concern that it may seek to extend its boundaries.[103] In 2006, the Park announced plans for a new building for the Erickson Corporation, contractor for some UMBC dormitories and donor of $5 million for the Erickson School two years earlier. The problem was that parking for that building would have encroached on a grass field used for athletics and intramural sports, despite the fact that campus maps showed that the field was safely outside the Park's boundaries. It turned out that the Park had obtained a zoning amendment for an additional five acres, but the campus maps had not been redrawn. A compromise was reached when the Park agreed to provide funding to develop another field in return for building on part of the contested site.[104]

Ellen Hemmerly has acknowledged, "There is a very strong demand. If we had more land, we would be, I'm sure, continuing to develop new buildings."[105] There is always the possibility in the future that some powerful politician or corporation may covet some piece of campus land. Of course, the trade-off might be good for UMBC and the State. Whatever the future holds for the boundaries of the Park and the campus, Richard Byrne summarized the past conflict:

> The land now shared by the research park and the CERA was the scene of a sustained and divisive battle unparalleled in UMBC's 40-plus year history. Vocal opposition to the research park developed—both on campus and off—and lawsuits held up the project for more than a decade.... Only a hard-won compromise between the administration, the research park advocates, and UMBC faculty finally pushed the project forward. But that compromise has paid dividends, creating space on the campus for creating companies and boosting UMBC's efforts in environmental research teaching and sustainability.[106]

President Hrabowski declared that all parties were victorious[107] because UMBC's tradition of "shared governance between various campus constituencies was the key to the deal ... The research park has become a major indicator of the value that we bring to this region. The CERA is a physical representation of our interest in the environment."[108]

By 2012, the bwtech@UMBC Research and Technology Park was host to more than 100 firms in 515,000 square feet of offices and was becoming the focus of the

103. Jamie Smith Hopkins, "UMBC Research Park on Roll: The complex almost seven years old, is meeting a need, growing, and realizing its potential," *Baltimore Sun*, April 4, 2007.

104. This issue was discussed in the minutes of a meeting of the Athletic and Recreation Policy Committee with Lynne Schaefer, Vice President for Administration and Finance and Arthur Johnson, Provost, December 6, 2006.

105. Hopkins, "UMBC Research Park on Roll," *Baltimore Sun*, April 4, 2007.

106. Byrne, "Best of Both Worlds." 1.

107. Hrabrowski formed a UMBC Presidents Advisory Board to address issues of concern to its neighborhoods and the campus. Jim Edwards, "UMBC strives to better relations with community," *Catonsville Times*, May 25, 1994.

108. Byrne, "Best of Both Worlds."1.

emerging cybersecurity industry in Maryland.[109] For many faculty and students, as interns and employees, the Park has provided collaborative opportunities.[110] The Park has also proved to be a benefit to its uncertain community host. In 2007, *Money Magazine* ranked Catonsville the forty-ninth best place to live in the United States saying:

> Once a quiet bedroom community outside Baltimore, Catonsville is undergoing a renaissance thanks in large part to the University of Maryland Baltimore County which has transformed itself from a commuter school into a dynamic research center.... In the process, the city has attracted a number of high-tech firms and the jobs they come with.[111]

D. Conclusions

Walking around the imposing UMBC campus today with its 3.6 million square-feet of space in 47 buildings valued at $1.5 billion, it is almost impossible to imagine the University's humble origins. John Blitz, a writer for University Relations, recalled opening day, September 19, 1966:

> Up from Wilkens Avenue, the cars and motorbikes came; first a few, then clusters and finally a steady steam, disturbed the morning stillness of the former farm land. They carried the final ingredient, the necessary spark to bring the University of Maryland Baltimore County campus into the world of higher learning.[112]

Six months earlier, opening day was less certain. Dr. Kuhn recalled that he frequently came out from the old grey farm building to assure parents and prospective students. "'Yes, it will be finished. It will be,'" (chuckles) And wondering myself if it would be. And the students saying, "'Do I dare enroll here? Are you really going to be finished?'"[113]

It was a close call. At the twenty-fifth anniversary celebration, Kuhn told an audience:

---

109. "bwtech@UMBC Helps Jump-Start Small Companies" UMBC homepage October 17, 2012. For a description of some of UMBC's cybersecurity activities, from protecting electronic ballot security to deflecting hacking from foreign-based computers, see Joab Jackson, "Battlefield Bits and Bytes," *UMBC Magazine*, Summer 2010. 31–35.

110. By 2014, the Park employed 105 students and 90 alumni. Email from Ellen Hemmerly to the author, December 22, 2014.

111. http://money.cnn.com/galeries/2007/moneymag/0707/gallery.BPTL_top_100.moneymag4.

112. John Blitz, "A Campus is Born," *Maryland Magazine*, Fall 1966. 10.

113. Albin O. Kuhn, interview by Edward Orser, February 4, 1994.17. To achieve the on-time opening bricklayers had to be paid double time for long shifts. Most of the chemistry labs weren't completed. The gym floor had not been laid, but early physical education classes could be held out of doors.

> The night before the students arrived, English professors worked next to physical plant employees, secretaries, athletic coaches, and Kuhn himself, hurriedly swept away sawdust, vacuumed dorm rooms and cleaned up construction.... The team that helped get the place open was the most wonderful team I've ever had to work with.[114]

Kuhn proudly remembered "We opened on the day we were supposed to, right on schedule. Buildings were ready to be occupied; sidewalks were installed; the faculty was here. There were blackboards and even chalk." There were, of course, Kuhn reflected, some doubts and minor glitches, but also some unanticipated help.

> No matter how good the plan, no matter how much you assure others that you'll open on schedule, inside you have to have some reasonable doubt. It would have been chaotic if we hadn't opened on schedule ... On the eve of opening day 20 people showed up and spent Sunday tidying up the buildings, including one lady who had read we were opening and just came down to see if anything needed dusting.[115]

The rest, as they say, is history.

---

114. Leslie Rice, "Pioneer spirit is recalled; UMBC marks its anniversary," *Catonsville Times*, September 25, 1991.

115. Albin O. Kuhn, interview by Edward Orser, February 4, 1994,17. See also a blog by grand daughter Julie Kuhn, titled "Scrubbing Bathroom Floors=True Dedication," October 18, 2011.

CHAPTER IV

Administration

This book is not organized around successive administrative regimes, the common pattern for academic histories. Still the success or failure of UMBC administrators was often a critical component in the growth and achievements of the campus. There have been so many dedicated and productive administrators at UMBC (and a few duds), that they cannot all be mentioned. This chapter will focus on five campus leaders, Albin O. Kuhn, Calvin B.T. Lee, John W. Dorsey, Michael K. Hooker, and Freeman A. Hrabowski III. (See photo section.) Their office was titled Chancellor until the 1988 creation of the USM organization, when the position was retitled President. At that time the USM chief then took on the title of Chancellor.

A. Albin O. Kuhn (1966–1971)

As the founding father of UMBC, Albin O. Kuhn will always have an iconic place in the history of the University. Its grandest building, the centerpiece of the campus, is the library and gallery named after him.

It was entirely accidental that this farm boy came to be the University founder. Raised on a 215-acre dairy farm in Woodbine, Maryland (Carroll County), it was natural for him to study agriculture at the University of Maryland. Study he did, receiving his B.S. in Agricultural Education in 1938, his M.S. in Agronomy in 1939, and his Ph.D., also in Agronomy, in 1948. In 1940, he was appointed an Instructor at his alma mater, working with agricultural extension services around the state, and a year later, he became an Assistant Professor. His academic trajectory was interrupted by two years of military service in the Pacific, principally as a deck officer on the attack transport USS *Clinton*. After the war, he returned to the University of Maryland as Associate Professor in 1946 and became Professor and Head of the Agronomy Department in 1948. Among other things he taught cereal crop production, plant breeding, and statistics in field crop research.

In 1955, Kuhn was appointed Assistant to President Wilson "Bull" Elkins, and in 1958 became his Executive Vice President. In these positions, Kuhn had wide-ranging responsibilities for budgets, capital improvements, the professional school's instructional programs, the University Hospital and, of course, agricultural programs. He also served as the University liaison to state commissions and chaired a committee considering the feasibility of consolidating the state teachers colleges and the University. Finally, in an extraordinary affirmation of his talent and energy, Kuhn was appointed to be the Chancellor for both the UMBC and the UMAB downtown professional school campuses from 1966 to 1971. After that he became the full-time leader downtown. He left that campus in 1979 to become Executive Vice President of the University of Maryland system before retiring in 1982, after a UM career spanning nearly a half century.

Kuhn was involved in the creation of UMBC almost from day one and apparently loved every moment of it. While major political disputes erupted around the location of the campus, Kuhn remembered the site selection issue in much simpler terms. One day in 1963, President Elkins said to his Vice President, "Well, just simply stop everything else and start visiting sites, and let's get the site selected." Kuhn recalled that for four or five weeks straight he just looked at possible alternative locations for the new campus:

> We had a lot of possibilities, people who thought it would be good if you developed here, up around Shawan for example, or around Towson and so forth. I must have visited, I guess, twenty or thirty different sites, and a lot of them were attractive, but they were almost all too small in my mind. You know when you locate a college, a university campus, it's there, if you will, forever.... a good many of them were a hundred, two hundred acre sites and they didn't seem adequate.[1]

A local real estate man who knew about land adjacent to Spring Grove State Hospital wrote to Comptroller Louie Goldstein, who then told Kuhn to look at the 465 acre hospital farm site which the state already owned. Kuhn assayed it had "lots of good characteristics." After the State Director of Mental Health agreed to turn over the land for a new campus, Kuhn called Elkins. The President came over that afternoon to survey the farmland himself and liked what he saw. Amazingly just a week later, the Board of Regents and the Board of Public Works approved the hospital farm as the site for the new University of Maryland campus.[2]

For Kuhn, their decision launched his new career. By 1965, Kuhn had spent ten years working for Elkins in various administrative capacities and was a bit bored with the routine of the annual cycle of duties. Interested in changing jobs, he pestered Elkins to let him go and develop UMBC. Elkins at first said no, pointing out that Kuhn's role as Executive Vice President was a more important job than creating a new campus. Kuhn disagreed, threatening to give up administrative work entirely and go back to being a tenured professor. So Elkins grudgingly relented, but the President struck a hard bargain. Kuhn recalled Elkins saying:

> But, if you persist, then, in fact, if you are willing to take on the responsibility for both Baltimore campuses, the oldest campus, medical school, den-

1. Albin O. Kuhn, interview by Ed Orser, February 4, 1994. 12.
2. Ibid., 13.

> tal school, pharmacy and nursing, school of social work, law campus, and develop a new campus, I'll recommend to the board that you get that job.[3]

Whether Elkins thought the twin campus responsibilities was a job description no prudent man would accept is unknown. Kuhn reflected later, "You know if you'd started out to do that, it would seem awfully presumptuous, but it was a happy marriage.... The half a day here [UMBC] could be chaotic at times, and the downtown was very stable, long time developing."[4] Given his professional background in agronomy, Kuhn clearly was more interested initially in converting UMBC's farmland into a campus than managing the feudalities of the City campus's professional schools.

In retrospect, Kuhn was an indispensable man during UMBC's critical formative years. He found a way to draw on the strength of UMCP's personnel without compromising the new campus's independence.[5] He had a passion for building the new institution and a temperament for dealing with practical issues such as the locating of utilities in tunnels that connected the buildings. He recalled "Good Lord, we lived every bolt and nut and screw, and everything that made up this campus for a good many years."[6] But he also saw the big picture in campus design, making major contributions to such key campus features as UMBC's loop road with large academic core buildings clustered within walkable distances. He delegated the complex educational issues to the academic leaders he selected and concentrated on building, building, and more building, while winning friends for the new campus. He knew almost every relevant leader in the state. Politicians in every Maryland county were familiar with the agricultural extension service. His four-decade University of Maryland career provided him with considerable credibility among its leaders and a reservoir of contacts on its campuses from which to tap talents and ask for help. As Chancellor of both the downtown and UMBC campuses, he had lunch with President Elkins weekly. Gregarious, pragmatic, and optimistic, above all, he was an "old boy" in the best sense of the term when that phrase fully captured the nature of Maryland governance.

There are many examples of Kuhn's connections and savvy, but one of the most important occurred as he maneuvered to get highway access to the campus. Governor Millard Tawes was initially not a supporter of financing the new campus, but Kuhn eventually turned him into a powerful advocate. A son of Crisfield, a small Eastern Shore crabbing town, Tawes grew up far from the UM main campus and had only a

---

3. Ibid.
4. Ibid.
5. Albin O. Kuhn, "University of Maryland Baltimore County (UMBC) Its Early Years of Development and Organization," unpublished manuscript, collection 107, Special Collections, University of Maryland Baltimore County. From UMCP, Kuhn brought in George Webber, physical plant, Mark Shumacher for campus planning and landscaping, Harry Fisher for budgeting, and Jim Boreson for campus life (pages 8–9). On the other hand, UMBC was given autonomy in the development of disciplines and, courses, selection of faculty and creation of a separate plan of organization. (13) Albin O. Kuhn, "University of Maryland Baltimore County.
6. Albin O. Kuhn, interview by Larry Wilt, January 4, 2001.

little more than a high school education. But convictions about the value of education and Kuhn's friendship converted him to UMBC's cause.

In an interview intended to compliment Governor Tawes, Kuhn also revealed how good he was at making the system respond to UMBC's many needs. Kuhn began:

> I hope that whatever we may record [about] the history of this institution, we show regard for Governor Tawes. Because I think he was one of the finest supportive persons we had that helped us get going.... And he did wonders in helping us establish this campus and have it really grow.[7]

Then Kuhn described "one little illustration." As the campus was being designed, the I-95 highway was not quite yet built.

> It was all laid out, it was all ready to go, contracts were ready to be put on the market. There wasn't any outlet for UMBC. There wasn't any outlet for Catonsville. There wasn't any way to get in here [UMBC] directly. You'd have to go into the Beltway and around and come around. And I told Governor Tawes ... we were going to get to be a pretty large campus one of these days, and this was sad to build a new highway beside it, a big highway, and not have an outlet that fed right into the campus. And I can remember after we talked for a while, he buzzed and asked for Mr. Funk.... he was the man responsible for pushing all the projects on the highway, on roads, that sort of thing. And Funk came in and.... Governor Tawes said, "How far along are you?"[Funk replied] "Oh, we're just about done; we don't want any more projects." He [Tawes] said ... "You're gonna have to put one in to, to have access to UMBC. Oh there was a fair amount of saying, "Governor, please don't ..." Governor said, "Can you do it?" He [Funk] said "Yeah, it can be done." ... So, Mr. Funk was resigned to doing it. He [Funk] said, "Now Governor, is this on the University's budget or mine?" Governor said, "Sure it's on your budget, don't worry about it, just go do it."[8]

In later years, under other Governors and other University leaders, UMBC had difficulty getting approval even for signs on the I-695 Beltway and on I-95 indicating directions to the campus.

As Kuhn focused on the physical development of the campus and cultivating its political allies, his new Dean of the Faculty, Homer W. Schamp, Jr., had the immense task of shaping the new academic enterprise. Schamp, who is now in the small town Sidney Ohio High School Hall of Fame, went on to receive an A.B. degree from Ohio's Miami University (1944) and a M.Sc. (1947) and a Ph.D. (1952) in physics from the University of Michigan. He joined the College Park faculty in 1952, becoming a full professor in 1960, specializing in thermodynamics and molecular physics. Perhaps a little tongue in cheek, Kuhn recalled how he first noticed Schamp striding

7. Albin O. Kuhn, interview by Joseph Tatarewicz, August 14, 2001. 22–23.

8. Albin O. Kuhn, interview by Edward Orser, February 4, 1994. 18–19. Other reflections by Kuhn about building the campus and some early pictures can be found in Louise White. "A School is Born," *UMBC Review*, 10, no.1, (Fall 1991).

across the UMCP campus wearing his beret and thinking that's "a real academic person." More to the point Schamp was the Director of the Institute for Molecular Physics and was frequently a member of the UM University Senate.[9] Kuhn noted Schamp got things done in the Senate and thought he would be the right person to recruit the new faculty at UMBC.[10] Although in the early stages, there wasn't much division of labor between Kuhn and Schamp, it was the latter's task to write the first catalogue and hire the initial faculty.

According to Kuhn, despite their scientific backgrounds, he and Schamp were both committed to making liberal arts, particularly the humanities, the centerpiece of the new university. They were influenced by Clark Kerr, the President of the University of California, who wrote about the role of universities in improving society as a whole. Kuhn believed:

> You can't do that with just science, you have to do that with understanding people, you have to do that with understanding that real drive that's involved in the humanities and the arts. And when you put it all together, you can be very forceful. Without all of it together you won't get there.[11]

In the 1960s, there was considerable ferment regarding the structure of universities. Some students and even some faculty were opposed to those symbols of hierarchy and oppression such as majors and grades. Kuhn admitted to being quite "conservative" about these matters, but did note that UMBC was innovative in creating a January mini-semester which still exists and a plan allowing a student to work with a single faculty advisor to work out an individualistic curriculum in order to graduate.[12] That arrangement no longer exists and maybe was never implemented, though there are echoes in the current, more structured Interdisciplinary Studies Program, one of the first of its kind in the country.

One of UMBC's biggest problems was working with the State Board of Higher Education (SBHE), which had the power to approve new majors and was skeptical about adding majors that were not in the original campus plan. On one hand, UMBC wanted to be cautious about the majors it said it would offer. Kuhn remembers feeling, "Hey, we're not offering this; we can't put it in the catalogue. We can't promise this to students if we are not doing it."[13] On the other hand, as the University's enrollment and academic capacity expanded in later years, the State Board and other institutions opposed adding new majors at UMBC, even those that were commonplace in other universities across the country. Sometimes it seemed that while the State had approved the new Catonsville campus, it wasn't sure it should have any programs that any other campus had or wanted. This hesitancy made it difficult for UMBC to balance traditional academic offerings with necessary curricular innova-

9. In addition to numerous scientific articles, Schamp was co-author (with J.T. Vanderslice and E. A. Mason) of the textbook, *Thermodynamics*, Englewood Cliffs, N.J.: Prentice Hall, 1966.
10. Albin O. Kuhn, interviewed by Joseph Tatarewicz, August 14, 2001.11.
11. Ibid., 24.
12. Ibid., 25.
13. Ibid., 27.

tions for its students and local businesses and industry. The challenges for new program approval have been a constant in UMBC's history and Albin Kuhn handled them as well as any leader of a new campus.

In his declining years, as his eyesight faded, Kuhn reminisced:

> Having the opportunity to be the team leader in finding and developing UMBC has been a once in a lifetime opportunity. The fact that the campus has prospered and become an important entity in the field of higher education has been and remains a special pleasure in my life.[14]

B. Calvin B.T. Lee (1972–1976/7)

Kuhn's successor as Chancellor, Calvin B.T. Lee, could not have been more different in origin, education, personality, or impact on the University. Lee was born in Manhattan to Chinese-American parents[15] and trained to be a lawyer. He published several books on law and higher education,[16] as well as a Chinese cookbook.[17] He graduated from Columbia University in 1955 and received his law degree from New York University in 1958. After practicing law for a few years and a short stint working for the U.S. Department of Education, he began an educational career at Boston University (BU), rising swiftly to become Dean of the College of Liberal Arts at age 36, then Executive Vice President, and finally Acting President. While he wanted passionately to be the permanent BU president and was one of the two finalists, its board eventually chose the controversial John Silber.[18]

Lee's brilliant resume reflected the training and achievement of a young man clearly a comer in higher education circles. Yet as it turned out his Chancellorship was not a happy one either for him or the University. All of Lee's experience had been in elite, well-funded, well-known private universities. UMBC was none of the above.

---

14. Albin O. Kuhn's Family "scrapbook," Collection 127. Special Collections. University of Maryland, Baltimore County.

15. The Black Coalition of the University, disappointed that a black Chancellor was not chosen to head UMAB, met with the Board of Regents asking them to name a black academic as Chancellor for UMBC. "New Chancellor appointed at UMBC," *The Afro-American*, February 2, 1971.

16. *One Man, One Vote: YMCA and the Struggle for Equal Representation*, New York: Charles Scribner's Sons, 1967; *The Campus Scene: Changing Styles of Undergraduate Life 1900–1970*, New York: McKay, 1970; *The Invisible College: A Profile of Small Private Colleges with Limited Funding* (with Alexander W. Astin and Ralph M. Besse), New York: McGraw Hill, 1974; and *Improving College Teaching*, Washington: American College on Education, 1976.

17. *The Gourmet Chinese Regional Cookbook* (with his wife Audrey Evans Lee) 1976, Lee also published *Chinatown, USA: A History and Guide,* New York: Doubleday, 1965. Lee came by his interest in Chinese cooking and community naturally. He was born in New York's Chinatown and his father owned Lee's restaurant at Peel and Mott Street.

18. Edward Kern, "Quest for a Silver Unicorn," *Life*, June 4, 1971. Lee was thought to be the first Asian-American to head a major university.

Nor did the political culture of Manhattan and Boston in the 1960s and 1970s much resemble that of the Old Line State. While Kuhn's hand fit perfectly into the glove of Maryland politics, Lee's could never quite grasp it. Once invited to sit in the President's box with the University's funders and politicians at a Terrapin football game, Lee came back complaining that it had been a waste of time because he had nothing in common with "those people." In the end it wasn't "those people," so much as his own faculty, he did not understand.

Lee began auspiciously by bringing in a prominent political scientist Morton S. Baratz as his Vice Chancellor.[19] The administration, however, was facing some difficult problems. Budgets were unusually tight. UMBC's enrollment and SAT scores were dropping precipitously.[20] To address these issues, Lee commissioned a consulting report by The Barton-Gillet Company in 1974. The news was not good.[21] The report conceded that eight years after its founding UMBC was only now becoming relatively well known in its surrounding counties, but barely known in Prince George's, Montgomery, or Carroll Counties. Further, what was known was often not very favorable. It had not established a distinctive mission in the eyes of many observers, leading some to question where the campus fit into the larger higher education system in the State. There was a high student attrition rate and, since the campus offered a limited number of majors, some of which were not of much interest to employers, there was some skepticism about the employability of UMBC graduates. There were problems with student life (e.g. some racial incidents, a lack of activities, no common gathering place), and a faculty more interested in research than teaching. Barton-Gillett concluded that most of all:

> the University lacks any real sense of community ... the Tenth Floor [top administration] seems to be going one way, the Divisions are headed on a course about 10 degrees off that and the faculty seem to be moving at right angles.... The University simply cannot afford to be less visible than its sister institutions in such an entrepreneurial situation than currently exists in the Maryland system.[22]

---

19. In partnership with Peter Bachrach, Baratz wrote one of the most prominent political science articles ever published, "Two Faces of Power," *American Political Science Review*, LVI, December, 1962) in which they argued elites not only influenced the outcomes of political controversies, but also whether issues ever made it to the public agenda. By 2005, the article had been cited over 500 times. (*American Political Science Review*,100, November 2006, 667). Their book, *Power and Poverty: Theory and Practice*, was published by Oxford University Press in 1970. Baratz survived Lee's departure from UMBC, until 1979 when he became General Secretary of the American Association of University Professors (AAUP) for one year. He still maintained an attachment to UMBC and was a member of the President's Club with a $10,000 plus gift in 2000–01.

20. See Figures M and O in Chapter VIII.

21. Barton-Gillett Report on UMBC Campus Communications and External Relations, September 30,1974, Box 35, Folder 10, President's Office records. Collection 50. Special Collections. University of Maryland Baltimore County.

22. Ibid., 9, 13–14. The report noted that "UMBC is still an idea for which there are few labels."

In short, without the political finesse and clout in its leadership of an Albin O. Kuhn, UMBC was a very vulnerable campus.

Lee's most immediate challenge was the resurrection by the Maryland Council for Higher Education (MCHE) of the State University of Metropolitan Baltimore Area or SUMBA concept. It was not a new idea, but MCHE had put it on the table again in 1974. Under this scheme, the four Baltimore area undergraduate campuses would be treated as though they were specialized colleges with Towson concentrating on education, the University of Baltimore on business and law, Morgan on the social sciences as they relate to urban problems, and UMBC on the other sciences.[23]

It fell to Lee to defend UMBC against a plan that would have removed the campus from the University of Maryland system and leveled all campuses in the Baltimore area. The tricky thing was to demonstrate the legitimate difference in UMBC's aspirations, if not its current achievements, from other Baltimore campuses without denigrating them. Lee used the mantra that UMBC was a university within a university (i.e. UM), but it is not clear anyone was persuaded by that phrase.[24] To distinguish UMBC from other potential SUMBA institutions, he pointed to the campus emphasis on faculty qualifications, particularly in research; budding relationships with UMAB professional schools; and on some new program developments he thought might be attractive. But Lee was most effective in joining the other Presidents in trashing the basic SUMBA concept. While conceding that SUMBA had "a sort of slick logic to it," Lee went on: "Speaking very frankly, it seems to me that this Commission and other committees are being asked to solve nasty political and inter-personal problems by devising structural changes that will only complicate the matter, if not make it worse."[25]

Attacking the motives of Maryland politicians may never be a good strategy for a public university leader, but Lee was at his strongest when he outlined the practical

23. Calvin B. T. Lee, "Presentation to the Commission on the Structure and Governance of Higher Education," December 24, 1974. (Rosenberg Commission) (UMBC archives) No specialization was identified for Coppin. See also, Calvin B.T. Lee, Presentation to Maryland Council for Higher Education's Committee to Study Higher Education in the Baltimore-Metropolitan Region," October 29, 1974. Box 14, Folder 25. President's Office Records. Collection 55, Special Collections. University of Maryland, Baltimore County.

24. Ibid. He elaborated that UMBC was a new kind of university because it was not a comprehensive university in competition with College Park He argued "this State is too small to afford more than one large comprehensive state university if it wants to have quality." (p.14), but that "UMBC was not a university in name only as was the case for converted teachers colleges who had adopted the university name." [The scorned name changers were not named].

25. Ibid. The year after the SUMBA proposal was defeated, another report, this time by the Governor's Study Commission on Structure and Governance of Education in Maryland, (Rosenberg Commission) was released. The report recommended a new centralized structure which was strongly opposed by the Maryland Regents. See their response dated September 2, 1975. Richard W. Case, at one time member of the Regents, described the Rosenberg proposals as a "mill which will grind all public higher education into a homogenized mass." *Baltimore Sun*, June 14, 1975. Because the threat was to the whole University of Maryland organization, UMBC did not play a central role in that debate.

problems with the SUMBA concept. First, he pointed out that many students do not have a clear or realistic idea of their academic aspirations when they enter college and should spend their first years engaged with the liberal arts. Second, he noted these first two years are often difficult to teach and require more than a bare-bones faculty in the non-specialized curriculum areas. The faculty in the de-emphasized areas, feeling they were second-class citizens, would seek positions at other universities where their talents could flourish. Third, he argued that a university should be an academic community and not just "an impersonal filling station for students." Finally, Lee declared bluntly that "The public transportation system in the Greater Baltimore area is so bad that it will defeat any program or structure which will require going to more than one institution in any given semester."

SUMBA was dead. It had no visible support from any Baltimore campus, but by 1976, both Lee and UMBC were facing difficult times. Although UMBC's enrollment had been projected to be 10,000, it seemed stalled at about 5,200. Budget cuts eliminated fourteen positions and faculty raises were only 2.5 percent. Many senior faculty felt the Chancellor was personally aloof and administratively inconsistent in following promotion and tenure policies. Most of all, they feared, he was not effective in advocating UMBC's interests in College Park or Annapolis. For his part, Lee had earlier that year sought, without success, the presidency of Tufts University, a Boston area private institution.[26] UMBC seemed stuck with a Chancellor who didn't really fit its leadership position and who knew it.

One of the perennial problems in any academic structure is managing change among top administrators, who typically do not serve for fixed terms. Chancellors and presidents theoretically work for a board of regents or trustees who have the legal power to hire and fire them, but these boards are usually dependent on the administrative chain of command for information. While in Maryland there is a student Regent, there is no regular procedure for the Regents to seek or receive faculty input from any campus. Further, the unpaid political appointees on the Board do not welcome public controversy and have no means to deal privately with faculty concerns even when they know about them. Finally, Regents' policies are carried out in practice by the same administrators who may be part of the problem. It is one thing for individual faculty to criticize administrators. The traditions of academic freedom usually protect that speech, but seeking to oust top leadership is a risky endeavor for most faculty. The only option is collective action, but faculty consensus about any course of action is notoriously hard to obtain.

As the frustration increased on the Catonsville campus, the UMBC Senate's Faculty Affairs Committee (FAC) took a step apparently unprecedented on Maryland campuses. It organized a no confidence vote. On March 3, 1976, all faculty received a ballot with a cover sheet that read:

> In recent months, the faculty attention at UMBC has been increasingly drawn to the subject of institutional leadership. The Faculty Affairs Com-

26. Mike Bowler, "2 here still vie for job at Tufts," *The Baltimore Sun*, January 28, 1976.

mittee which bears the responsibility to represent faculty opinion at UMBC has been reluctant to express itself without further clarification of the faculty viewpoint. Consequently, in response to requests by many of our colleagues, we are distributing the enclosed questionnaire. This secret ballot will be counted by the [Senate] Organizational Committee and that count will be made public.

We hope this procedure will prevent the further growth of rumors and facilitate an efficient decision-making process within the University.[27]

The ballot simply stated, "Given UMBC's current situation and probable future needs, my opinion of Chancellor Lee's ability to provide the appropriate leadership is best described as one of:

( ) Confidence

( ) No Confidence

( ) No Opinion

( ) I wish to abstain from voting"

Faculty ranks were to be indicated and the signed ballots were soon counted.

In retrospect at least, the FAC referendum was politically very astute. The FAC had the organizational mandate to represent the faculty and in theory all it was doing was asking for instruction based on faculty opinion. The FAC was a representative group, but small enough to reach consensus privately on a course of action. There was no lengthy public debate about the wisdom of the referendum. The cover sheet's language was not provocative and the ballot's choices clear. By turning over vote counting to another committee, there could be no charge that the outcome was being misrepresented.

That outcome was overwhelming. Of the 139 full-time faculty, 108 voted and the no confidence option was selected by a margin of seven to one. As promised, the vote totals were made public and there were stories about the referendum in the *Sun* and the *Chronicle of Higher Education*.[28] The FAC, however, decided not to talk to the press until it had a chance to report to the Senate, so the news stories were dominated by administrators and organizations that were willing to respond. Chancellor Lee told the *Chronicle* he would not resign, that the faculty's action "lacked legal status" and that "a no confidence vote is similar to a vote to unionize. Collegiality has been breaking down since the early 1970's, when harder times hit." From Lee's perspective, the issue was all about money and the faculty's impression that he was not an effective table pounder, but, "Pounding on people's tables doesn't solve the problem."[29]

---

27. The referendum papers are in the UMBC archives. UMBC historic documents collection, Special Collections, University of Maryland, Baltimore County.

28. Mike Bowler, "Chancellor loses confidence vote," *The Baltimore Sun*, March 12, 1976.

29. Gael M. O' Brien, "Maryland Professors Vote No Confidence in Chancellor," *The Chronicle of Higher Education*, March 27, 1976.

Speaking to the Faculty Senate which he chaired, Lee's comments were more pointed:

> I can only say, speaking for myself, having been in academic administration for 15 years, that I am profoundly disappointed in the manner in which the thing was done. I am not surprised about the vote or the size of the vote or anything like that. I was disappointed because I don't know whether to say people were naive, stupid or malicious to believe that to have a vote like this and not to have it leak out . . .[30]

The lawyer in Lee presented the situation as a due process issue in which he should have been presented with a bill of particulars to which he could have responded.

Refusing to resign and having labeled UMBC's faculty leadership as "naive, stupid or malicious," what was the next step? Lee's academic administrative career prospects were severely damaged. For its part, a few days later the FAC prepared a two and half page single space report to the faculty describing the situation from its prospective:

> In recording its judgment, the faculty acted with dignity. There was no campaigning, no emotional accusations, no attempt to arouse student discontent, no attempt to involve the press. We think it unfortunate that the issue was widely discussed in the media before the Senate met to consider the results of the referendum. The Committee did not take part in the media controversy.[31]

The FAC's report also provided a historical context, noting that as early as the fall of 1973, most of the full professors met with Chancellor Lee to discuss leadership concerns, but there was no response from his office. The next year, the UM central administration rejected most of UMBC's promotion and tenure (P&T) recommendations, although they had been endorsed by Lee. The faculty concluded that the Chancellor had lost credibility with the central administration and the P&T process needed to be reformed, but nothing was done. In 1975, a Middle States Task Force on Campus Governance and Faculty Rights and Responsibilities "found a massive lack of faculty confidence in the governance, promotion and tenure, and compensation procedures at UMBC." By late 1975, the FAC judged that the UMBC administration was in "deep disarray" and had "virtually ceased to function as a collegial decision-making body." In February 1976, after the Senate received the news that Lee had not been selected at Tufts and intended to remain at UMBC "for the foreseeable future," the President of the campus American Association of University Professors chapter suggested at a Senate meeting that Lee could no longer be effective at UMBC. The Chancellor, wielding the gavel, ruled him out of order. Fearing that individual faculty and administrators were intending to take the issue off campus to the press,

---

30. Transcript of remarks of Calvin B. T. Lee to the UMBC Senate, March 16, 1976. UMBC historic documents collection, Special Collections, University of Maryland Baltimore County.

31. "Report to the UMBC Faculty From the Faculty Affairs Committee of the UMBC Senate" 1. UMBC historic documents collection. Special Collections. University of Maryland Baltimore County.

the legislature, and the Regents, the FAC decided the better course was the referendum on no-confidence.

Addressing specifically Lee's view that there should have been a bill of particulars before the vote, the FAC responded:

> We respectfully disagree. First, a statement of charges at that point might have been seen as an attempt to influence the vote. Second, we believed then and we believe now that a debate over specific charges would unnecessarily damage the Chancellor, others in the administration and UMBC itself. The issues are solely those of quality of leadership and judgment. These are matters in which conclusive proof is not possible.... we think it inappropriate to talk in terms of due process in evaluating a Chancellor. This position is essentially political leadership. Its success depends on the confidence of a number of constituencies. If the Chancellor loses the confidence of the Regents or the central administration, he will be asked to resign without due process.
>
> The faculty does not possess such legal powers, but surely it is obvious that a campus cannot work effectively where there is no confidence in the leadership. The qualities that give UMBC its edge in excellence do not come from what the faculty has to do by contract, but stem from the extra effort the faculty volunteers in its teaching, scholarship and service. A continuing conflict between the Chancellor and faculty would erode that voluntary spirit and therefore the excellence we have achieved.[32]

The FAC's bottom line was to call for a month-long moratorium on off-campus public discussion of the controversy and to invite the Chancellor for talks with faculty leadership and ask about his plans to serve elsewhere next year or to take up his tenured faculty position. Should the Chancellor decline, the FAC said that after the thirty days it would draw up specific charges.

That threat proved unnecessary to carry out. While Lee received letters of support from two Regents and a few faculty members,[33] there was no action by the Board and no ringing affirmation from President Elkins. Indeed, Lee's previous interest in Tufts may have been encouraged by external campus leaders. In any event, Lee left UMBC a few months after the no confidence vote, with shove marks clearly on his back, to become a Vice President for training and development at the Prudential Insurance

32. Ibid., 2–3.

33. The UMBC black caucus disassociated itself from the vote, believing that the referendum should be directed against all the leadership of the university and that singling out the Chancellor might be an attempt "to hound Dr. Lee out of office because of his attempts to meet [desegregation] standards." Bowler "Chancellor loses confidence vote" March 12, 1976. The caucus received editorial support from the *Afro-American* newspaper which repeated the suggestion that Lee was "treated shabbily because he is a member of a minority group." March 20, 1976. For Vice Chancellor for Academic Affairs Morton Baratz's only qualified support of the Lee administration, see, Glen Fallin, "UMBC Chancellor's Support Called Hazy," *Baltimore News American*, March 15, 1976.

Company of America in Newark, New Jersey. Seven years later at age 49, Lee was dead. Even in death, his identification with the UMBC campus was tenuous. The *New York Times* obituary referred to him as a former Chancellor of the "University of Maryland."[34]

After Lee's abrupt departure, the Regent's selected one of their own, Louis L. Kaplan, the Regent's incumbent Chairman to be interim UMBC Chancellor. Kaplan, then age 74, was considered to be the grandfather of modern Jewish education in Baltimore. He founded Beth Am synagogue and established the Baltimore Hebrew University, serving as its first President. Given the perceived disarray at UMBC, Kaplan was a logical choice for the Regents to calm down the upstart campus. When he addressed them he said, "Please disabuse your minds of the fact that UMBC is down in the dumps. It is a campus that is moving ahead." Indeed he thought students from Prince George's and Montgomery counties should consider coming to the Catonsville campus. "The only thing we don't have to offer is a football team."[35]

C. John W. Dorsey (1978–1985)

Who would be Chancellor following Kaplan's interim year? Would it be an insider or an outsider? A search committee was formed and received 135 applications. That number may have been a bit surprising, since many thought UMBC was anything but a plum job. The *Evening Sun* wrote: "The new Chancellor, whoever he is, will take over a campus torn by faculty dissent and unsure of its mission in an era of slow enrollment growth and waning public support for higher education."[36]

The search committee for the new UMBC Chancellor was chaired by long-time UMCP administrator, R. Lee Hornbake, at that time its Vice President for Academic Affairs. Two of the final four candidates who were interviewed at UMBC were from College Park and the winner was John W. Dorsey. He had a strong Maryland background, born in 1936 in Hagerstown, growing up as a child in nearby Sharpsburg. He received his B.S. in Economics in 1958 from College Park, before moving on to Harvard for his M.A. (1962) and Ph.D. degree (1968). He also received a certificate from the London School of Economics. Dorsey started teaching at UMCP as an assistant professor and became the Director of the Bureau of Business and Economic Research on that campus in 1966. He then moved full time into administration as Vice Chancellor for Administrative Affairs in 1970. Dorsey was appointed to lead the College Park campus as acting Chancellor from 1974 to 1975. After that year, he returned to the economics faculty where he was not entirely comfortable, realizing that

---

34. "Calvin Lee, Education Planner for Employees at Prudential," *New York Times*, March 16, 1983.

35. Ellen I. James, "UMBC Campus That is Moving Ahead, Assures Kaplan, Interim Chancellor," *Baltimore Evening Sun*, August 19, 1976.

36. Michael J. Himowitz, "Dorsey Seen as Top Candidate for UMBC Post," *Baltimore Evening Sun*, May 2, 1977.

his administrative duties meant he was no longer in touch with the discipline's research frontiers.[37]

As UMBC welcomed its new Chancellor in 1978, the campus knew it was getting an experienced administrator with good College Park connections. Still there was a certain wariness.[38] Had the Regents picked Dorsey to quell the unruly UMBC faculty? While many of the early UMBC administrators at every level had come from College Park, UMBC was struggling to create its own identity and coming from UMCP no longer had an automatic cachet. After the selection, some UMBC faculty wondered whether Dorsey had been passed over for the UMCP Chancellorship and was made UMBC Chancellor as a consolation prize.[39] In the end, the selection of a quintessential UM insider had both its advantages and disadvantages.

Dorsey wanted to tap College Park administrative talent familiar to him to join his UMBC team. First, he asked George Callcott, who had been Vice Chancellor for Academic Affairs from 1970 to 1976 to come to Catonsville. Callcott, however, who later won UMCP's Distinguished Scholar-Teacher award in 1991, wanted to finish his career in College Park. Dorsey had a more short-lived success in getting Tom Day, who had been UMCP's Vice Chancellor for Academic Planning and Policy to come to UMBC as Vice Chancellor for Academic Affairs. Day said yes, but served at UMBC only about a year before becoming President at San Diego State University for eighteen years.[40] He was replaced by Walter Jones, a political scientist, who also came from UMCP.

Whether or not any of UMBC's problems were caused by mismanagement or benign neglect in the Lee administration, the problems were real and they had to be addressed. Enrollment and SAT scores had plummeted during the Lee years and grumbling could be heard among state political and educational leaders that creating UMBC might have been a mistake. A *Sun* columnist called UMBC a "white elephant" and pointed out that the State Board for Higher Education had rejected new doctoral programs on the Catonsville campus in favor of focusing doctoral work at College Park, UMAB, Johns Hopkins, and Morgan State.[41]

Dorsey responded quickly with three major internal reorganizations. He abolished the campus's original divisional structure in favor of a single dean of the faculty. The obsolete UMBC Assembly which had functioned something like a House of Lords requiring a two-thirds majority to approve "constitutional changes" in the campus

37. Some of these insights about Dorsey came from George Callcott, his longtime friend and author of two College Park histories, in an interview by the author, May 5, 2011.

38. See, for example, the skepticism expressed in the videotaped interview with Jonathan Finkelstein by Joseph Tatarewicz, April 16, 2013.

39. Himowitz had written "a feeling that UMBC was somehow a step child of the College Parks campus left many UMBC faculty members bitter."Dorsey Seen as Top Candidate for UMBC Post," *Baltimore Evening Sun*, May 2, 1977.

40. In a curious parallel, Elliot Hirshman, who was provost at UMBC from 2009–2011 also left to become President of San Diego State.

41. Michael J. Himowitz, "New Chancellor Plans A 'Fresh Breeze,' for UMBC," *Baltimore Evening Sun*, August 1, 1977.

by-laws was ended.[42] He also recruited Michael V. Mahoney, away from Towson University, as the new director of a restructured academic services office, combining admissions, registration, and financial aid. Previously, UMBC had had three admissions directors in three years, but Mahoney quickly reorganized and energized this area. In a combined organizational effort, UMBC enrollment increased from 5,346 students in 1977 to 9,740 in 1989.[43]

Whether it was the attention drawn to UMBC by the ouster of Calvin Lee, the campus's persistent enrollment deficits, Dorsey's connections with College Park power brokers or new UMS President John Sampson Toll, who enthusiastically supported expansion of all things connected to the University of Maryland is uncertain, but in November 1978 a plan was put forward that would have substantially increased UMBC's program portfolio.[44] Six months earlier, under the leadership of Michael J. Pelczar, Vice President for Graduate Studies and Research, the UM system completed a report reviewing the academic programs of the University for the purpose of "ascertaining the feasibility of relocating any program entirely or in part from one [UM] campus to another."[45]

UMBC, under Dorsey's leadership, reacted robustly to this invitation. The response articulated four goals: (1) supplementing UMBC's arts and sciences base with career-oriented programs; (2) utilizing existing and planned facilities at UMBC and other UM campuses with efficiency and economy; (3) increasing the number of upper division students to be more characteristic of a university campus; and (4) providing more extensive part-time graduate opportunities. These goals were premised, somewhat audaciously at that time, on the principles that UMBC should maintain academic standards equal to those at UMCP and UMAB and that, "Washington and Baltimore provide two separate spheres of influence, and UMBC and UMCP should relate to and benefit from the resources and challenges of two vital and differently oriented metropolitan communities."[46] The document also noted that all the existing UMBC doctoral programs have involved collaboration with UMAB or UMCP. Sometimes those affiliations were more for political cover, however, and did not involve regular academic interactions.

---

42. Michael J. Himowitz, "New Head Asks Changes at UMBC," *Baltimore Evening Sun*, September 3, 1977.

43. Mahoney who had seen many UMBC students transfer to Towson believed, "While the [campus] buildings are modern and functional, they lack warmth ..." that courses were scheduled at times more convenient to faculty than students, and that there were two few majors that led to clear cut career paths." Michael J. Himowitz, "New UMBC Official Wants to Add Personal Touch," *Baltimore Evening Sun*, December 12, 1977. By 1995, UMBC's SAT scores tied College Park's. But a gap returned, when UMCP used its far greater financial resources to offer more financial aid. David Folkenflik, "UMBC ties College Park in Freshman SAT scores," *Baltimore Sun*, February 21, 1995.

44. John Dorsey, John S. Toll, and B. Herbert Brown, "A Prospectus for the University of Maryland Baltimore County," (hereafter prospectus) November 17, 1978, UPUB P7-013, Box 2, University Publications, Special Collections, University of Maryland, Baltimore County.

45. University of Maryland Task Force Report, May 1, 1978.

46. Dorsey, Toll and Brown, Prospectus, 4.

So what did UMBC want specifically? In new facilities, the request was for a university center, which was constructed in 1982, and more residence halls (West Hill and Terrace apartments) which were built in 1981 and 1982. UMBC also wanted help in attracting and maintaining more minority students. There was not much controversy in those goals, but UMBC also proposed creating a Ph.D. program in Applied Developmental Psychology (jointly with UMCP), a doctorate in Instructional Systems Development, an M.M. in music, an M.A. in Geography, and an M.S. in Chemical Physics. That alone would be a substantial programmatic expansion, but UMBC's wish list went on. UMBC proposed that by the 1978–1979 academic years, the UMCP School of Business and Management be extended to UMBC, the extension of UMCP's education graduate programs to UMBC, the transfer of the UMCP Department of Information Systems Management to UMBC, and the creation of a School of Journalism at UMBC. These dramatic proposals caused deep rumbling of discomfort within and without UMS. Further, all these moves would have to be approved by the frequently unsympathetic SBHE.

The proposed creation of a UMBC School of Journalism, which would not have duplicated anything in Baltimore, never got off the ground either when it was opposed by Montgomery and Prince George's County interests who wanted to preserve College Park's monopoly in that field. The UMCP School of Education was not extended to UMBC and there is no undergraduate education major now on the Catonsville campus.[47] UMBC prefers to train teachers in their disciplines with thirty credit certificates in teacher training supplemented by field placements to enable professional certification. There is a substantial Education Master's program, enrolling 357 students in 2012. The Information Systems Management program, over some opposition at College Park, was transferred to UMBC and has flourished, enrolling 603 undergraduate majors, 357 M.S. students and 77 Ph.D. students in 2012.

Dorsey inherited a difficult situation in the aftermath of Calvin Lee's departure. Yet, he was able to stabilize the campus and reorganize its administration. During his years as Chancellor, enrollment grew by almost 3900 students and SAT scores increased by about 100 points, though still trailing the then national average. Of great long-term significance, since Dorsey had the confidence of the Regents and other UM administrators, UMBC was able to add thirty degree programs to its portfolio during his tenure. He neither sought nor attained much out-of-state visibility and fund raising remained stagnant. Dorsey appeared to be a quiet, taciturn insider leader, except when provoked as he was when the campus was threatened with closure and he discovered his inner Churchill.[48] His successor, however, was a gregarious, some would say flamboyant, outsider who vigorously set out to promote UMBC's and his own regional profile.

---

47. UMBC was one of the first universities to require prospective teachers to complete an academic major. Timeline-History of UMBC. http://lib.guides.umbc.edu/content.php?pid=417297&sid=3411009.

48. See Chapter II, p. 39.

D. Michael K. Hooker (1986–1992)

Born in Richlands, Virginia, son of a coal miner, Hooker was the first from his family to graduate from college.[49] He earned his B.A. with highest honors from the University of North Carolina, Chapel Hill in 1968 and then earned his M.A. (1972) and Ph.D. (1973) from the University of Massachusetts, all degrees in philosophy. Hooker taught at Harvard and then became an assistant professor at Johns Hopkins in 1975. He moved into administration as assistant Dean, associate Dean, and Dean at Hopkins, until 1982 when he was named President of Bennington College.[50]

Hooker's frequent mobility continued throughout his career, but moving, from Bennington, a tiny Vermont private liberal arts college, to UMBC was not a predictable career path. Nevertheless, Hooker had a deep commitment to public higher education and loved Baltimore. As UM system President John Toll said of Hooker at his installation as UMBC's fourth chancellor:

> Dr. Hooker has shown superb leadership as a dean of both undergraduate and graduate programs at a research university and has demonstrated success in building good cooperation between campus and community. As President of Bennington College, he had been on first name basis with students and faculty, inspiring each to his or her best effort, and has won the respect and support of trustees, donors, and national leaders for his dedication, high energy, academic judgment, and administrative effectiveness.[51]

Toll was famous for his enthusiastic upbeat style. He used to say when he visited the UMBC Faculty Senate that the only difference between UMBC and the University of California Berkeley (often considered the best public university in the country) was that Berkeley had a hundred year head start. By that he meant that both campuses were located at the periphery of their major urban centers and were related to public health science centers some distance away in the city. UMBC faculty who tended to notice other significant differences between the two universities, often rolled their eyes at such comparisons, but they were more than ready for aggressive positive leadership. Michael Hooker was ambitious and eager to assert a new role for UMBC.[52]

Hooker served as UMBC Chancellor from 1986 to 1992 and during that period both his political and personal skills were tested. One of Hooker's first initiatives was

---

49. Wolfgang Saxon, "Michael K. Hooker, 53, Chancellor with a Community Approach," *New York Times*, July 11, 1999.

50. Hooker's career path is chronicled in William Douglas, "Lofty wish list for a wunderkind," *Baltimore Evening Sun*, January 16, 1986.

51. UMBC public relations Hooker biography,1988.

52. Hooker began his advocacy for UMBC while he was still Chancellor-elect. Writing in the *Sun*, he praised its "first-rate faculty," increasingly talented students, and the merged UMBC/UMAB graduate school. He concluded: "Twenty years is not a very long time as the history of higher education goes, but UMBC's beginning is solid and its future enormously promising." *Baltimore Sun*, April 19, 1986.

to try to convince the Baltimore region's business and political elites that they needed UMBC, an idea that had probably never occurred to most of them.

As a signal that he intended UMBC to play on a wider stage, Hooker promoted Adam Yarmolinsky, who at that time was Regents Professor of Public Policy at UMBC to be his Provost. Yarmolinsky had been the former Bennington College Chairman of the Board and probably was the person who brought Hooker to the attention of the UM search process. In some respects, this was an unusual Provost appointment. Yarmolinsky did not have a Ph.D. or a conventional research track record. Instead his career followed a different trajectory. As a Harvard undergraduate and then Yale Law School alumnus, he went on to clerk for Supreme Court Justice Stanley F. Reed and then became an almost permanent advisor in the Washington establishment. He was one of Robert S. McNamara's Defense Department's "whiz kids," although he was increasingly skeptical of the Vietnam War. A quiet, intensely thoughtful man, he served as an advisor to Presidents Kennedy, Johnson, and Carter[53] and was reported to have 1000 names in his rolodex cards. When Yarmolinsky showed up in Catonsville first as Regents Professor of Public Policy and then as UMBC's new Provost, Baltimore noticed.

Hooker's philosophy was one that was widely welcomed in the abstract, but the details, when they were forthcoming, caused some hesitation and even fierce opposition. In his 1991 annual report on the occasion of the UMBC's 25th anniversary, he wrote:

> At UMBC, we envision the 21st century university as an interactive institution. The model we see replaces the 'ivory tower' at society's periphery with a 'glass power plant,' an open institution at the center of society generating and sharing knowledge to fuel a prospering healthy community.[54]

Hooker asserted "UMBC can shape and direct the region's economic and social development, as other research universities are doing in cities such as Pittsburgh, Seattle, and San Diego." Later, he escalated his vision, "UMBC has the potential to create the same kind of economic development for the Baltimore region that such institutions as Stanford University have created for the Silicon Valley."[55]

It was a message he carried to numerous, initially skeptical, but eventually welcoming civic, business, and political groups. A *Sun* editorial, "America's Biotech Future," quoted Hooker saying that the commercial application of the life sciences will be "the dominant technology of the 21st Century."[56] Of course, from his perspective UMBC

---

53. Neil A. Lewis, "Adam Yarmolinsky Dies at 77; Led Revamping of Government," *New York Times*, January 7, 2000.

54. Patrice Dirican, "Hooker Remembered as UMBC visionary," *Catonsville Times*, July 7, 1999.

55. See for example, Michael Hooker, "Advancing the Greater Baltimore Region: The Strategic Enhancement of UMBC," May 1990, p. 2. This white paper served as the basis for the Hooker campus agenda. UMBC historic documents collection, Special Collections, University of Maryland, Baltimore County.

56. "America's Biotech Future" *Baltimore Sun*, February 18, 1990.

would be a key player.[57] Tom Chmura, deputy director of the Greater Baltimore Committee, a booster organization that later adopted many of Hooker's ideas remembered: "A lot of people poohed-poohed it as futuristic nonsense. I don't think many people immediately buy into his ideas, but lo and behold, you look out a couple of years later and say 'Gee, a lot of that is on target now.'" Shaila Aery, Maryland Secretary of Higher Education, was even blunter: "Six years ago, people said this guy is nuts.' They would say 'All we want is for people to get along [in the status quo] not to be a model for the country.'" State Senator Barbara A. Hoffman, then perhaps the legislature's leader on higher education, put Hooker's impact in this perspective: "Some people didn't like him because he scared the pants off of them. He is not your typical low-key academic."[58] Hooker's vision of the modern university and UMBC's place in that new role meant enduring controversy, perhaps occasionally courting it.[59]

Creating a research park tied to the campus was a logical way to embody his glass power plant vision and Hooker vigorously championed that goal. As described in Chapter III, however, the actual plan to build such a park on unused land south of the campus Loop Road created substantial local opposition. Biotechnology experiments and the Catonsville lifestyle did not seem compatible. It took nearly a decade to overcome the procedural and financial obstacles and construction on the park did not begin until 1997, five years after his presidency ended.

Before Hooker's tenure, when the campus and the rest of the region wondered what UMBC was and what its future would be, the easiest explanation was that UMBC was the University of Maryland's undergraduate and graduate research university in the Baltimore region. Don't be misled by the County name, its adherents said, and don't confuse us with the University of Maryland at Baltimore, (UMAB), the professional school downtown in the City. Remember, instead, that Maryland higher education is organized like the University of California's three-tiered model with very clear distinctions about the roles of its top-tier competitive admission doctoral-granting research campuses, its second-tier of teaching-focused campuses with more open admissions standards, and its third-tier two-year community colleges. As long as Maryland followed this model and Johnny Toll could convince "the powers that be" that Maryland campuses could emulate their California peers,

57. Bill McConnell, "Region to Lead Biotech Rise: UMBC Head predicts Dramatic Economic Shift," *Daily Record*, June 7, 1990.

58. Thomas W. Waldron, "College chief's legacy: Hooker's vision enhances UMBC," *Baltimore Sun*, July 7, 1992.

59. At the very least, Hooker was an incurable enthusiast. In an interview the week after his installation, he declared, "... the whole Baltimore-Washington corridor will become the new Silicon Valley, largely dedicated to biotechnology, with Johns Hopkins at one end, the National Institutes of Health at the other and UMBC in the middle.... Cancer, Alzheimer's, dwarfism, and obesity will become things of the past." John Morris, "Anticipating UMBC's Future," *Catonsville Times*, November 5, 1986. See a more detailed statement by Hooker of this theme in "Fertile Baltimore/Washington corridor beckons biotechnology development," *Washington Board of Trade News*, June 1988. 13. Also see Hooker, "Education is the fire fueling our future economic growth," *Baltimore Business Journal*, January 28, 1989.

UMBC could explain to prospective faculty, staff, and student recruits that its future was bright and clear.

Then, two years after Hooker took office, the organizational structure which defined UMBC's place in Maryland higher education crumbled. New Governor William Donald Schaefer proposed consolidating the tier-one and tier-two schools into a new University of Maryland System. (UMS). Missions, status, funding, salaries, and workloads could all be affected by such a consolidation or leveling as it was perceived by the old UM campuses. That caused consternation at College Park, which was eventually assuaged by designating that campus as the "flagship" and guaranteeing enhanced funding. At UMBC, there was great alarm at the loss of its distinctive role and the faculty organized to oppose vigorously the consolidation, placing Hooker in a difficult position. He was personally against the Governor's plan, but he was appointed by the gubernatorally-selected Regents and being opposed to a Governor is not a tenable position for any Maryland academic administrator. As described in Chapter II, the compromise was that he quietly toed the party line, while faculty representatives testified, wrote newspaper opinion pieces, and plotted with other campuses to protect UMBC's interests. In this difficult time administration and faculty shared information completely and respected each other's predicaments.

After Schaefer achieved his consolidation in 1988, the proposal of a UMBC/UMAB merger which had been floated around for several years was put on the shelf. UMBC's status was still ambiguous. A UMBC/UB merger was studied in 1989, but was rejected by the Regents ostensibly on the grounds on the ground that the institutions were too incompatible. In 1991, UMBC and UMAB agreed on a new merger proposal with the support of new USM Chancellor Langenberg (replacing Toll, who did not survive the creation of USM). This merger won unanimous support from the Regents, but College Park supporters in the state Senate defeated the proposal without a vote.

During this tumultuous period, Hooker faced some difficult personal challenges. His concept of an enhanced UMBC role was not receiving statewide support. He was not opposed to a merger, which had substantial support among Baltimore elites and might speed up implementing the arrival of his twenty-first century university vision, but he did not want its consideration to detract from his immediate goals for strengthening his own campus. He also knew such a merger would probably cost him his job. So he announced to the press that "It was clear that I had become the issue.... The only way to get the merger forward was to get myself out of the picture."[60]

He interviewed for the leadership position at the University of Central Florida in Orlando without any outcome, but in the fall of 1992, Hooker returned to Massachusetts to become President of the five-campus, 51,000 student University of Massachusetts system. After his stint in the Bay State, he moved in 1995 to the chancellorship of his alma mater, the University of North Carolina, Chapel Hill. In many respects, Hooker's career was meteoric, but unfortunately, it ended prema-

60. Paul Lipowitz, "Merger would end Hooker's tenure," *Catonsville Times*, October 30, 1991.

turely in 1999 when he died at age 53 from non-Hodgkin's lymphoma. It was a shock to everyone who knew him. He had combined a high tech vision about educating students in the twenty-first century with a populist dedication to making the public university the servant of its state. UNC commemorated him by creating the Michael Hooker Research Center at the UNC School of Public Health, as well as an endowed professorship, and named a 5k annual race after him.[61]

In his brief six-year UMBC tenure, Hooker achieved some substantial gains for the campus. That certainly was his opinion. When a *Sun* reporter asked him to evaluate his accomplishments on the Catonsville campus, he responded, perhaps a bit puckishly, with one word "Fabulously," and then elaborated, "I accomplished everything I set out to accomplish in the beginning." In the article, the reporter alluded to Hooker's "remarkably robust ego and a preternaturally expansive vision."[62] Yet, as he departed, the *Sun's* editorial page saluted him:

> No one has set forth a better vision for Baltimore in the next century than Michael Hooker, President of the University of Maryland Baltimore County.... UMBC would be in the vanguard of Baltimore's knowledge-driven future.... This means not only creating knowledge at UMBC, but transferring it from laboratories to practical applications. So Dr. Hooker went about forming business and government partnerships for UMBC, focusing much of the campus' efforts on leading-edge pursuits such as biotechnology, photonics, robotics and artificial intelligence.
>
> He saw UMBC as the engine capable of turning Baltimore into a center for life science technologies. Corporate and government leaders bought into the idea....
>
> UMBC is a better campus than it was before Dr. Hooker's arrival. It is drawing more bright students, with an enrollment of 10,000. Contracts and grants stand at $18 million. It holds a prominent role in engineering, information and computer sciences, public policy and technology transfer.
>
> Replacing Dr. Hooker won't be easy. He raised UMBC to star status among peer institutions.[63]

Others also were concerned about the impact of Hooker's departure. The publisher of the *Warfield's Business Record* began hyperbolically and ended with a more accurate appraisal:

> Prior to his [Hooker's] arrival, UMBC appeared somnambulant, its profile so low, it couldn't even muster a negative image.... Hooker shook UMBC from its sleep and pointed it toward change.... He helped UMBC stake out

61. Scott Cline "Lasting Impact," *Inside Carolina Magazine*, Summer 2004, http://northcarolina scout.com/2/341518.html.

62. Thomas W. Waldron, "College chief's legacy: Hooker's vision enhances UMBC," *Baltimore Sun*, July 2, 1999.

63. "Mike Hooker's Vision," *Baltimore Sun*, May 21, 1992.

> territories on the graduate level where competition was limited and opportunities plentiful. He saw that through business, academic and other partnerships, UMBC could be the foundation for social and economic growth. He has left the institution prepared to build on that forward-looking vision.[64]

The *Sun* which previously had regarded Baltimore higher education as a mess and UMBC as a bit of a failure now lauded Hooker's for changing regional appreciation for the future role of universities and UMBC in particular. In the political trenches, the perspective might have been different. During Hooker's tenure, the State altered its higher education's governing structure by replacing the old 5 campus UM system with a new 12 campus USM system which threatened to diminish UMBC's future role. Furthermore, College Park, unaccustomed to seeing praise for any other UM campus and unwilling to see a UMBC/UMAB merger that would have immediately created a new nationally-ranked Maryland university, had decisively blocked such a merger. Commenting on these events, columnist Tim Baker wrote an opinion editorial titled, "As Hooker Goes, UM's Vision Goes With Him," complaining that the state's higher education establishment did:

> absolutely nothing to try to persuade him to stay. His decision to leave and their complacency at his departure tells a lot about the problems and prospects of higher education in this state.... His aspirations for UMBC threatened too many settled institutional relationships and his obvious ambitions for himself disturbed too many less obvious egos. But he still leaves behind the gift of a shining vision which others can implement.[65]

So, even as UMBC was achieving a new regional status under Hooker, national prominence still seemed unlikely. The conventional pathways for a public university to achieve that national recognition, consolidated political support, and major infusions of public and private money, did not seem possible for UMBC. No alternative path was then plausible. Still in Michael Hooker's short tenure, he had made UMBC the center of Baltimore's discussion about its economic future and higher education and he had shown that being UMBC's leader could lead to even larger responsibilities at better known universities. What was not recognized at the time was that Hooker's most important long-term contribution to the campus was to spot talent in an unlikely place and to mentor Freeman Hrabowski once he came to UMBC. As improbable as it might have seemed at the time, there was a roadway to national prominence and new leadership could build it.

---

64. Edward Warfield IV, "Baltimore's Institutional Leadership at a Crossroads," *Warfield's Business Record,* September 11, 1992.

65. Tim Baker, "As Hooker Goes, UM's Vision Goes With Him," *Baltimore Sun,* August 31, 1992. Baker's piece prompted a response from George V. McGowan, Board of Regents Chair, titled, "UMBC will survive the departure of Michael Hooker" which began "in what must be a genuine surprise to anyone reading Tim Baker's column, the sky has not yet fallen on the University System of Maryland," *Baltimore Sun,* September 19, 1992.

E. Freeman A. Hrabowski, III (1992–)

On the surface, the installation of Freeman Hrabowski represented all the traditions of those academic events. There was a ceremonial parade with faculty and dignitaries in colorful caps and gowns and representatives from more than forty colleges and universities.[66] But the celebration also broke with tradition. The *Sun's* headline read "Hrabowski chosen as new president of UMBC: Educator, 42, is first black to head predominantly white college in area."[67] It was a special moment for Baltimore's African-American community that in the past had sometimes viewed the Catonsville campus with suspicion. Rev. Vernon Dobson, civil rights leader and pastor of one of Baltimore's most influential black churches, described Hrabowski as "a son of the south and a great-great grandson of the motherland." Kurt Schmoke, Baltimore's first elected black mayor declared, "[Hrabowski] is a man who legitimately can be called a national treasure and a local hero."[68]

The new President wondered briefly about how some campus constituencies would respond to his youthful age and his race, but those doubts were quickly erased on both sides. He had been at UMBC for six years when he became its President and was both a well-known and well-liked figure.

Hrabowski's background was unlike any other previous UMBC administrator and maybe unlike any other research university president in the United States. Born in Birmingham, Alabama in 1950, four years before *Brown v. Board of Education*, and into its culture of rigid segregation, the African-American boy, an only child, with the unusual name remembers his parents always told him, "You don't have to be defined as a victim. You can define yourself."

Self-definition was not only difficult for blacks in that time and place, it could be dangerous. A seminal moment occurred when Hrabowski was twelve. He joined the Children's March organized by Rev. Martin Luther King, Jr. Freeman was arrested, spat upon by the fearsome Sheriff Eugene "Bull" Connor, and spent five days with other children in a Birmingham jail.[69] School integration did not begin in Birmingham until Freeman was in tenth grade and even then it was violently resisted. Freeman's parents were both college-educated teachers who also took on other jobs to help the family. A strong work ethic and constant intellectual challenges permeated

---

66. James Michael Brodie, "Installation of Hrabowski is historic event," *Jeffersonian*, September 3, 1993.

67. Thomas W. Waldron, *Baltimore Sun*, May 8, 1993. Hrabowski was not the *Sun's* first choice to lead UMBC. It preferred that UMAB's President Errol L. Reese fill the vacant Presidency at UMBC, governing both campuses as Albin Kuhn had done in the 1960s. This would have created a *de facto* merger of the two campuses which the *Sun* ardently desired at that time. "Mike Hooker's Vision," *Baltimore Sun*, May 21, 1992.

68. Quotes from Brodie, "Installation of Hrabowski is historic event."

69. These Birmingham events are portrayed in Spike Lee's 1997 documentary *Four Little Girls*. See also Byron Pitts interview with Hrabowski on CBS' *Sixty Minutes*, November 13, 2011.

the Hrabowski household.[70] They sent their thirteen year-old son to a summer program in Springfield, Massachusetts. Another summer was spent at a National Science Foundation-funded mathematics program at Tuskegee University for "smart kids" from public and private schools throughout the country. There Hrabowski learned he could compete with the best.[71]

At age fourteen Freeman was admitted to Morehouse College in Atlanta, but his mother thought he was a bit too young for that experience.[72] So he waited a year and went off to Virginia's Hampton Institute, a historically black university, where he received a Bachelor of Arts, (with high honors) in Mathematics at age nineteen.[73] In 1971, he chose the University of Illinois at Urbana-Champaign for graduate school. Typically the only black student in a class, there were social challenges, but he received an M.A. in mathematics and then his Ph.D. in higher education administration/statistics four years later at age twenty-four. Hrabowski's eye was clearly on the prize.[74] He began his professional career at Illinois with some teaching and administration and then returned to his home state for a one-year sojourn as Associate Dean of the Graduate School and Associate Professor of Statistics and Research at Alabama A&M University, another historically black university.

By 1977, Hrabowski, at age twenty-six, came to Baltimore as Professor of Mathematics and later became Dean of Arts and Sciences and Vice President for Academic Affairs at Coppin State College. He may have first come to UMBC's attention when Mike Bowler, the *Sun's* education reporter, wrote a story about Coppin State's recent progress.[75] Instead of the usual institutional overview with an emphasis on President Calvin Burnett, the story focused on Coppin's Vice President Freeman Hrabowski. He was featured in a four by six photo and the article stated that if there is a turnaround at Coppin, everyone attributed it to Hrabowski "who is a much more visible figure on campus than Dr. Burnett and in recent years has assumed more presidential duties." Publicity about Coppin was and is scarce in the Baltimore media and, like most Presidents, Burnett was not pleased to see the spotlight on a subordinate.

---

70. Childs Walker, "Freeman Hrabowski's UMBC legacy grows as he celebrates 20 years as President," *Baltimore Sun*, September 2, 2012. These facts and several others in this section come from the *Sun's* unprecedented treatment of an educational leader in its three page story about Hrabowski's life story and his impact at UMBC and national education issues.

71. Hrabowski's memories about this experience can be found in "Explorations in Black Leadership," with Julian Bond, http://www.virginia.edu/publichistrory/bl/index.php?uid+44, p. 6.

72. For a more campus-specific description of Hrabowski's background written when he was UMBC's interim President, see Louise White, "Profile of a Leader," *UMBC Review*, 11, no.1 (Winter, 1993).

73. He also had a year as a foreign exchange student at the American University in Cairo.

74. Hrabowski's family, church, and educational experiences from childhood to graduate student and his attitudes about race were discussed extensively in his interview with Julian Bond, http://www.virginia.edu/publichistrory/bl/index.php?uid+44.

75. Mike Bowler, "Coppin students express pride in rising standards," *Baltimore Sun*, December 16, 1984.

After almost a decade at Coppin, Hrabowski began to feel uncertain about his future there[76] and to consider other options. UMBC was located just seven miles from the Coppin campus and Michael Hooker knew a winner when he saw one. He made Hrabowski Vice Provost on the Catonsville campus, a new specially created position that ruffled some faculty feathers who objected to the ad hoc nature of the appointment without the traditional national search.[77]

Jackie Hrabowski, Freeman's wife, had an important professional career in her own right as Vice President for Community Relations at the Baltimore investment firm, T. Rowe Price. She also taught part time at UMBC before Freeman was appointed. When asked what he believed about UMBC when he was at Coppin, Hrabowski replied very carefully that he thought of UMBC as "very suburban" and maybe not as connected to "life" as Coppin. Then he switched the conversation to UMBC's international dimension, standing by the picture of the many country flags displayed in the Commons.[78]

Hrabowski was installed as the fifth President of UMBC on September 24, 1993.[79] Thirty years before, UMBC had been approved by the Maryland legislature, as the state's first non-segregated public university, coincidentally in that same year the twelve year-old Hrabowski had been jailed for protesting segregation in Alabama. The installation was a remarkable event in his life story and, as his career unfolded at UMBC, significant in the life of the nation. None of that future could have been predicted by the audience assembled to hear the forty-two year old President speak.

Installations include representatives of other academic institutions who come to pay tribute to the new President, as well as local dignitaries, and the UMBC community. After his six years as Provost, Hrabowski was already well-known to his own constituency, so he used the occasion, as he would so often in the future, both to tout the University's achievements and to define its future goals to the audience gathered before him. He began:

> To all of you, I proclaim it an honor and privilege to lead the University of Maryland Baltimore County. We are a university "on the move." We know who we are, what we want to become, and how to get there. We will work to become the best public research university of our size in the world and we are determined that our dream will not be deferred.[80]

Perhaps that particular "dream," looking at UMBC as it then existed, might have seemed a bit audacious to some in the audience. Others might have wondered just

---

76. Mike Bowler, interview by author, October 27, 2010.

77. William Rothstein, interview by author, May 6, 2013.

78. America East Conference on Campus, Season 6, Episode 1, Freeman Hrabowski, You Tube. http://www.youtube,com/watch?v=jdd-TwmtKFA.

79. He also had been serving as Interim President since the previous June.

80. Freeman Hrabowski III, "The Value of Community," Installation Address, September 24, 1993, Office of the President, http://presidentumbc.edu/selected-speeches/ UMBC Library Archives.

how much wiggle room there was in the phrase "of our size." Nevertheless, it was a bold proclamation and one in which Hrabowski clearly believed.

In his address, he linked the themes of character, connections, and community. To define UMBC's character, he proclaimed, "We are a research university that cares deeply about its students," a phrase that has become something of a mantra for the institution and frequently repeated in its press coverage. Describing UMBC's character, he pointed out numerous student service activities, along with measures of excellence such as national faculty fellowships and strong working relationships with top university laboratories involving both students and faculty. He also lauded the ethnic and other forms of diversity among UMBC's students and emphasized that every campus racial group was successful in achieving high academic goals. He noted connections with state and federal public agencies and private industry and the prospect of new research park that would enhance all. He also stressed the connections theatre and music had made with local and even international audiences, calling the arts and humanities the "soul of the campus." Finally he focused on community, pointing out that, while UMBC students came from forty-nine states and seventy-nine nations, they all shared the University's common goals of advancing science, technology, and public policy. He concluded with George Bernard Shaw's words which he had adopted as his own conviction. "My life belongs to the community, and as long as I live, it is my privilege to do whatever for it whatever I can. I want to be thoroughly used up when I die, for the harder I work, the more I live."[81]

There were many challenges to achieving these goals. The first UMBC strategic planning process occurred in 1986 in response to criticism by the Middle States Association of Colleges and Schools during an accreditation evaluation.[82] The University had grown so rapidly that its organizational structure and policies began to resemble a teenager who suddenly notices his pants are too short, his shoes too small, and who no longer wants cartoon characters on his pajamas. When Jo Ann Argersinger left the UMBC Provostship to become President of Southern Illinois University at Carbondale in 1998,[83] Hrabowski turned to a UMBC veteran whose academic field was public management. Arthur Johnson had been chair of Political Science, chair of the 1996 Middle States self study, chair of the UMBC Faculty Affairs Committee, and Assistant Vice President for Academic Affairs. He was appointed interim provost in 1998 and permanently to that position in 1999.

Johnson saw several problems that needed to be rectified. Although UMBC started out with five divisions, as enrollment did not reach initial projections, in 1978 it consolidated most management responsibilities into a single deanship for all thirty Arts and Sciences departments. Despite Dean Richard Neville's skills and personal charm,

81. Ibid.

82. Timeline-History of UMBC. aok.libumbc.edu/specoll/universityarchives.php.

83. "Jo Anne E. Argersinger Named Chancellor of Southern Illinois University at Carbondale," *Insights*, 12, no.3 (April 1998).

the management tasks were too many for one office.[84] Johnson proposed to redesign the single-college structure into three colleges (Arts and Sciences, Engineering and Information Technology, and Professional Studies, Education and Human Services).[85] After considerable debate, a three college structure did emerge (Arts, Humanities and Social Sciences, Natural and Mathematical Sciences, and Engineering and Information Technology), along with three schools (Erickson School, the Graduate School, and the School of Social Work). This structure was clearly an improvement, but the hope that the several deans could also be fund raisers was not realized when money was not available to support development staff for individual colleges.

In 1999, Johnson also created an Enrollment Management Task Force to give more precise definition to the balances that needed to exist between graduate and undergraduate students as UMBC sought to be the "best mid-sized public university in the United States."[86] The Task Force identified what it called UMBC's enrollment dilemma: how to continue to attract students to an "Honors University," while enrolling a substantial number of part-time students who needed to maintain some form of employment.[87]

A separate 1999 Task Force on Continuing Education was formed to develop UMBC's role in this field. This group realized that, "Continuing education, because of its flexibility, responsiveness to market needs, orientation toward non-traditional students, offers strategic potential to universities as they respond to these emerging challenges and opportunities."[88] On-line courses were created and, in 2000, UMBC began to develop an active presence on the UM Shady Grove campus in Montgomery County.[89] Also in 2000, the Report of The Honors University Task Force chaired by Angela Moorjani was released.[90] That led in 2003 to a "Proposal to Reform General Education" which established new rules for course distribution.

In 2002–03, a planning leadership team created a "Strategic Framework for 2016" which was the result of five years of planning intended to culminate in achieving UMBC's vision of "ranking in the top tier of research universities as defined by na-

---

84. In 1992, a UMBC College of Engineering was established when its engineering program became independent of UMCP. For a discussion of the general political controversy about the role of engineering on the Catonsville campus see Chapter VII.

85. Arthur T. Johnson, Provost to Cheryl Miller, President, Faculty Senate, "Organizational Structure of Academic Departments," September 6, 2002.

86. Enrollment Management Task Force, UMBC Provost Office, 1999. 10. UMBC historic documents collection, Special Collections, University of Maryland, Baltimore County.

87. Ibid., 2.

88. Continuing Education Task Force, Executive Summary, June 1999.

89. By 2012, UMBC offered undergraduate degree programs at Shady Grove in Management of Aging Services, History, Political Science, Psychology, and Social Work and graduate degree programs in Biotechnology, Cybersecurity, Geographic Information Systems, and Industrial/Organizational Psychology. www.shadygrove.umd.edu

90. "Educating Undergraduates in a Public Honors Research University in the Twenty-First Century," Final version, June 15, 2000. See also a memorandum from Arthur T. Johnson to the Faculty Senate, "Proposal to Reform General Education", November 11, 2003. UMBC historic documents collection, Special Collections, University of Maryland, Baltimore County.

tional standards," building "the size and quality of the undergraduate and graduate student bodies" and "more closely matching resource allocation and strategic priorities."[91] All of these reports led to the UMBC 2006 self study in preparation for seeking reaccreditation by the Middle States Commission on Higher Education.[92]

Provost Johnson and Vice Provost for Undergraduate Education, Diane Lee, were also responsible for articulating new standards for addressing issues of academic integrity for students, faculty, and staff, and for urging academic departments to build more assessment mechanisms into their courses.[93] None of these activities was likely to draw media headlines, but they represented necessary planning steps involving a wide variety of UMBC administrators, faculty, and staff to create intentionality and specificity to the lofty vision the campus had announced.

Figure A compares University statistics at the beginning of the Hrabowski era and as he celebrated his twentieth anniversary as President. It shows both the remarkable growth of UMBC during this period and that the University in 1992 had a solid foundation on which to build.

In this era, the tenure of university presidents tends to be short[94] and few qualify as transformational leaders. By any measure Freeman Hrabowski's UMBC presidency is unprecedented for the campus and perhaps for the nation. Historically, there have been some exceedingly influential University president's (Columbia's Nicholas Murray Butler, Chicago's Robert Hutchins, Harvard's James Bryant Conant, Dartmouth's John Sloan Dickey, and Harvard's Derek Bok),[95] but they led well-established institutions that already commanded wide-spread public attention. A very few others, such as Father Theodore Hesburgh, who during his twenty-five year tenure significantly changed the academic stature of his University, but Notre Dame was already well known with strong alumni and financial support.[96]

Hrabowski had none of those building blocks. It is a careless exaggeration to say, as many news articles did, that UMBC was just a sleepy commuter campus before Hrabowski.[97] The statistics in Figure A give lie to that caricature. Nevertheless, look-

91. "Framing the Future," 2003. UMBC historic documents collection, Special Collections, University of Maryland, Baltimore County.

92. UMBC was successfully accredited first in 1976 and then reaccredited in 1986, 1996 and 2006.

93. Minutes of the Faculty Senate Meeting, September 10, 2002, University Senate Records. University Archives, Special Collections, University of Maryland, Baltimore County.

94. Jeffrey O'Connell and Thomas E. O'Connell, *Five 20thCentury College Presidents: From Butler to Bok (Plus Summers)* (Durham: Carolina Academic Press, 2012), 113.

95. Ibid.

96. Michael O'Brien, *Hesburgh: A Biography* (Washington: Catholic University Press of America, 1998).

97. About 30 percent of UMBC students were resident in 1993 and "sleepy" was not an adjective its 1,171 employees would have used. The Wikipedia entry on Hrabowski states, "Hrabowski transformed a no-name commuter university into a research institution recognized as one of the most innovative in the country."

Figure A
Changes in UMBC during the Hrabowski Era

University statistics	1992	2012
Headcount enrollment	10,393	13,637
Full time Freshmen	1,000	1,547
Full-time Transfer	898	1,134
Graduate degree seeking	1,309	2,684
Out-of State	751	1,074
White	70 percent	50 percent
Minority	30 percent	50 percent
Residential	30 percent	40 percent
Freshmen Average SAT scores	1083	1222
Degrees Bachelors Awarded	1,555	1,905
Degrees Masters Awarded	161	582
Degrees Ph.D. Awarded	27	97
Full-time faculty	384	659
Part-time faculty	239	281
Full-time staff	548	1,195
Campus buildings	29	48
Building square feet	2,089,404	3,703,185
Endowment	$1.7 million	$57.8 million
Research and Development funding	$7.6 million	$91 million

ing from the inside, UMBC has become a very different place during his twenty-year tenure and the dramatic change in its external reputation has exceeded most people's wildest dreams. Hrabowski would be the first to concede that many faculty and staff should share the credit for the internal improvements, but UMBC's current external image is substantially due to its President. Robert Hutchins once said, "If the faculty is the backbone of the University, the President is its vocal cords...."[98]

98. O'Connell and O'Connell, *Five 20thCentury College Presidents: From Butler to Bok (Plus Summers)*, 46.

Like many metaphors, there is both a truth and oversimplification in that message. Hrabowski always affirms he did not write on a blank slate when he became President. As he noted in his installation address, most senior faculty were hired before he arrived and were already committed to the difficult task of conducting cutting-edge research, while actively nurturing undergraduate students. Very few classes at UMBC were taught by graduate students as was common in other research universities. Yet Hrabowski added some new dimensions to the campus compact. He personified diversity and emphasized the value of inclusion, particularly emphasizing staff involvement in university policies. He brought a moral dimension to the discussion of university activities that is not always common at public institutions. In addressing campus convocations Hrabowski will quote: "Watch your thoughts for they become words. Watch your words, for they become actions. Watch your actions, for they become habits. Watch your habits, for they become character. Watch your character, for it becomes your destiny."[99] Not all university leaders have the moral stature to speak that way.

Finally, he brought an almost unbelievable energy to reaching out to individual students and other members of the campus community asking about their progress and encouraging them to do their best.[100] That sort of role model encourages others to take extra steps to be engaged and helpful to students.

Hrabowski combined an inspiring life story with a message the nation was eager to hear. Despite substantial expenditures and intense efforts, creating academic excellence for African-American students has been challenging almost everywhere. He did not burnish a narrative of victimhood by simply blaming this problem on the history of slavery, the existence of racism or flaws in standardized testing as many others did. Rather this son of the Bull Connor era in Birmingham, Alabama insisted that properly prepared and motivated black students with structured programs and good mentoring could compete with anybody, even in the science, technology, engineering, and mathematics (STEM) fields. National press pundits were mesmerized at the demonstration of this reality at UMBC, an institution they previously had not noticed. In story after story in the *New York Times, Washington Post,* and CBS *Sixty Minutes*, reporters marveled at what they were hearing and at the man they were hearing it from.

Those stories led to impressive honors for UMBC's President as he became increasingly influential on the national scene. Hrabowski's national prominence might appear meteoric, but, in fact, his recognition was incremental, fueled by his extraordinary work ethic and his willingness to deliver his message to so many educational

---

99. Walker, "Freeman Hrabowski's UMBC legacy grows as he celebrates 20 years as President," *Baltimore Sun*, September 2, 2012. 21.

100. Many faculty members have a story about Hrabowski's involvement with students. One day I was talking to an outstanding UMBC tennis player who was also a fine student. He mentioned casually Freeman was tutoring him. "What do you two do?" I asked. "We read Cicero together," was the reply.

audiences, public bodies, and corporate leaders.[101] As early as 1996, in recognition of his Meyerhoff leadership, Hrabowski was honored by President Clinton with the U.S. Presidential Award for Excellence in Science, Mathematics and Engineering Mentoring. In the ensuing years, he has been awarded more than twenty honorary degrees,[102] usually when giving a commencement address. Restless audiences often make this genre difficult, but Hrabowski can be quite inspirational and these events yield valuable networking opportunities for him and a new awareness about UMBC in the greater educational community.[103] He also took the opportunity to publish his message in two books and forty articles.[104]

So it was not a total surprise when additional individual and institutional national accolades began to arrive. In 2008, *U.S News and World Report* named Hrabowski one of America's Best Leaders. In 2009, *Time* magazine named him one of America's 10 Best College Presidents and outdid itself in 2012 by selecting Hrabowski one of the hundred most influential people in the world.[105] In so doing, *Time* said, "When you think of the best science universities in the U.S., schools like MIT and Caltech may jump to mind. But perhaps, the most envied science program in the country is at the University of Maryland Baltimore County."[106]

---

101. In addition to speaking at various corporate events, Hrabowski has been on the boards of several Baltimore firms including Constellation Energy Group, Mercantile Safe Deposit and Trust Company, and McCormick & Company, as well as the charitable and non-profit boards of the Alfred P. Sloan Foundation, Carnegie Foundation for the Advancement of Teaching, France-Merrick Foundation, Marguerite Casey Foundation, Maryland Humanities Council, and The Urban Institute.

102. University of Maryland, Baltimore (2012), Harvard University (2010), Harvey Mudd College (2010), Georgetown University (2009), John Hopkins University (2009), University of Michigan (2009), Daniel Webster College (2009), North Carolina State University (2008), Haverford College (2007), Wheaton College (2007), Princeton University (2006), Goucher College (2006), Pace University (2006), University of Alabama-Birmingham (2005), Duke University (2005), University of Illinois at Urbana-Champaign (2004), Gallaudet University (2004), Franklin & Marshall College (2003), Roosevelt University (2003), Binghamton University (2002), Medical University of South Carolina (2002), Brooklyn College, The City University of New York, (2002), Mercy College (2001), and University of Mississippi (2001).

103. Readers interested in seeing and hearing Dr. Hrabowski expounding his optimistic message about STEM education and UMBC's role in that effort might view his Ted Talk "We must change the Culture of Science and Teaching." TEDxMid Atlantic, 2012. You will be joining over 712,000 other watchers and listeners.

104. Both of these books were coauthored with UMBC psychologists Ken Maton and Geoffrey Greif: *Beating the Odds: Raising Academically Successful African American Males* (New York: Oxford University Press, 1998) and also with Monica Greene, *Overcoming the Odds: Raising Academically Successful African American Young Women* (New York: Oxford University Press, 2002).

105. The Lincoln Center event to recognize the honorees was described by Bee-Shyuan Chang, "Influential And all In One Room," *New York Times*, April 26, 2012, E8. See also Erica L. Green "UMBC president named among world's most influential leaders," *Baltimore Sun*, April 18, 2012.

106. *Time* Magazine, http.:com./time/special/packages/article.0,28804,21119. "UMBC's quiet revolution in teaching science is earning the school extra credit." *Washington Post*, March 20,

In 2011, it seemed he was receiving new national recognition almost every month. In that year, the *Washington Post* and Harvard Kennedy School's Center for Public Leadership named him as one of the seven "Top American Leaders." Also in 2011, he received the TIAA-CREF Theodore M. Hesburgh Award for Leadership Excellence for demonstrating "innovative thinking, a positive impact on both higher education and society and a willingness to collaborate within and outside the university, all of which are embodied by Dr. Hrabowski's work,"[107] and the Academic Leadership Award by the Carnegie Corporation of New York for "demonstrating outstanding leadership and commitment to excellence and equity in undergraduate education, curricular innovation, the liberal arts, reform of K-12 education, and promotion of strong links between their institutions and their local communities."[108] No mere rhetorical tribute, the award came with a $500,000 grant to be used for academic initiatives. The Freeman A. Hrabowski Fund for Academic Innovation is used as seed money for educational innovations in departments across the University. The next year the Heinz Family Foundation honored Hrabowski with its Human Condition Award, adding $250,000 to the UMBC innovation fund carrying his name.[109]

On November 13, 2011, CBS's *Sixty Minutes* profiled Hrabowski, UMBC, and the Meyerhoff Scholars program. The program was broadcast twice and was an enormous public relations coup for the University. Freeman proclaimed to a national audience that "We have to teach Americans of all races, from all backgrounds, what it takes to be the best. And at the heart of it is the same thing we saw when we were kids—hard work.—I don't care how smart you are. Nothing takes the place of hard work."[110] These were hardly distinctive sentiments, but Hrabowski's life story added powerfully to their authenticity.

Consequently, in 2012 he chaired the National Academy of Sciences committee that crafted the report, *Expanding Underrepresented Minority Participation: America's Science and Technology Talent at the Crossroads.*[111] He well deserved that role because, according to a *New York Times* editorial, "UMBC produces more minority scientists than any other predominantly white institution in the country."[112] A few months later,

---

2012. See also Joni E. Finney, "Identifying Talent and Nurturing Its Success: An Interview with Freeman Hrabowski," *Change Magazine,* May–June, 2009.

107. http://www.tiaa-cref.org/public/about/press/about_us/releases/pressrelase375.html.

108. Elyse Ashburn, "Carnegie Corporation Honors UMBC President Freeman Hrabowski with 2011 Academic Leadership Award," *UMBC News,* November 3, 2011.

109. Lauren McEwen, "Freeman Hrabowski wins 2012 Heinz Award for Human Condition," *Washington Post* September 17, 2012.

110. Sixty Minutes Transcript, CBS, November 13, 2011.

111. The National Academies Press, http://www.nap.edu/openbook.php?record_id+12984&page=R1.

112. Brent Staples, "The Country Can Learn a Lesson From These Students," *New York Times,* December 8, 2010.

President Obama picked Hrabowski to chair his new initiative the President's Advisory Commission on Educational Excellence for African-Americans.[113]

Hrabowski's political savvy has been very helpful to the campus. His national visibility and personal affability have won him and UMBC entrance into Washington funding circles, though large national private foundation grants have not been forthcoming. In Maryland, he developed an extremely close relationship with Chancellor Britt Kirwan and more recently UMB President Jay Perman. He has been able to get legislative support, particularly for highly competitive building priorities. Thirteen new buildings and twelve major additions and renovations have been completed during his administration. Despite his focus on the problem, however, he has not been able to reduce the per-student funding gap in state support UMBC faces in relation to UMCP, Morgan, and Coppin.

In October 2012, political, corporate, foundation, and educational leaders from around the State assembled at a $250 a plate dinner at the Baltimore Waterfront Marriot Ballroom to honor Hrabowski's twenty years as UMBC's president. Event planners had hoped optimistically for an audience of 400, but more than 900 came together on that evening. Chancellor Kirwan was master of ceremonies and tributes poured out from the podium and on large screens around the room. An announcement was made that $5.5 million had been raised by the event.[114] Then, Hrabowski and the audience were surprised by a long distance phone call patched in from comedian Bill Cosby who joshed the honoree a bit, while a picture of him and Freeman posing by the sculpture of the Retriever dog mascot filled the screen. The two of them had bonded earlier over their joint message that young African-Americans could meet high education standards, if these challenges were taken seriously.

It was an extraordinary, deeply moving occasion displaying the University at its finest. By the time Hrabowski took the stage after earlier volleys of standing ovations, he was so moved for a moment he almost seemed at a loss for words. Of course, that did not happen, but after the speech when the UMBC Camerata sang a specially arranged version of Langston Hughes poem, "Hold Fast to Dreams," the President's face showed and the audience felt the passion that has propelled the University forward over thc last two decades.

While others introduce Hrabowski by extolling his personal achievements, he rarely mentions them in addressing campus audiences. His most single frequent sentence is "Give them or him or her a hand," drawing attention to others. Freeman is so accessible and generous in sharing credit; the campus largely took his national honors in stride without paying too much attention to how unlikely his personal saga and their new institutional status were. A campus on the move must still be looking forward. As Hrabowski is fond of saying, "Success is never final."

---

113. UMBC Press Release, "President Obama Appoints UMBC President as Chair of National Education Commission," July 26, 2012.

114. Philip Rous memo to UMBC Community, "Warm Support for the Hrabowski Fund for Innovation," October 23, 2012.

F. Staff

While this chapter has focused so far on the top leadership position at UMBC, "the" administration is much larger and more complex than one person or even the top academic leadership of Provosts, Deans, and Departmental chairs. In 2012 there were 659 full-time faculty teaching at UMBC, but 135 person in executive and management roles, 549 in other professional categories, 221 in clerical positions, 25 maintenance workers, 49 in skilled crafts and 137 in technical paraprofessional jobs. The salaried professional staff and the hourly professional or non-exempt employees are represented in their own Senates, while other employees are members of the American Federation of State, County, and Municipal Employees (AFSCME) and work under a collective bargaining agreement.

Some of these persons have had major influences on the University. Without their leadership, the hard personnel, budgetary, and program development decisions that led to the development of UMBC might not have been made. Marty Schwartz, Hugh Graham, Dick Neville, Adam Yarmolinsky, Scott Bass, Larry Wilt, Mark Behm, Lamont Tolliver, John Martello, John Jeffries, Arthur Johnson, and Charles Brown are just a few administrators who over the years played major roles in new campus initiatives. Many more than these persons including current top administrators, Philip Rous, Lisa Akchin, David Gleason, Greg Simmons, Diane Lee, Janet Rutledge, Robert Deluty, Ellen Hemmerly, Dale Bittinger, Lynne Schaefer, and Nancy Young, would merit discussion in this book, if there were no page limitations.

Another group of growing importance is the university staff members who operate the library, student services, physical plant, public relations, athletics, admissions, public safety, public relations, institutional advancement, and alumni relations to name some of the most important. No university can operate without them, but unless there are problems they rarely receive much publicity or create records on which their contribution to UMBC history could be developed.

Making generalizations about the enormous variety of people who work for a university is extremely difficult. But it is a fact that in the annual survey *The Chronicle of Higher Education* makes of "Great Colleges to Work For" UMBC was on the Honors list in 2010, 2011 and 2012, tied for fourth in the country in the large university category. The University ranked high in collaborative governance, confidence in senior leadership, professional/career development programs, respect and appreciation, supervisor/department chair relationships, tenure clarity, and process and work/life balance.[115] This represents a remarkable vote of confidence in UMBC by its employees who after all had suffered from furloughs and salary freezes during this same period. As Freeman would say, "Give them a hand."

115. "The 2012 Honor Roll," *The Chronicle of Higher Education*, August 10, 2012. A5.

CHAPTER V

Budgets and Benefactors

A. Introduction

During UMBC's relatively brief existence, the scope and economic foundations of American higher education have undergone enormous change.[1] As Derek Bok, former Harvard President, once noted, it took the Harvard Library 275 years to accumulate its first million books, but then only five years to acquire its next million.[2]

Some changes advantaged the new UMBC campus; others did not. Whatever the causes, universities have become much more expensive, with more complex and more corporate-like administrative structures.

Like other public universities, UMBC's principal revenues come from four sources: student tuition and fees, state appropriations, research grants and contracts overhead, and private gifts. The relative sources of institutional support have varied substantially over the years. In 1991, for example, of UMBC's total budget of about $101 million, 45 percent came from state appropriations, 8 percent from federal research grants and other funding, and 21 percent from tuition and fees. In 2001 of UMBC's budget of about $239 million, 28 percent came from state appropriations, 15 percent from federal funding, and 20 percent from students. By 2011, UMBC's budget surpassed $355 million of which 25 percent came from state appropriations, 20 percent from federal funding, and 28 percent from students. In the year 2004, University income from students (and their families) exceeded state appropriations for the first time in UMBC history.[3] The trend is more likely to accelerate than be reversed.

---

1. A useful overview of these changes can be found in John R. Thelin, *A History of American Higher Education*, (Baltimore and London: The Johns Hopkins University Press, 2004); Roger L Geiger, (*American Research Universities Since World War II*, New York: Oxford University Press, 1993); Bruce L.R. Smith, (*American Science Policy Since World War II*, Washington, D.C.: Brookings Institution, 1990) and Christopher P. Loss, *Between Citizens and the State*, (Princeton: Princeton University Press, 2012).

2. As quoted in Peggy Gordon Elliott, *The Urban Campus*, (Phoenix: Oryx Press, American Council on Education, 1993), 65.

3. These data come from "UMBC budget information, 1969–2102." UMBC historic documents collection, Special Collections, University of Maryland, Baltimore County.

B. Tuition and Fees

About 25 percent of UMBC income has historically come from tuition and fees, ranging from about 15 percent in 1969 to 28 percent in 2011. According to USM policy, Maryland residents should have access to System institutions at an affordable cost, but:

> Since the students benefit from the education they receive, they should pay a reasonable share of the costs through tuition. Since Maryland benefits from having an educated citizenry, the state also has a responsibility to bear a substantial portion of the costs through tax payer support.... Students [from other states and countries] should pay an additional amount of tuition, which at a minimum offsets the State's cost contribution intended to subsidize the education of all its residents.[4]

The Regents' policy continues that tuition policy should "provide students with a quality education and enable the System to move toward its legislatively-mandated goal of achieving and sustaining national eminence."[5]

Determining the request for annual tuition and fees levels begins on each campus. The Regents must approve campus proposals for tuition levels which are supposed to be based on "mission, program offerings, general funds per-full-time-equivalent student, facilities and other factors." Published tuition costs for UMBC students (minus financial aid, if available) are the highest of any Maryland state university.[6]

As President Hrabowski explained to the Maryland legislature in 2000, "UMBC's heavy reliance on tuition revenues is necessitated by the need to address the gap between State funding and the basic cost of offering a curriculum reflecting the institution's mission, focusing heavily on science, engineering and technology-related areas."[7] In 2003, he returned to this theme making a new argument. Hrabowski noted that "UMBC's ability to attract and retain high achieving students is especially significant because we have the highest tuition in the System among traditional campuses." In the preceding two years, UMBC had cut $7 million and 106 positions out of its budget, while enrolling additional students and opening new programs and buildings.[8] He warned:

---

4. USM Regents Policy on Tuition, VIII-2.01, as amended June 22, 2005.

5. Ibid.

6. "Annual Tuition and Fees at Colleges and Universities 2012–2013," *Chronicle of Higher Education*, November 2, 2012. 35. Among other public institutions, College Park's tuition is about $800 less than UMBC's, though St Mary's College tuition is considerably higher at $15,018. In addition, UMBC students pay one of the highest fees in the country. "How student fees boost college sports amid rising budgets," *USA Today*, October 6, 2010.

7. Freeman Hrabowski, III, "2000 Legislative Testimony." UMBC historic documents collection, Special Collections, University of Maryland, Baltimore County. 13. UMBC struggled to reduce its dependence on tuition in FY 1998–2001 from 51.2 percent to 46.9 percent, but it still exceeded the Board of Regents benchmark of 45 percent.

8. For a description of the impact of budget cuts on various aspects of UMBC's operations, Freeman Hrabowski, III. "2004 Legislative Testimony." UMBC historic documents collection, Special Collections, University of Maryland, Baltimore County. 9–10.

> We are seriously concerned that if State support is further reduced and our percentile of guideline funding continues to decline, we will be under further pressure to increase tuition. We are also concerned that many more of Maryland's best and brightest students will once again consider studying out-of-state to avoid higher costs and diminished services.[9]

There are other factors as well. As new university UMBC's endowment is low and some UMBC administrators believed that a high tuition signified status in the world of higher education

Much of the UMBC's high tuition problem, however, is caused by the way the state funds individual campuses. If a Maryland public campus chooses to set a lower tuition, the state will sometimes compensate it with higher state funding. To take only one example, in 2012, Coppin State charged $5,720 tuition to each in-state student, while similar UMBC students paid $9,764. The state compensated Coppin by providing $11,997 per student in funding, while UMBC only received $8,673 per student. That gap cannot be explained by differences in mission or program offerings, since UMBC is a doctoral research campus. This persistent structural deficit hampers UMBC in competing nationally for the most talented faculty and staff.[10]

Since as a practical matter, the Governor's budget is decisive for Maryland public campuses, tuition rates can easily become a political issue. Under Republican Governor Robert L. Ehrlich, Jr. (2003–2007), the general policy was to rely on user fee increases rather than state appropriations wherever possible. Consequently, according to *Baltimore Sun* reporter Childs Walker, Ehrlich "relied on tuition increases to help dig the state out of record deficits it faced when he came into office." Walker estimated that tuition went up about 40 percent during Ehrlich's four years.[11] Maryland was not unique. Nationally, raising tuition became part of the strategy for coping with economic downturns. On average tuition went up 8 percent nationally in 2008, including 15 percent increases in Florida and New York and an increase of more than 30 percent in California.[12]

Governor Martin O'Malley, facing an even more difficult economic environment after the 2007–08 recessions, took a different approach. He froze tuition at USM schools for four years. As a consequence, Maryland public higher education tuition which was the sixth most expensive in 2005, ranked twenty-first by 2009.[13] From FY 2008–FY 2013, the increase in average tuition at Maryland state higher education in-

9. Freeman Hrabowski, III. "2003 Legislative Testimony." UMBC historic documents collection, Special Collections, University of Maryland, Baltimore County. 3 and 5.

10. Freeman Hrabowski, III. "2004 Legislative Testimony." 12–13.

11. Childs Walker, "O'Malley to use tuition freeze as issue in re-election effort," *Baltimore Sun*, June 7, 2009, 1.

12. Childs Walker, "O'Malley to promote tuition freeze during campaign," *Baltimore Sun*, June 6, 2010.

13. William E. Kirwan, "A Message from Chancellor William E. Kirwan to the University of Maryland Community," February 18, 2010. For another view on tuition freezes see, Eric Kelderman, "Calculating the True Cost of Tuition Freezes at Public Colleges," *Chronicle of Higher Education*, May 15, 2009.

stitutions was $176 dollars, the lowest in the nation, compared to about $2200 per student in neighboring Virginia and Delaware, for example.[14] Initially, O'Malley was able to increase state appropriations to compensate for the loss of tuition, but as the recession endured, that was no longer possible.

Governor O'Malley, who pumped millions of extra dollars into the state's university system to fulfill a campaign promise to keep tuition flat, hoped that investment would pay dividends at the ballot box.[15] In a high school commencement address he pointed out:

> we've chosen—alone among the 50 states—to freeze in-state tuition for four years in a row. As a result, those of you who enroll in a state college or university this fall will not have to pay one of the most expensive tuitions in America—that wasn't true four years ago.[16]

Public higher education administrators did not want to publically criticize the Governor and some were effusive in their praise.[17] University System Chancellor, William E. Kirwan, said "his colleagues across the country 'are literally in a state of disbelief' when he describes the Maryland situation at national conferences." Kirwan said that the Governor should promote his higher education record during the campaign. "It is an applause line everywhere he goes."[18] Terry Hartle, Senior Vice President of the American Council of Education, referring to the Maryland tuition freeze, agreed. "It is such an extraordinary achievement that it would be surprising if Governor O'Malley didn't talk about it during his campaign. Nobody else in the country has done it in this century."[19]

There were some dissenters. Other Democrats, including Senate President Thomas V. Mike Miller and House Speaker Michael E. Busch, "both worried that the freeze had gone too far in 2009, saying that it diverted funds from community colleges and set the state up for a potentially huge tuition increase down the line."[20] Republican Ehrlich running again for Governor in 2010 said through his campaign spokesperson, Andrew Barth, that he "regards the four-year freeze as a blunt tool that gave economic breaks to families that could have afforded to pay more and did not do enough for those who needed the most help."[21]

---

14. Phil Oliff, Vincent Palacios, Ingrid Johnson, and Michael Leachman for the Center on Budget and Policy Priorities, "Recent Deep State Higher Education Cuts May Harm Students and Economy for Years to Come," March 19, 2013. Figure 4. http://wwwcbpp.or/cms/index.cfm?fa=view&id+3927.

15. Walker, "O'Malley to use tuition freeze as issue in re-election effort," *Baltimore Sun,* June 7, 2009.

16. Walker, "O'Malley to promote tuition freeze during campaign," *Baltimore Sun,* June 6, 2010.

17. Kayvan Vakili, "USM leaders laud Governor O'Malley on college affordability," *Retriever,* November 6, 2010.

18. Walker, "O'Malley to promote tuition freeze during campaign," *Baltimore Sun*, June 6, 2010.

19. Ibid.

20. Ibid.

21. Ibid.

Overall, however, the tuition freeze turned out to be politically popular. The unscientific, but conservative leaning "What Maryland Thinks" poll in the *Sun* reported that 58 percent of the electronic respondents thought the tuition cuts helped USM universities, while 28 percent said it hurt and 14 percent were not sure.[22]

In 2010, the USM Regents proposed a 5 percent tuition increase, but O'Malley came up with $16 million in new funding to avoid that necessity. Perhaps that was a staged political move. O'Malley agreed to a 3 percent increase in funding for 2011, with no more furloughs and a $750 onetime payment to each USM employee, while other states were still making substantial cuts to their higher education budgets.

UMBC's response to the tuition freeze, in addition to cutting back some services and furloughing some employees, was to increase enrollment keeping high the stream of tuition revenues.[23] Between the fall of 2008 and the fall of 2011, UMBC added 1,784 undergraduate students whose tuition partly allowed the University to absorb painful budgetary cuts.[24] Despite these increases, the instructional budget in those years slightly decreased and the financial aid budget was cut by 9 percent.[25] Increases in research awards during this period helped to stabilize the campus budgets. UMBC was doing more with less.

C. State Appropriations

Historically, Maryland lagged behind other states in support of higher education, particularly given the state's overall affluence. In 1977, the State Board for Higher Education (SBHE) seriously threatened to cap out-of-state enrollment at 15 percent on Maryland public campuses out of concern for a restricted operating and capital budgets.[26] The state funding problem persisted. In 1981, the State Board for Higher Education commented that:

---

22. "Tuition Politics," *Baltimore Sun* editorial, June 9, 2010, 19 and "What Maryland Thinks," poll, 18.

23. Such a strategy over time can be like a dog chasing its tale. Provost Adam Yarmolinsky described the dilemma, noting that though there were additional funds accrued through new tuition revenues: "The resulting marginal increases have been clearly insufficient to meet the full needs of the academic program, much less any needs of the campus' service structure. As a result, any additional funds made available to these support services have been allocated through the Working Budget process, on a case-by-case basis—often robbing Peter to pay Paul. Consequently, most services departments now find themselves in the unenviable position of not only having to respond to the increased demands of larger enrollments, which have compounded over several years, but being supported by as shrinking per capita level of funding." University of Maryland, Baltimore County Campus Plan Summary, February 2, 1988. 12 Special Collections, University of Maryland, Baltimore County.

24. UMBC, "Periodic Review Report," Middle States Accreditation, UPUB P12-017, Box 8, University Publications, Special Collections, University of Maryland, Baltimore County, 23.

25. Ibid, 21.

26. Edward Coltman, "Maryland backs off plan to limit college out-of state rolls," *Baltimore Sun*, February 5, 1977. One reason the cap proposal was not implemented was that the state's

> State funding of public higher education in Maryland has been modest by any measure chosen. This financing situation exists despite Maryland's relatively wealthy status and relatively high rate of taxation. Although there may be many reasons for this, a significant reason is that probably the relatively recent history of the public sector has served to limit the number of citizens served by that sector and, therefore, the numbers likely to have a strong commitment to supporting it.[27]

For example, in 1984–1985, average incomes in Maryland ranked 6th among the 50 states, but the state only was 38th in its higher education per student support.[28] In the mid-1990s, under the administration of Governor Parris Glendening, former UMCP Professor of Political Science, higher education funding increased annually, but in 2002 a $1.4 billion state deficit caused a 3.5 percent cut in the USM budget.[29]

So even after the substantial expansion of Maryland public higher education, including the growth of UMBC, Herbert C. Smith and John T. Willis in 2012 summarized the more recent history of state higher education financing:

> Lacking specific constitutional and statutory funding requirements, expenditures for higher education in Maryland have been often been subject to wild swings in the level of state support, dependent on the health of the state economy and state budget. Generous increases accompanied the reformulation of the governance structure of the state's colleges and universities in the 1980s, followed by double-digit losses of state funding during the recession of the early 1990s.[30]

In the last two decades, Maryland has done better in the national comparison of support of public higher education, but the overall trend has been negative.[31] This period has been one of decreasing state support for public higher education across the country. James Duderstadt, president of the University of Michigan from 1988 to 1996, described the budgetary revolution on his watch by saying his University was "state supported," then "state assisted" to "state related" and finally "state located."

Historically Black Colleges and Universities (HBCUs) had heavy out-of-state enrollments.

A useful description of the development of SBHE's role in the Maryland higher education budget process can be found in Sumler, "Life Cycle," 24–28.

27. SBHE, "Recommendations Concerning the Future Governance of Public Higher Education in Maryland," October 1981.14. A useful history of the Maryland financial support of higher education can be found in the SBHE report. 20–29.

28. Alan Rosenbaum, "Maryland's poor support of public universities," *Baltimore Evening Sun*, February 1986. Rosenbaum was then Director of the Maryland Institute for Policy Analysis (MIPAR) at UMBC. In this article he pointed out that the state did much better in funding its community colleges and was outstanding in its support of private higher education.

29. Abigail Green, "Maintaining the Momentum: Budget Cutbacks Challenge UMBC," *Generations*, Winter 2003.

30. Herbert C. Smith and John T. Willis, *Maryland Politics and Government: Democratic Government*, (Lincoln: University of Nebraska Press, 2012). 245.

31. Eric Kelderman, "State Support for Colleges Fall 7.6 percent in Fiscal 2012," *Chronicle of Higher Education*, January 23, 2012. The Maryland cut was only .1 percent, however.

The University of Michigan now receives less than 8 percent of its operating budget from the state.[32]

Since the start of the recession in December 2007, according to the Center on Budget and Policy Priorities, forty-three states cut their higher education budgets.[33] One reason is that states have more legal flexibility and political support for trimming higher education than in other areas. Public K-12 education is relatively protected by its state constitutional status and by judicial oversight of school finance. Public schools, existing in every legislative district, have widespread support from parents and politically potent teachers unions. Maryland polls, taken every year between 1992 and 2006, show a general public support for higher education spending, but at much lower levels than for public education.[34] There are only limited steps states can take to control public safety and health costs, so in hard times university budgets seem vulnerable. It is not that cutting higher education expenditures is popular. The Pew Research Center found that only 31 percent of the public concurred with cuts to higher education budgets, but there was even more resistance to curtailing healthcare or public schools expenditures.[35]

There is another political factor whose impact has not yet been fully measured, the exponential growth of for-profit higher education. Enrollment in the for-profit sector has grown nationally from 300,000 in 1986 to 2,360,000 in 2011 or from 2.8 percent of the market to 9.2 percent.[36] Most for-profits deliver their instruction electronically, often to a student body heavily dependent on federal Pell grants to pay tuition. These students and their families may have little interest in paying additional state taxes to support traditional campus-based higher education.

Another rapid cycling of Maryland budget increases and decreases occurred in the middle to late 1990s (up) and 2003–2004 (down). Since campus costs are fairly fixed, the only way UMBC and other public institutions could respond was to raise tuition, increase enrollment, freeze new hires and salaries, and furlough existing employees. These were painful choices for a new campus growing in almost every dimension.

Unlike some states, Maryland, however, still provided most of the money for capital expenditures. For a campus such as UMBC, that policy was particularly important. From 1990 to 2003, over $300 million in capital expenditures were made, resulting in the opening of very important academic buildings (Physics, Information

32. Howard H. Peckham, *The Making of the University of Michigan 1817–1996* (Ann Arbor, MI: The Millennium Project, 1998).20. See also "Cash Strapped State Schools Forced to Privatize," *Time*, April 23, 2009.

33. Center on Budget and Policy Priorities, "An Update on State Budget Cuts," February 9, 2011.

34. Smith and Willis, *Maryland Politics and Government,* Table 4-2. 92.

35. Kristina Dell, "State Universities face deepening cuts," MSNBC.com, March 3, 2011.

36. Center for College Affordability and Productivity, "For-Profit Higher Education," July 2010. 2011 data from the National Center for Education Statistics, "Enrollment in Postsecondary Institutions," Fall 2011, Nces.ed.gov/pubsearch/pubsinfo.asp?pubid=2012174.

Technology/Engineering, and Public Policy), even in years when operating budgets were cut.[37]

In 2004, a special legislative committee found that Maryland's support for higher education lagged behind national averages as a percentage of state budget and income.[38] In 2007, a new dedicated source of higher education funding was created from a portion of an increase in corporate income taxes.[39] About 15 percent of the Maryland state budget now goes to support higher education.[40]

Figure B shows the history of state annual appropriations to UMBC both in terms of the raw amount of state support and the percentage that support represents of the campus annual budget.

Figure B
Annual Total State Appropriations to UMBC

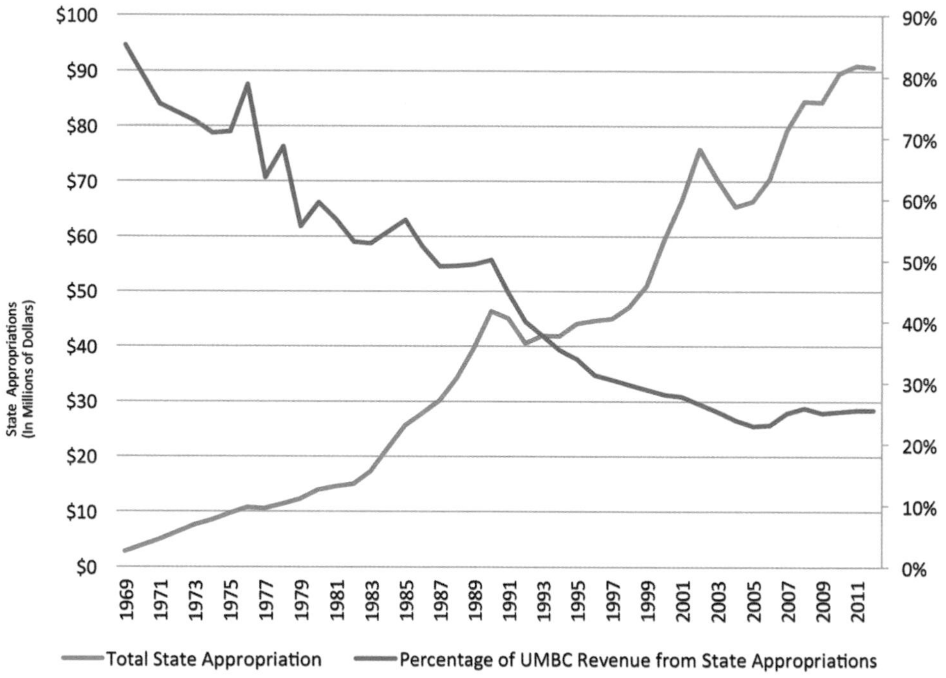

Source: UM System summary budgets.

37. Freeman Hrabowski, III, State of the University Address, September 5, 2003, Office of the President, http://president.umbc.edu/selcted-speeches/. 2.

38. State of Maryland. Department of Legislative Services, Special Commission on Higher Education Affordability and Access, "Final Report to the Maryland General Assembly," February 2004. 8, 11 and 13.

39. Smith and Willis, *Maryland Politics and Government.* 245.

40. Ibid.

While the raw amount, in fits and starts, has steadily risen as the University has grown, the numbers are best understood in context. As a percent of the total campus budget, the state contribution has plummeted from 81 percent in 1970 to 25.5 percent in 2011.To some extent that decline is just a reflection of the over-investment any new public campus must receive from government, but the halving of state support from 1990 to 2011 probably reflects national trends and UMBC's political weakness in the state.

The national recession that began in 2008, of course, affected the state, USM, and UMBC. In a single year FY 2009 to FY 2010, the state budget was reduced by almost $750 million, with reduction of $67.7 million in higher education.[41] Water and budget cuts flow downhill and the UMBC state appropriations budget was cut from $84,488,263 in 2008 to $77,416,858 in 2010.[42] Between FY 2008 and FY 2013, Maryland cut about $1500 per student in public institution budgets.[43]

Faced with a cut in state appropriations and a tuition freeze, UMBC, like other public institutions, had to reduce expenditures. For a growing campus with a number of required increases in costs, this was a considerable challenge. Between 2007 and 2011, there were a total of $23 million in reductions in state funding including a $13 million reduction in campus reserves.[44] To cope, UMBC achieved $18.7 million in saving by "efficiencies" and absorbed another $4.5 to pay for unfunded mandates. Twenty-two staff members were laid off, forty-four vacant positions were eliminated, faculty and staff absorbed $3.8 million in salary reductions and furloughs, scholarships were reduced by $1 million, and another $1 million in maintenance was deferred.[45]

Some other campus cost savings were made, but that could only go so far. If a university announced it was reducing classes, staff, library hours, or maintenance, it would diminish its attractiveness in the fierce competition of the academic marketplace. So the strategy is usually to continue whistling a happy tune, while reducing expenditures in a relatively invisible manner to the outside world. In the fall of 2011, the *Retriever* featured UMBC's various recognitions by *U.S. News and World Report* in its front page left story, while on the right the headline read, "Library to make journal cuts."[46]

At UMBC, as elsewhere in the USM, the major administrative choice was to impose temporary salary reductions (TSRs) for faculty and furloughs for staff. TSRs

41. William E. Kirwan, "Kirwan on Budget," The Faculty Voice, October 2009.23, no.1.

42. Harvard Graduate School of Education, "Institutional Advancement and Strategic Planning at the University of Maryland Baltimore County," November 2, 2010. 21.

43. Ibid., Figure 2.To put this budget cut into context, 38 states made greater per student cuts.

44. Freeman Hrabowski, III, "State of the University Address," August 19, 2010. Office of the President, http://president.umbc.edu/selected-speeches/. 2.

45. Freeman Hrabowski, III, "2011 Legislative Testimony," March 2011. Office of the President, http://president.umbc.edu/selected-speeches/. 2.

46. Olivia Ignacio, "We're #1 yet again," and Molly Bradtke, "Library to make journal cuts," *Retriever*, September 13, 2011.

meant that faculty were expected to continue working full time and teaching all classes. Staff could take their assigned furlough days off campus, though not all chose to do so. Salaries for both faculty and staff were reduced on a graduated scale. For example, those making $40,001–$60,000 were furloughed for five days or lost equivalent salary, while those earning $150,000 or more endured ten days of furloughs or lost salary.[47] At UMBC, in testimony to the generally high campus morale, that painful choice worked. There was a consensus that widespread furloughs and salary reductions were better than focused lay-offs, so that basic campus services continued with few hitches.

It was a painful experience, but it also highlighted a reality about UMBC's values. The academic and staff personnel core and its *esprit de corps* were preserved. As President Hrabowski wrote in *The Retriever* to faculty and staff:

> While dealing with campus budget reductions and furloughs and temporary salary reductions over the past three years [you] have resolutely put students first. I want to thank [you] publically ... for your continued passion for teaching our students, involving students in [your] research and giving them the support they need to succeed and thrive.[48]

While recessions do not last forever, the campus faces a longer-term problem in terms of the relative amount UMBC received per capita from the state compared to other Maryland public institutions. Figure C shows the consequence of the state funding calculated by the amount of subsidy per student. The College Park campus is the clear leader, followed by Coppin, Morgan State, then UMBC, and trailing is Towson University.

In this comparison, UMBC ranks fourth of ten, but it also has the highest percentage of students in more expensive STEM fields, as well multiple labor intensive doctoral programs which, except for College Park, other campuses do not have. UMBC trails UMCP by $4,272 per student and even Coppin by $3,324 and Morgan by $2,694. One consequence of UMBC's limited state funding is that as Figure C shows UMBC often has one of the highest public university tuitions in the state. Not only does that burden the students UMBC enrolls, but it causes some students to choose its less expensive competitors. Further, the State subtracts a portion of estimated tuition revenues from the funds it actually provides campuses.

Another reflection of state funding patterns is the substantial difference in faculty salaries between UMBC and its peers. Despite the higher cost of living in the

47. Valerie Thomas, "Temporary Salary Reduction Plan," UMBC Memo, June 22, 2010. Nevertheless, the furloughs were painful. Jenifer R. Ballengee, "State faculty treated unfairly: decreased support for public university faculty hurts all Marylanders, *Baltimore Sun*, November 5, 2010. For UMBC response to the FY 1991 budget cuts see: Michael Hooker, to UMBC Community, "Strategic Redeployment and Retrenchment Plan, March 27, 1991.

48. This quote is from Hrabowski, "State of the University Address," 2010. 2.

Figure C
State Appropriations and Tuition Per Capita FY 2010 and 2011

Institution	State Appropriation per FTEs (2010)	Tuition (2011)
U.M., College Park	$12,945	$6,763
Coppin State University	$11,997	$3,633
Morgan State University	$11,367	$2,204
U.M., Baltimore County	**$8,673**	**$6,679**
U. M., Eastern Shore	$8,271	$4,235
Bowie State University	$7,800	$4,415
Frostburg State University	$7,042	$5,150
University of Baltimore	$6,580	$5,484
Salisbury University	$5,208	$4,960
Towson University	$5,056	$ 5,336
St. Mary's College of Maryland	NA	$11,325

Source: UMBC Budget Overview FY 2011, UMBC historic documents collection, Special Collections, University of Maryland, Baltimore County. no page.

Baltimore-Washington area, in 1996 UMBC faculty salaries were next to last among its national peers.[49] More recently in 2012, the average salary of a full professor at UMCP was $136,300, while at UMBC the average at that rank was $111,800.[50]

Another way to look at funding is the gap between how Maryland aspires to fund its public campuses and the reality. Deciphering why those results exist requires an understanding of the objective and subjective process by which Maryland allocates money to its public campuses.

Prior to 1968, the state had not devised a higher education funding formula and, even after its creation, implementation was slow.[51] The first funding formula, oper-

---

49. MHEC Report, "Institutional Performance Accountability," October 18, 1996.

50. "Almanac of Higher Education 2012," *The Chronicle of Higher Education,* April 13, 2012.

51. This overview of the development of Maryland higher education funding is taken from Defendants' Memorandum in Support of their Motion for Summary Judgment Regarding Intentional Discrimination and Maryland Funding of Public Institutions of Higher Education Under *Fordice*, in *The Coalition for Equity and Excellence in Maryland Higher Education, et.al. v. Maryland Higher Education Commission, et.al.* February 11, 2011. (hereafter *Coalition* case.) See Chapter XII for a full discussion of this case.

ating from early 1970 until 1989, was based on a number of factors at each institution: (1) fixed cost for administration; (2) variable costs for teaching; (3) level of sponsored research required to be funded by the State; (4) library costs; and (5) research space.[52]

After the 1988 reorganization of higher education under Governor Schaefer, Maryland used a more ad hoc methodology based primarily on campus roles and missions. In 1999, the State tried to implement "an objective, mathematical" funding system based on how "peer" institutions are funded adjusted by the number of full-time equivalent (FTE) students.[53] The State was supposed to provide funding at the seventy-fifth percentile of an institution's peers FTE funding.[54] That number would then be multiplied by the FTEs on a particular Maryland campus, with a subtraction for the expected tuition and fee revenues generated by the institution itself.[55] Presto, changeo that would yield the magic state appropriation number; no politics need be involved.

The object in the peer selection game was to pick peers that bore a certain similarity to your institutional mission and curricular offerings and most importantly were in states that funded higher education well.

While the UMBC/UMAB full merger proposal ultimately died in the State Senate, an agreement had been made that, given the 1985 merger of graduate schools on those campuses, for the purpose of establishing peers the combined characteristics of both campuses would be the measure. Ostensibly, the rationale was that finding peer campuses for the UMAB's six-professional-school-constellation would be difficult. A more important purpose was that, by including well-established universities with medical schools in the peer list, UMBC would be helped. Figure D shows those peers.

The combined UMAB/UMBC peers were a glittering group, not coincidentally in states which at that time funded education well. In the previous four-campus University of Maryland system, UMAB/UMBC had the clout to seek those peer advantages. When the ten-campus USM was created in 1988, however, there were objections to the potential benefits the combined UMAB/UMBC peer list might create for those Baltimore institutions. So under the new governance arrangement, UMBC was asked to create its own peer list, in the context of a warning from Chancellor Toll that MHEC would be scrutinizing these peer lists and might at some point hold a campus accountable if it had fallen behind the achievements of its suggested

52. MHEC, "Consolidated Budget & Fact Book, Fiscal Year, 1990," December 1988. 10–11.

53. MHEC, "Operating Funding Guidelines and Formulas for Institutions of Higher Education in Maryland," June 4, 2007. 7–8.

54. James E. Lyons, Sr. memorandum to MHEC Finance Committee, October 16, 2008.

55. MHEC, "Operating Funding Guidelines," November 10, 2010, 11.The stated reason for subtracting tuition revenues is that it encourages institutions to moderate tuition rates and removes the incentive to take out-of-state students. Whatever the rationale is, it helps HBCUs more, since they charge the lowest tuition in the state.

Figure D
Combined UMAB/UMBC Peers (circa 1986)

Current Peers	Enrollment
University of North Carolina, at Chapel Hill	20,228
University of Connecticut with medicine	24,457
University of Virginia	17,981
University of California, San Diego	15,418
University of California, Davis	18,421
University of California, Irvine	13,998
SUNY Stony Brook with medicine	16,166
University of Illinois at Chicago	24,560
UMAB/UMBC	20,301

peers. Thus the peer list could be a double-edged sword. On one hand, it could be a source of increased funding, but, on the other, it could function as a high bar for institutional accountability. While UMBC might like to be funded like the University of California, San Diego, would it be so eager to be held to the same standards for federal research grants or Ph.D. production?

The important process of determining "peers" was not fully objective. There were many variables and many exceptions granted. The first step was for an institution to nominate peers. They needed to be within the same or nearest two Carnegie classifications for degree and research productivity. The institution had the choice of how many peers to include, but they should have been geographically as close to Maryland as possible. Other variables to be considered were size (headcount, FTE, degrees); revenues minus state appropriations; student characteristics (undergraduate, part-time, minorities); programs mix; and distance from an urban center.[56]

For UMCP, its peers were permitted to be aspirational, not actual. For UMAB, the formula was based on composite peers for each of its six professional schools, since that configuration is unique. Nor did the University of Baltimore have close peers because, until recently it had a distinctive arrangement of offering only the last two years of undergraduate education, accompanied by relatively low cost professional schools in business and law. Then there was St. Mary's College, a unique public liberal arts institution. All the HBCUs argued for supplemental funding, claiming they bore the costs of their additional mission to provide remedial education to their frequently underprepared undergraduates. Morgan was particularly effective, making

56. Ibid., 5.

not only the remedial argument, but also seeking increased funds because of its doctoral mission and because it was an urban university.[57]

Of course, UMBC had claimed the title "An Honors University in Maryland," though its more persuasive case for additional funding might be the added costs of its curricular focus on science, engineering and technology. By 2012, about 65 percent of its entering freshmen intended to major in these disciplines.[58] Over the years, UMBC's peers changed as the university's status evolved. In peer selection was there a difference in what UMBC wanted and what it received in state dollars?

In 1988, the solution for UMBC was to fend off adding some less attractive institutions to its list, while moving some institutional "stretches" to the category of aspirational peers. The Universities of Kentucky and Mississippi were excluded from a preliminary list. The Universities of Hawaii and New Mexico were deleted because in their mix of programs they granted two year Associate Arts degrees. The University of Colorado Boulder and the University of Tennessee at Knoxville were eliminated because less than one percent of their degrees were in health-related majors, and UMBC successfully subtracted the University of Utah because it was in a low cost standard of living metropolitan area. In the end UMBC was successful in retaining most of the schools from the previously combined list, though the University of West Virginia and Wayne State University were added.

In 1999, USM again asked each campus to identify new peers that might create a model for state funding guidelines, faculty salary, and productivity comparisons.[59] As it was on other campuses, this matter was a great concern to UMBC. President Hrabowski's response made some general methodological comments, but he also urged that private institutions be included as potential peers because UMBC competed with such for students, faculty and private giving.[60] That plea was not heeded.

UMBC's 1999 final list of peers were the University of Arkansas Main Campus, University of Delaware, University of California-Riverside, University of California-Santa Cruz, Mississippi State University, SUNY-Albany, Oklahoma State University, University of Rhode Island, Clemson University, and the University of Wyoming. Its aspirational peers were the University of Connecticut, Georgia Tech University main campus, SUNY Stony Brook, and the University of Massachusetts, Amherst.[61] UMBC was successful, however in eliminating certain state schools others had proposed to

57. Morgan's state appropriation included nine unique and favorable variables, not available to other institutions. State opening argument, *Coalition* trial. 46.

58. UMBC Office of Institutional Research, "UMBC New Freshman Headcount Enrollment Trends by Primary Plan." OIR Databook, 2012.

59. Donald Langenberg to Presidents, "Missions, Peers, and Performance," February 6, 1999.

60. Freeman Hrabowski letter to Donald Langenberg, "Peers and Performances," February 22, 1999.

61. Connie Pierson, Assistant Director of Institutional Research, UMBC, email to the author, October 31, 2012.

add to its peer list such as Southern Illinois University, University of South Carolina, Ohio University, Kent State University, and University of Wisconsin-Milwaukee.

In 2008, another round of peer negotiations with MHEC took place involving UMBC's top financial officers and USM officers.[62] Figure E displays that outcome.

If the image of some of these institutions is shaped by their sports prowess, UMBC's inclusion among them (i.e., Arkansas, Clemson, Oklahoma State) might

Figure E
UMBC Peer Institutions (2008)

Current Peers	**Enrollment**	**Endowment**
University of Arkansas Main Campus	19,849	$856,049,000
University of California Riverside	19,364	$122,590,000
University of California-Santa Cruz	19,675	$81,552,000
University of Massachusetts Amherst	27,016	NA
Mississippi State University	18,601	$280,711,000
New Jersey Institute of Technology	8,840	$70,638,000
Oklahoma State University Main Campus	23,033	$617,028,000
University of Rhode Island	16,389	$88,028,000
Clemson University	19,111	$421,299,000
University of Wyoming	12,427	$298,527,000
Aspirational Peers		
University of Connecticut	25,029	$328,132,000
Georgia Tech University main campus	20,291	$320,151,000
Stony Brook University.	24,681	$113,204,000
University of Pittsburgh	28,328	$2,333,602,000
UMBC	**12,870**	$57,294,264
Average Current Peers	18,142	$315,158,000
Average Aspirational Peers	24,582	$773,772,250

Source: UMBC Office of Institutional Research August 2010, National Association of College and University Business Officers (NACUBO) Endowment Study 2008.

62. James E. Lyons, Sr., "2008 Funding Guidelines Peer Reselection and Adjustments," MHEC memorandum, October 16, 2008, which discusses the outcome of the negotiations between MHEC and UMBC and other state campuses regarding peer selection.

seem a bit odd. But, of course, it was not athletics, but academic factors such as a focus on the STEM disciplines that drove the peer selection. Nevertheless, UMBC is considerably smaller in enrollment than most of its peers. It not only had the smallest endowment, but, in many instances, is dwarfed by the endowment of some of its "peers."

Whatever the peer formula and political modifications to it were, the end result did not work out well for UMBC. Peer selection, however, does not automatically lead to any particular funding outcome. In short, despite Maryland's attempt to be objective and mathematical in distributing higher education operating costs, it was not possible to exclude political judgments from these funding decisions. Figure F reflects actual state funding for USM institutions compared to what the state accepted peer calculations suggest it should be.

For those responsible for UMBC's finances, the facts captured in Figure F were sobering.[63] First, though Maryland is the wealthiest state in the Union, it funds its

Figure F
Maryland Peer Guideline Attainment—FY 2012 (Public Universities)

	Peer Calculation	Actual State Support	Percentage of State Support to Peer Calculation
Coppin State University	34,239,249	37,943,492	110.8
Morgan State University	94,201,019	73,001,828	77.5
U.M., College Park	555,279,637	413,391,061	75.1
U.M., Eastern Shore	44,855,208	32,112,536	71.6
Bowie State University	50,751,578	35,637,462	70.2
U.M., Baltimore	268,271,598	184,525,799	68.8
Frostburg State	48,532,380	33,321,923	68.7
Towson State University	138,144,474	90,924, 480	65.8
Salisbury State University	62,553,750	39,596,615	63.3
U.M., Baltimore County	**154,551,763**	**95,569,552**	**61.8**
University of Baltimore	65,405,783	30,321,428	46.4
State Totals	1,625,402,390	1,133,361,914	69.7

Source: Defense Exhibit 25 from *Coalition for Educational Equity v. Maryland Commission on Higher Education*, January 3, 2012.

63. In President Hrabowski's 2003 legislative testimony, he pointed out that UMBC was funded at only 64 percent of its designated peers. February 2003. Office of the President, http://president.umbc.edu/selected-speeches/. As Figure F shows the situation is now worse.

higher education institutions at only about seventy percent of their designated peers. Second, even at this diminished ratio, UMBC ranked 10th of Maryland's eleven public universities.

D. Endowments and Private Funding

The other traditional sources of revenue for a university are endowments and private giving, but they are always a challenge for a new campus.

Assembling a substantial endowment is every academic institution's ambition. Endowments can provide funding for special projects or can be used to smooth out budgets when money from other sources temporarily decreases. No institution is ever satisfied with the size of its endowment. Wealthy private universities staged endowment campaigns, even during the recent recessionary period, with goals in the billions.[64] Generally, private institutions have much larger endowment income per student than their public counterparts. Older universities usually have higher endowments than newer schools. Like their northeastern neighbors, Maryland's public campuses were late in the game of raising endowment funds. As a new Maryland public university, UMBC was disadvantaged on both counts.

Figure G shows the UMBC endowment and private giving between 1988 and 2012.

Apparently before 1993, UMBC's endowment amount was negligible. By 2008 UMBC's endowment reached $57 million, but those investments fell substantially when the economy went into recession in that year. The $15 million loss was painful for a new campus, but in endowments everything is relative.[65] Yale University's endowment, for example, temporarily lost $6.2 billion in that period and the institution even took some modest austerity measures as a result.[66]

One way to look at the size of the UMBC's endowment of almost $60 million is to compare it to other Maryland institutions. Not surprisingly, Johns Hopkins is the leader at about $2.6 billion. UMCP is next at $285 million,[67] followed by Goucher at $188 million, Washington College at $173 million, Loyola University at $165 million, St. John's College at $130 million and McDaniel College at $88 million.[68] These fig-

64. See for example: Yale University, "Annual Report 2010–2011: A Year unlike Any Other," www.yale.edu/honor/financial.html (accessed October 28, 2013).

65. During this period the University System of Maryland Foundation lost 28 percent of its investment pool. That was worse than the national average of a 23 percent recent decline. Goldie Blumenstyk, "Average Returns on Endowments Is Worst in Almost 40 Years," *The Chronicle of Higher Education*, January 28, 2010.

66. Yale Endowment update, investments.yale.edu/images/documents/Yale-Endowment-09.pdf.

67. This figure included endowments managed by the University System of Maryland Foundation and the separate The University of Maryland, College Park Foundation. "USM Foundation 2011 Annual Report," 1.

68. "College and University Endowments, 2011–2012," *Chronicle of Higher Education*, April 10, 2013.

Figure G
UMBC Endowment and Private Giving

Year	Total Private Giving	Book Value of Endowment
1988	$705,672	$132,618
1993	$1,085,470	N.A.
1994	$1,289,843	$1,656,280
1995	$1,220,051	$2,338,357
1996	$4,318,036	$3,517,251
1997	$8,958,126	$5,374,260
1998	$6,301,271	$8,502,465
1999	$9,656,317	$12,579,000
2000	$7,924,871	$14,003,106
2001	$10,793,216	$17,365,562
2002	$10,490,887	$17,099,562
2003	$8,030,793	$19,146,600
2004	$10,825,536	$25,653,960
2005	$15,162,714	$32,041,264
2006	$15,038,515	$42,273,516
2007	$13,244,625	$54,391,056
2008	$14,052,606	$57,295,264
2009	$13,495,047	$42,221,530
2010	$8,363,318	$47,602,603
2011	$11,605,904	$57,840,556
2012	$11,776,124	$59,995,583

Sources: Amy Clark and Matthew Miller, "Institutional Advancement at the University of Maryland Baltimore County (A)," (Cambridge, MA: Harvard Graduate School of Education, 2001): see also, UMBC Office of Institutional Advancement, "UMBC Historic Giving Values, FY 1983–FY 2012." UMBC historic documents collection, Special Collections, University of Maryland, Baltimore County.

ures make the advantages of private institutions, even small liberal arts colleges, in the amount of endowment per-student very obvious.

UMBC administrators, particularly those in the Office of Institutional Advancement, were, of course, very aware of the University's low endowment. The Harvard

University School of Education has come twice to UMBC to do case studies on the latter's institutional advancement efforts.[69] At first glance, it is not clear what researchers from a University whose endowment is counted in billions wanted to learn from a University whose endowment has barely topped $50 million in good years, but there are more up and coming, though still struggling campuses, than there are Ivy League members.

By 1991, as President Hooker left UMBC to become President of the University of Massachusetts System, the state of Maryland was in a deep recession. Since the State constitution requires its annual budget to be balanced, there were eight successive rounds of cuts between the fall of 1990 and the winter of 1992 that pared USM's funding by 20 percent.[70] At UMBC, that meant that the campus had to go through an excruciating process of program review and reduction described in Chapters VII and IX.

UMBC's philosophy in hard financial times has been to protect the faculty academic core, so cuts to UMBC's administrative staff were much deeper. Some administrative functions were transferred to System offices, but other on-campus activities were decimated. As the Harvard study reports:

> During the early 1990s, the UMBC Office of Institutional Advancement was virtually eliminated. The Vice President for Institutional Advancement vacated his position in 1991 and was not replaced. Likewise, the directors of alumni and development left UMBC and no replacements were sought. Staff for the entire advancement area was trimmed to six people, three of whom worked part-time.[71]

Thus, UMBC was placed in a "Catch-22" position. At the very time its state budget was being drastically cut, the campus appeared to lose the staffing ability to raise private money.

Fortunately, UMBC scored its first fundraising coup in 1988 which provided entree and hope in the dire years of the early 1990s. UMBC's new Vice Provost, Freeman Hrabowski, had won the hearts and minds of Robert and Jane Meyerhoff to establish what would become their nationally famous Meyerhoff Scholars program. (see Chapter VIII for a description of the Scholar's program). Obtaining what would be eventually $5 million in gifts from one of Baltimore's most prominent philanthropic families was an important entree to other fundraising opportunities. The initial Meyerhoff donation doubled UMBC's endowment and was widely noted by USM leaders and the national press. As Doug Pear, long-time chief staff aide to several UMBC Presidents, recalled: "the Meyerhoff [grant] was so successful, so quickly, that

69. Amy Clark and Matthew Miller, "Institutional Advancement at the University of Maryland Baltimore County (A)," (Cambridge, MA: Harvard Graduate School of Education, 2001). According to the authors these case studies are created for class discussions "rather than to illustrate either effective or ineffective handling of an administrative situation."

70. Ibid., 3.

71. Clark and Miller, "Institutional Advancement," 3.

you couldn't help but notice it. It reflected the donors' vision, Freeman's capabilities, and the University's commitment to minority education."[72]

If the Meyerhoff gift altered the general perception of UMBC, it also changed Hrabowski's reputation. According to Pear:

> When Freeman made the Meyerhoff program happen, people saw him as someone who could elevate our awareness of possibilities. He raised the bar at UMBC and in the process, made people believe the institution could advance to the next level, even though we weren't really sure what the next level meant for us.[73]

After Hrabowski became President, one of his first priorities was to improve the physical appearance of the campus. The Harvard study quotes him as saying:

> In addition to demonstrating my loyalty and commitment to UMBC's academic programs, I felt we had to make the campus more aesthetically appealing. How could we expect to become a first rate-research institution and attract the kind of financial support needed to attain such aspirations if our physical plant was uninviting and unattractive? UMBC had to take care of these core issues before we could get excited about raising serious money.[74]

That meant hard lobbying with the Chancellor's Office, the Regents, and the state legislature to get in the funding queue. This was a game Hrabowski has played very well during his time at UMBC. Out of his efforts came new buildings Physics (1999), The Commons, (2002), Information Technology and Engineering (2003), Public Policy, (2003) and Performing Arts and Humanities (2012), among others.

Nevertheless, capital expenditures are no substitute for the operating funds and private gifts that are essential for new initiatives. After a national search, Hrabowski hired Sheldon Caplis, the former Vice President for Institutional Advancement at the University of Baltimore, to manage fundraising, marketing, public relations, and alumni affairs.

The last category represented a quandary for UMBC. About 85 percent of UMBC's alumni then lived in Maryland, but Caplis decided that:

> UMBC was so new and its alumni body so young, we knew that creating corporate partnerships would represent a major part of our early activity. Our alumni group just wasn't sufficiently established professionally to warrant directing activity in that direction.[75]

---

72. Ibid., 4.
73. Ibid.
74. Ibid., 5.
75. Clark and Miller, (Appendix C). 6. Alumni giving had increased from $45,058 in 1993 to $422,644 in 1999. While this was a substantial percentage increase, the cash value was very modest. By 2011, giving by UMBC's more than 50,000 alumni reached only $411,031, with 2,154 donors. UMBC Office of Alumni Relations, "UMBC by the Numbers: Alumni & Giving," 2011. alumni.umbc.edu/s/1325/images/editor_documents/boardlinetoolkit/alumni_flyer.pdf (accessed May 15, 2013).

From Caplis' perspective, a more productive and profitable approach was to invigorate UMBC's Board of Visitors. While the Board of Regents has legal and political authority over all system campuses, each Maryland public higher educational institution was also required by the legislature to create a Board of Visitors which it hoped would relieve the demands for public subsidies with private support. As their name suggests the Visitors do not have management responsibilities, but they may be useful in garnishing a campus with their personal prestige, providing some perspective on campus issues, interpreting the university's external environment, and, of course, in fundraising. On the other hand, before they become an asset, they must be selected carefully and the relationships regularly nourished.

At the time Hrabowski assumed the Presidency, the Board met irregularly, sometimes with as few as three members, and was virtually moribund.[76] Caplis and Hrabowski set out to revitalize it and by 1994, it had some 20 members, most of them prominent members of the Baltimore business and community leadership. The key recruit was Jim Brady, a Managing Partner at Arthur Andersen, who served as chair. In 1995, he became Maryland Secretary of Business and Economic Development under Governor Glendening. He was replaced as Chair by Earl Linehan, co-founder of Meridian Healthcare and founder of Woodbrook Capital Investments, who after a rooftop tour with Freeman, recognized that UMBC was not "simply a satellite campus of UMCP."[77] As their relationship grew, Linehan and his wife Darielle, impressed by the Meyerhoff Program, became interested in creating an Artist-Scholars Program and started it with a million dollar gift.

The rebuilt Advancement staff, including Lisa Akchin, Kady Burke, and Sandra Dzija, came on board just in time. In 1994, USM mandated that each system campus undertake a five-year capital campaign to begin in the fall 1997. Each campus was required to "develop clear strategies for increasing philanthropic support with the goal of doubling alumni gifts and endowment gifts by 2002."[78] This requirement forced UMBC to speed up its fundraising efforts. Marts & Lundy, a specialized consulting firm, was hired to advise campaign. There were two levels to this effort. The first, was identifying "top-end" donors and the second was even more fundamental—creating an overall institutional plan. As a young ambitious institution, overcoming one challenge after another, UMBC never had formulated an overall strategic plan.[79] The consultants concluded:

> All campaign priorities are dependent upon private support in order to be funded ... Fund raising priorities should be consistent with the academic

76. In FY 1989, private gifts and grants to UMBC totaled about $1.2 million or about 1.5 percent of the University budget. UMBC "Mission Statement," 6, April 11, 1990.

77. Clark and Miller. "Institutional Advancement." 7.

78. Ibid., 8.

79. "Currently, there is no program or structure to support the identification, cultivation and solicitation of major donors." Marts & Lundy, Inc. *Internal Assessment and Campaign Planning Issues,* March 1996. 6. The consultants acknowledged that UMBC fund-raising activities were severely understaffed. UMBC historic documents collection, Special Collections, University of Maryland, Baltimore County.

> priorities specified in the mission statement and reflected in programmatic emphasis. In addition, it is important to recognize that certain types of funding opportunities are more appealing to donors than others.[80]

The consultants began to consider 1996, the year of UMBC's 30th Anniversary, as a possible link to fundraising. At first, President Hrabowski wondered: "Who celebrates a 30th anniversary?" But his skepticism was overcome and the 30th Anniversary celebration turned out to be a major success. Lisa Akchin remembered: "Freeman didn't think we could do it. But we did it, even if we didn't realize in the beginning how big it would become." Ultimately, it amounted to a UMBC "coming out party," and a way to be becoming better known throughout the region. It was the first time the campus was identified to the corporate community as an honors university. Akchin recalled:

> There were more suits in attendance than we had ever seen at a UMBC function. The *Baltimore Sun* covered the event extensively, and Steve Case, the AOL founder, gave a keynote speech that further established us as a "techie" campus. Our birthday party also attracted 1,200 alumni, the largest number ever to return for a single campus event.[81]

Accompanying the birthday bash was an effort to reach out to corporations, foundations, alumni, and parents.[82]

In planning the 1997 case statement for the capital campaign, the administration asked Professor Diane Lee (Education) to join Akchin as leaders of faculty focus groups. Lee, who later became Vice Provost and Dean of Undergraduate Education, agreed that, "Senior leadership involves faculty here. Very little can be accomplished top-down. We have a strong faculty—shared governance is essential and very much alive."[83] She hoped a skeptical faculty, which was not asked to formally approve the case statement, would feel appropriately involved. In addition to a list of University accomplishments and ambitions, the case statement tried out some new slogans. "UMBC is a university that knows how to win" (set on the background of a chess board), and UMBC "Hands on from the Start," reflecting the University's commitment to undergraduate research and internship experiences were two such attempts.

Not all faculty were enamored with the outcome. James Grubb, Professor and Chair of the History Department, spoke for many in the humanities when he called the case statement a "utopian marketing document." He continued:

> the mission statement presented here is what UMBC thinks it wants to be; it isn't what we actually are. The image doesn't fit the reality.... We need a

80. Ibid., 17.
81. Clark and Miller, "Institutional Advancement," 10.
82. For a chronicle of UMBC's achievements in the first 30 years, see "Marks of Excellence," *UMBC Magazine*, Summer 1997. For a description of the 30th anniversary fundraising, see Eleanor L Cunningham, "The Campaign for UMBC: keeping and getting the very best," *UMBC Magazine*, Spring 1998.
83. Clark and Miller, "Institutional Advancement," 12.

> more sophisticated balance of images. We need to recognize excellence more broadly.... A few areas of excellence are pounded over and over again, while others are never mentioned at all. Our emphasis on science and technology is leading to declining enrollments in other fields due to self-selection by students.... Humanities scholars and arts scholars are as important as Meyerhoff recipients. The history department may not need as much money to do research, but our teaching and scholarly output is equally as important and, I might add, equally as impressive.[84]

In part, the Grubb *cri di coeur* was part of a vigorous debate heard on most research university campuses where it is so much easier for institutions to sell their activities supporting businesses, medicine, farmers etc., than to convince the public that literature, history, and art may be as important to society's wellbeing as biochemistry and engineering.[85] In part it was also an appeal to President Hrabowski's sensibilities, who is a fine pianist and can recite poetry for almost any occasion. The rest of Grubb's objection to overstating UMBC ambitions is understandable.

Yet like all case statements, *The Campaign for UMBC: Keeping and Getting the Very Best*, emphasized the positive and UMBC has always been a university whose reach exceeded its grasp or its resources. Without that optimism and energy, far less would have been accomplished.

The campaign goal was $50 million which the Harvard writers thought UMBC "was positioned to reach." A stretch it was. In 1988, twenty-two years after UMBC was founded, its endowment was $132,000.[86] You read that right. By 1999, it was $12.5 million. The growth in percentage terms was impressive, but the cash on hand was not. Nevertheless, the 30th Anniversary capital campaign was a success, achieving an overall $66 million sum, including one eight-figure pledge from a UMBC alumnus.[87]

There were setbacks along the way. David Oros, UMBC class of 1985, had become President and CEO of Aether Systems, a wireless data systems firm. The company, once called the darling of Baltimore's "New Economy," had more than 1,000 employees and had a market capitalization of nearly $7 billion. Its ambition was no less than "to lead a shift from the city's old-line buttoned-down central business district to the new, tech-savvy 'Digital Harbor.'"[88] The talk of the town, UMBC took notice of its math major alumnus David Oros. After a Hrabowski rooftop tour and some other

84. *Ibid.*, 13–14.

85. Frank Donoghue, "Can the Humanities Survive the 21st Century," *The Chronicle for Higher Education,* September 10, 2010, B4. Donoghue argues that "universities have had no choice but to function increasingly as corporations and to form partnerships with corporations and this turn of events fundamentally alters their institutional dynamic." B5.

86. Clark and Miller, "Institutional Advancement," Appendix B.

87. Clark and Miller "Harvard update," November 2, 2010.4.

88. Tim Finin, "Aether Systems, once Baltimore's dot.com favorite, leaving the city," http://ebiquity.umbc.edu/blogger/2006/06/08/615/. Stacy Hirsch and Laura Smitherman, "Remaking self: Aether to leave City," *Baltimore Sun,* June 8, 2008.

cultivation, Oros made a pledge of over $10 million to finance a new center in mobile wireless computing and add to other applied research centers and labs.[89] Caplis viewed this pledge as a philanthropic coup; possibly the first of many from thirty something UMBC alumni entrepreneurs.

There was only one problem. Although Oros gave UMBC $510,000 in cash for wireless curriculum development in 2000,[90] the main gift was to be in Aether stock. At its height in March 2000 that stock traded at $345 a share, before it collapsed in the dot.com stock bubble and ended at $2.25 a share in 2002.[91] Aether announced it was leaving the wireless industry in 2004 to move into that surefire moneymaker:—mortgage-backed securities. That timing proved less than fortuitous and the company eventually morphed into NexCen brands owning various consumer product brands. The dream that the Aether gift would transform certain parts of the campus was dead.

Another outside investment in the campus seemed to be on more solid footing. John Erickson had built a nationwide empire of high-end retirement campuses. One site, called Charlestown, where his Catonsville company was headquartered was about three miles from the University. Erickson had manifested a previous interest in UMBC by building several dormitories in return for capturing rents for a number of years to pay off the mortgage. These dorms were constructed more quickly and with more amenities than those that could be built through the traditional state construction process. Now he recognized another new venture which could be fulfilled by a partnership with UMBC.

The retirement home industry was booming and, as America aged, demographic trends promised a bright future for those businesses. As these facilities grew more lavish and more complex, however, there was a growing need to find skilled managers. Consequently, Erickson suggested a partnership with UMBC to create a new professional school focused on the management of aging services. President Hrabowski responded enthusiastically. It was a good niche in what looked like a growth market with an attractive public service component. To launch the school, Erickson gave $5 million and the state provided $4 million. Additional support was promised from the lead donor and the Erickson School was launched. There was some faculty opposition by those who thought that, in the quick start, the process for program development had not been followed.[92] The new School appeared to some

89. At one point, Oros proposed moving his company to the technology park at UMBC where he hoped to create an institute of wireless technology. Andre Ratner, "Catonsville park is preferred over Inner Harbor site," *Baltimore Sun*, June 23, 2001.

90. "Aether Systems and UMBC Form Computing Partnership," UMBC press release, May 10, 2000. President Hrabowski declared, "The Aether-UMBC partnership will grow to attract the best minds in wireless and mobile computing, making our region a force in a field that is already changing the lives of people around the world."

91. Stacey Hirsh, "Aether founder Oros to give up NexCen post," *Baltimore Sun*, March 24, 2007.

92. See videotaped interviews with Arthur Johnson (April 16, 2013), John Jeffries (May 3, 2013), and Kevin Eckert (May 7, 2013) by Joseph Tatarewicz for discussions about the controversy over the creation of the Erickson School and some of its continuing problems.

as a fait accompli by a donor who wanted to buy a school named after him and by an over eager administration. Others thought neither the cash in hand nor the planned size of the enterprise were enough to warrant calling the new unit a School.

What neither side anticipated was the recession that began in 2007. The Erickson corporate model was to ask its guests/customers to pay hefty buy-in amounts in exchange for retirement housing with continuous care and many recreational and health facilities. The model worked well when aging couples could sell their houses and use the proceeds to buy into their new retirement home. When the housing market collapsed, Erickson's target audience could no longer sell, at a sufficient price or at all, to move into a company facility. The Corporation went bankrupt and John Erickson was ousted as CEO.[93] There would be no more gifts to the School from that source. Consequently there were sharp cuts in staff and enrollment, although the School survived.[94]

Nevertheless, in less than four years, UMBC exceeded its campaign goal, raising $54.3 million. Most of that money was in research contracts, however. The most important funding was still coming from the state in the form of new buildings and per-student funding.

In all these efforts, public and private, it was widely acknowledged that Freeman Hrabowski was the key player. Caplis was surprised at the ease of recruiting new Board of Visitors' members:

> We pursued what I jokingly called a "Friends of Freeman" strategy when building the Board of Visitors. Freeman had attended a leadership program sponsored by the Greater Baltimore Committee and Maryland Chamber of Commerce with a host of movers and shakers from throughout the region, so many of our initial asks were people he met during those experiences. We emphasized the very real opportunity to shape the future of an up-and-coming institution from the ground up. We said that UMBC was well positioned. Given Freeman's exciting vision for the place, many people wanted to support him.[95]

Hrabowski was always upbeat:

> We have many people here, myself included, who like asking for money. We enjoy talking about the place. We enjoy saying, 'you really ought to help us out.' It makes a difference. It is a big joke in business circles; they see me coming and say, 'Put your hands in your pocket, here comes Freeman.' I take

93. Jay Hancock, "Erickson's Smart Bets Soured Along With Nation's Economy," *Baltimore Sun*, October 21, 2009. After its Chapter 11 filing, the company was sold to Redwood Capital Investments which replaced its management team, "Erickson Retirement Emerges from Bankruptcy," *Baltimore Sun*, April 16, 2010. The final straw was an allegation in federal court that the Erickson family had enriched itself at the expense of the welfare of the corporation, Jessica Anderson, "Erickson retirement founder faces lawsuit," *Baltimore Sun*, June 5, 2011.

94. Stephen Kiehl, "UMBC Shrinks School of Aging," *Baltimore Sun*, April 15, 2009

95. Clark and Miller, "Institutional Advancement," 6–7.

people to baseball games and they want to give me money just so I'll shut up and let them watch the game.[96]

One person who quickly responded to that vision was alumnus Scott Rifkin. After the traditional rooftop tour, Rifkin joked that Freeman's passion about UMBC might cause him "to throw me off the roof if I didn't agree to show my financial support in some way."[97] Instead, Rifkin, a prominent physician, received the UMBC Outstanding Alumnus of the Year Award in 1995 and was asked to join the Board of Visitors. In 1999, he pledged the largest single alumni donation in UMBC's history and remarked. "There is no subtlety in Freeman. He can get away with asking you for anything."

Still UMBC's endowment remained at a modest level. Partly that reflects trend in modern philanthropy. As Anthony Deering, former CEO of the Rouse Corporation, UMBC Board of Visitors member and donor, explained endowment gifts are dead money to be used in the future for "who knows what, who knows when."[98] Many contemporary donors prefer to give for specific immediate and visible purposes. They often view their first gift as seed money to be supplemented over the years if the initial donation bears fruit.

As UMBC approached its 40th birthday in 2006, it publicly launched another capital campaign, this time for $100 million. President Hrabowski called this goal "beyond stretch,"[99] but the timing was not auspicious as the national recession set in a year later.[100] Nevertheless, when the "Exceptional By Example Campaign" ended on in June 30, 2011, $115 million had been raised and the endowment had increased from $17.3 million to $57.8 million.[101]

Although the UMBC Alumni Association was founded in 1970 and there are an estimated 50,000 alumni of the University, for most of its institutional history investment in alumni giving was moribund and their response was commensurate. Under the leadership of Greg Simmons '04 that relationship has been reinvigorated. By 2012, the number of donors, particularly among young alums had increased significantly, including a remarkable 42 percent of all athletic alumni. Still the bottom line in alumni giving for that year was only $300,000.[102]

For the foreseeable future, UMBC's income will come from the traditional sources (tuition, state appropriations, endowment and gifts). Most of those sources will

96. Ibid., Appendix C,.14.

97. Ibid., 7.

98. Anthony Deering interview by the author, August 18, 2011.

99. Clark and Miller, "Institutional Advancement,"8.

100. The difficulty of raising money for Maryland universities during the recession is described in Childs Walker, "Colleges, universities feel the pain," *Baltimore Sun,* July 20, 2009. A number of different constituencies contributed to the Campaign including Faculty and Staff ($679,000), Parents, ($1,200,000), Alumni, ($3,500,000), Corporations, Foundations and Friends, ($70,000,000), Gifts-in-Kind, ($8,500,000) and from Grants and Contracts. Jenny O'Grady and Meredith Purvis, "Measure of a Mission, *UMBC Magazine,* Fall 2011.

101. See Figure G.

102. UMBC's Alumni Community, http://retirement.

change only incrementally, although perhaps in different proportions. One of Albin Kuhn's favorite sayings was "hold fast to your dreams." Whether one of those dreams, that a breakthrough donor will emerge in some future year will come true, remains to be seen.

CHAPTER VI

Faculty

In all the turbulent periods of UMBC's history, there has been a general recognition of the strengths of its faculty. How did that happen? For many years, the Catonsville campus was, at best, an uncertain place to build a career.

For most of its existence, the University of Maryland was simply a branch of state government, which meant its employees served under the rules and regulations of the State Department of Personnel. Its purchasing and contracting activities were supervised by the State Department of Budget and Procurement. The priorities and practices of the burgeoning University after World War II, however, did not always mesh well with those existing departmental procedures.

The University wanted more independence from the state bureaucracy and so moved to buttress its legislative support. Tuition "scholarships" were provided for two constituents recommended by each state senator and one for each delegate. Then there was football. George Callcott describes a 1948 "special session" of the General Assembly when "a full quorum of legislators appeared at College Park for a luncheon and football game, with their meals and tickets paid for by the University and thus indirectly by the state treasury."[1] In the elections of 1950 and 1952, the University's alumni and farm extension mailing lists were lent to Democratic candidates running for election. These efforts paid off. The University's operating budget quadrupled from $4,800,000 in 1945 to $21,000,000 in 1954. On the playing field, after several conference championship seasons, the Terrapins won the national football title in 1954 to much legislative acclaim.

Still, the University chafed at the existing bureaucratic rules under which it operated. Questions were raised about some institutional accounting practices and some legislators were annoyed that University tuition money was being used for expenditures the General Assembly had rejected. President H.C. "Curley" Byrd, former UM football coach and athletic director, and the Regents responded by lobbying the General Assembly to pass what became known as the University of Maryland "Autonomy" Act giving UM the purchasing, personnel, and curriculum authority held by prominent universities in some other states. The potential loss of power was resisted by the state officials, however, and Governor Theodore R. McKeldin vetoed the Act, only to see his action overridden by the Legislature.

---

1. George A. Callcott, *A History of the University of Maryland* (Baltimore: Maryland Historical Society, 1966). 342. The author describes the "autonomy" fight pages 342–345.

There was only one glitch. "Autonomy" as defined in the Act only applied to existing campuses, so in its initial development and first year of operation, UMBC had to be very conscious of bureaucratic agendas and procedures that no longer affected other campuses. After Spiro T. Agnew, former Baltimore County executive, was elected governor, support among the his new appointees and the public for granting UMBC the autonomy granted other state campuses was such that legislation was passed to that effect in 1967. Lucy S. Wilson, who served as assistant to Albin Kuhn for twenty years, asked for the signing pen and it now resides in the UMBC library, which years later was named for the founding Chancellor.[2]

While having the normal independence that American universities enjoy from state bureaucracies was important to UMBC's development, a policy reserving most campus decisions to UMBC faculty and administrators was of critical significance. Was UMBC to be a free-standing university with its own distinctive characteristics, seeking its own forms of excellence, or a branch of College Park serving overflow students that could not be accommodated on the older campus? So many curricular, budget, and personnel decisions would turn on the answer to that question. Fortunately the decision was made clearly before the new campus even opened.

Faculty senates, representing all academic departments on a campus, can play a key role in the concept of university shared governance. Approval of new programs and rules for recruitment and retention of faculty, for example, usually require faculty senate affirmation. The elaborate structure of faculty committees is created by the senate and these committees in turn report to it. Senates do not make most university policy decisions, but they are an important check and balance in the process. If the faculty neglects its governance role or is ignored by administrators, there may be little professorial buy-in regarding decisions by others.

In 1965, the University of Maryland had a combined faculty Senate with representatives from both College Park and the Baltimore professional school campuses. Consequently, there was some logic simply to add a UMBC representative or two to the existing Senate. UM policies would affect UMBC and, furthermore, membership in that Senate might have conferred some status on the new enterprise. On the other hand, the myriad issues affecting the fledgling campus would have been afterthoughts in the combined faculty Senate.

According to Dr. Kuhn, UM President Elkins had a strong belief, "that a new campus, if we could get one formed, would have the authority to really develop as a part of the University of Maryland, not as a branch, not as a segment off here controlled by headquarters."[3] So, Elkins weighed in against the combined Senate concept, saying, "This new campus must have its own faculty administrative Senate, not be under the University umbrella ..." He also told UMCP chairs they could not pick UMBC faculty, though some department chairs wanted that power. Regarding UMBC fac-

2. A description of the autonomy acts was written in long hand in October 1999 by Dr. Kuhn and is now in the A.O.K. Library. I: //Admin/Friends/University of Maryland Autonomy.doc.

3. Albin O. Kuhn and Homer Schamp, interview by Larry Wilt, January 4, 2006. 4–5.

ulty appointments, Elkins came to the combined faculty Senate and urged, "There's no reason why the faculty here at College Park should be saddled with that responsibility."[4] He then called for a vote which reaffirmed that principle.

In addition to Elkins' vision, there were strong pragmatic reasons for granting UMBC substantial autonomy. The College Park campus had just increased by more than four thousand students from one year to the next. Kuhn concluded, "The faculty there, the leaders there, the administration, everybody was wanting to help, wanting a new campus, not worried about what the new campus might do to the old campus."[5] Moreover, Kuhn had been on committees in other states that looked at proposals for a number of branch campuses without any autonomy and he didn't like what he saw. Edward Orser, UMBC Professor of American Studies, interviewing Kuhn, remarked that the decisions that UMBC should have its own Senate and faculty appointment power were essential in freeing UMBC from being "sort of an extension campus or satellite campus."[6]

A. Assembling a Faculty

Kuhn's first decision was to hire an academic Dean. For that choice, he turned understandably to the UMCP faculty and he selected Homer Schamp, a molecular physicist. Kuhn had been observing Schamp's work for some time and his appraisal was that Schamp:

> was just the kind of ideal person who would come in, could be completely free to do the job of finding the right kind of faculty to start UMBC, and would do an excellent job. [My] job was to be sure I could talk him into doing it. He had a very peaceful life at College Park, compared to what he had after he got appointed to UMBC.... fortunately Homer was at the right stage where he thought another challenge would be fun.[7]

Before UMBC had departments, it created an organizational structure composed of four Divisions. Their chairs were Robert G. Shedd (1966–67) and then Lawrence Lasher, Humanities; Richard C. Roberts, Mathematics; Walter A. Konetzka, Sciences; and David T. Lewis, Social Sciences. There were several reasons for this arrangement. Some of it was a pragmatic response to the small number of faculty in each field, but there was also a pedagogical purpose. Kuhn's experience with agriculture, where entomologists, biologists, and agronomists needed to engage problems as a team, led him to support a divisional structure because he wanted UMBC to encourage interdisciplinary research.

That approach worked for a while. Kuhn remembered:

---

4. Ibid., 5.
5. Ibid.
6. Albin O. Kuhn, interview by Edward Orser, February 4, 1994, 4.
7. Albin O. Kuhn, interview by Joseph Tatarewicz, August 14, 2001, 11.

> Well, one of the interesting things in the early days when we were busy recruiting faculty was a very clear understanding about divisions. And kind of an interest in it among most of those we were recruiting. But the moment they got here they'd say, 'Where is my department'?[8]

The issue of divisions versus departments was mostly faced after Kuhn had moved on.

Choosing the first divisional chairs was critical because they would have the paramount influence in the development of the curriculum and in recruiting and hiring faculty. Kuhn reflected:

> Boy, you know the old multiplication thing. If you have one good person now, you're probably going to have a lot of good persons in that area. If you get a bad one, you may be in for some problems. But we were very fortunate. The division chairmen, the four were good people, very good people.[9]

From the beginning UMBC was ambitious about the kind of faculty it wished to employ. Three months before the campus opened, the *Sun* commented that UMBC's new faculty, "although young and comparatively inexperienced, have been chosen for the promise they have shown in research and graduate level instruction."[10]

Nevertheless, recruiting top flight faculty to the new campus was not always easy. Jay Freyman, one of the builders of the Ancient Studies department, remarked that UMBC's new professors were largely "fresh out of graduate school, marching into the ranks of academia 'amidst three buildings and a sea of mud.'"[11] Even later, UMBC seemed to some a risky choice. In 1980, after earning his Ph.D. from the State University of New York at Buffalo, Robert Deluty, psychologist and later a prolific poet, received offers for a tenure track assistant professor position from the University of Virginia and UMBC. His mentors (one of whom thought UMBC was a radio station) were stunned when he chose Catonsville over Charlottesville. Deluty felt he "could get in on the ground floor and really make a difference in shaping the department and the undergraduate and graduate programs."[12] After deciding to come to UMBC because "the challenge of new school appealed to me," the more senior Fred Gornick, then a tenured associate professor at Virginia, was told by his colleagues that he was "mad" for leaving Mr. Jefferson's university.[13]

---

8. Ibid., p. 37.

9. Albin O. Kuhn interview by Edward Orser, February 4, 1994. 20.

10. Gene Oishi, "New Ideas, Methods Slated at U.M. Catonsville School," *Baltimore Sun*, July 23, 1966.

11. Ivan Kramer, a physicist with a new Ph.D. from Berkeley decided to come to UMBC because it "was better to be mired in mud than in bureaucracy." For a description of UMBC's first faculty and a group picture, see "If you want to be pioneers, come with us," a recruiting pitch attributed to Albin O. Kuhn, *UMBC Magazine*, Summer 1997.

12. Robert Deluty email to the author, May 29, 2013. In 2008, Deluty became Associate Dean of the Graduate School.

13. Looking back after 30 years at the Chemistry Department he did so much to build, Gornick's appraisal was that "The department's done remarkably well in developing a recognized research faculty ... a result of the faculty's determination to pursue research from the very be-

In his typically understated manner, Albin Kuhn recalled in recruiting that:

> it was interesting to study the reactions of individuals when they came face to face with the realization that the contractors were still busily constructing the buildings and would have them ready just in time for school and that the Administration occupied an old gray house on the UMBC site. Generally speaking those with a tendency toward enjoying a new adventure seemed to gain momentum in their interest in UMBC as the visit progressed, and others who were not so adventuresome were turned off early in the course of the visit.[14]

So the UMBC faculty recruitment effort went on the road. Homer Schamp and Dave Lewis:

> went to New York because we had a number of [faculty] applicants from around there.... ordinarily you invite someone to the campus and they see what kind of people are here. We don't have any people on the campus, so we sought to show them what kind of people we are looking for. So we went up and took a suite at the Algonquin Hotel and invited everyone [eight people] to lunch.[15]

Despite the Algonquin gambit, only one faculty member was appointed from that trip. William Rothstein, a scholar in the social history of medicine and medical schools, however, taught sociology for forty-seven years at UMBC.

So it was decided that applicants had to be invited to Baltimore. The campus, what there was of it, was not much of a drawing card, nor was an impressive meal to be had in the adjacent suburbs or along Route 40. Kuhn recalled:

> We didn't have a lot of campus to show new recruits when we brought them [in]. We had a lot of land, but we didn't have a lot of finished buildings and we kind of played up the historical aspects of Baltimore City and its good food. You'd have thought it was about as good as New Orleans.... Well, we deliberately made a very careful listing of the top six or seven restaurants in the city and we tried to ferret out when we were recruiting different individuals what type of food they liked best. We did a pretty good lot of work on that.[16]

Maybe the UMBC faculty was built on the enticement of future crab cake dinners.

But more likely, as Kuhn noted with the zeal of a Marine recruiter, we talked to them "about the pioneer spirit of coming here and you weren't going to be in regular departments. You could develop this campus in a way, and it could be a different campus, and it depends on you. You know you can do your part."[17]

---

ginning which was unusual for a school of that size." "If you want to be pioneers," *UMBC Magazine*, Summer 1997.

14. Albin O. Kuhn, "University of Maryland Baltimore County (UMBC) Its Early Years of Development and Operation," UMBC historic documents collection, Special Collections, University of Maryland, Baltimore County. no date.

15. Albin O. Kuhn and Homer Schamp, interviews by Larry Wilt, January 4, 2006, 73.

16. Ibid., 58 and 60.

17. Albin O. Kuhn interview by Edward Orser, February 4, 1994, 20.

That spirit was also embodied in the messages by senior faculty as they recruited new colleagues. For example, in April 1966, Walter A. Konetzka, Professor of Bacteriology at Indiana University, who had committed to moving to UMBC to build a Biology program, wrote Robert Burchard, at that time a young professor at the University of Ife in Nigeria. He assured Burchard that UMBC would be an autonomous university comparable to the new campuses being established by the University of California. The intention was to create a full graduate program offering a Ph.D., though there would be challenges. Nevertheless, Konetzka urged:

> The campus offers many possibilities for combining teaching and research, and possibilities for combining traditional values with new approaches.... we are looking for the best young faculty that we can find. I cannot promise you that it will be an undemanding place to work, that its facilities will be complete and extensive during these first few years, nor that the position will not require stamina and energy, but I think it will be an exciting place to work for anyone who is ambitious and who wants to help in the development of an excellent institution.[18]

Burchard answered that challenge in 1967 and remained at UMBC until 1999, active as a scholar and eager to improve the University community on a variety of issues.[19]

Walter Sherwin, who taught ancient studies at UMBC for over forty years, was also one who responded to the challenge. He remembered: "We were all risk takers coming into a new venture.... People who wanted to get in the beginning of a venture, not to go to an established place and fit in, but create programs." Faculty members, he recalled:

> would go away during those early years on weekend retreats and become engaged in dynamic discussions about the future course of UMBC. There was great rapport. It affected the programs, to be sure, in the camaraderie we shared and passed to the students.[20]

Ability to recruit outstanding faculty was the cardinal achievement that got UMBC off on the right foot. Among those who made the greatest investment in the new campus was this group of pioneering faculty. For those holding their first teaching positions, there was the allure of shaping a new institution and of earning a regular paycheck. For those coming from more senior ranks elsewhere, there was also the exciting possibility of institution building. Nevertheless these jobs were also combined with the risk that UMBC's ambiguous status in Maryland's higher education environment might lead to an institutional and a personal professional dead end. Of the thirty-eight founding faculty, including lecturers and part-timers, twelve (Evelyn Barker-Philosophy; William Bettridge-English; Frank Burd-Political Science;

18. Letter from Walter Konetzka to Robert Burchard, April 27, 1966, UMBC historic documents collection, Special Collections, University of Maryland, Baltimore County.

19. In 2012, Burchard was in emeritus status, but still active in assisting the AOK library and supporting campus environmental efforts.

20. Patrice Dirican, "UMBC marks 30 years," *Catonsville Times*, 1996.

Lawrence Lasher-English; David Lewis-Sociology; Augustus Low-History; Richard Roberts-Mathematics; Alice Robinson-Speech and Drama; William Rothstein-Sociology; Homer Schamp-Dean and Physics; Robert G. Shedd-English; and Walter Sherwin-Comparative Literature and Classics) each gave at least twenty years of their careers to UMBC.[21]

There were still major uncertainties about what external forces would demand of the campus. John Jeffries, a historian, who came to UMBC in 1973 and later became UMBC's first Dean of the College of Humanities, Arts and Social Sciences in 2005, recalled discussions in the mid-1970's around the questions:

> What would UMBC's future be anyway? ... would it be merged with somebody else? Would it fundamentally change? There were some times when it wasn't clear what the founding vision of the university or the changing vision of the university by some was going to be able to get done in the vagaries or the politics of higher education in the state of Maryland.[22]

There were also difficult internal debates. Should interdisciplinary divisions or traditional departments control promotion and tenure decisions and what should the criteria and standards be? Historian Joseph Tatarewicz remembered:

> as the new faculty that you hired approached tenure decisions ... at that point disciplines rear their heads. Disciplines are tough entities in the University. And you may try to be innovative, and you may try to foster interdisciplinary work, but, in a certain sense, because academic disciplines exist in strong social locations outside the University, they have to be contended with.[23]

Many of these debates focused on who would be the permanent or tenured faculty of the university. Tatarewicz commented:

> That is one thing the university is going to have to grapple with in its own history because it does perceive itself as having been very experimental in the earliest years, at having accomplished a great deal in a precocious way by starting up the place and making it a place with good teaching and everything. And they hired a lot of people who were risk takers, who put a lot of themselves into teaching, and in certain sense the rules of the game changed under them. And that is not just in the history department but everywhere.[24]

In other words, the University had not thought through the relationship of its new hires to the standards it would eventually enforce in its promotion and tenure process. Historian Joseph Arnold remembered:

---

21. The list of original faculty and a brief biographical statement for each can be found in the Origins box, UMBC historic documents collection, Special Collections, University of Maryland, Baltimore County.

22. John Jeffries interview by Joseph Tatarewicz, July 18, 2006. 56.

23. Ibid., 36.

24. Joseph Tatarewicz commenting in Jeffries interview, Ibid., 52–53.

> the intensive pace of life in the early UMBC. Because there were no set policies and procedures for anything—from the curriculum to the color of the classroom walls—faculty were involved with many of the major decisions that helped shape the University as it is today. We spent hours, days, months on seemingly endless committees and commissions. All those things that today are long settled and occasionally reviewed had to be developed from scratch because we were all committed to building a unique and different kind of institution.[25]

Despite the necessary huge investment of time in department service, curriculum building, and teaching by faculty in any new campus, by the mid to late 70's being tenured at UMBC began to require a demonstration of substantial research productivity. According to Jeffries, in the history department there was: "Dismay. Distress. Anguish. Yeah, it was bloody sometimes."[26] Jeffries went on:

> Depending on how you counted, five of ten or six of twelve failed (to get tenure) in those first five years (73–78), which made life interesting for an untenured member in that department when you saw the kind of carnage that was going on with your friends.... one signal that was sent that this department was shaking out and this department was going to be one where first rate scholarship was expected and required, and that teaching mattered as well.[27]

Was the "shake out" necessary? History is written by the victors, so from the perspective of the UMBC's current profile as a research doctoral institution, the tough scholarship standards probably were necessary. Was it fair? Jeffries had mixed emotions and was uncertain how much warning the pioneer faculty had or what they were told when hired:

> I am not sure, in some respects, they were dealt with altogether justly, and they were hired under one set of expectations—at least in the history department whose expectation had changed by the time they came up for tenure. I think it was essential for the department to do that.... But we lost some good people who had been good teachers and good members of the department, and I think that was sad in that respect....[28]

At least one important evaluator thought UMBC took the right, if harsh, path. The 1976 Middle States accreditation report said:

> The usual pattern of steady and extensive growth being used to justify a watering down of faculty quality is not apparent at the University of Maryland Baltimore County. This quality is a tribute to its faculty, its two successive administrations and to its parent University system.[29]

---

25. Albin O. Kuhn,"If you want to be pioneers," UMBC Magazine, Summer1997.
26. . John Jeffries interview by Joseph Tatarewicz, July 18, 2006. 42.
27. Ibid., 49.
28. Ibid.,52.
29. "Middle States Report," 1976.1. UMBC historic documents collection, Special Collections, University of Maryland, Baltimore County.

While off to a good beginning, by 1975 external forces had begun to affect the campus negatively. There was a national slowdown in the economy, followed by disenchantment with higher education by a variety of public and private funding agencies. Nationally, there was a drop in the number of students entering college and that trend hit hard on the very vulnerable new campus.[30] UMBC's admission standards plummeted between 1973 and 1977; a mere decade after the campus had opened with so much flourish and high expectations.

Middle States also commented that UMBC:

> has had to face a significant reorientation of its priorities. It is clearly the impression on campus that barely three to five years ago UMBC was authorized to develop a galaxy of graduate programs, many of them replicating what was offered on the College Park Campus, and continue growing in its undergraduate admissions. Now undergraduate admission demand has declined and system headquarters has had to reconsider the development of graduate programs. This shift is seen by faulty and staff members at UMBC as both sudden and inexplicable.[31]

Other chapters tell the story of the external politics and administrative turmoil during the 1970s and 1980s. Sometimes it was unclear whether the most talented of UMBC's faculty would stay the course.

B. Faculty Composition

Overall, the UMBC faculty did remain invested in the campus in good times and bad. During the 1970s, both the process and standards for evaluating UMBC faculty replicated those at the best American research universities. For graduate faculty, a UM system-wide committee had to approve graduate school membership, until that was decentralized to each campus after 1988.

With very few exceptions, American research universities choose faculty from a national pool of applicants, organize them around disciplinary departments, and follow American Association of University Professors' guidelines governing promotion and tenure. In those respects, UMBC follows the model. The University insists that faculty members be measured by their contributions to teaching, research, and service. Those are across-the-board requirements, but the emphasis can vary by department and by the role a person plays within the department. Generally, no one is promoted or tenured on the basis of service alone, and a weak record either as teacher or researcher will be fatal. Students participate on promotion and tenure committees and write separate reports on teaching performance. External anonymous referees from other major universities are used to evaluate research significance

30. Ibid.
31. Ibid., 1.

and productivity. Departmental chairs weigh in with separate evaluative reports, as do deans and the campus-wide University Faculty Review Committee. All this material is evaluated by the Provost; and the results, at least, cross the desks of the President and the Regents. Candidates can write responses to their evaluations at every stage. These elaborate procedures and multiple evaluations are designed to create a rigorous, but fair, procedure for choosing the faculty, which are the key decisions that shape the long term character of the university. The current process is generally accepted and the kind of protests over faculty selection seen in the early days of the University has virtually disappeared.

While the concept of tenure in higher education has its critics,[32] its protections at UMBC has enabled the faculty to play a vigorous role in governance, from the vote of "no confidence" on Calvin Lee in 1976, to the development of the joint UMBC/UMAB graduate school in 1985, to active opposition to a UMCP/UMB merger in 2011/2012. At UMBC, there have always been some faculty leaders who, like the Roman Cincinnatus, temporarily left the scholarly fields they were tending, to defend the University's status and aspirations, before returning to a normal faculty life.

In 2012, as Figure H shows, there were 1001 persons who held UMBC faculty positions, but the composition of that faculty is far different from the faculty of earlier eras. For one thing, currently only half are full-time instructional faculty.[33] About 30 percent were part-time instructional faculty, while 20 percent were "research" faculty.

Figure H
Faculty, Instructional and Research by Rank (Fall 2012)

	Full-Time		Part-Time	
	Instructional	Research	Instructional	Research
Professor	154	11	2	9
Associate Professor	148	31	6	8
Assistant Professor	97	36	74	2
Instructor	12	0	127	0
Lecturer	86	0	123	0
Other	0	120	14	8
Total	497	198	279	27

Source: UMBC Office of Institutional Research databook. 2012.

32. Mark C. Taylor, *Crisis on Campus: A Bold Plan for Reforming our Colleges and Universities* (New York: Knopf, 2010).

33. Still this figure may be higher than the recent national norm. According to an American Federation of Teachers report, at doctoral-granting public universities, the percentage of full-time tenured or tenure track faculty members dropped from 34.1 percent in 1997 to 28.9 percent in 2007. AFT Higher Education, *American Academic: The State of the Higher Education Workforce*

Teaching assistants, usually in the process of earning their Ph.D.s and who often have considerable course responsibilities, are not counted at all in the above percentages. These categories are not entirely static. Instructional faculty do research regularly. Persons sometimes go in and out of full-and part-time status, and research faculty occasionally teach a class, but the configurations do show a dramatic shift in faculty make-up. Tenured full professors, the backbone of any faculty, who most establish the reputation of the university and who should be most responsible for faculty governance, are now only about 15 percent of the faculty total. This pattern is not likely to change soon or perhaps ever.

As the percentage of university budgets coming from state governments continually declines and there are political or market restrictions on tuition increases, universities with limited endowments, like UMBC, have only two choices. They can shift more instruction to part-time instructors or even graduate students, and/or they can seek to support more institutional expenses though income from grants and contracts. There are some advantages in efficiency and creativity in these trends, but there are also some costs. Some part-time faculty, usually paid $3000–$4000 a course, have specialized knowledge acquired from their full-time jobs in high-tech industries or government agencies. Others are just finishing their graduate training or are caught in the cruel glut of aspiring faculty in many disciplines and just teach part-time while hoping for a break that will make their dreams of an academic career a reality. Some part-timers have cobbled together a number of course assignments, sometimes at multiple campuses, in order to earn a meager living. The percentage of courses taught by instructors who have not gone through the rigorous selection procedure for full-time faculty has increased.

The increase in research faculty who do only a little teaching raises other opportunities and problems. They may provide valuable specialties not available in the full-time faculty. Their research jobs may end, however, when their grants expire, so they are always on a treadmill seeking new money. Shifts in agency or foundation priorities may open or close doors. Naturally the greatest focus of research faculty must be on the goals of their funders. For research faculty, the sustained development of students, their career choices and extra-curricular activities, or even the affairs of the larger university in developing curriculum, new programs, and new facilities, cannot be their focus or responsibility.

The trend toward part-time faculty is a national phenomenon. UMBC is not unusual in its employment pattern,[34] but it is a cause for some concern. Sometimes part-time faculty work out very well, and UMBC is advantaged because of the plethora of very talented, well-educated people with highly specialized skills in the Washington-Baltimore area. However, dependence on part-timers can undermine

---

1997–2007, https://www.aft.org/pdfs/highered/aa_highedworkforce0209.pdf, 2009 (accessed February 19, 2013).

34. Audrey Williams June, "Adjuncts Build Strength in Numbers: the new majority generates a shift in academic culture," *The Chronicle of Higher Education,* November 9, 2012.

the instructional quality and the intellectual vigor the University depends on faculty to provide. It is unreasonable to ask part-time faculty who receive only modest stipends to evaluate multiple drafts of research papers, guide independent studies, mentor student organizations, and participate in faculty committees or governance. Those necessary tasks fall to full-time professors who every year constitute a smaller proportion of the instructional faculty.

In one sense, professors at any university, given their emphasis on different disciplines and methodologies, are diverse. In recent years, the underrepresentation of certain minorities, and sometimes women, in faculties generally, as well as in some specific areas of study has become a concern to educators, accreditors, foundations, and political caucuses. That concern used to be expressed in terms of the need for affirmative action, but now the emphasis is on diversity, though in most cases the groups focused on are the same.

How should diversity be defined and how should its results be measured?[35] It is a question that has plagued higher education institutions and the courts. Because the pursuit of employment diversity in the modern university almost always involves seeking outcomes based on racial, ethnic, and gender classifications, difficult legal questions are raised. The Equal Protection Clause of the Fourteenth Amendment declares no state (or public university) may "deny to any person within its jurisdiction the equal protection of the laws." Executive Order 101925 which President John F. Kennedy signed and whose substance is still in effect, states that all contractors with the federal government should be race neutral and required them "to take affirmative action to ensure that applicants are employed, and that employees are treated during their employment *without* regard to their race, creed, color or national origin."[36] Title VI of the 1964 Civil Rights Act which covers students states, "No person in the U.S. shall on grounds of race, color, or national origin be excluded from participation in, be denied the benefits of, or be subjected to discrimination under any program or activity receiving Federal financial assistance."[37] Title VII, the employment provision of the 1964 Civil Rights Act, contains a flat prohibition against discrimination in "compensation, terms, conditions, or privileges of employment, because of an individual's race, color, religion, sex, or national origin."[38]

This legal structure would seem to suggest that the use of the ethnic, racial or gender preferences in employment would be illegal, but the problem is more complicated than a simple prohibition would suggest. The Supreme Court has struggled with mixed success to draw the lines between permissible and impermissible diversity-seeking behavior in higher education, though its academic cases deal only with admissions, not employment.

---

35. For a view of the development of the diversity concept in higher education see, Thomas Woods, *Diversity: The Invention of a Concept* (San Francisco: Encounter Books, 2003).

36. Executive Order No.10925, 26 FR 1977 (1961).

37. 42 U.S.C. § 2000d. (1964).

38. 42 U.S.C.§ 2000e-2. (1964).

In its first affirmative action case, *Board of Regents of the University of California v. Bakke*, (1978) which involved the use of race and ethnicity as a separate factor in admission to the Medical School at the University of California, Davis, the Court was divided 4–4. Justice Lewis Powell was the deciding vote ruling that particular admissions process violated the Fourteenth Amendment, but that considering diversity might be a compelling interest for a university in selecting students. Powell held that:

> The file of a particular black applicant may be examined for his potential contribution without the factor of race being decisive when compared, for example, with that of an applicant identified as Italian-American, if the latter is thought to exhibit qualities more likely to promote beneficial pluralism.[39]

Creating an admissions process where minority candidates were shielded from competition from non-minority candidates, however, was found to violate Title VI.

Twenty-five years later, the Supreme Court took up the diversity issue again, ruling on two different admissions' procedures at the University of Michigan. A deeply divided Court found that a point system which created a bonus for being a member of a racially under-represented group in undergraduate admissions was unconstitutional, while approving a racial "plus" used in the Law School's admission process. Justice Sandra Day O'Connor cast the positive deciding vote in the law school case because she believed its process conducted an individualized review of all candidates, while giving some advantage to candidates identified with underrepresented groups. In other words, the advantage was not to be an absolute or quantifiable preference.[40]

Part of the problem is that there are mixed motives in seeking diversity. Some educators see diversity as a tool to create role models who will unleash the potential of persons from underrepresented groups. Some, such as Justices Powell and O'Connor, saw diversity as providing other educational values. From this perspective the purpose of diversity is to ensure that the dialogue in academic communities is enriched by multiple perspectives, enhancing the educational experience of all. The implication of that concept is that diversity should be defined broadly, including at least a concern for religious, political, and ideological diversity. Others see a political value in diversity as a societal change agent. From this perspective, diversity is a device for increasing access for underrepresented groups, almost always defined in the old affirmative action categories. Only lip service is paid to measuring diversity in other categories. Finally, diversity may be a useful tool in satisfying legislative caucuses or other stakeholders interested in seeing that their groups are more fully represented in universities. Or

---

39. *Regents of the University of California v. Bakke*, 438 U.S. 265, 317. (1978). The personal qualities Powell though appropriate to consider were "exceptional personal talents, unique work or service experience, leadership potential, maturity, demonstrated compassion, a history of overcoming disadvantage, ability to communicate with the poor, or other qualifications deemed important."

40. *Grutter v. Bollinger*, 539 U.S.306 (2003). For an extended discussion of these issues from the author's perspective, see George La Noue and Ken Marcus, "'Serious Consideration' of Race Neutral Alternatives in Higher Education," *Catholic University Law Review*.57, no.4 (Summer 2008).

more bluntly, diversity may be a political tool within the university to increase group representation to leverage other demands or to influence administrative personnel appointments. From this perspective, search committees should reflect the groups powerful enough to require a seat at the table and it is expected these representatives will screen candidates to be certain of their attitudes towards diversity. This process, of course, has an impact in screening out more conservative candidates, so that administrators on elite campuses do not hold very diverse opinions on diversity.

In its mission statement and in its public image, UMBC is strongly committed to diversity:

> The University of Maryland Baltimore County (UMBC) has established a commitment to diversity as one of its core principles for the recruitment of faculty and retention of faculty, staff and students. Diversity is defined at UMBC in its fullest scope, embracing not only racial and ethnic groups and individuals who are or have been underrepresented in higher education, but also including religious affiliation, sexual orientation and gender identity, disability, foreign nationality, non-traditional student status and other important characteristics.[41]

There is no reference to political, ideological or intellectual diversity in UMBC's statement.

Some have said diversity is in UMBC's DNA. Most major universities share that commitment. Christopher Loss has asserted:

> Aside from shaping the student body the idea of diversity also shaped the organization of knowledge, the structure of the extracurriculum, and perhaps more important, how academic administrators and faculty sought to convey the economic, social, and political value of higher learning to the diverse publics their institutions served—publics that increasingly doubted affirmative action but professed to value and support diversity.... And since the 1960s, educating students in the name of diversity has been what colleges and universities do.[42]

But what does diversity actually mean? As a practical matter, for universities the question is not aspiration, but implementation. Data are gathered and measurement made in only some categories of diversity.

The selection procedures for full-time faculty described earlier may be fair and reasonably objective, but at UMBC and most universities around the country, they do not result in faculties that are demographically representative of students or the state population generally in the conventional terms of race, ethnicity and gender, Figure I portrays trends in the UMBC faculty. Like almost all public universities, UMBC gathers no data on the religious, political or sexual orientations of its faculty.

---

41. "UMBC Progress Report on Institutional Programs of Cultural Diversity," UMBC Office of the Provost, February 26, 2010.

42. Christopher P. Loss, *Between Citizens and the State* (Princeton, N.J.: Princeton University Press, 2012), 232–233.

Figure I
UMBC Full-Time Faculty Racial and Gender Diversity by Percentage, 1980–2012

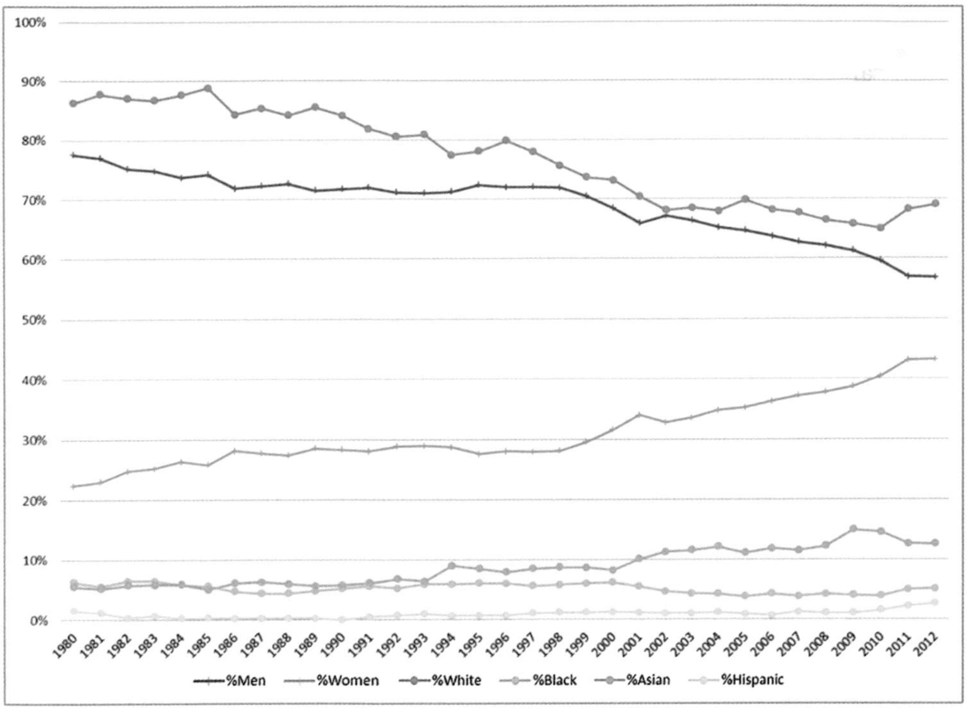

Source: UMBC Office of Institutional Research databook. 2012.

As Figure I illustrates there has been a dramatic increase in the percentage of women at UMBC from about 22 percent of faculty in 1980 to about 43 percent in 2012. In part, this is a national trend reflecting changes in the gender composition of Ph.D. holders and, in part, it is caused by some special efforts UMBC made, particularly in recruiting female STEM faculty.

At least twice, UMBC has sought to increase the number of faculty from underrepresented racial and ethnic backgrounds by setting aside positions for them.[43] In 2008, the university counsel found that the so-called "Opportunity Hires," where permission to hire persons of those backgrounds would be given to departments which otherwise did not have open lines, were not legally sound. In 2013, a Post-Doctoral Program for Faculty Diversity was announced after being vetted by the Maryland Attorney General's Office and the University's General Counsel.[44] Modeled after the Meyerhoff Program and other UMBC initiatives, candidates did not have to be from

43. For a description of the various efforts to increase UMBC employment diversity see: Freeman Hrabowski and Philip Rous, "Focusing our Resources for Results: Mid-Year Update on University Priorities," April 12, 2012. UMBC historic documents collection, Special Collections, University of Maryland, Baltimore County.

44. Autumn Reed to George La Noue, email April 4, 2013.

any identified groups, although applications were encouraged "from individuals who are members of groups that historically have been underrepresented in the professoriate" and "are committed to diversity in the academy."[45]

C. Teaching

When universities focus so intensely on developing their research capacities, undergraduate instruction may be neglected. That is a common accusation about American higher education. Has this trade-off characterized UMBC? In an earlier era, some UMBC students and faculty believed so. But now there is evidence that a more useful synergy of teaching and research has developed on campus.

Andrew Hacker and Claudia Dreifus, after their rather idiosyncratic tour of higher education institutions, pronounced in their book: "Of all the research universities we visited, UMBC was the place that we thought had most capably connected its research functions with undergraduate schooling."[46] They attributed their conclusion to "Dr. Hrabowski's leadership style" because "He sets a tone from the top that says teaching undergraduates is important, and the faculty knows he means it."

There is some other support for the view that UMBC takes undergraduate education seriously and does it well. The *U.S. News & World Report* recent annual surveys placed UMBC consistently in the top ten nationally in that category, ahead of many universities with much higher tuitions and older pedigrees.

Some higher education critics and reformers are not impressed with any of the above evidence.[47]A powerful movement to require campuses to assess learning outcomes empirically has arisen from the federal government and accrediting associations. From their perspective, it is not what anyone thinks is happening in classrooms and labs, but what measurable information, insights, and skills, have been added after a semester or four years of instruction. Lurking behind this imperative is the shadow of the accountability movement now so prevalent in K-12 education after No Child Left Behind. As one commentator wrote: "The specters of homogenization and government control are often invoked, and for good reason. It is not hard to imagine the consequences of assessment done wrong."[48]

---

45. Vice Provost Patrice M. McDermott, "2013 UMBC Postdoctoral Fellows for Faculty Diversity—Selection Process" UMBC historic documents collection, Special Collections, University of Maryland, Baltimore County.

46. Andrew Hacker and Claudia Dreifus, *Higher Education? How Colleges Are Wasting Our Money and Failing Our Kids and What We Can Do About It* (New York: Times Books, 2010), 224.

47. Richard Arum and Josipa Roksa, *Academically Adrift: Limited Learning on College Campuses* (Chicago: The University of Chicago Press, 2011).

48. Kevin Carey, "Without Assessment, Great Teaching Stays Secret," *The Chronicle of Higher Education*, October 15, 2010. A96.

In higher education, the ability to measure before and after learning outcomes depends considerably on the particular course. All instructors routinely evaluate examinations, papers, and other performances to reach some overall grade assessment for individual students, but no one would assert that there is uniformity in those assessments from instructor to instructor or course to course. Ideally, assessments would be given pre- and post-class and that can be done in classes where the goals are clear cut and quantitatively measurable, for example mathematics, languages, and introductory courses in other subjects. But in classes where learning goals are much more nuanced, students may exhibit different forms of strengths and take different paths to reach the goals. Then standardized learning assessments are more difficult. How has UMBC approached assessment?

In the fall of 2010, Kevin Carey, policy director of the Washington think tank Education Sector, came to see firsthand why UMBC was a major part of the national discussion about innovative teaching. He concluded the campus was "fairly standard, with clusters of dorms encircling a compact group of grassy lawns and academic buildings."[49] But he went on to assert that the most radical thing at UMBC "is that it appears to have substantially organized itself around the task of helping students learn" and that "bright students in Maryland are flocking to UMBC, and people in the know cite it as a university to watch."[50]

Carey cited as an example Chemistry 101, a class that across the nation often terrorizes hopeful scientists and pre-med students. In 2000, William LaCourse, then professor of Chemistry and now Dean of the College of Natural and Mathematical Sciences, became concerned that the gateway class in his discipline had become a yawning pit for too many entering students. So the course was completely redesigned away from the standard two hour lecture/recitation model to a discovery-centered model where students in four-person teams collectively solve problems. Attendance increased, and, despite more rigorous grading, the pass rate went up from 70 to 85 percent.[51]

In 2012, the *Washington Post's* education writer, Daniel de Vise, followed the science teaching story by asserting that, "UMBC is an insider's university, a place professors send their children, an academic brand as familiar to presidents and provosts as it is unfamiliar to the general public," though he conceded national recognition in *U.S. News and World Report* and elsewhere was changing that imbalance.[52]

Still Carey and others are wary of basing too much on personal observation or external reputation and he used his UMBC visit to urge the development of more objective assessment in higher education generally. He wrote:

---

49. Carey, "Without Assessment."

50. Ibid.

51. Steve Kolowich, "Group Chemistry," *Inside Higher Ed.com,* October 2, 2009. See also, Jeffrey Mervis, "Better Intro Courses Seen as Key to Reducing Attrition of STEM Majors," *Science*, 330, no 6002, (October 15, 2010). 306. For a detailed description of classes in the Chemistry Discovery Center, see, Ann Griswold, "An Elemental Education," *UMBC Magazine,* Fall 2010. 14–21.

52. "New science class formula brings UMBC extra credit," *Washington Post,* March 21, 2012.

> UMBC specializes in the task every parent, pundit, and lawmaker in America wants universities to accomplish: teaching young people to become great scientists and engineers. It may already be better at this than the Ivies and Research I universities that everyone knows. But without reliable, public assessment information to prove that to the world, UMBC has few ways of elevating its standing to a level that matches the quality of its academic work.[53]

There are about 1300 classes and 400 subsections (i.e. labs and discussion groups) taught in recent years at UMBC, so generalizations are difficult. In almost every class, two types of evaluation by students have been used for decades. A computer coded 23-item SCEQ (Student Course Evaluation Questionnaire) on white paper and a narrative evaluation form printed on blue paper are required in all courses. The results of the SCEQs are posted online for all to see and are an essential part of promotions and tenure considerations. The "blue sheets" are for the instructors' eyes only, and no one knows how carefully their comments are considered. According to the SCEQs, at least UMBC students think they are well taught. In 2010, the median score on the question "How well would grade the overall teaching effectiveness [in this class]?" And "Were the instructor's lectures well prepared?" on a five point scale were 4.09 and 4.38 respectively.[54]

Assessment of student learning is one aspect of the overall accountability movement that has had so much influence in all levels of education in the last two decades. In the 1988 legislation creating UMS, each institution was required to develop an accountability plan and to report annually on its goals and objectives.[55] The guidelines for implementing these objectives contained thirty-seven different items to be measured, including eleven for student performance.[56] The problem was that the one size-fits-all measures did not reflect the realities of the different statuses and missions of Maryland institutions. Further, none of them had the data or the money to acquire the information to meet the guideline measures. Like other unfunded mandates, these accountability requirements withered away. When UMBC departments were asked to list their student learning assessments, they mostly replied restating major requirements, some of which were rigorous and some not.[57]

The push for a more uniform process of learning assessment at UMBC begun in 2006–2007 when Arthur Johnson was Provost. UMBC had been an early adopter of the National Survey of Student Engagement (NSSE) program which assesses the time and effort students put into their classes and the way institutions organize their cur-

53. Carey, "Without Assessment."

54. In an earlier era (1988–1993) about 85 percent of UMBC students surveyed expressed satisfaction with their job preparation and about 98 percent were satisfied with their graduate or professional school preparation. Institutional Performance Accountability MHEC Report, October 18, 1996.

55. Arthur O. Pittenger, Dean of Arts and Sciences, "Accountability," memorandum to Department Chairs and Program Directors, July 11, 1989.

56. MHEC, "Guidelines for the Performance Accountability Plans," January 30, 1989.

57. Dick Neville. "Accountability Update," memorandum to Department Chairs and Updates, December 4, 1989.

riculum and encourage student participation in a variety of activities related to learning.[58] With continued pressure from the federal government and regional accrediting bodies, many higher education institutions, including UMBC, began to examine how they could assess learning outcomes in specific courses.

The campus earlier had a statement on general education competencies which focused on developing in students skills in oral and written communication, scientific and quantitative reasoning, critical analysis and reasoning, technological competency, and information literacy.[59] Under the direction of Linda Hodges, Associate Vice Provost and Director of the Faculty Development Center, UMBC began to train part-time and full-time faculty in assessing student learning. Developing specific goals for student learning and carefully assessing them seems entirely appropriate. In some courses which cover fixed amounts of information, that task is clearly feasible. For other classes, which focus on critical thinking and research, creating uniform learning assessment is more complicated and time consuming. Designing a valid learning assessment instrument, administering it, and evaluating it take considerable effort. More sophisticated forms of learning assessment are still in their infancy at UMBC and at most universities, but this will be a continuing issue for all institutions of higher education.

58. http://nsse.iub.edu. This information is taken from an e-mail from Arthur Johnson to the author, October 30, 2010.

59. "UMBC General Education Functional Competencies," August 2005. UMBC historic documents collection, Special Collections, University of Maryland, Baltimore County.

CHAPTER VII

Academic Programs and Research "UMBC Produces"

Americans expect many things from their universities. We intend for them to be accessible to students from all parts of the complex mosaic of our society. We insist these varied students have equal opportunity and, sometimes, think equal results should emerge from their educations. We want our universities to do research that will engage global challenges, protect US military superiority, increase economic competitiveness, mitigate environmental problems, and cure all the diseases that afflict us, while also figuring out an equitable system for paying for higher education. Oh yes, on the side, or maybe in 100,000 seat stadiums, we desire to be thrilled with athletic prowess garbed in school colors, while also being artistically enlightened in smaller, more cultured venues. Some of what UMBC produces in these various categories will be depicted elsewhere in this book. This chapter describes the University's basic academic and research programs.

After the 1988 creation of the University Maryland System (UMS) merging the University of Maryland campuses with the former state teachers colleges, many political and some educational leaders thought the time had come to rationalize the diverse missions and curriculums then offered throughout the state. There was a recognition that Morgan State University and St. Mary's College of Maryland would remain independent from this effort and that UMCP would remain as the State's comprehensive flagship campus (except for some Baltimore-located professional schools) and that UMUC could offer courses around the state wherever there was demand. So the focus for creating a more "efficient" order in higher education targeted the Baltimore area where there were four comprehensive USM campuses (Coppin, Towson, the University of Baltimore, and UMBC) all jockeying for position. Getting an approved mission statement was the vehicle for defining this competition. UMBC's mission statement was a firm assertion of its ambitions in this uncertain environment. It read a bit defensively:

> UMBC's mission is to serve the Greater Baltimore region as its public university for research and doctoral education in the arts and sciences, engineering, and selected professional areas. Together with UMAB, through the two campuses' jointly administered graduate and research programs, it is one of the State's two principal centers for research and doctoral-level teaching. Envisioned by the State of Maryland as a public doctoral and research university, UMBC has remained firmly committed to that mission since its founding in 1966. Recognized nationally as an emerging institution, UMBC

continues to plan all aspects of its development on the basis of that vision and its original mission.[1]

In more detail, UMBC's mission statement articulated the campus' proposed contributions to regional economic development, social, and public educational concerns, cultural and intellectual needs, and its intent "to transform the campus in five to seven years, from being moderately selective to highly selective, by emphasizing recruitment of more students in the top 10 percent of their class graduating class."[2]

There were no serious objections from other USM Baltimore institutions to UMBC's claim to the sciences, engineering, mathematics, information and computer sciences turf, but the social sciences, humanities, and arts were more contentious terrains. UMBC tried to solve that problem by pointing to its already existing graduate Policy Sciences program and adding public policy to its mission statement.[3] Expansion in the latter fields, as this chapter and chapter IX document, was more troublesome, since economic development and employment demands are more difficult cases for the arts and humanities to make to approval authorities.

A. Academic Departments

Many campus decisions are made through a process called shared governance which means a variety of stakeholders contribute to university policy. The strength of shared governance varies from campus to campus, decision to decision, and on the philosophy and ability of administrative and faculty leadership. The building blocks of governance are academic departments, usually but not always, organized around disciplines. *De facto*, though not *de jure*, they have the power to select, retain, promote, tenure, and determine the criteria of the reward structure for faculty, while also creating curriculum and major program requirements. None of these powers can be exercised unilaterally. All departmental decisions are subject to approval by deans and provosts, though, if departmental leadership is strong and the department is meeting its university goals, its decisions will not often be overturned.

By 2012 UMBC had 42 undergraduate majors, 41 minors, and 17 certificate programs. At the graduate level it offered 37 masters degrees, 24 doctoral degrees, and 21 certificates. Most of these programs are organized in departments, though the

1. "University of Maryland, Baltimore County Mission," April 11, 1990. 1. UMBC historic documents collection, Special Collections, University of Maryland, Baltimore County.

2. Ibid., 3.

3. Michael Hooker for example argued that "UMBC's existing Policy Sciences doctoral program is emerging as one of the largest and most innovative programs of its kind in the country," but that UMBC needed to add a M.A. in Applied Economics, a Ph.D. in Institutional and Policy History and a Ph.D. in the Sociology of Health and Aging to flesh out its policy contributions. "Advancing the Greater Baltimore Region: The Strategic Enhancement of UMBC," May 1990, 13–14. This white paper served as the basis for the Hooker campus agenda. UMBC historic documents collection, Special Collections, University of Maryland, Baltimore County.

Honors College and the Interdisciplinary Studies Program draw faculty participation from around the University. Figure J shows the configuration of UMBC undergraduate departments and the number of majors they serve. Figure K displays the configuration of programs at the graduate level.

Figure J
UMBC Undergraduate Headcount Enrollment by Major (Fall 2012)

College of Arts, Humanities and Social Sciences	
Africana Studies 5	History 260
American Studies 34	Media and Communications Studies 208
Ancient Studies 40	Modern Language and Linguistics 145
Asian Studies 22	Music 134
Dance 39	Philosophy 37
Economics 193	Psychology 941
Financial Economics 353	Political Science 355
Emergency Health Services 91	Sociology 156
English 280	Cultural Anthropology 62
Gender and Women's Studies 27	Health Administration and Policy 266
Geography 47	Theatre 50
Environmental Sciences 154	Acting 20
Environmental Studies 63	Visual Arts 468
College of Natural and Mathematical Sciences	
Biological Sciences 1485	Chemistry Education 7
Bioinformatics and Computational Biology 29	Mathematics 223
Chemistry 124	Statistics 21
Biochemistry and Molecular Biology 418	Physics 112
	Physics Education 8
College of Engineering and Information Technology	
Chemical Engineering 278	Information Systems 603
Engineering 142	Business Technical Administration 239
Computer Engineering 288	Mechanical Engineering 527
Computer Science 796	
The Erickson School	
Management of Aging Services 48	
Provost/Academic Affairs	
Interdisciplinary Studies 145	Undergraduate Education 538
School of Social Work	
Social Work 357	

Figure K
UMBC Graduate Headcount Enrollment by Major (Fall 2012)

College of Arts, Humanities and Social Sciences

- Economics
  - Masters: 19
- Education
  - Masters: 357
- Emergency Health Services
  - Masters: 28
- Geography
  - Masters: 41
  - Ph.D.: 16
- History
  - Masters: 49
- Language Literacy and Culture
  - Ph.D.: 61
- Modern Language, Linguistics and Intercultural Communications
  - Masters: 34
- Psychology
  - Masters: 94
  - Ph.D.: 90
- Public Policy
  - Masters: 40
  - Ph.D.: 100
- Sociology
  - Masters: 61
  - Ph.D.: 15
- Visual Arts
  - Masters: 16

College of Engineering and Information Technology

- Chemical, Biochemical and Environmental Engineering
  - Masters: 361
  - Ph.D.: 36
- Computer Science and Electrical Engineering
  - Masters: 330
  - Ph.D.: 139
- Information Systems
  - Masters: 10
  - Ph.D.: 77
- Mechanical Engineering
  - Masters: 34
  - Ph.D.: 38

College of Natural and Mathematical Sciences

- Biological Sciences
  - Masters: 17
  - Ph.D.: 64
- Chemistry
  - Masters: 4
  - Ph.D.: 45
- Mathematics
  - Masters: 47
  - Ph.D.: 70
- Physics
  - Masters: 1
  - Ph.D.: 45

The Erickson School

- Aging Management and Policy
  - Masters: 10

Source: OIR Databook, 2012.

Many of these departments and programs have interesting stories to tell. Their sheer number, however, makes it impossible to treat each separately, short of writing an encyclopedia, even if the research capacity existed to investigate each one.[4] There

4. Very few UMBC departments have recorded their histories. In connection with the UMBC history project, some undergraduates did write histories of various academic programs. See for example, Amanda Hickey, College of Engineering and Information Technology, David Bennett,

are some departmental stories, however, that do fit into the general "Saga" political thesis of this book. While Figures L and M show an impressive array of programs for a campus less than 50 years old; in fact, it is a rather small portfolio for an institution of UMBC's size. What the Figures do not show is the extensive time faculty and administrators devoted to creating these programs. Nor does it portray that for many of its departments, there were long, often bitter, struggles to create new programs and sometimes even to keep existing ones.

B. The Politics of Intercampus Curricular Competition

Since UMBC was created largely to solve a problem of over enrollment at College Park, little thought was given to what specific programs should be developed there, except that the new campus would have both an undergraduate and a graduate role. It was an unarticulated assumption, however, that as a University of Maryland campus, UMBC would have all the standard programs common to public universities. In 1966 when the campus opened, UMBC was approved to offer bachelor's degrees in American Studies, Ancient Studies, Biological Sciences, Chemistry, Economics, Geography, History, Option II (later Interdisciplinary Studies), Mathematics, Modern Languages, Philosophy, Physics, Political Science, Psychology, Sociology, Theatre, and Urban Studies, but no professional or graduate programs. In short, UMBC opened with the program configuration of a small liberal arts college. Eight years went by before another undergraduate major (Africana Studies) was approved.[5] Expectations were for many more programs.

As new students came to the three-building campus, a *Sun* story reported: "By 1985, an enrollment of 20,000 students is expected. U.M.B.C. (sic) will offer full-scale graduate programs within a few years."[6] Achieving that enrollment proved impossible, later undesirable, while adding a full panoply of new programs frequently encountered political barriers. At first, UMBC's enrollment went through a rapid growth spurt, though never coming close to earlier projections. Then several things happened. The good fiscal times did not last, and college enrollments trended downward in the state.

Other unforeseen developments affected UMBC. The extension branch of the University of Maryland (University College), formerly best known for its overseas'

Social Sciences, and Nimit Bhatt, Theatre and Music, This research is housed in UMBC historic documents collection, Special Collections, University of Maryland, Baltimore County.

5. See Appendix B for the chronology of UMBC program approvals which now numbers 141 separate degrees. Some of them were approved expeditiously, some after considerable negotiation, and some after overcoming opposition.

6. Gene Oishi, "New Ideas, Methods Slated At U.M. Catonsville School," *Baltimore Sun*, July 23, 1966.

campuses serving the American military, began to open new centers in Maryland, including metropolitan Baltimore. Some College Park departments became unsettled at UMBC's graduate ambitions. The University of Baltimore, in jeopardy as a private institution, became public in 1975. Morgan, now facing competition from two new public campuses and an expanding Towson State, became anxious about its future. In 1988, the four University of Maryland campuses were merged with the six state college and university campuses into a single system, so UMBC's special status as a UM campus was threatened. In 1992, the Supreme Court ruled in *Fordice v. Mississippi* that awarding duplicative programs to white campuses, which already existed at black campuses, might impede desegregation and violate Title VI of the Civil Rights Act.[7] So during the quarter century after UMBC was born with a limited programmatic slate, constant conflict occurred as the new campus sought to protect or add programs. Sometimes it seemed governing authorities were saying, while we are glad to build a new campus, we just don't think UMBC should have any programs anyone else wants.

Of course, there are other perspectives. Any program at a state institution costs the taxpayers' money. If too many programs are approved, none may grow to be of sufficient stature, leaving behind derelict structures of tenured faculty. Furthermore, the market may have perverse outcomes given the asymmetry of knowledge most students have in selecting academic programs. While students may flock to a particular campus for reasons of accessibility, cost, convenience, or reputation, they may not make wise choices in terms of the quality of specific programs.

On the other hand, if governing boards use political criteria to distribute programs, they may find that their choice cannot be implemented by existing faculty or will not be selected by potential students, who can always attend private institutions or go out of state if they reject what state campuses provide. Given the recent expansion of online education, their choices are now even greater.

Colleges are constantly competing for students, even as they limit enrollment. There are never enough of the brightest, most talented, and affluent students to meet the demands of academically ambitious institutions. In UMBC's early days, the question was whether it could recruit students in numbers sufficient to meet its state-fixed enrollment goals. As the campus matured, the issue became whether UMBC could add the programs it needed to create the academic environment for the new students it sought to recruit. Since, unlike many other of the new wave urban public universities, UMBC had no geographic monopoly; there were almost always other campuses that could offer the programs the new campus wished to add.

The first conflict came from an unlikely source. When the University of Maryland University College (UMUC) began to extend its offerings in-state, as its overseas military market seemed unlikely to grow, it had strong political support within and with-

7. 505 U.S. 717 (1992).

out the UM system.[8] Establishing educational alternatives for servicemen and women was an admirable enterprise. The stateside courses created options for students who could not afford the time or did not have the traditional academic credentials to be admitted at College Park. So a parallel educational universe was created. UMUC classes listed with College Park course numbers were frequently offered on the latter campus in the evening, often taught by moonlighting College Park faculty. The arrangement was attractive because it provided extra income to that campus and its faculty, without formally increasing enrollment. Invitations to attend overseas UMUC graduation ceremonies were also a welcome perk for some UM administrators and politicians.[9] But most of all UMUC was popular with state government. Here was a University of Maryland education without the burdensome investment in libraries, tenured faculty, or research facilities. Whether the stateside education always was equivalent to that offered by other UM campuses was an issue difficult to determine.[10]

What was a useful synergy between UMCP and UMUC was a threat to the enrollment needs of UMBC. Since most of the new institution's students were commuters with only a marginal interest in campus life, why not take courses in Catonsville from UMUC instead of UMBC? A decade after UMBC opened, it was easy to find posters in its administration building advertising UMUC courses. They paralleled existing UMBC courses and were offered in the evening on the UMBC campus. UMBC administrators were petitioned by faculty to put a stop to that practice and it ended. Later, there was friction when UMUC wanted to offer an engineering management masters programs on the UMBC campus. The fledgling UMBC Policy Sciences Graduate Program thought it should offer the management courses in a combined engineering management program, but UMUC resisted. Gradually UMUC's programs disappeared from the UMBC site altogether, though they are offered on other state campuses.

In UMBC's first catalogue, new students were promised that a College of Business and Public Administration would be developed. In 1970 when faculty considered

8. Sharon Hudgins, *Never An Ivory Tower: University of Maryland University College The First 50 Years* (Adelphi: University College, 2000), 33. In 1970, UMUC was given the status of a separately accredited UM institution with its own chancellor. Prior to that time it was a component of the College Park campus.

9. Kuhn reported that when John Toll was building up the UMCP physics department he wanted financial support for four new positions. State budget director Jim Renny was resistant to the entreaties of the UMCP delegation and said to Dr. Elkins, "You know, there is nothing in my makeup that will let me go with you on that one. I'll tell what I will do. I'll get the phone and you talk with him [the Governor]." ..."Well, Governor McKeldin had just been on a trip to Europe with Dr. Elkins for ten days attending the Heidelberg Graduation of the University of Maryland, and they had a grand chat. And the Governor said, 'put Jim on.' And we got our budget." Albin O. Kuhn and Homer Schamp interview by Larry Wilt, January 4, 2006. 66.

10. According to Callcott, the Middle States Evaluation Report for 1953 concluded that UMUC's "standards of instruction and student performance in overseas classes would be at least as high and very probably higher than the standards achieved in the same classes on campus." *A History of the University of Maryland.* 349.

whether to implement that pledge, they decided to defer. Some wondered whether the study of business was compatible with their vision of a liberal arts university.[11] Later, as business became a very popular undergraduate major, UMBC had cause to regret its earlier decision. But it was too late.

In 1978, Rudolph Lamone, Dean of the UMCP College of Business and Management, proposed to the Regents that the College's undergraduate and graduate programs be extended to Catonsville with courses taught by resident UMBC faculty. Part of the motivation was that the UMCP College intended to reduce its enrollment by 2,000 undergraduate students. If these students attended classes in Catonsville, the total business College enrollment would still remain the same. At the Master of Business Administration (MBA) level, UMCP was receiving 1,200 applications for 100 slots, forcing most students to go out of state.[12] The UMCP business school was the only state institution accredited by the American Assembly of Collegiate Business Schools. Highlighting that reality was not calculated to endear the move to other campuses.[13] Creating at UMBC a business program, the bread and butter of many local schools, drew immediate opposition.[14] The Presidents of Loyola, Morgan State, Towson State, and the University of Baltimore all testified before SBHE that permitting UMCP to extend its program to UMBC "would be extremely costly ... and clearly duplicative."[15] SBHE agreed with the opponents and the concept of a full-scale business program at UMBC has never been resurrected, though there is a B.S. financial economics program on the campus.

Under continuing pressure to increase enrollment, while forbidden to create a conventional business program, UMBC, under the leadership of economics professor Chuck Peake, began to explore alternatives. The first step was to offer introductory accounting courses.[16] That was not sufficient to meet the student demand, so the campus negotiated an agreement with nearby Catonsville Community College (CCC)

---

11. Albin O. Kuhn, "University of Maryland Baltimore County (UMBC): Its Early Years of Development and Operation," unpublished manuscript, UMBC Historic Documents Collection. Special Collections, University of Maryland, Baltimore County. 14,28.

12. Statement by Dr. Rudolph P. Lamone, Dean of the College of Business & Management at the Board of Regents Meeting, October 31, 1978, "Regarding the Proposal for the Extension of the Undergraduate and Graduate Programs of the College of Business & Management (UMCP) to UMBC." The proposal was to maintain "the same level of faculty and program quality on both campuses." In addition, the UMBC program would add a focus on "International Trade and Transportation, a program designed to take advantage of UMBC's proximity to a city increasing in its importance as major world trade and distribution center." See also Tom Kapsidelis, "Transfer of programs' just talk: Regents to form UMBC study group," *Diamondback*, November 17, 1977.

13. Ibid., 10. All local business programs are accredited now.

14. David Simon, "Missing: Baltimore's Great University," *Baltimore Magazine*, September 1982.

15. Michael Sagalnik, "Four College Heads Fight UMBC Plan," *Baltimore Sun*, November 22, 1978.

16. The history of accounting, administrative sciences, and financial economics at UMBC can be found in a September 18, 2013 memo from Chuck Peake to the author. UMBC historic documents collection, Special Collections, University of Maryland, Baltimore County.

which would offer the advanced accounting courses. UMBC students could then obtain an accounting certificate, but this practice was an inversion of the normal arrangement where community colleges offer introductory courses and universities offered advanced classes. The University of Baltimore saw this arrangement as a threat to its existing accounting business program. After UB President Mebane Turner called the CCC President challenging its right to offer advanced courses, UMBC was left without a partner. So UMBC decided to offer its own advanced courses leading to an accounting certificate, staffed with part-time faculty. That program flourished, and for several years UMBC graduates led all state institutions on the pass rate on the Certified Public Accountant (CPA) examination. In 1989, Don Blair, UMBC *magna cum laude* graduate in economics, won the Elijah Watts Sells Gold Medal Award for the nation's highest score on that year's CPA examination.[17]

Building on this success, UMBC decided to create an Administrative Sciences program offering five certificates in Managerial Sciences (Accounting, Finance, Managerial Economics, Personnel and Industrial Relations, and Systems Analysis and Operations Research). Since the then existing state coordinating body did not have the power to control certificates, the Administrative Sciences program was successful. The Regents' Vision II policy, however, forced campuses to give up programs considered extraneous to their mission or just coveted by other institutions. Administrative Sciences was one of UMBC's casualties, to the relief of some economics faculty who were not pleased with its pragmatic focus and dependency on part-time instructors.[18]

UMBC and Chuck Peake, however, were not finished in their attempt to provide an opportunity for UMBC students to learn business related skills. In 1999, the Financial Economics major, the first in the country, was launched at UMBC. This major reflects the growing professionalization of work related to the pricing of bonds, stocks, and other assets and the financing of corporations and governments. Because it was distinctive enough, Financial Economics did not create objections from any other institutions. An MBA or even an undergraduate major in business, however, is not likely in UMBC's foreseeable future.

Although containing the role of UMUC on the UMBC campus and the limitations put on UMBC's business offerings were matters of consequence, the competition with Morgan State University over doctoral programs was an institution-defining conflict.

In Baltimore, where two historically black public institutions (HBIs) were a few miles from three traditionally white institutions (TWIs) and UMBC, there was bound to be conflict over program expansion. UMBC and Morgan found themselves pitted against each other several times in competition for history and engineering programs.

Within a decade of its founding, UMBC had assembled a remarkably distinguished and productive history faculty. In 1975, Bob Webb had come from Columbia

17. Mr. Blair, after working for KPMG and Goldman Sachs, became a managing director for Raymond James Investments in Tampa.

18. Some of the certificates were later transferred to the Information Systems Management program which created a B.A. degree in Business Technology Administration at UMBC in 2004.

University and the editorship of the *American Historical Review (1968–1975).* Gus Lowe, a founding father of the Department, was the editor of the *Journal of Negro History* and *Encyclopedia of Black History.* There were many other faculty with national reputations. As the Department considered its graduate future, there were two realities. There was a decreasing market for traditional academic historians, and College Park already had a fine program serving that need. On the other hand, without any graduate program, it would be hard for History to keep up with other UMBC departments and some of its talented scholars would leave for campuses where the apparatus of graduate scholarship was in place. The solution was to work out an accommodation with College Park to offer a UMBC Master's Program that focused on the history of policy and social issues, rather than on traditional history. UMBC would train historians who mainly would work for government agencies and museums rather than compete for academic positions. That strategy was largely successful and the M.A. in Historical Studies, begun in 1978, had a reasonable enrollment.[19]

By 1985, the History Department wanted to add a Ph.D. program in Institutional Policy and Public History, but it was killed by the MHEC bureaucracy without formal consideration. In 1992, UMBC resurrected its History Ph.D. aspirations. Though the College Park History Chair had been supportive of the earlier proposal, at the UM President's Advisory Council for Graduate Studies, the three UMCP representatives had to be outvoted 7–3 to pass the proposal. Morgan proved a more formidable opponent in this instance and it objected to the UMBC plan. On May 24, 1994, Shaila Aery, MHEC Secretary, citing the U.S. Supreme Court *Fordice* decision, announced that the UMBC proposal was "substantially similar" to a revised Morgan proposal which was then awarded Baltimore's public campus Ph.D. history franchise.[20] According to John Jeffries, UMBC historian and later Dean of the College of Arts, Humanities and Social Sciences:

> Morgan's production of Master's students and subsequently of Ph.D. students was very small whereas our production of master's students was relatively high. And we thought that we could in fact do what we said we wanted to do in the [UMBC] Ph.D. proposal and they [Morgan] weren't able to do it. So there was a good deal of frustration and irritation, perhaps some anger, at the outcome.[21]

Moreover, some at UMBC thought that SBHE's rigid bifurcation of Maryland campuses into HBIs and TWI's was inaccurate and unfair. UMBC phrased the issue this way:

---

19. Franklin Mendals and Gary Browne, "Evaluation of Program in Historical Studies 1978–1985," unpublished ms. UMBC History Department files. Between 1978 and 1984, the UMBC History faculty published 22 books and 120 articles.

20. Eugene W. Goll. "Academic Program nixed by MHEC," *Cumberland Times-News,* July 16, 1994. MHEC's staff concluded UMBC 's program "would most probably reinforce the racial identifiability of UMBC" and would not foster integration.

21. The accounts of UMBC's History's graduate ambitions come from John Jeffries, interview by Joseph Tatarewicz, August 4, 2006. 28–36. In what Jeffries called "a consolation prize," History developed a policy history track inside existing Public Policy (nee Policy Sciences) Ph.D. program. Such tracks do not require off-campus approval and it enabled a few doctoral students to write history dissertations at UMBC.

> UMBC was not part of the old segregated system of higher education in Maryland and since its inception has been at the forefront of state and national public institutions in achieving racial diversity among faculty and students alike. UMBC's most recent minority achievement reports document the university's striking success in attracting and graduating highly-qualified minority undergraduate and graduate students and in recruiting and promoting minority staff. Arguably, indeed the state should support program development at UMBC in order to enhance and sustain a record of minority achievement and student diversity that is unique in the state and exceptional in the nation.[22]

The most contentious competition took place over the creation of an engineering program at UMBC.[23] The issue developed after a special commission appointed by Governor Hughes in 1982 urged that the state rejuvenate its industrial base by attracting high-tech industries. Specifically the commission recommended "preeminent engineering, and business programs at the university level."[24] Nothing unusual there, it was a concept that attracted many states as they sought to stay ahead of the economic development curve. What was unusual was how Maryland struggled with the decision.

There were no engineering courses at UMBC until eleven years after the campus was founded. After that, a number of pre-engineering classes were offered with the expectation that students would transfer to UMCP to earn their degrees. As the focus of the Baltimore business elites turned to the role of science and technology in the future economy, an obvious gap was that none of Baltimore's public campuses had strength in those areas. UMBC's initial ability to offer engineering courses across a wide variety of fields was because its program was considered an extension of UMCP's School of Engineering which in turn shaped the curriculum, offered some of the classes, and helped recruit a strong Catonsville-based faculty who otherwise might not have joined the fledgling program.

Since College Park already had a well-developed engineering school, the State Board of Higher Education's first decision was simply to support that school's Baltimore outreach.[25] Morgan, however, also was given a yellow light to develop a Baltimore-based engineering program when it showed it could manage one by implementing some administrative changes. This qualified support displeased Morgan President Andrew Billingsley who wanted an immediate affirmation.[26] On the other

22. Draft response to Shaila Aery, May 10, 1994, "Letter Denying History Ph.D. History," History Department files.

23. The history of the effort to bring engineering to UMBC is discussed in a videotaped interview of Schlomo Carmi, former Dean, by Joseph Tatarewicz. April 23, 2013. A description of these events from one SBHE's official's perspective can be found in Sumler, "Life Cycle," 90–102.

24. Joel McCord and David Simon, "Tight budget scuttles engineering plans at Morgan, UMBC," *Baltimore Sun*, June 6, 1983.

25. McCord and Simon. SHBE was the predecessor to MHEC.

26. Morgan's civil rights argument to obtain Baltimore's engineering franchise was summarized by Clarence Mitchell in "Engineering" *Baltimore Sun,* June 26, 1983.

hand UMBC, which by that time had 370 engineering students enrolled on the Catonsville campus for three years before transferring to College Park for the fourth year and their degree, appeared to be shut out from ever developing its own engineering school.[27] "An unnamed UMBC source" called the SBHE decision "a blow to the heart" and predicted the decision would "lead to hostile back biting among Baltimore-area colleges."[28]

SBHE's action created an immediate negative response among Baltimore leaders. The *Sun* responded with an acerbic editorial: "The Baltimore metropolitan region has been firmly consigned to the back of the education bus." While supporting the Morgan proposal, the *Sun* also commented,

> For UMBC, the decision is even more devastating. The state panel made a joke of its own planning procedure by throwing out a three-year-old master plan giving UMBC the right to start an engineering school. The Catonsville school once again has been told not to aim for greatness.[29]

SBHE's decision was not to be the final word. The state's legislative Black Caucus was not pleased. *Sun* columnist Barry Rascovar wrote: "[UM President] Toll never conceded defeat for UMBC. He mobilized the board of regents and found allies who were upset by the engineering school decision."[30] Support for UMBC came from Baltimore area politicians, such as Melvin Steinberg, state Senate President, and Ben Cardin, state House Speaker. Letters poured in from the Baltimore business community, including one from the general manager of Martin Marietta Aerospace who said his firm would need 250 engineers the next year alone.

Engineering programs are expensive requiring extensive facilities and a faculty that can compete for research grants. In this political atmosphere, however, academic considerations were not paramount. The issue pitted Morgan's civil rights claims versus the UMBC's more promising academic environment, particularly since it could borrow faculty and other resources from UMCP.[31] The UM position was that, given the economic demands, engineering schools at both UMBC and Morgan should be created. John Slaughter, College Park's Chancellor and an African-American, opined that UMBC would be "complementing not competing with Morgan." Clarence M. Mitchell, Jr., from the distinguished Baltimore civil rights family and a UM Regent,

---

27. For a detailed description of the political context of SBHE's decision and support for UMBC, see Barry Rascovar, "Baltimore's Talented Stepchild," *Baltimore Sun*, June 20, 1983.

28. Joel McCord and David Simon, "Tight Budget.".B.8.

29. "What about Baltimore?" *Baltimore Sun,* June 5, 1983. See also, Michael Hirten, "Baltimore needs engineering school," *Baltimore Evening Sun,* June 8, 1983.

30. Barry Rascovar, "Encore," *Baltimore Sun*, September 5, 1983. At the June 1983, UMBC graduation, President Toll used the term "a disgraceful double-cross" to describe SBHE actions on engineering and affirmed that "attempts to undermine UMBC will not succeed," drawing a robust round of applause from his audience. *Baltimore News-American*, June 6,1983,

31. David Simon, "Morgan presses bid for engineering school," *Baltimore Sun*, September 2, 1983. See competing letters from Morgan President Andrew Billingsley and UMBC's John W. Dorsey, *Baltimore Sun*, September 29, 1983 and October 5, 1983.

however, threatened that a program at UMBC "may well lead to litigation, which could disrupt the flow of federal funds."[32]

Both sides lobbied intensely and threats were made to the funding of the rival institutions. Morgan supporter, J. Harrison Ager and a SBHE board member, decried UM President Toll's efforts on behalf of UMBC saying he "ran around the state determined to undermine the work and integrity of the Board and, on this issue, he has gotten his way." Ager added ominously, "one day soon this individual will run out of fuel."[33]

In the end, SBHE split the undergraduate baby giving electrical, civil, and industrial engineering to Morgan and chemical, biological, and mechanical programs to UMBC, as well as a license to propose graduate programs in Catonsville in all engineering fields.[34] Sheldon Knorr, State Commissioner of Higher Education, conceded, "In terms of the politics of the decision, I admit it was emotional. But in terms of the decision, I think it was a good one." Not everyone agreed. The *Sun's* editorial "Engineering a Monster" declared that "the SBHE decision ... will give the region two half-engineering schools, neither capable of attaining prominence with its truncated offerings."[35] Several legislators introduced resolutions deploring the cost of two separate Baltimore engineering programs. Senator John Cade (Anne Arundel-R) urged SBHE to investigate the feasibility of merging the programs under a single administrative head. Other powerful legislators threatened to delete the SBHE from future budgets over dissatisfaction at the way the engineering issue was handled.[36]

A part of the problem was like many regulatory agencies SBHE, and later MHEC saw its function as creating a level playing field by giving each institution under its purview a special niche (except flagship College Park) and then preventing duplication. Competition that might create clear-cut differences in quality would not lead to harmony and broad political support for the regulators, Not only was an ambitious growing UMBC a threat to this regulatory mindset, but SBHE's leveling perspective was not shared by the UM system top leadership. The engineering issue was just an example of conflicts that emerged on many fronts. David Sumler, SBHE Director of Planning and Academic Affairs, wrote:

> Deep wounds in the Maryland higher education community were opened by the engineering dispute. John Toll emerged as a tireless and unyielding opponent of the State Board's authority. Toll did not accept a decision by the State Board that was adverse to one of his campuses. He did not recognize limits on the ambitions of the University.[37]

---

32. Becky Todd York, "Morgan, UMBC square off to offer engineering degree," *Baltimore News American*, September 16, 1983.

33. Antony Pipitone, "Morgan, UMBC get OK to split engineering program," *Baltimore Evening Sun*, November 4, 1983.

34. Ibid.

35. "Engineering a Monster," *Baltimore Sun*, November 8, 1983.

36. Gwen Hill, "Lawmakers want to end education unit," *Baltimore Evening Sun*, January 26, 1984.

37. Sumler, 102.

In 1985 in an effort to defuse the animosity the engineering competition had created UM and Morgan signed a five-page treaty to cooperate in educating Baltimore engineering students. They agreed to share faculty, computers, research, instructional television, and library privileges. UMBC offered to extend its microwave signal to Morgan, so that the Instructional TV it generated itself and also received from College Park could be relayed to Morgan.[38] In 1988, the Accreditation Board for Engineering and Technology (ABET) accredited UMBC's B.S. programs in Chemical and Mechanical engineering. UMBC also was providing courses at Aberdeen Proving Ground, and Harford and Hagerstown Community Colleges.[39]

Nevertheless, the operation of engineering programs by Baltimore campuses remained contentious for the next fifteen years.[40] In 1990, when state higher education secretary, Shaila Aery proposed granting UMBC authority to offer electrical, industrial and civil engineering for undergraduates, MHEC (SBHE's successor) signaled it opposition.[41] By this time, UMBC had accumulated some influential allies. The Greater Baltimore Committee [GBC] had begun to see how important the campus could be to economic development in the region. Chancellor Langenberg, a physicist, was willing to up the stakes beyond engineering program approval. He wrote on a Sun opinion editorial:

> I agree [with the GBC] that we should establish at that institution [UMBC] a complete engineering school. But I think we should aim for something even more ambitious, a type of institution the University of Maryland presently lacks. I envision UMBC evolving into a medium-sized comprehensive institute of technology along the lines of Georgia Tech or an MIT. Something we might call the University of Maryland Institute of Technology.[42]

In the meantime little brother was growing up and taking some measures into its own hands.[43] By 1992, UMBC formed its own College of Engineering with its own Dean, Duane Bruley, while his faculty chaffed at their inability to offer electrical engineering at the undergraduate level to supplement its graduate offerings in that field. The College noted UMBC was the only accredited engineering school in the country that could not offer undergraduate electrical engineering. Morgan, however, still opposed and Shaila Aery, now heading MHEC eventually rejected UMBC's proposal.

---

38. Mike Bowler, "Engineer pact set at 2 colleges," *Baltimore Sun*, January 8, 1985.

39. James Milani, Director of Administrative Affairs, COEIT, interview by the author, April 2, 2013.

40. See chapter XII for a description of the eventual litigation regarding this conflict.

41. Melody Simmons,"'Separate but equal' schools complaint to be reviewed." *Baltimore Evening Sun*, August 17, 1990.

42. Donald N. Langenberg, "A Canary Sings of the Future of Education," *Baltimore Sun*, November 28, 1990.

43. In 1991, three UMBC engineering professors, Jayavant Gore, Jay Humphrey, and Govind Rao were named Presidential Young Investigators by the National Science Foundation. Timeline-History of UMBC. http://lib.guides.umbc.edu/content.php?pid=417297&sid=3411009.

Ostensibly, the rejection was only a delay to study,[44] but as that "delay" lengthened to nearly a decade, UMBC renewed its effort to get permission to offer undergraduate electrical engineering.

In 1996, UMBC developed a proposal for an undergraduate program in computer engineering, while acknowledging there was some overlap between that field and electrical engineering; it insisted they were separate fields. Morgan again opposed, but this time MHEC approved.

The penultimate stage of the engineering battle took place in 2000. UMBC had had a successful graduate program in electrical engineering since 1986 and it wanted to add a full undergraduate program in that field where the greatest marketplace demand existed. The first step was relatively easy when the UM Regents approved UMBC's petition to add an undergraduate electrical engineering major. Then, Morgan protested to MHEC that the new program would be competitive with its own and therefore harm integration in violation of the *Fordice* rule. UMBC countered that of Morgan's engineering students only one percent were white and President Hrabowski pointed out that the two campuses served different populations because Morgan "enrolls students with lower SAT scores and high school rankings than did UMBC." If the decision had turned on the availability of faculty resources and equipment, the verdict for UMBC would have been clear. But Maryland had been trying without success since 1969 to end the Office for Civil Right's (OCR) oversight of State educational decisions. So after MHEC signaled it would not approve the UMBC program, the State believed that action would lead to a quick OCR approved overall desegregation agreement. A temporary agreement was signed, but a decade later a final desegregation resolution had not been achieved.[45]

By 2009, UMBC engineering enrolled 1058 undergraduate students in four programs including a B.S. in Computer Engineering, but not Electrical Engineering, and 354 graduate students in M.S. and Ph.D. programs in Civil, Computer, Chemical and Biological, Electrical, Mechanical, Systems, Management Engineering programs. Morgan enrolled 708 undergraduates in three programs and 106 graduate students in three M.S. and Ph.D. programs. Both schools programs face competition from Johns Hopkins' off-campus engineering programs.

UMBC was not the only campus to have program expansions opposed by Morgan. It successfully objected to a masters program in History and a doctoral program in Education at Towson and a graduate business program at University of Baltimore.[46]

---

44. "Maryland delays engineering programs over desegregation order," *Chronicle of Higher Education*, September 2, 1992.

45. Michael Hill, "Temporary peace for UMBC and Morgan: Civil rights inquiry played a role in decision to drop degree request," *Baltimore Sun*, September 16, 2000 and "U.S. colleges reach a desegregation pact," *Baltimore Sun*, October 27, 2009.

46. Jason Song, "Morgan's President again fights building competitor: Opponent of Towson MBA has squelched 4 programs," *Baltimore Sun*, June 13, 2005. In 2012, Morgan and Towson clashed again, this time over the creation of a satellite campus in Harford County. Childs Walker, "Harford seeks college growth," *Baltimore Sun*, March 26, 2012.

In 2005, Towson and UB reached an agreement to extend UB's MBA program to the Towson campus. Morgan objected, since its MBA enrollment had dropped from 263 students (including 54 white students) in 1975 to 28 students (no whites) in 2004.[47] MHEC approved the new joint program, but the Black Caucus succeeded in getting a bill though the legislature which would have forced MHEC to reconsider and permitted public colleges to sue one another over programmatic conflicts. Governor Ehrlich vetoed that bill, but the State gave Morgan $800,000 to strengthen its MBA program.[48] In 2009, Morgan opposed the creation of Ph.D. program for aspiring community college administrators that UMUC wanted to offer on-line. MHEC blocked UMUC from offering its program in-state.[49] It will not be the last such conflict and the issue of program duplication in Maryland higher education is now in litigation (see Chapter XII).

Competition does not always characterize the curricular relationships among Maryland universities. In 1982, the UMBC Modern Languages and Linguistics (MLL) Department learned that Morgan and Towson were preparing a joint proposal for a M.A. in foreign languages and urged SBHE to let it participate. By 1985, an agreement had been worked out for a Baltimore Graduate Consortium in foreign languages and linguistics.[50] All M.A. students were to take a common core of nine credits, including one course on each of the three sponsoring campuses. Certain resources, including UMBC's capacity to receive satellite television programs from countries around the world and Morgan's multilingual word processor were to be shared. Optimism reigned as the proposal was described as "... a remarkable example of academic cooperation designed to broaden opportunities to graduate students in the Baltimore area, while simultaneously conserving the resources of the State by reducing duplication...."[51] The program brochure included a one and a half inch square map of the 695 Beltway region with three dots for each campus location. It looked simple, but perhaps the cartographer had never actually driven the Beltway at rush hour. By 1990, the requirement that student actually take courses at multiple campuses was phased out.[52] Three years later, the cooperative language program was dead. Chancellor Langenberg wrote the Towson and UMBC presidents to advise their students that they would no longer be required to take courses on other campuses. In his view, the political purpose of the joint program to gain approval of master's programs in this curriculum area,

47. Song, "Morgan's President."

48. Gail Dechter, "Opponents face off in MBA war: Bill aims to dismantle Towson's program in favor of Morgan State's," *Baltimore Sun*, March 27, 2007.

49. Jonathan Pitts and Childs Walker, "Morgan wins fight with UMUC over online program," *Baltimore Sun*, October 22, 2009.

50. Letter from David S. Sparks, Vice President for Graduate Studies and Research, University of Maryland, to Sheldon H. Knorr, Commissioner, SBHE, February 8, 1985.

51. Ibid.

52. Letter from Jack Sinnigen, Coordinator of Graduate Studies, UMBC Modern Languages and Literature to Stephen Max, Acting Vice President for Graduate Studies and Research "Change in Consortium Agreement," November 11, 1990. UMBC historic documents collection, collection 55, Special Collections, University of Maryland, Baltimore County,

where SBHE had been skeptical, had been achieved.[53] Currently the UMBC MLL Department offers both a M.A, in Intercultural Communication and a Ph.D. in Language, Literacy, and Culture as stand-alone programs.

Some intercampus programs involving UMBC do exist.[54] UMBC and the UMB School of Nursing (UMSON) have created a combined pathway to a Bachelor of Science in Nursing degree and a Clinical Nurse Leader status. Every year UMBC students from Catonsville and Shady Grove campuses have thirty seats secured at UMSON. UMBC Bachelor's degree program in Social Work is offered in affiliation with the UMB School of Social Work. The most important collaborations reflect UMBC's work with the UMB campus as a partner in the University of Maryland Graduate School Baltimore. At the Ph.D. level, the Biochemistry and Molecular Biology program as well as the Gerontology Program (involving the UMB schools of medicine, law and nursing) are joint programs. The biostatistics track within the UMBC statistics graduate program requires courses from both campuses and faculty from each chair dissertations. A track within the UMBC Emergency Health Systems program requires UMB courses in the Medical School.

Other collaborative programs are multi-campus. The M.S. and Ph.D. programs in Marine, Estuarine, and Environmental Sciences involved faculty from five University of Maryland campuses. A grant from Howard Hughes Medical Institute to develop a competency-based curriculum in the life sciences for pre-medical students included UMBC, UMCP, Purdue University, and the University of Miami. UMBC collaborates with Towson, Johns Hopkins, and UMCP to offer a Post-Baccalaureate Certificate in Arts Integration. Faculty from multiple UM campuses frequently work together on research projects and twelve faculty from UMBC's College of Engineering and Information Technology hold appointment in UMB's health care schools. Still as logical as the rationale for intercampus activities might be, so long as promotion, tenure, and budget decisions remain on individual campuses, making collaborative programs work is often challenging.

C. Research

Even though much of the original motivation for UMBC's founding was to reduce enrollment pressure on College Park, from the beginning of the new campus there was the intent to create a research university. This particular form of higher education, first flourished in the United States when it was brought from Germany by Baltimore's Johns Hopkins University late in the Nineteenth Century, and then was

53. Letter from Donald H. Langenberg to Towson President Hoke L. Smith and UMBC President Freeman Hrabowski, "Cooperative MA in Foreign Languages," March 5, 1993. UMBC historic documents collection, Special Collections, University of Maryland, Baltimore County

54. UMBC Office of the Provost, "UMBC Inter-Institutional Collaboration Inventory," December 6, 2011.

emulated by the great private and public universities across the country. Robert Rosenzweig, president of the American Association of Universities from 1983–1993, wrote that the research university was:

> A form of social organization barely known elsewhere in the world has so clearly demonstrated its value in the United States that the wisdom of sustaining it is almost beyond serious debate. We chose to combine basic research, a fair mixture of applied research, training for research and undergraduate education in the same place, done by the same people, frequently at the same time.[55]

This concept he said was a "volatile mixture." It is easy to short change one of the functions and not every campus that has tried it has been successful.

Although in the early days, there was conflict over faculty teaching and research priorities, by the Eighties, UMBC had reached a consensus that its faculty would do both. There were several reasons. First, as a member of the prized University of Maryland family, research was the distinguishing characteristic of UM campuses compared to the state teachers colleges. Second, creating research opportunities was an absolute necessity for recruiting the faculty UMBC sought. Faculty trained at the top graduate schools expect that research and publishing will be central to their careers. Third, as a growing and chronically underfunded campus, research awards carrying overhead money, particularly from the federal government, were necessary to pay for laboratories and graduate assistantships. Finally, UMBC was created in the era when the explosion of new knowledge and technologies was first fully acknowledged. Students required training to think beyond textbooks and examinations through multiple choice tests. They needed to focus less on regurgitation of facts (which computers can do so much better) and more on inquiry, synthesis, and communication. Becoming a lifelong learner was not just cliché, but a requirement in a world where jobs could evolve into new skill demands or oblivion very quickly, and in which most students could expect to live twenty years or more beyond retirement.

Of course, no new institution could fully compete with the behemoths of the university research world, but by 1990 there was some evidence that UMBC was becoming successful. In their book, *The Rise of the American Research Universities: Elites and Challengers in the Postwar Era,* Hugh Graham, UMBC history professor and Graduate School Dean, and Nancy Diamond, UMBC Policy Sciences Ph.D. student, developed a new technique for measuring research productivity by measuring output per capita rather than just aggregated campus output. In the past, university research status had been compared by the sum of research dollars awarded or by reputational surveys. The first measure reflected institutional size and the second often age. The per capita productivity method leveled the playing field somewhat. The authors divided 151 public research universities into four tiers and examined the research and development

---

55. As quoted by Hugh Graham and Nancy Diamond, *The Rise of the American Research Universities: Elites and Challengers in the Postwar Era* (Baltimore: Johns Hopkins University Press, 1997), 1.

funding and publication citation index measures per capita for full time faculty. In the top tier, it was not unexpected to find five of the top six campuses were members of the University of California system, but most academics would have been surprised to see that the Riverside and San Diego campuses ranked slightly ahead of the Los Angeles and Berkeley campuses on per capita measures.[56] UMBC did not appear until the third tier, placing ahead of Auburn, but behind Connecticut. The authors noted that UMBC was the only metropolitan campus of the baby-boom era to have moved out of the fourth tier.[57] When the authors measured the social sciences and the arts and humanities separately and combined those fields with the sciences, UMBC looked even better tying for 4th place among the 23 third tier institutions, many of which were state flagships universities.[58] Most of the other tier three institutions were established in the 19th century and many were land grant institutions which should have meant that their research facilities were better established.

Figure L shows UMBC's development in terms of research dollars awarded.[59] As Figure L demonstrates, UMBC has experienced a dramatic growth in research funding and expenditures, particularly in the fierce completion for federal awards.

Figure L
UMBC Research Expenditures by Year

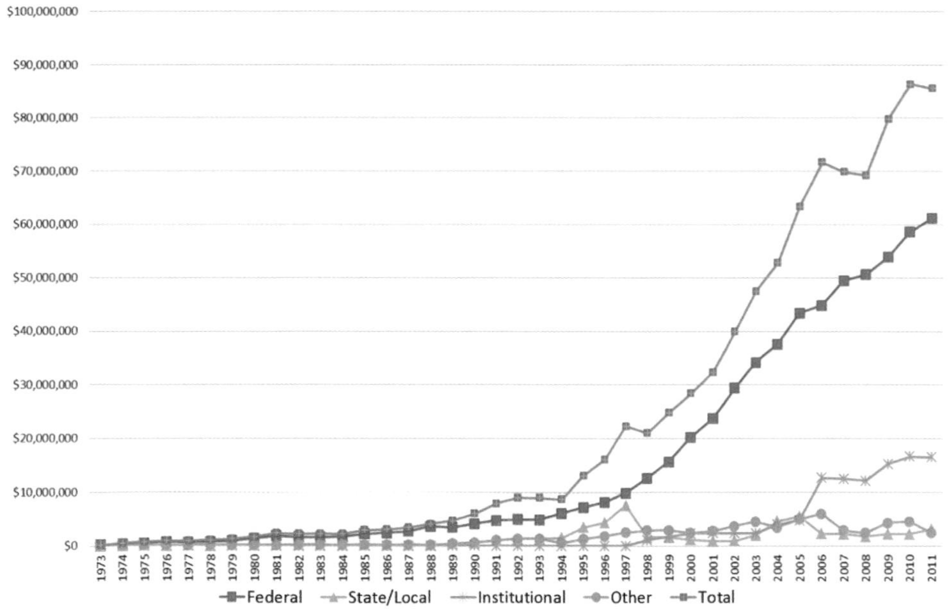

Source: National Science Foundation Datahttps:webcaspar.nsf.gov/ (accessed October 24, 2013).

56. Ibid.146. On this list UMCP was a very creditable number 26.
57. Ibid, Table 6.5, 161.
58. Ibid., Table 6.9, 170.
59. Since many research awards and contracts are awarded once, but may cover multiple years, expenditures are a better indicator of campus trends than awards.

UMBC's grant award success was quite purposeful. UMBC's first chancellor, Albin Kuhn confided:

> I think that basically in most departments where there are opportunities to gain considerable grant and contract support, the university is going to strengthen those departments and those departments are going to be more prominent than the departments where those opportunities are very limited.[60]

Consequently, an initial strategy was to "push biology" because the field was burgeoning and because UMBC had a close proximity to UM's medical school, while College Park's activities were fragmented in two different Colleges.[61] This approach paid off. UMBC's Applied Molecular Biology program was the first in the country and by 1981 a *Sun* headline read, "Respected biology department emerges at UMBC."[62] The article described the role Martin Schwartz, Biology's chair, played in this development. Joining UMBC in 1969, after teaching at the University of Chicago and the University of Pennsylvania, Schwartz set about recruiting "young minor leaguers with can't miss label" about them. A dozen years later, of the 18 members of the department, 16 had received a total of 32 competitively awarded national research grants.

After Schwartz's death in 1982, the Maryland House of Delegates and the Senate passed a resolution remembering him because he organized "one of the finest biology programs in the country at the University of Maryland Baltimore County and propelled it to international prominence." A faculty-led movement emerged to name the UMBC biology building after him. The UM administration, while sympathetic, was bound by a Regent's policy that naming opportunities be used for fund raising.[63] Faculty were not deterred, however. A House of Delegate's bill was introduced by a friend of UMBC, Charles Avara from Arbutus, who had played a role getting financing for the biology building, to name it retroactively after Schwartz. Though the UM administration sent witnesses to testify against the bill, UMBC Professor of African American Studies Willie Lamousé-Smith testified passionately on its behalf declaring, "He [Schwartz] cared as much for achieving excellence in athletics, the arts, the humanities, and the social sciences as he did for the natural sciences."[64] The bill became law and today a brass plaque that reads "He dedicated his life to Excellence for UMBC" stands outside Martin Schwartz Hall.

Working in such sophisticated and productive laboratories paid off for UMBC students too. In 1994, biochemistry professor Michael Summers became the only Howard Hughes Medical Investigator at a public university in Maryland. With his students, Summers' research on HIV proteins contributed to new pharmaceutical

60. Kuhn/Schamp interviews by Larry Wilt. January 4, 2006. 67.

61. This was Homer Scamp's explanation. Ibid., 68.

62. Albert Sehlstedt, Jr., "Respected biology department emerges at UMBC," *Baltimore Sun*, April 19, 1981.

63. Letter from John S. Toll to Michael K. Hooker, July 18, 1986. "Policy for the Naming of Buildings Board of Regents, January 26, 1979.

64. Willie B. Lamousé-Smith testimony before the Constitutional and Administrative Law Committee, Maryland House of Delegates in support of House Bill 1397. March 8, 1988.

treatments for AIDS as well to the installation of an 80-megahertz nuclear magnetic spectrometer, the largest at that time in any U.S. academic research facility. By 2009, UMBC had the highest percentage of science and technology bachelor's degree recipients (45 percent) among all state and private research institutions in Maryland.[65]

Since program approval proved so difficult, UMBC frequently had to go ahead and begin programs with no new money. STEM programs are expensive to operate, however, so faculty and students must enter and frequently win national grant competitions. UMBC has been increasingly successful in garnering wining external funding in rigorous competition. Behind each of those awards is often an exciting story of perseverance and discovery. While at this young campus, no one has won a Nobel Prize or cured a type of cancer, every year there is the creation of new knowledge that not only increases the learning experience of students, but provides benefits to the state, the nation, and the world.[66] There is room here for only three diverse contributions, all of which received media attention in 2011.

World population growth has placed a heavy burden on our oceans in a variety of ways. Among the most acute problems is the insatiable food demand for fish and other salt water creatures. An obvious alternative is aquaculture, but fish farming has its own problems of pollution, disease transmission, and the reluctance of fish to breed in confined quarters. After fifteen years of research, Dr. Yonathan Zohar, Chair of UMBC's Department of Marine Biotechnology at its Columbus Center facilities in the Baltimore Inner Harbor, may have found some solutions. Discovering a hormone that stimulates reproduction and using larger tanks and microorganisms to clean recirculating water, Dr. Zohar hopes to raise at least 100,000 pounds of sea bass or sea bream a year in his tanks.[67] So the next time, you sit down for dinner in the Inner Harbor or Little Italy and order a "European" or "Chilean" sea bass for dinner, you may in fact be eating an aquaculture neighbor which is actually much better for the environment.

In the referendum election of 2012, the glitter of gambling expansion and the lure of jobs and taxes swept aside the opposition. There is, however, a darker side to gambling for those who are pathologically addicted. In 2011, UMBC's Maryland Institute for Policy Analysis and Research (MIPAR) conducted a telephone survey for the Maryland Department of Health and Mental Hygiene of state residents to see how many gambled and what the characteristics of this population were. It turned out that about 90 percent of Marylanders have gambled at least once in their lifetime and

---

65. The Naval Academy was the single exception. "UMBC: Innovation is Our Culture." www.umbc.edu/excellence.pdf, accessed April 16, 2013.

66. In 2009, UMBC ranked 2nd nationally in NASA university research grants and cooperative agreements, 3rd nationally in citations for research citations in geosciences, top ten rankings in information systems and public policy research productivity, and 13th nationally among public universities in per capita Fulbright, Guggenheim, and Mellon awards. Timeline-History of UMBC. http://lib.guides.umbc.edu/content.php?pid=417297&sid=3411009.

67. "The future of fish: Sea bream and sea bass," *Baltimore Sun,* August 2, 2010. See also, Anthony Lane, "Fishing without a Net," *UMBC Magazine*, Winter 2011.

almost 22 percent within the last year. More than 15.3 percent gambled weekly and about 3.4 percent were "pathological" or "problem" gamblers.[68] Gambling occurred among all income brackets, but more frequently among smokers, drinkers, those with poor health, high school education or less, incomes of less than $15,000 a year, and African-Americans.[69] In short, as a producer of revenue, gambling taxes are very regressive. The MIPAR study conducted before the first casino opened in the state led to an increased awareness of the need to help problem gamblers.[70]

In the mosaic of American history, one of the lesser known episodes was the fate of Chinese laborers who came to California as a part of the nineteenth century Gold Rush. Christopher Corbett, UMBC Professor of Practice in the English Department, used an obscure woman to illuminate the economic and racial tensions of that era. Though called Polly Bemis, her anglicized name, she was in fact imported from China to work as a prostitute. Her impoverished parents had sold her for a bag of seeds, before she was resold in California for the handsome sum of $2500 in the gold fields. Eventually she was won in a card game by one Charlie Bemis, thus the book title, *The Poker Bride: The First Chinese in the Wild West.*[71] After living with Bemis for almost half a century and nursing him back to health from a nearly fatal wound, he broke convention and married her. Corbett follows her life and those of other Chinese immigrants struggling for existence and recognition in that Western winner-take-all environment, and we are reminded of the historical relationships of poverty and the sex trade that still exists in the modern world.

Some research awards went to individual scholars working in labs or libraries or, not infrequently, wherever they had access to computers, but other grants were the product of research engines in the form of the centers and institutes the University established. Some of their characteristics and achievements are discussed below.

Research centers transformed many science activities at UMBC because they permitted a fairly small university to compete for large research awards that otherwise would have been impossible to win.[72] These new organizations moved UMBC's national rankings as a research campus up by 50 slots. As President Hrabowski reported in 2006, although the academic consensus was that research universities change very

68. Judith Shinogle, Donald Norris, Dwan Park from UMBC, Rachel Berg from Gemini Research, and Donald Haynes and Eric Stokan from the Schaefer Center for Public Policy, "Gambling Prevalence in Maryland : A Baseline Analysis," MIPAR 2011.

69. Ibid., Tables 4-8 to 4.20. 23–28.

70. DHMH, "Approximately 1 in 30 Maryland Adults Have a Gambling Problem: Baseline Study Will Help with the Design of Prevention and Treatment Services," June 13, 2011. See also a story in the *Washington Post* by Patricia Sullivan, "One in 30 Marylanders has gambling problem, state study finds," June 20, 2011 and an editorial in the *Baltimore Sun*, "Maryland gamblers: A studied look," June 15, 2011, about the MIPAR gambling research.

71. (New York: Atlantic Monthly Press, 2011). For a story about Corbett's career as journalist and his earlier book on the Pony Express titled *Orphans Preferred,* see Rafael Alvarez, "Chasing Tales," *UMBC Magazine*, Summer 2010. 22–29.

72. Ray Hoff, Professor of Physics, interview by the author, April 9, 2013.

slowly over time, by measuring federal research expenditures between 1993 and 2003, UMBC's rise in the rankings led all other major research universities in the nation.[73]

A model was developed by Scott Bass, then Vice President for Graduate Studies and Research; Geoff Summers, his successor as Vice President for Research and then chair of Physics; Mark Behm, Vice President for Administration and Finance; and Harvey Melfi, who worked at the Goddard Space Flight Center and was hired as a full professor at UMBC. This team recognized that neighboring federal science bureaucracies employed large numbers of highly productive research scientists who might value a relationship with university colleagues and the opportunity to do some teaching. Though Johns Hopkins University is the clear national leader of this sort of activity,[74] the UMBC team saw an entrepreneurial opening. If relevant centers could be developed, it could increase UMBC's visibility, attract new graduate students and faculty, and not coincidentally produce substantial overhead funds that would support campus research activities more generally. The competition for such federal funding is fierce, however, and sometimes politics more that scientific productivity can influence awards.

The obvious target for a new center and federal partnerships was the Goddard Space Flight Center located about twenty miles from the campus. The Center for Space Science and Technology (CSST), the Goddard Earth Sciences and Technology Center (GEST), and the Joint Center for Earth Systems Technology (JCET) eventually emerged from this cooperation.

Center for Space Science and Technology (CSST)

CSST administers the grant for UMBC's portion in the CRESST (Center for Research and Exploration in Space Science and Technology) consortium, which also includes the University of Maryland, College Park and the Universities Space Research Association (USRA). This consortium entered into a cooperative agreement with NASA's Goddard Space Flight Center in September 2006. Initial research of the CRESST program was focused on black holes, neutron stars, and extremely hot gases. CRESST also focuses on increasing the involvement of minorities and females in space science research, and increasing undergraduate research involvement.

Goddard Earth Sciences and Technology Center (GEST)[75]

In 2000, a grant was awarded by the NASA Goddard Space Flight Center to UMBC for the establishment of a research center in the earth sciences. UMBC then

73. Freeman Hrabowski, III. "2006 Legislative Testimony." UMBC historic documents collection, Special Collections, University of Maryland, Baltimore County. 5. Citing the Lombardi report. "The Top American Research Universities." (2004).

74. Daniel de Vise, "Hopkins tops U.S. in R&D," *Washington Post*, October 16, 2009.

75. GEST annual reports can be found at http;//gest.umbc.eud/media/media.html.

organized collaborative research programs with Hampton University, Howard University, Caelum Research Corporation, and Northrop Grumman in all areas of earth sciences.[76]

From 2001 to 2011, about 160 scientists were associated with UMBC's GEST and during this period $148,201,575 in research funding came to the campus, 20 percent of which was overhead money. As is customary in 2012, a ten-year review of the project was conducted by the sponsoring federal agency. The NASA reporter concluded, "Given what I know today about the Contractor's [UMBC] ability to execute what they promised in their proposal, I would probably award to them today given that I had a choice."[77] But it was not to be.

In the next round of competition, NASA received four submissions: UMBC, UMCP, the National Institute of Aerospace, and the University Space Research Association[78] (in this instance principally Johns Hopkins and Morgan State). In a competition in which both UMBC and UMCP were contenders, USM lobbyists could not take sides. Nor did Maryland Senators want to weigh in to support USM institutions in the selection, when Hopkins and Morgan entered the ring.

Among GESTAR's technical evaluation factors was the ability to "connect with and leverage innovative efforts ... with historically black colleges and minority institutions."[79] The Congressional Black Caucus, a persistent advocate for more federal funding for Historically Black Colleges and Universities (HBCUs) favored Morgan. NASA's selection process put Congressman Elijah Cummings in a difficult position, since his district includes both Morgan and UMBC. Ultimately, he supported Morgan and his colleagues in the Congressional Black Caucus, but all the factors that played into the transfer of this major research project from UMBC to Morgan may never be known.[80] NASA pointed out that UMBC personnel, including GEST researchers, were included in state mandated salary freezes and furloughs then in effect, and that there was no "permanent rectification giving a very low confidence that current morale and retention issues will be handled effectively."[81] Morgan is also a state institution and had the same salary constraints, but its USRA partner promised cre-

76. Consistent with the mandate followed by federal agencies, there had to be minority institution participation in the project. Hampton and Howard are historically black institutions and Caelum is a black-owned 8(a) firm.

77. Denise Y. Sydnor, "Contractor Performance Assessment Report," May 5, 2012. UMBC historic documents collection, Special Collections, University of Maryland, Baltimore County.

78. USRA is a non-profit corporation that packages research submissions on behalf of 300 various universities that can benefit from its expertise and flexibility. "About USRA," http://www.usra.edu/about/ (accessed April 15, 2013).

79. In the UMBC submission, no new HBCUs were added, but further working relations with the University of Georgia, Colorado State University, and Penn State University focusing on minority and underrepresented participants were promised. Peter H. Hildebrand. "Selection of Contractor for the Goddard Earth Sciences Technology and Research (GESTAR) Studies and Investigations." March 1, 2011. 2–3.

80. Ray Hoff, Professor of Physics, interview by the author, April 9, 2103.

81. Peter Hildebrand, "Selection of Contractor. 4.

ative approaches, including the "use of visiting scientist and honoraria mechanisms to manage any compensation and retention issues that might arise."[82]

The loss of the GEST contract was a major blow to UMBC amounting to about 3 percent of the University's budget at a time when state funds were also being cut. On the campus, the loss was met with silence and no clear explanation about the cause. It was not the result of any academic deficiency. Indeed, Goddard retained its other partnerships with UMBC. Many of GEST's former faculty members, however, had to depart to work on other projects: the GESTAR project as faculty at either Morgan or USRA; the JCET project at UMBC; or the Goddard Planetary Heliophysics Institute (GPHI), a new Goddard-UMBC project.[83] The visiting fellows programs previously administered through GEST were discontinued at the end of the UMBC agreement, and summer internship programs in the earth sciences were transferred to JCET for management.

Joint Center for Earth Systems Technology (JCET)[84]

The Joint Center for Earth Systems Technology was founded in 1995 under a cooperative agreement with the NASA Goddard Space Flight Center to work towards developing new environmental remote sensing technologies. JCET focuses on research themes aligned with NASA's priorities in Earth Sciences research such as atmospheric sciences, climate and radiation concerns, atmospheric chemistry, and engineering among others. In 2012, JCET had 19 research professors serving as affiliated faculty in UMBC departments of Mathematics and Statistics, Physics, Geography and Environmental Systems, Chemistry and Biochemistry, Computer Engineering, Computer Science, and Electrical Engineering. JCET also had an additional 12 research scientists and 4 research associates.

JCET also administers a number of student programs, including the Graduate Student Summer Program for research at NASA Goddard, the JCET Earth Science Explorers Program for undergraduates to conduct research at either UMBC or Goddard, and the Summer Institute in the Earth Sciences for undergraduate research at Goddard or UMBC's campus.

Among JCET's most publicized projects is research by Jeffrey Halverson, UMBC Associate Professor of Geography and Environmental Systems, about predicting when and where hurricanes are likely to develop. While Hurricane Katrina garnered

---

82. Ibid., 14.

83. Childs Walker, "Morgan, Hopkins to be part of team receiving $95.8 million from NASA," *Baltimore Sun*, April 5, 2011. Morgan's share of the grant was $28.5 million. Among the objectives of the GESTAR team was to "increase the involvement of minority and women scientists in earth science research." "Morgan State Receives Major NASA Grant to Study Earth Sciences," MSU Press Release, April 6, 2011. Earlier President Barack Obama announced that Morgan would be part of a research team receiving a $129 million dollar federal grant to improve energy efficiency in buildings around the country.

84. JCET annual reports can be found at http://jcet.umbc.edu/media/.

national attention for the damage done to the Gulf coast, Hurricane Isabel caused $955 million damage to the Delmarva region in 2003. Accurate projections of a storm's trajectory can create precious hours in which lives and property can be saved.[85]

Center for Advanced Sensor Technology (CAST)

CAST began as an ad hoc group of research faculty and students at two other University of Maryland centers: the University of Maryland Biotechnology Institute and the Center for Fluorescence Spectroscopy at the University Of Maryland School Of Medicine. This group moved to the Technology Research Center in 2001, and began operating within the UMBC Department of Chemical and Biochemical Engineering in 2006. In 2007, CAST became an official campus center with affiliated faculty from a number of different departments and centers.

CAST is a multidisciplinary group focusing on research and development of sensing technologies of particular use to biotechnology, medicine, environmental science, and homeland security. The group has three main purposes: research, sensor technology development, and education. Currently, some 25 different technologies are under development. The Center has created a number of technologies that have been licensed or are available for licensing and has obtained patents for approximately 15 new specialized technologies. The Center works closely with the Office for Technology Development and Office for Sponsored Programs to develop collaborative agreements. The Center also assists on Small Business Innovation Research and Small Business Technology Transfer (SBIR/STTR) grant projects. CAST has obtained funding from many agencies and corporations, including the National Science Foundation, National Institute of Health, Juvenile Diabetes Foundation, Maryland Technology Development Corporation, State of Maryland, Maryland Industrial Partnerships, Artisan, DuPont, Fluorometrix, Genentech, Grace, Merck, Pfizer, and Sartorius-Stedim.

Center for Advanced Studies in Photonics Research (CASPR)

CASPR is funded partially through a NASA grant which began in June 2002. The Center focuses on several specializations within photonics research, including quantum optics, sensors lasers and detectors, high capacity optical fiber communication, nanotechnology, and biophotonics. The Center seeks to provide opportunities for businesses and researchers looking to create commercial applications for new inventions in the photonics field.

---

85. Jack Williams, "Storm Stalker," *UMBC Magazine*, Summer 2011, 14–19.

Projects and research are conducted within relevant departments and laboratories: Physics, Computer Science and Electrical Engineering, Mathematics and Statistics, and Chemical and Biochemical Engineering.

Center for Urban Environmental Research & Education (CUERE)

Funding and support for CUERE initially were provided by the U.S. Department of Housing and Urban Development and the U.S. Environmental Protection Agency, but the Center has expanded to include a number of collaborators such as the United States Department of Agriculture Forest Services, the Baltimore Department of Environmental Protection and Resource Management, the Baltimore Ecosystem Study, the Institute of Ecosystem Studies, and Princeton University. The Center focuses on providing assistance to K-12 education in the environmental research, staging conferences, symposia and forums, and supporting postsecondary teaching efforts. The Center works with degree-granting academic departments at UMBC that focus on the environment, as well as programs that can involve environmental science such as Engineering, Public Policy, and Economic Policy Analysis.

Center for Women and Information Technology (CWIT)

Founded in July 1998 to address the problem of underrepresentation of women among information technology professionals and to address the distinctive needs of women as technology users, the Center has created a number of community and K-12 education programs. It partners with other organizations to hold events such as Computer Mania Day to help interest women in pursuing careers in information technology and computing. CWIT's efforts also include the administration of the CWIT Scholars Program (described in chapter VIII on students), which is open to all students interested in increasing the representation of women among the IT professions.

Howard Hughes Medical Institute (HHMI)

The HHMI laboratory at UMBC is a member of a national network of laboratories at over 70 U.S. research universities which collectively employ approximately 330 principal investigators, 700 postdoctoral students, and over 1,000 graduate students. The HHMI UMBC site includes one principal investigator, several postdoctoral fellows, and a substantial number of graduate and undergraduate students engaged in medical and biomedical research. Dating back to 1983, researchers from the Howard Hughes Medical Institute @ UMBC have published over 100 papers in scholarly and medical journals.

A 2002 grant from HHMI funded the creation of the UMBC HHMI Scholars program, modeled after the Meyerhoff program, to increase the number of minority students achieving M.D./Ph.D.s in biomedical fields. The HHMI Scholars program includes intensive focus on research experiences.

Not surprisingly, most of UMBC research centers are in the hard sciences, but the campus also hosts important centers in the social sciences and the humanities.[86]

Alex. Brown Center for Entrepreneurship

The Alex. Brown Center for Entrepreneurship was founded in 2000 after the receipt of a $1 million dollar gift from the Alex. Brown Foundation. The Center works with leading members of Baltimore's business community to instill an entrepreneurial spirit on the campus. This is done through the provision of educational and practical opportunities, including the Raymond V. Haysbert, Sr. Entrepreneurship Lecture Series, CEO Chats, an Entrepreneurship Club, Faculty Institutes, Business Plan Competitions, and undergraduate and graduate credit and non-credit coursework.

The Center is designed to be useful to both the campus (students and faculty) and the business communities by facilitating communication among and providing resources to both. The Center works with the Shriver Center to provide students with internship placements in early-stage companies. The Center works with bwtech@umbc.edu to give access to the Idea Lab, which provides necessary resources for students and faculty to develop and execute plans for high-tech businesses.

The Center also has a number of resources for faculty, including a Faculty Fellows program with three three-year appointments, a Faculty Development Institute held yearly, and Department and Faculty Innovation Grants to encourage interdepartmental collaboration and entrepreneurial skills in curricular development.

In 2007, the Alex. Brown Center was awarded a $2 million grant from the Ewing Marion Kauffman Foundation which funds entrepreneurship programs at colleges and universities available to students regardless of major or field of study. This funding joined a $1 million grant from Constellation Energy Group and $1 million grant from the Herbert Bearman Foundation (2005), which was used to establish the Bearman Family Chair in Entrepreneurship.

Center for Aging Studies

This Center is housed in the Department of Sociology and Anthropology and works with the joint UMBC/UMB Doctoral Program in Gerontology. The Center has had more than $21 million in research projects and works on quality of life, transitions, social relations, medical care, autonomy, employment, bereavement, and suffering issues for the elderly. The research is conducted in independent and assisted

86. The descriptions of the Center for Art, Design & Visual Culture (CADVC) and the Imaging Research Center (IRC) are in Chapter IX on the arts.

living, nursing homes, active adult and continuing care retirement communities with a special focus on ethnography as a lens for understanding the complex socio-cultural dimensions of aging in different residential settings.

Dresher Center for the Humanities

In 1989, Virginia and her (late) husband Jim Dresher established the Dresher Foundation to provide grants for projects focusing on community and educational opportunity in Baltimore City, Baltimore County, and Harford County. UMBC had a Center for the Humanities founded in 1996 that was renamed in 2007 after gift of $500,000 from Dresher Foundation. The Center was created to promote interdisciplinary research and scholarship in the humanities among faculty, students, and staff.

The new Dresher grant encourages the Center to bring national attention to humanities scholarship at UMBC and administers both the Humanities Scholars program and Humanities Forum series. The Center also sponsors a brown bag research series, hosts grant writing workshops (financed by the Vice President for Research and the Dean of CAHSS) and provides Center Summer Fellows to allow faculty to develop proposals to obtain external funding for research grants or fellowships.

The Hilltop Institute

The Hilltop Institute was established in 1994 as the Center for Health Program Development and Management (CHPDM) through a partnership between UMBC and the Maryland Medicaid program of the Maryland Department of Health and Mental Hygiene. CHPDM's original mission was to provide advice to the state's Medicaid administration on the development and management of new health programs.

In 2008, in recognition of the evolution and growth of its research activities, the Center changed its name to the Hilltop Institute. Today, the Institute has a much broader mission of instigating research and using data to create better health outcomes for vulnerable populations. While it still maintains a Maryland focus, it has worked in Idaho, Massachusetts, Michigan, and New Jersey and with a number of local agencies and non-profit organizations.

Maryland Institute for Policy Analysis & Research (MIPAR)

MIPAR was one of the earliest UMBC research centers, established in 1982 to help connect UMBC social science research capabilities with research needs throughout the state, region, and nation. MIPAR conducts research on public opinion, policy analysis, and program evaluation, as well as the organization of symposia addressing pressing public policy needs. The staff includes several dedicated administrators and one research scientist, though several associated faculty have been involved with conducting research. MIPAR has worked with national, state, and local organizations and agencies to conduct their research. In addition, MIPAR has the responsibility for administering a number of grants for the Maryland Department of Health and Mental Hygiene.

Since 1989, MIPAR has been awarded $96 million in external grants and contracts, the largest from the National Institute of Health to the UMBC Center of Aging Studies and from the Maryland Department of Health and Mental Hygiene. These and other grants support about 25 graduate research assistants a year.

While it is easy to portray the growth of UMBC research activities in quantitative or organizational terms, it is almost impossible to describe the cumulative effect of UMBC researchers on the enlightenment, wellbeing, and security of students, scholars, and citizens of Maryland and the world.

There is a UMBC special emphasis on developing undergraduate research skills and the campus funds an undergraduate research journal and fifty $1,500 grants for undergraduate researchers.[87] One of the greatest on-campus intellectual feasts is a visit to the annual undergraduate and graduate research days. In 2012, about 230 undergraduate students presented to audience of about 2,000 their research projects ranging the implications of the Arab Spring for women's rights in the Middle East, to "Modified Carbocyolic Nucleosides as Antiviral Agents," to the design of low cost incubators to aid families in India and Ethiopia with premature babies.[88] There in the form of posters or electronic presentations were the products of collaboration of scores of UMBC students and faculty on cutting-edge research on every subject the university touches. The atmosphere is one of bubbling genius and the research skills learned and displayed will have impacts for many generations.

The standards for the classification of American universities and colleges are set by The Carnegie Foundation for the Advancement of Learning. In 2000, the Foun-

87. The first undergraduate research day was held in 1996. Timeline-History of UMBC. http://lib.guides.umbc.edu/content.php?pid=417297&sid=3411009.

Many individual departments also sponsor undergraduate student research. For example, since 1993 every Interdisciplinary Studies' student must write a Capstone paper under the supervision of two faculty from different academic advisors and an INDS program advisor. After the completion of the project, the students make a public oral presentation which is now captured on YouTube. A recent external evaluation found "As members of the Board of the Association for Integrative Studies, we are familiar with recent developments in interdisciplinary studies curricula around the country. We are convinced that INDS practice at UMBC is exemplary in its developmental and inquiry-based approach to building student familiarity with key IDS concepts and methods. The capstone project is highly structured and provides substantial opportunity for students to integrate multiple disciplinary perspectives into a new intellectual formation. Program emphasis on public presentation of research outcomes moves students into situations where they need to be able to demonstrate transferable competencies and build self-confidence in articulating personalized learning outcomes." James. T. Hall and Karen Moranski, Academic Program Review Report, March 7–8, 2011. Historic documents collection, Special Collections, University of Maryland, Baltimore County.

88. Childs Walker, "Annual Conference showcases UMBC's focus on undergraduate research," *Baltimore Sun*, April 26, 2012.

dation moved UMBC from its 1994 classification in the Doctoral II category[89] to the top tier Doctoral/Research University Extensive status.[90] Only 146 universities were in that elite category out of the country's 3,500 higher education institutions. UMBC was one of five nationally to make that leap between 1994 and 2000. The criteria were that a university had to award at least 50 doctoral degrees in at least 15 disciplines.

In 2008, the Carnegie Foundation engaged in reclassification of the expanded category of doctoral institutions, then numbering 294. In the new order, there are three subcategories: "very high research," "high research," and "research." UMBC was placed in the middle "high research" tier. That rating is based on a number of factors, including science and engineering (S&E) research dollars garnered and the number of Ph.D.'s awarded in a wide variety of fields.[91]

UMBC set its sights on the new "very high research" classification. At the time, those goals seemed like a mountain too high. But in 2011 UMBC received roughly $85 million in S&E dollars, more than double the median achievement for schools in the middle tier. That same year, there were 97 UMBC Ph.D.'s awarded, also higher than the median for comparable schools, so this mountain appears now to be scalable.[92]

---

89. In UMBC's 1996 Middle States Self-Study Report, it was asserted that UMBC's Doctoral II classification was obsolete before it was even published. The Report went on to identify a number of Doctoral I, Research II, and even Research I institutions where UMBC exceeds the productivity of the average for each grouping, "despite receiving substantially lower levels of financial support from the State." 5.

90. Karen Baxter, "UMBC Moves Into Top Tier of Research Universities," *Insights*, September 2000.

91. Carnegie Foundation for the Advancement of Learning, Detailed Descriptions of the Carnegie Classification Methodology, http://classifications.carnegiefoundation.org/methodology/basic.php (accessed October 21, 2013).

92. Freeman Hrabowski and Philip Rous, "Focusing our Resources for Results: Mid-Year Update on University Priorities," April 12, 2012. UMBC historic documents collection, Special Collections, University of Maryland, Baltimore County.

In the UMBC tradition, undergraduate research made a major contribution to this book. 2010 UMBC history team front row, Alexia van Orden, Yasmin Karimian, George La Noue, Amber Spry, back row Amanda Hickey, Jessica Pitman, Namit Bhatia, David Bennett, Matthew McNey, Bridgett Flynn, Grant Foerkolb. Team member Surewna Ehrameni is not pictured. P. xiii. Photo by Patricia La Noue.

Above: UMCP campus in its full Georgian splendor. Below: UMBC campus barely a hole in the ground, p. 34. From George A. Calcott, *A History of the University of Maryland*, Baltimore, Md.: Maryland Historical Society, 1966. Photographer unknown.

Albin O. Kuhn, the master builder, p. 68. Courtesy of Special Collections, the University of Maryland, Baltimore County.

UMBC's first two first buildings, 1966, p. 73. Courtesy of Special Collections, the University of Maryland, Baltimore County.

UMBC campus 2012, p. 93. Courtesy of UMBC Facilities Management.

"UMBC Closing Protested," March 3, 1981. Photo J. Pat Carter. Used by arrangement with *The Baltimore Sun*, p. 53.

UMBC chief administrators. Freeman A. Hrabowski, Michael K. Hooker, John W. Dorsey, Louis L. Kaplan and Albin O. Kuhn. (Not pictured: Calvin B. T. Lee), p. 132.

Robert Meyerhoff and Freeman Hrabowski celebrating their collaboration, p. 229.

UMBC's production of *Spring's Awakening* at the American College Theatre Festival in 1987. Director Sam McCready, set design and costumes, Elena Zlotescu, light design Terry Cobb. p. 353.

After trailing 11–2 in the 2008 America East lacrosse championship game, Alex Hopmann leads the cheers in the Retriever's final 14–13 win. Don Zimmerman, AEC Coach of the Year. p. 406.

CHAPTER VIII

UMBC Students

When students chant "We are UMBC" at a game, in many respects they are right. There are, of course, many more of them than any other University constituency, and their energy, ambition, and success provide important markers reflecting the achievements of UMBC.

Located in a region rich in college choices and in a state that traditionally sent a very high proportion of its best-prepared and more affluent students to out-of-state, usually private colleges, UMBC found itself in tough competition for the students it wanted to admit. When UMBC opened in 1966, there were literally dozens of college choices within a day's drive and the much better developed Catonsville Community College was just one mile away.

So how did UMBC survive that competition, finally begin to prosper, and by 2009 become one of the top campuses in the nation for both undergraduate teaching and research?[1] *U.S. News and World Report* ranked UMBC a breathtaking number one among "up and coming" universities in the United States in 2009, 2010, 2011, and 2012. Perhaps more significant in several recent years, UMBC was the top-ranked public university in its commitment to undergraduate teaching. It was often the only public campus in that category where prestigious, well-funded private universities dominated the list. In 2009, for example, UMBC was the fourth ranked university tied with Yale University in that teaching commitment. Additionally, UMBC was included in that magazine's unranked list of twenty universities that provide the best research opportunities for undergraduates. This chapter tells the stories that led to that impressive achievement and of some of the staff, students, and organizations that made them happen.

Of particular interest are the students themselves, without whom the University would not exist. From UMBC's earliest days to the present, students have shaped every facet of the University. When the new campus opened to receive students in 1966, who were those students who sometimes called themselves pioneers?

1. *U.S. News & World Report*, "America's Best Colleges," 2009 edition.

A. Student Pioneers

Little is known about the academic or demographic characteristics of the 760 students who enrolled at UMBC in the fall of 1966. After the long and sometimes frenetic planning period, Albin Kuhn was eager to see them arrive. He wrote:

> We welcome the new students, for a campus does not come alive until it has a student body. We look forward to the way in which you will become a part of the activities on the campus and will begin to develop the traditions that are so important to college life. We do not expect UMBC to be quite like any other campus.... Collectively, you are a different student body from any previously assembled. In working with the faculty and staff of UMBC, make the most of this opportunity to help create a center of learning in which those who give their best in the laboratory and on the playing field develop a brilliance that is the mark of their efforts and the UMBC environment.[2]

High hopes to be sure, but why did students choose this three-building campus when it first opened? Some may have thought the very underdeveloped UMBC stood for "U Made a Bad Choice," but there was also a feeling of excitement in knowing these pioneer students could write the first words on the campus blank slate. What were those early days like? Bob Dietrich, an Arbutus native who came to the campus as a freshman and in a sense never left, recalled that while some of his high school peers were enrolling in big name institutions across the country, he chose the newest, nearest campus possible.[3] He said:

> You couldn't beat the location and the tuition was inexpensive, but what I think was most attractive was the fact that we would be the first. There were no traditions established, there were no footsteps to follow. But at the same time we had no idea what we were getting into. We were all flying blind. Some of the professors even admit that now. We were all just making it up as we went along.[4]

The 1968 *Skipjack*, the student-edited yearbook, rhapsodized: "Without traditions and the weight of rigid sanctions, the opportunities for creative expression in a new university are limitless."[5] Boundless optimism was a perishable commodity in the 1960s. Abbie Hoffman, Yippie leader, was the featured participant in a "political/rock" demonstration on the campus in 1970. *Skipjack* photos show two stolid looking state policemen monitoring the crowd he drew. Indeed, twenty-four pages of that *Skipjack* were given over to pictures of various protests and the editors concluded:

---

2. Quoted from the notebook created for the UMBC 40th Anniversary.1. UMBC historic documents collection, Special Collections, University of Maryland, Baltimore County.

3. Dietrich worked at UMBC for several decades. His last job was Laboratory Facilities Manager in the Biology Department. Bob Dietrich, interview by Joseph Tatarewicz for the UMBC 40th Anniversary.

4. Cheryl Clemens, "First class event for UMBC's 25th," *Catonsville Times*, no date.

5. *Skipjack*, 1968.9.

> initiative and action formerly originated from the pool of experience concentrated in the administration at Hillcrest, but now the flow of energy is being reversed and the chains of energy of action are originating and being strengthened by the idealism and restlessness of the students on the campus below.[6]

Walter Sherwin, long time professor of Ancient Studies, noted the unusual environment the 1960s created for establishing a new university. It was "an era when kids were coming of age against a backdrop of sexual revolution, practicing 'mind expansion' through the use of psychedelic drugs, and voicing their convictions about the Vietnam War." Sherwin recalled, "We had the first generation students to a huge extent. Between them and their families, there was a remarkable appreciation." Then, as now, the majority of UMBC students worked while they attended school to pay for their college education. "That has always impressed me, how many hours students worked to put themselves through school."[7]

Charles "Tot" Woolston, who began his long and memorable career working in the Registrar's office in 1968 and rose to become Interim Vice Provost for Student Affairs in 1996, remembered UMBC's pioneer students wanted to make a difference and were more politically active than more recent students:

> This first group was made up of risk takers, by the simple fact that they came here. But it showed in many ways. The students back then questioned things and communicated in a way that was more discovery than confrontational. Today's students seem to be less risk takers. They are more cautious, more conservative. They have more respect for authority.[8]

Woolston was not certain whether it was the 1960's spirit or the fact that there were so many things to be decided on the new campus, but he reflected:

> We shared an experience almost no students or faculty member ever have because we all came together at a school with no history or tradition. Everything was open. It was probably the most unique educational experience any of us ever had. I often think how lucky I was to have an opportunity to be a part of that.[9]

B. Student Activism

Unlike many older universities, where nostalgic descriptions of campus life focus on football homecoming games, fraternity parties, May Queens, and Proms, UMBC had none of those activities. Its students were less privileged and less certain of their

6. *Skipjack*, 1970. 245.
7. Patrice Dirican, "UMBC marks 30 years," *Catonsville Times*, 1996.
8. Clemens, "UMBC marks 30 years."
9. Ibid.

places in society. Most were part-time or commuters who had little time for political causes or campus frolics. Still others, however, who could become more fully involved in the campus, were absorbed in participating in newly-formed musical ensembles, theatrical groups, athletics teams, or their studies. Nevertheless, UMBC was a child of the turbulent 1960s. In the first decades of UMBC's life, some of its students were greatly influenced by the protest movements sweeping over many of the nation's campuses.[10]

Demonstrations broke out at the University of California, Berkeley (1964, 1966), San Francisco State (1968–69), Columbia (1968), and Harvard (1969), as well as at lesser known campuses. The nation paid attention to student movements as never before or since. Sometimes these protests involved suspension of classes, occupation of buildings, whole campus shutdowns, and occasional property destruction and violence.[11] Other actions were quite peaceful marches or rallies. Some of the student protests were part of national movements in opposition to the Vietnam War or in support of civil rights causes. Other demonstrations were concerned about large educational issues, raising questions about the role of students in the overall governance of universities. Still other protests focused on more parochial campus concerns.[12] Some could best be explained as copy-cat "things to do in the spring" activities.

As a new campus forty miles from the nation's capital, UMBC students were not immune to these actions, though they were not leaders. In December 1967, military representatives visited the campus to answer questions about the Marine Corps Officer Training Program and to recruit those interested. After setting up shop in the cafeteria, the Marines drew attention from eight students who began to protest their presence and using a PA system announced their opposition.[13] They were in turn challenged by about one hundred students who began to harass the protestors and obtained their own PA system. As word about the verbal confrontation spread, still

---

10. In this section I am greatly indebted to a research paper written by Surena Ebrahimi, UMBC B.A. 2010. His independent study paper "The History of Student Activism at UMBC (1966–2010)" can be found in the UMBC historic documents collection, Special Collections, University of Maryland, Baltimore County.

11. Jack D. Douglas, *Youth in Turmoil: America's Youth Cultures and Student Protest Movements*, (Rockville, MD: National Institutes of Health, 1972); Phillip G. Altbach and Robert Cohen, "American Student Activism: The Post-Sixties Transformation," *The Journal of Higher Education*, (January–February, 1990) 32–49.

12. One of the more unusual controversies at UMBC occurred when a 1969 student magazine, "*The Red Brick*," published some "artistic" nude photographs. Some local politicians appeared to be incensed and a Baltimore County Councilman threatened in the *Baltimore Evening Sun* that if UMBC was to be an "institution of pornography" the state should reallocate unused campus land for faculties for the "mentally retarded and the elderly." Eighty-four UMBC faculty responded by pooling their own money for an *Evening Sun* ad arguing that a" university must cherish and defend the right of open and free expression within its faculty and student body." Caught between increasing pressures descending on his vulnerable institution, Chancellor Kuhn suspended that student publication. Richard Byrne, "Blow Up," *UMBC Magazine*, Winter 2012. 15–21.

13. "UMBC Students Sit-In," *The Retriever*, December 11, 1967. Steve Lesser, "Protesters Invade UMBC Campus: Oppose Recruiting," *Catonsville Times*, December 8, 1967.

other students came to join both sides and the shouting and haranguing lasted throughout the afternoon. But that was it and whether the incident discouraged or encouraged any young man about joining the ongoing war is unknown.

In April 1970, when the invasion of Cambodia and the Kent State shootings of students prompted a call for a national student strike, some at UMBC urged boycotting final exams. There was no consensus on the matter. Some students did refuse to take finals with the consequences left to the ideology and ethics of individual faculty graders, while others showed up to write in their blue books as usual.[14] Looking back on this era, doubtless many UMBC students marched in anti-war parades in Washington; but on campus anti-war demonstrations were rare.

Concerns about civil rights issues were more common on a campus founded only twelve years after the official desegregation of the University of Maryland. UMBC could not avoid the tense racial atmosphere of the era. In a sort of official apology, the State recently acknowledged that in 1968:

> Circumstances for black Marylanders were dramatically different then, not only in education but also in politics, business, employment, housing and virtually all areas of life. For example, in 1968 Maryland voters approved by a 55 percent majority, a referendum to nullify the State's first Open Housing Act, which had been passed in 1967. The State's population in 1968 was less than four million, and fewer than 18 per cent of Maryland residents were African Americans. In 1968, neither Maryland's highest court, the Court of Appeals, nor its intermediate appellate court, the Court of Special Appeals contained even one African-American judge. Only 13 of the 188 legislators in Maryland's General Assembly were African-Americans. At that time, Baltimore had never elected an African American mayor. Relatively few African Americans or other minorities attended Maryland's non-HBIs, least of all at the University of Maryland at College Park where black students made up less than 1 percent of the undergraduate population until the end of the 1960s.[15]

If all UMBC students were educational pioneers on the new UM campus, its African-American students may have felt they were racial pioneers as well. Some student actions were tied to larger national civil right issues, while others were provoked by incidents at UMBC with racial overtones that were misinterpreted or mishandled on the campus. These events may have reflected an uncertainty about the role of black students on the suburban Catonsville campus and the lack of mechanisms for promoting more constructive inter-racial dialogue. Whatever the explanation, these student protests led to some bad publicity for UMBC in Baltimore

---

14. Fred Pincus, interview by Surena Ehrahimi, January 26, 2010.

15. Defendant's "Memorandum in Support of Their Motion for Summary Judgment Regarding Intentional Discrimination and Maryland Funding of Public Institutions of Higher Education Under *Fordice*." *The Coalition for Equity and Excellence in Maryland Higher Education er.al. v. Maryland Higher Education Commission,* Case No. CCB-06-CV 2773. February 11, 2011. 2.

newspapers and television stations and continuing suspicion about the campus among some constituencies.

In 1969, the first of several seemingly minor incidents triggered a racial confrontation. An African-American student, who was under some financial pressure, went to the Office of Student Life to pick up an overdue check for some typing work she had done three months earlier for "*The Red Brick*" campus publication.[16] Student Activities Director, Betty Ammerman, insisted she did not have the authority to issue a check drawn on Student Government Association (SGA) funds and that the SGA Executive Board would have to resolve the matter when it met the following week. Fifteen other black students then confronted the Director of Student Life, Arthur Libby, asking him to process a check, but he claimed there were no emergency funds for that purpose. The students then posted "closed" signs on the Student Life office door and three students refused to leave until the twenty-six dollar check was paid. The tempest finally ended when SGA President Daryl Hagy gave the student the money owed her from his own pocket. Underlying issues of distrust were not so easily allayed, however.

In 1976, another racial incident captured the campus attention.[17] Cindy Hardy, a former secretary for the Office of Campus Affairs, was stopped by campus police for allegedly running two stop signs. According to Officer Glen Johnson, when asked for her license, Hardy conceded she had left it at home, though she did have her registration card. In an ensuing argument, Johnson alleged that Hardy had punched him in the stomach, and Hardy claimed that the officer had twisted her arm, frisked, and handcuffed her, before taking her under arrest to the Halethorpe District Court on an assault and battery charge. Forced to choose between the competing stories of its two employees, UMBC sided with its policeman.

These kinds of "police said, civilian said" incidents occur with unfortunate regularity in many urban areas, but on the campus the confrontation took on larger racial significance. Organized by a coalition of African-American groups, about 300–400 demonstrators, shouting "stop police brutality," started in front of the Administration Building and made their way to the office of the Director of Public Safety to demand that Officer Johnson be fired. Interim Chancellor Louis Kaplan was not persuaded, but the protest triggered a broader discussion of racial issues. Concern was voiced about racist graffiti in the bathrooms, and some black faculty spoke about the "dwindling presence of blacks" in upper-level campus positions and noted that nine of the seventeen total black faculty held their positions in the African-American Studies department.

---

16. Larry Thomas, "Black students hold Student Life Office," *The Retriever*, November 18 1969. In the spring of that year, Chancellor Kuhn prohibited on-campus solicitation by off-campus groups, in this case the Black Panthers, and some students staged a protest in the cafeteria. A bomb threat was phoned in to the state police and a half hour later state and county police cleared the building. John Adams, "To gain solicitation rights: Students, Libby in confrontation," *The Retriever*, March 16, 1970.

17. This incident was described in Jeanne Saddler, "Blacks protest UMBC Arrest," *Baltimore Sun*, October 16, 1976 and Kevin Estis, "Demonstrators Protest Hardy's Arrest," *The Retriever*, October 25, 1976.

In 1979, the campus again drew unwelcome notoriety for racial grievances. On April 6th, a group of students organized by the Black Student Union (BSU) occupied the lobby of Chancellor Dorsey's office and shouted for a meeting with him.[18] The students had several demands, including that they be represented on the search committee for a new financial aid officer, noting that the position had not been advertised in black academic journals, and that a dorm lottery proposal be retracted. This proposal would have given the lowest priority to students who lived within eight miles of the campus, a measure that encompassed much of Baltimore City. The protestors feared that the proposal, whatever its intent, would force inner-city students off campus to depend on the vagaries of an uncertain bus system. The protestors also called on the campus to create an affirmative action program and to reinstate the Office of Minority Recruitment and Retention.

The Chancellor refused to meet with the students, though they did meet with other administrators. Gradually the confrontation drew the attention of the press and television, as well as some non-campus demonstrators. Armed guards were brought in to create minimal security. Although students were warned that the police might be called, the demonstrators focusing on the Financial Aid office replied, "This is our office, this is our money, and we're tired of this. We're not moving." Public attitudes about student protests by then had become less tolerant than in the 1960s and Dorsey issued a written statement:

> Any further action which will disturb or prevent the orderly conduct of the activities, administration or classes of this institution will not be tolerated and any persons participating in such actions will not only be subject to campus judicial proceedings, but also to civil authority.[19]

Fifteen, mostly black, students were charged with violations of school rules (being in an off-limits area containing confidential student records) which created another demonstration of about 150 students. The rally for the "UMBC 15" (echoing the earlier antiwar group, the Catonsville 9) focused on minority rights.[20] The charges were quietly dropped the next August.[21]

Two years later, UMBC suffered another round of racial recriminations. Some black students claimed that BSU posters were defaced with racial slurs and that a student-run event featured a slave auction and mock hangings. Some white students believed that the culprits were few in number and that BSU exaggerated the incidents.[22] The tensions climaxed when two senior members of the Athletic Department admitted they used racial slurs and the Director of Human Relations recommended one be fired and the other reprimanded. Vice Chancellor Walter Jones refused to dis-

---

18. Alex O'Brien, "Students Take Over Admin," *The Retriever*, April 9, 1979.
19. Alex O'Brien and Tena Satterwhite, "Students Continue Occupations," *The Retriever*, April 23, 1979.
20. "150 students demonstrate to back minority rights," *Baltimore Sun*, May 12, 1979.
21. Alex O'Brien, "Admin drops charges against UMBC 15," *The Retriever*, August 31, 1979.
22. Joel McCord, "UMBC officials ignore mounting racial tension," *Baltimore Sun*, March 26, 1981.

cuss what he thought was appropriate discipline, but it was evident termination was not involved.[23] This triggered rallies and protests throughout the spring.[24]

In 1986, a dorm fight between a black and white student in which the black student was suspended from the dorm, led to rallies and an Administration Building sit-in.[25] A few months later, a shanty was constructed between the library and the biology building to protest South African apartheid and urge the University of Maryland to divest in companies doing business in that country. The shanty was defaced with a racial slur and physically damaged. No vandals, on or off campus, were ever identified, but the incident added to racial tensions.[26]

By 1987, Michael Hooker had become Chancellor and Freeman Hrabowski had become Vice Provost.[27] They were determined to improve the image and the realities of race relations on campus. Although 15 percent of UMBC's students were African-American by 1987, some still saw the campus as not welcoming.[28] After another sit-in of administrative offices, joined by some students and faculty from other campuses and the President of the Baltimore County NAACP, the protestors chanted, "Hooker, you better fear, we won't take another year."[29] Consequently, the Chancellor held an open press conference to announce several important decisions. An Office of Minority Affairs was to be established, an initiative to recruit and retain minority faculty was created, a formal role for the BSU in student judicial proceedings was granted, and reprimands were given to two administrators.[30] Hooker stated that he respected the student's right to protest and later met with several of the protestors who had taken over his office.[31]

---

23. Ronald Hubes, "Jones takes action on discrimination," *The Retriever*, April 8, 1981.

24. Sherri Conyers, "Students speak out against discrimination," *The Retriever*, April 8, 1981, and "Students picket lacrosse game," *The Retriever,* April 29, 1981.

25. Joan Michaels, "Hundreds of students protest racism," *The Retriever*, April 22, 1986.

26. Alden Knisbacher, "Shanty heightens protest," *The Retriever*, December 16, 1986; "Protest," *The Retriever,* March 3, 1987 and James R. Polchin, "Students rebuild protest shanty," *The Retriever*, March 10, 1987.

27. The story of the evolution of UMBC's relationship to its African-American students is told in Freeman A. Hrabowski, III, "Creating a Climate for Success," *The Presidency* (American Council on Higher Education), Winter 1999.

28. Samuel L. Banks, "Why UMBC is inhospitable to blacks," op-ed in *Baltimore Evening Sun*, December 18, 1987. Constance Beims, executive assistant to Chancellor Hooker, wrote an op-ed response to Banks, noting among other things that UMBC's retention rate was higher for black students than for whites. "UMBC is fighting racism." *Baltimore Evening Sun*, December 29, 1987.

29. A description of the sit-in and negotiations that followed can be found in William Douglas "Talking ... but not talking: Black sit-in enters 7th day at UMBC." *Baltimore Evening Sun,* April 21, 1987.

30. "UMBC to make changes after racial charges," *Carroll County Times*, April19,1987. Juan C. Ordonez and James R. Polchin, "Rickard resigns after week-long sit-in by protesting students," *The Retriever*, April 29, 1987.

31. Gail Anderson, "Chancellor and Coalition reach agreement," *The Retriever*, April 29, 1987; Gail Anderson and Arun Gupta, "Students stage sit-in outside Chancellor's office," *The Retriever*, April 21, 1987, and Gail Anderson, "A student gives a day-to-day report of protest," *The Retriever*, April 21, 1987.

A few months later UMBC put out a press release boasting that black student applications in a year had risen by 13.1 percent and SAT scores for entering African-American students were up 52 points.

The fall of 1988 brought the first funding for the Meyerhoff program, at that time exclusively for black males, which received favorable national attention.[32] Locally, the Baltimore *Afro-American* featured two full-page stories, one titled. "UMBC: A State University undergoing a racial renaissance" and a second "Freeman Hrabowski: UMBC Vice President is proud of his institution."[33] The tide of negative press had turned.

The 1987 sit-in marked the last of the major student protests concerning race at UMBC. The temper of the times and the student body had changed.[34] While there were no short-term solutions to feelings of racial isolation or animosity, finding ways to be inclusive and to promote multi-cultural dialogue have become major objectives at UMBC which is now one of the most diverse campuses in the country.

During this period, UMBC students also demonstrated concern about more purely educational issues. In April 1970, some UMBC students participated in a week-long sit-in to protest the emphasis on research and publication in faculty tenure decisions and the release of four professors who did not meet those standards.[35] About seventy students went to the Vice Chancellor for Academic Affairs' office and occupied it for three hours. The next day they marched to the Hillcrest building, where the administration was then located, with a plan to create a students-faculty Promotion and Tenure Review Board. A resolution advocating for such a Board was presented to the Faculty Senate, but it was ruled to be out-of-order. So the protesting students settled in for a night on Hillcrest's linoleum floors. The day after, the students won the support of the Student Government Association Senate which might have called a general strike. Consequently, they received an audience with Chancellor Kuhn. The first two-hour meeting with Kuhn needed a follow up the next day, so the students decided to sleep in the carpeted and air conditioned faculty office building instead of Hillcrest. The subsequent meeting attracted nearly half of UMBC's 2300 students, a remarkable number for a commuter school, and a sign of how seriously these students took university governance and the quality of their education at the four-year-old campus. Another two-hour session resulted in an agreement that there would be no general student strike and that the issues would be reviewed in

32. This funding was celebrated in an article in "Black Men in Science and Technology Targeted: Precedent Setting Grant to UMBC," *Black Issues in Higher Education, 5, no 18* (October 27, 1988).

33. Both stories by Jill P. Carter, August, 1988.

34. Andrea Thomas, "Few students aware of UMBC's history of protest," *The Retriever*, May 16, 2009. See Neil Howe and William Strauss, *Millennials Rising: The Next Great Generation,* (New York: Vintage, 2000), who argue that this generation is much more willing to work with existing structures and rules to achieve personal success.

35. "Students protest faculty tenure policy: Week-long sit-ins show dissent," *The Retriever*, April 28, 1970. Antero Pietila, "UMBC Unrest, Hopkins Strike Quieted," *Baltimore Sun,* April 24, 1970; Charles P. Kochakian, "UMBC Protest Continues," *Baltimore Sun*, April 25, 1970.

the regular administrative and faculty process. The next day, the Faculty Affairs Committee called an emergency meeting, which was also attended by 800 students and many faculty. The three-hour debate did not result in a particular agreement, nor did the subsequent meetings held in the following weeks. Then the semester ended and with it the specific causes of action.

The issue of standards for promotions and tenure and student participation in those decisions, however, did not go away and erupted again in 1974[36] and 1977.[37] When five popular professors were faced with dismissal in 1978, a rally of 200–300 students in the cafeteria led to a march on the Administration building and a confrontation with Chancellor Dorsey. The Chancellor initially refused to speak to what he described as a mob, but eventually admitted three leaders for a ten-minute discussion. Those outside were not mollified and pounded on the door and wall of his office, chanting "We want Dorsey." After it was clear the students were not leaving, Dorsey came out of his office to address them. He denied that ideology played any role in the decisions about the five professors the students had championed and reminded them that faculty personnel decisions were based on peer judgments. Students had "the right to provide advice, but not to make the decisions," but he did promise to review the promotion and tenure process and suggested the guidelines might be revised in the future.

Although the student protests during the 1970s to achieve a voice in faculty personnel decisions and to weight them more heavily toward teaching did not immediately prevail, their values are reflected in current procedures. Virtually every UMBC class is evaluated by students. In faculty promotion and tenure decisions, two student representatives write a report on teaching based on surveys of their peers and then have both voice and vote on the teaching section of the evaluation report. Although a candidate for UMBC tenure will not be successful with a mediocre research and publication portfolio, a poor record in teaching will be a considerable, perhaps decisive liability.

For the next few years, there were several student petitions, but no organized student protests. Then in the fall of 1975, UMBC students became concerned about system-wide tuition increases and organized the Student Committee Against the Tuition Hike (SCATH).[38] The November meeting of the Board of Regents, which rotates among campuses, was scheduled to be at UMBC. The Board convened for a campus "show and tell" performance in the auditorium of the new Fine Arts building. The theatrics, however, took on a different tenor. Once inside, the Board was surrounded by hundreds of students from UMBC and other UM campuses who eventually filled

36. David Bostwick, "Rally protests P&T," *The UMBC Retriever*, March 25, 1974.

37. Jackie Toback, "Promotion-Tenure Criticized at Speakout," *The UMBC Retriever*, May 2, 1977 and Joe Kerger, "Committee Presents Platform at P&T Rally," *The Retriever*, May 8, 1978. A history of sorts of early UMBC P&T conflicts can be found in Steve Miller, "P&T Disputes First Incarnation," *The Retriever*, May 1, 1978.

38. Tom Shipley, "Student Movement Forms Against Tuition Hikes," *The Retriever*, October 20, 1975.

the building. Joined by some faculty members, the students displayed placards and banners, while picketing the building. Eventually, the protestors began to pound on the doors of the meeting room shouting "No hike, No way," and more poetically made a very 1970s chant "They got the money, we're no fools, take it from the ruling class and give it to the schools."[39]

The Regents, who, if there were a Maryland ruling class, would certainly be represented, decided dialogue would be useful and invited two student leaders to address them. SGA Vice President, Jack Neil, took off his jacket and rolled up his sleeves, but said in a reasonable tone, "The students here don't mean to be disrespectful. They are just scared. They are scared that they won't be able to continue their education."[40] Both the SGA and other campus groups were concerned that the University was pricing itself out of the reach, not only of the lower class, but also the middle class.[41]

No decision was made that day, but later the Regents voted for an 8.5 percent tuition increase from $698 to $758. But it was not enough, and the new budget called for reduced library services. In March, former Senator Joseph Tydings, then chair of the Regents' Budget Committee, came to give a lecture and found hundreds of students who interrupted his speech shouting: "Stop the hike! No cut, no way! They say cut back, we say fight back."[42] Tydings reminded the students that this was a difficult year economically and urged them to take their grievances to the General Assembly in Annapolis. A week later, they did, and joined by faculty, graduate assistants, and classified employees, a rally was held to protest the double harm of tuition increases and budget cutbacks.[43]

Watching the first wave of student protests and trying to be the middleman between state authorities and campus activism was Chancellor Kuhn. Initially, he had to confront his own emotions. He remembered that:

> The first year [at UMBC] was great, students, faculty, staff and administrators all seemed on the same page with great cooperation toward a solid progressive and noteworthy beginning.... The pioneer spirit ran through 1967–70, even though we ran headlong into the student revolution that was rampant in the nation.... Some wondered if we had picked a good time to start a university campus.[44]

---

39. Jim Vidmar, "Student Protestors Take Their Gripe to Regent Tydings," *The Retriever*. March 1, 1976; Charles Lean, "Tuition Hike Protestors Storm Regents Meeting," *The Retriever*, November 24, 1975 and Mike Bowler, "Students protest UMBC tuition rise," *Baltimore Sun*, November 22, 1975.

40. Lean, "Tuition Hike."

41. Patricia Cote, "Unity Isn't Revolutionary: A Cry for Unity is Next Step in Tuition Protest," *The Retriever*, March 8, 1976.

42. Charles Lean, "It Don't Come Easy," *The Retriever*, March 1, 1976 and Jim Vidmar, "Student Protestors Take Their Gripes to Regent Tydings," *The Retriever*, March 1, 1976.

43. Areta Kupchyk, "Students Take Cutbacks, Tuition Gripes to Annapolis," *The Retriever*, March 8, 1976.

44. Albin O. Kuhn family "scrapbook." 6.

Using his agricultural extension contacts he spoke around the state about the new university campus and, of course, there were questions about student unrest. He replied:

> the students through their discussions and through their ideas of what universities ought to be and what society ought to be, helped bring some of us into a lot broader, better, total thinking ... got us out of our narrow-minded ways of thinking about things.... A lot of good things have come out it.

Some of his listeners who had known Albin O. Kuhn for decades said, "Good Lord, you've changed a lot. What have you been doing? You're not the person, facing some of this in the way I thought you would."[45]

Still there were limits. Kuhn remembered:

> Students were smart, they didn't want to talk to anybody but the Chancellor.... So I was invited to a number of meetings, and many discussions were held about whether we couldn't change this or that and why we were doing this and I remember one day in which a student made a very good speech about the fact that students really ought to establish exactly what the university did, rather than the faculty or the administration, or the Board of Regents....[46]

Kuhn responded to the students:

> We are a wholly owned corporation of the State of Maryland and the State of Maryland has given the Board of Regents the responsibility for running the university, and we shall continue operating that way. And so, I guess the more we got pounded on, the more we tended to retreat to things that were long standing, if you will.[47]

According to Kuhn, the most painful part of student unrest was that, while political support for higher education in the country had been good, the turmoil made it difficult to get additional money for campuses. For a new campus with a small reservoir of trust and money, the timing could not have been worse. Kuhn recalled:

> The greatest effect on UMBC, and on the rest of public higher education in Maryland in the student unrest days, was the fact that we were coming through an era where we were expanding rapidly, where the legislature, the Governor, everybody was in tune to support very well higher education, and then all of the sudden, we, those in charge of campuses couldn't control our own students. The next year, if you went down to the legislature, you faced some really hostile people about increasing appropriations or about doing new things in which you needed more money. The biggest thing was it took higher education off the pedestal and put them down into the rat race with

45. Albin O. Kuhn, interview by Joseph Tatarewicz, August 14, 2001. 31

46. Ibid., 27–28.

47. Ibid.

> the prisons.... other state agencies for money attention and support.... All of the sudden everybody you depended upon sort of got angry with you....[48]

It was an emotional time for the campus founder: "But I think the toughest thing for some of us who had been part of developing UMBC; you get very possessive of the campus. Why would someone do that to my campus, you know? Sit in, do this, do that. You get over it, but it was painful for a while.[49]

But there was no violence. Kuhn reminisced:

> we had four or five retired Baltimore City policemen on the campus security force ... they were old-timers really accustomed to things. And they'd say, "Doc, don't you worry about that. You know, we will keep things calm." And they'd go around and wear these flowers that students made up that had fuzz on them.... First thing you had to teach is that you don't arrest anyone, you know. You learn to relax.... The students here were not violent in their reactions. It wasn't fun though.[50]

It is easy in hindsight to dismiss campus protests thirty years ago as tempests in teapots. But the passions were real and the issues were important, even if the tactics used and the solutions advocated were sometimes simplistic. In the modern university, UMBC included, with its well-trained student personnel officers and elaborate problem solving and disciplinary procedures, sustained student protest movements are unlikely. But perhaps those officers and procedures are in part a legacy of those who marched and shouted to show concern for racial sensitivity, student participation in personnel decisions, and college affordability, UMBC is better for that legacy. Students then showed a vigorous emotional commitment to shaping the University, which now many contemporary students take for granted. After all, the largest demonstration in UMBC's history occurred when UMBC was threatened with closure.[51] One thousand students rallied to defend the University they had criticized in the past.

C. Enrollment Challenges

UMBC survived the campus protest era with only a few scars. After the first decade, however, there were still serious problems in recruiting and maintaining an

48. Ibid., 30–31. An extended discussion of the student protest movement which Kuhn saw as bringing to an early and abrupt conclusion a period that had been a golden era in higher education in this nation, can be found in Albin O. Kuhn, "University of Maryland Baltimore County (UMBC) Its Early Years of Development and Operational History," 40, unpublished manuscript, Box 2, Folder 10, UMBC historic documents collection, Special Collections, University of Maryland, Baltimore County.

49. Albin O. Kuhn, interview by Ed Orser, February 4, 1994. 24.

50. Ibid.

51. See Chapter II. Sherri Conyers, "One thousand jam quad to defend campus, protest closing proposal," *The Retriever*, March 4, 1981.

appropriate student body. UMBC had only a very local reputation and was largely a commuter school with almost no public transportation to its suburban campus. Part of the difficulty in attracting full time students was that UMBC had very little dormitory space. In 1971, after Chesapeake Hall opened there were still only 309 beds available and the on-campus facilities for student life were poor. The 1976 Middle States accreditation report referred to the "relative desertion of the campus after 4:30 P.M."[52] Students complained about the absence of lockers or lounges or places to get coffee and snacks. Nor was there any central student gathering place, a student "union" or commons. Some of those problems would be solved with the opening of the University Center in 1982, but there was another issue that would take much longer to resolve.

The Middle States Accreditation Report described that issue in stark terms:

> ... the [Middle State's] team's sense that there was serious mismatch between faculty aspiration and expectation, and the needs of the students UMBC draws to itself. There is a downward accent placed on the words "commuter" and "commuting student" in the self study, in reports and statements that UMBC makes about itself, and in discussions team members had with individual administrators and faculty members. At times the same accent is heard in the mouths of students. It is clearly pejorative, and at times patronizing.
>
> The students struck the team as having very real assets. Not the least of these was a touching and naive faith in the value of higher education. Many of the students appeared to be first generation college goers and to have the urgency and conviction that the status brings with it. They impressed the team members with their sense of courtesy, both to visiting foreigners like ourselves as well as to other members of the UMBC community. They also impressed all of us as deserving respect, despite the fact that the needs they bring to the college are great. The statistics available at UMBC indicate that its students are a solid notch better prepared than the national average. Despite this, there seems to be a general feeling among faculty and administrators, that UMBC students are in many cases too deeply underprepared for the institution to be able to cope with their needs.[53]

Despite the team's assurance that the students were a "solid notch" above national norms, the admission criteria were in fact quite modest as their own report shows. Maryland residents were admitted if they had a C average and stood in the top half of their classes or had a predicted GPA of 1.75. The class of 1977 had an average 435 verbal and 475 mathematics SAT scores, or about 120 points below the national median. The student body was also quite parochial geographically with only 1.5 percent out-of-state and 1.8 percent foreign. None of these statistics were very surprising for

---

52. Middle States report 1976. 28. UMBC historic documents collection, Special Collections, University of Maryland, Baltimore County.

53. Ibid., 3.

a new public university, but UMBC administrators and faculty and the Middle States visitors viewed the data from different perspectives.

Part of the problem was that the accrediting team reflected a faction in the larger national debate about the role of urban universities.[54] Some thought of these institutions as serving a residual function in higher education by enrolling first-generation, minority, and immigrant students who had few other choices and who would need considerable remedial help. There was no thought that these campuses would grow to be comparable to preeminent private universities or state flagships, even in some of their programs. The new wave urban universities were apparently to be second class, but it was a noble mission.

From UMBC's perspective, its role had to be defined in part by its geographic niche and the faculty it had recruited. It could not serve many parts of the city's population as well as Morgan, Coppin, and the University of Baltimore could, and it was now staffed by faculty who were neither trained nor aspired to do much remedial work. Nor did UMBC want to be defined by its immediate suburban context. The author of the American Council of Education monograph *The Urban Campus* wrote approvingly, "The name University of Maryland-Baltimore County says 'We are the University of Maryland operating in support of and in cooperation with a context that is Baltimore County.'"[55] In fact, that interpretation of UMBC's mission was never widely held either on or off campus. Before residence halls were built, there were limits to how far students could commute, of course; but by 2012, less than 15 percent of the full-time freshmen were from Baltimore County. (Montgomery County was the leading source.) The faculty had always been recruited nationally and even internationally, and their research perspectives were equally as broad.[56]

The Middle States team did not imagine that UMBC could or should remake its student body to fit its academic aspirations. From their perspective it was commendable for UMBC to recruit a "faculty that comes from the best graduate schools," but the student body it had was the student body it would always have and perhaps deserved. Therefore, from the team's perspective it was patronizing to lament the mismatch. But possessing "a touching and naive faith in the value of higher education," in the team's words, does not itself create the basis for the synergy between students and faculty that builds a great research university.[57]

There always were, of course, many fine students at UMBC, even among the pioneer classes. The problem was to create a critical mass of such students. Over the

---

54. See for example, Peggy Gordon Elliot, *The Urban Campus: Educating the New Majority for the Next Century* (Phoenix: American Council of Higher Education, Oryx Press, 1994)

55. Ibid., 28.

56. The most local of the faculty research centers is the social science applied research arm, the Maryland Institute for Policy Analysis and Research (MIPAR), but as its name implies it has a more statewide than county focus and does research on some national policy issues as well.

57. Quotes are from the 1976 Middle States report. 3.

Figure M
UMBC Headcount Enrollment, 1974–2012

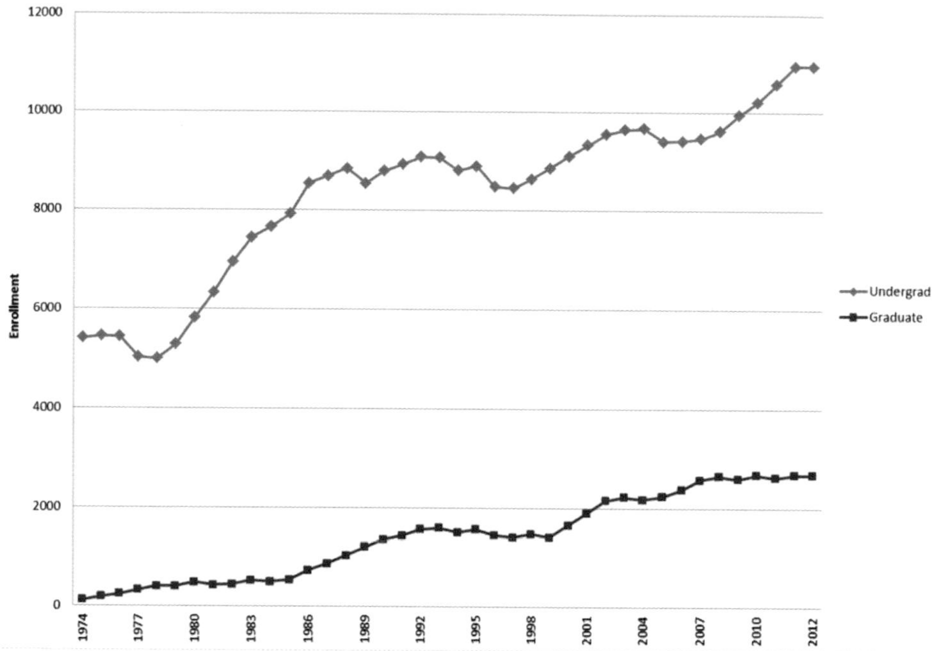

Source: UMBC Office of Institutional Research databook. 2012.

next decades, the student body evolved significantly in size, quality, and diversity.[58] As Figure M shows, except for a few difficult years in the late 1970s, enrollment growth has been relatively consistent.[59]

In 1983, UMBC's Vice Chancellor for Administrative Affairs announced that the campus would have to use a waiting list for qualified applicants because "Our rate of growth has far exceeded the rate of growth of the state general fund" and the state had asked for an enrollment cut back. UMBC has become increasingly more selective, since that turning point. By 2012, there were 10,953 undergraduates. Full-time undergraduates numbered 9,371 and part-timers 1,582 or about 15 percent of the total undergraduate enrollment. As recently as 1992, part-timers accounted for 29 percent of all undergraduates, but the percentage of full-time students has increased almost every year since then.

Another significant trend is the growth of graduate enrollment. Despite UMBC's ambitions to be a research university, which requires a critical mass of graduate stu-

58. A good discussion of UMBC's admission strategies can be found in the "Report of the UMBC Enrollment Management Task Force," January 28, 1999. UMBC historic documents collection, Special Collections, University of Maryland, Baltimore County.

59. UMBC's administrative and financial problems under Chancellor Lee in those years are described in Chapter IV.

dents, twenty years after its founding, graduate students made up less than 8 percent of the campus enrollment. That was not the profile of a research institution. UMBC's graduate enrollment was lower than other state campuses that saw their mission as primarily teaching. As Figure M shows, since 1986 there has been a dramatic increase in graduate students, who numbered 2,684 by 2012 or about 20 percent of the total enrollment.

A key part of UMBC's admission's strategy was turning the University into more of a residential community. The first problem UMBC had to overcome was to change the University from a "park car, take notes, and leave" place to a "live, grow, and contribute to a community" environment. As Figure N shows from 1987 to 2012, UMBC began to close the gap between commuter and residential students, though the economic downturn may have a reverse effect in some recent years. But within those overall statistics was a more dramatic change. In those years, UMBC moved from a university where 59 percent of the full-time freshmen were commuters to a campus where 76 percent of those freshmen were in residence halls. After that first year, in a common pattern nationally, many students move to private apartments that surround the campus. Residential Life estimates that about 1,500 students now live in nearby apartments, and although they are not commuters in the ordinary meaning of that word, they are still counted as such in Figure N and other calculations. So, while UMBC is still often thought of as a "commuter campus," the reality has changed significantly.[60]

UMBC also wanted to change the academic preparation of admitted students. Part of its motivation was to improve its retention rates by becoming more selective. James Vaillancourt, then Assistant Provost for Enrollment, reported that most students who drop out do so in the first two years and that by increasing admission standards more admitted students would actually graduate. Consequently UMBC admitted 14 percent fewer applicants in 1987 than in 1977.[61] That change was reflected in rising SAT scores on the campus.

SAT scores are only one measure of the quality of a student body. Some institutions have even made SATs optional. But in an era when high school grade point averages have become even more difficult to compare, UMBC's consistent requirement of this national test shows the increase in the selective nature of the student body.

Figure O reflects the overall rise in SAT scores at UMBC. In 1972, the combined SAT scores of new freshman were 946 or 93 points below the national average and then in the next six years the scores plummeted almost 100 points. In 1989, UMBC freshmen first surpassed the national average for SAT scores, while more recent classes have substantially exceeded that norm.[62] By 2012, UMBC freshmen exceeded

60. Chapter III describes the development of campus housing policy and the building of dormitories at UMBC.

61. Stacey Colino, "The Great Admissions Competition," *Baltimore Sun*, May 8, 1988.

62. In 1995, UMBC SAT scores rose to become even with UMCP's, but then the flagship campus allocated a few more dollars to merit scholarships and pulled away in subsequent years. David Folkenflik, "UMBC ties College Park in freshman SAT scores," *Baltimore Sun*, February 21, 1995.

Figure N
UMBC Resident and Commuter Students, 1987–2012

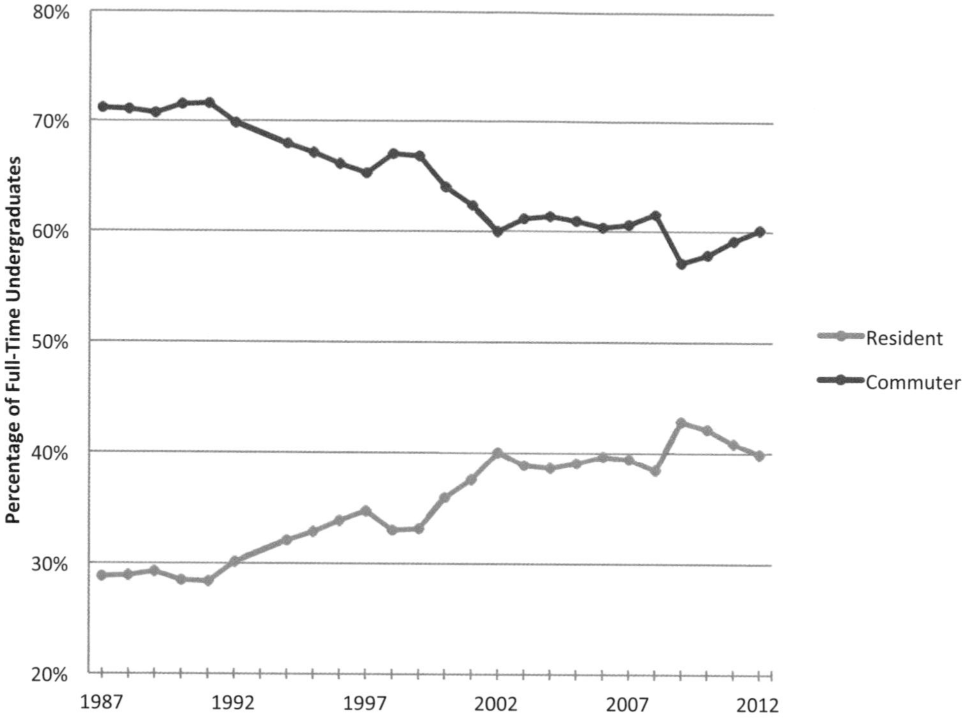

Source: UMBC Office of Institutional Research databook. 2012.

the national SAT average on the verbal section by 100 points and on the mathematical section by 112 points. The ten year running average for both sections was a combined 1200 plus or more than 200 points above the national norm.

There are many reasons for the growing academic strength of UMBC students. Figure P shows that applications have tripled from 1977 to 2012, while the size of the freshman class has increased 19 per cent. A decade after its founding, UMBC was virtually an open admissions university, admitting almost 90 per cent of its undergraduate applicants. Now it admits about 60 percent (a rate stable for the last ten years) which is still a high number for a competitive campus. Unlike some other institutions, UMBC does not encourage large numbers of applications to create rejection rates that enhance reputations for selectivity.[63] Rejecting large numbers of Marylanders who wish to attend their state university is not a winning political strategy.

The other important statistic is the steady decline in the percentage of accepted students who actually enroll (the yield rate). In 1977, if UMBC said "yes," about 70 percent of those admitted applicants later enrolled. By 2012, only 30.4 percent sent

63. Eric Hoover, "Application Inflation," *Chronicle of Higher Education*, November 12, 2010. 1.

Figure O
UMBC and National SAT Scores

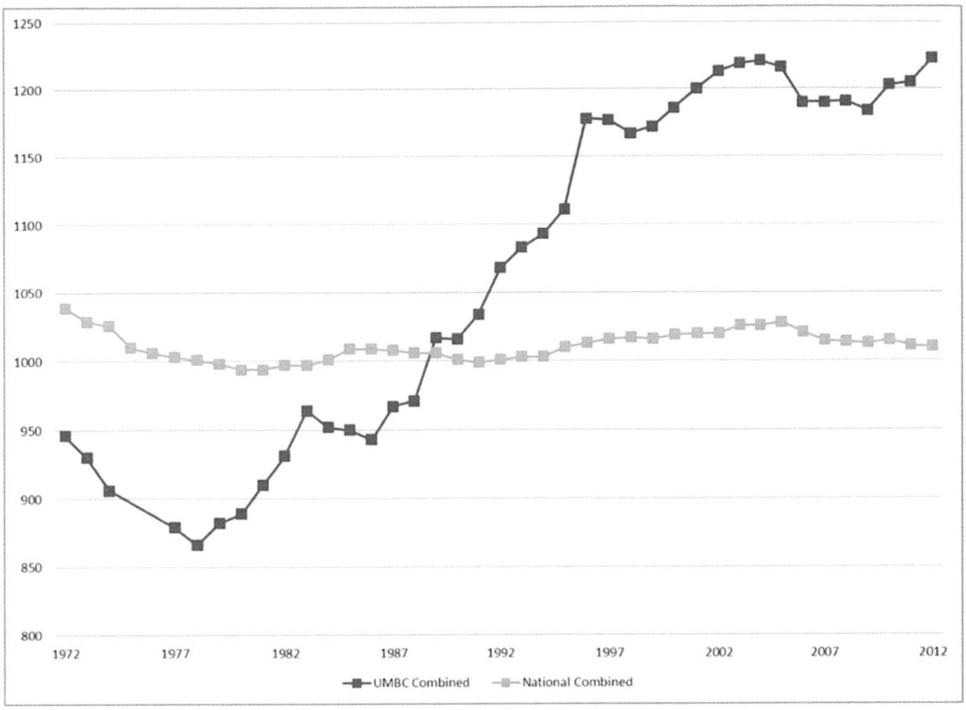

Source: UMBC Office of Institutional Research databook. 2012.

in their enrollment deposits and showed up at the beginning of classes. There are several reasons for this trend. Nationally, high school seniors are applying to many more colleges than before in order to increase their chances because admission has become more competitive at selective institutions. Further, multiple acceptances may increase the probability of bargaining for a favorable financial aid package. As students considering UMBC increasingly have better high school records, higher SAT scores, and more interest in a residential campus, they also expand the geographical scope of their search, so the chances of actually enrolling them decreases.

Why then did the quality of UMBC freshmen rise so significantly? There are three plausible hypotheses. First, the academic rigor of the University, called after 1996 the Honors University in Maryland, began to be recognized at least in-state, particularly in Montgomery and Howard County. Second, UMBC became substantially more residential and more attractive to students who wanted a more traditional campus experience. Third, UMBC established a network of very competitive merit scholarship programs that attracted substantial numbers of the best and brightest students. UMBC, like most universities, has long awarded financial aid to some students with strong academic credentials, but in the early years these awards had no particular name or cachet. Now several of its named scholarship programs are widely known and sought after.

Figure P
UMBC Undergraduates Applicants Accepted, Enrolled

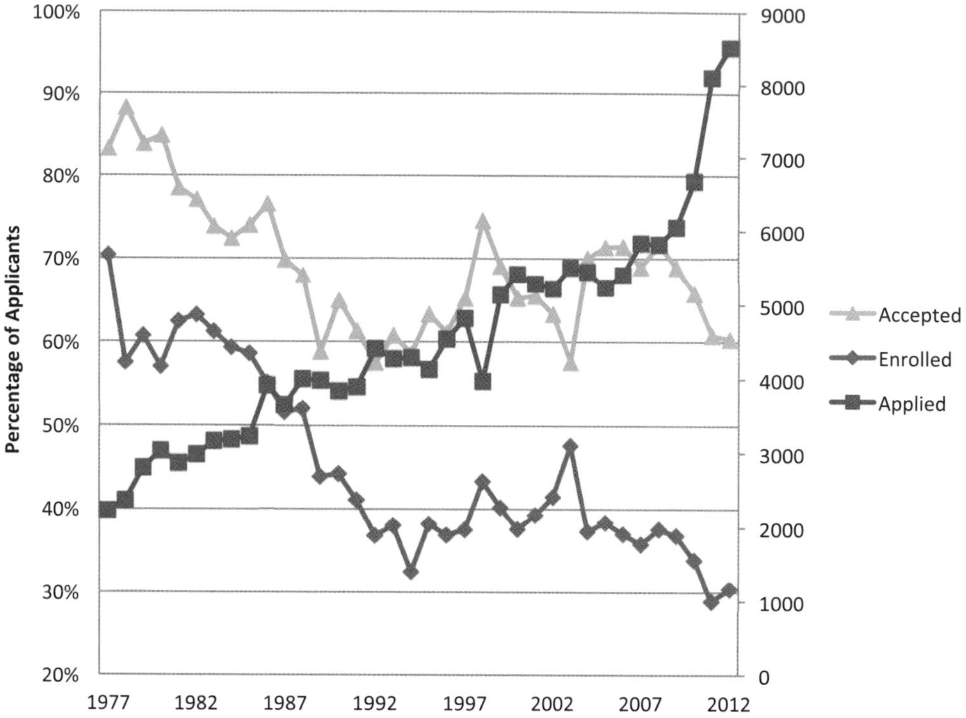

Source: UMBC Office of Institutional Research databook. 2012.

D. UMBC Merit Scholarships and Fellowships

Meyerhoff Scholarship Program

The most famous of these scholarships is the Meyerhoff, which has developed a national reputation.[64] The origin of the Meyerhoff Scholars is most unusual. Robert and Jane Meyerhoff were the victim of a mugging which unfortunately is not an uncommon occurrence in downtown Baltimore. What happened next, however, was quite unpredictable. The Meyerhoff family had already established a reputation in the City as a major source of philanthropy, funding among other things the symphony hall that bears their name. They also, more quietly, were supporting some of their African-American employees in obtaining educations at UMCP, and so were determined to turn this assault into something positive.

64. Joye Mercer, "Guiding Black Prodigies: U. of Maryland scholarships help me succeed in science and engineering," *The Chronicle of Higher Education*, June 22, 1994; The Today Show August 12, 2002; Brent Staples, "Why American College Students Hate Science," *The New York Times*, May 25, 2006; and National Public Radio, "Need to Know," February 21, 2011.

Robert Meyerhoff contacted Freeman Hrabowski, then the newly appointed UMBC Vice-Provost, and together they explored how a major gift to the University might benefit African-American males. (See photo.) Hrabowski, a mathematician, had long been concerned about the paucity of blacks in the fields of sciences, technology, engineering and mathematics, thus depriving the nation of their talent and young African-Americans of well-educated role models.[65] So in 1988 with a grant of $522,000[66] from the Robert and Jane Meyerhoff Foundation, the Meyerhoff Scholars program was created to provide funding and extensive mentoring for black males who wanted to earn doctorates in the STEM fields.[67]

Originally, the goal was to award ten Meyerhoff scholarships, but as Hrabowski searched the state for African-American male talent, he found twenty-six young men who met the high Meyerhoff standards.[68] UMBC found money to double the size of the original goal.[69] It was quite unlike any other existing programs and not at all a certain bet for success, but then Freeman Hrabowski was quite unlike any other college administrator. In a few short years, UMBC emerged from a fairly troubled racial history to become a competitor for the best black college students in the country, and Hrabowski became a familiar name in higher education circles.[70]

---

65. Hrabowski chaired a National Academy of Sciences report, "Expanding Underrepresented Minority Participation: America's Science and Technology Talent at the Crossroads," (Washington, D.C. The National Academies Press, 2010).

66. Since that initial gift, the Meyerhoffs have made even more substantial contributions. The Program also has received support from six federal agencies, the state of Maryland, and a wide array of corporations and foundations.

67. The special problems facing black males in higher education have been a continuing national concern. See Peter Schmidt, "Colleges Seek Key to Success of Black Men in Classroom," *The Chronicle of Higher Education,* October 10, 2008. The Meyerhoff program is cited as an exemplary program in this article. Hrabowski was also committed to improving the college-going pipeline for disadvantaged students interested in science. After a proposal by Governor William Donald Schaefer to create a Math and Science Academy was defeated in the State Senate, his office and UMBC worked to create a summer residential program for forty-five Eleventh and Twelfth grade students on the Catonsville campus. The plan had not been approved by the Regents or more importantly by Senate President Thomas V. Mike Miller who was annoyed to be surprised at the proposal. He said other institutions should have input into the plan and that "Politics should be divorced from higher education as much as possible." Patricia Meisol, "Math-Science academy resurfaces as UMBC plan," *Baltimore Sun,* June 11, 1989.

68. For an early view of the creation of the Meyerhoff Scholars program see, Marcia Hope Ames, "The Meyerhoff Scholars: Names You'll Hear in Maryland's Future," *UMBC Review,* 9, no.2 (Fall 1990). Hrabowski commented, "Some minority students need special support because the environment is predominately white. Even though they are accustomed to doing well in this kind of environment, it is very easy to feel somewhat isolated." 3.

69. Garland Thompson, "Why Hrabowski Chuckles," *Baltimore Sun,* June 1, 1989.

70. An AP report trumpeted, "Md.-Baltimore County winning top students." The wire service told the story of a 16-year-old honors student, Chris Goodwin, from Fort Davis, Alabama who was on his way to MIT, until he heard about the Meyerhoff program. Chris' mother, reflected, "I like the idea of him growing up among strong people who look after him and care for him, teaching him how to be a black male with a positive image in addition to an education." Hrabowski was quoted in the piece that Meyerhoff scholars "are in the top 1 percent of black students nationwide," *Salisbury Times,* September 12, 1990.

Over the years, the program has evolved and expanded. Since Maryland has an equal rights provision in its state constitution, in 1990 the scholarships were opened to African-American women. In 1996, after the Fourth Circuit Court of Appeals found the University of Maryland, College Park's all-black Benjamin Banneker Scholarship Program to be a violation of the Fourteenth Amendment Equal Protection clause,[71] UMBC opened the Meyerhoff Program to students of any race[72] who "are committed to increasing the representation of minorities in science and engineering."[73]

The program has expanded in size as well. Annually about 1,900 students are nominated for the Scholarship by high school teachers and guidance counselors. About 100 students are offered the award and roughly half accept UMBC's offer, a very high percentage given the glittering alternatives these candidates have available. In 2012, there were 268 Meyerhoff Scholars on campus. In that year the alumni of the program numbered 70 Ph.D.s, 25 M.D/Ph.D.s, 80 M.D.s and 85 other graduate degrees, while another 300 still were in graduate and professional degree programs.[74] A National Academy of Sciences report found that UMBC was a national leader in preparing underrepresented minorities in sciences and engineering. Among predominately white institution, UMBC was the top university in preparing African-American undergraduates in those fields.[75]

Beyond these statistics are the remarkable stories of the Meyerhoff Scholars who are now doing brilliant work in so many areas of American society. In one case, the venue was the Johns Hopkins Cardiology Care Unit and the patient was Jane Meyerhoff herself. She needed major heart surgery and one of the attending physicians was Andrew Atiemo, a Ghanaian immigrant, who after graduating from UMBC went

---

71. *Podberesky v. Kirwan*, 38 F. 3d 147 (1994). "Black scholarship case stirs review, *Capital*, June 19, 1995.

72. Some criticized this UMBC decision as diluting the original purpose of the program, but Janet Rutledge, Graduate Dean and Vice Provost, took the position that broadening the program "turned out to be wonderful thing—because what we are getting is students from across the spectrum who have a full understanding of the importance of diversifying the science work force." As quoted in David Glenn, "What Universities Can Do to Graduate More Minority Ph.D.'s" *The Chronicle of Higher Education*, December 4, 2008. See also, Scott A. Bass, Janet C. Rutledge, Elizabeth B. Douglass and Wendy Y. Carter, "The University as Mentor: Lessons Learned from UMBC Inclusiveness Initiatives" (Washington, D.C: Council of Graduates Schools, 2007).

73. About half of the Meyerhoff Scholars are now African-American. There is also a graduate version begun in 2002 of the Meyerhoff Program at UMBC financed by National Institute of General Medical Science open to U.S. students and permanent residents interested in the advancement of underrepresented groups (i.e. African-Americans, Hispanics, and Native Americans) in the biomedical and behavioral sciences. http://www.umbc/meyerhoff/graduateprograms historystatistics.html.

74. Harvard Graduate School of Education, "Institutional Advancement and Strategic Planning at the University of Maryland Baltimore County," November 2, 2010. 3.

75. National Academy Report, "Expanding Underrepresented Minority Participation." 166. From 2005–2009, 48 African-Americans who earned UMBC bachelor's degrees went on to earn doctorates in science and engineering. Daniel de Vise, "UMBC's quiet revolution in teaching science is earning school extra credit," Washington *Post*, March 20, 2012.

on to Harvard Medical School. When it came time for Robert to sign a permission form for a complex cardiac assessment procedure for his wife of nearly fifty years, Atiemo told him that he would be "honored to participate in your wife's care in any way I can, because you have done so much for me and many others." When Meyerhoff realized that Atiemo was also a Meyerhoff Scholar, Robert reflected, "It was just wonderful, the idea that it came home, that it would come back to us like that."[76]

There are three keys to the Program's success.[77] These are, first, a careful philosophy; second, an array of well-coordinated program of services; and third, Freeman Hrabowski.

The underlying theory of the Program is that, with hard work and support, students from groups that have not traditionally been successful in the STEM disciplines can meet the highest achievement standards.[78] When young students have frequent interaction with Meyerhoff alumni who have excelled at the most distinguished graduate schools and now have successful careers, and with the University president who himself personally exemplifies all the Program's values, it is easy to believe in success. Failure rarely occurs, and students who receive only a C in a course must repeat it.

The Meyerhoff program provides financial aid, full tuition and fees, as well as $1000 annually for expenses such as books, paid summer internships, and some extracurricular travel. That kind of financial support for these prized students would often be available elsewhere. But there are also comprehensive support services from the moment the Scholars arrive on the campus in the summer to attend a Bridge Program specifically designed to prepare them for college life. They also develop a strong team spirit, including a lot of group studying and other activities, individual tutors, and a welcome into the advanced laboratories of the University, government, and corporations.[79]

Hrabowski's passion for the Meyerhoff Program's purpose and his active role in seeking funding, recruiting new scholars, mentoring students, and taking the program's message to national audiences who are sometimes in awe of its achievements has been crucial.[80] The year after the Program's creation, he contacted nearly every

---

76. Joe Burris, "Bound by Generosity; For at least one Meyerhoff Scholar, a chance to return the favor." *Baltimore Sun*, November 2, 2005.

77. Freeman A. Hrabowski, III, Kenneth I. Maton, and Geoffrey L. Grief, *Beating the Odds: Raising the Academically Successful African American Males* (New York: Oxford University Press, 1998) and Freeman A. Hrabowski, III, Kenneth I. Maton, Monica L. Greene, and Geoffrey L. Grief, *Overcoming the Odds: Raising the Academically Successful African American Women* (New York: Oxford University Press, 2002).

78. For a description of the operation of the Meyerhoff Program see, *Beating the Odds*, 170–186.

79. Hrabowski and several Meyerhoff students were interviewed on CBS "*60 Minutes*," November 13, 2011. The summer program was described as a boot camp with no cellphones, no Facebook no headphones. See also, "Meyerhoff Scholars Nurturing Excellence in Science and Engineering," *Black Collegian*, October 1, 2007. Tyron Gadson, "Student Success: An Interview with Freeman Hrabowski," *Educational Policy Institute*, April 2010.

80. Brent Staples, "Preaching the Gospel of Academic Excellence," *New York Times*, June 5, 2000. This article is focused on the success of the Meyerhoff Program which National Science

high school principal in Maryland to find talent to compete for the Meyerhoff awards. He persuaded sixty to apply. Six years later, ten times that number applied and he has been an indefatigable recruiter ever since.

A question often asked is whether the Meyerhoff program has demonstrated anything other than that elite African-American students can perform well when carefully identified[81] or whether its particular leadership and program mix have made a difference in the quality of that performance. The question has been carefully evaluated. When a control group of students who were invited to be Meyerhoffs, but who declined and attended other institutions were compared with matriculated Meyerhoff students, both groups made similar grades and graduated at similar rates. The UMBC Scholars, however, were twice as likely to be awarded a science or engineering degree and were 5.3 times as likely to go to graduate schools. Meyerhoffs were about twice as likely to earn science and engineering degrees as Asian, Caucasian, and non-Meyerhoff African-American UMBC students with similar interests and preparation. Moreover, the Program seems to have increased dramatically the interest of UMBC underrepresented minorities generally in science and engineering majors, even though those students are not in the Program.[82] These results seem to substantiate the idea that the Program does not just concentrate on promising minority talent on one campus, but expands the pool and improves their chances of success, benefitting the whole society.

In 1996, UMBC received the Presidential Award for Excellence in Science, Mathematics and Engineering Mentoring from President Bill Clinton.[83] As the *New York Times* said about UMBC's performance in science education generally, but with a particular emphasis on the Meyerhoff program:

> The University of Maryland Baltimore County opened for business in a former cow pasture not far from downtown just 40 years ago. Still in its infancy as universities go, U.M.B.C. *(sic)* is less well-known than Maryland's venerable flagship campus at College Park or the blue-blooded giant Johns Hopkins. But the upstart campus in the pasture is rocking the house when it comes to the increasingly critical mission of turning American college students into scientists.[84]

While the Meyerhoff program is the largest and most visible of UMBC's academic scholarships, there are a number of other programs that fund promising students in

---

Foundation Director Rita Colwell hailed as a model that "needs to be replicated all over the United States."

81. Peter Schmidt concluded in the *Chronicle of Higher Education* that, "Unfortunately for other colleges, the Meyerhoff program's success depends largely on its ability to bring high achieving minority students together" and that there were not enough of those students to go around. June 1, 2007.

82. Michael Summers and Freeman A. Hrabowski III, "Preparing Minority Scientists and Engineers," *Science*. 311 (March 31, 2006).

83. http://www.umbc.edu/meyerhoff/program_history.html.

84. Staples, "Preaching the Gospel."

other curricular areas. UMBC views these programs as creating a cultural change on campus. Provost Elliot Hirschman and Freeman Hrabowski wrote in 2011:

> accomplishing our goals may require cultural changes within our institutions and the integration of these changes with our planning process. At the University of Maryland-Baltimore County, we view the culture of the institution as manifesting itself in every aspect of our daily life on the campus.[85]

CWIT and SITE Scholars

The CWIT/SITE scholars program, begun in 2002 and managed by The Center for Women & Information Technology (CWIT), is focused on increasing the numbers of women in information technology and engineering professions.[86] These scholarships, however, are open to men if they "support women's full involvement in information technology." In 2009, 28 percent of the CWIT and 39 percent of the SITE (Scholarships in Information Technology and Engineering) scholars were men. The program has proved to be a great academic success. Since its inception in 2002, the 86 CWIT Scholars have achieved a 3.5 GPA in a rigorous curriculum. Over 90 percent of the CWIT and SITE scholars have graduated or are still studying, and their list of internships, graduate school admissions, and job placements is very impressive.

Linehan Artist Scholars Program

Artistically inclined students can sometimes feel overwhelmed on a campus with such a strong STEM focus, so since 1995, the Linehan Scholars have been invited to join a community of artists composed of their peers and faculty. These four-year scholarships, supported by a gift from Earl and Darielle Linehan, are used to provide a window for talented high school students to experience all of the opportunities in the arts at UMBC. In their freshman year, the Scholars participate in a seminar to discuss contemporary art, participate in workshops, and collaborate with other artists. In the fall, they visit New York to see museums and attend performances, while in the spring, Washington, D.C. is the site of their exploration. The Linehan Scholars can also apply to live in the Visual and Performing Arts Living Community in Harbor Hall.[87]

---

85. "Meet Societal Challenges by Changing the Culture on Campus," *The Chronicle of Higher Education*, January 16, 2011.

86. Anam Salman, "CWIT: Changing the status quo in STEM fields," *The Retriever*. February 2, 2007.

87. http://www.umbc.edu//las/description. html. UMBC has several living learning communities (LLCs) designed to create clusters of otherwise diverse student who have common intellectual interests. The LLCs may take classes together, form study groups, participate in community service, plan on-campus events and take field trips. In addition to the Visual and Performing Arts Living Community, there are LLCs for Aspiring Teachers, Center for Women and Information Technology, Exploratory Majors, Honors College, Humanities Floor, Intercultural Living Exchange, Shriver Living Learning Center, Visual and Performing Arts and

Sondheim Public Affairs Scholars Program

This program, begun in 1999, is named after Walter Sondheim, Jr., businessman and a distinguished Baltimore civic leader.[88] For decades, he served his community by advising mayors and governors, by overseeing the desegregation of the Baltimore schools, and by his role in the development of the Inner Harbor. His statue now stands outside the UMBC social sciences building which was renamed the Janet and Walter Sondheim Hall. At its dedication, President Hrabowski said, "Walter Sondheim embodies the values that the UMBC community treasures most. He is a visionary leader who cares deeply about children, families, and education in Baltimore."[89] Sondheim Scholars, drawn broadly from the social science disciplines, focus on studying important urban problems though research, service learning, and internships. The goal is to create a new generation of leaders in the mold of their namesake.

Sherman STEM Teacher Education Scholars

The Sherman Teacher Education Scholars Program was created in 2006 with a grant from George and Betsy Sherman to address the shortage of highly qualified math and science teachers and to reduce the achievement gap that exists between low income families and others. UMBC's strengths in teacher preparation, experiential education, and leadership development and its curriculum in the STEM disciplines help to produce new teachers in high-needs schools, particularly in Baltimore City.

Humanities Scholars

The Humanities Scholars Program was begun in 1992, and is now administered by the Dresher Center for the Humanities which was dedicated in 2007. After a career in business, Jim Dresher and his wife Virginia created the Dresher Foundation in 1989. The Humanities Scholars program provides awards to students who want to study the "great thinkers of the past and present in the light of modern scientific discoveries, popular culture, and current social issues."[90] These scholars are not only active in exploring their local communities, but also participate in taking a required freshmen seminar and then study abroad for a semester.

Women Involved in Learning and Leadership. http://www.umbc.edu/bestcolleges/programs.html.

88. "At 94, still humble, still vital," *Baltimore Sun,* June 30, 2003.

89. Charles Rose, "For Sondheim and UMBC, Shared Values Set in Stone," *UMBC Insights Weekly*, May 2, 2005. The Sondheim Scholars program is supported by gifts from the France-Merrick Foundation, the Abell Foundation, the Jacob and Hilda Blaustein Foundation, and the Annie E. Casey Foundation, among others.

90. http://www.umbc.edu/dreshercenter/scholars_program.html.

Phi Beta Kappa

Founded in 1776 at the College of William and Mary, Phi Beta Kappa (PBK) is the most prestigious of the national honorary societies. UMBC was particularly eager to be awarded a chapter because the organization requires campuses where its chapters reside to have a strong liberal arts program. UMBC is sometimes stereotyped as being excellent only its STEM disciplines. Further, as the *Sun* once noted, "when [UMBC] added a logo to its welcoming sign designating itself 'an honors university,' some scoffed, viewing the title as a badge of self-importance."[91] A PBK chapter might redress both those images. UMBC first submitted PBK applications in 1979 and 1982. In addition to possibly being perceived as a bit of a brash move for a campus founded in 1966, PBK faulted UMBC's low SAT scores, as well as its lack of a firm foreign language requirement, and absence of an Honors Program. UMBC was not deterred, however. It corrected its deficiencies and under the leadership of Professor Jay Freyman, Ancient Studies, applied again in 1994. The new three-year-long review involved an application the size of two telephone books and numerous question and answer sessions and campus visits. This time, in the words of PBK executive director, Douglas Foard, UMBC passed with "flying colors [a]nd the society could not be more delighted."[92] When UMBC was awarded a chapter in 1998, only about a quarter of the other new wave universities had won that honor.[93]

Honors College

Although UMBC is a mid-size university, there was a need to create a special program for those talented students who might be seeking the experiences of a smaller liberal arts college. While an honors program had existed since 1981, the University in 1989 created a more selective and more focused Honors College "offering talented students a challenging and interdisciplinary academic program within the broader university."[94] The Honors College features small classes which bear the Honors designation and an Applied Learning Experience requirement which can be an approved research project, internship, study abroad, service or teaching activity. To build an

91. Melody Simmons, "UMBC begins a new chapter: Elite Honor society established at college after lengthy review," *Baltimore Sun*, May 26, 1998, 1.B.

92. Ibid.

93. Other UMBC campus-wide honorary societies include Phi Kappa Phi, Golden Key, National Society of Collegiate Scholars, Sigma Alpha Lambda, Tau Sigma, Omicron Delta Kappa. Departmentally based honoraries include Alpha Kappa Delta (Sociology), Gamma Theta Upsilon (Geography),Omicron Delta Epsilon (Economics), Phi Alpha (Social Work), Phi Alpha Theta (History), Pi Mu Epsilon (Mathematics), Pi Sigma Alpha (Political Science), Psi Chi (Psychology) Sigma Phi Omega (Gerontology and Aging Studies) Sigma Pi Sigma (Physics), Sigma Tau Delta (English), Tau Beta Pi (Engineering), and Upsilon Pi Epsilon (Computing Science). In addition, departments have councils of majors with elected officers.

94. Honors College homepage, http://www.umbc.edu/honors/.

esprit de corps, the 540 Honors students have lunches with faculty, work on service projects, and even have their own social event, the annual Mirror Ball.

E. Student Diversity and Organizations

While the quality of UMBC freshmen has risen sharply by conventional measures, keeping students in school until graduation has been a more difficult challenge. The average six year graduation rate for 1997–2002 entering classes has been 55.3 percent.[95] To a partial extent that figure reflects that some campus programs, such as nursing, are structured so that students must complete their degrees at the downtown professional school campus. UMBC's unusually small number of majors also forces some students to finish their degrees elsewhere. Nevertheless, the University has devoted considerable energy to improving graduation rates and there has been some success. By 2011, the six year the graduation rate has increased by eleven points to 66.8 percent.[96]

In one area, however, UMBC's graduation performance has been outstanding—the graduation of African-American students. Graduation success for black students has been a national problem. The national six-year graduation rate average is 43.3 percent for black students and 59.9 percent for white students. At other urban research institutions, the gaps are much worse. For example, at the University of Illinois at Chicago the gap was about 21 points with only 28.8 percent of black students graduating; at the University of Cincinnati, the gap was 24 points with only 31.3 percent of black students graduating; at Wayne State University, the gap was 34 points with only 9.5 percent of the black students graduating.[97] At Maryland's four HBCUs, in 2010 the six year graduation rates for all students were Bowie State, 39 percent; Coppin State, 16 percent; Morgan State, 32 percent; and the University of Maryland Eastern Shore, 32 percent. UMBC, however, graduated 59.4 percent of its African-American students entering between 1997–2002, along with 56.9 percent of its white students and 54.1 percent of its Asian students.[98]

---

95. Graduation rates can be calculated in several different ways. The statistics in this section are based on the percentage of full-time, first-time freshman who graduate from their original campus in six years. Many UMBC students who are transfers and commuters do not fit that model. If a more flexible definition is employed, the graduation percentages would rise for all campuses.

96. Freeman Hrabowski and Philip Rous, "Focusing our Resources for Results: Mid-Year Update on University Priorities," April 12, 2012. UMBC historic documents collection, Special Collections, University of Maryland, Baltimore County.

97. Kevin Kiley, "Wayne State's Graduation Gap Reflects Detroit Schools Struggles," *The Chronicle of Higher Education*, October 2010. A13.

98. "UMBC Progress Report on Institutional Programs of Cultural Diversity," February 26, 2010, and Childs Walker, "Towson and UMBC praised for minority success," *Baltimore Sun*, August 11, 2010.

Another UMBC characteristic is its unusual student diversity. That diversity would exist by almost any cultural measure, but as is common in higher education, counting is mostly done by race and ethnicity.

Figure Q displays UMBC's trends in racial and ethnic diversity. Of course, such diversity is now a primary objective in higher education,[99] but UMBC achieved it before it became *de rigueur*. In 1975, UMBC's undergraduate enrollment was 81 percent white, 17 percent African-American, about 1 percent combined for Asian-American, Hispanic, and Native American students, and less than 2 percent were foreign. By 2012, whites were about 50 percent, African-Americans 18 percent, Hispanics 6 percent, Native Americans, 0.22 percent and foreign students 5 percent. The dramatic growth was in Asian-American students who increased from 13 students or .24 percent in 1975 to 2194 students or 22 percent in 2012.

One of the earliest efforts to achieve student diversity was the creation of the Office for Minority Recruitment in 1971, headed by Reginald Lawrence. Using an affiliation with radio station WWIN, lectures by prominent African-American politicians and

Figure Q
UMBC Students by Race, Ethnicity and International Origins, 1975–2012

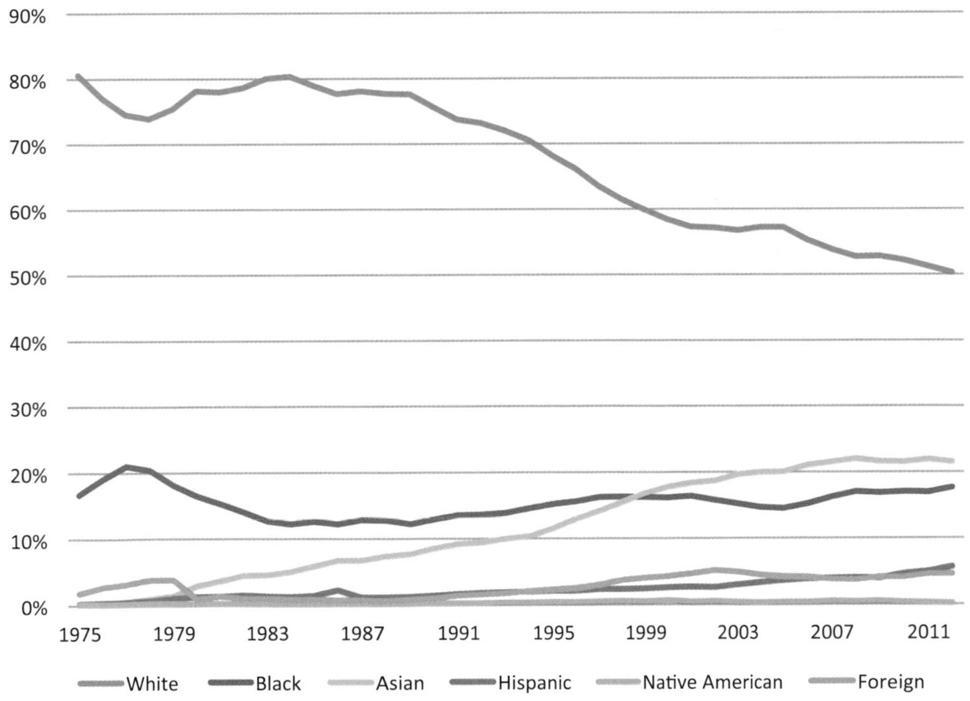

Source: UMBC Office of Institutional Research databook. 2012.

99. Peter Woods, *Diversity: The Invention of a Concept* (San Francisco: Encounter Books 2003).

educators, and scholarship funds, UMBC increased its minority enrollment from 7.5 percent to 10.6 percent in two years.

That tradition of diversity has continued and there are now more students from Asian origins than African backgrounds.[100] There never has been a distinctive recruiting or scholarship program at UMBC for Asian students. Having large numbers of Asian students is not unusual at competitive universities and students from varied Asian backgrounds are clearly attracted by the University's reputation, prominent faculty, and state-of the-art facilities, principally in science and technology. UMBC does not, however, stand for "U Must Be Chinese." The Asian students are themselves highly diverse, represented at UMBC in separate clubs for students from Bangladesh, China, Korean, Japan, Pakistan, Persia, Philippines, South Asia, Taiwan, and Vietnam.[101]

In 2009, UMBC ranked second in the country in racial and ethnic diversity among universities, according to data compiled by the Princeton Review.

Figure R
Most Diverse Universities

1. Baruch College, City University of New York
2. **University of Maryland Baltimore County**
3. Brooklyn College, City University of New York
4. University of Alabama at Birmingham
5. Temple University

Source: Princeton Review, The Best 368 Colleges-2009 edition.

This list suggests just how remarkable is UMBC's student demography. The other ranked campuses are largely non-residential in the center of large urban areas well served by public transportation. But UMBC is now a majority residential campus adjacent to largely white suburbs. Few students can walk to campus, and there are no subways or trains that directly serve it.

This diversity is also reflected in the composition of some of the University's degree programs. For example, the American Society for Biochemistry and Molecular Biology ranked UMBC 1st nationally in the total number of undergraduate chemistry and biochemistry degrees awarded to African-Americans, 4th in the award of such degrees to Asian-Americans, and 7th in overall undergraduate chemistry and biochemistry degrees.[102]

Why did this diversity occur? One reason is that UMBC was begun after the end of the segregation era that afflicted every other public campus in the state. Indeed,

100. The diversity issue was first seen in black and white terms. "Toward an Ethnic Balance at UMBC," *UMBC Now,* 1973. But see Figure Q which shows different trends.

101. Like all non-competitive campus clubs, these organizations are open to all UMBC students and some have members who are not ethnically affiliated, but just are interested in the cultures represented.

102. Annual survey 1998–99, For more recent surveys, see http://www.asbmb.org/asbmb/site.nsf/Sub/Graduation Survey?Opendocument.

UMBC is the only Maryland public campus that was never segregated. Attendance by African-American students is high at UMBC considering there are two historically black universities (Coppin and Morgan) a few miles away in Baltimore City. Certainly the presence of the Meyerhoff Program and President Hrabowski provided important role models. The growth in Asian students seemed to be caused by UMBC's reputation in the STEM disciplines.

Student organizations centered on specific racial and ethnic identities can sometimes have a downside on a campus. Scholars who have studied campus cultures have formulated two contending hypotheses about the impact of these organizations. The Ethnic Segregation hypothesis suggests that student membership in campus racial and ethnic organization enhances in-group identification and leads to increased perception of discrimination, ultimately causing more segregation. Conversely, the Peer Socialization hypothesis suggests that, while minority students may initially join ethnic student groups to increase their level of comfort by associating with others similar to their background, eventually such membership causes students to become more interested in cross-cultural experiences and encourages more use of campuses services.[103] In UMBC's first two decades, there were obvious racial tensions on the campus. Initially, the SGA was reluctant to recognize the Black Student Union officially or to provide it funding, fearing the organization would cause disunity and undermine the growing, but fragile, UMBC identity. Given the current campus diversity and the fact that UMBC will soon become a majority-minority community, it is worth asking how this demographic change has worked out.

In 2010, there were twenty-two racial and ethnic organizations on campus. Examination of their constitutions, their activities, and interviewing their leaders demonstrates that UMBC's diversity has few exclusionary characteristics. Instead the mosaic of their identities has culturally and intellectually enriched the campus. Several factors may contribute to that outcome. UMBC does not discriminate in admitting undergraduates and does not have segregated housing. Recognized student organizations must be open to all students,[104] and many see themselves more about sharing a culture than reflecting immutable characteristics. Events are planned to attract non-members. For example, the Pakistani Student Association (PakSA) Constitution includes the statement that "the diffusion of different cultures enriches all of our lives, and for this purpose, PakSA will attempt to provide a positive exposure to the lifestyles of the people of Pakistan."[105] Such intercultural exposures can have many positive benefits. After the 2010 Pakistani flood, the South Asian Student Organization, the Chinese Student Organization, and the Black Student Union part-

---

103. I am indebted here for a paper written by Amber Spry, UMBC political science major, titled "UMBC Ethnic Student Organizations: Impact on Diversity," January 2011, 4–5. UMBC historic documents collection, Special Collections, University of Maryland, Baltimore County.

104. Some persons have argued that this provision undermines diversity of opinion on the campus at large and student First Amendment rights, but the Supreme Court upheld open membership requirements in *Christian Legal Society v. Martinez*, 130 S.Ct. 2971 (2010).

105. Pakistani Student Association, Constitution. (2008).

nered with the PreMed Society, a traditional sorority (Delta Phi Epsilon), and a new multi-cultural fraternity (Sigma Beta Rho), to raise funds for the relief of victims.[106] Similarly, the Persian Student Association aims to eliminate "all kinds of prejudice by promoting cultural diversity at UMBC and the community at large," and it sponsors a splendid celebration of the Persian New Year and Winter Solstice open to all.[107] Though each group seeks to preserve or even "positively promote" a particular cultural identity on campus, they appear to be equally concerned with engaging the community outside the boundaries of ethnicity. The Japanese Culture Club (JCC) exists to "connect students interested in Japan with one another."[108] In 2010, its president, Mary Igoe, was white and she explained that the use of the term culture club was purposeful so that students from many backgrounds would be welcome. JCC members come together to practice language skills, to immerse themselves in Japanese culture, to find a support network among other Japanese students, and to eat sushi. In an event that might take place only on a campus, the Student Union of Arabs co-hosted with the Jewish Student Union a screening and discussion of the documentary, *Trembling Before G_D*, which is about Orthodox Jewish gays and lesbians trying to reconcile their sexual and religious identities.

Administrative leadership, for example, Nancy Young, Vice President for Student Affairs, and, of course, President Hrabowski encourage an inclusionary ethos. In response to the Princeton's Review's recognition of UMBC's unusual diversity, he declared: "It is a guiding principle at UMBC that living, studying and interacting with diverse groups strengthen us as people. We challenge our students to reach beyond their comfort zones and connect with others different from themselves."[109]

Another form of diversity is the percentage of students from out-of-state. In 1977, only 3 percent of UMBC undergraduate enrollment was from outside Maryland. While that percentage doubled to 6 percent by 2007, the University has made continuing efforts to increase U.S. geographical diversity. It has been a tough sell. Perhaps that is because a rising university's reputation lags beyond its current reality. Perhaps the County name is unhelpful with those from other states. Or perhaps the expensive out-of-state tuition rate compared to in-state tuitions at competitor public universities in potential feeder states is a cause.[110]

106. Yasmin Radbod, "UMBC Pakistan relief efforts are making progress." *The Retriever*, September 20, 2010.

107. Persian Student Association, Constitution (2007).

108. Japanese Culture Club, Constitution (2009).

109. *UMBC Watch: UMBC named one of nation's most diverse universities.* August 8, 2008, Retrieved from http://www.umbc.edu/NewsEvents/Watch/08-08-08.html.

110. As President Hrabowski pointed out in response to a question from a legislative analyst UMBC had to increase its out-of state tuition and fees by 33 percent between FY 2003 and FY 2007. As a consequence, a New York resident would have to pay $26, 300 in tuition and fees to attend UMBC as compared to $11,600 at SUNY-Binghamton. Freeman Hrabowski, III. "2008 Legislative Testimony."15. UMBC historic documents collection, Special Collections, University of Maryland, Baltimore County. See also the President's response to this issue in his 2009 legislative testimony. 17–18.

On the other hand, UMBC has been very successful in attracting international students. Over 100 countries are represented in the student body; and particularly at commencement ceremonies for the graduate school, listening to the names of the students crossing the stage is like hearing a roll call at the United Nations.

Race and ethnicity are only two measures of campus diversity, and maybe not the most important ones intellectually, though politically that is what is always counted. Another way to examine diversity at UMBC is to highlight the extraordinary roster of recognized student organizations on the campus, other than those identified by race and ethnicity. In 2010, there were 25 academic clubs connected to departments, 11 related to arts and performances, 12 career and professional, 5 governance, 15 graduate organizations, 25 Greek fraternities and sororities, 20 hobby, 7 honor societies, 6 intellectual sports, 5 media, 4 political, 23 religious or spiritual, 24 service, and 27 sports and recreation clubs. These clubs rarely receive much off-campus attention, but they are important manifestations of diversity and participation for many students. There are some exceptions, however, where clubs have received considerable external recognition.

UMBC Chess

The most famous and, for a brief period the most notorious, of UMBC student clubs is the chess club.[111] Consistent national and even international champions, UMBC chess success fit the image of a new university more interested in intellectual pursuits than fraternities and football.[112] How big time chess came to UMBC is an intriguing tale spread across several continents.[113]

---

111. UMBC has also excelled on other "intellectual sports." In 2009, the UMBC Society of Automotive Engineers Mini Baja team ranked 7th out of 100 teams in the Baja East race. Timeline-History of UMBC. http://lib.guides.umbc.edu/content.php?pid=417297&sid=3411009.

UMBC also has had strong debate teams, mock trial protagonists, Ethics Bowl competitors, and Model United Nations (MUN) participants. The latter program began in 1994 and been led by Cynthia Hody of Political Science. The MUN teams have been ethnically and discipline-diverse. Over the years UMBC MUN has represented Poland, Austria, Ukraine, Israel, Egypt, Mongolia, Sweden, Angola, Democratic Republic of the Congo, Sudan, Japan, United Kingdom, Liberia, Luxembourg, China, Cameroon, Jamaica, Pakistan, Antigua, Uzbekistan, Solomon Islands, Germany, France and Lebanon. Cynthia Hody, "A Brief History if UMBC's Model UN Chapter." UMBC historic documents collection, Special Collections, University of Maryland, Baltimore County.

112. Chess has also contributed to a certain mythology about UMBC. A *Washington Post* writer concluded a piece about teaching and minorities at UMBC by stating, "Hrabowski, protective of the school's intellectual image, has famously rejected fielding a football team. Instead, UMBC has won several national championships in chess. And school cheerleaders perform at the tournaments," Daniel de Vise "New science class formula brings UMBC extra credit," March 21, 2012. In fact, football was first rejected by the faculty in the Albin Kuhn era and has never seriously been considered since then. UMBC cheerleaders, dancers, and pep band mostly perform at basketball games.

113. This section is heavily dependent on a thirteen-page history titled "The Story of Chess at UMBC 1990–1997," written by the team's long time faculty advisor, Professor of Computer

Prior to 1990, chess was a fairly well organized activity at UMBC, but not exceptional compared to other universities that took the game seriously. Several faculty, including John Bell (Mathematics and Statistics), Slobodan Petrovich (Psychology), and Alan Sherman (Computer Sciences/Electrical Engineering)), were serious players and there were several on-campus matches with students. When UMBC first entered international competition in the 1990 Pan-American (Pan-Am) tournament at Harvard, the underfinanced team was driven to Cambridge by a player's father and finished 26th out of 27 teams.

In the spring of 1991, Sherman accepted the position of faculty advisor to the chess club, and his energy and ambition changed everything. He recalled: "Eventually, I realized I was the right person, at the right place, at the right time, to make some significant contributions to college chess, while helping students, the community, and UMBC along the way."[114] Like all coaches, Sherman knew the first step in building a strong team was recruiting. He began by examining applicants to the UMBC computer science program and contacting those who mentioned a chess background. That effort yielded former Sri Lankan chess champion Ishan Weerakoon and a Senior Master Craig Jones. Soon UMBC had assembled a team of five players and appealed to Freeman Hrabrowski for funding to send the team to Florida to play in the Pan-Am games. Since the President was himself a mathematician and more significantly a tireless promoter of UMBC, it was not a hard sell. UMBC made its mark in the tournament tying for third place.

The Pan-Am success only whetted Sherman's and UMBC's chess ambition. In 1994, Sherman convinced Bella Belegradek from Moscow to enter the computer science Ph.D. program, while building a local pipeline to the best young players in Philadelphia. He also discovered Chess Master Igor Epshteyn, former coach of international teams from Belorussia, then living in New Carrollton, who agreed to coach the University chess team. This created the chess infrastructure on the campus and the framework for recruiting even stronger players. A "Man vs. Machine" (computer) competition was instituted. UMBC began to host the Maryland Scholastic Chess Championship, bringing 250 students to the campus and offering a four-year tuition scholarship to the winner. Sherman sent direct mail to the top 100 finishers in the National Scholastic Championships and took out an ad in *Chess Life* extolling the academic program on campus and, of course, the chess team.

All these activities were within the range of normal, if chess recruiting had such a range. Then UMBC Chess began to stretch the envelope. Sherman made contact with William "The Exterminator" Morrison, who frequented New York's Washington Square Park, playing for money. Sherman found Morrison intelligent, charismatic, and without a college degree. A scholarship was offered and accepted. Later that year, Sherman received a call from Israeli Grandmaster Ilya J. Smirin, ranked 28th in the

Science, Alan Sherman. http://www.umbc.edu/studentlife/orgs/chess/storyof. Sherman describes this story as one of "serendipity, determination, organization, recruiting, coaching, coordination, vision, perseverance, teamwork and good fortune."

114. Ibid., 3.

world, who was willing to come to UMBC to study computer science. There were problems of tuition money and immigration status,[115] but these were overcome and UMBC had its Grandmaster. After arriving on campus, Smirin once played a simultaneous exhibition against the six finalists in the UMBC chess championship and never lost a game, while mostly concentrating on reading a book about his idol, Al Pacino.

While recruiting luminaries to compete in international tournaments, UMBC was also developing the game in the region and the United States. The Chess team worked to create the Intellectual Sports Council of various campus groups engaged in those kinds of competitive performances, a 500-volume collection on the game in the AOK library, a summer chess camp for Baltimore area youth, various competitions and exhibitions, an online Master Preparation Chess course, and a barrage of publicity about chess in newspapers.[116]

As in other sports, recruiting is never ending. Oxana Tarassova and Gregory Shahade (1996 National High School Co-Champions) accepted UMBC awards for chess prowess. Hrabowski told Sherman that the goal was to win the 1996 Pan-American tournament. Since Smirin had decided to return to Israel, after finding that being a student and an international professional chess player were not compatible goals, Sherman set his sights on identical twin brothers, Valery and Dmitry Atlas from Belorussia. They were good students and received graduate assistantships.

As UMBC Chess entered the 1996–97 season, it scheduled a fall match against Harvard, five time Pan-Am champions in the AOK Library Seventh Floor. Marching in with their newly acquired chess team jackets, the Retrievers vanquished the Crimson 5–1 and garnered a *Baltimore Sun* headline, "Harvard outclassed by tough UMBC chess team." Ahead was the major goal, the Pan-Am tournament, hosted by UMBC at the Baltimore Harbor Renaissance Hotel. With sponsorship by Southwest Airlines, Uptronics, and Pizza Hut, the tournament was a major success, though with an unusual climax. At the end of the competition, UMBC team A was tied with UMBC team B for the leader position and in the playoff match team A won. UMBC chess was not only strong, but had a deep bench. That led to an unparalleled streak of victories in national and international competition. UMBC won the Pan-American Intercollegiate Championship in 1998 and 1999, then tied for first place in 2000–01, before winning again in 2002. The *Sun's* headline gushed, "Maryland's No.1 team; UMBC chess: School's honors reputation rises even higher with another championship" The story continued:

> The Terps didn't culminate their dream football season with an Orange Bowl victory. But the state — the Baltimore area in particular — still has reason to

115. To be eligible for a UMBC chess scholarship, Smirin would have to be a permanent resident of the United States. Sherman studied immigration policy and wrote what he described as a lengthy, well-documented petition arguing that Smirin should be granted immediate permanent status because of extraordinary chess ability. Ibid., 6.

116. For example, Dan Fesperman, "Putting the Pieces together; Teamwork: Chess aces from as far away as Kazakstan and Belarus are being recruited with scholarships to a world class organization — at UMBC," *Baltimore Sun*, December 8, 1996.

> celebrate a collegiate championship.... In recent years, UMBC has pounded the Ivy Leaguers and other schools in this game of brains, not brawn.... It all adds up to amazing success on the chessboard, which solidifies UMBC's reputation as an honor's university.[117]

Then in 2003, the accolades turned sour. The *Sun's* new headline read, "UMBC chess star remains in Ala. jail on sex counts; Former med student 32 was on full scholarship."[118] The story went on to say, "The case brought new attention to the UMBC chess team which [Alex Sherzer] led to its first ever victory in the national collegiate chess championship last month." Sherzer, a Grandmaster, had completed a medical degree in Hungary, but enrolled at UMBC to obtain a bachelor's in emergency health services. After winning the best player award at the Pan-Am tournament, Alan (aka The Surgeon) Sherzer left the campus before the end of the spring semester to take up a medical internship in Louisiana, before he was arrested on charges that he had solicited a fifteen year old girl in a juvenile detention center for sex. UMBC insisted that Sherzer met the eligibility standards both academically and as a player. He was later acquitted of the charges against him because of police entrapment, but it was an uncomfortable moment for the University.

In the world of intercollegiate football and basketball, athletes leaving before graduation and getting into legal difficulties are not all that unusual. In the small world of intercollegiate chess, where there had been few, if any, eligibility regulations, there was an increasing feeling that the rules for competitors needed to be re-examined to eliminate overage vagabond players with no real commitment to earning a degree. In 2003, the U.S. Chess Federation approved a requirement that competitors must take at least two classes in the semester in which a tournament is held, maintain a 2.0 G.P.A. average, not play for longer than six years, and not be older than twenty-six.[119] UMBC has buttressed those standards by requiring a 3.0 and 100 hours of community service to hold a chess scholarship.[120]

UMBC's meteoric rise in the chess world was one of the motivations for these rule changes, so how would the UMBC chess fare in the new order? Just fine as it turned out. The Retrievers won the Pan-Ams in 2005 and 2009, while finishing second in

117. *Baltimore Sun* Editorial, January 4, 2002.

118. Alec MacGillis, *Baltimore Sun*, May 14, 2003.

119. Ann Zimmerman, "For Aging Knights of College Chess, Endgame is near" *The Wall Street Journal*, July 10, 2003 A. 1. "A growing number of collegiate chess players and advisors are looking to tighten the lax rules governing player eligibility, believing they've been rooked by competing college teams that buy their way to victory." Buying one's way to win is hardly unknown in the academic or athletic competition in American universities. Perhaps the problem was which universities had become new chess competitors. See Luke Mullins, "Rah! Rah! Block that Rook!," *The American Journal of the American Enterprise Institute*, November 9, 2007. "Small no-name colleges have become powerhouses in intercollegiate chess, trying to attract top quality applicants and alumni money."

120. For a general discussion of the world of chess scholarships and UMBC's place in it, see Dylan Loeb McClain, "Good Opening can be a Scholarship," *The New York Times*, December 27, 2006. Those holding chess scholarships are currently called Chess Fellows. Email from Alan Sherman to the author, November 6, 2013.

2004, 2007, 2008, and 2010 and third in 2006. UMBC also won the President's Cup in 2009 and 2010.[121] The *Sun* headlined: "UMBC chess takes its place as a dynasty." The story continued: "In basketball it's UCLA. In hockey, it's Michigan. In baseball, it's Southern Cal. And now in chess, the dynasty, the champion of champions is the University of Maryland, Baltimore County."[122]

There is nothing accidental about UMBC prominence as a chess power. Alan Sherman's own prowess as a player, his willingness to tirelessly recruit, raise money, and seek publicity for chess is central to the University's team rise. By challenging the murky recruiting rules that had existed in intercollegiate chess, he has, perhaps inadvertently, improved the game on a national basis. None of this could have occurred without the support of Freeman Hrabowski, who saw chess as a natural form of competition for the University he envisioned. In 1996, as UMBC chess was entering the national stage, he said: "Chess is, quite frankly, symbolic of the mind-set here which says nobody is more prestigious than people who do really well in intellectual pursuits."[123] That is the chess club's legacy.

Graduate Students

While recruiting a talented undergraduate student body was challenging for a new campus and took several decades, building graduate education was even more difficult. Because of its proximity to UM's downtown cluster of professional schools, UMBC could not launch any conventional professional programs, which might have given the campus more visibility as a place for post-baccalaureate degrees. There were also many other fine graduate programs in the Washington-Baltimore corridor. Gaining approval from state coordinating boards to create new graduate programs was always arduous. It often required UMBC departments to seek niche degrees, because some other nearby institution was offering more traditional programs.[124] Institutions with established research programs, a broad range of programs, and recognized prestige do better in recruiting students and winning research awards. UMBC, of course, had none of those advantages during its early years. Moreover, there is often little change in the institutional pecking order from decade to decade.[125]

---

121. Joe Burns, "At UMBC, Chess is King, with Queens and Bishops, They Rule the Final Four," *The Sun*, April 5, 2008. A.1. A chess pep rally was held as a prelude to the President's Cup Final Four complete with pep band, cheerleaders, dancers, mascots and six foot tall chess pieces.

122. Josh Mitchell, *Baltimore Sun*, December 31, 2005. At one point, Sherman had hoped that the chess club would become a club sport under the auspices of the Athletic Department, as it is in some eastern European and former Soviet countries. There was not much sympathy in the Department for that idea as chess became increasingly described in the press as UMBC's most successful sport's team.

123. Fesperman, "Putting the Pieces together," *Baltimore Sun*, December 8, 1996.

124. UMBC's first graduate program was in applied mathematics where the first Masters degree was awarded in 1973 and the first Ph.D. in 1976.

125. Graham and Diamond, *The Rise of the American Research University*, 2–3.

Most of all graduate education is expensive. Full-time graduate students require financial aid and doctoral students may need it for several years. New programs should, at least, be competitive in fellowships with established programs, but UMBC had little money for such purposes. That frequently meant UMBC faculty had to be successful in rigorous grant competition to acquire the funds to support their graduate students. Yet the stakes were great. If UMBC could not sustain credible graduate programs, its future as a research university was uncertain and, if it failed to produce research in a wide range of fields, the rationale that distinguished it from other local public institutions would be undermined. Despite these challenges, graduate education at UMBC has been a success and is now internationally recognized. From a base of 121 graduates students in 1974 in a just a handful of programs, by 2012 there were 2,684 graduate students studying in 47 programs.

Graduate education has some distinctive characteristics. Generally graduate education is a much more decentralized activity than undergraduate education. Admissions decisions are made by individual departments with only a limited review by the graduate school. Graduate students rarely take courses from other departments away from their home department.[126] Graduate students in Psychology do not associate often with their peers in Physics. Graduate students, though welcome, tend to be less well integrated into clubs, sports, and other extracurricular activities. All graduate students must face several high stakes exams and there is more uncertainty about how long it will take to get a degree than for undergraduates. Graduate students are also more dependent on the support, approval, and evaluation of a few or even a single advisor than are undergraduates.

At UMBC, part-time students have been a majority of the graduate school since 1976 and in most years have been about 60 percent of that total. Graduate study can be a lonely activity and many students do not persevere to earn degrees. These problems afflict graduate study generally, but UMBC has taken national leadership in trying to improve the situation, not only for underrepresented minorities and women, but for all students. In *The University as Mentor: Lessons Learned from UMBC Inclusiveness Initiatives*, published by the Council of Graduate Schools, Scott Bass, former Graduate Dean, and Janet Rutledge, current Graduate Dean, describe a number of campus programs to support graduate students and to increase graduation rates. Many of them are influenced by the success of the Meyerhoff program. Among the initiatives were involving more faculty in the recruiting process, creating better bonding between new students and faculty research priorities, providing extensive orientation for new graduate students, re-evaluating the mentoring process, improving record keeping about student progress and attrition, clarifying financial aid policies, creating periodic recognition ceremonies of progress, developing programs to engage students from underrepresented groups, strengthening graduate student organizations, and preparing professional development plans for post-degree careers. All of

126. There are two major interdisciplinary graduate programs at UMBC, Public Policy and Language, Literacy, and Culture.

these policies have come out of UMBC campus experiments. From 1999 to 2012, the number of UMBC Master's degrees awarded annually increased from 270 to 605 and the number of doctoral degrees from 55 to 72.

F. Alumni

The 1974 Barton-Gillet report suggested that UMBC "intensify its efforts to communicate with its rapidly growing alumni body and to win them to the habit of regular and increasing financial help to the institution."[127] Of course, that is the goal of almost every academic institution, but carrying it out at UMBC has been more difficult than for most. The first UMBC Alumni Association was not formed until 1979.[128] As a young campus, most of its alumni were focused on finding jobs, building careers, starting families, and buying houses. Furthermore, a survey taken in 1989 of 1980–1981 UMBC alumni found over two-thirds of them continued their education within six years of graduation.[129]

There was little discretionary money of any kind for these young alumni and UMBC might not have been high on their priority list anyway. Nor was there much in the way of class identifications as there are at some private institutions where most students live on campus and expect to graduate with their peers in four years as member of the class of 1978, 1979, etc. UMBC students took courses at the pace their wallets and off-campus jobs permitted and graduated whenever they could. Many of the earlier students were commuters and spent as much time in their cars as in campus buildings that were not classrooms. There wasn't much that was glamorous or prestigious about the UMBC campus or brand. There was no tradition of giving to what might have seemed to some like a sterile campus with little sign of philanthropy or a caring environment. Some alumni just merged their identities with the larger University of Maryland (how about those Terps?) and others just moved permanently beyond their college years with little further thought. On the other hand, some alumni retained strong UMBC identities and had begun distinguished careers.[130]

127. Barton-Gillett Report on UMBC Campus Communications and External Relations, September 30,1974. Box 35, Folder 10, President's Office records, Collection 50, Special Collections, University of Maryland, Baltimore County. 23.

It wasn't until eighteen years later that UMBC produced the first directory of its alumni. James Michael Brodie, "UMBC, directory coming of age." *Catonsville Times*, July 1, 1992. Barbara Quinn, Director of Alumni Affairs told the reporter, "We have worked under the illusion that we are a young university. But on your 25th anniversary, you start to look and see that you want to do more traditional things."

128. Timeline-History of UMBC. http://lib.guides.umbc.edu/content.php?pid=417297&sid=3411009.

129. UMBC Office of Institutional Research, "UMBC Long-Term Follow-Up Survey of Bachelor's Recipients: 1980–81 Alumni," June 1989. Over 80 percent of this sample still resided in Maryland.

130. For thumbnail sketches of twenty-seven of them, see "UMBC's Lasting Legacy: Our Alumni." *UMBC Magazine*, 1997.

It also takes money to raise money. Minds must be engaged and flesh must be touched before pocket books are opened. Successful alumni relations require regular communications, campus events, and off-campus meetings. All this costs money and on a perpetually cash-strapped campus that needed every dollar to meet the needs of its current students, there was little left over for alumni events. The alumni staff was caught in a Catch-22 situation. In order to get a share of the UMBC budget, they had to show they could raise alumni giving, but to increase giving they had to have an adequate budget. So not much happened. There were few alumni events or publications. Alumni had little role in governance or any other activity. Alumni were not really a part of the UMBC community despite the pretense to the contrary.

The University always knew it wanted to do better. Things began to change noticeably by 2003. In that year, UMBC purchased a fine looking brick house on Wilkens Avenue and the Alumni Office had a home. In 2008, the University hired Richard Byrne to produce the kind of glossy campus-focused magazine so common in higher education.[131]

The Alumni Office also began to tackle the long-term problem of creating a culture of giving on a campus where the bricks and mortar evidence of that tradition was largely lacking. Most UMBC buildings and their interior spaces do not reflect any private gifts. To encourage the development of a giving culture among current students, during the 2012 UMBC Homecoming Week, the Alumni Office posted signs on the main walkways of the campus that read:

- Alumni gave back more than $300,000 to UMBC this year.
- 63 percent of first time donors graduated in the last 10 years.
- 216 Faculty and Staff gave back to the UMBC community this year.
- 42 percent of UMBC Athletic Alumni gave back to their alma mater this year.
- Parents of current UMBC students gave $123,678 to the university this year.
- 518 donors made their first gift to UMBC this year.
- UMBC has 45 student Phonathon callers!
- Alumni and parent gifts built the Retriever Learning Center.
- You can name your own seat in the new Performing Arts and Humanities building theater!

It is a beginning, but whether a culture of giving back to UMBC financially will emerge, only the future will tell.

In the early days of the campus, many students had an ambiguous identity with UMBC. When one of the first UMBC basketball teams showed up to play at Mount St. Mary's College, they were greeted by a sign mocking them as "UMBC, University of Migratory Bird Catchers" (aka Retrievers). Long-time athletic director, Dr. Charles

---

131. The magazine has already won a number of regional and national awards for overall design and staff writing. Email from Richard Byrne to George La Noue, September 5, 2013.

Brown, remembers having to go to Chancellor Michael Hooker in 1989 to ask the campus book store to sell clothing with UMBC colors and logos, rather than reflecting its perceived local market with apparel from Notre Dame, Georgetown, and Maryland.[132] Those days are long gone. Athletes and non-athletes can be seen everywhere on the campus wearing black and gold with UMBC logos now. In 2012, the UMBC bookstore sold $435,000 in UMBC licensed clothing.[133]

---

132. Kevin Cowherd, "Retiring UMBC AD Brown has helped drive changes," *Baltimore Sun*, May 15, 2013.

133. Bob Somers, book store director, interview by the author, June 6, 2013.

CHAPTER IX

The Arts

Shorthand descriptions of UMBC usually focus on its prowess in science and technology, with an occasional nod to the social and policy sciences; though, in fact, the University has always had flourishing arts programs. By overcoming inferior spaces and meager financial resources, UMBC arts have survived, like determined saplings growing in rocky crevices, and sometimes thrived with considerable distinction. With the completion of the $153 million Performing Arts and Humanities Building in 2013–14, UMBC arts will enter a new era.[1] The history of their turbulent past, however, should be preserved.

UMBC has spent much of its existence in an era of steadily shrinking percentages of state contributions to public university budgets. Federal higher educational funding, however, has generally increased in this period. Chapter VI describes UMBC's achievements in competing for these funds. Federal funds, however, are disproportionately available for some university activities, but not others. In FY 2010, the $138 million budget for the National Endowment for the Humanities (NEH) was about 3 percent of the National Science Foundation's $5 billion budget and barely 0.5 percent of the National Institutes of Health's $31 billion budget. Much of the NEH budget goes to museums, historical societies, ethnic and cultural awareness programs, and teacher training.

The imbalance in federal and other public budgets means that arts' activities on college campuses are often underfunded. Yet, arts education is labor intensive, requiring hands-on training, and frequently dependent on expensive equipment such as musical instruments, theatrical sets and costumes, and sophisticated computers to create complex graphic manipulations. Some revenues can be generated from box office receipts, but UMBC has lacked venues to attract large crowds, creating a constant scramble for the resources to create quality performances reflecting the faculty and student talents on the campus.

In recounting the history of the arts at UMBC, it is important to remember that faculty sponsored activities are only a part of the picture. Student sponsored performances can also be significant. The acapella singing groups, the male "Mama's

1. In addition to housing classroom and performance spaces for three of the four arts departments (Visual Arts will remain in the Fine Arts building) PAHB will be home to the Departments of Ancient Studies, English, and Philosophy as well as the James T. and Virginia M. Dresher Center for the Humanities, the Dresher Humanities Scholars Program, and the Linehan Artist Scholars Program.

Boys," the female "The Stilettos" and the coed "Cleftomaniacs" are popular on campus and have achieved external reputations.

Most of the University's artistic efforts are focused in the theatre, music, dance, and visual arts departments. In UMBC's first years, artistic performances took place in a variety of settings, including the library, classrooms, auditoriums, and dormitories. In 1973, the Fine Arts building was completed. From an architectural and user perspective, this building is probably the least successful on the campus. Its performance and practice spaces are inadequate and its interior arrangements are not conducive to socialization by those interested in the arts. Overcoming space limitations, perceived uncertain administrative support, and external political opposition to a UMBC arts role have been persistent problems.

A. Theatre

Dim the house lights. Curtain Up! UMBC Theatre is playing at the Kennedy Center in Washington as an invitee of the American College Theatre Festival (ACTF) in 1974. And again in 1976, 1987, 1988, 1997, 2004 and 2011.[2] Figure S displays this amazing record.

Figure S
UMBC American College Theatre Festival Performances[3]

Year	Title	Director
1974	You're a Good Man Charlie Brown	Craig Montgomery
1976	Samuel Beckett plays	Xerxes Mehta
1987	The Importance of Being Oscar	Sam McCready
1988	Spring's Awakening	Sam McCready
1997	The Diary of a Scoundrel	Sam McCready
2004	Buried	Colette Searle
2011	Las Meninas	Eve Muson

Theatre's achievements have not relied on substantial facilities or fiscal support, but on amazing talent and energy. With meager budgets, UMBC theatre has created some magical performances. While Kennedy Center invitations are just one facet of a stunning record of success by national standards, what makes these performances even more remarkable is that for more than forty years UMBC theatre had to work

2. By 2011, the only other theatre program with more KCACTF appearances was Boston University. Richard Byrne, "Finding Their Light," *UMBC Magazine*, Summer 2011. 20–29.

3. http://www.umbc.edu/lasmeninas.

and perform in spaces that would shame an affluent high school. From 1999 to 2011, the UMBC theatre was housed in a building shared with various administrative services. Although located in the middle of the campus, the one-story building has all the charm of a small town bus station. Further, in 1993, the UMBC theatre department had to survive a near death encounter with the UM Regents.

Theatre was introduced to the campus when Alice Robinson was hired in 1967, fresh from earning a Stanford Ph.D. In her second semester at UMBC when she was the "whole theatre and speech department," she drafted students from her speech class and put on a comedy, *Scenes by Four Playwrights* in Lecture Hall I.[4] A few months later, she ambitiously directed James Thurber's *The Male Animal*, as well as designed UMBC's first set. Over the next three years, she had a hand in almost all UMBC theatre productions, including *Bus Stop* (1968) *Antigone* (1969), *Galileo* (1969), and *Spoon River Anthology* (1970).[5] In her 33-year UMBC career, she directed eleven productions. What made this ambitious introduction to theatre on campus so extraordinary was that originally student participation was just an extra-curricular activity. A student organization, the Sage players, anchored the program.[6]

In 1970, William (Bill) T. Brown brought his prodigious talents to UMBC as chair of a combined speech and theatre program. Brown had extensive theatre experience as a professor at Howard University and at the University of Ibadan, Nigeria. His mission was to hire new faculty, find a new facility to produce shows, and gain departmental status for the theatre program.[7] He was successful in the latter task in 1971. He also created a summer stock program for training students in every aspect of production, from stage design to props and costumes, and for two years, was able to raise scholarship money for his charges until funding ran out.

Over his twenty-seven-year UMBC career as director, set designer, and chair, he received credits for over fifty productions. In 1971, with Brown as set-designer and Will Hicks directing, the UMBC production of *The Lark* by Jean Anouilh was selected for regional competition by the American College Theatre Festival. Begun in 1969, this rigorous competition now involves about 600 theatre programs and 18,000 students from around the country. The ultimate goal is to be one of the five or six performances invited to the Kennedy Center in Washington. First, a production has to win one of eight regional competitions which the UMBC theatre program accomplished a mere four years after the first full plays were staged on campus. Three years

4. "If you want to be pioneers, come with us," *UMBC Magazine*, Summer 1997.

5. Terry Cobb has put together a UMBC Department of Theatre Production History, Timeline. http://userpages.umbc.edu/~cobb/p/1970s. which has been very helpful in writing this section. "UMBC at 40 Timeline," lib.guides.umbc.edu/umbctimelines.

6. "Sage Players Success With P.R.; Will Become First Campus Frat," *The Retriever*, February 10, 1969.

7. Bill Brown, interview by Nimit Bhatt, December 14, 2010. I am indebted to UMBC undergraduate Nimit Bhatt's research paper on the development of the campus Theatre and Music Departments for much of the material in this section. UMBC historic documents collection, Special Collections, University of Maryland, Baltimore County.

later in 1974, UMBC actors trod the stage of the 1160-seat Eisenhower Theater at the Kennedy Center for the production of *You're a Good Man Charlie Brown.* Suddenly, UMBC theatre was winning national publicity for the new campus. In the summer of 1976, UMBC hosted the New Theatre Festival, "a concentration of experimental [theatre] companies from around the country and the most well-known experimental theatre festival at the time."[8]

In 1976, Xerxes Mehta, who had been at New York University, accepted the chair's position in the Theatre Department. Although intrigued by the freedom of working at a new university, he remembered telling his wife who asked what the campus was like: "Well, I don't know because all I saw were freeways."[9] Mehta was innovative and ambitious. He and the faculty changed the curriculum from a fairly traditional department to one in which reading, researching, and writing about plays became viewed through the prism of performance. Most of all, he wanted to create an acting M.F.A, a terminal degree in the arts. He believed that having a corps of more seasoned graduate theatre majors would greatly benefit undergraduates just learning their craft. He was convinced that:

> There would not have been a M.F.A. program of comparable quality anywhere between New York and Atlanta if we had been allowed to do it. We had the faculty that could have done it extraordinarily well. We could have done it better than anyone else in the region given our faculty and students.[10]

In 1989, under the leadership of Bill Brown, then departmental chair, Theatre put forth a full proposal to create an M.F.A. in acting and was willing to offer it jointly with Towson State University.[11] Despite garnering support from local theatre companies, community colleges, and the Baltimore County Commission on Arts and Sciences, the UMBC proposal became quite controversial.[12]

The location of new graduate programs is not decided in Maryland solely by the quality of a faculty or by their external recognition. It is often a political decision. In 1992–1993, the Regents became fascinated by the idea that the solution to the problem of the multiplicity of public institutions in Baltimore was to give them each a distinctive programmatic specialty. UMBC was to be the STEM campus and Towson would be awarded the Arts franchise. That doomed UMBC's aspirations for a theatre M.F.A. After that divisive concept eventually collapsed, a decade later in 2002 UMBC was awarded an important consolation prize, the only B.F.A. program in the state.

Wendy Salkind came to UMBC from California in 1979, and has stayed for more than thirty years. In addition to her acting and directing talents, she served as De-

8. Xerxes Mehta, interview by Nimit Bhatt, December 15, 2010.

9. Ibid.

10. Ibid.

11. Memorandum from William T. Brown, Chairman UMBC Theatre Department to Gertrude Eaton, Associate Vice President for Academic Affairs, USM, August 30, 1989. UMBC historic documents collection, Special Collections, University of Maryland, Baltimore County.

12. "Letters of Support," Appendix A to the UMBC M.F.A. proposal. UMBC historic documents collection, Special Collections, University of Maryland, Baltimore County.

partmental chair for twelve years, faculty chair of the new Performing Arts and Humanities Building planning committee, and was awarded the Presidential Teaching Professor from 2010–2013.

In 1984, a year after he immigrated to the United States, Sam McCready, Irish actor, teacher, director, and writer joined the Theatre Department. He directed three Kennedy Center selection performances, *The Importance of Being Oscar*, (1986), *Spring's Awakening*, (1987) (see photo) and *The Diary of a Scoundrel* (1996) and delighted campus and Baltimore audiences with his versatile acting skills.[13]

Elena Zlotescu came to UMBC also in 1984 from the National Theatre in Bucharest, Romania where she had won awards for costume and set design. In her UMBC career, spanning more than twenty years, she had dressed up or down actors in over 110 performances.

While this stellar cast was being put in place, the narrative on campus was dominated by the continuing frustration of this ambitious and talented faculty, on the edge of true national prominence, with the lack of institutional resources to support them.

One low-budget UMBC theatrical innovation was Shakespeare on Wheels, a concept based on an earlier Rockefeller-funded Nigerian experiment that Bill Brown had directed. Every summer for a decade, the Bard was presented on a forty-foot flatbed trailer which could be moved from public parks to other locations in the Baltimore and Washington region to delight audiences, sometimes in the thousands, and to create wonderful growth opportunities for UMBC actors.[14] Then, in 1995, UMBC decided it could no longer subsidize these performances.[15] That administrative action created some bitterness among those such as Brown and McCready who had put so much effort into building the summer tradition. In its ten-year history, the program had appeared at the Kennedy Center and had won awards from the Council for the Advancement and Support of Education and the Maryland Association of Higher Education.[16]

The most significant problem faced by the Department was the lack of a suitable on-campus venue for performing.[17] The Fine Arts building had a 450-seat lecture hall, but the seating was on a flat plane. The "stage" was an acceptable 14-foot by 20-foot teaching size, but unsuitable for complex performances. When the opera, *Marriage of Figaro*, was performed in the recital hall, with singers on stage, there was not

---

13. Eleanor Lewis, "Sam McCready to Retire from UMBC," *Insights*, 15, no.7 (April 2001), 2.

14. Ron Engle, Felicia Hardison Londre and Daniel J. Watermeier, eds., *Shakespeare Companies and Festivals: An International Guide* (Westport, CT: Greenwood Press, 1995). 171–4. Zoe Ingalls, "From Parks to Prisons, Traveling Theater Brings Shakespeare to the People," *Chronicle of Higher Education*, September 11, 1991. B5.

15. "Travels with the Bard Come to an End," *UMBC Magazine*, Spring 1996.

16. Ibid. Ironically at about the same time the 1000 member Shakespeare Association of America moved its headquarters to UMBC.

17. "Arguments to Support Funding, for a Theatre at UMBC," University Archives, Special Collections, University of Maryland, Baltimore County.

sufficient room for the orchestra to play in front and the lighting was too inflexible to spotlight the drama. So the theatre was eventually moved to a space in the student union, sharing a wall with the university bookstore. With no rehearsal space, only one production could be worked on at a time. Another obstacle was the lack of fly, wing, or storage space. Props had to be moved almost daily from the Fine Arts building 250 yards away. The 13-foot ceiling was under a tin roof with no soundproofing and poor acoustics. The only other venue option was an open air amphitheater. An outdoor production of *Lysistrata* was attempted in 1977, but the Gods were not amused and a windstorm nearly ruined the show.

In the spring of 1980, Xerxes Mehta recognized that an appropriate state funded on-campus theatre was unlikely, so he began to think "outside the Loop." He wrote a proposal suggesting that his faculty would "investigate the possibilities of acquiring a building in downtown Baltimore and renovating it into a comprehensive performance/teaching/ research space." This space was to be used for three to five major theatre productions a year, three to four full symphonic or choral concerts, and performances by IMPETUS, the UMBC Dance Company. It would give Baltimore "art of great quality and diversity" and Mehta hoped to find larger, more sophisticated audiences downtown and more media coverage.[18]

His memorandum was an opening gambit intended to be kept within the University community. Talks began with College Park officials who were supportive. Their architecture department drafted a $60,000 feasibility study for the new building and sent it to construction companies for comment. USM President John Toll and UMBC Chancellor John Dorsey proclaimed their support, but with three caveats about the realism of the project. It would need, they noted, backing from the community, including other local universities; approval from state and local authorities; and non-UMBC funding.[19] Political responses seemed initially positive. State senators, Congresswoman Barbara Mikulski, and Mayor William Donald Schaefer all made supportive comments. Mehta said Schaefer promised to find a building to turn over to the project for one dollar. The Mayor wanted to create what he called the University of Maryland School for the Arts to be used by several institutions and performance companies. The proposed location was to be in downtown Fells Point overlooking the water.

Then the tide turned. Some Fells Point community representatives voiced concern about traffic and noise. More significantly most of the other Baltimore higher education institutions' presidents vigorously opposed the project. While their letters were often couched in procedural objections noting that UMBC had not gone first for approval to the State Board for Higher Education, their real opposition was to UMBC's territorial expansion. UMBC had "its place," of course, but it should not be in the City. President H. Mebane Turner of the University of Baltimore, which had at that time a very limited arts program, wrote:

18. Ibid.

19. Memorandum from John Toll, President of USM and John Dorsey, Chancellor of UMBC, July 17, 1982, University Archives, Special Collections, University of Maryland, Baltimore County.

> I think you can assume that each one of [the institutions in the Baltimore area] will vigorously oppose the move of UMBC's Theatre Department or any branch of the University of Maryland Baltimore County into the City. UMBC has a major campus in Baltimore County, where UMBC says more students are needed, and to move activities from that campus into the City would be totally contrary to the State's efforts to see that campus more fully utilized.[20]

Towson's President Hoke L. Smith could hardly play the City versus County card, but, he weighed in "We are apprehensive about this project because Towson State University has been designated by the State Board for Higher Education as the university to concentrate in the arts."[21]

Faced with this opposition, the project was killed.

Nevertheless, UMBC theatre decided to make lemonade from the political lemons it had been handed. Mehta founded the Maryland Stage Company in which UMBC faculty and some students performed classical and other works at Center Stage on St. Paul Street in downtown Baltimore.[22] While this alternative did not give UMBC theatre the name recognition it sought or full control over productions, it did provide a venue for the use of their talents and delighted Baltimore audiences.

So the theatre space problem moved back to being a campus issue.[23] In 1988, UMBC made funding for a theatre its top campus building priority, but it was later dropped from the budget.[24] The UMBC administration, fully aware of Theatre's need for a new performance space,[25] entertained a petition from Theatre to move into space being vacated by a student center and the book store which had moved to the new University Center. It was decided, however, that the priority was to move Academic Services (registration and advising) from the Administration building to the new space. It wasn't until 1999 that a new theatre space was built as a wing of the

---

20. Memorandum from University of Baltimore President H. Mebane Turner to Baltimore City Mayor William Donald Schaefer, September 11, 1981. (UARC 1999–03) University Archives, Special Collections, University of Maryland, Baltimore County.

21. Memorandum from Towson State University President Hoke L. Smith to Baltimore City Mayor William Donald Schaefer, September 24, 1981. See also similar letters from Coppin President Calvin W. Burnett, September 16. 1981 Maryland Institute College of Art President Fred Lazarus, IV, September 16, 1981 and Morgan State University President Andrew Billingsley, October 19, 1981. All can be found in the University Archives, Special Collections, University of Maryland, Baltimore County.

22. Between 1987 to 2002, the Company performed at least sixteen plays in the Baltimore region as well as touring performances in France and Germany.

23. Bill Brown wrote a series of memos on the theatre space issues from 1973 to 1975. University Archives, Special Collections, University of Maryland, Baltimore County.

24. See memorandum from Bill Brown to Robert Burchard, "Theatre Frustration," November 2, 1989. University Archives, Special Collections, University of Maryland, Baltimore County.

25. Memorandum from Sergei P. Tschernisch, Theatre Chair to Richard Neville, Dean of Arts and Sciences, "Space Needs for the Theatre Department (Old Student Center-Bookstore)" July 30, 1981. University Archives, Special Collections, University of Maryland, Baltimore County.

Academic Services building. This theatre's 170 seats (with folding chairs) created an intimate venue where audience members felt they could easily give the actors a hug or a push, though that was generally not encouraged. The stage area was small and the ceilings only sixteen-feet high which greatly limited the size of moveable sets. At least, the new accommodations had storage space for props and for the making of Elena Zlotescu's marvelous costumes.

While the new Theatre was small, it did give some stability to the program. A more sinister possibility loomed, however. At the end of 1992, as the state grappled with a difficult economy, UMS struggled to absorb a loss of $123 million or about 8 percent of its total budget. For UMBC, the hit list included two arts programs, the Ethnomusicology Masters and Ph.D. programs and the undergraduate Theatre major.[26] The latter was a kick in the gut to the UMBC community because, if a program with such a record of distinction as Theatre could be extinguished, excellent achievement would not protect any campus department.

The struggle to save UMBC Theatre was fought not on numbers or cost-savings, but on quality grounds. By many measures, it was the best program in the region, and it had attracted many admirers. They turned the threat into a teachable moment and UMBC Theatre received substantial favorable mentions in the press and arts circles. Theatre ultimately lost $100,000 from its budget, but it survived. Four years later UMBC was back in the Kennedy Center representing the State in the ACTF staging *"Diary of a Scoundrel,"* with no particular reference to any Maryland personage.

In 2011, the intrinsic worth of UMBC Theatre, overcoming its still inadequate facilities, was demonstrated once again. Director Eve Muson, with an imaginative set and costumes by Elena Zlotescu and technical direction by Greggory Schraven, took *Las Meninas,* a highly innovative production about a seventeenth century affair between French Queen Marie-Therese and an African dwarf named Nabo to the ACTF finals. It played to sold-out houses in the Kennedy Center and was the seventh such ACTF "final four" achievement in UMBC's theatrical history.[27]

In retrospect, had the Fells Point arts center project materialized, it would not have been possible for President Hrabowski's decade-long campaign for the Performing Arts Center and Humanities Building to have achieved success. As they say, the "show must go on" and now it will do so in UMBC's sparkling new 275-seat proscenium theatre and 120-seat black box theatre. Looking ahead, Mehta believes UMBC "... is slowly coming to the realization that a university is an organic entity. All parts are interdependent." Reflecting on the tribulations of the earlier era, Mehta, now professor emeritus, recalls:

---

26. The Regent's view was that eliminating UMBC theatre would save $375, 000, eliminate unnecessary duplication, and sharpen institutional mission. UMS was then spending about $2.5 million on theater programs, about half in the Baltimore area. UMBC's program was the most expensive (and ambitious). Chancellor Langenberg opted to preserve the program, but cut its budget. Freeman Hrabowski memorandum to the UMBC Community, "Chancellor's Recommendation on UMBC Program Appeals."

27. Richard Byrne, "Finding Their Light," *UMBC Magazine*, Summer 2011. 20–29.

> All of us tried to do our best to create theatre according to our own visions of how theatre should be. All of us worked like dogs for up to 60 hours a week. We worked as teachers, professional artists, fund raisers, floor-sweepers, and administrators. We did whatever needed to be done in order to do something that was really, in our view, terrific or worthwhile.[28]

B. Music

Music classes, mainly introductory or with a cultural focus, were offered at UMBC in 1967, the year after the campus opened. Gradually the University added some distinguished faculty and began several performance groups, the UMBC chorus, and an ambitious Community Orchestra, consisting of music students and other regional musicians.[29] Musical performances became campus cultural highlights.

None of these activities required formal off-campus approval. In 1972, however, the University announced its intention to offer a full-fledged music major enrolling forty students and providing more advanced performance courses. That brought UMBC's music activities squarely within the purview of the Maryland Council for Higher Education (MCHE) which had the authority to approve new programs in both the public and private sector. Already alarmed at what it viewed as the new campus' insatiable desire to begin programs and its cavalier view of the MCHE's prerogatives, the Council decided to hold hearings on UMBC's proposed music program. Of course, institutions with established music programs did not welcome a competitor. Although UMBC argued its program had more of a liberal arts orientation than a desire to produce professional musicians, MCHE did not agree.[30] Eugene Stanley, the Council's Senior Specialist, concluded that UMBC's proposed music major duplicated existing majors at the University of Maryland, College Park, Towson State University, Morgan State University, and the private Peabody Conservatory of Music. In its ultimate ruling, MCHE asserted that a new program at UMBC had to meet the test of, not only "duplicating" programs at local public universities, but also of not infringing on public and private institutions elsewhere in the state.

While consideration of duplication is one legitimate facet in the approval process, overreliance on these criteria can lead to programmatic monopolies which stifle new

28. This quote and the one above come from the Xerxes Mehta interview by Nimit Bhatt, December 15, 2010.

29. "Concert Slated Tonight," *UMBC Retriever*, December 11, 1972.

30. MCHE reported, "... data secured from the Maryland Department of Employment Security do not indicate a demand for graduates [in music] at a rate faster than that currently provided by programs already in operation in the state. If, then, the state is already doing its share in the field of music, the approval of an additional program would constitute an uneconomical use of the state's limited resources, and make counter-productive other efforts by the Council to secure positive responses from institutions." "Major in Trouble: Duplication Cited in Music," *UMBC Retriever*, December 11, 1972.

initiatives. Campuses are not likely to propose new program for which there will be no student market, but regulatory bodies often function to protect their existing clientele from new competitors. The brute logic of MCHE's position as applied to UMBC was that whatever the Board of Regents' reasons (which were never persuasive to the Council in the first place) for creating a Catonsville campus in 1966, it should not be permitted to develop majors other institutions regarded as duplicative. This position would be a difficult hurdle for any new campus and influenced UMBC program development toward emerging fields (public policy), niche programs (medical sociology) or areas clearly related to state economic development (life sciences, computer science, and engineering).

MCHE's decision came as a bitter disappointment to Arthur Tollefson, Music's departmental chair, who had spent two and half years hiring new faculty, developing courses, and recruiting students.[31] Losing the music major meant courses had to be reduced, but all five faculty were retained. Despite the uncertainties surrounding the future of the music program and limitations in facilities, several distinguished faculty were attracted to UMBC. Robert Gerle, a concert violinist of international stature,[32] and his wife, pianist Marilyn Neeley[33] joined the department in 1972. Two years before, the couple had won an Emmy Award for recording the complete Beethoven violin and piano sonatas. After they came, Gerle created the UMBC Symphony[34] which he directed until 1989. Mantle Hood, the founder of the Institute for Ethnomusicology at UCLA, moved to UMBC in 1980. This new field combined the study of the cultural context of music with performance on instruments, often from non-Western cultures. A Fulbright Scholar and Ford Foundation Fellow, Hood and his wife Hazel Chung, musician and performer of Indonesian and African compositions, created the ill-fated ethnomusicology Ph.D. program at UMBC. During this period, the campus was treated to parades and performances of musicians in colorful garb playing international music rarely heard in Maryland.

Given the MCHE's pointed suggestion that other institutions had the capacity to absorb UMBC's music majors, the music department faced a situation of losing the students it had already recruited and seeing new applicants dry up. Two options were created in response. Some students switched majors, but continued their music study, while others designed an Interdisciplinary Studies major permitting them, with the permission of the Bachelor of Arts committee, to develop their own course of study. These stop-gap measures stemmed the flow of musicians from the campus and saved the UMBC Community Orchestra, much to the relief its creator Robert Gerle.

Almost two decades after state authorities decided against a music major at UMBC, MHEC approved such a program in 2001. By 2012, the UMBC music de-

31. "Music Department Upset," *UMBC Retriever*, December 12, 1973.

32. "Robert Gerle: Concert Violinist: 81" Obituary, *San Diego Union-Tribune,* November 8, 2005.

33. Ms. Neeley was awarded "Woman of the Year" by the *Los Angeles Times* in 1963.

34. UMBC 40th Anniversary notebook, UMBC historic documents collection, Special Collections, University of Maryland, Baltimore County. 11.

partment had 13 full-time faculty and 31 part-time faculty, with 160 music majors and 50 minors. After passing a rigorous audition process, a student may select concentrations in composition, instrumental and vocal performance, music education in both choral and instrumental performances, jazz, and technology on their way to a Bachelor of Arts in Music. They participate in a wide range of musical expressions, including the Symphony Orchestra, the Jazz Ensemble, the Camerata,[35] the Wind Ensemble, the Jubilee Singers, Chamber Players, Classical Guitar Ensemble, Jazz Guitar Ensemble, Collaborative Piano, Collegium Musicum, Flute Ensemble, Jazz Guitar Quartet, Jazz Small Groups, New Music Ensemble, Percussion Ensemble, Saxophone Ensemble, Opera Workshop, UMBC Gospel Choir and, dating back to the Mantle Hood era, the Gamelan Angklung.

Some music on the campus is student led and has received considerable external recognition. The acapella group "Mama's Boys," began in the basement of Potomac Residence Hall, started to entertain for various campus events, branched out into regional shows, and then to international competition.[36]

After several early attempts, a pep band was started in 1998 led by Jari Villanueva, an accomplished musician with twenty-three years-experience in the United States Air Force Band and one of the nation's top buglers.[37] To commemorate UMBC's 40th anniversary, Villanueva wrote and arranged an alma mater, *Our UMBC,* played win or lose after basketball games and more formal occasions. Band members choose songs and when to play them, except for the mandatory playing of *The UMBC Riser*[38] when the Retrievers take the basketball court, score lacrosse goals or otherwise need inspiration. The Band, which typically has about fifty members, has received some media recognition. Tony Kornheiser, *Washington Post* columnist declared, "They never played the same song twice, they were great, they were loud. . . ." which is a good review for a pep band. ESPN's Kurt Whelliston added, "No other school can match the rich repertoire of the Down and Dirty Dawg Band, easily the tightest brass section in the [AEC] league."[39]

UMBC music has come a long way from MCHE decision in 1972 that the state had no more room for additional university trained musicians. In 2012, the music department established a two year post-baccalaureate certificate program in Music

35. In the summer of 1994, the Maryland Camerata embarked on three week European tour, singing in Austria, Germany and Italy, including a performance at Rheingau Music Festival in Wiesbaden. *UMBC Review,* Summer 1994.

36. www.umbcmamasboys.org. Nayana Davis, "Mama's Boys shame competition at Festivus Acappelius. *Retriever Weekly.* November 15, 2009. Gaby Arevelo, "Mama's Boys Prepares for International Championship" *Retriever,* March 10, 2010. To hear them sing visit www.youtube.com/user/umbcmamasboys.

37. http://www.umbc.edu/music/faculty/villanueva.php and http://www.umbc.edu/pepband/index.php/page/jari.

38. George La Noue wrote the words and music to *The UMBC Riser* in 1991.

39. Corey Johns, "The Down and Dirty Dawg Band" *Retriever,* March 10, 2010. A CD "Dancing with the Dawgs" featuring the 2006–2007 band's music is available at UMBC bookstore.

Entrepreneurship in collaboration with the Baltimore Symphony Orchestra (BSO). Given the proliferation of ways to obtain free music in this era, the music certificate program trains persons in the management skills necessary to create and sustain new organizations and new audiences. Emerging from a Kaufman Foundation grant to encourage entrepreneurship generally at UMBC, the certificate program is the first of its kind nationally in pairing the resources of a major symphony orchestra and a research university. This grant extends work done earlier with the BSO in creating the successful OrchKids program which trains children to play musical instruments, while adding to their academic and social skills.[40]

Marin Alsop, Music Director of the Baltimore Symphony Orchestra, declared:

> As programs like OrchKids flourish and expand in America, the need for qualified teachers and administrators will grow exponentially. This important program and partnership between UMBC and the BSO is a major step toward serving that need. I couldn't be more pleased.[41]

As the Department prepares to move into the new Performing Arts and Humanities Building with its 350 seat concert hall, instrument ensemble rooms, and a recording studio, it is apparent that UMBC music's best days are still ahead.

C. Dance

The smallest of the UMBC arts programs is a vigorous Dance department with more than 50 majors.[42] In 1972, Elizabeth Walton came to UMBC to develop a nascent dance program then administered by theatre. Walton served as chair for twenty-three years. A pre-med major and graduate of Brandeis University, she spent some time working in a Boston hospital. Finding that not to her liking, she enrolled in the dance program at Julliard. Once in New York, she became a part of the Paul Taylor Dance Company which brought his version of modern dance, not only to the United States, but to Europe, Latin America, and Asia. It was a heady, if exhausting, seven-year experience for the twenty-something Walton. She began teaching at Adelphi University in New York and then Baltimore's Peabody Conservatory, before taking on the challenge of developing a dance program at UMBC.

Ten years later, Carol Hess-Vait joined as the second full time dance professor.[43] Hess had been a math major at Barnard College before beginning to see her mother's

---

40. This Baltimore program is the largest American version of El Sistema (the System), the world renown Venezuelan program. CBS News did a "60 Minutes" Report on the original program. "Changing Lives Through Music," July 16, 2008. http:www.cbs.news.com/2012-18560-162-4009335html?tag.

41. Thomas Moore, "UMBC Announces Nation's First Post-Baccalaureate Certificate Program in Music Entrepreneurship," *Insights*, July 2, 2012.

42. A pictorial display of Dance Department activities, "Extend and Elevate," can be found in the *UMBC Magazine*, Winter 2011. 20–29.

43. Carol Hess-Vait, interview by the author, May 18, 2011.

vocation in dance as her own. She began performing with the Hannah Khan and Dancers group while teaching tap and modern dance in New York City. Leaving New York, she migrated to teach at Southern Oregon State College. Seeking a full-time position, she crossed the continent again to join the UMBC faculty in 1982, though compared to Ashland, Oregon the Catonsville campus seemed industrial and virtually treeless.

As it turned out a decade later, Hess-Vait played a key role in protecting all the arts at UMBC. In 1991–92, when the Chancellor and the Regents were proposing that all campuses, except College Park, "tighten their focus," meaning UMBC might lose most of its arts programs; Hess-Vait was the President of the UMBC Faculty Senate. As it happened, in the normal campus rotation, a key Regents' meeting was held at UMBC. The meeting room was packed, and many who hoped to attend could not get in. Outside the room, however, UMBC arts students, led by dancers were in full demonstration mode. The Regents were treated to a mock funeral for the threatened programs, attended by strange apparitions tearing out their hair. Inside at the meeting, Hess-Vait quietly and adeptly defended the role of the arts in a liberal arts education, a position that ultimately prevailed.

Establishing a dance major at UMBC continued to be challenging, not only because of a chronic lack of funding. When the first proposal for that major was created in 1974, it drew objections from Goucher College and the Peabody Conservatory. Consequently, the proposal was redesigned to become the Visual and Performing Arts major which included the visual arts and music, as well as dance. Since that combination was distinctive, it passed two years later. In 2001, dance became an independent major and department, when MHEC finally began to realize that to educate whole persons, campuses could not be restricted to non-duplicative programs.

A major boost to the dance department has been the Linehan Scholars Program. It not only adds three or four new dancers with impressive backgrounds to the department each year, but the audition process displays arts opportunities at UMBC to a much wider audience. For a decade (1983–1993), the Phoenix Dance Company flourished and more recently it morphed into the Baltimore Dance Project. These companies have performed at various colleges, but also at the Kennedy Center and Lincoln Center.

Dance, like all the UMBC arts, has struggled to overcome space problems, but with the arrival of the second phase of the new PAHB, it will have its own performance space, as well as several studios. The future seems quite optimistic.

D. Visual Arts

The newest of UMBC's arts programs, the Department of Visual Arts, was the result of some innovative conceptualization, entrepreneurial and aggressive leadership, and creating a new niche in the array of existing arts programs in the Baltimore area.

There was no possibility that UMBC could acquire a collection of old masters or fine examples of modern art such as grace the Yale and Stanford campus museums. Instead UMBC found a niche in collecting about two million photographs, slides, and digital images, often with social significance.[44] Other forms of expression collected by UMBC were pulp science fiction and mystery magazines, as well as literature on radical social movements which had been ignored by other campuses.[45]

The Maryland Institute College of Art (MICA) had established a national reputation for teaching painting and sculpture. So UMBC had to find a different path in the visual arts. That direction took the campus away from the past of classical forms to future formats using computers, digital arts, and videos.

Founded in 1999, the Department of Visual Arts at UMBC now offers both a Bachelor of Arts (B.A.) and a Bachelor of Fine Arts (B.F.A.) degree at the undergraduate level, as well as a Masters of Fine Arts (M.F.A.) in Imaging and Digital Arts. The undergraduate programs emphasize the interdisciplinary connections between the history, theory, and context of visual arts in areas such as animation, film, graphic design, photography, video, and print media.[46]

Graduates of the Visual Arts department have earned a number of prestigious awards, most notably in 2008. That year, Steven Fischer (B.A. 1998), Scott Mueller (B.A. 1999) and Renee Shaw (M.F.A. 2005) all won awards at the Rosebud Film and Video Festival, a yearly competition that honors "the innovative, unusual, experimental and deeply personal" in regional film making.[47]

The academic entrepreneur responsible for much of the burgeoning work of the Department was David Yager, Wilson Elkins Professor of Visual Arts and Chair of the Department, for twelve years. Yager, who had been at the University of South Florida, was a challenging recruit for UMBC. He was hired first as a consultant and identified the need for an arts gallery, a laboratory with new equipment, an undergraduate arts education component, and a hiring plan focusing on more diverse faculty who would exhibit their work regularly. To accept the position, he insisted that all the above conditions be met, though he remembers UMBC never had the bankroll to fulfill his entire package.[48] Nevertheless, Yager became a transformational leader in his program, dramatically increasing the scope of its offerings and majors on campus, and chairing the key Faculty Senate Appointments, Promotions and Budget Committee for nine years.

Yager's personal arts field was photography. His work was exhibited nationally and is in the permanent collection of the Art Institute of Chicago and the Museum of Modern Art, but he quickly saw the potential of electronics to make new types of

---

44. http://aok.lib.umbc.edu/specoll/photog.php.

45. http://aok.lib.umbc.edu/specoll/popcul.php.

46. UMBC Visual Arts Website, Undergraduate Program, http://art.umbc.edu/undergraduate/index.php, accessed on August 25, 2012.

47. Rosebudfestival.org/rose4.html, accessed August 25, 2012.

48. David Yager, interview by the author June 20, 2012. In 2009, Yager moved to the University of California, Santa Cruz to become Dean of the Visual Arts Division.

images. Consequently, the Department of Visual Arts is home to two important centers involved in expanding the limits of the visual arts medium, the Imaging Research Center (IRC) and the Center for Art, Design and Visual Culture (CADVC).

The IRC, founded in 1987, utilized what were then cutting-edge 3D graphics to create visualizations of reality that were otherwise beyond human observation, from biological processes too small to see with the naked eye to ancient or even hypothetical architectural structures. The IRC works with the Department of Visual Arts to create partnerships between undergraduate and graduate students working with scholars, researchers, artists, and members of industry in a public and visually appealing way. For example, the IRC has worked with the UMBC's Theater and English departments to present Shakespeare's work through a combination of live-action and animated staging processes. The IRC has collaborated with a number of local and community organizations and presented in different venues including the Baltimore Museum of Art, the National Academy of Science, the Dallas Museum of Art, the British Broadcasting Corporation, the Discovery Channel, and the Learning Channel (TLC). Nearly thirty researchers from UMBC and other institutions work with the IRC.

As computer imaging advanced to the point where "visualization capabilities have become all but limitless," the IRC has sought to develop new forms of these possibilities.[49] Perhaps the mostly widely seen of IRC's images were the original Angry Birds or six animated ravens who cavort on the giant RavensVision screen in M&T Bank stadium.[50] Other projects have been more scholarly. For example, the IRC created a visualization of Washington DC circa 1814 for a PBS documentary; an interactive map called "USDemocrazy," developed with UMBC artist-in-residence Kevin Kallaugher (KAL) to teach American politics to school children; and an interactive virtual tour for the Baltimore Museum of Art.[51] In 1950, the Cone sisters donated their collection of French art and furniture, considered one of the finest collections of that period in the world, to the BMA. The IRC project recreated how the sisters had integrated this large collection into their early twentieth century home, highlighting the way they presented their collection to guests in a non-museum setting. The virtual tour allows visitors to the BMA to see this important collection in a new and different way, something that would be impossible to replicate in the real world.[52] One of the most innovative of the IRC's projects was a collaboration between professors Anne Sarah Rubin (History) and Kelly Bell (Graphic Design). The project was funded with a grant from the American Council of Learned Societies and entitled "Sherman's March and America: Mapping Memory."[53] When General William

49. IRC About webpage, http://www.irc.umbc.edu/about/, accessed on August 25, 2012.

50. Kristen Campbell, "The Raven Raps on the IRC's Door," *Insights*, 13, no.1. (September 1998).

51. Ibid.

52. "Virtual Tour: The Cone Sisters Apartment," http://www.irc.umbc.edu/2005/10/01/cone-sisters/.

53. Scott McLemore, "Marching into the Future," *UMBC Magazine*, Winter 2011, 14–19. See also www.shermansmarch.org.

Tecumseh Sherman led Union troops on their destructive path from Atlanta to Savannah in 1864, the impact was different for Yankee soldiers, Confederate adherents, newly freed slaves, and the citizens of each town. The Sherman's March project permits viewers to follow the campaign with short videos based on the particular events in highlighted towns.

The Center for Art, Design and Visual Culture (CADVC) began in 1989 as the Fine Arts Gallery of UMBC. Fourteen years later, this Center became a non-profit entity "dedicated to organizing comprehensive exhibitions, the publication of catalogs, CDs, DVDs, and books on the arts," while promoting educational and community outreach projects.[54] In addition, the CADVC works with local educators to incorporate visual images in classroom settings. Teachers can organize tours through the Center or make use of the many classroom resources created by the Center over the years in cooperation with local and visiting artists.[55] Education programs include partnerships with over thirty K-12 schools in Baltimore City and Baltimore County since 2003 and prominent museums and art institutions in Baltimore City. Recent projects and initiatives of the CADVC have investigated the relationships between science and the arts, gender and politics, and race and culture.[56]

CADVC maintains a 4,200 square foot museum space in the Fine Arts building where it can showcase art designs, and exhibitions created by UMBC students and faculty. They have also produced traveling exhibitions appearing at the Warhol Museum, the Berkeley Art Museum, the Cincinnati Center for Contemporary Art, and the Barbican Centre (London), among many others.

In 2010, the Center partnered with the Smithsonian National Museum of African American History and Culture to create the exhibition "For All the World to See: Visual Culture and the Struggle for Civil Rights." Initially funded by the National Endowment for the Arts, the project eventually attracted funding from the Maryland State Arts Council, Communities Foundation of Texas, the Trelis Fund, and the St. Paul Travelers Corporation. This exhibition brought together images from magazines, film, television and newspapers to trace the history of the Civil Rights movement in the U.S. from the 1940's through the 1970's. It displayed photographs and artifacts portraying the images that reinforced racial stratification in the United States and then gradually began to change them. The exhibition will be shown at sites throughout Maryland and around the country from 2012–2017.

For All the World to See" was a true multimedia experience, with a traveling exhibition in New York, Washington, and Boston, a website, an online film festival, and a successful companion book published by Yale University Press, each taking a

54. "About CADVC" webpage, http://www.umbc.edu/cadvc/about/, accessed on August 25, 2012.

55. CADVC's K-12 Teacher/ Student Resources, http://www.umbc.edu/cadvc/education/resources.php, accessed on August 25, 2012.

56. www.umbc.edu/blogs/foralltheworld/neh-on-the-road/.

different approach to telling this complex and important story.[57] The exhibit's creator and project director, Dr. Maurice Berger, Senior Research Scholar at the UMBC Center and Senior Fellow at the Vera List Center for Art and Politics of the New School in New York, received a curatorial award from the Association of Art Museum Curators in 2011, and was nominated that same year for an Emmy award based on his PBS Sunday Arts Segment.

When UMBC was conceived in 1963 for the very pragmatic reasons of relieving over enrollment pressures at College Park, strengthening economic development in the Baltimore region, and preparing students for the downtown professional schools, there was not a lot of thought given by legislators to the role of the arts on campus. It is worth repeating that Albin Kuhn, UMBC's first Chancellor, and Homer Schamp, its first Provost, though both scientists, were convinced that you couldn't have an excellent university based on those disciplines alone. Kuhn said: "You can't do that with just science, you have to do that with understanding people, you have to do that with understanding that real drive that's involved in the humanities and the arts."[58] They would have been very proud to see their vision of the complete university come to life in the strength of UMBC's contemporary arts programs and now embodied in the Performing Arts and Humanities Building.

57. *For all the World to See*, Homepage, http://www.umbc.edu/cadvc/foralltheworld/index.php, accessed August 28, 2012.

58. Albin Kuhn, interview by Joseph Tatarewicz, August 14, 2001. 24.

CHAPTER X

UMBC Athletics

As a fledgling commuter institution founded in the 1960s, it was not a foregone conclusion that UMBC would engage in intercollegiate athletics, let alone take them seriously. Still, unlike universities in the rest of the world, for better or worse, intercollegiate sports competition is a distinguishing characteristic of American higher education.[1] It comes as a surprise to many people that the university with the most varsity teams is Harvard[2] and that Stanford is a perennial winner of the Sports Director's Cup, emblematic of fielding teams with the cumulative highest rankings in NCAA Division I competition.

There are dramatic differences in the intensity with which universities pursue athletic goals. In many Division III institutions intercollegiate competition is only one step up from club and intramural sports and the perceived benefits are mainly for those students who participate. At the Division I level, however, athletics serve a more institutional purpose and, if pursued successfully, can add to the university's quest for status, publicity, and funding. Of course, there is a financial and, sometimes, an academic price for such ambitions.[3]

A few of the new wave urban institutions, such as the University of California at Santa Cruz, the University of Massachusetts at Boston, and the University of Texas Dallas play NCAA Division III schedules against mostly local competition. The University of Missouri-St Louis and the University of California, San Diego are in the limited athletic scholarship Division II. Others such as the University of Central Florida and the University of South Florida are big time Division I powers. What choice would UMBC make?

---

1. For discussion of the distinctive role of competitive athletics in American universities and an empirical analysis of the costs and benefits of such programs, see Charles T. Clotfelter, *Big-Time Sports in American Universities* (New York: Cambridge University Press, 2011). James J. Duderstadt, *Intercollegiate Athletics and the American University: A University President's Perspective*, (Ann Arbor: University of Michigan Press, 2003), provides a good balance of the positives and negatives in big time college athletics from a more political viewpoint.
2. Harvard has 41 intercollegiate teams and an extensive House or intramural sports program. Richard Bradley, *Harvard Rules: Lawrence Summers and the Battle for the World's Most Powerful University* (New York: Harper Collins, 2003).220.
3. Sometimes, scandal can strike even in such an unlikely place as the American East Conference's Binghamton University, "Down and Out in Division I," *Inside Higher Education*, October 6, 2009. Also Clotfelter, "Big-Time Sports," 177–9.

A. Early Days

Since intercollegiate sports cannot be played without a mascot, the first month after the campus opened, UMBC held a contest to pick a new campus symbol. No commonplace animals, warriors, or mythological beings would do. In an October 30, 1966 dedication ceremony, the new campus's unique choice was unveiled: the Chesapeake Bay Retriever, the state dog.[4]

On November 4, 1966, about two months after the University's doors first opened, the men's soccer team played UMBC's first intercollegiate game losing "with high praise" 4–1 to a team (probably B squad) from University of Maryland, College Park (UMCP). In the spring of 1967, under coach Tom Rider, the Retrievers played six baseball games and won one. Almost a year later, the men's basketball team played its first varsity game, losing by 10 points to Catonsville Community College and a few days afterward losing by 57 to Bowie State. At least the travel costs were low. Then, on January 8, 1968, UMBC won its first varsity game beating Eastern College of Commerce.[5] If UMBC wanted to have a greater athletic profile, it needed to upgrade its opponents and its facilities. A crucial first step was to join a conference.

B. Finding a Conference Home

In theory, UMBC had many choices about the role of athletics on campus, but, in fact, there were significant restrictions on its options. Although beginning at the Division III level was a financial and logistical necessity, it was not a long-term solution. Conference affiliation is useful for both the competition it offers and for facilitating scheduling. UMBC's academic inclinations might have led it to follow the path of such distinguished private urban research universities as Brandeis, Case Western, Carnegie Mellon, Chicago, Emory, New York, Rochester, and Washington-St. Louis which together make up the Division III University Athletic Association. These universities have chosen to co-habit with their academic peers in low-level competition, even if it means spending on team travel what they forgo in expenditures for athletic scholarships. An invitation to such august academic company, at that point of UMBC's development, however, was on the impossible side of unlikely.

---

4. Tom Berlin from Catonsville submitted the entry. For some reason, the mascot was called "Sam" in its earlier years. Later, he was christened "True Grit" and amazingly he discovered a sister in 2007 called Trudy Grit who sometimes appears at games. In 2008, the campus acquired a Retriever puppy with proper pedigree, though it came from the farther reaches of the Chesapeake in New Jersey. Unlike another state mascot, True Grit is at least warm-blooded. "So fear the turtle if you must, but love the dog."

5. This abbreviated history is taken from "UMBC 40-Year History" in various 2006 athletic department media guides. The Eastern College of Commerce was a part of the merger that created the University of Baltimore.

In the mid-Atlantic area, most Division III schools are private liberal arts colleges.[6] Membership in the Maryland-Pennsylvania-based Centennial Conference (Swarthmore, Haverford, Gettysburg, Franklin and Marshall, Western Maryland [now McDaniel], and others) might not have been offered or accepted. So for the first decade or so of UMBC sports, team schedules were a potpourri of schools from all three NCAA divisions. Although a few Retriever teams experienced some success in this ad hoc arrangement, it was not a substitute for finding the right conference.

From 1970–1978 and again from 1983–1986, the best available conference choice was the currently mostly defunct Mason-Dixon Athletic Conference (MDAC).[7] It was composed at one time or another of such local rivals as Towson, the University of Baltimore, Loyola, Mount St Mary's, Salisbury, and Washington College. The MDC offered competition only in a few sports and its membership was unstable as some members attained Division I status and others drifted away to other conference affiliations.

For its first eleven years, UMBC was a Division III, no-athletic-scholarship-competitor, but in 1978 it began offering very limited financial aid in a few sports and moved to Division II. The Retrievers found some success in that Division, winning the 1980 National Collegiate Athletic Association (NCAA) Men's Lacrosse championship; and in 1979 and 1980 men's basketball was in the NCAA South Atlantic regionals. There was no appropriate Division II conference, however, and that made it difficult to put together a balanced multi-sport program.[8]

In March 1985, Vice Chancellor Warren Phillips appointed a twelve-member committee to examine the role of athletics on the campus. Partly out of the need to find a stable, attractive conference and partly reflecting a growing sense that UMBC's overall visibility was not keeping up with its actual accomplishments, this group pushed for the University to seek Division I status.[9] Otherwise, the Committee concluded that there was a "very real possibility that UMBC will be lumped in the public mind into the same category as the Division II schools with low or virtually non-existent academic standards." Consequently a recommendation to petition the NCAA for Division I status was sent to Chancellor Michael Hooker who won approval for that move from the Regents in 1986.

---

6. In Maryland, Frostburg, Salisbury, and St. Mary's College are public Division III schools, while Bowie State is in Division II. Coppin, Morgan, Towson, UMES and, of course, UMCP are all Division I.

7. The conference, begun in 1936, still survives holding annual track and field and cross country competitions for Division III regional institutions. http://www.themasondixonconference.com/.d5.html (accessed, July 1, 2009).

8. For a while the Mason-Dixon Conference was reformatted as a Division II conference composed of Liberty Baptist, Longwood, Randolph-Macon, Mount St. Mary's, University of Pittsburgh at Johnstown, and UMBC.

9. In an option uniquely open in men's lacrosse, in 1981 UMBC joined Division I, reflecting its previous success and future ambitions, but which required offering athletic scholarships in that sport. It is a choice also exercised by Johns Hopkins and Hobart College, otherwise Division III schools. By the time of UMBC's transition to Division I, Towson, Loyola, Morgan State, and the University of Baltimore had already made that move.

This decision meant UMBC again had to find a new conference. The Mason-Dixon Conference was informed rather abruptly that the Retrievers would be leaving, triggering a chain of events that caused the eventual disintegration of that association. Form letters by UMBC Athletic Director (AD) Rick Hartzell were sent to the Division I Atlantic 10, Colonial Athletic, and the ECAC-Metro conferences.[10] Despite portraying UMBC's academic and athletic achievements in their most favorable lights, the letters drew no positive responses for the upstart Division I member.

In intercollegiate athletics, the path from Division II to Division I has many pitfalls. After examining several case studies, Grant Wahl and George Dohrmann concluded:

> The vast majority [of schools that move to Division I] soldier away in obscurity, negotiating a treacherous landscape that features chronic losing, uninterested fans, wacky conference affiliations (or even worse none at all) and, not least, crushing financial deficits.[11]

By 1986, however, the die was cast and the Retrievers were Division I in all sports, sort of. Although the planning committee stated bluntly "To move [to Division I] without adequate planning and resources would be to invite disaster," except for the easy generalization that more money would be necessary, the financial implications were not fully considered. In 1988, the UMBC athletics budget was less than $1 million (80 percent from student fees) and most teams did not have full time coaches.[12]

Locating other than a "wacky conference" affiliation seemed no easier. It was difficult to find a multi-sport conference of similar institutions with reasonable travel costs. UMBC joined the now defunct East Coast Conference (ECC) (Brooklyn, Buffalo, Central Connecticut, Delaware, Hofstra, Rider, Towson, and others) for the 1990–1991 and 1991–1992 seasons. In its second membership year, the Retrievers impressively won the Presidents Cup, emblematic of overall team success. Then the ECC dissolved. An option for some sports was the East Coast Athletic Conference (ECAC), an ad hoc arrangement for schools which did not have a traditional conference home or played particular sports their regular conference did not sponsor.[13] The ECAC, however, did not have the coherence or stature to be a comfortable long term solution for UMBC.

---

10. President's Office Records Series III, 8 Box 50, Folder 88. University Archives, Special Collections, University of Maryland, Baltimore County. See also memo "Re: Division I status, 1986–87." From Rick Hartzell AD, to Warren Phillips, Vice Chancellor, November 21, 1985. Bob Clark, "Hartzell must get UMBC ready for Division I," February 20, 1986, newspaper article found in Dorsey papers, Series II.B50 F88.

11. Grant Wahl and George Dohrman, "Welcome to the Big Time," in Scott Rosner editor, *The Business of Sports.* (Boston: Jones and Bartlett Publishers, 2004).

12. Charles H. Brown, "UMBC Athletics Division I Summary" unpublished document, was written to compare 1988 with 1998. In that decade, the athletics budget increased to $3.6 million fueled by an increase in student fees from $106 dollars a year to $376. All teams had full time coaches. Larger squads or sports of emphasis now possessed assistant coaches as well.

13. This conference is distinctive in that it currently includes institutions in all three NCAA divisions.

After the demise of the ECC, the only possible alternative appeared to be the Big South Conference (BSC), which despite its moniker was dwarfed by the attention and level of competition of the Atlantic Coast Conference (ACC) occupying the same region. Having added Towson and UNC-Greensboro as members, the BSC approached UMBC about joining. Since a conference affiliation was a necessity, in 1992 the Retrievers suited up for competition against Campbell, Coastal Carolina, Charleston Southern, Liberty, UNC-Asheville, Radford, and Winthrop, enduring some painfully long road trips. It was not an attractive choice and, in a few years, the conference search began again.[14]

The next available option was the Northeast Conference (NEC) which awarded UMBC membership in 1998. Travel would be decreased and UMBC would be facing north toward more potential students and away from the ACC-dominated territory where the Maryland Terps played. Despite this logic, the NEC (Central Connecticut State, Fairleigh Dickinson, Long Island University, Monmouth, Quinnipiac, Mount St. Mary's, Robert Morris, the St. Francis twins in Pennsylvania and New York, and Wagner) was not the right choice either. There were no natural rivals. Most of the schools were private and small without the research graduate school profile UMBC was attaining. The Retrievers were able to dominate the conference, winning the all-sports trophy five times in five years which meant championships and NCAA experiences for its athletes. For the rest of the campus, however, the feeling of "so what?" was hard to suppress.

So by 2002 the conference search was on again. UMBC considered the Colonial Athletic Association (CAA), even though the financial commitment would have been substantial. After some initial probing, including a phone call by President Hrabowski to the President of the College of William and Mary, the answer was always the same. Without football, the CAA would not be interested. Delaware, Hofstra, and Towson were admitted to the CAA instead and left the America East Conference (AEC).

Doors close; doors open. In a call from UMBC athletic director Charles Brown to the athletic director at Stony Brook about a personnel recommendation, the question was raised about UMBC's interest in the AEC which was feeling a bit vulnerable after losing three members in the musical chairs of conference affiliations. The AEC was a very attractive affiliation. At that time, among the AEC's nine members there were three private universities, (Boston, Hartford, Northeastern), three state flagship universities, (Maine, New Hampshire and Vermont), and three New York public research universities, (Albany, Binghamton, and Stony Brook), which also happened to be on UMBC's academic peer list. In terms of the size, academic aspirations, and athletic profile of the other members, the America East Conference was clearly a de-

14. Roch Eric Kobatko, "UMBC eyes bigger market, enters Northeast Conference. Move from Big South Effective in 1998," *Baltimore Sun*, June 20, 1996. Charles Brown was quoted in this article, "When we went into the Big South, there were no other options. The Big South has been good to us, but it was time to look for a better geographic fit."

sirable affiliation for UMBC, but would the affection be reciprocal? AEC conference expansion seemed imperative, but would the new member be the Retrievers? Located in the middle Atlantic region, UMBC presented some considerable additional travel costs for the other northeastern conference members and it would not bring significant athletic prestige to the table, though its academic profile was certainly acceptable. Again some conference members preferred a football school.

Consequently, it took a campaign to persuade the other presidents that UMBC was the most attractive candidate to become the AEC's tenth member. President Hrabowski had spoken at the Binghamton Commencement and received an honorary doctorate from that institution. He also had taken UMBC faculty to Stony Brook to see research facilities, so he used those relationships and contacted other presidents to make the case for AEC membership.[15] Dr. Brown was in extensive communication with conference athletic directors. On February 21, 2003, UMBC received an official invitation to join the AEC, and on April 2, President Hrabowski wrote the acting head of the NEC conference to inform him that UMBC had found a new athletic home.[16]

Because UMBC had been the most successful athletic program and was probably the most prominent NEC academic institution, there were likely some mixed emotions when the Retrievers departed. More concretely, there was a $250,000 penalty for early withdrawal from the NEC. So after UMBC paid the AEC conference initiation fee of $250,000, that conference in turn paid a penalty of $200,000 to the NEC, while UMBC paid the other $50,000. UMBC had found the right conference both academically and athletically, but it also had a new debt in its athletic program and had to make considerable improvements in the quality of its teams and facilities to be competitive.

C. Athletic Directors and Facilities

UMBC athletics are distinctive in at least two regards. Unlike most large American universities, UMBC combines the responsibility for managing intercollegiate competition, club sports, intramurals, and physical education in one department. Furthermore in its forty-five year history, it has had only two athletic directors for ninety percent of those years.[17] In 1967–1968, UMBC began to play men's and women's basketball, baseball, and men's lacrosse, before it had residence halls or athletic facilities. The stature of both the opponents and UMBC's competitive success was modest. But in 1967, E. Richard (Dick) Watts was recruited both as athletic director and men's

15. Doug Pear email to the author, September 25, 2009.

16. Dr. Freeman Hrabowski letter to Dr. George Hansen, Chair, NEC Executive Committee, April 2, 2003.

17. W. Richard Mentzer was Athletic Director from 1966–1968. Rick Hartzell was Athletic Director from 1985–1988.

lacrosse coach with a mandate to broaden the intercollegiate program and to win some lacrosse games. Even then, UMBC administrators had divined that lacrosse had a special status among Baltimore elites. Watts played football, lacrosse, and had wrestled at Johns Hopkins and had coached multiple sports at Baltimore Friends School and Kenyon College.

Beginning an athletic program virtually from the ground up was a daunting task. The major source of the athletic budget came from the campus requirement that every student take two physical education courses which received state reimbursement. The course instructors would also coach; equipment such as basketballs could be recycled from the state budget to various teams. One thing that Watts insisted on was that any UMBC sports activity, no matter how minor, got some press mention. He was keenly aware that much of the public did not understand the difference between UMBC and GBMC (Greater Baltimore Medical Center) or CCC (Catonsville Community College).[18]

Watts added six sports (field hockey, women's volleyball, men's and women's golf, and men's and women's track and field), to the UMBC portfolio and undertook to find adequate places for them to play. It was an exceedingly difficult task. There were no private donors eager to contribute to this new, mostly commuter, campus. Moreover, Maryland state policy, unlike many other states, does not generally permit the use of tax funds to build student housing, recreational, or athletic facilities. This policy handicaps all state campuses, though College Park can mitigate most of its effects with football and basketball ticket sales, television fees, and revenues from its ACC membership and frequent post-season play. The Maryland legislature has also made special appropriations for Terp athletic facilities. For other campuses, facilities funding must come largely from state bonds, which must be repaid by student activity fees. Competition for access to the bond funds is frequently fierce and bad feelings can develop as campuses jockey for position.

For the first six years of intercollegiate competition, UMBC played home games in the eponymous Gym 1, which had a grand total of 500 bleacher seats. Outdoor sports such as lacrosse and baseball were played on what are now recreational fields, while track and field used Catonsville Community College facilities. In his twenty-four year tenure, Watts also oversaw construction of several key facilities. In 1973, UMBC opened a new gym, now a part of the Retriever Activities Center (RAC), with seats for about 4000 spectators, providing a venue for men's and women's basketball and volleyball. Adjacent to the RAC, an indoor pool was opened in 1977 which has become the main facility for the stellar UMBC swim teams.

After moving from flat recreational fields, Retriever fans, what there were of them for outside sports, sat on the grassy steppes above a field carved from a hollowed out hillside. When the weather was good, that could be a pleasant experience, but November soccer or March lacrosse severely tested spectator endurance. In the early 1970s, after UMBC thought it had approval to build a stadium with fixed seats and

18. Dick Watts, interview by the author, August 3, 2011.

rest room facilities, UMCP convinced authorities that the state's athletic bond money should be used to add luxury seats at Byrd Stadium. So the construction of a UMBC stadium was postponed until 1976.

Dick Watts relinquished the athletic directorship in 1985, while remaining as lacrosse coach. A national search led to the hiring of Rick Hartzell from Northwestern University with a mandate from Chancellor Hooker to seek Division I status. Although Hartzell only served as Athletic Director for three years, before taking a similar position at Bucknell University, he approved UMBC's swimming and diving program and oversaw the Department's transition to Division I.

After still another national search, Dr. Charles Brown, previously Athletic Director at Hunter College in New York City, where he also coached the wrestling team, was hired.[19] Although Watts and Brown had in common blue-collar backgrounds and a fierce competitiveness, Watt's retirement as AD marked the end of an era. No longer could UMBC athletics be run by someone who also had head coaching responsibilities in a major sport.

Brown's mandate was to upgrade the stature of UMBC athletic competition and the quality of its athletic physical plant. In 1986, UMBC was in theory Division I, but its gym was outclassed by several high schools, its stadium had no lights, and its track team had no track. During his tenure, spanning more than two decades, Brown remedied some of these facilities problems by adding an outdoor swimming pool that is the envy of many institutions, lights and a new artificial turf field for UMBC Stadium, a track and field complex, the Bermuda grass Retriever Soccer Park with lights that seats 1,500, a new baseball Alumni Stadium with lights and seats, a softball diamond, an $8 million RAC expansion with new seating, modern scoreboards, expanded weight room, coaches office space, training facilities and locker room renovations, a $5,000,000 UMBC stadium locker room expansion, new lighted tennis courts, and several new fields for club and recreational sports. The UMBC stadium has hosted several NCAA tournament events, as well as annual state high school lacrosse and soccer championships. UMBC also was a co-sponsor of the NCAA basketball and NCAA lacrosse championships in downtown Baltimore venues. Under Brown's direction, the program's staff tripled and the amount of athletic scholarships also tripled to above $4 million.

Still, for competition in the AEC, UMBC has some significant facilities problems. The RAC is now 36 plus years old and it does not have the seating capacity or amenities some rivals possess. Nor is it a very suitable venue for University graduations, convocations or other non-athletic events. Yet constructing a new arena out of student activity fees is challenging without major external donations. Moreover, as the university expands its enrollment and research portfolio, there is constant pressure to divert existing athletic and recreational facilities to other purposes. Whether UMBC will be able to remain competitive in athletic and recreational facilities is a major uncertainty.

---

19. Charlie Brown, interview by the author, November 30, 2009.

There is no single story of UMBC athletics because each team has its own history and special character. The following is a very brief profile of UMBC's 19 existing teams as they play schedules from fall to spring.

D. Teams[20]

Volleyball

UMBC has played women's volleyball since 1970. From 1973, for the next sixteen years, volleyball was coached by Kathy Zerrlaut who also doubled as women's lacrosse coach during that period. Moving to administrative duties, Zerrlaut is now Senior Associate Athletic Director.[21] In her long career as coach and administrator, Zerrlaut has made unequaled contributions to UMBC athletics and is a member of the UMBC Athletics Hall of Fame. A local girl from Lansdowne High School, she earned her Bachelor's and Master's degrees from Frostburg State after a career there as a multi-sport athlete. Immediately upon graduation, she was offered a position at UMBC coaching the fledgling lacrosse and volleyball teams. The challenges were formidable. Women's intercollegiate athletics were just emerging from what was a *de facto* club sport level, yet some schools were beginning to invest in these sports and to ratchet up the professional qualifications of their coaches. UMBC was interested in women's athletics, but did not have the space or the budget to implement its ambitions. Zerrlaut had no recruiting budget, no full time assistants, and her volleyball and lacrosse players wore the same jerseys during their different seasons. Nevertheless, the foundation Zerrlaut built for UMBC women's athletics endures today.

Like other UMBC sports, volleyball began at the Division III level and for the first four years played a schedule of other local schools. Coach Zerrlaut's teams were often quite successful, winning about 70 percent of their matches between 1975 and 1979. After UMBC volleyball became a Division I sport, the season wins fell from 27 in 1985 to 11 in 1986. By 1990, new coach Catherine Lavery had the Retrievers playing a more national schedule with considerable success wining 67 percent of their matches between 1990 and 1998 and having only one year where her teams did not win 20 games. Her Retrievers won the ECAC championship in 1994, the BSC title in 1995, as well as an NCAA play-in game against the University of Central Florida. In 1998 her team won the NEC with a perfect conference record and garnered UMBC's first and, so far only, volleyball regular NCAA bid. That earned the Retriev-

---

20. Much of this team specific material came from the splendid media guides produced by Steve Levy, Associate Athletic Director/Director of Athletic Communications and UMBC alum. The guides are available on the web at umbc.retrievers.com. In addition, Charlie Brown has put together five scrapbooks of UMBC athletics newspaper clippings from 1989 to date which are now housed in the University Publication Collection, UMBC Special Collections and in the RAC Room 325.

21. Kathy Zerrlaut, interview by the author, January 20, 2010.

ers a first round trip to the University of Southern California, the hotbed of the sport, where they were a bit overwhelmed.

Ian Blanchard took over the coaching reins in 2005 and broadened the recruiting base as the Retrievers were facing increasingly tough AEC competition. In his second year, he built a consistently winning team that made it to the AEC tournament in 2006 and then in consecutive years from 2008–2012. The conference championship and an NCAA bid have just barely eluded his squads.

Volleyball at UMBC has had a distinguished history both on the court and in the classroom. In their 27 year Division I volleyball history, the Retrievers have won .556 percent of their matches. In 2009, the NCAA recognized UMBC women's volleyball for being in the top 10 percent among all Division I volleyball teams in the country in multi-year APR rates.[22]

Women's Soccer

Twenty-one years after UMBC started a men's soccer program in 1967, Retriever women began to play the game. After a winning record as an independent for three years, under Coach Dave Kelley, the program made the move to the Division I BSC conference in 1991. Under Coaches Jamie Watson (1991–1995) and Amanda Cromwell (1996–1997), UMBC had winning records, but no championships. Then in 1998, UMBC moved to the NEC, where the competition in women's soccer grew tougher and, in 2003 joined the AEC, where it was even more difficult. Perhaps that is why UMBC had four women's soccer coaches in seven years from 2005–12.

Men's Soccer

UMBC's oldest sport also has been one of its most successful. Under Tom Rider's tutelage in 1967–1972, the Retriever puppies were 31 wins and 27 losses. Ed Veit had a very successful tenure from 1973 to 1980 as the Dawgs grew up to go 69–39 in those years. In 1977, his 15–2 team became the first to ever wear UMBC colors in an NCAA soccer tournament. In ten seasons (1981–1990), John Ellinger's teams finished over .500 four times.

As the Retrievers looked for a coach who could compete in increasingly tougher leagues and schedules, they found their man in Pete Caringi, Jr., a native Baltimorean. He graduated from the University of Baltimore where he was a two-time soccer all-American and is still UB's all-time leading scorer. Caringi came to UMBC after a ten-year stint at Essex Community College, where he compiled a stunning 170-27-8 record and was National Junior College Athletic Association Coach of the Year in 1984 and 1985. He also had several years of professional coaching experience.

Beginning in 1991, he has coached at UMBC for more than two decades, winning at a .600 rate. His Retrievers won the ECC in his first year, the BSC in his second,

22. APR is a NCAA mandated calculation measuring graduation rates.

the NEC in 1998 and that league' regular season title in 2002, the AEC regular season title in 2003 and its tournament championship in 2010 and 2012. Based on this performance, Caringi has been honored multiple times as Coach of the Year (NEC, 1999 and 2002, South Atlantic Region 1999 and AEC in 2005).

During his UMBC career, he has produced more than 75 all-conference and all-region players and more than a dozen who went on to professional careers. Giuliano Celenza, NEC Player of the Year in 1999 and 2000, is only one of the many Retrievers who made the Baltimore Blast an indoor soccer professional power. In 2010, Levi Houapeu was drafted by the Philadelphia Union of outdoor Major League Soccer.[23] The next year UMBC teammates Andrew Bulls was drafted by the Columbus Crew and Matt Watson by the Vancouver Whitecaps.

Caringi's most outstanding season during this period was in 1999 when the Retrievers were nationally ranked with a 19-1-2 record, the best in the nation. Tough at both ends of the field, they were ranked 6th in defense and 11th in scoring. Their reward was UMBC soccer's first trip to the Division I NCAA soccer tournament. The NEC was not entitled to an automatic bid, so UMBC had to play Lafayette College, the Patriot League champion in a playoff match. After four overtimes, the Retrievers edged the Leopards 6–5 in penalty kicks.

No one would have predicted another overtime game in the NCAA opening round because, even though UMBC was undefeated in the regular season, the Retrievers drew the nation's top-ranked Duke Blue Devils in Durham. During the hard fought game, UMBC was ahead 3–l, an often insurmountable lead in soccer, but Duke came back to win 4–3 in overtime. That is what the box score said, but the action on the field was even more dramatic and controversial. At 11:14 of overtime, Duke was awarded a corner kick which means that a player can take an uncontested kick toward the goal about 100 feet away. The typical strategy is to loft the ball into a pack of opposing players in front of the goal with the hope that in the ensuing melee, an unpredictable short header or deflected kick will beat the goalie. Scoring on the original kick is unlikely, since there is no angle to the goal and the keeper has unimpeded vision and plenty of time. On this play, however, the Duke kicker tried to angle the ball directly into the goal which ordinarily would have been an easy save, except in a flagrant foul, the UMBC goalie was knocked into the back of the net and left helpless to defend. UMBC protested and later sent game films to the NCAA and Soccer Referees Committee, but that box score will never change.

Perhaps Caringi's best coaching job was in 2009. In the preceding year, UMBC soccer had an uncharacteristically bad season, finishing last in the AEC. Expectations were low for 2009 as well, but Caringi blended a host of new recruits with veterans who had something to prove to create an outstanding 14–6 record. Midway in the season, the team was nationally ranked and it ended up playing for the conference championship, earning Caringi's 200th victory along the way. The 2010 season was

23. Giuliano Celenza was an All-American in 2000. Levi Houapeu, an All-American, was the nation's leading scorer in 2009 and 2010.

even better. UMBC won the AEC Championship in a dramatic shoot-out to gain an NCAA berth. In the opening tournament round, the Retrievers eliminated #10 Princeton 2–1, before losing to #9 William and Mary in another penalty kick shootout.

In 2012, UMBC returned to the NCAA tournament again. Powered by Pete Caringi, III (ECAC Offensive Player of the Year), Liam Paddock (First Team Academic All-American, NCAA Post-Graduate Scholarship winner), and Phil Saunders (MVP AEC Championship) the Retrievers won the America East Championship with a penalty kick victory over New Hampshire. Then UMBC won a first round tournament match against host Old Dominion University, again with penalty kicks. For the second round, the Dawgs had to travel to Chapel Hill to play the defending national champion University of North Carolina. Once more after 110 minutes, the score was 0–0. This time the Tarheels won the penalty kick shootout, 3–2.

UMBC soccer has been a regional power for many years. The Retrievers have beaten such teams as Air Force, Georgetown, Navy, Maryland, North Carolina State, Penn State, Virginia Tech, Vanderbilt, and West Virginia. At the end of the 2012 season, the team was ranked nationally for both its athletic and academic performance. Soccer now has its own stadium, very strong student support, and the promise of a future as bright as it's past.

Cross Country and Track and Field

The aggregate team records for cross country and track and field are not as comprehensive as for other Retriever sports, partly because their events are often not well publicized. The father of the two sports is quite clear. Jim Pfrogner coached both teams for a remarkable thirty years from 1971–2001. In 1998, he was BSC Coach of the Year and, in his last five years of coaching, UMBC cross country teams won the Baltimore Metro meets five times. The campus provided ample grounds for long cross country runs, but UMBC athletes did not have a modern track until 1996, practicing at Catonsville Community College instead. Pfrogner was elected to the UMBC Hall of Fame[24] and has the unusual honor of being the only member of the UMBC staff to have an athletic facility (in this case the stadium press box) named after him.

In the fall of 1997, David Bobb, UMBC alumnus, became head track coach for the women and three years later, added responsibilities for the men. Bobb was an ideal replacement to fill Pfrogner's big shoes, since he was UMBC's first Division I track All-American. Winning that award as a sprinter five times, he placed third in the 55 meter and 200 meter dashes in the 1996 NCAA indoor championships and finished second in the 100 meter at the NCAA outdoor championships in 1997.

---

24. Only a handful of the luminaries who have graced UMBC athletics can be mentioned in these pages, so the reader may wish to visit the UMBC Hall of Fame web site and check out Appendix H in this book to get to know them better.

Two Retriever All-Americans from other countries have also distinguished themselves. Cleopatra Borel was born in a small fishing village on the east coast of Trinidad and Tobago. She became a three-time All-American winning the 2002 NCAA indoor shot put for UMBC and then represented her native country in many international competitions. She finished 4th in the 2002 Commonwealth Games, later won the bronze medal in several meets (the 2006–07 Commonwealth Games, the Central American and Caribbean Games, and the Pan American Games). A three-time Olympian, she finished 10th in the 2004 Athens Olympics, 17th in the 2008 Beijing Olympics and impressive 6th in the 2012 London Olympics. In 2002, Huguens Jean, who was born in Haiti, placed fourth in the high jump at the NCAA outdoor championships.[25]

Track and field is a quintessentially individual sport, but Coach Bobb has been successful in moving UMBC up in AEC team competition. In 2003 the Retrievers hosted their first AEC championship with the men finishing third. By 2010–2011, there were 45 men and 27 women running, jumping, and flinging for UMBC.

Swimming and Diving

In only one sport could UMBC be called a dynasty and that would be men's and women's swimming and diving. Pool records, conference championships, and even success in international competitions characterize the UMBC swimming tradition. Swimming is a sport that is heavily dependent on facilities and UMBC's are first-rate, serving varsity athletes as well as community swimmers of all ages. The UMBC Natatorium was opened in 1977 and the 50 meter outdoor pool in 1996. In 1997, Michael Phelps, swimming for a local club, set the still-existing indoor pool record in the 100 and 200 meter backstroke, before he went on to upgraded Olympic competition.

The swimming and diving program was begun in 1986 under Sid Burkot who coached for 15 seasons and gradually built a powerhouse, winning almost 200 meets and the ECAC championships and NEC Conference championships in 1988–1989, 1999–2000, and 2000–01.

In 2001–2002, Chad Cradock became head swimming and diving coach. Raised in Barrie, Ontario, Cradock is a son of UMBC. As an undergraduate, he won the Matt Skalsky Outstanding Scholar Athlete award and was the team's most valuable athlete for two years. He swam middle and long distance events and held three UMBC records, only recently broken by athletes he himself coached. He swam at the U.S. open and in the Canadian Olympic Trials. As a coach, Cradock built on a strong tradition and has taken the program to new heights.

Division I competition requires hard work for any athlete, but swimming can be particularly grueling, requiring long hours in the pool competing against former personal best times. On meet day, races are often won and lost in fractions of seconds against multiple competitors recruited from around the world. It is a team sport with fierce personal competition.

---

25. UMBC Track and Field Guide 2008.

Coaches like to say there is no "I" in team, but it might be a temptation to accept that perspective in swimming and diving.

In this environment, Cradock has not only produced record holders, but an assembly of swimmers and divers who regard themselves as a team with an usual communal *esprit de corps*. They root for each other intensely. By 2011, the men had won seventeen conference championships (NEC and ECAC in 2001–2002 and 2002–2003 and in the AEC an incredible eight in a row from 2003 to 2011, while the women have won NEC championships in 2001–2002 and 2002–2003 and the AEC in 2006, 2008 and 2010–11). Not surprisingly, Cradock has been named Conference Coach of the Year in 2001–2002 and 2002–2003 and he and his staff have been picked as the AEC best in 2005–2006, 2006–2007, and 2010–2011. Overall by 2011, Cradock's dual meet record was an astounding 83–17 for men and 78–32 for women. Moreover, the 2011 team was named a Scholar All-American team by the College Swimming Association and two of its stars (Keilan Freeman and Brad Reitz) were awarded Division I Scholar All-American status.

All dynasties end someday, but UMBC swimming and diving has had a very long run. In 2012, the Retrievers finished behind Boston University in the AEC championships, but three members of the team: Mohamed Hussien (Egypt); Pierre De Waal (South Africa); and Patrick Husson (USA) earned Olympic try-outs.[26]

Tennis

UMBC first fielded men's and women's tennis teams in 1970, but those records are not well preserved. The considerable modern success of Retriever tennis is the result of Coach Keith Puryear who built the program over his twenty-year UMBC career. In 2009 he departed to begin the women's tennis program at the Naval Academy, but leaving UMBC was a tough decision. A UMBC alumnus, Puryear played at UMBC for a year, before serving a four-year stint in the Marine Corps, and then returning for his economics degree in 1990.

In his two-decade UMBC career, he was conference Coach of the Year in the BSC 1997–1998 (women), NEC 1998–1999 and 2002–2003 (women), 2000–2001 and 2001–2002 (women and men), and AEC 2006–2007 (women and men). His overall winning record for men was 226–179 (.558) and women 207–129 (.616). Between 1997 and 2003, Retriever men won four conference championships and the women a remarkable seven conference titles in a row to make multiple NCAA appearances. In 2007, UMBC men won their first AEC championship.

UMBC's total tennis facilities consist of six courts for its two teams and more than 14,000 students. Lights were not installed until 2005. So it was not the grandeur of the infrastructure that accounts for Retriever success. As his accolades signify, Puryear was a talented coach and player, but his quiet, almost laconic personality, helped to recruit players from around the world, most of whom had never seen the campus

26. Hussein made the Egyptian team, joining as an Olympian former Retriever swimmer Mehdi Addadi, who swam for the Algerian team during the 2000 games.

before they arrived. His 2007–2008 team included athletes from Brazil, Estonia, France, Ontario, Quebec, Poland, and Romania.

When Puryear left for Navy, he was replaced by Rob Hubbard, a native Baltimorean (Calvert Hall alumnus), former professional player, and an experienced tennis coach (Goucher College and the University of Texas-Pan American). Hubbard continued broadening the recruiting base and strengthening the schedule. In 2009, the Retriever men were 12–7 in individual matches and in 2009–2010, they went 17–6. The women's tennis team was 7–7 in 2009, 15–8 in 2010, 10–9 in 2001 and 15–8 in 2012. Both the men's and women's teams have consistently made the AEC tournament, but a conference title has eluded them.

Tennis also has been a sport with strong academic performers. Oscar Lopez was an Academic All-American in 1998–2000. Lana Khvalina, an Academic All-American in 2003 and 2004, was her class Salutatorian and won UMBC's first NCAA Post-Graduate Scholarship. Three UMBC women's tennis players were named 2010–2011 Intercollegiate Tennis Association Scholar athletes.

Women's Basketball

A year after men began to play intercollegiate basketball, UMBC women took up the sport in 1968. Over the winter break, twenty girls formed a basketball team, though originally, it did not have a coach. As with all UMBC sports, it was tough sledding at first. In 1970, the Retriever women lost to Catonsville Community College 35–69. By 1980, when Sue Furnary took over as the program's fifth head coach in twelve years, UMBC had lost at least 68 of the 104 games it had played as a Division III school and in some years complete records of scores were not preserved. Furnary coached thirteen years at UMBC, spanning the Division III to the Division I era. Beginning in 1984–1985 to 1986–1987 in Division II, UMBC had an unprecedented three straight winning years. As member of the Mason-Dixon Conference in 1985–1986, Furnary won twenty games and lost only nine. But after UMBC became a Division I school, the increased competition resulted in only one winning season in its first seven years of competition at that level. Nevertheless, Coach Furnary was in many respects the founding mother of UMBC women's basketball and, by the time she left, the Retrievers were playing and beating teams such as Delaware, Hofstra, and Richmond.

Kathy Solano (1993–1994 to 1997–1998) and Jennifer Bednarek replaced Furnary, but, although they could get their teams into BSC and NEC tournaments, they could not win them. Enter Phil Stern in 2005, the first male coach of the women's team and its eighth coach in thirty-seven years. Stern, a successful Division II coach at Dowling College and University of South Carolina-Aiken, was an advocate of the Princeton offense. This precision passing attack requires recruits who want to play it and even then it takes a while to master. In his first year, Stern took a senior laden team to the NEC championship game, but in the next year he had to play without those seniors just as UMBC entered the much tougher AEC. Only four games were won in 2003–2004 and eight the next year. In the meantime, not only was the conference schedule more difficult, but there were road trips to the University of North Carolina and Maryland.

By 2005–2006, there were tangible signs of improvement at 15–13, AEC 5–7, but the real drama was in the 2006–2007 season. In that season UMBC (AEC 5–7) entered the conference tournament as the 5th seed, but the Retrievers upset Stony Brook and then beat Vermont the day after. Now they would play the formidable Hartford Hawks (15–1), by far the dominant team in the league. And play they did, leading 48–39 with an excruciating six minutes left. UMBC would not score again. As time wound down, Hartford mounted a ferocious rally on their home court, but a Hawk three point buzzer-beater to win bounced off the basket rim, instigating a delirious Retriever celebration.[27]

A characteristic of the NCAA tournament is a nationwide broadcast announcing the seeds and first round games. A novel experience for the Retrievers, UMBC went all out to imitate its more experienced foes. As the team gathered in the Retriever Sportszone room of the Commons surrounded by athletic paraphernalia from all the UMBC teams, the pep band, dance teams, cheerleaders,[28] and packed-in fans, the audience waited impatiently to hear their team's name called. In reality, UMBC was almost certain to be the 16th seed in the sixteen team regional competition. No matter, few people in the room believed these women would have ever arrived at this moment. When the ESPN announcer intoned UMBC would play Connecticut, winner of five previous NCAA championships, in Hartford, no less, the room exploded with cheering and not a little impromptu dancing. The women would be the first UMBC basketball team to go to the NCAA Division I Tournament. Except for the players, the actual game was a bit anti-climactic, abandoned by network television early on. The Huskies were taller, faster, and stronger than the Retrievers. Though the final scoreboard showed a 33–82 defeat, it was an unforgettable experience for the University and it set a bar for future achievements.

By 2010–2011, another trend was evident—academic excellence. In the past, there had been some women's basketball stars who were also academic stand-outs. Matea Pender (2001–2006), a former member of the Croatian national team and one of UMBC's all-time leading scorers, received her Ph.D. in Public Policy in 2010. By 2009–2010, the UMBC women's basketball team GPA was 3.58, ranked 3rd nationally among all Division I teams. All eleven team members had at least a 3.0 and seven had 3.5 GPAs or better. There was nothing accidental about that achievement. Coach Stern asserted "Ever since I got here, we've targeted student-athletes who understand that academics are our top priority," which turns out has helped recruiting. Meghan Collabella, 2010–11 team captain and high school New Jersey Distinguished Scholar, graduated from UMBC magna cum laude in three years and finished her playing career by studying for a Master's degree in Historical Studies,

27. The moment can still be savored in a You Tube video "Magic Moments First Taste of Big Dance, A New Future for UMBC Athletics."

28. For descriptions of these very energetic athletic support groups, see three stories by Corey Johns, *Retriever*, March 5, 2011.

which she earned in 2012. Center Dana Lewis, a high school valedictorian from Wisconsin, chose to become a Retriever because "The team's academic reputation played a huge role in me choosing UMBC. Some of the other schools that I was looking at had [team] average GPAs of 2.8–3.0, and that was not up to my standards."[29] In 2010 and again in 20ll, UMBC women's basketball was recognized as one of the top 25 academic teams in the country.

In 2010–2011, the academically proficient Retrievers showed they could also score on the court, winning twenty games and the regular season AEC championship. Advancing to the Women's National Invitational post-season tournament, they lost in a competitive first round game to the University of Florida in Gainesville. The next year the Retrievers won seventeen games and played for the AEC championship.

Men's Basketball

For schools ambitious to make an impact on the sports world, there is no more tempting target than men's basketball. Its tournament, "the Big Dance," has become a national obsession. Make the sixty-eight team tournament and, as long as you survive, you are a national story. Furthermore, the cost-benefit ratio looks propitious. Recruit just a couple of high school "stars" and you can be nationally competitive. It is, of course, not that easy. These "stars" have pro career stars in their eyes and that means they seek a big national stage with lots of media publicity, which is difficult for "mid-major" institutions in non-power conferences to generate. Unlike baseball, lacrosse, or soccer, no UMBC basketball player has ever played in the sport's major league, the NBA, though some have appeared briefly for European professional teams.[30]

Then there are academic issues. Many of the best high school basketball players have poor academic skills and indifferent scholastic motivations. Like all of its athletic rivals UMBC does accept a few athletic "individual admits" whose SATs or high school GPAs are below the University norm, though still acceptable by NCAA rules, in basketball and other sports. Once admitted they are closely monitored with supervised study halls and individual tutoring. Away from home and high school culture, some flourish and some perish. UMBC has no "jock" majors and no willingness to cut educational corners. Still UMBC casts covetous glances at what basketball success might look like and for one brief shining moment the Dawgs danced.

Men's basketball began in 1967, the year after the school opened. Not surprisingly it was tough going. The team won four games that year, five in each of the next two and three in 1970–71. In 1969–1970, the Retrievers lost to St. Mary's Seminary by a point. By 1972–1973, under Coach John Frank, however, the team won the Potomac Conference tournament beating Gallaudet, George Mason, and Coppin in three successive games.

---

29. Jessica Bernheim, "UMBC Women's Basketball: A Team of Student Athletes," *UMBC 2011 Gameday.* 14–15.

30. Andrew Feeley, class of 2005, played on four continents, Asia, Europe, North America, and South America in six professional seasons.

UMBC men's basketball fortunes and its competition began to improve in 1974 with a new arena (now called the Retriever Athletic Center or RAC) and a new coach, Billy Jones. The first African-American player in the Atlantic Coast Conference, Jones began to recruit better athletes. In 1977–1978, ten years after beginning the sport, UMBC had its first winning season. The next two years were the highlights of the Jones era, as the team won 21 and then 23 games. As a reward, it was invited to the Division II South Atlantic regionals the first year and was the regional runner-up the second. Jones coached twelve years at UMBC, leaving with a 143–179 record and the distinction of creating a very competitive Division II program that was being taken seriously for the first time on campus.

UMBC moved to Division I in 1986, only sixteen years after losing to the St. Mary's hoops-playing seminarians. With this move, the University signaled its intention to step up its basketball profile by hiring Jeff Bzdelik, who had been an assistant coach at Northwestern. Bzdelik coached only two years in the RAC before moving on to a career as head coach of the Air Force Academy, the University of Colorado, and later the National Basketball Association's Denver Nuggets. He did not have winning seasons at the Retrievers helm, but UMBC, in the manner of hopeful mid-majors, began to sprinkle its schedule with bona fide basketball powers (Georgetown, Maryland, Miami, North Carolina State, Northwestern, and Ohio State). These were always away games and the Retrievers always lost; but the financial guarantees were lucrative and the schedule spoke to the school's new aspirations. Bzdelik's teams did beat some good mid-major teams (American, East Carolina, Florida International, Navy, and Northern Arizona).

In Bzdelik's brief tenure, he raised the profile of UMBC basketball and there were 125 applicants for his vacated job. In 1988, the basketball reins were passed to Earl Hawkins, a very successful high school coach. Hawkins, who coached at UMBC for seven years, while competing in the ECC and BSC conferences won with Bzdelik's players in 1988–1989, but after that victories were hard to come by.

Tom Sullivan, former assistant at Seton Hall, took over in 1995 for a nine-year run in the BSC and NEC. His best year was in 1998–1999 when he compiled a 19–9 record and won the regular season NEC championship. In 2001–2012, he became the first UMBC Division I men's basketball coach to win twenty games in a season. UMBC had become the dominant power among Baltimore's five Division I basketball teams, winning the Battle of Baltimore tournament four straight years from 2000–2003. Other local coaches then gave up on that tournament concept. In UMBC's first year as an AEC member, however, there were only seven wins in that season and a last place finish in the conference. It was time for a change, but none of UMBC's previous six men's basketball coaches had had overall winning records.

The new choice to replace Sullivan was an unusual one for a not very successful program. UMBC promoted its long-time assistant coach, Randy Monroe as the new head man. Monroe had been an assistant at Cheney State, his alma mater, before moving to LaSalle, and then to Vanderbilt. He joined the UMBC staff in 1994 and in 2003 he was chosen the AFLAC National Assistant Coach of the Year. Monroe was ready to have his own team. His "Monroe doctrine" sought to make UMBC basketball a part of the community, rekindle alumni pride, ensure the long-term success of student-athletes, create a UMBC basketball family, and outwork the competition. It was a tall order.

Success was not immediate as the Retrievers twice finished eighth in the nine-team AEC. But there were signs of progress. UMBC won a conference tournament game in 2005, 2006, and 2007. In the climax of the 2008 season, Monroe took the Retrievers to new heights. Combining the talents of three transfers with some home grown stars, UMBC finished the regular season at 21–8. Expectations were high for the AEC tournament and the team did not disappoint, dispatching Stony Brook and Vermont. That meant the conference championship, with an NCAA bid on the line, would be played in the RAC. The campus began to experience an unprecedented Retriever fever, as students became excited by the kind of consequential game they had only watched on television before. The RAC was sold out four days before the game. As the ESPN2 crews began to set up, students donned their gold shirts, painted their faces, and prepared to do some serious barking. Again the opponent was Hartford, but the Hawks never had a chance as the Retrievers went on a twenty point run in the first half and won a convincing 82–65 victory. With a comfortable lead, the delirium began early. When students rushed the floor before the buzzer went off, nobody objected.

At last, a favored UMBC basketball team had played magnificently on a big stage and now would advance to the biggest one, the NCAA tournament. March Madness, as the tournament is called, is probably the most publicized athletic event in the United States. UMBC found itself on the cover of *USA Today* and a picture of its diminutive guard, Jay Greene was shown in the *CBS Special* "One Shining Moment." Even after drawing the perennial power Georgetown Hoyas in the first round at Charlotte, hopes were high; but the superior height and athleticism of the Big East foe prevailed 66–47.

Graduation took its toll, but the 2008–2009 Retrievers were still tough. They ended a long Nebraska home game winning streak by defeating the Cornhuskers and played again for the AEC championship, losing it to a scandal-stained Binghamton Bearcats team.

Basketball is a sport in which only a few players can be decisive and UMBC's recruiting well abruptly ran dry. The 2009–2010 team won only four games, none at home, and the 2010–2011 team prevailed in only five games, a dismal record followed with just four wins in 2011–2012. On October 10, 2012, Randy Monroe resigned a month before the start of the season, taking with him some memorable highlights, but an overall 85 win 160 loss record

Baseball

Begun in 1967, baseball was initially coached by Tom Rider who did double duty by also handling men's soccer in the fall. The team struggled, until John Jancuska was brought in to coach in 1977. That began the longest and one of the most successful coaching tenures in UMBC history. In his thirty-four year reign, Jancuska won 673 games, and coached his team to five NCAA appearances. During this period he led the Retrievers to the NCAA II Middle Atlantic Regional tournament twice in his first two years (1978–1979), the NCAA II South Regionals in 1986, the Division I East Regionals in 1992, and again in 2001. The 37–11, 1992 season was particularly special, even though the Retrievers lost 3–1 to Miami, a national power, in the NCAA tournament.

Jancuska has been Coach of the Year in all three Division I Conferences in which the Retrievers have played (Big South 1993, Northeast 2000, and America East 2008). Aided by 15 year assistant Bob Mumma, UMBC alumnus and home run record holder, the program has produced twenty players who signed professional contracts. In 2004, when San Diego played San Francisco, former UMBC players Wayne Franklin (7 years in the majors) was in the bullpen for the Padres and Jay Witasick (16 years in the majors) was pitching for the Giants. Four Retrievers hardballers have become Academic All-Americans.

In 2011, Mumma moved up to become head coach. Like other sports, entrance into the AEC has toughened the schedule considerably, but the combination of new coaching and improved facilities may be enough to build on the program's long history of success.

Softball

Begun in 1991, twenty-four years after baseball, softball has been a successful sport at UMBC. Unlike baseball, it has had five different coaches in a much shorter time frame. In 2000, Michele Neveling won the Northeast Championship, but softball's greatest success has been under Coach Joe French, hired in 2002. French was a veteran who has coached in more than 1000 games spanning tennis, women's basketball, and, of course, softball. In his first year, the Retrievers won 47 games, the NEC championship and a play-in game to advance to the first round of the NCAA tournament. The next year, the Retrievers were the NEC regular season champions and then the team entered the AEC. Their conference record fell from 19–3 in the NEC to 3–17 in the AEC. Coach French has been successful, however, in building an AEC competitor, with a winning conference record each year from 2005–2011. Overall his record is 346–276 at UMBC. A number of his players have won all-conference and all-regional honors. Possibly the most distinguished was Melanie Denischuck who was AEC Player of the Year in 2006 and selected as a top-twenty-five finalist for the USA Collegiate Softball Player of the Year award.

Women's Lacrosse

The year after the woman's lacrosse program began; Kathy Zerrlaut became its head coach in 1973. In 1984, Zerrlaut's team won the Division II ECAC championship and in an outstanding twenty-four years as head coach, she won 150 games for an overall .510 record. Zerrlaut was the Intercollegiate Women's Lacrosse Coaches Association Coach of the Year for Division II in both 1985 and 1986.

In 1987, women's lacrosse gained Division I status. Ten years later, after Zerrlaut took on more administrative responsibilities, UMBC had four head women's lacrosse coaches in a span of fourteen years. Monica (nee DiCandilo) Yeakel won the regular season NEC Championship in 1998, 1999, 2000, 2002, and 2003. Three times as NEC tournament champions, UMBC women went to the NCAAs in 1999, 2002, and 2003.

But winning in the AEC conference presented much more formidable challenges. AEC teams are frequently nationally ranked and the women's game had changed. Partly because of Title IX and partly because of the natural attractiveness of women's lacrosse, programs were started at Florida, Louisville, Cincinnati, Cal-Berkeley, Stanford, Oregon, Northwestern, and Vanderbilt, all schools with substantial resources. The one thing all the new programs had in common was that they loved to recruit in the Baltimore area, absolutely plundering the region for its highly talented players. Naturally, that impacted recruiting at UMBC. Nevertheless, in 2006, Courtney Connor's team beat 11th ranked Boston University, leading to a share of the AEC regular season title and an AEC Coach of the year award for Connor.

Three years later, Connor was gone, replaced by Kelly Berger, a two time All-American, most valuable player in the 2007 North/South game, nominee for the Tewaaraton Trophy (lacrosse's Heisman award) and a member of the 2011–2012 USA national team. Her assistant coach, Amy Appelt won the 2004 Tewaaraton Trophy and was a four time All-American leading Virginia to a national championship in that year. Success was instantaneous for the new Retriever staff. UMBC beat the regular season AEC champion and nationally-ranked Albany in the semi-finals of the conference tournament, before a heartbreaking 11–10 loss to Boston University in the title game in 2010. Again in 2011 and 2012, the Retrievers advanced to the title game, only to come up short against Albany's undefeated and nationally-ranked Great Danes.

Men's Lacrosse

The arrival of Dick Watts to UMBC in 1967 almost immediately made men's lacrosse a force to be reckoned with. In his twenty-two years as head coach, Watts coached forty-eight players who earned All-American status. In 1975, his no-athletic scholarship Retrievers beat Syracuse (as part of a four-game winning streak against the Orange), Navy, and Virginia in games watched by fans sitting on the hillside before the current UMBC stadium was built. The Navy game was played in a downpour, but all that water did not help the nationally-ranked Mids who lost a tight 10–9 contest. To add insult to injury, the Navy bus got stuck in the mud above the field, like a marooned ship, and the Navy team had to find another way back to Annapolis. In 1986, Watts's UMBC team beat Princeton, Virginia, Cornell, Penn State, and Georgetown in a single season. His teams won four MDC championships, but his greatest success was in the NCAA tournaments. From 1974 to 1980, he coached the Retrievers into the Division II–III tourney each year. His team was runner-up in the 1979 Division II NCAA tournament. The next year UMBC won the 1980 national championship before an appreciative home crowd and national television audience. It has been UMBC's only national championship team.

Recruiting to a new campus that offered only a few majors and had even less on-campus social life, while competing against national lacrosse powers required a special approach. Watts remembers that he instructed his ace recruiter Charlie Coker to focus on fine athletes who were overlooked or out-of-position in high school. The strategy worked. Gary Clipp had been a high school goalie, but his speed earned him an All-American defenseman award and a position on the USA national team in 1982. George McGeeney, who became the best defenseman in America and played on the 1986 and 1990 USA national teams, had been a football player before coming to UMBC. Rick Wey, another All-American, never faced off before coming to UMBC, but became nationally dominant in that skill after becoming a Retriever.

In 1981, Watts moved men's lacrosse into Division I status. Although they were consistently competitive with ten wins in 1991 and 1992, the going was tougher and it was not certain UMBC could be a nationally-ranked or even a tournament team in Division I. Replacing Dick Watts as lacrosse coach whose overall record was 176–144 was a daunting task. In 2008, Watts was elected to the U.S. Lacrosse Hall of Fame.

Fortunately, the ideal candidate was only a few miles away with roots in Johns Hopkins University's storied lacrosse program. Don Zimmerman had been an All-American midfielder at Hopkins. Returning to his alma mater as head coach in 1984, he led the Blue Jays to a national championship in his first year and repeated again in 1985 and 1987.[31]

When "Zim" moved to UMBC in 1994, lacrosse had begun to emerge into the high profile sport it is today. By 1994, the national championship game was watched by 20,000 fans or more and broadcast by ESPN. Universities such as Duke, Georgetown, Ohio State and Notre Dame that had treated lacrosse as a minor athletic activity began to invest in the sport and seek national prominence. Keeping UMBC in the top echelons of the lacrosse world had become much more difficult. In Zimmerman's first three years, victories were tough to come by, but in his fourth year the Retrievers were 9 and 3. Then in 1998 and 1999, UMBC made its first appearances in the Division I NCAA tournament losing by one goal to Georgetown and Delaware respectively. Nevertheless, his 1999 team beat Navy, Cornell, North Carolina, and Maryland.

In its first two years in unexpectedly tough AEC lacrosse competition, UMBC was knocked out twice in the league tournament. But from 2006 until 2009, UMBC won the AEC East regular season and tournament championship in three out of four

---

31. Zimmerman's coaching career at Hopkins and UMBC was chronicled in an article, Kevin Heitz, "Don Zimmerman: Lacrosse Engineer," *Pressbox*, Issue 146, February 2010, http:w.w.w.pressboxonline.com/story/ 5909/.

years. For their achievements in 2006, Zimmerman was voted Coach of the Year, Brandon Mundorf was conference player of the year,[32] Justin Berdeguez, defensive player of the year, and Jeremy Blevins, rookie of the year. From 2006–2009, Zimmerman coached the Retrievers back into the NCAA tournament for four consecutive years. A loss to Princeton in the 2006 NCAA tournament took only a little luster off this wonderful 10–5 season. In 2007, the Retrievers were co-regular season AEC Champion, but they lost the tournament championship by a goal. They still were awarded at "at-large" invitation to the NCAA tournament which set the stage for their most dramatic NCAA contest, a 13–9 tournament victory over the Maryland Terrapins. The next year, UMBC was back in the NCAA tournament, (see photo of the dramatic comeback win against Albany) but lost a nail-biting 10–9 game to #2 Virginia in Charlottesville. Four Retrievers from that team were named to All-American teams. In a back and forth 2009 NCAA struggle in steamy Chapel Hill, the Tarheels prevailed 15–13, in what was a bitter disappointment for the Retrievers. Although UNC was the higher ranked team, UMBC expected to win after a brilliant 12 and 3 season.

In almost every sport, there are ups and downs in talent flows and 2010, 2011, and 2012 were unusual low points for the Retrievers. Playing a very tough 2012 schedule, UMBC lost in one-sided contests to national finalists Loyola and Hopkins, but beat the national semi-finalist Maryland. The #4 Terrapins had tried to avoid playing UMBC that season. Perhaps they sensed their fate because they lost the game 8–7, when the Retrievers scored five unanswered goals in the fourth quarter.[33]

Except for Johns Hopkins, UMBC has beaten all the major lacrosse powers at one time or another with players who were rarely the top-ranked recruits. Two-thirds of Retriever All-Americans were produced by Watts and Zimmerman. Men's lacrosse and men's soccer, both mentored by veteran coaches, are UMBC's only sports where consistently beating nationally ranked teams is often not an upset.

Club Sports

For every varsity athlete at UMBC, another person wears the black and gold playing club sports. These teams, which offer no financial aid to participants and have volunteer or part-time coaches, nevertheless provide their athletes with the benefits of physical fitness, team comradeship, and competition. Begun in the early 1990's, by 2011, UMBC sponsored club teams in twenty-five sports (aikido, badminton, bowling, ballroom dancing, crew, cricket, cycling, fencing, field hockey, jujitsu, sailing, skiing and snow boarding, tae kwon do, tennis, ultimate frisbee, and men's and

32. Mundorf went on to play professional lacrosse with the Denver Outlaws (outdoors) and New York Titans (indoors) achieving all-league status. He and teammate Drew Westervelt were selected to the 2010 United States National Lacrosse team. For a description of Mundorf's storied career, see Jeff Seidel, "The Mask," *UMBC Magazine*, Winter 2013. 23–26.

33. UMBC previously had beaten higher ranked Maryland lacrosse teams five times, including the #1 Terrapins in 1998 and three straight years between 2007 and 2009.

women's rugby, lacrosse, soccer and volleyball) involving about 1000 athletes. As club sports, men's ice hockey, cricket, and wrestling have been nationally ranked.

E. Conclusions

The public view of the health of intercollegiate athletics, like its view of many other subjects, is distorted by television. Packed stadiums and arenas are not the norm among the more than 3,000 United States higher education institutions. The public does not see the indifferent students and communities and the constant cut backs of "non-revenue" sports that are characteristics of many campuses. Those realities are an important context for a school such as UMBC with a history of no bowl games or NCAA Division I championships and which does not dominate even a local sports market. Does anyone care about Retriever athletics? Should anyone care?

Intercollegiate athletics at the so-called "mid-major" Division I universities rarely make money. Unlike the major conference schools whose contests may enthrall entire states and are frequently on national television, mid-major games may appeal to niche audiences in the community and find their way occasionally into local cable television. Consequently, they are often a hard sell to modern students who do not come to universities to be audiences at uncool unpublicized events. In an era when students have ever-available electronics as a completely pliant companion, the sense of community and bonding athletics can provide often does not happen on such a diverse and, sometimes, austere seeming campus as UMBC. In a media market so overdosed on professional sports that it barely notices Baltimore collegiate teams, generating on-campus enthusiasm for sporting events that television often ignores is difficult.[34]

Competitive athletic programs also can be costly in several ways. Academic scandals are not uncommon among the big-time schools. No one at UMBC ignores that price or would be willing to pay it. In recent years despite the intensive time demands of playing a Division I sports, Retriever athletes have been more likely to graduate by about ten percentage points than the average UMBC student and the University has always exceeded NCAA academic requirements for every team.[35] More than half of all varsity athletes have 3.0 GPAs or better and there have been twenty-five Academic all-Americans.[36] Cornelia Carapcea was a two-time Academic All-American tennis player and the co-salutatorian of the class of 2009 with a 4.00 GPA. No surprise, she won a national competition to be one of the ten best English speakers in her native Romania.

34. George R. La Noue, "The Muddled Future of Mid-Major Athletics," *The Chronicle of Higher Education* (on line) December 4, 2014.

35. NCAA certification reports are public documents. UMBC was one of the first five Division I program in the country to be certified by the NCAA.

36. See Appendix H.

But the other cost, financial, is unavoidable.[37] In 2011, the UMBC's athletic budget was more than $12 million,[38] though as Figure T shows that is one of the smaller budgets in the AEC.[39]

Figure T
America East Conference Athletic Total Revenues

University at Albany	$14,638,810
Binghamton University	$11,773,318
Boston University	$27,788,714
University of Hartford	$11,948,177
University of Maine-Orono	$16,636,706
UMBC	$12,514,970
University of New Hampshire	$22,716,355
Stony Brook University	$22,038,328
University of Vermont	$16,319,000

Source: UMBC athletic department from America East Conference reports.

In comparison, for example, the University of Maryland College Park athletic budget in 2011 was about $65 million. Unlike the major powers which can count on substantial gate receipts, TV contracts, advertising and generous fan donations, Division I schools with lesser profiles cannot depend on those sources.[40] At UMBC, where by Maryland law tax funds cannot support intercollegiate competition, student

37. Libby Sander and Brad Wolverton, "Debt Loads Weight Heavily on Athletics Programs," *The Chronicle of Higher Education*, September 28, 2009, p.1 ff. The USM Regents have required the University of Maryland, College Park, Bowie State University, Coppin State University and UMBC to submit a plan to reduce their athletic department debt. UMBC's debt was caused principally by the costs involved in joining Division I and later the America East Conference. Priyanka Oza, "UMBC Athletics: In debt but worth it." *The Retriever Weekly*, December 8, 2009.

38. That amount is roughly equivalent to the combined compensation of the three Southeastern Conference head football coaches, but then in 2009 that Conference signed a $3 billion television agreement with ESPN and CBS. Brad Wolverton, "A Powerful League Piles Up Its Advantages," *The Chronicle of Higher Education*, September 4, 2009. A1, 26.

39. Some AEC rivals have made heavy investments in expensive sports such as football and/or hockey, so expenditures by UMBC and conference competitors in sport by sport comparisons may be similar.

40. By 2011, UMBC had three or four regular season men's basketball games televised and about the same number for men's lacrosse. The cost per game was about $25,000 with the station recouping about half through commercials and UMBC paying for the other half.

fees that are over $800 a year keep the program afloat.[41] For part-time students and others putting themselves through college on minimum wage jobs, the fee can be painful. UMBC families also contribute voluntarily to upgrading facilities, subsidizing road trips, and replenishing calories just expended by sons and daughters with after game food feasts. More recently, the Athletic Department has had some success in becoming more entrepreneurial, raising about $1.25 million a year in camps, corporate sponsorships, and five figure donations.

Nevertheless, partly for financial reasons, UMBC has had to give up on five intercollegiate sports. None of them generated much public interest. Gymnastics competed from 1971 to 1978. Varsity wrestling existed for a few years before being resurrected as a club sport. Fencing was a varsity sport from 1972 to 1980. Field hockey was played at the varsity level from 1977 to 1987, when it was replaced by women's soccer, and then reestablished in 2000. The program was not successful and the AEC had decided to emphasize three sports (basketball, soccer, and lacrosse) with the goal of making them nationally competitive, so something had to give. Despite a passionate effort by its supporters and a hearing by the Women's Caucus in the Maryland legislature, UMBC varsity field hockey played its last game in 2005. It is now a club sport. Men's and women's golf were more competitive, with the men winning three straight NEC championships (1999–2001), but these squads played their last varsity rounds in 2002.

Then, there is the phantom sport which UMBC has not played and, perhaps, never will because it is so expensive. It is "remembered" only on t-shirts with the ironic slogan "UMBC football-undefeated." In 1967, Albin Kuhn reserved $50,000 to start football which he viewed as a normal program in a university. Along with a new football program, a proposed ROTC unit was also on the 1968 Faculty Senate agenda.[42] Since this was the Vietnam era, there was a long debate in the Faculty Senate. The young UMBC faculty had little sympathy for either proposal and the vote was a resounding "no" on both.[43] Several decades later, a local businessman approached UMBC with an offer to put up some money for a football team, but President Hrabowski said no. Given the struggle to support existing teams at a Division I level, maybe deferring on football was the right answer. The existing stadium, seating only 4,500, would have made that sport a money-losing proposition, draining resources from other sports. There is, however, a definite vacuum on the campus when most universities have autumn rituals revolving around football.

---

41. In 2011, about 31 percent of student fees went for to athletics and recreation purposes, but those funds provided 71 percent of the athletic budget. UMBC, "FY 2011 Annual Report on Intercollegiate Athletics to the USM Board of Regents," April 2012.

42. Chancellor Kuhn wrote to Senate Faculty leaders, "Although, as I mentioned in the last Senate meeting, I strongly favor this development [ROTC] at UMBC, I believe it is a matter that should be decided by the faculty and I will no way attempt to unduly influence the outcome." Albin O. Kuhn to Alvin Meckler, memorandum April 9, 1968. Formal pro and con position papers were developed before the May 1968 Senate negative vote. Historic Documents, Special Collections, University of Maryland, Baltimore County. Exactly forty years later, President Hrabowski welcomed the establishment of a UMBC ROTC unit.

43. Rudy Storch, emeritus professor, email to Freeman Hrabowski, November 14, 2011.

Currently UMBC supports 19 varsity teams, 10 for women and 9 for men which is a fairly large number in this era of budgetary constraints. Fully compliant with Title IX, in 2011, UMBC provided 83 equivalent athletic scholarships to 186 women athletes and 67 such scholarships to male athletes, even though men are about 54 percent of the enrollment.

Athletics at UMBC have not become the juggernaut that has developed at many universities. For many institutions committed to ever more expensive intercollegiate programs, athletics has become an exercise in riding the proverbial tiger. Too risky to ride and too dangerous to dismount.[44] At UMBC, there are no celebrity coaches who earn many multiples of the salary of the university president and whose fate often appears to be the most important decision that the campus CEO and Board can make. No local economy depends on UMBC game day crowds. There are no loud, demanding booster clubs whose attachment to the university is as fickle as a face-off outcome. UMBC is still more likely to receive major press coverage for its academic than its athletic prowess.

UMBC's athletic path has very much followed its academic trajectory. From Division III to Division II to Division I in twenty years and from the Big South Conference to the Northeast Conference to the America East Conference in eleven years, UMBC has gone from an obscure local sports school to a University playing strong opponents in its region and recruiting nationally and internationally. Sustained success against increasing competition is a goal rarely achieved in intercollegiate athletics. Particularly in the early years, recruiting quality student-athletes who had many other choices was not an easy task. The rumor that UMBC had no student life was never true, but recruitable athletes were not equipped with stethoscopes to detect its sometimes faint pulse.

Unlike the initial intention that UMBC should be a research university, it cannot be said UMBC's athletic development was always in the plan. Athletic growth occurred incrementally with a number of critical decisions made over the years. Administrators and coaches do not win races or bury shots, but they do raise money, make budgets and schedules, enforce rules, recruit athletes, hire assistants, organize practices, and make countless game day decisions. UMBC has attracted a number of outstanding administrators and coaches (Brown, Caringi, Craddock, Jancuska, Kubiet, Levy, Maier, Pfrogner, Puryear, Watts, Wohlstetter, Zerrlaut, and Zimmerman) who made long-term commitments to program building and they have been essential to the Retrievers' success.

Intercollegiate athletics cannot be evaluated just by the benefits accorded varsity athletes or by win-loss records. There are many markers of the increasing importance of UMBC athletics to the University. Perhaps the most significant is that Retriever teams have sometimes become a catalyst for creating the kind of spirit that brings

---

44. For a critique of the place of the athletics as a business enterprise in the university, see Derek Bok, *Universities in the Marketplace: The Commercialization of Higher Education* (Princeton, N.J.: Princeton University Press, 2003), chapters 3 and 7.

people together on the highly diverse UMBC campus. Some students, alumni, and community members care and root passionately for the Black and Gold. Basketball games feature the famous Down and Dirty Dawg pep band, dancers, cheerleaders, baton twirlers, and sometimes tumblers. It is quite a show. Win or lose, singing the alma mater, only composed in 2006, as the final act after a game, does not seem strained any more. The words of the UMBC Riser, written in 1991, but now played regularly, "Rise up and cheer UMBC, Forward to another Victory ... Stand Up and Roar, Make Echoes ring from the Mountains to the Shore" gets the crowd clapping in rhythm.[45] Pictures of happy students captioned "We are Retriever Believers" shouting out their approval of the 2007 victory that propelled UMBC to its first NCAA women's basketball tournament were featured for a long time in University publicity. This spirit, commonplace on some other campuses, did not come quickly, easily or consistently to UMBC.

The road ahead is uncertain. The NCAA seems committed to acquiescing to the demands of power conference schools who are willing to spend whatever it takes to win. Mid-majors Division I schools such as UMBC cannot provide comparable salaries or facilities. Students are changing. They are more diverse in almost every way with a bewildering array of specialized interests and formats for their activities. Fewer of them see attendance at mid-major games to be an essential part of their college experience. For the true sport's junkie, there is ESPN, ESPN 2, ESPN 3, ESPNU, and host of other cable and internet opportunities to watch all sports all the time. Actual attendance for mid-major games, particularly in metropolitan markets, is diminishing.

Nevertheless, in an era when the term student-athlete can have a slightly sarcastic implication when used by the media, UMBC has built an athletic program that reflects the University's values of competitive performance, rules adherence, community service, and academic expectations.

In 2011–2012, the year was marked by some outstanding individual performance and one huge collective achievement. In soccer Andrew Bulls scored 30 goals and made 30 assists in his senior season, while Dan Louisignau was AEC Goalkeeper of the year. Abby McKinney won six swimming gold medals at the AEC championship after amassing 215 points in her career, while on the men's side Junior Mohamed Hussein, the AEC's most outstanding swimmer, qualified for the London Olympic Games for the Egyptian team. Lacrosse featured two seniors Alicia Krause and Emily Coady who each scored 100 career goals. Combining athletic and academic excellence, Michelle Kurowski, not only scored 1,690 points, the second highest in school history, but was chosen for the NCAA Division I Scholar Athlete women's basketball team and was a finalist for the national Lowes Senior Class Award.[46] Joe Adewumi, who won 100 tennis matches for the Retrievers in four years, earned a 4.0 GPA on

45. The alma mater and fight song lyrics are in Appendix I.

46. Kurowski holds several UMBC all-time records (most starts, 118, minutes played, 4,131, and free throws made 383), while finishing second all-time in field goals made (577) and free throw percentage, .857.

his way to medical school and was a national Arthur Ashe Scholar Award recipient. Also winning that award was Iman Kennedy who's 3.90 GPA will lead her to dental school, while on the volleyball court she was a team leader in blocks, kills, and hitting percentage. Both Adewumi and Kennedy received the 2012 Matt Skalsky awards as UMBC's outstanding Scholar-Athletes.

These athlete-scholar exemplars also reflected a superb collective academic performance by UMBC athletes. The combined team GPA exceeded 3.0 for the first time ever. Over 62 percent of UMBC athletes received a 3.0 or better, while 96 earned at least a 3.5, with 31 of the latter group achieving a 4.0. This senior class earned an 88 percent NCCA graduation rate which is considerably above the nation's and the University's average. Women's' cross country (3.39 GPA), women's volleyball (3.37 GPA) and women's basketball (3.26 GPA) were nationally ranked for academic achievement in their sports.

Perhaps the most interesting sign of the changed role of UMBC athletics is the evolution: some might say conversion, of President Hrabowski. As a young administrator, he had been a considerable skeptic about intercollegiate athletics. But gradually he began to see the value of the spirit, community building, and leadership training that athletics could provide. He led cheers at the pep rally held before the 2008 AEC men's basketball championship game. He sat at that game with several politicians and fundraisers who probably never before had come to a campus event. These are conventional public roles college presidents sometimes feel the need to perform whether they like them or not.

But a few people saw the private man after the 2009 AEC men's lacrosse championship game. Earlier that year, the President played a major role in persuading Coach Don Zimmerman to reject a probable offer to become head coach of the University of North Carolina Tarheels. UNC supports one of the most successful intercollegiate sport programs in the country and Zimmerman had been an assistant coach at Chapel Hill for four years during which time the team won two NCAA national titles. The Tarheels' athletic resources and their potential to win national championship were immense, but Zimmerman decided to stay at UMBC, raising eyebrows everywhere in the lacrosse world.

On the AEC championship evening, the President wanted to be there, flying back from the University of Michigan where he had that afternoon received an honorary degree. After a tough victory, Hrabowski entered the locker room and waded into the crowd of half-dressed players. It was an exuberant happy moment. He gave a short speech saying basically what would be expected in such a moment. "The University is proud of you both for what you have accomplished on the field this season and for what you give to our community academically and in service all year long." Slowly the players, pungent with what Hrabowski later called the "aroma of victory," circled the President and started to chant. At first all that could be heard was the low primeval noise that males may have made for millennia in times of triumph. Then there was a single word cheer and the circle broke with a beaming President inside. As he emerged from the locker room, Freeman was asked what the word was. "Family" he replied with a huge smile.

CHAPTER XI

UMBC Service

A. The Service Tradition of American Universities

Higher education is designed to produce skilled graduates who replenish and expand the supply of talent upon which the world depends and the research that enlightens all the activities of modern civilization. Universities are also expected to provide various services to the communities that support them. The triumvirate of university activities is often labeled teaching, research, and service.

The earliest American colleges provided a classical education in Greek, Latin, history, and theology to men preparing for the ministry or for lives in the gentry where such knowledge was prized.[1] Though Benjamin Franklin, of a more practical and secular bent, later argued for "a more *useful* culture of young minds" that would produce "an inclination joined with the ability to serve,"[2] this new kind of institution did not take root until the middle of the 19th Century. Tempered by the lessons of the Civil War, President Lincoln signed the Morrill Land-Grant College Act in 1862, which provided federal support for higher educational institutions in each state. "[W]ithout excluding other scientific and classical studies" the purpose of this statute was to establish "such branches of learning as are related to agriculture and the mechanic arts."[3] The Act revolutionized American higher education by creating a new emphasis on public education and by changing curriculums everywhere. Today, flagship campuses with "state" in their names such as Penn State, Michigan State, and Iowa State are likely to be the progeny of the Morrill Act, though others such as Auburn, Purdue, and Clemson fit that category as well. In Maryland, the USM campuses at College Park and Princess Anne are both land-grant institutions.[4]

---

1. Ira Harkavy, "The Role of Universities in Advancing Citizenship and Social Justice in the 21st Century," in *Education, Citizenship and Social Justice*, no.1 (2006).

2. Benjamin Franklin, "Proposals relating to the education of youth in Pensilvania," (Philadelphia 1749), 8.

3. George Works and Barton Morgan, *The Land Grant Colleges* (Washington: United States Government Printing Office, 1939), 8.

4. In 1890, Congress passed the Second Morrill Act which provided funding for colleges open to people of color in the states with formerly segregated higher education. To receive the funds, states had to prove that their colleges would not use race as the criteria for admission or they had to create separate colleges for people of color. Maryland chose the latter alternative which is why the historically black University of Maryland Eastern Shore receives land-grant

One of the differences between the land-grant colleges and their more traditional sisters was a commitment to provide service beyond the campus, indeed to every corner of their states. The most visible form of that service was the "cooperative extension" which provided assistance to farmers in animal husbandry, crop management, and cultural support for rural peoples. The passage of the Smith-Lever Act in 1914 was intended to "foster agricultural extension work in the States and to coordinate the extension of the land-grant colleges and the United States Department of Agriculture."[5] By 1919, 75 percent of the counties in the country had such programs.

Land grant universities are not typically located in urban areas, but it was quickly recognized that cities also needed university services. In 1876, Johns Hopkins's first president Daniel Coit Gilman, called on universities to, "make for less misery among the poor, less ignorance in the schools, less bigotry in the temple, less suffering in the hospitals, less fraud in business, less folly in politics."[6]

One implementation of the aspiration to provide help beyond the campus was the "service-learning" concept where various forms of community activities helped students to become change agents in their communities.[7] In the early 1970s, federal initiatives such as the National Center for Service Learning and the University Year of Action were created. In 1985, a consortium of campus presidents signed the Campus Compact to advance "the public purposes of colleges and universities by deepening their ability to improve community life and to educate students for civic and social responsibility."[8] UMBC's President Michael Hooker was a founding member. That initiative led to the creation of the Student Literacy Corps in 1989 in which federal grants supported literacy tutoring programs where students would receive academic credit.[9] In 1993, President Clinton took another step in that direction by sponsoring the National Service and Trust Act establishing the Corporation for National Service which made a number of Learn and Serve Grants to those campuses encouraging service-learning.[10]

Despite this flurry of federal programs, as well as some state level policies, by the 1990s, there was a realization that there had been some over-promising about the potential of university engagement with their communities. Derek Bok, president of Harvard and the person responsible for spending its multi-billion dollar endowment, criticized American universities for failing to "help our country cope more effectively with a formidable array of problems."[11] Ernest Boyer, president of the Carnegie Foun-

---

funds. See "7 USC § 323—Racial discrimination by colleges restricted" at http://www.law.cornell.edu/uscode/text/7/323.

5. Harkavy, *The Role of Universities,*" 12.

6. Ibid., 10.

7. Allen J. Wutzdorff and Dwight E. Giles, Jr., "Service-Learning in Higher Education," in *Service Learning*, ed. Joan Schine, (Chicago: National Society for the Study of Education, 1997) 107.

8. http://www.compact.org/about/history-mission-vision/.

9. Wutzdorff and Giles, "Service-Learning," 108.

10. Ibid., 109.

11. As quoted by Harkavy, *The Role of Universities,*" 28.

dation for the Advancement of Teaching, concluded that, "higher education's historic commitment to service seems to have diminished."[12] One response to these concerns was a National Conference on Higher Education and Civic Responsibility to find ways "to strengthen higher education's civic role in both educating students and institutional service to communities."[13] That was the crux of the problem. Community needs sometimes seem inexhaustible, but university time and money are definitely not.

Given this historical context, what service roles would the new UMBC campus play? The land-grant college role was taken in Maryland and there were already a number of service activities by existing Baltimore universities. The UMBC mission statement was clear that the three main goals of the campus were "high-quality teaching, advanced research, and social responsibility."[14] When UMBC faculty members are considered for promotion and tenure, their performances are evaluated in service as well as in teaching and research, and faculty must make annual reports about their paid and unpaid service. These individual reports reveal a cornucopia of service activities which benefit the metropolitan region, the nation, and the world community. Their students also work in internships for government, businesses, and non-profit organizations.

Collective university service activities take many forms. This chapter will focus on two of the most visible UMBC service activities, providing assistance to disadvantaged persons and supporting economic development.

B. Shriver Center

The largest student service programs at UMBC are located within the Sargent and Eunice Kennedy Shriver Center. The Center has a national reputation, and many of its programs have been emulated at other institutions across the country. How the Shriver Center came to UMBC and the services it offers are stories worth telling.[15]

In 1976, realizing that many of its students needed to earn money or at least acquire job experience, UMBC created a Cooperative Education Program (Co-Op), supported with federal funding under the leadership of John Martello, himself a

---

12. Ernest Boyer, "Creating the New American College," *Chronicle of Higher Education*, March 9, 1994.2.

13. Ibid., 3.

14. UMBC Mission Statement, http://www.umbc.edu/provost/planning/Mission_statement_dec.2000htm, accessed December 5, 2010.

15. The best description of the founding and development of the Shriver Center can be found in John Martello and James R. Price, III, "The Shriver Center: Lessons in the Creation of a Setting." *University and Community Schools*, 5, no. 1-2 (1997). The author is greatly indebted to Bridget Flynn, political science undergraduate and member of the UMBC History team, for her research on the Shriver Center and other forms of service on the campus. Her paper is titled "A History of Service at UMBC," UMBC historic documents collection, Special Collections, University of Maryland, Baltimore County.

UMBC graduate. This program "integrates classroom learning with real-world experience by allowing students to alternate semesters of full-time study with semesters of full-time work." The Co-Op program's philosophy is that with a well-designed work experience for students "the theories taught in the classroom will be challenged, improved, and perhaps disproved." The program remained very successful, receiving federal funding and student placement slots from the Social Security Administration and the Maryland Department of Transportation. Research labs, corporations, public schools, and hospitals also welcomed UMBC students. Currently, the Center provides about 2,600 Co-Op, internships, research and service-learning opportunities in hundreds of businesses and agencies.

When Co-Op federal funding ended in 1980, UMBC decided to support the campus program on its own. The 1984 UM annual Presidential report pointed out that UMBC had the largest Co-Op program in the state with a success rate of 100 percent of its alumni going to graduate schools or gaining employment. In 1987, Governor William Donald Schaefer created the Governor's Internship program, and UMBC was chosen to administer it.

Two years later, UMBC began a relationship with the Choice Program serving at-risk Baltimore youth. This program was founded in 1988 by Mark Shriver, one of five children of the illustrious Shriver family. Mark was educated at Georgetown Prep and the College of Holy Cross and after graduation he returned to Maryland to work as an intern for Governor Schaefer, no doubt to work his way up the ladder to a political career.[16] During his time as aide to Schaefer's Chief of Staff, Shriver observed first hand problems in the juvenile justice field and the state's inadequate response. He wrote: "I have experienced the frustration of a youth being arrested and the joy of seeing a youth going to school ten days in a row, as well as the difficulties from dealing with seemingly uncaring bureaucrats."[17] He left government, and in the family tradition secured funding for a delinquency prevention initiative that he called the Choice Program. There was no better site for such work than Baltimore with its high crime and huge public school drop-out rate. The program depended on recent college graduates who established intensive mentoring relationships with children whose families were often troubled. The mentors are available seven days a week to work with families and schools, to assist with employment skills development, and to monitor curfews. As a free standing non-profit agency, Choice constantly had to scramble for funds from private charities and government agencies and it was floundering.

After discussions with Provost Adam Yarmolinsky, Vice Provost Freeman Hrabowski, and John Martello, who was managing UMBC's Service Learning pro-

16. Mark Shriver served two terms in the Maryland House of Delegates representing Montgomery County from 1994–2002, but then narrowly lost in the 2002 Democratic Congressional primary to Chris Van Hollen.

17. From Shriver's application to UMBC's Public Policy Program (nee Policy Sciences) April 2, 1990. (used with permission) Shriver completed 15 hours in the program before moving to Boston to be with his fiancée, and earning a Master's degree in public administration at Harvard University in 1993.

gram, the decision was made in 1990 to bring Choice to UMBC, where Shriver later became a graduate student. The program evolved under UMBC's stewardship with considerable success. During their participation in the Baltimore program, 83 percent of the Choice youth did not commit another offense or otherwise recidivate and at a cost of $4,500 per youth compared to the $40,000 it cost to house a young person in a juvenile detention setting.[18] The UMBC seedling was later adopted in San Diego, Hartford, and Syracuse.

All these programs were operated by the Office of Professional Practice which sounded vaguely like a CIA front, so Director John Martello thought a new name was necessary. His first try in 1990, the Center For Learning Through Work and Service, was not much more euphonious and a bit East German. Then as Martello recalled:

> all of a sudden you had this hub of programs that as we stepped back and could see collectively were the way the university was now engaged with the community. And I got this crazy idea to name it the Shriver Center.... I thought, let's put it together and give it a name, and from my research [on the Shriver family] I was very excited about a named center that would inspire the values of public service and what Eunice used to call contemplative reflection[19]

Probably there could be no more distinguished or appropriate names for UMBC's programs in service learning for its own students and Baltimore's at-risk students than Sargent and Eunice Shriver. Appropriate or not, linking the Shriver name to UMBC seemed improbable.[20] While Mark introduced Martello to his parents, their impression of the then twenty-five-year-old public campus operating a variety public service programs out of several strapped-together trailers must have been underwhelming.[21] Their public service had been played out in national, and, even, international arenas. After directing key parts of John F. Kennedy's presidential campaign in 1960, Sargent Shriver became the first Director of the Peace Corps from 1961–1968, then the first Director of the Office of Economic Opportunity (the "War on Poverty"), as well as Ambassador to France for two years.[22] He returned to the United States to run as a Vice Presidential candidate with George McGovern in 1972 and then as a candidate himself in the 1976 Democratic Presidential primary. While UMBC was certainly honored to have such a politically distinguished person give his name to its activities, it was the family's particular social contributions that made the

18. Choice Program website, www.choiceprograms.net, accessed on Dec. 12, 2010.

19. John Martello, interview with Bridget Flynn, October 20, 2010.

20. For a history of the process of linking the Shriver family to UMBC's service initiatives, see Louise White, "The Shriver Center," 12. no.2 (Summer, 1994).

21. Michele Wolff, interview by Bridget Flynn from Flynn's paper "A history of UMBC service," 13.

22. His life is portrayed in two biographies, Mark Shriver, *A Good Man: Rediscovering My Father, Sargent Shriver* (New York: Henry Holt and Company, 2012) and Scott Stossel, *Sarge: The Life and Times of Sargent Shriver* (Washington, D.C.: Smithsonian Books, 2004) and a PBS documentary "American Idealist: the Story of Sargent Shriver," 2011, http://americanidealist movie.com/.

naming of the Center so appropriate. In addition, to his political achievements, Sargent founded Head Start, Volunteers in Service To America (VISTA), the Job Corps, Community Action, Upward Bound, Foster Grandparents, the National Clearinghouse for Legal Services, the Indian and Migrant Opportunities program, and Neighborhood Health Centers. Perhaps most visibly identified with his family were the Special Olympics, an international program where persons with intellectual disabilities can demonstrate their will to compete and to overcome. Sargent served as President and then Chairman of the Board of that program for many years.

It was Eunice's special concern for persons with disabilities, however, that focused the family's attention on this cause. She was founder and Honorary Chair of the Special Olympics. Earlier as head of the Joseph P. Kennedy, Jr. Foundation, she organized its mission around the prevention of intellectual disabilities by identifying its causes and by improving society's response to these persons. That led to the eventual formation of the National Institute for Child Health and Human Development (1962) and changes in Civil Service regulations to allow persons with disabilities to be hired based on their abilities rather than on test scores. She also sponsored centers at Harvard and Georgetown on medical ethics (1971), and the "Community of Caring" programs (1981–1997) to reduce intellectual disabilities among babies of teenager.[23]

Obviously there were great demands on Sargent's and Eunice's time and already a number of initiatives had been named after them. Why create a new affiliation with UMBC? Yale and Stanford had approached their alumni with plans to enshrine the Shriver name on their campuses, as had Johns Hopkins, Loyola, George Mason, and Harvard. So why did UMBC finally win this academic courtship? The other suitors were willing to name a building or a public policy program after the Shrivers, but the family wanted something less conventional. Yet unlike the other more affluent institutions, providing matching grants to endow the Shriver's goals was not possible at UMBC.

Despite his national and even international prominence, Sargent Shriver's ties to Maryland were very deep. He was born in Westminster about twenty miles from the UMBC campus to an old Maryland family descended from David Shriver, who signed the Maryland Constitution and Bill of Rights in 1776. Still like many children of blue-blood families, he was sent out of state for high school (Canterbury in Connecticut), undergraduate college (Yale), and law school (Yale). Eunice was a part of the Massachusetts' Kennedy clan and was educated at Stanford University. So when it came time to locate their many non-profit public service activities, it was not clear a Maryland location, much less UMBC, would be selected. Indeed, the family's first choice as a campus in the area for future activities was Georgetown University, which in addition to its other assets appealed to the family's strong Catholic convictions. The Shriver Peaceworker Program began at Georgetown, but never flourished there.

---

23. These details of Eunice Kennedy Shriver's career are taken from the citation accompanying the award of an honorary Doctor of Public Service degree by UMBC, May 21, 1999.

According to Martello:

> The Shrivers were drawn to the idea of a center that would lead the country in engaged scholarship and UMBC was the perfect place because it was near a deeply troubled city. Furthermore, UMBC was a young school that was willing to pursue progressive new ideas, and 'what both Shrivers realized is that even though we were new, even though we were largely unknown outside of Maryland, this was a fabulous up-and-coming university.'[24]

As a result of many conversations between Martello, Yarmolinsky, and the Shrivers, the family's initial caution turned to enthusiastic consent. UMBC had turned its liabilities into an asset.

It helped, of course, that there were some personal connections. A few years before the decision to create the Shriver Center, their son Mark was working on the Choice Program at UMBC and Adam Yarmolinsky, then UMBC's Provost, had been a longtime Shriver family friend, working on the creation of the Peace Corps for President Kennedy, and then as principal drafter of President's Johnson's War on Poverty.[25]

After obtaining the Shriver's consent to use their name, the next step was to design the new center and craft a mission statement. There was still some skepticism about the academic seriousness of service learning and concern that promoting virtue among young people might become proselytizing. Shriver turned to his friend, Ernest Boyer, the President of the Carnegie Foundation and former Secretary of Education, who saw the possibility of creating a national model at UMBC and drafted a mission statement that is still in use:

> The Shriver Center at UMBC promotes the integration of civic engagement, teaching, learning, and discovery on campus, regionally, and nationally so that each advances the others for the benefit of society.

The Shriver Center strives to:

- Engage students and faculty in applied learning linked to academic study;
- Develop socially engaged citizens with the commitment and experience to serve responsibly in their communities, the state and the nation;
- Harness the resources of the University to strengthen our communities, and to build their capacity to meet the needs of civil society through the development and leadership of community-based service delivery programs.[26]

Boyer continued to promote the Shriver Center, lauding it in the *Chronicle of Higher Education* as a "bold new initiative that will focus a rich array of academic re-

---

24. Martello, interview by Bridget Flynn, October 20, 2 010. As paraphrased and quoted by Flynn's "A history of UMBC service," 11.

25. Remarks by the Honorable Sargent Shriver at a Memorial for Adam Yarmolinsky," transcription, UMBC Albin O. Kuhn Library Gallery, May 4, 2000, 6. UMBC historic documents collection, Special Collections, University of Maryland, Baltimore County.

26. Shriver Center Mission Statement www.shrivercenter.umbc.edu/about/ (accessed on September 17, 2012).

sources on [Baltimore]."[27] He also had a hand in recruiting for the Center's National Advisory Board which he chaired and which included government luminaries (a former Secretary of Defense, a former U.S. Congressman, and a former ambassador), directors of non-profit organizations, experts in children's and urban issues, as well as members of the Shriver clan, including Mark Shriver, Timothy Shriver, Maria Shriver, and Arnold Schwarzenegger. The UMBC Faculty Advisory Committee for the Center was chaired by Adam Yarmolinsky. Suddenly, UMBC, "largely unknown outside of Maryland," had begun to forge a national reputation as a campus model for civic engagement.

Behind this glittering assembly of supporters was a less glamorous reality. When it began in 1993, the Center had no permanent space, and was housed in one trailer after another. Michelle Wolff, the current director of the Center, remembers beginning her work in a temporary building made up of the strapped-together trailers. "They tried to make them as comfortable as possible, but from the terrible ventilation and moldy smells, to the unbearably noisy wall units we had for heat and air, you could tell you were in a converted trailer."[28] A decade later, when the Shriver Center finally moved to brick and mortar quarters on the first floor of the new Public Policy building, Martello recalled: "Our move from trailers to a building signified that we were mainstream, and central as opposed to marginal ... You put things in the trailers that you don't think will last. But we did last. We prospered."[29]

Even more significant than location for the Center's future was success in the quest for project funding. UMBC did not have the money itself to prevent a constant scrambling for grants and contracts to continue the Center's work. While there has been some public funding, the majority of the Center's budget has come from competitive awards for particular service projects and more general funding from foundations. These opportunities fluctuated with the changing economy and political priorities. In 1994, the Center had an annual budget of slightly above $4 million, peaking at about $12 million in 2000. By 2012, the Center had garnered over $70 million in foundation grants and contracts coupled with about $1 million in university funding.[30] The Center has survived what the Civic Index called a "civic depression" in the economic downturn after 2007 when 72 percent of respondents polled had cut back on civic engagement and volunteerism grants.[31]

The initial vision for the Center was to be the coordinating hub for service learning projects from all of the Baltimore area colleges and universities. At the opening ceremony of the re-christened Center, Sargent Shriver spoke of "a whole metropolitan

27. Boyer, "Creating the New American College," 3.

28. David Hoffman, "Real People Profiles: Michele K. Wolff," Co-Create UMBC (blog), March 25, 2010, http://cocreateumbc.blogspot.com/2010/03/real-people-profiles-michele-wolff.html, (accessed February 18, 2013).

29. Martello, interviewed by Bridget Flynn, October 20, 2010.

30. Flynn, "A History of Service at UMBC." Figure C.22.

31. The Shriver Center, Annual Report, 2008. UMBC historic documents collection, Special Collections, University of Maryland, Baltimore County.

area dedicating itself to the study and to the service of the city and its population."[32] A Shriver Higher Education Consortium and President's Council was chaired by Freeman Hrabowski, and composed of the executives of virtually all Baltimore-area higher education institutions. The hope was to centralize and make more visible service learning opportunities for students at all twelve consortium schools as the Shriver Center had done at UMBC. Most service activities previously had been ad hoc, sponsored by academic departments or student groups. In 1994, the Center received a substantial grant from the Corporation for National Service. The money was used to strengthen the new consortium by making sub-grants to member institutions and faculty to foster service learning on their campuses. Over the duration of the Shriver Center's Corporation for National Service funding, the Center awarded eighty grants. After the Corporation's funding ended in 2000, most of the energy in the consortium shifted to more campus-based service learning projects which the Shriver Center helped incubate and grow. For its own UMBC service-learning projects, however, the Center received grants from the Joseph P. Kennedy, Jr. Foundation and the Kauffman Foundation. By 2010, the Center was enrolling about 700 students a year in these programs.

One of the most prominent of the Center's activities and a direct legacy of its namesake is the Shriver Peaceworker program. Founded in 1985 to meet the need for optimum reintegration of returning Peace Corps members, it creates graduate school opportunities that combine "community service, academic training, and ethical reflection." The Peaceworker program was originally located at Georgetown, but the family was not pleased with its growth and moved it to the newly created UMBC Shriver Center. In 2001, the UMBC Peaceworker program was made an officially recognized affiliate of the USA/Peaceworker Fellows. An average of ten Peace Corp volunteers return to Baltimore each year, and by 2012 over 100 volunteers had earned graduate degrees at UMBC or other consortium schools.[33] A 2008 survey of Peaceworker graduates found that 100 percent were in public service careers and 74 percent remained in the Baltimore area.[34] Although the Shrivers had many biological grandchildren, Sargent felt that former Peaceworkers were his social grandchildren. John Martello recalled Shriver always wanted to talk to returned Peace Corps members:

> He was like a grandfather with his grandchildren. It was always his idea that they would take what they had learned in the Third World and apply it to the First World, here in the U.S. He carried a message of such enthusiasm and hope. He could make your spine tingle.[35]

---

32. Shriver's remarks can be found in *The Shriver Center.* 20, no. 2 (Spring/Summer, 1994).

33. "Program History and Description," The Shriver Center at UMBC, http://www.shrivercenter.org/pw_history.html, accessed December 4, 2010.

34. "Results" The Shriver Center, http://shrivercenter.umbc.edu/about_results.html, accessed December 4, 2010.

35. Childs Walker, "UMBC center carries Shriver name, spirit," *Baltimore Sun*, January 20, 2011.

The Shriver Center and its programs have been widely recognized as models. In 1997, the Choice Program was recognized as "among the nation's most successful graduated sanctions programs" by the Office of Juvenile Justice and Delinquency in the U.S. Department of Justice. In 1999, *The Templeton Guide* described the Shriver Center as the prototype for urban education in the 21st Century. In 2000, the Choice Middle School program received the Crystal Star Award for Excellence from the National Dropout Prevention Network. In 2008 and 2009, the Center's applied learning program received a national Best Practice Awards, and UMBC won a place on President George W. Bush's Higher Education Community Service Honor Roll, largely because of the Shriver Center's achievements. UMBC has received this Presidential Award every year since. In 2007, the Maryland State legislature established the Walter Sondheim Public Leadership program headquartered in the Shriver Center.

C. Student Organizations[36]

A considerable part of UMBC's reputation as an innovative public service university is due the Shriver Center's work, but the University's service extends beyond the Center. The service ethic is often inculcated in students by their families, religious organizations, and high schools before they arrive on campus. For early UMBC students, who were almost all commuters, often working long hours on outside jobs and sometimes unprepared and struggling to meet the growing academic requirements the campus imposed on them, community service was usually an unaffordable luxury. Still the seeds of volunteerism were sown in that period; and after the student body and campus evolved to be more typical of research universities, a number of service organizations and activities were created by UMBC students. In all these programs, it is not just the service provided that is beneficial, but the awareness created in the formation of young minds of needs beyond the campus and the role models students identify that may have lifetime significance.

Despite the difficulties many of the first UMBC students faced in finding the time and money for community involvement, the reform fervor of the 1960s impacted the campus. Within weeks after opening day, according to *The Retriever*, twelve UMBC students and their dates took twenty-five orphans from the St. Vincent Infants Home for a picnic and a day at the zoo.[37] By 1968, student leaders were identifying with larger issues. Daryl Hagy, an early Student Government Association President, argued: "We at UMBC have the opportunity to lead our generation and peers. We are a new school, unshackled by old tradition and old ways of doing

---

36. This section like the previous section on the Shriver Center greatly benefitted by the work of Bridget Flynn, "A history of Service at UMBC," UMBC historic documents collection, Special Collections, University of Maryland, Baltimore County.

37. "UMBC Students Plan Orphans' Picnic Outing," *The Retriever,* October 3, 1966.

things."[38] He urged students to take on greater responsibilities for the world around them in a school newspaper article:

> The problems which are now frustrating the United States are not separated from this university by ivy covered walls. They are just down the street. We have demonstrated against them. We have marched. We have protested—but what have we offered as solutions to them and how deep is our commitment to work toward their solutions?[39]

Hagy put his rhetoric into to action by creating the College Council on Human Relations, which became a forum for Maryland universities to "pool the wealth of knowledge and research ability of the University in order to directly serve the poor and uneducated in the state." Perhaps this was a bit of an audacious agenda for the student leader of a two-year-old campus, presaging the creation of the Shriver Center by almost two decades, but committees were formed to discuss integration, the Biafra War, poverty in Appalachia and Baltimore, and lowering the voting age to eighteen.[40]

There were a number of other student groups concerned about the world outside the campus. In the 1970s, the politically active Black Student Union (BSU) created the Tutorial Project to help elementary school students improve their reading skills and their self-confidence. The BSU, working with the Black Caucus of Faculty and Staff, collected food and money for African famine relief.[41] Other students focused on self-help programs for adolescents being treated at nearby Spring Grove State Hospital and later extended their activities to work with adults in special education.[42]

Organized concern about the environment was evident as early as 1974, when UMBC students audited campus energy use and operated reclamation centers. The modern successor to these efforts, Students for Environmental Awareness, is still very active today.[43]

By 2010, there were twenty-four service organization recognized by the Office of Student Life. They range from focused groups such as UMBC Habitat for Humanity (founded in 1994) to activities sponsored by Greek organizations, particularly, the Golden Key Honors Society. The latter group, formed in 1995, has already won national awards for its service contribution in tutoring, mentoring, the AIDS Walk Day, and the Relay for Life.[44] To coordinate and nurture all these activities, the Student Involvement Center, a "gateway for involvement and leadership opportunities at

---

38. "With Student Government Assoc. Hagy Outlines Work to Date," *The Retriever*, September 3, 1968.

39. Ibid.

40. John Adams, "Various Committees Assigned to Stimulate Student Participation," *The Retriever*, October 8, 1968.

41. "African Relief Efforts Planned," *The Retriever*, October 1, 1973.

42. "Students Help Out in Spring Grove Training," *The Retriever*, February 22, 1972 and Feb 11, 1974.

43. Dale Nitzberg, "Mary PIRG Cites Energy Waste at UMBC," *The Retriever*, May 13, 1974.

44. "About the UMBC Chapter of Golden Key," http://www.umbc.edu/studentlife/orgs/gknhs/info.html (accessed on December 4, 2010).

UMBC" was established in 2002.[45] UMBC Serves is a University-wide student group that publicizes and coordinates student service activities.

Perhaps it is surprising, given their challenging schedules, that UMBC athletes are among the most prominent students in service activities.[46] Most coaches make some sort of service a team activity. There are several tutoring programs. The America East Conference sponsored "College for Every Student" program which led UMBC athletes to form a partnership with the local Arbutus Middle School. The "Make a Difference Mentoring Program" pairs a UMBC athlete with an elementary or middle school student on a one-on-one basis to promote academic and personal growth. Some programs work with persons who have disabilities. The "League of Dreams" program provides baseball and softball opportunities for individuals who are wheelchair bound or wear leg braces. The Special Olympics Program uses eight-week periods to teach hand and eye coordination skills to two to seven year-old disabled children, so that they learn confidence in their ability to do physical tasks and play games. In the Ride with Pride Program, UMBC athletes assist trainers in horseback riding lessons for children with disabilities. UMBC athletes also help out in the Maryland Food Bank in packaging and distributing food. There are a number of fund-raising programs related to health: Passionately Pink and Power in Pink for the Susan G. Komens Breast Cancer Foundation; the Great Prostate Cancer Challenge, a 5k race whose proceeds benefit cancer research; Light the Night Walk for the Leukemia and Lymphoma Society; and the Christmas toy drive for the Children's Home in Catonsville. The UMBC women's basketball team plays a game as a fundraiser for the Kay Yow Cancer Fund, and the men's lacrosse team plays a game for the Autism Awareness program with proceeds donated to the Kennedy Krieger Institute. After Hurricane Katrina, the UMBC women's basketball team went to New Orleans in 2006 to build houses with Habitat for Humanity.

None of these activities would be considered as newsworthy to the wire services as one of the too frequent scandals involving intercollegiate athletics, but they are actually more characteristic of athletes and, in the long run, more important to society than the misbehavior of a few.

D. Research Park

The decade-long controversy over the creation of the UMBC research park, now called bwtech@umbc, was recounted in Chapter III, but it is useful to revisit the Park to examine its current activities, particularly as a part of UMBC's service. It may

---

45. Jennifer Leigh Gibbons, "UMBC's Student Involvement Center Considered a Model for Other Universities," *Insights*, February 3, 2003.

46. Information for this section was drawn from an interview with Lisa Gambino, Coordinator of Student-Athlete Affairs, by Bridget Flynn, October 8, 2010, and from the author's work with Jessica Hammond, Assistant Athletic Director.

seem odd to discuss the role of a research park as a university service, but the Park sits on 71 acres of University land on which it pays no rent and adds some traffic congestion. On the other hand, its existence produces jobs and taxes for the County and the State, creating some amount of goodwill among Maryland politicians because UMBC is doing its bit for the state economy.[47]

By 2012, the Park housed nearly 90 technology and life sciences companies in five building encompassing 500,000 square feet employing 135 persons who produce $200 million of sales annually. Earlier predictions about the size and impact of the Park were more modest.[48] Other claims that the Park would produce many jobs for UMBC students and research opportunities for faculty may have been a bit oversold, although there have been some of these benefits. About 100 UMBC students work in the Park annually, but that number might not be very different if the Park tenants had been located in one of the surrounding counties.

Some Park occupants are just devoted to typical corporate activities of producing goods for profit, while generating jobs and tax revenues.[49] Other occupants have created more synergy with the campus and contribute to its service role. For example, the Maryland Clean Energy Technology Incubator (CETI) houses early-stage companies working on issues of solar power, wind power, biofuels, electric grid, energy maintenance, and storage.[50]

The National Security Administration (NSA) and the Department of Homeland Security jointly have bestowed two honorary designations on UMBC, as a Center of Academic Excellence in Information Assurance (2001) and as a Center of Excellence in Research (2008). These designations place UMBC faculty in a position to lead research teams implementing policies recommended by the 9/11 Commission. UMBC students will also be advantaged in applying for Department of Defense Information Assurance Scholarships and the Federal Cyber Service Security Program.[51]

A few months after these designations, the research park created an agreement between Northrop Grumman and UMBC called project "Cync."[52] This project was designed to assist start-up companies in the field of cybersecurity by offering them free office space and acccss to Northrop's clients. After the first year, five such companies, all with customers and revenues, were being nurtured on the bwtech@umbc campus.[53] By 2012, bwtech@umbc was home to 33 cybersecurity companies.

---

47. Richard Byrne, "Best of Both Worlds," *UMBC Magazine*, Fall 2009.

48. Memorandum from Adam Wasserman to Baltimore County Council, February 11, 1995.

49. Sometimes the Park falls victim to business cycles just as any other commercial enterprise. In 1999, the Park attracted a major tenant, RWD from Howard County, but a few years later RWD was bought by GP Strategies which left the Park and created an empty building.

50. http://www.bwtechumbc.com//programs/ceti.html.

51. Chris Cook, "UMBC leads in cyber security research and education," *The Retriever*, March 3, 2010.

52. Marjorie Censer, "Northrup joins other companies in teaming up with universities on cyber security research," *Washington Post*, November 15, 2010.

53. "Northrup Grumman and UMBC City Progress after Cyber 'Cync' Program's First Year." News release. http://irconect.com/noc/press/pages/news_releases.html.

Maryland, the home of the National Security Agency together with other installations at Fort Meade, is positioned to become the national center for cybersecurity research. In the summer of 2010, the Science Applications International Corporation (SAIC) noticed that 20 of their 42 summer interns came from UMBC and a few months later, SAIC formed a new partnership with the campus.[54] That outcome is not surprising, since UMBC is the largest producer of IT graduates in Maryland, Washington D.C., and Virginia and the 4th largest among U.S. research universities.[55]

In the ever continuing struggle to protect military, economic, and other data, the twenty-first century electronic lifeblood of so many activities, UMBC will play a role. The key to expanding this field is the preparation of newly trained graduates in the exotic skills of cybersecurity. In the fall of 2010, UMBC announced a unique new master's degree in cybersecurity and a graduate certificate in cybersecurity and policy. In addition to technical skills, these UMBC educated cyberwarriors will be trained in law, management, and public policy.[56]

As has been described, UMBC service extends from serving at-risk and disabled youth and children in the Baltimore region to producing cybersecurity on a global basis, but there is much more that has not been detailed previously. Only a few examples can be cited here. UMBC's Psychology Department teaches courses at the Kennedy Krieger Institute which seeks to improve the lives of children and adolescents with developmental and injuries. The Center for Urban Environmental Research and Education supports environmental education at a variety of K-12 schools. The History Department's Center for History Education also works with many local K-12 teachers to improve the teaching of American history. The Maryland Institute for Policy Analysis and Research serves many state and local agencies to solve problems as diverse as deer management in Howard County to evaluating alternative voting technologies for the state of Maryland. The recently established Orser Center for the Study of Place, Community, and Culture at UMBC (named after UMBC professor Edward Orser) will use humanities tools to respond to issues identified by communities in the greater Baltimore region. The service ethic is a core value at UMBC.

54. Censer, "Northrup joins other companies" *Washington Post*, November 15, 2010.

55. "Assured Information Security, Inc. to Open New Office at UMBC," News release, April, 2012.

56. Emma Marston, "UMBC introduces a new Master's degree in cybersecuity," *Retriever*, September 21, 2010.

CHAPTER XII

UMBC 2011–2012: Living in Interesting Times

Most changes in large universities are incremental. Enrollments, budgets, and personnel ordinarily do not experience dramatic year-to-year alterations. In 2011–2012, two events threatened to have major negative impacts on UMBC. The ancient Chinese curse, "May you live in interesting times" seemed to dominate Maryland higher education policy during that period.

A. Miller's Merger

In the spring of 2011, Senate President Thomas V. Mike Miller sought to attach an amendment to the State's budget bill that would have required the USM Regents to complete a plan by December 15 of that year to merge the University of Maryland, College Park with the University of Maryland Baltimore (the downtown professional and graduate school campus). Given the potential impact of such a merger, it might have been expected that Senator Miller would have wanted hearings and considerable publicity about the proposal, but there were none. When the House leadership discovered the amendment, the Delegates intervened to change the requirement from a merger mandate to a study of the pros and con of such a merger. House Speaker Pro Tem Adrienne Jones, UMBC '76, who grew up in the tiny Cowdensville neighborhood, a virtual stone's throw from the campus, was the pivotal figure in making the change.

Senator Miller, the longest-serving state Senate President in the country, may be the second most powerful politician in the state, after only the Governor. He has the authority to appoint all committee chairs and committee members in the Senate, a power that is life and death to aspiring politicians, and to those invested in the fate of particular bills.[1] In 1992, a potential merger of UMBC and UMB (then UMAB) was supported by both campuses, the Baltimore business community, and the Regents. The proposal passed in the House of Delegates overwhelmingly, but Miller refused to let the proposal even have a hearing in the Senate. He told the Secretary of

1. Laslo V. Boyd, *Maryland Government and Politics* (Centerville, Md.: Tidewater Publishers, 1987), 64. The current Senate office building is named after Mr. Miller.

Higher Education Shaila Aery that a UMBC/UMB merger would occur, "not this year, not next year, not ever."[2]

Why then did Miller almost unilaterally push for a merger for UMCP and UMB? His public statements originally focused on the advantage of combining College Park's $545 million research portfolio with Baltimore's $567 million in research funding which would have moved the merged entity up to tenth place in the national rankings from the mid-forties where UMCP by itself then resided. The tangible consequences of those ranking placements, however, are hard to measure once a critical mass is reached. He also argued that it was necessary for the flagship campus to have its own medical school, though there are no medical schools on the campuses of the University of California, Berkeley, the University of Texas at Austin, or the University of Nebraska, Lincoln, among others.

In a debate on radio station WYPR with Robert Embry of the Abell Foundation, Miller elaborated on the proposed merger benefits.[3] It would be good for Baltimore, because the *Baltimore Sun* could have UMCP Journalism students as interns and Whiting Turner Construction Company could have UMCP engineering student interns. What he did not explain was why the State needed a campus merger to achieve those internship benefits. Later in the debate, interning turned out to be a sideshow to Miller's proposal to move a substantial number of UMCP undergraduates to live and study in Baltimore. The problem, as he explained it on the WYPR broadcast, was that the Prince George's County permit process was so slow that UMCP needed to move upperclassmen out of its dorms to house incoming freshmen. Therefore, Miller's solution was to take those "empty buildings downtown" in Baltimore and create a new campus where UMCP "students could live, study, and work." In Miller's words, "Wouldn't it be neat to have these students safe and sound walking through the harbor in downtown Baltimore, buying in shops and eating out, and at the same time working there?"

Obviously, there were a number of questions that needed answers. How much would a new campus cost? How many UMCP students would be sent to Baltimore to finish their education? Would that assignment be voluntary? What majors would be offered? Who would do the teaching? Where would the library and computing facilities be located? How would UMCP's new satellite campus in Baltimore affect other higher education institutions already serving the region? What would be the effects of such a plan on the State's already struggling efforts to complete its desegregation obligations?

During the summer and early fall, the University System of Maryland engaged in a full-fledged examination of the merits of the merger proposal to meet its legislative mandate,[4] A number of questions were identified for further study. Experts, includ-

---

2. *Baltimore Sun* editorial, "Troubled UM Merger," March 3, 1992. For a description of the struggle over the UMBC/UMB merger, see Chapter II.

3. WYPR broadcast, June 1, 2011.

4. http://usmd.edu/regents/UMCP-UMB (accessed October 15, 2012).

ing former USM Chancellor Donald Langenberg, who warned that merging institutions was a long and difficult process, were invited to provide input.[5] Teams of representatives from UMB and UMCP met to consider common ground and answer the questions the System had raised. As the tension grew between those two campuses, however, the expected report was delayed.

Behind the scenes, there was fierce politicking. UMCP President Wallace Loh, having just completed his first year at College Park, professed publicly for many months that he was still neutral, even as his campus mobilized its formidable lobbying resources to support the merger. In his second State of the Campus address, however, Loh elaborated on the merger stakes which he saw as monumental. He declared that once merged with UMB:

> We will be able to paint ourselves as a global educational and research powerhouse situated to win the future because the competition will not be with other universities in the system; the competition is with rising universities in Asia, in Brazil and in Europe. That is the future. If we want to out-educate, out-innovate, out-compete, we have to have the resources to do that, and we have to be this global powerhouse.[6]

UMB President Jay Perman, also just beginning his second year, began to realize that what was being sought was not a merger of equals, but rather the adding of UMB's schools to the flagship campus administration's portfolio. Given UMB's $1.5 billion budget, the diverse missions of its professional schools and hospital, and its huge investment in redeveloping Baltimore's Westside, having future decisions made in Prince George's County did not seem desirable.

From the beginning, UMBC's faculty and administrative leadership saw the Miller proposed merger as a threat to Baltimore, the University System of Maryland, and their campus.

The threat placed President Hrabowski in a difficult position. As the senior campus president in the USM, many saw him as the natural leader to oppose the potential merger, and he communicated frequently with Chancellor William E. "Brit" Kirwan about the difficulties he saw in the proposal. As UMBC's president, however, he could not afford to antagonize Senator Miller and jeopardize other campus priorities or have the press characterize the debate over the merger as a personal fight between the two of them. Consequently, he appointed a shared governance committee of two vice presidents and two faculty (Lisa Akchin, Lynne Schaefer, Tony Norcio, and George La Noue) to monitor events and to be the public face of the campus in system discussions and testimony. Using decades of educational policy experience and his national reputation as an educational leader, he began to contact others, principally to point out the downside of the merger for Baltimore.

---

5. Langenberg had previously been involved with the merger of the University of Illinois Chicago Circle campus and the University's medical school campus four and a half miles away.

6. Yasmin Abutaleb, "Loh pledges support for merger," *Diamondback online*, November 9, 2011.

Pieces began appearing in the press that presented the case against the UMB/UMCP merger, though it cannot be known for sure who influenced whom. News commentator Barry Rascovar warned that: "The powerful senator [Miller] wants to impose a hostile takeover of the university system's Baltimore campus, so College Park can get its hands on the law school and school of medicine."[7] C. Fraser Smith, long-term political analyst, began his *The Daily Record* column by asserting that the merger:

> would be akin to the departure of a Fortune 500 company—as if Baltimore had any more Fortune 500 companies to lose. It would be a grievous blow in prestige, comparable to or greater than Baltimore's loss of the Colts. It would damage efforts to attract new industry and to retain and broaden the tax base.[8]

Smith concluded, "What is proposed here is a kind of a shotgun wedding—without the usual compelling argument for such unions. All you have here is the shotgun-wielding father figure with no real reason for his unhappiness." Smith graciously did not name the gunman in this case.

The next day Laslo Boyd, former professor at the University of Baltimore, interim secretary of Higher Education, and in 2011 interim chief of staff for Towson University's new president, wrote in the *Montgomery Gazette* that the merger would have several negative effects. First, it would cause the Baltimore professional schools to be subject to decision-making at College Park, geographically forty miles away and culturally much farther. Second, the "new merged behemoth" would cause "collateral damage" to other Maryland universities, "which would be left in the shadow of the new super university." Third, the merger would undermine the USM system, which was intended to reduce political interference in higher education policy. According to Boyd, "the solution is for the Board of Regents to carry out its own responsibilities and not be bullied by the Senate President."[9]

This was tough talk and gradually, members of the Baltimore political and business elite began to signal their opposition. Mayor Stephanie Rawlings-Blake, Don Fry of the Greater Baltimore Committee, Robert Embry, Abell Foundation President, and Rick Berndt, former Regent and prominent lawyer, all began to use their influence to oppose this particular merger, though almost two decades earlier the Baltimore elites had championed the UMBC/UMAB merger.

A climactic moment occurred at a retreat for the Regents and campus presidents on October 6 and 7, 2011 where the proposed merger dominated the agenda.[10] Pres-

---

7. Barry Rascovar, "UM merger deserves scrutiny," *Community Times*, April 5, 2011. See also Rascovar, "Flagship Maryland? Merger has many outstanding issues," *Montgomery Gazette*, gazette.net, April 1, 2011.

8. C. Fraser Smith, "UMB-UMCP merger—just say no," *The Daily Record*, October 13, 2011.

9. Laslo Boyd, "E.F. Hutton and Mike Miller," *Montgomery Gazette*, October 14, 2011.

10. There were, of course, no minutes taken during this retreat meeting, so this account is taken from the immediate recollections of several participants.

ident Loh began by discussing "facts" which supported the proposal, including an assertion that the transportation of UMCP students living in Baltimore, who needed to get to College Park regularly would not be difficult if bus routes were established. President Perman raised questions about the proposal, but then President Hrabowski gave an impassioned speech against the merger. When he finished, there was dead silence in the room. After a few moments, President Bogomolny of the University of Baltimore stated that he agreed with everything Hrabowski had said and that the other Presidents also concurred. Regent Norman Augustine, former Lockheed Martin CEO, commented he had been through a number of mergers and it was very difficult process in the best of circumstances. He declared that Miller's proposal was like creating a system of Snow White and nine dwarfs and to break the tension, he said he didn't see Freeman as a dwarf. The meeting broke up in laughter. Afterward Hrabowski was surrounded by well-wishers and several presidents even gave him a hug. President Loh, who perhaps was learning some lessons about the politics of higher education in Maryland, was essentially isolated after the meeting.

After that meeting, the Regents and most of the State's political and educational elite knew that all campus leaders, except those at UMCP, were opposed to the merger. Yet the public was largely in the dark. Newspaper coverage was slim.[11] The real story, largely missed, was that the only support for the merger was from Prince George's County politicians, and a few corporate leaders dependent on that campus, while the merger was fiercely opposed by their Baltimore counterparts.[12] No campus President was willing to be quoted in the press and risk offending the powerful Senator Miller. Furthermore, USM was in the midst of its mandated study, so the official line was that no campus leader would reach a position until the study was complete.[13]

The Regents scheduled hearings on October 21 and 28, 2011. Consequently, a long line of outside experts, advocates, surrogates, and some student leaders testified, even though almost none of them had read the various USM study group reports which were not released until the day of the Regents final vote.[14]

Senator Miller sat through both hearings and in Baltimore was the lead witness urging support for the merger, arguing for the necessity of a combined University of

---

11. An exception was Childs Walker, "Debate intensifies over UMB-College Park Merger," *Baltimore Sun,* October 20, 2011.

12. On November 9, 2011 the *Washington Post,* in an editorial, "Why merging two Maryland universities makes sense," favored a merger by arguing it would create a "research juggernaut," while noting "bitter resistance" from Baltimore "which regards a merger as a hostile takeover by College Park." Actually, the *Baltimore Sun* also supported this merger for largely the same reasons. Editorial, "A research powerhouse: Combining the University of Maryland with the University of Maryland-Baltimore would boost prestige—and offer some practical benefits." March 24, 2011.

13. Some Presidents still found ways to get their message across. President Perman, while stressing he had no official position on the merger, still gave an interview to *Washington Post* education writer, Daniel de Vise, in which he summarized his faculty's opposition. "Five arguments against a University of Maryland merger." *College Inc. blog.* October 24, 2011. President Hrabowski also spoke to the press, but always off the record.

14. Interview by the author with *Baltimore Sun* reporter Childs Walker, December 15, 2011.

Maryland to compete with flagship institutions in other states. The cumulative size of research awards seemed to him to be the decisive factor in that competition.[15] In this argument, he reversed the position he had taken earlier when he opposed the 1992 merger of UMAB and UMBC. Regarding that merger, Miller had stated:

> Another benefit of the proposed merger also crumbles upon inspection.... the federal government awards research grants on the quality of the faculty, not whether the faculty member's institution is of a certain size. So the argument that the merger will lead to an increase in federal dollars is poppycock.[16]

Unlike the later College Park hearings, where most witnesses favored a merger, most witnesses in Baltimore were opposed. Sensing hostility to his proposal, Miller suggested maybe the merged institution might have two presidents, though there are no precedents for that arrangement anywhere in the United States and the idea was never taken seriously. Former Chancellor Langenberg commented later in the hearings that merging an institution, while retaining two presidents made about as much sense as having two Maryland Senate presidents, drawing a snicker from much of the audience.

Meanwhile, within USM confidential reports responding to the legislature's study mandate were slowly being formulated. The most significant was the report of the "blue" group whose ten members were evenly divided between UMCP and UMB and assigned to studying the pros and cons of a merger of their institutions. Not surprisingly, they could not come to a consensus, so their report described the assets and liabilities of a merger, as well as a new concept they called a "Strategic Alliance" without making a recommendation. Some saw the "Alliance" as having intrinsic merit and others saw it as a face-saving alternative for Senator Miller, who still would have a powerful influence on USM regarding every campus operating and capital budget, regardless of the merger outcome. The "Alliance" concept did not include much detail, but it was essentially a kind of intercampus treaty to conduct certain joint activities. It would be more flexible than a merger and for certain activities might expand to include other campuses. Unfortunately, because the document was not yet released, none of the witnesses at the Regents' hearings knew or were able to testify about the "Alliance" so the public did not know that proposal was being considered.

On October 28 and then again on November 4, 2011, the System convened a meeting of the "purple" group composed of high level leaders of the campuses who would be excluded from a UMB/UMCP merger as well as members of System groups

---

15. An effective analysis of mergers and ranking was published in an op-ed piece by David Salkever, UMBC Professor of Public Policy. Salkever argued that in some ranking systems the proposed merger would not result in combining research dollars because the two campuses would still be counted separately, while in other rankings every USM campus could count in the combined total without any merger. In short, pursuing actual competitive excellence through rankings could be a chimera. David Salkever, "UM Merger false premise," *Baltimore Sun*, November 9, 2011.

16. "Mike Miller lambastes merger in Baltimore," opinion editorial, *The Faculty Voice*, 7, no.1, (October 1992). See also, Miller, "The Case Against a UMAB-UMBC Merger," *Baltimore Sun*, June 16, 1992.

representing faculty, staff, and students.[17] Chancellor Kirwan skillfully presided over what were tense encounters. During the first "purple" group meeting where the UMB/UMCP "blue" group presented their report, the other campus representatives commented mostly by asking pointed questions. At the second meeting where only the "purple" group members attended, the frustrations, anxieties, and hostilities to the proposed merger were expressed with a vehemence rarely heard in multi-campus academic gatherings. Almost every representative of the "excluded campuses" and the System personnel groups were against the merger and said so unambiguously. Some of their objections were focused on money. The "blue" group had made it clear that implementing a merger would be difficult, protracted, and cost a lot of money. They were also firm that merger funding had to be new money, because they did not intend to reallocate existing funds for that purpose. In a period of very tight state higher education budgets, including three years of faculty and staff furloughs and almost no merit pay, an expensive two-campus merger was not a popular idea in the "purple" group. Further, given the System's Strategic 20/20 plan, which promised to achieve a 55 percent goal for Marylanders to attain bachelor's degrees, new money was needed for several campuses to expand to meet those goals, though neither UMB nor UMCP was slated for enrollment expansion.[18]

The "excluded campuses" from the merger were also concerned about the concentration of political power the new entity might create in the Regents and the General Assembly. Some speculated the merger might destroy USM. The "excluded campuses" might not wish to stay as USM members, if the merged campuses always had a veto. The merged institution, probably with Senator Miller's blessings, also might withdraw, if its priorities were frustrated by other System institutions.

Certainly Chancellor Kirwan, though officially neutral on the merger proposal, was aware of the threat to the System and to his job. In the middle of November, USM asked all of its campuses to detail the already existing inter-institutional cooperative arrangements.[19] Not surprisingly, since UMBC and UMB had created a joint graduate school in 1985, most of the inter-institutional programs and joint research projects were between those campuses. The list of joint publications, collaborative research project and cooperative mentoring of students between the two campuses was substantial. At least thirteen UMBC faculty had joint appointments in the UMB School of Medicine. Major capital facilities projects at UMBC are managed by UMB officials. There was a worry that the decade's long pattern of UMB/UMBC cooperation might be undermined by a merger of UMCP and UMB.

17. The author was one of UMBC's representatives on the purple group and attended those meetings and had access to all the task force reports.

18. USM, "Powering Maryland Forward: USM's 2020 Plan for More Degrees, A Stronger Innovation Economy, A Higher Quality of Life." adopted December 3, 2010, 10. UMBC historic documents collection, Special Collections, University of Maryland, Baltimore County.

19. See "UMBC Inter-institutional Collaboration Survey" and "UMBC Faculty Inter-campus Collaboration." Both documents are dated December 6, 2011. UMBC historic documents collection, Special Collections, University of Maryland, Baltimore County.

Finally, there was concern about future status and branding, particularly at UMBC. The Catonsville campus began as one of the four University of Maryland campuses and flourished under that arrangement's protection. It had adopted the standards for faculty selection and promotion of UM research campuses. In 1988, all the research campuses were wary of merging with the state colleges to form UMS, and the lines between the doctoral-granting research campuses and the teaching campuses, in fact, have become a bit blurred.

The proposal to merge UMB and UMCP would raise even more serious questions about UMBC's identity. Paradoxically, just as UMBC was receiving great national recognition for its new achievements, a UMB/UMCP merger might undermine the public perception that UMBC was really a major University of Maryland campus. Would student and faculty recruits need considerable reassurances that the Catonsville campus had a serious role in the state's higher education plans? Would the campus need to change its name? Would UMBC need to find a merger partner? Would President Hrabowski stay? If the state had decided to downgrade UMBC's status with the UMB/UMCP merger, Hrabowski would have immediately made the "A" list of any public flagship or elite private campus in the country with a presidential vacancy. Powerful state players suggested he could replace USM Chancellor Kirwan, who was nearing retirement age, or that he should have become the College Park president when that position was open the year before. Hrabowski's loyalty to UMBC was unfathomable to them, since he was not playing the conventional move-up-the-status-ladder game. When asked about other career alternatives, the national Hesburgh and Carnegie award winner for outstanding Presidential leadership, replies simply, "I have UMBC in my blood."

While UMBC's governing bodies were briefed on developments about merger politics, there was very little open discussion of that possibility on the campus. Students were largely unaware and uninformed. The *Retriever* carried a single story.[20] President Hrabowski worked very hard to solidify opposition to the merger, while he carefully avoided appearing or being quoted in the press. UMBC Faculty Senate President Tim Nohe led Faculty Senate presidents from UMB, Coppin, Towson, and the University of Baltimore to create a joint statement opposing the merger, but the authors decided that it should not be publicly released until the Regents voted.[21] Professor Carlo DiClemente, on behalf of the UMBC Research Council, put together a white paper detailing the $1,000,000 in current joint projects with UMB that might be jeopardized by a two campus merger that excluded the Catonsville campus.[22]

---

20. Ruth Umoh, "Board continues to study merger of MD universities, *Retriever*, November 8, 2011.

21. Letter to Orlan M. Johnson Regents Chair from Timothy Nohe, (UMBC), Richard Y. Zhao, (UMB), Nicholas Eugene, (Coppin), Timothy Sullivan, (Towson), and Ordeana R. Neal (UB), November 30, 2011. UMBC historic documents collection, Special Collections, University of Maryland, Baltimore County.

22. Letter to Freeman Hrabowski and Lynne Schaefer from Carlo DiClemente, "UMBC Research Council Concerns about UMB-UMCP merger," November 21, 2011. UMBC historic documents collection, Special Collections, University of Maryland, Baltimore County. An expanded version of UMBC/UMB collaboration paper was prepared for a February 20, 2012 meeting with

By the end of November the tide had turned. It became accepted wisdom that the Regents would not vote to support any merger. Some thought the vote count might be a lop-sided 12–4. A Regents' meeting was scheduled for December 2, but then postponed until December 9, when in an unusual move the proceedings were streamed so they could be watched on campuses around the state. The vote turned out to be an almost anti-climactic unanimous "no," though the actual sentiments on the Board were not that one-sided.[23] The official language was that "The Board is convinced that maintaining these two exceptional institutions as separate entities is in the best interest of the state." Kirwan added, "A merger to be successful has to have unified support across the two organizations. And we didn't have that."[24]

The Board, however, did approve a version of the "Strategic Alliance" concept, first articulated in the "blue" task force report as an alternative to merger, but which was not actually released prior to the final vote. What the actual implementation of the "Alliance" would look like was left to further negotiations by the two campuses with a report due to the legislature by March 1, 2012. Among items to be discussed were joint programs in bioscience, biomedical research, public policy, law, sociology, and social services. Some joint appointments might take place, and a new center to commercialize medical innovation was considered. Everyone was in favor of more inter-campus collaboration. UMBC took comfort in language the Board attached to its Alliance proposal that it expected "the Alliance to reach out to the other USM universities as well as other institutions within Maryland and beyond to build synergistic collaborations whenever and wherever they can advance the mission and impact of the institutions."[25]

Still there were concerns. How would the proposed joint UMB/UMCP programs fit with the existing UMB/UMBC joint programs, particularly the existing University of Maryland Graduate School Baltimore? Would something be created that would give UMCP undergraduates privileged admission to UMB graduate and professional programs, making other USM campuses less attractive to potential students? Would the cost of Alliance activities be such that it would crowd out other priorities? The same day of the Regents vote, the State reported that tax revenues would be $120 million less than expected.[26] After the vote, UMCP President Loh declared, "I have a

---

Chancellor Kirwan who was also treated to recitations by UMBC administrators about the virtues of their work with UMB colleagues.

23. Childs Walker, "Merger given a 'no' by regents," *Baltimore Sun*. December 10, 2011. The editorial page of the Sun lamented the loss of the merger referring to the "self deprecating and parochial" views of city leaders that College Park would inevitably have the upper hand in a merger.... "UM's nonmerger," Baltimore *Sun,* December 13, 2011.

24. Walker, "Merger given a 'no' by regents."

25. Board of Regents Report on the Study Examining the Advantages and Disadvantages of Merging the University of Maryland, College Park and the University of Maryland, Baltimore, December 9, 2011. 30–31. UMBC historic documents collection, Special Collections, University of Maryland, Baltimore County.

26. Annie Linskey, "State cuts revenue estimates by $120 million," *Baltimore Sun,* December 10, 2010.

philosophy that no money equals no mission. I think if you are going to do a new collaboration with new things, it is going to cost money."[27]

About two months before the Regents were to report on how they defined the details of the "Strategic Alliance," Senator Miller laid down his markers for that enterprise. It wasn't so much that the two campuses had different goals for their participation in the "Alliance," but Miller made it clear that he was "prepared to force the issue through legislation if necessary." and that he wanted eventually to work toward a complete merger. House Speaker Michael Busch replied that while he supported collaboration, he did not believe legislation was necessary. Chancellor Kirwan repeated his position that substantial benefits could be achieved through collaboration, but that the "Alliance" would not be a step toward full merger.[28]

Chancellor Kirwan visited UMBC on February 20, 2012, to meet with the Faculty Senate Executive Committee and an array of campus administrators, major and minor, to allay any fears about the impact that a new relationship between UMB and UMCP might have on UMBC. Kirwan suggested some doubt about whether the enhanced UMB/UMCP collaboration would be called a "Strategic Alliance" or have any special name at all. Perhaps the new agreement should be viewed as simply an incremental step in the existing pattern of collaboration among USM campuses and, in any event, he assured his audience that it would serve to strengthen collaboration between all USM campuses.

On March 1, 2012, the Regents announced the details of what was now called a "structured collaboration" between UMB and UMCP.[29] As the creation of the phrase "MPowering the State" in the title of the announcement suggests, there was considerable attention to "optics" of the plan. Among its specifics were combining research and educational programs on the Montgomery County Shady Grove campus, creating some collaborative graduate public health programs, establishing a program to promote technology transfer and commercialization, as well as more joint research, grant submissions and faculty appointments. At UMBC, after the initial relief that the campus was not going to face a merged academic goliath, the question now was how the "structured collaboration" would affect its institutional interests? There were closed UMB/UMCP negotiations over the terms of the alliance/collaboration on one hand, while UMBC and UMB were also discussing future joint activities.

After what has become a national annual competition to have Freeman Hrabowski as a spring commencement speaker, the UMBC President chose to accept UMB's invitation, thus sending a message about future cooperation to both campuses and the

27. Childs, "Merger given a 'no' by regents."

28. Michael Dresser and Childs Walker, "Miller tries again to join UM campuses," *Baltimore Sun*, January 6, 2012. Toward the end of the merger consideration, USM took the step of trying to catalogue existing cooperation among USM campuses. That document was not released during the merger debate.

29. "USM Regents Approve University of Maryland: MPowering the State: Bold Collaboration for Leveraging UMB and UMCP Resources," http://www.usmd.edu/newsroom/news/1070?t+print.php.

audience beyond. President Perman reciprocated by being the keynote speaker at the UMBC fall 2012 retreat. While he, of course, affirmed his intentions to carry out the terms of the collaboration with College Park, Perman spoke with great warmth of past and future activities with UMBC and his goal of strengthening the joint UMB/UMBC graduate school. Some UMBC administrators speculated the campus might have been helped by the merger debate, since it energized UMBC/UMB cooperation and reaffirmed the Regents' commitment to USM as a collection of diverse campuses. Other feared that the new UMB/UMCP role at Shady Grove might be used to diminish UMBC's presence there. In December 2012, UMBC Professor Julia Ross, Chair of Chemical, Biochemical Engineering and Environmental Engineering was appointed "Special Assistant to the Provost for Inter-Institutional Research Initiatives." With her counterpart, Bruce Jarrell, UMB's chief academic and research officer and Senior Vice President and Dean of the Graduate School, they will administer a five year SEED program to provide funding for faculty at either campus to develop grant proposals for external competitions.

Those on the losing side of the merger proposal made public relations lemonade out of the lemon the Regents handed them. Senate President Miller smiled: "It's a great first step; it is a grand first step. I'm totally pleased."[30] President Loh averred: "Whether it is called a merger or a strategic alliance, who cares. Let's get it done."[31] At UMBC, the campus statement about the new arrangement emphasized the earlier Regents' position that, "current collaborations would stay in force, other institutions would not be negatively affected, and collaborations between the Alliance and other institutions would be encouraged by the Board."[32] That sentiment, however, was not explicitly affirmed in the Regents' March 1 statement on the new UMB/UMCP arrangement.

In the fall of 2012, UMB and UMCP announced the design of a "collaborative" School of Public Health. It will involve some joint faculty appointments, coordinated research, and opportunities for students on both campuses. UM's work in public health had long been overshadowed by the Bloomberg School of Public Health at Johns Hopkins. Senator Miller again prophesied that "A complete merger" of UMB and the flagship campus would take place. It might not happen in my lifetime, but it will happen."[33]

It is too soon to tell what the long term impact of merger controversy and the resulting UMCP/UMB "Strategic Alliance" or "structured collaboration" will be.[34]

---

30. Childs Walker, "UM regents approve alliance for College Park and Baltimore campuses," *Baltimore Sun*, March 1, 2012.

31. Ibid.

32. Freeman Hrabowski, and Philip Rous, "UMBC Collaborations with USM Partners, March 9, 2012 (unpublished paper). UMBC historic documents collection, Special Collections, University of Maryland, Baltimore County.

33. Nick Anderson, "U-Md. Officials announce new joint public health school," *Washington Post*, September 25, 2012.

34. UMB President Jay Perman discussed his view of that alliance in *The Faculty Voice*, April 10, 2013.

B. The Coalition for Educational Equity and Excellence Lawsuit

After the Regents' vote on December 9, 2011, it appeared that UMBC and the System had avoided a major, potentially fatal challenge to the existing governance arrangements under which both had prospered. A week later, however, attention turned to another issue as a long-lingering legal problem advanced in court.

In 2006, HBCU (Historically Black Colleges and Universities)[35] supporters formed The Coalition for Equity and Excellence in Maryland Higher Education, Inc. to engage in "community organizing and awareness campaigns."[36] Shortly, thereafter, they began a lawsuit in federal court against the Maryland Higher Education Commission (MHEC). This litigation did not raise the classic southern states issue that African-Americans had been first shut out and then discouraged from attending white schools. That had happened among existing Maryland higher education institutions prior to the Supreme Court's landmark *Brown v. Board of Education* decision in 1954.[37] The Coalition conceded, however, that what were now called TWIs, or traditionally white institutions, were now fully open to qualified black students. Nor were there issues raised about employment discrimination.[38] What the Coalition argued was that white students still were not attending HBCUs in significant numbers, reflecting the State's failure to fully desegregate. From their perspective the remedy was more public money and some program monopolies that would encourage additional white enrollment, while preserving their historic institutional identities as HBCUs.

While the lawsuit created issues for all USM institutions, UMBC was a particular target. Among the many plaintiffs' allegations was #47 which stated: "In 1965, however, rather than encourage integration at Morgan State, Maryland established the University of Maryland Baltimore County (UMCB) [*sic*]. UMBC was a complete duplication of Morgan State's entire institution, not just its programs." From UMBC's perspective, however, its campus was established after the segregation era and as previous chapters have shown it had become a national model of diversity. UMBC did not believe it was fairly labeled as a TWI or that any litigation remedy should punish it.

---

35. An alternative name HBI (Historically Black Institutions) is sometimes used since most former colleges have now become universities. In this book, the traditional nomenclature HBCUs will be used, except when quoting others who use the term HBIs.

36. *The Coalition for Equity and Excellence in Maryland Higher Education, Inc. et.al., v. Maryland Higher Education Commission, Civil no.MSJ-06-2773.* Joint Proposed Pre-Trial Order, November 30, 2011. 1 (hereafter Pre-trial order). There are no public reports on who the members of the Coalition are, its funding or decision making process. A history of the SBHE and MHEC attempts to resolve Maryland's desegregation problem, mostly by providing additional resources to HBCUs, can be found in Sumler, "Life Cycle," 80–89.

37. 349 U.S. 483 (1954).

38. There had not been a judicial finding of discrimination against African-American students or employees in Maryland higher education for at least fifty years.

For this very expensive litigation, the Coalition was able to attract the services of Kirkland and Ellis, a large national law firm, and the Lawyers Committee on Civil Rights.[39] The plaintiffs essentially argued that the State's HBCUs were not equal to their TWI counterparts and that those inequalities were rooted in the State's pre-*Brown* segregation era. The plaintiffs asserted that HBCUs were underfunded compared to TWIs, had more limited missions, and were being subjected to unnecessary duplication of their programs. The Coalition wanted the Court to impose compensatory remedies in capital and operating expenditures, and in the allocation of programs. Those familiar with pre-trial negotiations mentioned that the plaintiff wanted $1 billion to remedy the identified problems. Dr. Robert Toutkoushian, a University of Georgia economist and plaintiff's expert on operating funds, calculated that $2.73 billion would be necessary to compensate HBCUs for operating fund deficiencies going back to 1990.[40] To put that number into context, the proposed Maryland state FY 2013 budget for all public and private higher education was $1.6 billion.

The defendants, represented by the State Attorney General's (AG) office replied that the pattern over the last several decades was to favor HBCUs on average over TWIs for both capital and operating expenditures. The exception was UMCP, whose special status as a flagship campus made it non-comparable with any other campus.

One theory for enhancing HBCUs was that new facilities and programs would attract non-black students to their campuses and thus would increase integration system wide. By the time of the trial, there was little evidence that this strategy was working in Maryland or other states. That reality led to a debate in the case over whether the failure of HBCUs to enroll non-black students was caused by their "inferior" institutional status and by the proximity of alternative programs at TWIs, as the plaintiffs claimed, or whether it was a reflection of choices HBCUs made in the way they presented themselves to the larger community which the defendants suggested. As Supreme Court Justice Clarence Thomas noted in his *Fordice* concurring opinion, HBCUs "have succeeded in part because of their distinctive histories and traditions; for many historically black colleges have become 'a symbol of the highest attainments of black culture.'"[41] Maryland pointed out that, while its HBCUs complained about their difficulty in attracting white students, they "embraced their history as historically black schools and highlight in their mission statements and their websites and other marketing tools their continuing commitment to operate as HBIs."[42] The State then quoted the district court in *Knight v. Alabama,* "The desire of an HBI to maintain racial identifiability extracts an intangible, but very real cost in the desegregation process. It makes it very difficult to recruit white students to the

39. According to its website, this international firm was the eighth largest law firm in the United States with approximately 1500 lawyers. http://www.kirkland.com.

40. *Coalition* trial testimony, January 17 and 18, 2012. 5.

41. *Fordice*, 505 U.S., 717, 748–749.

42. Pre-trial order, page 21, fn. 17.

college."[43] While the Partnership negotiations between Maryland and OCR seemed to be in an indeterminate limbo, by the end of 2011, the conflict over the State's responsibilities towards HBCUs had been moved into the judicial process.

These kinds of cases inevitably are very fact intensive. In the long discovery grind, there were 42 depositions and for trial the plaintiffs proposed eighteen fact, four expert, and six hybrid (fact/expert) witnesses. The defendants responded with forty-five fact, three expert, and six hybrid witnesses. The witness lists looked like a who's who of Maryland higher education, including the USM Chancellor, public campus Presidents, MHEC Commissioners, Higher Education Secretaries, and Regents, among others.

Five years after the complaint was filed, hearings on motions for summary judgment finally took place on May 11, 2011. The Baltimore federal courtroom was packed with so many HBCU supporters and Kirkland and Ellis lawyers that some had to sit in the empty jury box. With Judge Catherine Blake[44] presiding, both sides made opening arguments, but the first sign of her evaluation of the case did not come until June 6. Then, she dismissed the issue of unequal capital expenditures, because "the Coalition had not presented a genuine issue of material fact," meaning that she was not persuaded that unequal capital funding had occurred.[45] But the Judge reserved ruling on the issues of operating expenses, limited missions, and program duplication.[46]

Subsequently, she told the parties to the *Coalition* lawsuit that, if the remaining issues were not settled by December 15, 2011, they should be prepared for a long trial shortly after that deadline. That is usually judge talk for saying, "I don't want my courtroom dominated by an interminable trial and I expect the parties to get me a settlement I can approve."

A trial of that magnitude also would not be an attractive proposition to the plaintiffs' lawyers who were probably working on a contingency arrangement without immediate payment nor to an over burdened state's attorney staff. Furthermore, Attorney General Douglas Gansler even then was raising campaign funds for a gubernatorial run and had to be aware of the political ramifications of antagonizing black voters before the 2014 Democratic primary. When a misleading *Baltimore Afro-*

43. 900 F. Supp. 272, 314 (N.D. Ala. 1995). For a recent discussion of the ambiguity HBCUs face about whether to be fully integrated, see Johnny C. Taylor, Jr. CEO of the Thurgood Marshall College Fund who argued that more racial diversity, maybe 70 percent black might be a good thing, but "at the end of the day ... we're chartered and our mission is to educate African-Americans and we will hold true to that." Dr. R. L'Heureaux Lewis agreed, "diversity is a great thing, but if we make diversity the end goal, making sure that HBCUs look like other schools, as in not composed of predominantly of African-Americans or with a target of educating and uplifting African-Americans, we lose an important cultural institution in the higher education landscape." Interview by John Hockenberry, *The Take Away*, August 26, 2011.

44. Judge Blake attended Radcliffe College before graduating from Harvard Law School in 1975. Leaving her native Massachusetts, she joined the U.S. Attorney's Office in Maryland in 1977 and was nominated by President Clinton to be United States District Court Judge in 1995.

45. Pre-trial order, 19, fn.13.

46. Judge Catherine Blake letter to Counsel, June 27, 2011.

American article claimed that the State believed HBCUs were no longer needed, Gansler's office responded immediately asserting that: "[O]ur Office has always been committed to support their [HBCU] goals.... Our Office has been tasked with defending the State, and has been arguing that the State has in fact worked hard to erase any vestiges of discrimination in its higher education system."[47] Of course, to win the lawsuit, the State had to show not only that it had "worked hard to erase any vestiges of discrimination," but that, in fact, it had succeeded in that goal.

At stake was both the money the HBCUs demanded as compensation for remedying the effects of previous segregation and stricter rules protecting them from competing or duplicative programs at TWIs. A substantial monetary payment temporarily might disrupt Maryland higher education budgeting, but a court order about program duplication would have unpredictable consequences and its effects might last for decades.

Once litigation goes into settlement negotiation, the discussions are protected by secrecy, so UMBC had no formal role, though USM did participate. Three of HBCU USM's institutions (Bowie, Coppin, and UMES) would be beneficiaries of a favorable settlement, but other System campuses might view any award as a loss to them, given the difficult economic times that restricted new spending in the state budget. Certainly Freeman Hrabowski did not fail to point out at opportune times that Morgan and Coppin already received $1,700 more per student from the State than did UMBC. That added up to about a $20,000,000 annual loss for UMBC, if it had been similarly funded.

To make any sort of monetary settlement offer, the defendants had to have a commitment from Governor O'Malley and then get approval from the Board of Public Works. The AG's lawyers had some difficulty getting the Governor's staff to focus on the issue and to come up with a number. Finally a number was determined and Chancellor Kirwan stated publicly that the HBCUs had been offered a "very generous" financial settlement (probably about $20 million, though that figure was never released), but they had turned it down. The two sides were far apart on every issue. As negotiations between the two parties staggered along, retired magistrate Judge Paul Grimm was brought in to mediate, but that approach was not successful either.

After settlement negotiations collapsed, Judge Blake received a fifty-three page joint proposed pre-trial order on November 30, in which, among other things, both sides sought to exclude many of each other's experts. The Judge's earlier decision to remove the capital expenditure issue was a bitter loss to the plaintiffs, since that would have been one of the easiest and most desirable remedies, and they sought to reopen it. It was clear, however, that the trial, predicted to last six weeks, would focus on operating costs and program duplication.

The trial over the allocation of operating expenses, mission scope, and unnecessary program duplication began on January 3, 2012. For what many called a historic

---

47. "Attorney General Gansler Issues Statement on *Coalition....* Case," press release, May 26, 2012.

case, the courtroom was again packed, largely with HBCU supporters. The plaintiffs had somewhat unusually begun their advocacy with a pretrial opinion piece in the *Sun* arguing their case.[48] In the courtroom, they were staffed with seven lawyers from Kirkland and Ellis and the Lawyers Committee on Civil Rights. On the other side, the state added to two African-American attorneys from Venable, LLP, a prestigious 600-member law firm with Baltimore roots, to the three lawyers and supporting staff from the State Attorney General's office.[49] The state budgeted $900,000 for lawsuit expenses for 2012 alone.[50] Both sides had prepared long and hard for what they knew would be a protracted battle.

Opening arguments revealed the overall trial strategies of the two sides. *Coalition* lawyers drew upon the State's long history of segregation and attempts to remedy it. There was little doubt that a satisfactory remedy for HBCUs had eluded Maryland, despite a number of Commissions and reports on the matter.[51] In the end, the plaintiffs wanted the court to accept the concept that the rights in the case were institutional rights and that the language in the 2000 Partnership Agreement, calling for HBCUs to be made "comparable and competitive" to TWIs, should be enforced.

After stating that Maryland was committed to "ensuring equal access to high quality education for all of the State's citizens regardless of race, color or national origin," which is the legal requirement, in the Partnership Agreement the State had made a further pledge which was not a constitutional or a statutory requirement. It declared, "Central to this commitment is the continuing contributions of the State's four HBCUs and the necessity of ensuring that these institutions are *comparable and competitive* with the State's TWIs in all facets of their operations and programs."[52] (emphasis added) To achieve this goal, additional funding was pledged, particularly for new buildings and infrastructure, so that "facilities which serve similar functions at HBCUs and TWIs should be comparable in scope and quality." Moreover, HBCUs were to receive money to have "lower student-faculty ratios appropriate to support their missions" of serving underprepared students who needed substantial amounts of remedial services.

However attractive or glib, depending upon one's viewpoint, the slogan "comparable and competitive" might be, what would it mean in practice? Would the State be required to duplicate the professional schools at UMB at an HBCU? Or create a second flagship campus comparable to UMCP? Or an HBCU liberal arts honors college comparable to St. Mary's College? If Towson or UMBC were the models HBCUs sought

48. Michael Jones and Jon Greenbaum, "MD Fails to Keep its Promise to HBCUs," *Baltimore Sun*, December 29, 2011.

49. http://w.w.w.venable.com/overview/ (accessed January 11, 2012).

50. Maryland Higher Education Fiscal Budget Overview, January 2012. 4.

51. Commission to Develop Maryland Model for Funding Higher Education, "The Panel on the Comparability and Competitiveness of Historically Black Institutions in Maryland," Final Draft Report, Oct. 27, 2008. 1–5. See also Commission to Develop the Maryland Model for Funding Higher Education (Bohanan Commission report) iii.

52. Higher Education Commission, "Maryland Report and the Partnership Agreement between the State of Maryland and the U.S. Department of Education Office of Civil Rights (OCR)," October 1999.

to emulate, HBCUs already had a substantial funding advantage over these institutions, so what else could the state do to make HBCUs comparable and competitive? In 2008, the HBI panel, a subcommittee to the Bohanan commission, given the task of further defining "comparable and competitive," decided to operationalize the phrase by arguing that the goal should be attaining equal graduation rates at HBIs and TWIs.[53] Figure U shows statistically the dimensions of the graduation rate problem.

Figure U
Comparative Graduation Rates and SAT Scores of Entering Freshmen at Maryland HBIs and TWIs (2010)

Institution	4-year Graduation Rate	6-year Graduation Rate	Average SAT
HBIs			
Bowie State University	15.4	40.2	884
Coppin State University	7.6	22.0	850
University of Maryland Eastern Shore	23.7	45.1	827
Morgan State University	15.5	39.3	937
TWIs			
Frostburg State University	23.1	58.9	1010
St. Mary's College of Maryland	76.7	85.5	1219
Salisbury University	47.7	74.5	1118
Towson University	35.5	68.1	1094
University of Maryland, Baltimore County	34.4	65.0	1200
University of Maryland, College Park	54.0	79.8	1244

Based on graduation rates and SAT scores for 2001 entering cohort. "Institutions," June 2010; "Trends in Average Combined SAT Scores of Entering Freshmen Public Four-Year" Source: Maryland Higher Education Commission, "Retention and Graduation Rates at Maryland Four-Year Campuses 1996–2005."

As Figure U demonstrates, the task of creating equal graduation rates for Maryland's HBIs and TWIs, as long as admission practices and policies varied so widely, is formidable. There were wide gaps in the six-year graduation rates at HBIs compared to TWIs.[54] Graduation rates are influenced by a number of factors: the major or program a student chooses; whether students are part-time or full-time; public

53. Bohanan Commission report, 24.

54. For campuses that educate a large number of part-time students, the six-year graduation rate is thought to be a fairer measure of institutional performance than the four-year rate.

financial aid; expectations and monetary support from families; the number of AP credits a student brings from high school; and the degree of preparedness and academic ability of a entering student.

Some of these factors can be influenced by the decisions students and institutions make after enrollment, but a major influence is the characteristics of the students a university admits in the first place. For example, national data show that students with "A" grade averages in high school and over 1200 SAT scores graduate at more than a 70 percent rate in six years. Students with "B-" averages and less than 900 SAT scores graduate at less than a 40 percent rate in six years.[55] TWIs admit students with stronger academic backgrounds than do HBCUs, which see reaching out to underprepared students as essential to their mission. Therefore, it is not surprising HBCU graduation rates are substantially lower. The Bohanan Commission, however, recommended that HBCU's be funded at the 80th percentile of their peers with a supplement of about $1,400 per student to underwrite remediation at those schools.[56] In many respects, the State honored that commitment, insofar as enhanced funding could solve the problem. For example, the Coppin campus was dramatically transformed physically, and overall funding at the HBCUs exceeded that of TWIs from 1984 to 2010.[57]

The dilemma HBCUs face was evident on the first day of trial in the testimony of Morgan State's new President David Wilson. He insisted Morgan had two missions. First, Morgan believed an important part of its purpose was to admit underprepared students, thus its freshman combined SAT scores then averaged 909 and its six-year graduation rate was about 35 percent. Second, it aspired to be a doctoral research university with fifteen doctoral programs in place and nine more approved, while waiting for staffing. Combining those two very different missions creates very difficult personnel decisions. Teaching remedial courses and advancing the frontiers of a discipline are not the same skills and often not found in the same person. President Wilson admitted that he found several Morgan programs to be "houses of cards" when he took office. When asked on cross examination whether he knew of any other universities that combined such divergent missions, he said "yes," but declined to name any.

As the supporters of HBCUs attended the Coalition trial day after day, their passion born out of disappointment was certainly understandable. They had been promised in the 2000 Partnership Agreement and the Bohanan report that the State would make HBCUs "comparable and competitive" with TWIs. That hadn't happened in a

55. A thorough exploration of these issues can be found in Linda DeAngelo, et al. "Completing College: Assessing Graduation Rates at Four-Year Institutions," www.heri.ucla/heri.prev/DARCU/CCReportpressCopy.pdf. The statistics in the text are modified from Table 7. 16.

56. Bohanan Commission report. xi.

57. The rest of the Bohanan report received the rhetorical affirmations that most recommendations to support education do in Maryland, but the $760 million proposal had little chance of becoming law because the state was facing the need to cut the budget in the darkening 2008 fiscal climate. Gail Decter, "More funds urged for colleges; leaders voice support for MD. Panel's $760 million proposal," *Baltimore Sun*, December 11, 2006.

decade or more, even after enhanced investment, and the frustration of HBCU leaders was palpable. By supporting the "comparable and competitive" criteria for institutions with dramatically different admissions requirements, the State had created an unreachable goal in the same way No Child Left Behind legislation had promised that all children would be academically proficient by 2014. From that perspective, the State had inadvertently triggered the *Coalition* lawsuit by committing to a goal it could not achieve. Better prepared students, regardless of race, are more likely to graduate than students who need substantial remedial work.

Once locked into litigation, the State had to articulate its civil rights obligation in a different way. Maryland argued that rights belonged to individuals, not institutions. The Fourteenth Amendment guarantees equal protection to persons, and Title VI of the Civil Rights Act forbids discrimination against persons on the basis of race. By the individual rights standard, it was clear that for several decades, based on their academic credentials, Maryland students of any race were admissible to any of its state universities. The Attorney General's office prepared slides showing that the number of black students at TWIs was substantial and, in general, growing. The defense attorneys also prepared several slides showing the State's relative financial support for HBCUs and TWIs. They showed that HBCUs received a higher amount of dollars per student than TWIs.[58] In looking at a twenty-six year period since 1984, the State showed that HBCUs received $1,874 more per student than TWIs.[59] As Figure F in this book's budget chapter shows of the top five Maryland best-funded campuses compared to their peers, four were HBCUs, joined by UMCP. Coppin was at an astounding 110 percent compared to its peers, while UMBC was 61.8 percent. In general, as Figure V shows, Maryland funded HBCUs significantly better than it funded TWIs.

So the question was less about contemporary funding and more about whether HBCUs had deficits traceable to the segregated era. The answer to that question is complex.

Figure V
Comparison of Maryland HBCU and TWI Funding*

	Per student State funding**	Percentage of State Support to Peer Calculation
HBCUs	$9858	82.5
TWIs	$7600	63.5

* excludes professional schools at UMB
** institutional median funding Source: Defense Exhibit 25 from *Coalition for Educational Equity v. Maryland Commission on Higher Education*, January 3, 2012.

58. See Defense Exhibit 25 and the discussion on page 25 xx of the budget chapter.
59. Defense exhibit 26.

In its "Proposed Finding of Facts and Conclusions of Law," the State argued that prior to the trial, the plaintiffs conceded that Maryland, unlike Mississippi in the *Fordice* case, had integrated its non-HBCU campuses in students, faculty, and staff and that there was no discrimination in various inter-campus agreements.[60] Further, the Court asserted in its pre-trial order that it found no intentional discrimination in capital funding, but also none in student recruitment, admissions, retention, and graduation. From the State's perspective, the boundaries of the case had shrunk considerably, but important issues of operational funding, the scope of institutional missions, and program duplication were still undecided.

The Coalition replied that the current status of Maryland higher educational institutions was the result of the *de jure* segregation era. Citing financial statistics from 1926 to 1936, the plaintiffs sought to demonstrate the origins of institutional inequality. The Coalition asserted that sixty-five programs at TWIs were unnecessarily duplicative of programs at HBCUs and that the remedy was for the judge to order that HBCUs have exclusive offerings by developing new programs and transferring some existing programs from TWIs to HBCUs.[61]

Obviously, UMBC had a keen interest in the direction the Court might go on any of these issues. All of the State's institutions indisputably are now open to students, staff, and faculty of all races and have been for decades. It is doubtful UMBC should even be defined as a TWI, since it was never segregated and as Figure W shows the campus is almost perfectly balanced between white and minority students. Dr. Hrabowski refers to UMBC as a HDI, a Historically Diverse Institution. The Figure W data bear out his contention.

By 2009, 59 percent of African-American students attending Maryland public universities were at non-HBCUs.[62] Institutional racial identifiability, however, particularly among HBCUs, was still evident with undergraduate enrollments only about 1 to 3 percent white.[63] What to do about that latter issue, if anything, was far from certain, and there was no consensus among either black or white leaders.

One of the problems for historians of contemporary policies is that conflicts may not conclude before a book goes to press. So in the single exception to this book's rule to terminate its description of events affecting UMBC at the end of 2012, notice must be taken here of Judge Blake's October 7, 2013 memorandum in the *Coalition* case. In a pre-trial ruling, she found that the plaintiffs had not justified their complaint that they had been discriminated against in the State's allocation of capital expenditures. In her post-trial sixty-page, rather discursive, opinion, she held that the plaintiffs had not proven any discrimination in the State's per student HBCU funding

60. Proposed Findings of Facts and Conclusions of Law," June 6, 2012.

61. Scott Jaschik, "Federal judge gets ready to decide suit by supporters of Maryland historically black colleges," *Inside Higher Education*, October 22, 2012.

62. Considering all public and private four year institutions and community colleges, 81 percent of African-American students attend non-HBCUs. Ibid., 8.

63. Pre-Trial order. 18, fn. 18.l. Only UMES was higher with about 13 percent white students.

Figure W
UMBC Race, Ethnicity, Enrollment Trends

Year	Total Enrollment	White Percent	Minority Percent	Other Percent
2002	11,711	55	33.8	10.4
2003	11,872	55.0	34.7	10.3
2004	11,852	55.6	34.7	9.8
2005	11,650	55.8	34.6	9.6
2006	11,798	54.5	36.0	9.5
2007	12,041	53.4	37.0	9.6
2008	12,268	52.0	38.1	9.9
2009	12,870	51.9	37.7	10.4
2010	12,888	49.7	37.8	12.5
2011	13,199	49.6	38.4	12.0

Minority defined as Asian, Black, Hispanic, Native American and Pacific Islander. Other defined as foreign, unknown or after 2010 multiple races. Sources: USM data arranged by Childs Walker, "Bigger Purposes" *Baltimore Sun*, September 2, 2012. 20.

either. She found that "under the current funding formula. Maryland's HBIs are not 'underfunded' by the State relative to the TWIs."[64] Nor had the State had restricted their missions relative to TWIs, since "HBIs ... have independence and flexibility in crafting mission statements."[65] Nor did she find any fault with the integration of black students at TWIs which, of course, was the problem the original civil rights movement sought to address.

She did find, however, that a number of academic programs at TWIs duplicated programs at HBCUs and that might cause students not to enroll at HBCUs, thus deterring their integration. The issue of what is a duplicate program in higher education is complex. All universities must offer core majors, but in the emerging twenty-first century higher education new academic programs are developing constantly. Program development at HBCUs or TWIs largely turns on faculty initiative who must add to their regular teaching and research assignments to take on the strenuous activity of launching a new curriculum area. Thirty years ago, no campus would have offered a program in photonics such as the one UMBC developed in 2002 with a NASA grant.[66] On the other hand, UMBC had seen its attempts to establish programs in the arts delayed; its engineering college deprived of offering

64. Judge Catherine C. Blake, "Memorandum," *Coalition* case, October 6, 2013.38.
65. Ibid., 25.
66. The UMBC Center for Advanced Studies in Photonics Research (CASPER) is composed of sixteen professors and post-doctoral scientists and a similar number of graduate students in

an undergraduate major in electrical engineering in order to give Morgan a Baltimore area public monopoly in that field; and a flat denial of the permission to offer a business administration major.[67] Nor was the issue that HBCUs could not get their programs approved. As Laslo Boyd wrote: "From 2005–2012, the four HBCUs had 49 new degree programs approved, including six doctorates, and another 16 certificates."[68]

The State's lawyers focused on the money and mission matters, where they prevailed, but did not put on an expert to testify on program duplication issues. Yet, although the plaintiffs clearly wanted more funding, they also hired Clifton Conrad, a professor at the University of Wisconsin, who Judge Blake regarded as the "nation's preeminent scholar" on the issue of program duplication. In the end, his testimony and other evidence convinced her that the State and MHEC had not done enough to control unnecessary program duplication, and she ordered a mediator to sort out where programs at TWIs should be closed, merged, or transferred. She quoted another plaintiff's expert who identified environmental studies, computer science, aging studies, and health care facilities management as fields that might be possible new programs for Maryland's HBCUs. All of these programs were well established at UMBC, enrolling about 3,300 graduate and undergraduate students.[69]

Transferring programs from TWIs to HBCUs or just closing them at TWIs to increase white student enrollment at HBCUs is a speculative remedy at best. Unlike public K-12 education where central authorities can reshuffle students and staff to achieve their goals, universities exist in a much different environment. The higher education marketplace does not function as a zero-sum game between HBCUs and TWIs. If a UMBC program were transferred to Morgan or Coppin, for example, students might elect to enroll instead at another Maryland TWI, or an out-of an state university or a private, profit-making, or on-line institution.

Judge Blake did not suggest any rule about what percentage of white students at HBCUs would constitute sufficient evidence of desegregation. If the first round of program transfers did not produce the enrollment percentage she might have in mind or if they did not remain stable, would a second or even third round of program transfers be judicially ordered? The growing number of Maryland's Asian-American and Hispanic students did not seem to enter into her calculus at all.

---

the Physics, Computer Sciences and Electrical Engineering, Mathematics and Statistics and Chemical and Biochemical Engineering departments.

67. See Chapter VII and IX for descriptions of UMBC program approval conflicts.

68. Laslo Boyd, "Muddled and Misguided Court Decision," October 16, 2013, www.centralMaryland.org/blog. For a different perspective see Jose Anderson, UMBC graduate and now University of Baltimore Professor of Law, "Judge Blake Issued a Bold, Risky and Wise Opinion," *The Afro-American*, October 23, 2013.

69. George R. La Noue, "Antiquated ruling on desegregation," *Baltimore Sun*, October 27, 2013. For other views on this case, see Roye Templeton, "Where's the Diversity?," and by former Chancellor Donald N. Langenberg, "Let Maryland's college compete." both in *Baltimore Sun*, November 2, 2013 and Barry Rascovar, "The new segregation in Maryland colleges," marylandreporter.com November 5, 2013.

Nor did the Judge seem to consider the impact program transfers might have on faculty. Would professors, research infrastructures, and library resources also be transferred? Would faculty recruited to teach black and white students with SAT scores above 1200 be effective teaching students whose scores were 300 or 400 hundred points less and who required extensive remediation? In their new setting would these faculty remain competitive for national research awards? Would program transfers cause Maryland to lose some of its best and brightest research scholars? For example, if UMBC's computer science program were closed or transferred would that campus maintain its pre-eminent status in the burgeoning cyberspace field? Its potential loss might undermine a very promising opportunity for the state and even affect national security.

Judge Blake's memorandum added considerable complexity to Maryland higher education politics. By the time it was issued, Attorney General Douglas Gansler was formally campaigning to win the 2014 Gubernatorial Democratic primary against a formidable candidate, Lt. Governor Anthony Brown, an African-American. Governor Martin O'Malley was widely considered to be positioning himself to be a candidate for the Presidency in 2016. He would not want to be criticized in primary debates as the politician in charge of Maryland higher education during a period when a federal judge found the state had not lived up to its desegregation obligations.[70]

Higher education elites were also caught in cross currents. USM Chancellor Brit Kirwan was a long-time champion of the rights of African-Americans in higher education and three of his USM institutions (Bowie, Coppin, and UMES) would have been beneficiaries of any program transfers from TWIs to HBCUs. On the other hand, he was well aware of the steps, including financial advantages, USM had taken already to benefit HBCUs. Further, the current chairman of the Board of Regents, James L. Shea, was also a senior partner of Venable LLC, the firm which had furnished attorneys to defend the State's and USM's actions. The three USM member HBCUs were also affected by cross-pressures. On one hand, they depended for much of their political support on the state legislative black caucus, which was generally elated at what it saw was a judicial confirmation of their long-standing grievances about the lack of equal status of Maryland HBCUs. However, as members of the USM family, HBCU presidents were quick to understand that insisting that TWIs transfer programs to their campuses was not a winning strategy in the long run. On the other hand, Morgan State, which had vigorously maintained its independence from USM, saw Judge Blake's decision as an opportunity to acquire some long coveted programs. The different goals among the institutions represented by the Coalition must have created some difficulties for the plaintiff's attorneys as they approached the mandated mediation.

---

70. Carrie Wells, "Maryland universities unnecessarily duplicated the programs of black colleges, judge says," *Baltimore Sun,* October 8, 2013. In that article, the Governor's spokeswoman said he was pleased that the court "recognized our commitment" to correct funding imbalances for HBCUs, but that he respectfully disagreed "with the court's conclusion regarding duplication."

On the UMBC campus the politics of responding to the judicial findings were also complex. Despite his stature as an education leader and his particular moral authority on racial issues, President Hrabowski decided to make no public comments about Judge Blake's decision.[71] He said he did not want her ruling to become a personal issue between him and Morgan's leadership. Also in the last year he had invested considerable effort attempting to resuscitate and restructure HBCU Coppin State University.[72] Further, in 2012, he had been appointed by President Obama to chair "The White House Initiative on Educational Excellence for African Americans," which among other things was charged with "strengthening the capacity of institutions that serve large numbers of African American students, including ... HBCUs."[73] Instead, he told his staff, the Faculty Senate Executive Committee, USM leadership, and the Regents that UMBC would give up no programs in any mediation process. He pointed out that the monopoly in undergraduate electrical engineering given to Morgan twenty-five years earlier had resulted in only a two percent white enrollment in that program.[74] Program monopolies without institutional transformation do not succeed.

The possibility of an immediate appeal to the Fourth Circuit Court of Appeals was also considered.[75] Others in the UMBC administration, however, were concerned that telling a federal judge that the mediation she had ordered would be pointless was a dangerous strategy. The faculty senate also decided to make no public statement, ostensibly because the case was a "legal matter," even though Blake's decision might have a very negative impact on UMBC's academic program and faculty tenure. In this atmosphere of general campus silence, *The Retriever* also considered the case was not worth a story.

On October 31, 2013, a spokeswomen for Governor O'Malley's office announced that the State would seek to mediate the issues again before retired Judge Grimm, who had presided over the earlier failed mediation process. Now, however, he had new instructions to focus on program duplication which Judge Blake said would likely involve "the transfer or merger of select high demand programs" from TWIs to HBIs.[76] By November 6, USM had decided it would oppose program transfers and

71. He did make many speeches around the state stressing that UMBC had never been a segregated university and was instead a TDI (Traditionally Diverse Institution). He also wrote an opinion editorial for the *Baltimore Sun* which did not mention the Coalition case directly or use the terms TWI or HBCU, but did vigorously point out UMBC's history as a successfully integrated university. Freeman A. Hrabowski III, "50 Years in American educational equity, November 24, 2013.

72. Tricia Bishop, "Panel pushes changes at Coppin; Report calls for enrolling higher-caliber freshmen, focusing transfer students," *Baltimore Sun*, May 13, 2013.

73. White House press release, "President Obama Signs New Initiative to Improve Educational Outcomes for African Americans," July 26, 2012.

74. Remarks to the UMBC Faculty Senate, November 12, 2013.

75. Interview with Freeman Hrabowski by the author, October 25, 2013.

76. Erica L.Green and Carrie Wells, "Maryland's HBCUs, state head to mediation," *Baltimore Sun*, November 1, 2013. Some believe the Coalition ruling on program duplication will have national implications. Eric Kelderman, "4 Other States Could Be Affected by Desegregation Ruling in Maryland." *The Chronicle of Higher Education*, October 18, 2103.

arranged that each campus would have a line of communication with the Attorney General's office during the mediation process. By year's end, the mediation process had not yet begun as both sides prepared their negotiating positions.

At this writing, it is not possible to predict how long mediation might take or what its outcome might be. In mediations between adversaries involving monetary issues, compromises can usually be found; but when the issues are child or program custody, conciliation may impossible and a forced outcome may have bitter consequences. If mediation fails, Judge Blake will probably hear new arguments about her proposed remedy. If she does not change her mind about required program mergers, transfers, or closures, an appeal is likely. The policies of a new Governor and Attorney General after the 2014 election are often unknown. So in the *Coalition* case, like the issue of campus mergers and strategic alliances, UMBC's saga will continue to be influenced by outside forces in which the University's influence is limited.

CHAPTER XIII

Conclusions: "Success Is Never Final"

In the competitive environment of American higher education, it is a great advantage to be an old institution. "Founded in...." is always touted as an asset by those whose charters are antiques. To be established before the American Revolution is the best of all (Harvard, 1636; William & Mary, 1693; Yale, 1701; Pennsylvania, 1740; Princeton, 1746; Columbia, 1754; Brown, 1764; Rutgers, 1766; and Dartmouth, 1769). Occasionally a nouveau riche university with a very wealthy sponsor (Vanderbilt, 1873; Johns Hopkins, 1876; Chicago, 1890; and Stanford, 1891) has broken into the esteemed circle. Surveying higher education, scholars Claudia Goldin and Lawrence Katz concluded, "Something profoundly altered higher education around 1890, so that almost all of today's noteworthy U.S. universities and colleges were founded before 1900."[1]

Vanderbilt historian Paul K. Conklin asserted:

> It takes at least a century for a university to reach early adolescence, to gain a relatively stable identity. By then, some basic character traits have already been established, but any rapidly growing university retains the impressionability of adolescents, their openness to new goals and new self understanding. For a historian, writing a biography of an adolescent has its challenges and rewards. The early, rapidly changing years of a university are always exciting, full of soaring dreams and great hopes as well as great dangers and bitter disappointments. But the hazards are intimidating. Only in the light of a mature, if not completed life, can one locate the more enduring and significant facets of childhood and youth.[2]

A. UMBC's Historical Context

In 1965, a year before UMBC had completed its first building or enrolled its first student, a university publicist wrote a story on the new campus titled, "UMBC strives

---

1. Claudia Goldin and Lawrence Katz, "The Shaping of American Higher Education: The Formative Years in the United States 1890–1940," *Journal of Economic Perspectives.* 13, no.1, 1999.39.

2. Paul K. Conklin, *Gone with the Ivy: A Biography of Vanderbilt University* (Knoxville: University of Tennessee Press, 1985), 1.

for excellence." Without wealthy benefactors, an architecturally distinctive campus, nationally prominent alumni, a variety of professional schools, or consistent regional or statewide political support, UMBC's ambition to achieve "excellence" might have seemed laughable.

UMBC not only had to overcome the handicaps particular to its situation, but it could not avoid the national trends that created strong headwinds. In "The Stunted Career of the Second Flagships," section of their book, *The Rise of American Research Universities*, Hugh Graham and Nancy Diamond described the changing environment in the 1970s that dampened the optimism that had created the new urban universities in the 1960s. Only a few, notably the University of California campuses at Irvine and San Diego and the University of Illinois at Chicago escaped these trends. For the others, including UMBC, the authors wrote:

> The new urban universities, lacking alumni support and the political and business ties of established institutions, and the financial magnet of a medical center, were especially vulnerable to the academic recession of the 1970s. Flagship university administrators and faculty rallied to protect their exclusive degree programs and their privileged state appropriations against aspiring claims from newer schools. State colleges, winning university status by mobilizing their political resources, objected to program expansion at the new research campuses.... The ambitions of upstart challengers often prompted a combined assault by resentful ... state colleges and universities, established private institutions and by the flagship campus itself....[3]

Maryland's higher education politics created additional problems for UMBC. The long-standing rivalry between the UM Board of Regents and the various statewide coordinating boards often sent conflicting and inhibiting signals to the new campus. Further, none of the other new wave urban universities faced so many local public competitors. The University of Missouri-Kansas City, the University of North Carolina at Charlotte, the University of Wisconsin-Milwaukee and many others were launched in geographical niches starved for public education. These campuses garnered critical political and business support almost immediately. Their virtual geographical monopolies meant they rarely had to struggle with local competitors for program approval. Most of them were free to become the center of public professional and graduate school education in their regions.

For a new campus, building an attractive portfolio of programs was an absolute necessity, but getting approvals may have consumed more political energy at UMBC than in any other new wave urban university. Not only was there the gauntlet to be traversed through the USM procedures, but the statewide coordinating boards were very sensitive to both private and public competitor's objections to UMBC proposals.

---

3. Hugh D. Graham and Nancy Diamond *The Rise of American Research Universities: Elites and Challengers in the Postwar Era* (Baltimore: Johns Hopkins University Press, 1990), 164.

Then there were the special problems of civil rights mandates. Though about half of the new wave institutions were in southern or border states covered by desegregation requirements, with a few exceptions, those new institutions were not located close to public Historically Black Colleges and Universities (HBCUs). Maryland has an exceptionally large number of public HBCUs, including two in Baltimore, so program duplication issues were certain to be fiercely contested. The State has struggled to meet the Office of Civil Rights' (OCR) ambiguous desegregation mandates which have caused constant battles as UMBC sought to create or expand programs. These complex racial issues have meant that the impact of federal decision makers on UMBC and the rest of Maryland higher education has lasted for over four decades.[4] The State had not been released from OCR oversight and, as Chapter XII describes in 2013, the federal district court in Baltimore published memorandum in the *Coalition for Equity and Excellence in Maryland v. Maryland Higher Education Commission* case contains a several possible threats to UMBC's current and future programs. Judge Blake has ordered mediation on these issues before making a final decision. If the State decides to take her post-mediation ruling to the United States Fourth Circuit Court of Appeals, civil rights policies in Maryland higher education will not be decided for years.

The case's significance for UMBC's future can be gleaned from the assertion in the plaintiff's opening brief that the State should not have created UMBC in the first place, let alone established it as "a research institution and proceeded to provide it with better funding, facilities, and better academic programs than Morgan State, a pre-existing research institution in the same metropolitan area."[5] Although no final ruling in this case will threaten UMBC's existence, it might jeopardize program development and require continuation of the pattern where Maryland HBCUs have been funded more generously than non-HBCUs since 1984. UMBC trailed Coppin State in state per capita student funding by $3,600 and Morgan State by $2,700 in 2010.[6]

B. The Enigma of Success

Given these conditions and others, UMBC is a most improbable upstart. The new campus was created to respond to excess student demand at College Park, but ten years after its founding the situation had changed. Enrollment all across the state had leveled off. The *Baltimore Sun,* however, was quick to seize on the fact that UMBC's enrollment had plateaued, far from its predicted 12,000–15,000 goal. In a 1978 article

4. George R. La Noue and Alexia Van Orden, "Dual Sovereignties: The Four Decade Struggle between the U.S. Office of Civil Rights and the State of Maryland over the Desegregation of Higher Education," presented at the Policy History Conference, Richmond, Virginia, June 2012.

5. Plaintiff's Statement of the Case and Statement of the Issues to be considered at Trial. Civil No. 06-2773-CCB, October 10, 2010. 6.

6. Defendant's Statement of the Case and Statement of the Issues to be considered at Trial. Civil No. 06-2773-CCB, October 29, 2010. 19–20.

titled, "The academic Camelot that never came about," the *Sun's* education writer conceded UMBC's faculty credentials were impressive because 94 percent of its professors held doctoral degrees, the highest percentage among state campuses, which averaged 50 percent. Nevertheless, he focused on the "cold" and "severe" campus architecture and quoted a UMBC professor that after morning classes, "Around 2 or 3 o'clock this place looks exactly like the surface of the moon. Buildings have been thrown up, but they stand there empty."[7]

Although there were no public undergraduate universities in the Baltimore area at UMBC's birth in 1966, the state acquired the University of Baltimore in 1975 and later converted Towson and Morgan from undergraduate colleges into universities. Those moves increased competition in the region and in 1979 the *Sun* criticized UM Chancellor John Toll and UMBC:

> He [Toll] is not responsible for Baltimore having five public campuses and only enough students to fill four. And the more desperately he struggles to find a future for UMBC, the more apparent he makes it seem that UMBC should not have been built in the first place.[8]

In 1991 the *Sun* returned to this theme in evaluating UMBC's 25th anniversary, but with a grudging acknowledgement that it might have been wrong:

> Critics began to say UMBC was a mistake. It was chronically under-enrolled. Although the school had hired many bright young scholars when it began, it was described as having a graduate school faculty and a community college student body. In the cutthroat competition for state resources—not only dollars, but programs now allocated by a state board—UMBC could not call on influential alumni or other constituency groups with clout.[9]

But the *Sun* went on to say that by 1991, UMBC had not only survived but thrived, praising its growth in quantitative and qualitative terms, citing rising student SAT scores, retention rates, and research grants.

Less than twenty years after that assessment, UMBC had attained unprecedented recognition as a nationally significant university in *U.S. News and World Report*, *Newsweek*, and *Time*, among others. The *Sun* began to reappraise the campus it had so vigorously disparaged during its growing pains. In 2011 a *Sun* editorial, "A model institution," applauded UMBC's innovative approach to undergraduate teaching, but also made some broader points:

> As the state's honors university with a particular focus on science, technology, engineering and math, UMBC enrolls some of the best prepared high school graduates of any institution in the University System of Maryland.... The UMBC president and faculty turned the entire school into a giant ex-

---

7. M.William Salganik, "The academic Camelot that never came about," *Baltimore Sun*, May 28, 1978.

8. "Dr. Toll's Desperation," *Baltimore Sun*, March 29, 1979.

9. "UMBC: 25th Birthday—and Last?" *Baltimore Sun*, September 19, 1991.

> perimental laboratory for testing innovative teaching methods and instructional strategies.... That is something the rest of the country is rightly taking notice of. It's also an approach that could well serve as a model for the entire University of Maryland system.[10]

Whatever the intrinsic merit of institutional rankings in higher education, almost everyone agrees they have real world consequences. Regardless of their private posture, most universities and colleges take the public relations value of their rankings very seriously. UMBC's 2009 national accolades seemed to have an immediate payoff in admissions numbers. By January 2010, applications were up 27 percent overall in a single year. Perhaps most hopeful was an increase of 17 percent in out-of-state applications, an area of long-term concern for the University.[11] When the freshmen finally enrolled in September, their average SAT scores were up twenty points. In a bad economy, a state public university with a rising reputation seemed like a good choice for many Maryland families.[12]

How did UMBC move from the ranks of academic wannabes and underachievers to an institution that has maximized its assets and made a real mark in higher education? In a sense that is the question this book tries to answer. Looking back, as historians do, what factors contributed to UMBC's improbable success? The danger for an historian is to seize upon a particular theory and fit the facts to that explanation.[13] Reality, however, is much more complex.

As this book illustrates, success and failure exist simultaneously in many different areas in a university. It is clear there was no magic bullet; no foolproof formula. Instead, UMBC, as it approaches its half-century birthday, is the product of many interwoven forces. Every day in the University there are victories and failures in a variety of arenas. On the campus, some classes are taught that shape careers and lifelong values, while other lessons are swiftly obliterated by the crescendo of social networking messages impacting students as they step outside the classroom door. From the time students are admitted, they compete with varying amounts of success, until they hear from graduate or professional schools or employers, pending graduation. Professors receive evaluations about long-sought research awards, foundation grants, and publishing contracts. Some messages contain fulsome praise and new opportunities, while others communicate pro forma regrets. Directors design art exhibitions, theatrical productions, and musical performances that exceed expectations or end up mediocre and forgotten. Months of discipline and determination can lead athletes

---

10. "A model institution: UMBC pioneers an innovative approach to undergraduate teaching," *Baltimore Sun* editorial, December 17, 2011.

11. Childs Walker, "Applications jump at 3 Md. Schools," *Baltimore Sun*, January 17, 2010. 2.

12. The numbers of new out-of-state students actually enrolled declined a bit, possibly because UMBC cut the amount of merit scholarships it awarded by $840,000 to fill in other budget holes.

13. Margaret MacMillan, *Dangerous Games: The Use and Abuse of History* (New York: Modern Library, 2009).

and coaches to victory, but the most careful preparation is not always a shield against defeat. Staff find creative ways to help students and faculty solve complex problems or they let opportunities slip by. No single theory or explanation can encompass all these events, but hindsight can provide some insights about why, on balance, UMBC has been so successful.

It turned out that UMBC's location has been a major asset. The Baltimore metropolitan area's $131 billion gross domestic product is the 76th largest in the world.[14] The University really is in the center of Maryland, accessible by all forms of transportation. Its surrounding communities, Catonsville, Ellicott City, and Columbia, are attractive places to live and raise children, particularly for two-professional families.[15] For the more adventurous, Baltimore has every variety of neighborhoods. It can be a tough commute, but the capital of the world is only forty miles away in Washington. More immediately, although UMBC's campus does not inspire the architectural awe that Yale, Stanford, or Notre Dame might, it is safe, expansive, yet walkable, and maturing with some graceful elements and some spectacular new buildings.

Maryland is a well-educated, wealthy state whose government and citizens have produced a general improvement in the state's public K-12 education in recent decades,[16] so there have been more good admissible students available. UMBC was a beneficiary of this rising tide that lifted the test scores of almost all Maryland universities and colleges.

For years, however, Maryland families sent their most promising sons and daughters out of state, often to private universities. In 1981, the State Board for Higher Education lamented, "Large numbers of Maryland's high ability high school seniors leave the State to attend college.... This exodus of well qualified students hinders Maryland's efforts to improve the quality of its public institutions and gain increasing public support."[17] Consequently, there was an underserved market for a mid-size public campus whose graduates would be competitive nationally for graduate and professional schools and employment. UMBC filled that important niche.

UMBC has also been blessed with good neighbors. In its nearby environment are a cluster of major federal agencies and one of the largest pools of Ph.D.s, MDs, JDs and other talented people in the world.

---

14. Real Time Economics, "U.S. Cities with Bigger Economies than Entire Countries," *Wall Street Journal,* July 20, 2012.

15. Columbia/ Ellicott City area was ranked 2nd and Catonsville placed 49th on the "Best Places to Live in America" list by *Money Magazine,* July 2010.

16. Liz Bowie, "Md. seniors rank No.1 in passing AP exams," *Baltimore Sun*, February 5, 2009. Liz Bowie, "Md. Students leading the nation in tests," *Baltimore Sun*, July 17, 2012 Between 1992 and 2011, Maryland led the nation in overall achievement gains. Part of the reason for Maryland's overall high ranking is that when the 2007 recession hit, the state largely preserved or even increased K-12 funding, while cutting state appropriations to higher education. Phil Oliff and Michael Leachman, "New School Year Brings Steep Cuts in State Funding For Schools," Center for Budget and Policy Priorities, October 7, 2011. 6.

17. SBHE "Recommendations Concerning the Future Governance of Higher Education, October 1981.6.

UMBC's geographical advantages would not have been decisive, however, if it were not for the remarkable number of persons attracted to the campus who were committed to institution-building as well as to their own careers.

None of UMBC's successes would have happened without a strong faculty dedicated to both research and teaching. UMBC's pioneer faculty were hired in a job market that gave the University many fine choices. But it is also true that, in the early years, application of rigorous tenure standards by senior professors and administrators, particularly regarding published scholarship, meant that many of the original faculty did not survive. They were replaced by new hires with a clearer expectation about how high the University's requirements would be. These faculty were engaged in launching graduate programs and competing for grants and contracts at a national level. UMBC faculty had to have an unusual concern with institutional development, if their own careers were to flourish. Serving on committees to design and approve new curricula, programs, laboratories, performance spaces, and buildings were all essential parts of the job for UMBC professors, in ways not so prevalent at more mature campuses.

As John Jeffries, who came to UMBC as an Assistant Professor of History in 1973 and later became departmental chair and then Dean of the College of Humanities, Arts, and Social Sciences, reflected:

> UMBC was built from the bottom up. It wasn't that there was any particular president or provost who made UMBC what it was. There was the sense that when Michael Hooker became president and then got UMBC on the map, that Michael Hooker had somehow built or vitalized this university that had sort of been slumbering. Well, what Michael did was to have the good sense to recognize when he got here just how strong some of the faculty and programs were and to make the best of that in terms of publicizing it.... There are a handful of people with real energy and insistence upon excellence and upon building UMBC who I think were mostly responsible. There are department chairs, maybe some deans responsible for building UMBC, but it was much more from the bottom than it was in any way from the top down. And that's been a part of what's been good about being at UMBC, that you were able to build something, certainly down through the mid to late 1990s, as much from internal dynamics.... the excellence of UMBC, though often enabled and sometimes directed from the top, but the building has really been at the faculty level and to some degree, at the division or college level.[18]

Faculty are given considerable flexibility in how they spend their time. The quality of universities is built hour by hour through laborious faculty decisions on hiring, tenure and promotion, and graduate admissions, and grading thousands of exams, papers, and theses. This time-consuming work is rarely cause for external notice. But, if there is not careful internal attention to these professorial duties, over time the standards on a campus deteriorate, and the new normal is mediocrity. The expectations of chairs and deans often play a role in outlining and enforcing these standards.

---

18. John Jeffries interview by Joseph Tatarewicz, August 4, 2006. 51.

None of this is to suggest that top administrators don't play critical roles. UMBC benefitted enormously from the support of UM leaders Wilson Elkins, John Toll, Don Langenberg, and Brit Kirwan and, generally, the Regents, who protected the new campus from various conflicts with state coordinating boards and from being smothered by College Park. These leaders insisted that they were in charge of a system and that their headquarters at Adelphi was not an adjunct to College Park. Although a young campus, they believed UMBC had a promising future that should be respected and nurtured.

Two UMBC Chancellors, Albin Kuhn and John Dorsey, both of whom came from College Park, were completely dedicated to the new campus's welfare. As the founding father, Kuhn's values, contacts, and judgments were indispensable. He worked virtually on a blank slate and his vision was expansive and valid. Dorsey had a very different task. Arriving to take over the leadership reins after the faculty had deposed his predecessor was a difficult challenge. He had to assure nervous Regents that patricide would not become a UMBC tradition, while calming a suspicious and rambunctious faculty by affirming his loyalty to their campus. Ironically, the State Board for Higher Education's threat in 1981 to turn the campus into an industrial park produced the occasion that united every UMBC constituency and John Dorsey rose to that challenge.

The only clear administrative failure, Calvin B.T. Lee, in a curious way, also made an important contribution. By demonstrating that the campus could not always depend on its administrators to overcome UMBC's political liabilities, the faculty began to develop a sense of ownership and responsibility that energized shared governance for at least two decades.

Michael Hooker, bright, charming, and visionary, was the first UMBC chancellor who engaged the attention of Baltimore elites and made UMBC a player in both economic and higher education discussions. He encouraged his faculty and administrators to think in grander terms and he believed that UMBC could achieve some prominence on the national stage. Even though he was not successful in effecting the UMBC/UMAB merger, the proposal was serious, and the negotiations proceeded on equal terms. When Hooker left to become President of the University of Massachusetts System and later moved to become the Chancellor of the University of North Carolina at Chapel Hill, people noticed that it was UMBC that was the launching pad for his high profile career.

Perhaps the most important thing Hooker did for UMBC was to recruit Freeman Hrabowski to the campus as Vice Provost in 1987. As Hooker's successor as President, Hrabowski has had an almost unbelievable ascent to the heights of personal acclaim and as leader of an institution that has become a national role model. For most of UMBC's history, knowledge of UMBC's President or even of the University's existence would not have been a concern at Harvard. Yet, on the banks of the Charles River in May 2010, Freeman A. Hrabowski III was given an honorary degree with a Crimson hood. Harvard President Drew Gilpin Faust remarked at the graduation ceremony that Hrabowski "has been a galvanic force in his university's ascent."

Hrabowski characteristically turned the honor into a compliment for his institution by saying "The respect our colleagues at Harvard have for UMBC as a research institution is clear."

As for the "galvanic force," sorting out to what extent Hrabowski created the now nationally recognized achievements at UMBC, and to what extent he was the eloquent publicist for those achievements is a fruitless chicken and egg argument. The twenty honorary degrees he has been awarded would not have occurred without the synergy of his outstanding personal characteristics and the institutional rise of UMBC. There is no doubt that Hrabowski's insistence on high academic performance for students of every background has inspired UMBC faculty and other administrators to uphold those values. Further, his public speaking prowess and up-beat message have won him a platform to spread the UMBC story at professional associations and graduation ceremonies across the country. In garnering the attention of the national media, education leaders, and federal and state office holders, Hrabowski's interpersonal skills, message, and character have been indispensable.

UMBC's new recognition has not come because of a well funded advertising campaign. There have been no full-page ads in the *Chronicle of Higher Education*. Hrabowski at the microphone before rapt audiences across the nation, giving interviews to the press, or one-on-one on the administration building's rooftop have been the catalyst for UMBC's new recognition.

C. UMBC's Future

One of President Hrabowski's contributions has been to imprint the aphorism, "Success is never final" into the UMBC ethos. What will be UMBC's future? Questions about the future make historians tremble. The past is prologue, but to what? The advantages of UMBC's location are secure. The quality of the faculty, staff, and students in higher education institutions increases or deteriorates over time. Given the macro trends in American culture and demography, a metropolitan, inclusive, multi-ethnic, secular university such as UMBC should be well-positioned to maintain or even increase its market shares. Leadership continuity is harder to predict. Institutions usually cannot count on a succession of charismatic leaders, but the job will now attract top talent when new leadership is necessary. There will always be fierce competition for the best, but UMBC can now compete.

The demand for post-high school education will continue to rise. The Georgetown Center on Education and the Workforce projects that 62 percent of all jobs will require some college education in 2018, up from 28 percent shortly after UMBC was founded.[19] The Regents' plan for USM in 2020 should enhance UMBC's importance

---

19. Oliff, et.al. "Recent Deep State Higher Education Cuts," 10.

to the state.[20] The ten-year plan proposes to add 45,000 students to system campuses, redesign introductory courses to reduce dropouts, increase by 40 percent its graduates in science, technology, engineering and mathematics, double its research funding to more than $2 billion, and develop more ties with industry and businesses.[21] Although UMBC does not wish to grow to be the size of College Park or even Towson, which would deprive the state and students of a mid-size campus option, it will grow, particularly at the graduate level. Given its existing prowess in the STEM disciplines, UMBC should greatly benefit from state plans to increase the focus on them and proposals to create more scholarships and tuition waivers in those fields. The goal of increasing research space and linking campuses more closely with economic development should mesh well with UMBC's room for expansion and research park experience. UMBC has already pioneered improvements in introductory STEM courses to decrease attrition.[22]

Fostering closer connections with institutions whose primary goals are not educational can run some risks. There are often different values in government agencies which must respond to ever changing political signals and in corporations whose attention must always be on the financial bottom line.[23] While the dangers of having STEM scientists conducting research funded by pharmaceutical or energy corporations may be obvious, social science research sponsored by government or foundations may have ideologically-driven agendas as well. Increasingly, faculty social scientists, like their STEM counterparts, are expected to demonstrate a record of external grant support to be hired or obtain tenure.

Driven by the unceasing need to raise money in an extremely competitive market, universities have adopted many corporate characteristics. There is an intense concern with institutional branding, managing the flow of information, political correctness, internal auditing, and top-down uniform policies.[24] When carefully-selected politicians or community and business leaders are brought to campus at all, it is often on ceremonial occasions as dignitaries, where they are sheltered from any open engagements about their policies. Depriving students of valuable lessons about the intelligent questioning of authority, a fundamental citizen skill, campuses appear to be more ideologically homogeneous than they actually are. The academic value of serious self-evaluation is being replaced by a corporate value of relentless self-praise. Transparency

---

20. Childs Walker, "Regents OK 10-year plan for state universities." *Baltimore Sun*, December 4, 2010. 5.

21. USM Strategic Plan, 2010–2020, adopted December 3, 2010. 10–12.

22. Daniel de Vise, "UMBC's quiet revolution in teaching science is earning school extra credit." *Washington Post*, March 20, 2012.

23. See Derek Bok, *Universities in the Marketplace: The Commercialization of Higher Education* (Princeton: Princeton University Press, 2003); Jennifer Washburn, *University, Inc, The Corporate Corruption of Higher Education* (New York: Basic Books, 2005); and Ellen Schrecker, *The Lost Soul of Higher Education: Corporatization, the Assault on Academic Freedom and the End of the American University* (New York: The New Press, 2010).

24. Greg Lukianoff, *Unlearning Liberty: Campus Censorship and the End of American Debate* (New York: Encounter Books, 2012).

in internal decision making is declining, while fostering and expressing diverse or controversial viewpoints that can threaten the institution's public image are not encouraged. A service ethic is emphasized for students and faculty, but few campuses anymore are the centers for the great policy debates about America's future.

Harvard's President Drew Gilpin Faust has written:

> Universities are meant to be producers not just of knowledge but also of (often inconvenient) doubt. They are creative and unruly places, home to a polyphony of voices. But at this moment in our history, universities might well ask if they have done enough to raise the deep and unsettling questions necessary to any society.... have universities become too captive to the immediate and worldly purposes they serve? Has the market model become the fundamental and defining identity of higher education?[25]

In the corporate model, academic research that affects economic development is widely publicized, whereas breakthrough discoveries in the social sciences and humanities are often slighted. Yet the recent economic recession was not caused by technological failures or a dearth of patentable products. It was caused by the failure to examine new highly complex statistical models in historical perspective and by the stain of human greed that the classics texts have illuminated for centuries.

Another driver of corporatization is the dramatic increase of regulations emanating from state and federal governments. Some of these new rules are attached to funding, but others are unfunded mandates. In these instances, the compliance task will be assigned to some university administrative office.[26] There is little incentive for campus debate about a policy, if its outcome is dictated by law or a "Dear Colleague" letter from the Office of Civil Rights or some other government agency.

The corporatization of universities, however, is not just an administrative problem. Faculty typically do not protest when search firms locate transient professional hirelings, aka big-time athletic coaches, who come with hugely disproportionate salaries, to create branding for their universities. Nor do the full-time faculty usually object to the pauperization of part-time faculty who bear heavy teaching loads, so the regulars can pursue tenure and more lucrative research opportunities. After all, that is what the market will bear and the arrangement does create institutional status. UMBC is not unaffected by some of these corporatizing national trends.

The great unknown is whether UMBC can continue to compete at the national level without the financial resources of its wealthier competitors. This is not a newly recognized problem. The 1996 UMBC Middle States Self Study Report concluded:

> It is unrealistic to expect UMBC to continue such a high level of performance into the next century if adjustments in its funding base are not made

25. Drew Gilpin Faust, "The University's Crisis of Purpose," *The New York Times Book Review,* September 6, 2009.

26. Benjamin Ginsberg, *The Fall of the Faculty: The Rise of the All-Administrative University and Why it Matters,* (New York: Oxford University Press, 2011).

> to ensure greater equity between UMBC and other UMS campuses, to achieve a level of funding that recognizes the inherent costliness of UMBC's mission emphasizing science and engineering, and to acknowledge its productivity relative to many of the of the leading institutions in the nation.[27]

As we are now firmly in the "next century," those funding inequities have not been improved, but UMBC still is progressing. The past record would suggest UMBC can continue to levitate its performance above its funding base, but that might be a dangerous illusion. The appeal of being a pioneer for faculty and students will no longer suffice. There will be new programs to be sure, but the institution's basic structure is in place. Key gifts that established the Meyerhoff Scholars, Linehan Artist Scholars, Sherman Teacher Education Scholars, and Sondheim Public Affairs Scholars have proven critical in attracting the best students. UMBC has begun to develop a small cadre of endowed, named professorial chairs[28] in an academic world where such positions are becoming more common as a faculty recruitment and reward strategy.[29] In time, growing professorial stars internally may not be enough. Great departments often require money to raid other universities for talent; and, with limited means, UMBC may be more often the victim rather that the victor in those captures. As Maryland universities are expected to be even more productive in grant competition, money for start-ups and creating research teams will grow in importance.

Although the stability of annual infusions of Maryland state funds is important to UMBC, every prediction suggests a decreasing share of public university budgets will come from state coffers, no matter who is governor.[30] The National Science Foundation (NSF) reported that in the years between 2002–2010, all but seven states

---

27. 1996 UMBC Middle States Self Study Report. 6.

28. In 2012, there were six such chairs: The Bearman Foundation Chair in Entrepreneurship (2004), held by Craig Saper, Professor of Language, Literacy, and Cultural Doctorate Program; the Willard and Lillian Hackerman Endowed Chair in Engineering (1997), Brian Read, Professor of Chemical, Biochemical and Environmental Engineering; the Robert and Jane Meyerhoff Chair in Biochemistry (1997), Professor Suzanne Ostrand-Rosenberg; the Lipsitz Professor of the Arts, Humanities and Social Sciences (1998), Ralph Falco, Professor of English; the Constellation Professorship in Information Technology and Engineering (1999), Julia M. Ross, Professor of Chemical, Biochemical and Environmental Engineering; the Oros Family Professor for Computer Science and Technology (2000), Anupam Joshi, Professor Computer Science and Electrical Engineering, and James T. Oates, Professor of Computer Science and Electrical Engineering. Unlike chairs at wealthier institutions, these "chairs" provide stipends, but not full support, and the occupants hold the positions for relatively short periods.

29. In her history of UC, San Diego, Anderson notes that Chancellor Richard Atkinson followed his philosophy that "You recruit the very best people, not always trying to fill in because you need a person here and a person there" by creating forty endowed professorships and offered new stars larger salaries, real estate loans, additional appointments in their subspecialty and possible employment for spouses. Nancy Scott Anderson, *An Improbable Venture: A History of the University of California, San Diego*. 234.

30. See Figure A in Chapter V. For a discussion of the funding problem from the state government perspective, see Peter A. Harkness, "Pass/Fail: The Greatest Public Universities in America are at the tipping point," *Governing*, June 2012.

cut their funding for higher education.[31] NSF predicted that trend was virtually certain to continue. Although the state budget cuts were not as draconian in Maryland as in some other states, they were substantial, amounting to 20 percent per student over those years. Only a 10 percent increase in total students enrolled gave relief in the form of additional tuition dollars to some campuses. The State may have learned a bad lesson, however, when tuition was frozen for five years between 2005 and 2010 to political and editorial applause. The mending tape and baling wire used to hold programs together during this period were not visible to the public. On the other hand, the State has been more supportive for capital expenditures, and the quality of UMBC's physical plant has continued to grow impressively.

The external environment will be increasingly competitive for UMBC and other campus-based universities. The traditional higher education economic model is being stress tested and found wanting. For-profit institutions, teaching mostly online, already have established a foothold in Maryland and will likely expand. In 2012, MOOCs or Massively Open On-line Courses, often offered by faculty from distinguished universities making their classes freely available on the internet, entered the education scene.[32] Although there are many problems yet to be solved in their business models, MOOCs mean that students from Glen Burnie or Hagerstown can take a course from a professor at Stanford or MIT without leaving their homes. Further, the American Council on Education and other organizations are recommending that some MOOC courses can be taken for credit. The United States Department of Education is urging higher education institutions to measure the competencies of incoming students and to grant credit for those skills. Some universities will offer tutorials to help students opt out of courses[33] and in California there is a movement to create a "faculty-free" public institution that awards degrees based only on examinations.[34]

Given the rising amount of higher education debt students and their families are accumulating, these non-campus based alternatives may be tempting. While there are some societal benefits in these trends, they may also create a race-to-the-bottom mentality as universities compete to offer degrees on ever more flexible terms. Right now, MOOCs and competency-based credits experiments are like the first gentle waves as part of an incoming tide. When fully developed, however, their surge may wash away many of higher education's sand castles.

---

31. Paul Basken, "NSF Raises Alarm over Falling State Support for Research Universities," *The Chronicle of Higher Education*, September 25, 2012. See also National Science Board, "Diminishing Funding and Rising Expectations: Trends and Challenges for Research Universities," July 12, 2012.

32. Katherine Mangan, "MOOC Mania: It's raising big questions about the future of higher education," *The Chronicle of Higher Education*, October 1, 2012.

33. Libby Sander, "U. of Akron to Help Students Test Out of Courses," *Chronicle of Higher Education*, April 12. 2013.

34. Allie Bidwell, "Under Calif. Bill, Faculty-Free 'Colleges' Would Award Exam-Based Degree," *Chronicle of Higher Education*, April 12, 2013.

Increasingly state universities must depend on grants, contracts and private funds.[35] The long term consequences of that trend are uncertain. But in the short run, more emphasis on the revenues research faculty can produce may diminish the focus on teaching and advising undergraduates. More classes taught by part-time instructors, who have little expectation of permanent employment by a university and, therefore, less loyalty to the institution or to their profession, seem inevitable.

Some national trends may be a particular problem for UMBC. In its relatively brief lifespan, UMBC has been an overachiever in the university world compared to its better funded peers. But how long can that last and what alternatives exist? UMBC alumni have a growing, but still tenuous, identification with the campus and little history of making substantial donations. Perhaps when a critical mass of them reach retirement age that pattern may shift. Philanthropists can make a decisive difference in the trajectory of a university, but who they are and what forms their gifts might take are unknowable.

So when the next history of UMBC is written, will its remarkable progress in the past decades seem like a golden era? Will UMBC slide backward to fit the norm of other underfunded institutions or will the solid foundation of its past create the basis for new achievements? In fact, the bar is being raised. In the conclusion of his 2012 speech at the glittering gala dinner honoring his twentieth year as UMBC's President, Freeman Hrabowski reiterated his vision for the campus. He quoted Aristotle, "Excellence is never an accident. It is always the result of high intentions, sincere effort and intelligent execution; it represents the wise choice of many alternatives—choice, not chance determines your destiny."

For UMBC, with uncertain political support, an awkward name, surrounded by well-established public and private competitors, and unable to launch its own professional schools, seeking excellence at its founding by following the traditional routes seemed most improbable. Instead, UMBC has developed a new model and, perhaps, the quest for excellence may be a permanent part of the UMBC culture. The only thing that can be known for sure is that the past cannot be changed, but the future depends on those who care for it.

35. Emma Roller, "State Budget Cuts for Research Universities Imperil Competitiveness," *The Chronicle of Higher Education*, January 17, 2012. See also Paul Fain, "Cuts Intensify Identity Crisis for Washington's Flagship Campus," *The Chronicle of Higher Education*," September 3, 2010. 1. Over a fifteen-month period, the University of Washington absorbed a 33 percent cut in core state dollars, but it raised $2.7 billion in private funds in a recent campaign. Cuts in state funding were also very severe at the University of California, the University of Illinois, and the University of Virginia.

Appendices

A. UMBC Time Line

Years	Governor	State Coordinating Board	University System	System Chancellor or President	UMBC Chancellor or President
1963–1965	J. Millard Tawes	Advisory Council on Higher Education	University of Maryland (UM)	Wilson H. Elkins	
1966					Albin O. Kuhn
1967	Spiro Agnew				
1968		Maryland Council on Higher Education (MCHE)			
1969–1971	Marvin Mandel				
1972–1975					Calvin B.T. Lee
1976		State Board for Higher Education (SBHE)			
1977	Blair Lee III (acting)				Louis L. Kaplan
1978				John S. Toll	John W. Dorsey
1979–1985	Harry R. Hughes				
1986					Michael K. Hooker
1987	William D. Schaefer				
1988–1989		Maryland Higher Education Commission (MHEC)	University of Maryland System (UMS)		

Years	Governor	State Coordinating Board	University System	System Chancellor or President	UMBC Chancellor or President
1990–1992				Donald N. Langenberg	
1993–1994					Freeman A. Hrabowski
1995–1996	Parris N. Glendening				
1997–2001			University System of Maryland (USM)		
2002				William E. Kirwan	
2003–2006	Robert L. Ehrlich				
2007–2012	Martin J. O'Malley				

B. Degrees Approved at UMBC

Year Approved	Degree Offered
1966	American Studies (BA)
	Ancient Studies (BA)
	Biological Sciences (BA, BS)
	Chemistry (BA, BS)
	Economics (BA)
	English (BA)
	Geography (BA, BS)
	History (BA)
	Interdisciplinary Studies (BA, BS)
	Mathematics (BA, BS)
	Modern Languages and Linguistics (BA)
	Philosophy (BA)
	Physics (BA, BS)
	Political Science (BA)
	Psychology (BA, BS)
	Sociology (BA)
	Theatre (BA)
	Urban Studies (BA)
1970	Applied Mathematics (MS)
1973	Biological Sciences (Ph.D., MS)
	Chemistry (MS)
1974*	Africana Studies (BA)
1974	Community Clinical Psychology (MA)
	Public Policy (MPP)
1975	Applied Sociology (MA)
1976	Instructional Systems Development (MA)
1977*	Visual and Performing Arts—Visual Arts (BA)
1977	Biochemistry and Molecular Biology (BA, BS)
	Health Administration and Policy Program (BA)
	Historical Studies (MA)
1978	Biochemistry (Ph.D.)
	Applied Mathematics (Ph.D.)
	Public Policy (Ph.D.)
	Marine Estuarine Environmental Science (MS)
1979	Information Systems (BA, BS)
	Applied Developmental Psychology (Ph.D.)
1980	Emergency Health Services (BS)

* UMBC does not have a record of when these programs were approved. These are the years in which the first degrees were awarded.

Year Approved	Degree Offered
1981	Computer Science (BS)
	Ethnomusicology (Ph.D., MA)
1982	Social Work (BA)
	Human Services Psychology (Ph.D.)
1983	Statistics (Ph.D.)
	Applied Molecular Biology (MS)
	Statistics (MS)
1984	Chemical and Biochemical Engineering (Ph.D.)
	Computer Science (Ph.D.)
	Electrical Engineering (Ph.D.)
	Civil Engineering (Ph.D.)
	Marine Estuarine Environmental Science (Ph.D.)
	Mechanical Engineering (Ph.D.)
	Toxicology (Ph.D.)
	Chemical and Biochemical Engineering (MS)
	Computer Science (MS)
	Electrical Engineering (MS)
	Emergency Health Services (MS)
	Civil Engineering (MS)
	Mechanical Engineering (MS)
	Toxicology (MS)
1985	Chemistry (Ph.D.)
	Intercultural Communication (MA)
1986	Applied Physics (MS)
1987	Information Systems (Ph.D.)
	Engineering Management (MS)
	Information Systems (MS)
1988	Molecular and Cellular Biology (Ph.D.)
1989	Africana Studies (MA)
1991	Chemical Engineering (BS, BSE)
	Mechanical Engineering (BS, BSE)
	Applied Developmental Psychology (MA, MPS)
	Human Services Psychology (MA)
	Imaging and Digital Arts (MFA)
	Molecular and Cellular Biology (MS)
1992	Applied Physics (Ph.D.)
1994	Applied and Professional Ethics (MA)
1996	Neuroscience and Cognitive Sciences (Ph.D.)
	Biochemistry and Molecular Biology (MS)
1997	Computer Engineering (BS)
	Language, Literacy and Culture (Ph.D.)
	Neuroscience and Cognitive Sciences (MS)
1998	Economic Policy Analysis (MA)

Year Approved	Degree Offered
1999	Acting (BFA)
2000	Cultural Anthropology (BA)
	Financial Economics (BS)
	Statistics (BS)
	Visual Arts (BA)
	Atmospheric Physics (Ph.D., MS)
	Gerontology (Ph.D., MS)
2001	Bioinformatics and Computational Biology (BS)
	Dance (BA)
	Environmental Science (BA, BS)
	Environmental Studies (BA)
	Music (BA)
	Information Systems—Online (MS)
2002	Computer Engineering (Ph.D., MS)
	MA in Teaching (MA)
2003	MA in Education (MA)
2004	Business Technology Administration (BA)
2006	Management of Aging Services (BA)
	Human Centered Computing (Ph.D., MS)
	Management of Aging Services (MA)
	Professional Studies (MPS)
	Professional Studies: Biotechnology (MPS)
	Professional Studies: Cybersecurity (MPS)
	Professional Studies: Geographic Information Systems (MPS)
	Professional Studies: Industrial Organizational Psychology (MPS)
2007	Gender and Women's Studies (BA)
	Media and Communication Studies (BA)
	Physics Education (BA)
	Geography and Environmental Systems (Ph.D., MS)
	Systems Engineering (MS)
2008	Chemistry Education (BA)
2009	*Instructional Systems Development—Online (MA)*
	Emergency Health Services—Online (MS)
	Mathematics Instructional Leadership (K-8) (MA)
	Teaching English for Speakers of Other Languages (MA)
	Teaching English for Speakers of Other Languages—Online (MA)
2011	Asian Studies (BA)
2012	Design (BFA)
	Language, Literacy and Culture (MA)
	Text, Technologies and Literature (MA)
2013	Global Studies (BA)

C. Faculty Award Winners

Presidential Research Professor

Name	Department	Term
Robert K. Webb	History	7/1/89–6/30/93
Paul S. Lovett	Biological Sciences	7/1/90–6/30/94
Elizabeth Ermarth	English	7/1/91–6/30/95
Ralph Pollack	Chemistry	7/1/92–6/30/95
Michael Broyles	Music	7/1/93–6/30/96
Peter Argersinger	History	7/1/94–6/30/97
Suzanne Rosenberg	Biological Sciences	7/1/95–6/30/98
Curtis Menyuk	Computer Science/Elect. Engr.	7/1/96–6/30/99
J. Leeds Barroll	English	7/1/97–6/30/00
Ram Hosmane	Chemistry	7/1/98–6/30/01
Michael Summers	Chemistry	7/1/99–6/30/02
Bimal K. Sinha	Mathematics & Statistics	7/1/00–6/30/03
Warren Cohen	History	7/1/01–6/30/04
Yung-Jui (Ray) Chen	Computer Science/Elect. Engr.	7/1/02–6/30/05
J.Kevin Eckert	Sociology & Anthropology	7/1/03–6/30/06
James Grubb	History	7/1/04–6/30/07
Joel Liebman	Chemistry & Biochemistry	7/1/06–6/30/09
Lena Orlin	English	7/1/07–6/30/10
Thomas Mathew	Mathematics & Statistics	7/1/08–6/30/11
Thomas Cronin	Biological Sciences	7/1/09–6/30/12
Ka-che Yip	History	7/1/10–6/30/13
Carlo DiClemente	Psychology	7/1/11–6/30/14
Timothy Finin	Computer Science/Elect. Engr.	7/1/12–6/30/15

Presidential Teaching Professor

Name	Department	Term
Jay Freyman	Ancient Studies	7/1/89–6/30/93
Slobodan Petrovich	Psychology	7/1/90–6/30/94
Eugene Parker	Geography	7/1/91–6/30/95
Thomas Field	Modern Languages & Ling.	7/1/92–6/30/95
Donald Creighton	Chemistry	7/1/93–6/30/96
Ka-che Yip	History	7/1/94–6/30/97
Warren Belasco	American Studies	7/1/95–6/30/98
Marilyn Demorest	Psychology	7/1/96–6/30/99
Diane Lee	Education	7/1/97–6/30/00
Ed Orser	American Studies	7/1/98–6/30/01
John Jeffries	History	7/1/99–6/30/02
Muddappa S. Gowda	Mathematics & Statistics	7/1/00–6/30/03

J. Lynn Zimmerman	Biological Sciences	7/1/01–6/30/04
Robert Deluty	Psychology	7/1/02–6/30/05
Alan Rosenthal	Modern Languages & Linguistics	7/1/03–6/30/06
Cynthia Hody	Political Science	7/1/04–6/30/07
Phillip Sokolove	Biological Sciences	7/1/06–6/30/09
Robert Reno	Physics	7/1/07–6/30/10
Tim Topoleski	Mechanical Engineering	7/1/08–6/30/11
Ram Hosmane (retired 1/2010)	Chemistry & Biochemistry	7/1/09–6/30/12
Wendy Salkind	Theatre	7/1/10–6/30/13
Lynnda Dahlquist	Psychology	7/1/11–6/30/14
Terry Bouton	History	7/1/12–6/30/15

D. Staff Award Winners

Presidential Distinguished Professional Staff Award

1999	John Martello, Shriver Center
2000	Lawrence Wilt, Library
2001	Betty Glascoe, Career Development Center
2002	James Milani, College of Engineering
2003	Charles Brown, Athletics
2004	Jack Suess, Office of Information Technology
2006	Joseph Hill, Facilities Management
2007	William-John Tudor, Ctr. For Art and Visual Culture
2008	Danita Eichenlaub, GEST/JCET
2009	Sandy Campbell, Institutional Advancement
2010	Jill Randles, Office of Undergraduate Education
2011	Connie Pierson, Office of Institutional Research
2012	Paul Ciotta, Physics
2013	Tim Lynch, Summer, Winter & Special Programs

Presidential Distinguished Staff Award, Non-Exempt (formerly Classified Staff Employee of the Year)

2000	Sally Hearn, Library
2001	Ann Pfrogner, Computer Science & Electrical Engineering
2002	Mary Hilton, Dept. of Professional Education & Training
2003	Jane Gethmann, Computer Science & Electrical Engineering
2004	Teresa Aylsworth, College of Arts and Sciences
2006	James Peach, Plumbing Shop
2007	Deborah Geare, MIPAR
2008	Ethel Haskins-Cotton, University Health Services
2009	Suzanne McMillian, Office of the Provost
2010	Dorothy Anderson, Institutional Advancement
2011	Michelle Howell, Erickson School
2012	Cheryl Johnson, Office of Grants and Contracts
2013	Peggy Major, The Honors College

University System of Maryland Board of Regents Staff Awards

Year	Name	Category
2001	Lettie Bratcher	Outstanding Service to Students
	Norma L. Green	Extraordinary Public Service to the Campus or Community
	David Langford	Outstanding Service to Students
	George Vitak	Exceptional Contribution to the Mission of UMBC
	Karen Wensch	Exceptional Contribution to the Mission of UMBC

Year	Name	Category
2002	James Milani	Exceptional Contribution to the Mission of UMBC
	Virginia Kellman	Outstanding Service to Students
2003	Andrea Spratt	Outstanding Service to Students
	Ramona Arthur	Extraordinary Public Service to the Campus or Community
	Gregory Bagwell	Exceptional Contribution to the Mission of UMBC
2004	Kathy Sutphin	Exceptional Contribution to the Mission of UMBC
2006	Cindy Kubiet	Outstanding Service to Students
2007	Cathy Bielawski	Outstanding Service to Students
	Dennis Cuddy	Exceptional Contribution to the Mission of UMBC
	Earnestine Baker	Extraordinary Public Service to the Campus or Community
	Karen Sweeney-Jett	Extraordinary Public Service to the Campus or Community
	Patty Martin	Exceptional Contribution to the Mission of UMBC
2008	Ralph Murphy	Exceptional Contribution to the Mission of UMBC
2009	Myrle Combs	Exceptional Contribution to the Mission of UMBC
2011	Jim Lord	Exceptional Contribution to the Mission of UMBC
2012	Janet Magruder	Exceptional Contribution to the Mission of UMBC
	Arlene Wergin	Exceptional Contribution to the Mission of UMBC

Jakubik Family Endowment Awardees

2008	Delana Gregg, Sondheim Scholars Program
2009	Lorie Logan-Bennett, Career Services
2010	Sally Helms, Public Policy
2011	Joyce Riley, Health Administration and Policy
2012	Michele Wolff, The Shriver Center
2013	Lee Calizo, Office of Student Life

PASO/PASS/PSS Presidents

1975–1976	Suzanne R. Kemp (Chairman) for Subcommittee on Status of Professional Associate Staff
1976–1977	Mary Leach
1977–1978	Dave Hollander
1978–1979	David Herman
1979–1980	Maxine M. Cote
1980–1981	Maxine M. Cote

1981–1982	John Martello
1982–1983	Charles (Tot) Woolston
1983–1984	George Preisinger
1984–1985	Tom Beck
1985–1986	Chris Keating
1986–1987	Larry Wilt
1987–1988	Harry Seideman
1988–1989	Jamie Washington
1989–1990	Greg Bean
1990–1991	James Milani
1991–1992	Linda Blankenship
1992–1993	Greg Roepke
1993–1994	Kyle Brookes
1994–1995	Arlene Wergin
1995–1996	Jose Barata
1996–1997	Jim Donlan
1997–1998	Jill Randles
1998–1999	Linda Brown
1999–2000	Tom Beck
2000–2001	Marie Yeh
2001–2002	Tim Ford
2002–2003	Diane Crump-Fogle
2003–2004	Jim Citro
2004–2005	Joe Hill
2005–2006	Jennifer Lepus
2006–2007	Delana Gregg
2007–2008	Brain Thompson
2008–2009	Anne Roland
2009–2010	Rehana Shafi
2010–2011	Timothy Sparklin
2011–2012	Stanyell Bruce
2012–2013	Carrie Sauter
2013–2014	Laila Shishineh

E. UMBC Valedictorians

Name	Year	Major
NL	1970	
NL	1971	
NL	1972	
NL	1973	
NL	1974	
NL	1975	
NL	1976	
NL	1977	
NL	1978	
NL	1979	
Thomas J. Duffy	1980	Mathematics
Lynn Ellen Schreiberg	1981	Geography
Barbara L. Phillips	1982	Information Systems Management
Philip A. Hausler	1983	Mathematics/Computers
Joseph E. Crouse	1984	Biological Sciences
Stephen Pui-Cheung Siu	1985	Economics
Bertina Bryant	1986	Ancient Studies
Beth Lynn Young	1987	Biological Sciences
Sarah Jean Curtis	1988	Political Science/Modern Languages and Linguistics
Stephen Lanier Godwin	1989	Biological Sciences
Suzanne Marie Wright	1990	American Studies
Deborah Marie Thompson	1991	Political Science
Bernadette Simone Thompson	1992	Psychology/Social Work
Carol A. Sennello and Julie A. Sennello	1993	Economics
Steven F. Geisz II and Priyadarshan K. Tulsi	1994	Biological Sciences/Philosophy, Biochemistry and Molecular Biology
Jennifer Michelle Carr	1995	Modern Languages and Linguistics
Yvonne Violet Shashoua	1996	Mathematics
Juliana K. Sander	Spring, 1997	Ancient Studies
Peggy Schaum	Winter, 1997	Social Work
Paul Adam Reichadt and David Adam Scheraga	Spring, 1998	Physics/Mathematics, English
Jamie Smith Hopkins	Winter, 1998	English
Ryan B. Turner	Spring, 1999	Biochemistry and Molecular Biology
Kimberly Welsh	Winter, 1999	Social Work
Steven P. Rowe	Spring, 2000	Biochemistry and Molecular Biology

Name	Year	Major
Tatyana Bushel	Winter, 2000	Mathematics
Steven J. Handy	Spring, 2001	Honors College
Elizabeth M. Mitchell	Winter, 2001	Computer Science
Ian Stucky	2002	Modern Languages and Linguistics
Erika Danna	2003	Biological Sciences
Anthony Hoffman	2004	Physics
Aaron Ralby	2005	English/Modern Languages and Linguistics
Amber McGuigan	2006	Economics
Stephanie Nunez	2007	Biochemistry and Molecular Biology
Simon Gray	2008	Chemical Engineering
Priya Mathews	2009	Psychology
Benyam Z. Kinde	2010	Biological Sciences
Alexandria V. Kening	2011	Mathematics/Statistics
Mary Beth Cole	2012	Biological Sciences/Sociology and Anthropology

F. UMBC Fulbright Scholar Winners, 2002–2013

Melodee M. Baines, English Teaching Assistantship, Germany, 2002
Justine D. Wagner, Economics, Costa Rica, 2004
Allison M. Kotenko, English Teaching Assistantship, Germany, 2004
Tavon H. Cooke, Social Work, Russia, 2005
Pamela M. Greenlee, Islamic Studies, Morocco, 2006
Asynith H. Palmer, Literature, France, 2006
Jessica M. Lewis, English Teaching Assistantship, Germany, 2006
Leonard P. Salter, English Teaching Assistantship, Malaysia, 2006
Vikas Behl, English Teaching Assistantship, Turkey, 2007
Allen P. McFarland, Economics, Canada, 2007
Joseph A. Maher, Environmental Studies, Chile. 2007
John O. Mullee, Economic Development, Argentina, 2008
Jessica Sadler, English Teaching Assistantship, Thailand, 2010
Michelle Ko, Wind Instruments: Flute, Italy, 2010
Anna Gitterman, English Teaching Assistantship, Argentina, 2010
Katrin Patterson, Anthropology, Botswana, 2011
James Mayhew, Installation Art, Iceland, 2011
Christina Briscoe, Virginia, Public Health, Brazil, 2011
Ryan Max, English Teaching Assistantship, Laos, 2012
Kimberly Mawyer, English Teaching Assistantship, Spain, 2012
David Anguish, Political Science, Mexico, 2012
Achsah Joseph, English Teaching Assistantship, Malaysia, 2012
Vivian Ekey, Education, Brazil, 2012
Madeline Hall, Environmental Studies, New Zealand, 2013
Andrew Holter, English Teaching Assistantship, Czech Republic, 2013
Hannah Kurlansky, English Teaching Assistantship, Slovakia, 2013
Alexandra Mills, English Teaching Assistantship, Malaysia, 2013
Yasmin Radbod, English Teaching Assistantship, Nepal, 2013

G. UMBC Student Government Association (SGA) Presidents

Name	Year	Name	Year
Doug Gordon	1966–67	Eric Carlton	1990–91
Paul Sekulick	1967–68	David Smith	1991–92
Daryl Hagy	1968–69	David Smith	1992–93
Daryl Hagy	1969–70	William Honablew	1993–94
William Soltesz	1970–71	William Honablew	1994–95
David Rowe	1971–72	Lamont King	1995–96
Dave Tibbetts	1972–73	Anya Thompson	1996–97
Bobby Thompson	1973–74	William Barnes	1997–98
Beth Wayne	1974–75	William Barnes	1998–99
Harry Johnson	1975–76	Alicia Hobson	1999–2000
Tim Kernan	1976–77	Kafui Dzirasa	2000–2001
Lisa Dickerson	1977–78	Suran DeSilva	2001–2002
Danny Blum	1978–79	D. Philip Shockley	2002–2003
Nate Chapman	1979–80	Scott Nicholson	2003–2004
Scott Rifkin	1980–81	Dominic Cirincione, Jr.	2004–2005
Terry Nolan	1981–82	Jordan Hadfield	2005–2006
Steven Gilliard	1982–83	Jordan Hadfield	2006–2007
Jeff Neuman	1983–84	Carrie Mann	2007
Mary Jo Werner	1984–85	Jay Lagorio	2007–2008
Mike Tkacik	1985–86	Steve Gilmore	2008–2009
Alvin West	1986–87	Gabriel Rettaliata	2009
Will Backstrom	1987–88	Yasmin Karimian	2009–2010
Jim Lotfi	1988–89	Yasmin Karimian	2010–2011
Chris Tkacik	1989–90	Catie Collins	2011–2012

H. Athletics

UMBC Athletic Hall of Fame

Jackie Abendschoen-Milani	(1984–88)	Field Hockey/ Lacrosse
Mehdi Addadi	(1998–2002)	Swimming & Diving
Angela Adams	(1984–88)	Cross Country/Track & Field
William Ahern	(1976–80)	Baseball
Jose Anderson	(1977–81)	Track and Field
David Andrzejewski	(1974–78)	Soccer/Lacrosse
Shannon Bagrosky-Hernandez	(1994–98)	Soccer
LaNae Baker	(1995–98)	Volleyball
Susan Fahrman Bathgate	(1975–79)	Lacrosse/volleyball
Jeff Berman	(1994–97)	Baseball
Cathy Bielawski	(1973–77)	Gymnastics
David Bobb	(1994–97)	Track & Field
Dick Bond	(1966–70)	Lacrosse
Lisa Boone	(1999–2003)	Softball
Jared Boyd	(1998–2002)	Baseball
John Burns	(1989–93)	Baseball
Chris Cain	(1988–91)	Lacrosse
Giuliano Celenza	(1999–2000)	Soccer
Lisa Cline Smith	(1995–98)	Volleyball
Gary Clipp	(1973–77)	Lacrosse
Marty Cloud	(1977–81)	Lacrosse
Jeff Crabill	(1984–88)	Baseball
Chad Cradock	(1993–97)	Swimming & Diving
Fran Daum	(1968–70)	Basketball/volleyball
Tom Dunlap	(1975–79)	Lacrosse
Greg Elliott	(1990–93)	Baseball
Ray Ford	(1977–80)	Soccer
Bill Gerhardt	(1976–80)	Baseball
John Goedeke	(1975–79)	Basketball
Kevin Goh	(1997–2001)	Swimming & Diving
Mark Gold	(1980–84)	Lacrosse
Mary Greenwalt	(1971–75)	Tennis/F. Hockey/Basketball
Jeff Hahn	(1967–71)	Lacrosse
Susan Herzog	(1987–89)	Swimming & Diving
Kirk Hewling	(1991–95)	Track and Field
Jack Kane	(1975–79)	Basketball
Kori Kindbom	(1982–86)	Basketball
Bob Jacobsen	(1975–79)	Baseball
John Jancuska	(1978–present)	Head Baseball Coach

Huguens Jean	(1999–2003)	Track & Field
Jennifer Jewell	(1991–95)	Volleyball/Softball
Ingrid Kilpe-Huber	(1993–97)	Swimming & Diving
Belinda Knisley	(1976–80)	Volleyball
Fritz Lahner	(1970–73)	Baseball
Craig Linthicum	(1978–81)	Lacrosse
Paul Loebach	(1986–90)	X Country/Track
Kevin Loewe	(1991–95)	Baseball
Monica Logan	(1995–99)	Basketball
Oscar Lopez	(1997–2000)	Tennis
Dan Marohl	(1996–2000)	Lacrosse
Steve Marohl	(1988–92)	Lacrosse
Tammy McCarthy	(1983–87)	Basketball
Carol McDaniel	(1981–85)	X Country/Track
George McGeeney	(1978–82)	Lacrosse
Michael Meyer	(1992–94)	Golf
Rick Moreland	(1979–83)	Basketball
David Miller	(1992–96)	Swimming
Shawn Miller	(1989–93)	Soccer
Bob Mumma	(1989–92)	Baseball
Reggie Nance	(1977–81)	Basketball
Kelly O'Brien-Hoch	(1990–94)	Volleyball
Shawne O'Connor	(1981–85)	Basketball/Lacrosse
Jim Pfrogner	(1971–2000)	Head Coach, X Country/Track & Field
Felice Pinkney	(1987–91)	Basketball
Jim Pirisino	(1968–72)	Soccer/Baseball
David Quattrini	(1977–81)	Men's Lacrosse
Michele "Missy" Quille	(1988–1993)	Basketball
Steve Rice	(1975–79)	Baseball
Robert Ritz	(1971–75)	Lacrosse
Jay Robertson	(1976–80)	Lacrosse
Breck Robinson	(1982–86)	Basketball
Laura Robinson	(1983–87)	Lacrosse
Gary Rupert	(1977–88)	Athletic Administration
Denise Schilte	(1991–95)	Soccer
Jackie Seboda Pfeiler	(1986–90)	Lacrosse
Loreta Saurusaitis	(1982–86)	Volleyball
Shawn Shugars	(1990–93)	Baseball
Emmerson Small	(1970–1973)	Basketball
Jason Smith	(1990–94)	Lacrosse
Larry Simmons	(1986–90)	Basketball/Soccer
Linda Lyall Sowers	(1966–70)	Basketball/Volleyball/Field Hockey

Michael Sterling	(1981–85)	Cross Country/Track
Robi Tamargo	(1978–82)	F.Hockey/Lacrosse/Track
Darius Taylor	(1988–91)	Soccer
Pam Lottes Tomczak	(1976–80)	Volleyball/Lacrosse
Steve Tomshack	(1996–99)	Baseball
Greg Usilton	(1981–85)	Baseball
Jeff Usilton	(1978–82)	Baseball
Deanna Vecchio	(1999–2002)	Softball
Ed Veit	(1973–80)	Men's Soccer Coach
Bobby Wagner	(1991–95)	Soccer
Karin Wagner	(1984–85)	Cross Country/Track
Terence Ward	(1997–2001)	Basketball
Dick Watts	(1967–1985)	Director of Athletics
Jennifer Webster	(1985–89)	Gymnastics
Angel Webb	(1988–92)	Basketball
Anne Wellington	(1988–92)	Basketball
Andy Wells	(1998–2002)	Soccer
Rick Wey	(1974–78)	Lacrosse
Amy Wolff	(1994–97)	Softball
Michael Woodard	(1974–78)	Soccer
Steve Zerhusen	(1975–1978)	Soccer
Kathy Zerrlaut	(1974–)	Administration/Head Coach

UMBC All-Americans (33)

Members of First, Second or Third Team All-America squads.

Men's Lacrosse—NCAA Division II (15)

Bobby Ritz	1974, 75	Defense	(First Team, First Team)
Scott Edmonds	1974	Midfield	(Third Team)
Jeff Benson	1975	Attack	(Second Team)
Joe Provance	1975	Midfield	(Third)
Gary Clipp	1975, 1976	Defense	(First, First)
Rick Wey	1976	Midfield	(First)
Boe Duffy	1978	Defense	(Third)
Tom Dunlap	1978, 1979	Goalkeeper	(Second, First)
Tony Pierotti	1978	Midfield	(Third)
Jay Robertson	1979, 1980	Attack	(First, First)
Craig Linthicum	1979, 1980	Midfield	(Second, First)
Marty Cloud	1979, 1980	Attack	(Third, First)
Dave Quattrini	1980	Attack	(First)
Steve Rodkey	1980	Midfield	(First)
Bruce Baldwin	1980	Defense	(First)

Men's Lacrosse—NCAA Division I (8)

Dave Quattrini	1981	Attack	(Third)
George McGeeney	1982	Defense	(First)
Mark Gold	1984	Midfield	(Second)
Steve Marohl	1992	Attack	(Third)
Chris Turner	1999	Attack	(Third)
Brendan Mundorf	2006	Attack	(Third)
Drew Westervelt	2007	Attack	(Third)
Terry Kimener	2008	Midfield	(Second)
Peet Poillon	2009	Midfield	(Second)

Men's Soccer—NCAA Division II (1)

Ray Ford	1978

Men's Soccer—NCAA Division I (3)

Bobby Wagner	1993
Giuliano Celenza	2000
Andrew Bulls	2009

Men's Track & Field—NCAA Division II (1)

Michael Sterling	1984

Men's Track & Field—NCAA Division I (2)

David Bobb	1996, 1997
Huguens Jean	2003

Women's Track & Field—NCAA Division I (1)

Cleopatra Borel	2001, 2002

Baseball—NCAA Division II (1)

Jeff Usilton 1980

Baseball—NCAA Division I (1)

Shawn Shugars 1992

UMBC Academic All-Americans (41)

Division II

John Goedeke, Men's Basketball, 1977–78
Jack Kane, Men's Basketball, 1977–78
Hank Schulz, Men's Basketball, 1977–78
Kori Kindbom, Women's Basketball, 1985–86
Doug Ward, Baseball, 1986

Division I

Jennifer Whiteside, 1987–88
Christina Mychajliw, Track & Field, 1989
John Burns, Baseball, 1991
Jennifer Fosnaugh, Swimming & Diving, 1992
Rob Magin, Cross Country/Track, 1992
Bob Mumma, Baseball, 1992
Laurie McGuire, Women's Lacrosse, 1994
Judy Jackson, Volleyball, 1995
Jennifer Jewell, Softball, 1995
Taryn McDonald, Softball, 1997, 1999
Sharese White, Track & Field, 1998
Kafui Dzirasa, Track and Field, 1999
Caroline Koncilja, Tennis, 1999
Ted Lawler, Soccer, 1999
Oscar Lopez, Tennis, 1999, 2000
Jen Ecker, Cross Country/Track, 1999, 2000
Kathryn Wheatley, Tennis, 2000, 2002
Eric Weltmer, Baseball, 2001
Angie Amedro, Softball, 2002
Cleopatra Borel, Track and Field, 2002
Jessica Graziano, Softball, 2002
Huguens Jean, Track and Field, 2002, 2003
Christy Sheppard, Softball, 2003
Karl Strauss, Swimming & Diving, 2003
Carlos Canepa, Swimming & Diving, 2004
Jennifer Davis, Volleyball, 2003, 2004
Lana Khvalina, Tennis, 2003, 2004
Jessica Young, Women's Soccer, 2005
Adam Grossman, Track & Field, 2006

Geza Szabo, Swimming & Diving, 2006
Dana Shepherd, Softball, 2006, 2007, 2008
Mary Hearin, Women's Soccer, 2006
Cornelia Carapcea, Tennis, 2008, 2009
Dominic Devaud, Track & Field, 2008, 2010
Alice Chen, Tennis, 2010
Keilan Freeman, Swimming & Diving, 2010, 2011

I. Music

Our UMBC

Hail alma mater! OUR UMBC,
Boldly bearing your colors, the whole world to see,
Striving together in true unity,
Black gold forever we're reminded of thee,
Proudly we hail to thee, OUR UMBC!

Throughout the ages, OUR UMBC,
Songs and memories still echo with true clarity,

Knowledge and wisdom and truth we found here,
Friendships we treasure that will last through the years,
Proudly we hail to thee, OUR UMBC!

Music by Matthias Keller
Words and Arrangement by Jari Villanueva

Retriever Riser (Fight Song)

Stand up and cheer, UMBC
Forward we go, to another victory.
Retrievers, be bold,
We back you as we stand,
Black and gold, the best in Maryland.

Rise up and sing, stand up and roar,
Make echoes ring, from the mountains to the Shore.
Baltimore's pride, our alma mater grand,
UMBC, the best in any land.

Music and words by George La Noue
Professor of Political Science and Professor of Public Policy

Bibliography

Books

Albin O. Kuhn's Family "scrapbook" Collection 127. Special Collections, University of Maryland Baltimore County.

Anderson, Nancy Scott. *An Improbable Venture: A History of the University of California, San Diego.* (La Jolla, CA: The UCSD Press, 1993).

Arum, Richard and Roksa, Josipa. *Academically Adrift: Limited Learning on College Campuses.* Chicago: University of Chicago Press, 2011.

Astin, Alexander W., Lee, Calvin B.T., and Besse, Ralph M. *The Invisible College: A Profile of Small, Private Colleges with Limited Resources.* New York: McGraw Hill, 1974.

Bachrach, Peter, and Baratz, Morton S. *Power and Poverty: Theory and Practice.* New York: Oxford University Press, 1970.

Berdahl, Robert O. *Statewide Coordination of Higher Education.* Washington, DC: American Council on Education, 1971.

Berrigan, Daniel, Andersen, Robin, and Marsh, James. *The Trial of the Catonsville Nine.* Boston: Beacon Press, 1970.

Bok, Derek, *Universities in the Marketplace: The Commercialization of Higher Education.* Princeton: Princeton University Press, 2003.

Boyd, Laslo V. *Maryland Government and Politics.* Centerville: Tidewater Publishers, 1987.

Bradley, Richard. *Harvard Rules: The Struggle for the Soul of the World's Most Powerful University.* New York: Harper Collins, 2005.

Callcott, George A. *A History of the University of Maryland.* Baltimore: Maryland Historical Society. 1966.

Callcott, George A. *The University of Maryland at College Park, A History.* Baltimore: Noble House. 2005.

Clotfelter, Charles T. *Big-Time Sports in American Universities.* New York: Cambridge University Press, 2011.

Committee on Underrepresented Groups and the Expansion of the Science and Engineering Workforce Pipeline. *Expanding Underrepresented Minority Participation: America's Science and Technology Talent at the Crossroads.* Washington, DC: The National Academies Press, 2011.

Corbett, Christopher, *Poker Bride: The First Chinese in the Wild West.* New York: Atlantic Monthly Press, 2011.

Conklin, Paul K. *Gone with the Ivy: A Biography of Vanderbilt University.* Knoxville: University of Tennessee Press, 1985.

Douglas, Jack D. *Youth in Turmoil: America's Youth Cultures and Student Protest Movements.* Rockville: National Institutes of Health. 1972.

Duderstadt, James J. *Intercollegiate Athletics and the American University: A University President's Perspective.* Ann Arbor, MI: The University of Michigan Press, 2003.

Elliott, Peggy Gordon. *The Urban Campus: Educating the New Majority for the New Century.* Phoenix: Oryx Press, 1993.

Engle, Ron, Londre, Felicia Hardison, and Watermeier, Daniel J., eds., *Shakespeare Companies and Festivals: An International Guide*. Westport, CT: Greenwood Press, 1995.

Franklin, Benjamin "Proposals relating to the education of youth in Pensilvania," Philadelphia, Pa. 1749

Geiger, Roger L. *Research and Relevant Knowledge: American Research Universities Since World War II*. New York: Oxford University Press, 1993.

Ginsberg, Benjamin, *The Fall of the Faculty: The Rise of the All-Administrative University and Why it Matters*. New York: Oxford University Press, 2011.

Graham, Hugh D. and Diamond, Nancy. *The Rise of American Research Universities: Elites and Challengers in the Postwar Era*. Baltimore: The Johns Hopkins Press, 1997.

Hacker, Andrew and Dreifus, Claudia. *Higher Education? How Colleges Are Wasting Our Money and Failing Our Kids and What We Can Do About It*. New York: Times Books, 2010.

Howe, Neil, and Strauss, William. *Millennials Rising: The Next Great Generation*. New York: Vintage, 2000.

Hrabowski III, Freeman A., Maton, Kenneth I., and Greif, Geoffrey L. *Beating the Odds: Raising Academically Successful African American Males*. New York: Oxford University Press, 1998.

Hrabowski III, Freeman A., Greene, Monica L., Maton, Kenneth I., and Greif, Geoffrey L. *Overcoming the Odds: Raising Academically Successful African American Young Women*. New York: Oxford University Press, 2002.

Hudgins, Sharon. *Never an Ivory Tower: University of Maryland University College, the First 50 Years*. Adelphi MD.: University College, 2000.

Jencks, Christopher, and Riesman, David. *The Academic Revolution*. Garden City, New York: Doubleday & Company, 1968.

Kaplan/Newsweek. *How to Get into College (2003 Edition)*. New York: Stanley H. Kaplan Educational Center, 2002.

Keidel, George C. *Colonial History of Catonsville*. Catonsville: The American Centennial Committee of Catonsville, 1976.

Lee, Calvin B.T. *Chinatown, USA*. New York: Doubleday, 1965.

Lee, Calvin B.T., ed. *Improving College Teaching*. Washington: American Council on Education, 1967.

Lee, Calvin B.T. *The Campus Scene: Changing Styles of Undergraduate Life 1900–1970*. New York: David McKay Co., 1970.

Lee, Calvin B.T., and Kanzer, Alan. *One Man, One Vote: YMCA and the Struggle for Equal Representation*. New York: Charles Scribner's Sons. 1967.

Lee, Calvin B.T., and Lee, Audrey Evans. *The Gourmet Chinese Regional Cookbook*. New York: Putnam, 1976.

Loss, Christopher P. *Between Citizens and the State*. Princeton, NJ: Princeton University Press, 2012.

Luger, Michael I., and Goldstein, Harvey A. *Technology in the Garden: Research parks and Regional Economic Development*. Chapel Hill: University of North Carolina Press, 1991.

Lukianoff, Greg, *Unlearning Liberty: Campus Censorship and the End of American Debate*. New York: Encounter Books, 2102.

Marks, Bayly Allen. *Hilton Heritage*. Catonsville: Catonsville CC Press, 1972.

MacMillan, Margaret. *Dangerous Games: The Use and Abuse of History*. New York: Modern Library, 2009.

Millett, John D. *Mergers in Higher Education: An Analysis of Ten Case Studies*. Washington, D.C: Academy for Educational Development, 1976.

Moos, Malcom, *The Post Land Grant University: the University of Maryland Report,* 1981.
O'Brien, Michael. *Hesburgh: A Biography.* Washington, DC: Catholic University Press of America, 1998.
O'Connell, Jeffrey and O'Connell, Thomas E. *Five 20th Century College Presidents: From Butler to Bok (Plus Summers).* Durham, NC: Carolina Academic Press, 2012.
Orser, Edward and Arnold, Joseph. *Catonsville: 1880–1940.* Norfolk, VA: Donning Company, 1989.
Peckham, Howard H. *The Making of the University of Michigan 1817–1996.* Ann Arbor, MI: The Millennium Project, 1998.
Pietilla, Antero *Not in My Neighborhood: How Bigotry Shaped a Great American City,* Chicago: Ivan R. Dee, 2010.
Princeton Review. *The Best 368 Colleges: 2009 Edition.* New York: Princeton Review, 2008.
Schrecker, Ellen. *The Lost Soul of Higher Education: Corporatization, the Assault on Academic Freedom, and the End of the American University.* New York: The New Press, 2010.
Shriver, Mark. *A Good Man: Rediscovering My Father, Sargent Shriver.* New York: Henry Holt and Company, 2012.
Smith, Bruce L.R. *American Science Policy Since World War II.* Washington, DC: Brookings Institution, 1990.
Smith, Herbert C. and Willis, John T. *Maryland Politics and Government: Democratic Government.* Lincoln: University of Nebraska Press, 2012.
Stossel, Scott. *Sarge: The Life and Times of Sargent Shriver.* Washington, DC: Smithsonian Books, 2004.
Taylor, Mark C. *Crisis on Campus: A Bold Plan for Reforming our Colleges and Universities.* New York: Knopf, 2010.
Thelin, John R. *A History of American Higher Education.* Baltimore and London: The Johns Hopkins University Press, 2004.
Vanderslice, J.T., Schamp, H.W., and Mason, E. A. *Thermodynamics.* Englewood Cliffs, N.J.: Prentice Hall, 1966.
Wahl, Grant and Dohrman, George."Welcome to the Big Time." In *The Business of Sports,* edited by Scott Rosner. Boston: Jones and Bartlett Publishers, 2004.
Washburn, Jennifer, *University, Inc.: The Corporate Corruption of Higher Education*, New York: Basic Books, 2005.
Wilson, Edward, N. *Morgan State College: A Century of Purpose in Action 1867–1967,* New York: Vantage, 1975.
Woods, Thomas. *Diversity: The Invention of a Concept.* San Francisco, CA: Encounter Books. 2003.
Works, George and Morgan, Barton. *The Land Grant Colleges.* Washington DC: United States Government Printing Office, 1939.
Wutzdorff, Allen J. and Giles, Jr., Dwight E. "Service-Learning in Higher Education." In *Service Learning*, edited by Joan Schine. Chicago: National Society for the Study of Education, 1997.

Articles

"150 students demonstrate to back minority rights." *The Baltimore Sun*, May 12, 1979.
"The 2012 Honor Roll." *The Chronicle of Higher Education*, August 10, 2012.
Abutaleb, Yasmeen. "Loh pledges support for merger." *Diamondbackonline,* November 9, 2011.

Adams, John. "Various Committees Assigned to Stimulate Student Participation." *The Retriever*, October 8, 1968.
Adams, John. "To gain solicitation rights: Students, Libby in confrontation." *The Retriever*, March 16, 1970.
Adams, Marcia. "On UMBC campus, student urges preservation." *The Jeffersonian*, June 2, 2005.
"African Relief Efforts Planned." *The UMBC Retriever*, October 1, 1973.
"Almanac of Higher Education." *The Chronicle of Higher Education*, April 13, 2012.
Altbach, Phillip G. and Cohen, Robert. "American Student Activism: The Post-Sixties Transformation." *The Journal of Higher Education*, 61, Issue 1, January–February, 1990.
Alvarez, Rafael. "Chasing Tales." *UMBC Magazine*, Summer 2010.
"America's Best Colleges, 2010 edition." *U.S. News & World Report*, September, 2009.
"America's Biotech Future." *The Baltimore Sun*, February 18, 1990.
Ames, Marcia Hope, "The Meyerhoff Scholars: Names You'll Hear in Maryland's Future," *UMBC Review*, 9, no.2 (Fall 1990).
Anderson, Gail. "A student gives a day-to-day report of protest." *The UMBC Retriever*, April 21, 1987.
Anderson, Gail. "Chancellor and Coalition reach agreement." *The UMBC Retriever*, April 29, 1987.
Anderson, Gail and Gupta, Arun. "Students stage sit-in outside Chancellor's office." *The UMBC Retriever*, April 21, 1987.
Anderson, Jessica. "Erickson retirement founder faces lawsuit." *The Baltimore Sun*, June 5, 2011.
Anderson, Jose. "Judge Blake Issued a Bold, Risky and Wise Opinion." *Afro-American*, October 23, 2013.
Anderson, Nick. "U-Md. Officials Announce New Joint Public Health School." *The Washington Post*, September 25, 2012.
"Annual Tuition and Fees at Colleges and Universities, 2012–2013." *The Chronicle of Higher Education*. November 2, 2012.
Arnold, Joseph. "A Signature Building—the Heart and Soul of the Campus." *UMBC Magazine*, Summer 1995.
"At 94, still humble, still vital." *The Baltimore Sun*, June 30, 2003.
Atwood, Liz. "Marine center sails on winds of trade-off." *Baltimore Evening Sun*, October 4, 1989.
Atwood, Liz and Dang, Dan Thanh. "UMBC scales back plans for technology park." *The Baltimore Sun*, March 31, 2000.
Babington, Charles. "Plan to Merge Md. Campuses Hits Snag: Senate President Says He will Kill Proposal." *The Washington Post*, March 3, 1992.
Bachrach, Peter and Baratz, Morton S. "Two Faces of Power." *American Political Science Review*, LVI, December, 1962.
Ballengee, Jennifer R. "State faculty treated unfairly: decreased support for public university professors hurts all Marylanders." *The Baltimore Sun*, November 5, 2010.
Baker, Tim. "As Hooker Goes, UM's Vision Goes With Him." *The Baltimore Sun*, August 31, 1992.
Baker, Tim. "Incubating Success." *The Baltimore Sun*, June 19, 1989.
Baker, Tim. "Questions While Waiting for the Regents: Why Not Two Top Universities?" *The Baltimore Sun*, May 15, 1989.
Banks, Samuel L. "Why UMBC is inhospitable to blacks," *Baltimore Evening Sun*, December 18, 1987.

Basken, Paul. "NSF Raises Alarm over Falling State Support for Research Universities." *The Chronicle of Higher Education*, September 25, 2012.

Beims, Constance, "UMBC is fighting racism." *Baltimore Evening Sun*, December 29, 1987.

Benjamin, Robert. "Knorr preparing new plans for consolidating state's colleges." *The Baltimore Sun*, February 24, 1981.

Berkowitz, Steve, McCarthy, Michael and Gillum, Jack. "How Student fees boost college sports amid rising budgets." *USA Today*, October 6, 2010.

"Best Places to Live in America" *Money Magazine,* July 2010.

Bidwell, Allie. "Under California Bill, Faculty-Free Colleges Would Award Exam-Based Degrees." *The Chronicle of Higher Education*, April 2, 2013.

Billingsley, Andrew. "Engineering School: A Continuing Debate." The *Baltimore Sun*, September 29, 1983.

Bishop, Tricia. "Panel Pushes Changes at Coppin." *The Baltimore Sun*, May 15, 2013.

Blitz, John. "A Campus is Born." *Maryland Magazine,* Fall 1966.

Blumenstyk, Goldie. "Average Returns on Endowments Is Worst in Almost 40 Years." *The Chronicle of Higher Education*, January 28, 2010.

Bostwick, David. "Rally protests P&T." *The UMBC Retriever*, March 25, 1974.

Boyd, Laslo. "E.F. Hutton and Mike Miller." *Montgomery Gazette*, October 14, 2011.

Boyd, Laslo. "Muddled and Misguided Court Decision." www.centralMaryland.org/blog, October 16, 2013.

Boyer, Earnest. "Creating the New American College." *The Chronicle of Higher Education*, March 9, 1994.

Bowie, Liz. "Hopkins' Bayview campus picked as 'incubator' site." *The Baltimore Sun*, February 14, 1992.

Bowie, Liz. "Md. seniors rank No.1 in passing AP exams." *The Baltimore Sun*, February 5, 2009.

Bowie, Liz. "Md. Students leading nation in test gains." The *Baltimore Sun*, July 17, 2012.

Bowler, Mike. "2 here still vie for job at Tufts." *The Baltimore Sun*, January 28, 1976.

Bowler, Mike. "Chancellor loses confidence vote." The *Baltimore Sun*, March 12, 1976.

Bowler, Mike. "Coppin students express pride in rising standards." *The Baltimore Sun*, December 16, 1984.

Bowler, Mike. "Engineering pact set at 2 colleges." *The Baltimore Sun*, January 8, 1985.

Bowler, Mike. "Students protest UMBC tuition rise." The *Baltimore Sun*, November 22, 1975.

Bowman, Tom. "Marine center's federal funding still in question." *The Baltimore Sun*, May 16, 1989.

Bradtke, Molly. "Library to make journal cuts." *The Retriever Weekly*, September 13, 2011.

Brodie, James Michael. "Installation of Hrabowski is historic event." *Jeffersonian*, September 3, 1993.

Brodie, James Michael, "Anti-research Park forces on offensive," *Catonsville Times*, November 17, 1993.

Burnett, Calvin W. "Why Coppin and Morgan Shouldn't Merge." *The Baltimore Sun,* July 16, 1991.

Byrne, Richard. "Best of Both Worlds." *UMBC Magazine*, Fall 2009.

Byrne, Richard. "Blow Up." *UMBC Magazine*, Winter 2012.

Byrne, Richard. "Finding Their Light." *UMBC Magazine*, Summer 2011.

"Calvin Lee, Education Planner for Employees at Prudential." *New York Times*, March 16, 1983.

Camper, John. "In academic circles, UIC is a big-league player." *Chicago Tribune,* August 30, 1987.

Carey, Kevin. "Without Assessment, Great Teaching Stays Secret." *The Chronicle of Higher Education*, October 15, 2010.
Case, Richard W. and Rosenberg, Leonard H. "Education Reform: How it Affects the U. of M." *The Baltimore Sun*, June 14, 1975.
"Cash Strapped State Schools Forced to Privatize." *Time*, April 23, 2009.
"'Cat Campus' Sprouting Rapidly." *Baltimore News American*, September, 1966.
Censer, Marjorie. "Northrup joins other companies in teaming up with universities on cyber security research." *The Washington Post*, November 15, 2010.
Chang, Bee-Shyuan. "Influential And all In One Room." *New York Times*, April 26, 2012.
Clemens, Cheryl. "First class event for UMBC's 25th." *Catonsville Times*, Date unknown.
Clark, Bob. "Hartzell must get UMBC ready for Division I," February 20, 1986, newspaper article found in Dorsey papers.
Clark, Gerald W. "Door is Closed to McKeldin Bid." *The Baltimore Sun*, December 15, 1963.
Clark, Gerald W. "New Agency is Divided on U.M. Site." *The Baltimore Sun*, September 21, 1963.
Clark, Gerald W. "U.M. Site Review is Rejected." *The Baltimore Sun*, November 27, 1963.
Cline, Scott. "Lasting Impact." *Inside Carolina Magazine*, Summer 2004.
Colino, Stacey. "The Great Admissions Competition." *The Baltimore Sun*, May 8, 1988.
Coltman, Edward. "Maryland backs off plan to limit college out-of-state rolls." *The Baltimore Sun*, February 5, 1977.
"Concert Slated Tonight." *The UMBC Retriever*, December 11, 1972.
Conyers, Sherri. "One thousand jam quad to defend campus, protest closing proposal." *The UMBC Retriever*, March 4, 1981.
Conyers, Sherri. "Students speak out against discrimination." *The UMBC Retriever*, April 8, 1981.
Conyers, Sherri. "Students picket lacrosse game." *The UMBC Retriever*, April 29, 1981.
Cook, Chris. "UMBC leads in cyber security research and education." *The Retriever Weekly*, March 3, 2010.
Cote, Patricia. "Unity Isn't Revolutionary: A Cry for Unity is Next Step in Tuition Protest." *The Retriever*, March 8, 1976.
Couturier, Brian J. "County OKs loan guarantee for UMBC's research park." *Baltimore Business Journal*, Oct. 23–29, 1989.
Cowherd, Kevin. "Retiring UMBC Ad Brown has helped drive changes." *The Baltimore Sun*, May 15, 2013.
Cunningham, Eleanor L. "The Campaign for UMBC: Keeping and Getting the Very Best." *UMBC Magazine*, Spring 1998.
Davis, Nayana. "Mama's Boys shame competition at Festivus Acappelius." *The Retriever Weekly*, November 15, 2009.
Dechter, Gail. "Opponents face off in MBA war: Bill aims to dismantle Towson's program in favor of Morgan State's." *The Baltimore Sun*, March 27, 2007.
Dechter, Gail. "Suit Seeks to toss out joint program at UB, Towson." *The Baltimore Sun*, October 14, 2006.
Dell, Kristina. "State universities face deepening cuts." *MSNBC.com*, updated March 22, 2011.
"Designs on College Park." *The Baltimore Sun*, November 7, 1977.
de Vise, Daniel. "Five Arguments Against a University of Maryland Merger." *College Inc. blog*. October 24, 2011, http://www.washingtonpost.com/blogs/college-inc/post/five-arguments-against-a-university-of-maryland-merger/2011/10/24/gIQAkzyTDM_blog.html (accessed on April 30, 2013).

de Vise, Daniel. "New science class formula brings UMBC extra credit." *The Washington Post*, March 21, 2012.
de Vise, Daniel. "Hopkins tops U.S. in R&D." *The Washington Post*, October 16, 2009.
de Vise, Daniel. "UMBC's quiet revolution in teaching science is earning school extra credit." *The Washington Post*, March 20, 2012.
Dirican, Patrice. "UMBC marks 30 years." *Catonsville Times*, 1996.
Dirican, Patrice. "Hooker Remembered as UMBC visionary." *Catonsville Times*, July 7, 1999.
Dirican, Patrice. "UMBC, opponents eye pact." *Catonsville Times*, February 23, 2000.
Donoghue, Frank. "Can the Humanities Survive the 21st Century." *The Chronicle for Higher Education*, September 10, 2010.
Dorsey, John. W. "A Giant Step Backward." *The Baltimore Sun*, October 5, 1983.
Douglas, William. "Lofty wish list for a wunderkind." *Baltimore Evening Sun*, January 16, 1986.
Douglas, William. "Big changes urged for college system." *Baltimore Evening Sun*, January 7, 1987.
Douglas, William, "Talking ... but not talking: Black sit-in enters 7th day at UMBC." *Baltimore Evening Sun*, April 21, 1987.
"Down and Out in Division I." *Inside Higher Education*, October 6, 2009.
Dresser, Michael and Walker, Childs. "Miller tries again to join UM campuses." *The Baltimore Sun*, January 6, 2012.
Dubas, Danielle, "Field of Dreams: Our Blueprint for the Future," *UMBC Review*, 9, no.3, (Spring 1991).
Edokpayi, Ashley. "UMBC Looks Back with Civil Rights Leaders." *The Retriever Weekly*, December 11, 2012.
Embry, Jr., Robert C. and Baker, Jr., Russell T. "An Outstanding Public University." *The Baltimore Sun*, December 20, 1987.
"Engineering a Monster." *Baltimore Sun*, November 5, 1983.
"Erickson Retirement Emerges from Bankruptcy." *The Baltimore Sun*, April 16, 2010.
Estis, Kevin. "Demonstrators Protest Hardy's Arrest." *The Retriever*, October 25, 1976.
"Extend and Elevate." *UMBC Magazine*, Winter 2011.
Fallin, Glen. "UMBC Chancellor's Support Called Hazy." *Baltimore News American*, March 15, 1976.
Fain, Paul. "Cuts Intensify Identity Crisis for Washington's Flagship Campus." *The Chronicle of Higher Education*, September 3, 2010.
Faust, Drew Gilpin. "The University's Crisis of Purpose." *New York Times Book Review*, September 6, 2009.
Finney, Joni E. "Identifying Talent and Nurturing Its Success: An Interview with Freeman Hrabowski." *Change Magazine*, May–June, 2009.
Folkenflik, David. "UMBC ties College Park in Freshman SAT scores." The *Baltimore Sun*, February 21, 1995.
"Freeman Hrabowski Entry" *The World's 100 Most Influential People: Time Magazine Special Issue*, April 18, 2012, http://www.time.com/time/specials/packages/article/0,28804,2111975_2111976_2112119,00.html (accessed April 17, 2013).
"The future of fish: Sea bream and sea bass." *The Baltimore Sun*, August 2, 2010.
Gibbons, Jennifer Leigh. "UMBC's Student Involvement Center Considered a Model for Other Universities." *Insights*, February 3, 2003.
Gilbert, Patrick. "Manley irks council by refusing to budge on rezoning issue UMBC proposal leaves her isolated." *The Baltimore Sun*, October 7, 1992.

Goldin, Claudia and Katz, Lawrence. "The Shaping of American Higher Education: The Formative Years in the United States 1890–1940." *Journal of Economic Perspectives*, 13 no.1, 1999.

Goldstein, Amy. "Blacks insist on autonomy for Morgan." *The Baltimore Sun*, September, 19, 1987.

Goldstein, Amy. "MD Regents Get Some Help From Schaefer." *Washington Post*, July 7, 1989.

Goldstein, Amy. "Reforms jeopardizes state colleges, professors charge." *Baltimore Sun*, May 22, 1987.

Goldstein, Amy. "Regents approve change in direction for U-Md., Bowie State." *Washington Post*, August 8, 1989.

Goldstein, Amy. "Steinberg opposes 1 board for colleges." *The Baltimore Sun*, September 27, 1987.

Goldstein, Amy. "U-Md. Regents Reject Baltimore Campus Merger: Business Community had Sought Major Research Center to Bolster City Economy." *Washington Post*, December 12, 1989.

Goll, Eugene W. "Academic Program nixed by MHEC." *Cumberland Times-News*, July 16, 1994.

Gormley, Mara. "Toll refutes stories of proposed closing." *The UMBC Retriever*, March 4, 1981.

Graham, Hugh Davis. "Be wary, Maryland officials, of the North Carolina 'model.'" *The Baltimore Evening Sun*, July 23 1987.

Graham, Hugh. "Educational monopolies are not the only way to excellence for universities." *The Baltimore Sun*, October 11, 1987.

Graham, Hugh Davis. "Structure and Governance in Higher Education: Historical and Comparative Analysis in State Policy." *Journal of Policy History*, 1, Issue 1, Winter 1989.

Graham, Hugh. "We Don't Need Superboards: It's Competition that has made U.S. Higher Education Great." *The Chronicle of Higher Education*, November 4, 1987.

Graham, Hugh Davis and La Noue, George R. "Let's form a Washington-Baltimore UM faculty consensus." *The Faculty Voice*, 2, No. 3, November, 1987.

Graham, Hugh Davis and La Noue, George R. "The case for a 3-campus merger in the Baltimore area." *The Baltimore Sun*, July 26, 1987.

Green, Abigail. "Maintaining the Momentum: Proposed Cutbacks Challenge UMBC." *Generations*, Winter 2003.

Green, Erica L. "UMBC President Named among World's Most Influential Leaders." *The Baltimore Sun*, April 18, 2012.

Green, Erica L. and Wells, Carrie. "Maryland's HBCUs, state head to mediation." *The Baltimore Sun*, November 1, 2013.

Griswold, Ann. "An Elemental Education." *UMBC Magazine*, Fall 2010.

Groer, Anne. "UM to Open New Unit: 750 New Frosh Expected." *The Baltimore Sun*, September 1966.

Gunts, Edward. "Firms study prospects for research park near UMBC." *The Baltimore Sun*, February 21, 1990.

Gunts, Edward. "Proposed marine center would have many facets." *The Baltimore Sun*, May 14, 1989.

Hancock, Jay. "Erickson's Smart Bets Soured Along With Nation's Economy." *The Baltimore Sun*, October 21, 2009.

Harkavy, Ira. "The Role of Universities in Advancing Citizenship and Social Justice in the 21st Century." *Education, Citizenship and Social Justice*, No.1 (2006).

Harkness, Peter A. "Pass/Fail: The greatest public universities in America are at a tipping point." *Governing,* June 2012.
Heitz, Kevin. "Don Zimmerman: Lacrosse Engineer." *Pressbox,* Issue 146, February 2010.
"Higher Education Mess (cont.)." *The Baltimore Sun,* February 15, 1978.
"Higher Educational Reform." *The Baltimore Sun,* September 21, 1987.
Hill, Gwen. "Lawmakers want to end education unit." *The Baltimore Evening Sun,* January 26, 1984.
Hill, Michael. "Temporary peace for UMBC and Morgan: Civil rights inquiry played a role in decision to drop degree request." *The Baltimore Sun,* September 16, 2000.
Himowitz, Michael J. "Dorsey Seen as Top Candidate for UMBC Post." *The Baltimore Evening Sun,* May 2, 1977.
Himowitz, Michael J. "Loyola Ruling on Doctoral Program Due." *The Baltimore Evening Sun,* June 3, 1977.
Himowitz, Michael J. "New Chancellor Plans A 'Fresh Breeze' for UMBC." *The Baltimore Evening Sun,* August 1, 1977.
Himowitz, Michael J. "New Head Asks Changes at UMBC." *The Baltimore Evening Sun,* September 3, 1977.
Himowitz, Michael J. "New UMBC Official Wants to Add Personal Touch." *The Baltimore Evening Sun,* December 12, 1977.
Hirsh, Stacey. "Aether founder Oros to give up NexCen post." *The Baltimore Sun,* March 24, 2007.
Hirsch, Stacy and Smitherman, Laura. "Remaking self: Aether to leave City." *The Baltimore Sun,* June 8, 2008.
Hirten, Michael. "Baltimore needs engineering school." *The Baltimore Evening Sun,* June 8, 1983.
Hooker, Michael. "Fertile Baltimore/Washington corridor beckons biotechnology development." *Washington Board of Trade News,* June 1988.
Hooker, Michael. "Education is the fire fueling our future economic growth." *Baltimore Business Journal,* January 2–8, 1989.
Hoover, Samuel H. "UMBC Provides Excellent Quality." *The Baltimore Sun,* January 5, 1980.
"How to Get into College: Five Schools with a Mission."
"How student fees boost college sports amid rising budgets." *USA Today,* October 6, 2010.
Hrabowski, Freeman, III. "Creating a Climate for Success." *The Presidency,* Winter 1999.
Hrabowski, Freeman, III, "50 years in American education equity," *The Baltimore Sun.* November 24, 2013.
Hubes, Ronald. "Jones takes action on discrimination." *The UMBC Retriever,* April 8, 1981.
"If you want to be pioneers, come with us." *UMBC Magazine,* Summer 1997.
Ignacio, Olivia. "We're #1 yet again." *The Retriever Weekly,* September 13, 2011.
Ingalls, Zoe. "From Parks to Prisons, Traveling Theater Brings Shakespeare to the People." *The Chronicle of Higher Education,* September 11, 1991.
Jackson, Joab. "Battlefield of Bits and Bytes." *UMBC Magazine,* Summer 2010.
Jackson, Joab. "The Power of Parallels." *UMBC Magazine,* Summer 2009.
James, Ellen I. "UMBC 'Campus That is Moving Ahead' Assures Kaplan, Interim Chancellor." *The Baltimore Evening Sun,* August 19, 1976.
Jacobson, Joan. "13 UM Deans rap centralized system." *The Baltimore Evening Sun,* October 30, 1987.
Jacobson, Joan. "College plan still a cauldron of controversy." *The Baltimore Evening Sun,* November 23, 1987.

Jacobson, Joan. "Doubts about Schaefer's college plan surface." *The Baltimore Evening Sun*, February 24, 1988.
Jacobson, Joan. "Heads of Maryland's public colleges urge 'superboard.'" *The Baltimore Evening Sun*, July 7, 1987.
Jacobson, Joan. "Schaefer at odds with Steinberg over higher education plan." *The Baltimore Evening Sun,* December 24, 1987.
Jacobson, Joan. "Senators skeptical of college reorganization." *The Evening Sun*, February 26, 1988.
Jacobson, Joan. "State superboard is proposed." *The Baltimore Evening Sun*, June, 1987.
Jacobson, Joan. "'Sublime mediocrity' rules here, educators told." *The Baltimore Evening Sun,* October 30, 1987.
Jacobson, Joan and Waldron, Thomas W. "Compromise quietly worked out on college 'superboard.'" *The Baltimore Evening Sun*, January 8, 1988.
"Jo Ann E. Argersinger Named Chancellor of Southern Illinois University at Carbondale." *Insights*. 12, No. 3, April 1998.
Johns, Corey. "The Down and Dirty Dawg Band." *The Retriever Weekly*, March 10, 2010.
Jones, Brent. "BCCC Set to Move on Renewal Plan." *The Baltimore Sun*, July 8, 2008.
Jones, Jennifer. "Hillcrest's rich history going to waste." *The Retriever*, December 12, 2006.
June, Audrey Williams. "Adjuncts Build Strength in Numbers: the new majority generates a shift in academic culture." *The Chronicle of Higher Education,* November 9, 2012.
Kapsidelis, Tom. "Transfer of programs 'just talk.'" *The Diamondback*, November 17, 1977.
Kelderman, Eric. "4 Other States Could Be Affected by Desegregation Ruling in Maryland." *The Chronicle of Higher Education*, October 18, 2013.
Kelderman, Eric. "Black Colleges See a Need to Improve Their Image." *The Chronicle of Higher Education*, July 2, 2010.
Kelderman, Eric. "Calculating the True Cost of Tuition Freezes at Public Colleges." *The Chronicle of Higher Education*, May 15, 2009.
Kelderman, Eric. "State Support for Colleges Falls 7.6 percent in 2012 Fiscal Year." *The Chronicle of Higher Education*, January 23, 2012.
Kerger, Joe. "Committee Presents Platform at P&T Rally." *The UMBC Retriever*, May 8, 1978.
Kerger, Joe. "Ralliers Take Protest To Chancellor's Office." *The UMBC Retriever*, May 1, 1978.
Kern, Edward. "Quest for a Silver Unicorn." *Life*, June 4, 1971.
Kerzel, Pete. "Blast Owner's UMBC arena plans 'premature.'" *The Catonsville Times*, April 18, 1990.
Kiehl, Stephen. "UMBC Shrinks School of Aging." *The Baltimore Sun*, April 15, 2009.
Kirwan, William E. "Kirwan on Budget." *The Faculty Voice*, October 2009.
Knisbacher, Alden. "Protest." *The UMBC Retriever,* March 3, 1987.
Knisbacher, Alden. "Shanty heightens protest." *The UMBC Retriever*, December 16, 1986.
Kobatko, Roch Eric. "UMBC eyes bigger market, enters Northeast Conference. Move from Big South Effective in 1998." *The Baltimore Sun*, June 20, 1996.
Kochakian, Charles P. "UMBC Protest Continues." *The Baltimore Sun*, April 25, 1970.
Kolowich, Steve. "American Council on Education Recommends 5 MOOCs for Credit." *The Chronicle of Higher Education*, February 7, 2013.
Kolowich, Steve. "Group Chemistry." *Inside Higher Ed.com,* October 2, 2009.
Kupchyk, Areta. "Students Take Cutbacks, Tuition Gripes to Annapolis." *The Retriever*, March 8, 1976.
Kuhn, Julie. "Scrubbing Bathroom Floors = True Dedication." UMBC Admissions Counselors' Blog. http://umbcadmissionsblog.wordpress.com/category/julies-posts/page/3/. October 18, 2011.

LaMotte, Lawrence A. "The college combination that would work in Baltimore." *The Baltimore Evening Sun*, January 7, 1988.

Lane, Anthony. "Fishing without a Net." *UMBC Magazine*, Winter 2011.

Langenberg, Donald N. "A Canary Sings of the Future of Education." *The Baltimore Sun*, November 28, 1990.

Langenberg, Donald N. "Let Maryland's colleges compete." *The Baltimore Sun*, November 2, 2013.

La Noue, George R. "Antiquated ruling on desegregation." *The Baltimore Sun*, October 27, 2013.

La Noue, George and Marcus, Ken. "'Serious Consideration' of Race Neutral Alternatives in Higher Education." *Catholic University Law Review*, 57, No.4, Summer 2008.

La Noue, George R. "The Muddled Future of Mid-Major Athletics," *The Chronicle of Higher Education* (on line) December 4, 2014.

Lean, Charles. "It Don't Come Easy," *The Retriever*, March 1, 1976

Lean, Charles. "Tuition Hike Protestors Storm Regents Meeting." *The Retriever*, November 24, 1975.

Lee IV, Blair. "The College Park Campus is Under Siege: They want to move it to Baltimore." *The Washington Post*, September 13, 1987.

Lewis, Neil A. "Adam Yarmolinsky Dies at 77; Led Revamping of Government." *The New York Times*, January 7, 2000.

Libowitz, Lisa. "When Business Speaks, UMBC Listens. Can We Talk?" *UMBC Magazine*, Fall 1994.

Liggett Meyer, Linda and Gilfoy, Nancy. "Views from the Tower." *UMBC Magazine*, Summer 1995.

Linskey, Annie. "State cuts revenue estimates by $120 million." *The Baltimore Sun*, December 10, 2010.

Lipkowitz, Paul. "UMBC plans $16.8 million multi-facility." *Catonsville Times*, October 11, 1989.

Lipkowitz, Paul. "Opposition to Project Mounts," *Catonsville Times*, January 2, 1991.

Lipowitz, Paul. "Merger Would End Hooker's Tenure." *Catonsville Times*, October 30, 1991.

Lynton, Ernest A. "What is a Metropolitan University?" *Metropolitan Universities: An Emerging Model in American Higher Education*, ed. by Daniel M. Johnson and David A. Bell, Denton, TX: University of North Texas Press, 1995.

"Major in Trouble: Duplication Cited in Music." *The UMBC Retriever*, December 11, 1972.

Mangan, Katherine. "MOOC Mania: It's raising big questions about the future of higher education." *The Chronicle of Higher Education*, October 1, 2012.

Marston, Emma. "UMBC introduces a new Master's degree in cybersecuity." *The Retriever Weekly*, September 21, 2010.

Martello, John and Price, III, James R. "The Shriver Center: Lessons in the Creation of a Setting." *Universities and Community Schools*, 5, No. 1-2, Fall–Winter 1997.

"Maryland gamblers: A studied look." *BaltimoreSun.com*, June 15, 2011.

McConnell, Bill. "Incubator Brewing Big Plans." *Baltimore Daily Record*, May 30, 1990.

McConnell, Bill. "Region to Lead Biotech's Rise." *Baltimore Daily Record*, June 7, 1990.

McCord, Joel and Simon, David. "Tight budget scuttled engineering plans at Morgan, UMBC." *The Baltimore Sun*, June 5, 1983.

McCord, Joel. "UMBC officials ignore mounting racial tension." *The Baltimore Sun*, March 26, 1981.

McCormick, Charles P. "Board Chairman Nods Approval of UMBC Faculty, Facilities." *UMBC News*. 1, No. 4, October 30, 1966.

McEwen, Lauren. "Freeman Hrabowski wins 20102 Heinz Award for Human Condition." *The Washington Post*, September 17, 2012.

McGowan, George V. "UMBC will survive the departure of Michael Hooker." *The Baltimore Sun*, September 19, 1992.

McLemee, Scott. "Marching Into the Future." *UMBC Magazine*, Winter 2011.

Meisol, Patricia. "Math-science academy resurfaces as UMBC plan." *The Baltimore Sun*, June 11, 1989.

"Merge Baltimore Campuses," *The Baltimore Sun*, 1987.

Mervis, Jeffrey. "Better Intro Courses Seen as key to Reducing Attrition of STEM Majors." *Science*, 330, No 6002, October 15, 2010.

Meyers. Linda Leggett, "What's In A Name? UMBC Review, 9, no.2 (Spring 1991).

Michaels, Joan. "Hundreds of students protest racism." *The UMBC Retriever*, April 22, 1986.

"Mike Hooker's Vision." *The Baltimore Sun*, May 21, 1992.

"Mike Miller lambastes merger in Baltimore." opinion editorial, *The Faculty Voice*, 7, No.1, October 1992.

Miller, Mike. "The Case Against a UMAB-UMBC Merger." *The Baltimore Sun*, June 16, 1992.

Miller, Steve. "P&T Disputes First Incarnation." *The UMBC Retriever*, May 1, 1978.

Miller, Sue. "Panel Is Studying Duplications at Area Colleges." *The Baltimore Evening Sun*, no date.

Mitchell, Clarence. "Engineering." *The Baltimore Sun*, June 6, 1983.

Morgan State College, "Joint Statement by the Presidents of the Black Colleges" *The President's Newsletter*, .2, No.8, May 1969.

"Morgan, UMBC: Peace at last." *Baltimore News American*, Jan. 10, 1985.

Morris, John. "Anticipating UMBC's Future." *Catonsville Times*, November 5, 1986.

"Music Department Upset." *The UMBC Retriever*, December 12, 1973.

Murray, Shannon D. "RWD Eyeing UMBC Facility." *The Baltimore Sun*, October 20, 1999.

"Negroes Demand Place on University Board," *Baltimore News American*, March 17, 1970.

"New Chancellor appointed at UMBC." *The Afro-American*, February 2, 1971.

Nitzberg, Dale. "Mary PIRG Cites Energy Waste at UMBC." *The UMBC Retriever*, May 13, 1974.

O'Brien, Alex. "Admin drops charges against UMBC 15." *The UMBC Retriever*, August 31, 1979.

O'Brien, Alex. "Students Take Over Admin." *The UMBC Retriever*, April 9, 1979.

O'Brien, Alex, and Satterwhite, Tena. "Students Continue Occupations." *The UMBC Retriever*, April 23, 1979.

O' Brien, Gael M. "Maryland Professors Vote No Confidence in Chancellor." *The Chronicle of Higher Education*, March 27, 1976.

O'Grady, Jenny and Purvis, Meredith. "Measure of a Mission," *UMBC Magazine*, Fall 2011.

Oishi, Gene. "New Ideas, Methods Slated at U.M. Catonsville School." *The Baltimore Sun*, July 23, 1966.

Ordonez, Juan C. and Polchin, James R. "Rickard resigns after week-long sit-in by protesting students." *The UMBC Retriever*, April 29, 1987.

Oza, Priyanka. "UMBC Athletics: In debt but worth it." *The Retriever Weekly*, December 8, 2009.

Perman, Jay A. "Message from the President," *The Faculty Voice*, April 13, 2013.

Pietila, Antero. "UMBC Unrest, Hopkins Strike Quieted." *The Baltimore Sun*, April 24, 1970.

Pipitone, Anthony. "Morgan, UMBC get OK to split engineering program." *The Baltimore Evening Sun*, November 4, 1983.
Pitts, Jonathan and Walker, Childs. "Morgan wins fight with UMUC over online program." *The Baltimore Sun*, October 22, 2009.
Polchin, James R. "Students rebuild protest shanty." *The UMBC Retriever*, March 10, 1987.
Pollack, Randi M. "UMBC educator: Chancellor Lee plans ahead to year 2000." *The Baltimore Sun*, April 26, 1972.
Popovich, Joseph. "Engineering School: A Continuing Debate." *The Baltimore Sun*, September 29, 1983.
Preston, Mike. " 'This is my home,' coach says of decision to withdraw from consideration for UNC job." *The Baltimore Sun*. June 11, 2008.
"Protest nets tenure study at UMBC." *The Baltimore Sun*, April 27, 1978.
Rascovar, Barry. "Baltimore's Talented Stepchild." *The Baltimore Sun*, June 20, 1983.
Rascovar, Barry. "Battling to a Standstill." *The Baltimore Sun*, December 6, 1987.
Rascovar, Barry. "Encore." *The Baltimore Sun*, September 5, 1983.
Rascovar, Barry. "Futures of UMBC, UMAB caught in state politics." *Cambridge Daily Banner*, June 18, 1992.
Rascovar, Barry. "The new segregation in Maryland colleges." marylandreporter.com, November 5, 2013.
Rascovar, Barry. "UM merger deserves scrutiny." *Community Times*, April 5, 2011.
Rasmussen, Dennis F. "Our Region's Missing Ingredient."
Raspberry, William. "Engineering Desegregation." *The Washington Post*, January 9, 1984.
Ratner, Andre. "Catonsville park is preferred over Inner Harbor site." *The Baltimore Sun*, June 23, 2001.
Real Time Economics, "U.S. Cities with Bigger Economies than Entire Countries," *Wall Street Journal*, July 20, 2012.
"Research Park Cooperation to be Encouraged, Not Required," *Insights*, 13, no7, April 1999.
"A research powerhouse." *The Baltimore Sun*, March 24, 2011.
Rice, Leslie Rice, "BIG RETURN: Early returns show major opposition to research park," *Arbutus Times*, February 20, 1991.
Rice, Leslie. "Pioneer Spirit is recalled." *Catonsville Times*, September 25, 1991.
"Robert Gerle: Concert Violinist: 81." *The San Diego Union-Tribune*, November 8, 2005.
Robinson, Lynda, "Catonsville envisioned as high-tech: UMBC, state seek extensive rezoning," *The Baltimore Sun*, November 12, 1987.
Roller, Emma. "State Budget Cuts for Research Universities Imperil Competitiveness." *The Chronicle of Higher Education*, January 17, 2012.
Rosenbaum, Allan. "Maryland's poor support of public universities." *The Baltimore Evening Sun*, February 1986.
Rothstein, William G. "Regents at Play: Carving up Campuses." *The Baltimore Sun*, January 3, 1993.
Saddler, Jeanne. "Blacks protest UMBC Arrest." *The Baltimore Sun*, October 16, 1976.
Sadler, Dan. "Prospective tenants for Research Park: Students, Staff Concerned with Layout of Buildings, Placement of Park Itself." Oct/Sept 1999.
Salganik, M. William. "The Academic Camelot that Never Came About." *The Baltimore Sun*, May 28, 1978.
Sagalnik, Michael. "Four College Heads Fight UMBC Plan." *The Baltimore Sun*, November 22, 1978.
"Sage Players Success With P.R.; Will Become First Campus Frat." *The Retriever*, February 10, 1969.

Salkever, David, "UM Merger False Premise," *The Baltimore Sun,* November 9, 2011.
Sander, Libby and Wolverton, Brad. "Debt Loads Weight Heavily on Athletics Programs." *The Chronicle of Higher Education,* September 28, 2009.
Sander, Libby. "U. of Akron to Help Students Test Out of Courses." *The Chronicle of Higher Education*, April 3, 2013.
Saxon, Wolfgang. "Michael K. Hooker, 53, Chancellor with a Community Approach." *The New York Times*, July 11, 1999.
Sehlstedt, Jr., Albert. "Respected biology department emerges at UMBC." *The Baltimore Sun*, April 19, 1981.
Seidel, Jeff. "Behind the Mask." *UMBC Magazine*, Winter 2013.
Shen, Fern. "U-MD Approves Wedding Baltimore Branches." *The Washington Post*, December 11, 1991.
Shipley, Tom. "Student Movement Forms Against Tuition Hikes." *The Retriever*, October 20, 1975
Shriver, Sargent. *The Shriver Center,* 20, No 2, Spring/Summer, 1994.
Silberholz, Elizabeth. "Gender-Neutral Housing Being Tested." *The Pretriever*, Issue #2, August 5, 2008.
Simon, David. "Missing: Baltimore's Great Urban University." *Baltimore Magazine*, September 1982.
Simon, David. "Morgan presses bid for engineering school." *The Baltimore Sun*, September 21, 1983.
Simmons, Melody. "'Separate but equal' schools complaint to be reviewed." *The Baltimore Evening Sun*, August 17, 1990.
Slagel, Kelley. "Hrabowski hopeful that programs can be saved." *The UMBC Retriever,* February 2, 1993.
Smith, C. Fraser. "UMB-UMCP merger--just say no." *The Daily Record*, October 13, 2011.
Song, Jason. "Morgan's President again fight building competitor: Opponent of Towson MBA has squelched 4 programs." *The Baltimore Sun*, June 13, 2005.
Staples, Brent. "The Country Can Learn a Lesson From These Students." *The New York Times*, December 8, 2010.
Staples, Brent. "Editorial Observer; Preaching the Gospel of Academic Excellence." *The New York Times*, June 5, 2000.
"State Notes." *The Chronicle of Higher Education,* September 2, 1992.
"State universities to cheer about." *Kiplinger's Personal Finance Magazine,* September 1998.
"A Step toward Consolidation." *The Baltimore Sun*, March 23, 1984.
Stewart, Michael. "Task Force Rejects UMES-Salisbury Merger." *The UMBC Retriever,* October 31, 1977.
Stigler, George J. "The Theory of Economic Regulation." *The Bell Journal of Economics and Management Science.* 2, No. 1, Spring, 1971.
"Students Help Out in Spring Grove Training." *The UMBC Retriever,* February 22, 1972 and Feb 11, 1974.
"Students protest faculty tenure policy: Week-long sit-ins show dissent." *The Retriever*, April 28, 1970.
Sullivan, Patricia. "One in 30 Marylanders has gambling problem, state study finds." *The Washington Post*, June 20, 2011.
Sunderland, Lowell F. "Catonsville Campus Opened." *The Baltimore Sun*, September 19, 1966.
Surock, Erika. "Professor Spotlight: Pete Caringi II." *The Retriever Weekly,* September 18, 2012.

Templeton, Roye. "Where's the Diversity?" *The Baltimore Sun*, November 2, 2013.
Thomas, Larry. "Black students hold Student Life Office." *The Retriever*, November 18, 1969.
Thompson, Garland L. "Why Hrabowski Chuckles." *The Baltimore Sun*, June 1, 1989.
Thomson, Andrea. "Few students aware of UMBC's history of protests." *The Retriever Weekly*, May 16, 2009.
"Three-Campus Powerhouse." *The Baltimore Sun*, July 22, 1987.
Toback, Jackie. "Promotion-Tenure Criticized at Speakout." *The UMBC Retriever*, May 2, 1977.
"Travels with the Bard Come to an End ..." *UMBC Magazine*, Spring 1996.
"Troubled UM Merger." *The Baltimore Sun*, March 3, 1992.
"Tuition Politics." *The Baltimore Sun*, June 13, 2010.
"UMBC Chancellor Lee." *The Afro-American*, March 20, 1976.
"UMBC strives for excellence." *The Diamondback*, December 10, 1965.
"UMBC Students Plan Orphans' Picnic Outing." *The Retriever*, October 3, 1966.
"UMBC Students Sit-In." *The Retriever*, December 11, 1967.
"UMBC to make changes after racial charges," *Carroll County Times*, April19,1987.
"UMBC's Lasting Legacy: Our Alumni." *UMBC Magazine*, Summer 1997.
Umoh, Ruth, "Board continues to study merger of MD universities." The *Retriever Weekly*, November 8, 2011.
"UM's Nonmerger." *The Baltimore Sun*, December 13, 2011.
"Unfortunate Competition." *The Baltimore Sun*, March 30, 2007.
"U.S. colleges reach a desegregation pact." *The Baltimore Sun*, October 27, 2009.
Vakili, Kayvan. "USM leaders laud Governor O'Malley on college affordability." *The Retriever Weekly*, November 6, 2012.
Vidmar, Jim. "Student Protestors Take Their Gripe to Regent Tydings." *The Retriever*, March 1, 1976.
Waldron, Thomas. "Battle to merge UMAB, UMBC still being fought." *The Baltimore Sun*, May 11, 1992.
Waldron, Thomas. "Hrabowski chosen as new president of UMBC: Educator, 42, is first black to head predominantly white college in area." *The Baltimore Sun*, May 8, 1993.
Waldron, Thomas. "Integration Cases Raise Doubts about Future of Black Colleges." *The Baltimore Sun*, April 25, 1993.
Waldron, Thomas. "UM Regents agree on $9.4 million cuts: Pressure saves academic programs." *The Baltimore Sun*, April 9, 1993.
Waldron, Thomas. "College chief's legacy: Hooker's vision enhances UMBC." *The Baltimore Sun*, July 2, 1999.
Walker, Childs. "Advance Degree: Loyola College officially celebrates its change to a university Friday." *The Baltimore Sun*, September 24, 2009.
Walker, Childs. "Annual Conference showcases UMBC's focus on undergraduate research." *The Baltimore Sun*, April 26, 2012.
Walker, Childs. "Applications Jump at 3 Md. Schools." *The Baltimore Sun*, January 17, 2010.
Walker, Childs. "Colleges, universities feel the pain." *The Baltimore Sun*, July 20, 2009.
Walker, Childs. "Debate intensifies over UMB-College Park Merger." *The Baltimore Sun*, October 20, 2011.
Walker, Childs. "Freeman Hrabowski's UMBC legacy grows as he celebrates 20 years as President." *The Baltimore Sun*, September 2, 2012.
Walker, Childs. "Generations of Students Attest to the role UMBC President Freeman Hrabowski and his Wife Have Played as One-on-One Mentors." *The Baltimore Sun*, September 2, 2012.

Walker, Childs. "Harford seeks college growth." *The Baltimore Sun,* March 26, 2012.
Walker, Childs. "Harvard Honors UMBC President Hrabowski." *The Baltimore Sun*, May 27, 2010.
Walker, Childs. "Merger Given a 'No' by Regents." *The Baltimore Sun*, December 10, 2011.
Walker, Childs. "Morgan, Hopkins to be part of team receiving $95.8 million from NASA." *The Baltimore Sun*, April 5, 2011.
Walker, Childs. "O'Malley to promote tuition freeze during campaign." *The Baltimore Sun*, June 6, 2010.
Walker, Childs. "O'Malley to use tuition freeze as issue in re-election effort." *The Baltimore Sun*, June 7, 2009.
Walker, Childs. "Regents OK 10-year plan for state universities." *The Baltimore Sun*, December 4, 2010.
Walker, Childs. "Towson, UMBC praised for minority successes." *The Baltimore Sun*, August 10, 2010.
Walker, Childs. "UMBC center carries Shriver name, spirit." *The Baltimore Sun*, January 20, 2011.
Walker, Childs. "UM Regents Approve Alliance for College Park and Baltimore Campuses." *The Baltimore Sun*, March 1, 2012.
"Walter Orlinsky Obituary." *The New York Times*, February 25, 2002.
Warfield IV, Edward. "Baltimore's Institutional Leadership at a Crossroads." *Warfield's Business Record,* September 11, 1992.
Wells, Carrie. "Maryland universities unnecessarily duplicated the programs of black colleges, judge says." *The Baltimore Sun,* October 8, 2013.
"What about Baltimore?" *The Baltimore Sun*, June 5, 1983.
"What Maryland Thinks." *The Baltimore Sun*, June 9, 2010.
White, Louise, "A School is Born," *UMBC Review*, 10, no.1, (Fall 1991).
White, Louise, "Profile of a Leader," *UMBC Review*, 11, no.1 (Winter 1993).
White, Louise, "The Shriver Center," 12, no.2 (Summer 1994).
"Why Merging Two Maryland Universities Makes Sense." *The Washington Post*, November 9, 2011.
Williams, Jack. "Storm Stalkers." *UMBC Magazine*, Summer 2011.
"With Student Government Asso. Hagy Outlines Work to Date." *The Retriever,* September 3, 1968.
Wolverton, Brad. "A Powerful League Piles Up Its Advantages." *The Chronicle of Higher Education,* September 4, 2009.
Yarmolinsky, Adam. "Crying Wolf Over College Park." *The Washington Post,* September 27, 1987.
York, Becky Todd. "Morgan, UMBC square off to offer engineering degree." *The News American,* September 16, 1983.

Reports

An Evaluation Team Representing the Commission on Higher Education of the Middles States Association, "Report to the Faculty, Administration, Trustees, Students of the University of Maryland Baltimore County," Collection 50, President's Office Records, Box 37, Folder 1, March 21–24, 1976.
AFT Higher Education. *American Academic: The State of the Higher Education Workforce 1997–2007.* https://www.aft.org/pdfs/highered/aa_highedworkforce0209.pdf, 2009 (accessed February 19, 2013).

Baltimore Department of Planning, "A Third Campus, A Statement of Need For an Undergraduate Branch of the University of Maryland Based on New Enrollment Projections," January 26, 1965.

Barton-Gillett Report on UMBC Campus Communications and External Relations, September 30, 1974. Box 35, Folder 10, President's Office records. Collection 50, Albin O. Kuhn Library. Special Collections, University of Maryland, Baltimore County.

Bass, Scott, Rutledge, Janet, Elizabeth Douglass, and Carter Wendy. "The University as Mentor: Lessons Learned from UMBC Inclusiveness Initiatives." The CGS Occasional Paper Series on Inclusiveness, 1. Council on Graduate Schools. 2007.

Black Coalition of the University of Maryland Campuses, "Position Paper," May 6, 1971.

Bennett, Daniel L., Adam R. Lucchesi, and Richard K. Vedder. "For-Profit Higher Education: Growth, Innovation and Regulation." Center for College Affordability and Productivity, July 2010.

Berdahl, Robert O. "Strong Governors and Higher Education: A Survey and Analysis." State Higher Education Executive Officers Association Archives, Recommended Readings. http://archive.sheeo.org/govern/strongpercent20governors.pdf. June 2004 (accessed July 12, 2013).

Board of Regents, University of Maryland System, "Achieving the Vision in Hard Times: II An Action Plan for Reinvesting the System's Resources," December 16, 1992. Also Report of the Regent's Ad Hoc Committee, December 11, 1992.

Cannon Designs, B&D Venues, Barton Malow, "Campus Events Center Study," Final Report, July, 2013.

Center for College Affordability and Productivity. "For-Profit Higher Education." July 2010.

Clark, Amy and Miller, Matthew. "Institutional Advancement at the University of Maryland Baltimore County (A)." Harvard Graduate School of Education, 2001.

Commission for Excellence in Higher Education, January 1986.

Commission for the Expansion of Public Higher Education in Maryland, *Public Higher Education in Maryland 1961–1975*. 1962.

Commission on the Needs of Higher Education in Maryland. 1955.

Commission to Develop the Maryland Model for Funding Higher Education, Final Report, Dec. 2008.

Commission to Study the Problem of Expansion of the University of Maryland, February, 1960. (Available in the UM Law School)

DeAngelo, Linda, Ray Franke, Sylvia Hurtado, John T. Pryor, and Serge Tan, "Completing College: Assessing Graduation Rates at Four-Year Institutions," Higher Education Research Institute, 2011.

Department of Legislative Services, Special Commission on Higher Education Affordability and Access, Final Report to the Maryland General Assembly, February 2004.

Department of Legislative Services, Office of Policy Analysis, "Maryland Higher Education Fiscal 2013 Budget Overview," January, 2012.

Dorsey, John W. John S. Toll. B. Herbert Brown, "A Prospectus for the University of Maryland Baltimore County," November 17, 1978, UPUB P7-031, Box 2, University Publications, Albin O. Kuhn Library Special Collections, University of Maryland Baltimore County

Executive Committee of the Baltimore Branch of the NAACP. "Position Paper of the Task Force on Reform of Higher Education in Maryland." October 19, 1987.

"FY 2001 Annual Report on Intercollegiate Athletics to the USM Board of Regents," April 2012.

Graham, Hugh D. "UMBC and Morgan State." June 15, 1977. Memorandum. June 15, 1977. Box 78, Folder 106, President's Office records, Collection 50, Albin O. Kuhn Library, Special Collections, University of Maryland, Baltimore County.

Hall, James T. and Karen Moranski, INDS Academic Program Review Report, March 7–8, 2011.

Higher Education Commission. "Maryland's Report and the Partnership Agreement between the State of Maryland and the U.S. Department of Education, Office for Civil Rights (OCR)." October, 1999.

Hildebrand, Peter H. "Selection of Contractor for the Goddard Earth Sciences Technology and Research (GESTAR) Studies and Investigations." March 1, 2011.

"Historical Perspectives on the Governance Structure of the University System of Maryland," Report of the Task Force to Study the Governance, Coordination of the University System of Maryland. January, 1999. http://mgaleg.maryland.gov/Pubs/CommTFWorkgrp/1998-tf-funding-usm.pdf.

Hooker, Michael, "Report to the Greater Baltimore Committee—UMBC: Responding to the Challenge" May 1989. UPUBI1-027, Box 7, University Publications, Albin O. Kuhn Library, Special Collection, University of Maryland, Baltimore County.

Hooker, Michael. "Advancing the Greater Baltimore Region: The Strategic Enhancement of UMBC." May 1990. UPUBI1-027, Box 7, University Publications, Albin O. Kuhn Library, Special Collection, University of Maryland, Baltimore County.

Hrabowski, III, Freeman. "2000 Legislative Testimony." UMBC historic documents collection, Special Collections, University of Maryland, Baltimore County.

Hrabowski, III, Freeman. "2003 Legislative Testimony," UMBC historic documents collection, Special Collections, University of Maryland, Baltimore County.

Hrabowski, III. Freeman "2004 Legislative Testimony." UMBC historic documents collection, Special Collections, University of Maryland, Baltimore County.

Hrabowski, III. Freeman "2005 Legislative Testimony." UMBC historic documents collection, Special Collections, University of Maryland, Baltimore County.

Hrabowski, III. Freeman "2006 Legislative Testimony." UMBC historic documents collection, Special Collections, University of Maryland, Baltimore County.

Hrabowski, III. Freeman "2007 Legislative Testimony." UMBC historic documents collection, Special Collections, University of Maryland, Baltimore County.

Hrabowski, III. Freeman "2008 Legislative Testimony." UMBC historic documents collection, Special Collections, University of Maryland, Baltimore County.

Hrabowski, III. Freeman "2009 Legislative Testimony." UMBC historic documents collection, Special Collections, University of Maryland, Baltimore County.

Hrabowski, Freeman and Philip Rous, "Focusing our Resources for Results: Mid-Year Update on University Priorities," April 12, 2012. UMBC historic documents collection, Special Collections, University of Maryland, Baltimore County.

Johnson, Nicholas, Phil Oliff, and Erica Williams. "An Update on State Budget Cuts: At Least 46 States Have Imposed Cuts That Hurt Vulnerable Residents and Cause Job Loss." *Center on Budget and Policy Priorities*, February 9, 2011.

Kirwan, William E. "University System of Maryland FY 2010 annual report." June 18, 2010.

Knapp, Laura G., Janice E. Kelly-Reid, and Scott A. Ginder. "Enrollment in Postsecondary Institutions, Fall 2011." National Center for Education Statistics, December, 2012.

KPMG Peat Marwick. "Study of the Proposed Merger Between the University of Baltimore and the University of Maryland, Baltimore County: Final Report." December 13, 1989.

Lee, Calvin B. T. Presentation to the Commission on the Structure and Governance of Higher Education, December 24, 1974.

Lee, Calvin B. T. Presentation to the Maryland Council for Higher Education's Committee to Study Higher Education in the Baltimore-Metropolitan Region, October 29, 1974. Box 14, Folder 25, President's Office records, Collection 55, Albin O. Kuhn Library, Special Collections, University of Maryland Baltimore County (Baltimore, MD).

Long, Matthew P. and Schonfeld, Roger C. "Ithaka S+R Library Survey 2010: Insights form U. S. Academic Library Directors." Ithaka S+R. 2010.

LDR International. "Design Guidelines: UMBC." 1992.

Maryland, "Access and Success: A Plan for Maryland's Historically Black Institutions."1997.

Maryland Higher Education Commission. "Consolidated Budget & Fact Book, Fiscal Year, 1990," December 1988.

Maryland Higher Education Commission. "Guidelines for the Performance Accountability Plans." January 30, 1989.

Maryland Higher Education Commission. "Institutional Performance Accountability," October 18, 1996.

Maryland Higher Education Commission. "Operating Funding Guidelines and Formulas for Institutions of Higher Education in Maryland." June 4, 2007.

Maryland Higher Education Commission. "Operating Funding Guidelines." November 10, 2010.

Maryland Higher Education Commission. "Operating Funding Guidelines and Formulas for Institutions of Higher Education in Maryland." June 4, 2007.

Marts & Lundy, Inc., *Internal Assessment and Campaign Planning Issues*, March 1996.

"Master Plan for Higher Education in the State of Maryland, Phase One." November, 1968.

Moos, Malcolm. "The Post Land Grant University: the University of Maryland Report." 1981.

Morgan State College. "Annual Report of the President for the year 1966–67." Baltimore, January, 1968.

Morgan State College, *The President's Newsletter*, 2, No.8, May 1969.

NAACP Executive Committee of the Baltimore Branch of the NAACP. "Position Paper of the Task Force on Reform of Higher Education in Maryland," October 19, 1987.

National Association of College and University Business Officers (NACUBO) Endowment Study 2008.

National Science Board. "Diminishing Funding and Rising Expectations: Trends and Challenges for the Public Research Universities." Arlington, Virginia. July 18, 2012.

New University Conference of the University of Maryland Baltimore County, "Racism in Maryland Higher Education with Special Reference to UMBC." (April 1970). UPUB H8-009, Box 2, Albin O. Kuhn Library Special Collections, University of Maryland, Baltimore County.

North Charles Street Design Organization. "UMBC Marketing Communications Plan." May, 1995.

Oliff, Phil and Leachman, Michael. "New School Year Brings Steep Cuts in State Funding For Schools." Center for Budget and Policy Priorities. October 7, 2011.

Oliff, Phil, *et al.* "Recent Deep State Higher Education Cuts May Harm Students and the Economy for Years to Come." Center for Budget and Policy Priorities. March 19, 2013.

RTKL, Inc. "Master Plan for the University of Maryland Baltimore County." Baltimore: publisher unknown, 1965 UPUB F3-001, University Publications, Digital Collections, Albin O. Kuhn Library, Special Collections, University of Maryland, Baltimore County

R. Christopher Goodwin & Associates, Inc. "Phase I and II Archeological Investigations for the UMBC Research Park and Playfield, Baltimore County, Maryland Final Report."

November 15, 1999. UPUB R2-001, Box 1, University Publications, Albin O. Kuhn Library, Special Collections, University of Maryland, Baltimore County.

"Report of the Principal Centers Task Force on the Consolidation of the UMAB and UMBC Graduate Schools, " Box 42, Folder 58, Other Campuses, UMBC Library. "Report of the Principal Centers Task Force on the Consolidation of the UMAB and UMBC Graduate Schools," 1983 Box 42, Folder 58, President's Office records, Collection 50, Albin O. Kuhn Library, Special Collections, University of Maryland, Baltimore County

Shinogle, Judith, Donald Norris, Dwan Park, Rachel berg, Donald Haynes, and Eric Stokan. "Gambling Prevalence in Maryland: A Baseline Analysis." Maryland Institute for Policy Analysis and Research (MIPAR), 2011.

Shriver Center. "Annual Report, 2008."

SBHE, "Maryland Statewide Plan for Postsecondary Education." July, 1978.

SBHE," Recommendations Concerning the Future Governance of Public Higher Education in Maryland." October, 1981.

Storch, Rudy "UMBC: The Early Planning," a report to Albin O. Kuhn UMBC Chancellor, August 31, 1970. (UMBC Founders Oral History Project, Interviewer Briefing Book, (UMBC library).

Sydnor, Denise Y. "Contractor Performance Assessment Report: UMBC and Goddard Space Flight Center." May 5, 2012.

Szanton, Peter L. "Baltimore 2000: A Choice of Futures." Goldseker Foundation. 1985.

Toll, John S. "President's Report 1987–88. UMBC historic documents collection, Special Collections, University of Maryland, Baltimore County. 3.

UMBC "A Prospectus for the University of Maryland Baltimore County." November 17, 1978.

"UMBC budget information, 1969–2102." UMBC historic documents collection, Special Collections, University of Maryland, Baltimore County.

UMBC, "Commission on Higher Education Periodic Review Report." September 30, 1981. UPUB P12-017, Box 7, University Publications, Albin O. Kuhn Library Special Collections, University of Maryland, Baltimore County (Baltimore, MD).

UMBC "Facilities Master Plan, Update 2009–2019, March 25, 2010.

UMBC Faculty Affairs Committee, "Report to the UMBC Faculty from the Faculty Affairs Committee of the UMBC Senate," 1976, Box 6, Folder 76, University Senate records, Collection 52, Albin O. Kuhn Library, Special Collections, University of Maryland, Baltimore County.

UMBC, "Middle States Self Study Report," UPUB-P12-016, Box 6, University Publications, Albin O. Kuhn Library Special Collections, University of Maryland Baltimore County (Baltimore, MD).

UMBC. "Institutional Performance Accountability Report." October 18, 1996.

"UMBC Inter-Institutional Collaboration Inventory," UMBC Office of the Provost, December 6, 2011, http://www.umbc.edu/provost/initiatives/COLLABORATION_INVENTORY_FINAL.pdf.

UMBC Office of Institutional Research. "UMBC Long-Term Follow-Up Survey of Bachelor's Recipients: 1980–81 Alumni." June 1989.UPUB I2-006, Box 1, University Publications, Albin O. Kuhn Library Special Collections, University of Maryland, Baltimore, County (Baltimore, MD).

UMBC Office of Institutional Research. "UMBC New Freshman Headcount Enrollment Trends by Primary Plan," OIR Databook, 2012.

UMBC Office of Institutional Advancement, "UMBC Historic Giving Values, FY1983–FY2012."

UMBC Office of the Provost. "Faculty Inter-Campus Collaborations." December 6, 2011.

UMBC Office of the Provost. "UMBC Inter-Institutional Collaboration Inventory." December 6, 2011.

UMBC. "Periodic Review Report to the Middle States Commission on Higher Education." October, 1981.

UMBC, "Periodic Review Report," Presented to: The Commission on Higher Education of the Middle States Association of Colleges and Schools, Pursuant to: Middle States Self-Study of 1996 and the Evaluation Team Visit, March 3–6, 1996, June 1, 2001, UPUB P12-017, Box 8, University Publications, Albin O. Kuhn Library Special Collections, University of Maryland, Baltimore County

UMBC, "Middle States Self-Study Report." January, 1996, UPIB P12-017, Box 7, University Publications, Albin O. Kuhn Library Special Collections, University of Maryland, Baltimore County.

UMBC, "Periodic Review Report," June 1, 2001, Presented to: The Commission on Higher Education of the Middle States Association of Colleges and Schools, Pursuant to: Middle States Self-Study of 1996 and the Evaluation Team Visit, March 3–6, 1996.

UMBC "Progress Report on Institutional Programs of Cultural Diversity." February 26, 2010.

UMBC Office of the Provost, February 26, 2010. http://www.umbc.edu/provost/PDFs/UMBCDIVERSITYPLANProgressReport22510.pdf.

UMBC "Report of the Enrollment Management Task Force, January 28, 2013.

UMBC "Report of the Honors University Task Force" June 15, 2000.

UMBC Office of Institutional Advancement, "UMBC Historic Giving Values, FY1983–FY2012."

United States Office of Civil Rights, "Revised Criteria Specifying the Ingredients of Acceptable Plans to Desegregate State Systems of Higher Education" 43 FR 6658, February 12, 1978.

United States Office of Civil Rights and the State of Maryland, "Partnerships Agreement," http://mhecmarylandgov/highered/ocrplan/index.asp#marylandreport.

USM Board of Regents, "Powering Maryland Forward: USM's 2020 Plan for More Degrees, A Stronger Innovation Economy, A Higher Quality of Life," Adopted December 3, 2010.

USM Board of Regents. "Board of Regents Report on the Study Examining the Advantages and Disadvantages of Merging University of Maryland, College Park and University of Maryland, Baltimore." December 9, 2011.

Warfield Commission. "A Plan for Expanding the University of Maryland." 1960.

Whitman Requardt &Associates, "The UMBC Events Center," December 16, 2013.

Working Group on Curriculum Priorities, Provost's Subcommittee on Campus Environment, "Statement of Opposition to Research Park," May 1996.

Cases

7 USC § 323-Racial discrimination by colleges restricted, www.law.cornell.edu/uscode/text/7/323.

Ayers v. Musgrove, 2002 U.S. Dist. Lexis 1973 (N.D. Miss. 2002).

Brown v. Board of Education, 347 U.S. 483 (1954)

Grutter v. Bollinger, 539 U.S.306 (2003).

*Mandel v. United States Department of Health, Education and Welfare.*411 F. Supp.542 (D. MD 1976).

Regents of the University of California v. Bakke, 438 U.S. 265 (1978).

The Coalition for Equity and Excellence in Maryland Higher Education, Inc. v. Maryland Higher Educational Commission, Civil No. MJG-06-2773.

Trustees of Dartmouth College v. Woodward, 17 U.S.518 (1819).
United States v. Fordice, 505 U.S. 717 (1992).

Unpublished Manuscripts

Bennett, David, "History of UMBC Social Sciences," 2010. UMBC archives.
Bhatt, Nimit, "History of UMBC Theatre and Music," 2010. UMBC archives.
Ehrahimi, Surena. "The History of Student Activism at UMBC (1966–2010)," 2010. UMBC archives.
Flynn, Bridget. "A History of Service at UMBC," 2010. UMBC Archives.
Foehrkolb, Grant, "The Research Park at UMBC," 2010. UMBC archives.
Hickey, Amanda, "History of the College of Engineering and Information Technology," 2010 UMBC archives.
Spry, Amber, "UMBC Ethnic Student Organizations: Impact on Diversity,"2010. UMBC archives.
Hrabowski III, Freeman and Philip Rous, "UMBC Collaborations with USM Partners, March 9, 2012 (unpublished paper).
Kahn, Ernest M. "Universities and Urban Affairs: Case Studies of the Colleges and Universities in the Baltimore Area in the 1960's" Ph.D. dissertation, University of Maryland Graduate School, 1972.
Kuhn, Albin O. "University of Maryland Baltimore County-Its Early Years of Development and Operation." UMBC Historic Documents Collection #107. UMBC University Archives.
Box 2, Folder 10, Albin O. Kuhn Library Special Collections, University of Maryland, Baltimore County
Mendals, Franklin and Browne, Gary. "Evaluation Program in Historical Studies 1978–1985." History Department files.
Popovich, Joseph. "Higher Education Development in the Absence of Statewide Planning: A Case Study of the Creation of the University of Maryland Baltimore County." Unpublished paper, Revised February, 2010.
Mendals, Franklin and Browne, Gary. "Evaluation Program in Historical Studies 1978–1985." History Department files.
Popovich, Joseph. "Higher Education Development in the Absence of Statewide Planning: A Case Study of the Creation of the University of Maryland Baltimore County." Unpublished paper, Revised February, 2010.
Seiple, G. Stewart. "A History of Hillcrest," March 21, 2002. UPUB H2-002, Box 1, University Publications, Albin O. Kuhn Library Special Collections, University of Maryland, Baltimore County.
Sumler, David E. "Life Cycle: The History of a State Higher Education Board" date unknown. Baltimore County.
Van Orden, Alexia. "Desegregation of Higher Education in Maryland." Ph.D. Dissertation. In progress.

Emails, Letters, and Memoranda

(All these documents are in Historic Documents, Special Collections, University of Maryland, Baltimore County.)

"Arguments to Support Funding, for a Theatre at UMBC," UMBC Archives (UARC 1999–03).

Kuhn, Albin O. to Faculty Senate leaders, "ROTC," April 9, 1968. See also memos "Argument in Favor of ROTC Program on Campus" and "Argument Against ROTC Program on Campus," April 30, 1968.
Blake, Catherine, Judge, to Counsel in the Coalition on Equity and Excellence in Higher Education litigation, June 27, 2011.
DiClemente, Carlo to Freeman Hrabowski and Lynne Schaefer. "UMBC Research Council Concerns about UMB-UMCP merger." November 21, 2011.
Day,Thomas to John W. Dorsey, "MCHE Action on Pear Committee Report," memorandum, December 19, 1974, Box 14, Folder 26, President's Office records, Collection 55.
Elkins, Wilson H. to Harry L. Phillips, letter, November 25, 1974, Box 14, Folder 27, President's Office records, Collection 55.
Graham, Hugh D, "UMBC and Morgan State," Memorandum, June 15, 1977, Box 78, Folder 106, President's Office records, Collection 50.
Hooker, Michael to UMBC Community, "Strategic Redeployment and Retrenchment Plan, March 27, 1991.
Hartzell, Rick memorandum to Warren Phillips, Vice Chancellor, "Re: Division I status, 1986–87," November 21, 1985.
Hornbake, R. Lee to Wilson H. Elkins, "Maryland Council for Higher Education action on the Special Committee report," memorandum, December 23, 1974, Box 14, Folder 26, President's Office records, Collection 55.
Hornbake, R. Lee to Philip Pear, memorandum, December 13, 1974, Box 14, Folder 26, President's Office records, Collection 55.
Hrabowski, Freeman, III, Interim President, to the UMBC community, September, 1992.
Hrabowski, Freeman to the UMBC Community, "Responding to the Regents' 'Action Plan' " January 29, 1993.
Hrabowski, Freeman to the UMBC Community, "Chancellor's Recommendation on UMBC's Program Appeals." April 8, 1993.
Hrabowski, Freeman to the UMBC Community, "Final Action," May 20,1993.
Hrabowski, Freeman, III to Donald Langenberg. "Peers and Performances," February 22, 1999.
Hrabowski, Freeman, III to Dr. George Hansen, Chair, NEC Executive Committee, April 2, 2003.
Jeffries, John to John Dorsey, "Two Principal Centers task Force Report," December 23, 1983,Box 42, Folder 58, President's Office records, Collection 50.
Johnson, Arthur email to author, October 30, 2010.
Johnson, Arthur to Cheryl Miller, "Organizational Structure of Academic Departments," memorandum, September 6, 2002.
Johnson, Arthur to the Faculty Senate, "Proposal to Reform General Education", November 11, 2003.
Kaplan, Louis L. letter, to Hugh Graham, June 23, 1977.
Kirwan, William E., "A Message from Chancellor William E. Kirwan to the University of Maryland Community," February 18, 2010.
Konetzka, Walter letter to Robert Burchard, April 27, 1966.
Langenberg, Donald H. to Presidents Hoke L. Smith and Freeman Hrabowski. "Cooperative MA in Foreign Languages," March 5, 1993.
Langenberg, Donald H. to Presidents, USM "Missions, Peers, and Performance." February 6, 1999.
Lee, Calvin B.T. to Wilson H. Elkins, letter, September 30, 1974, Box 14, Folder 25, President's Office records, Collection 55.

Lyons, Sr., James E. "2008 Funding Guidelines Peer Reselection and Adjustments." MHEC memorandum, October 16, 2008.

Mitchell, Gust, Chair of Social Work to UMBC Community," Social Work fact sheet," memorandum, December 28, 1992.

Neville, Dick memo to Department Chairs and Program Directors, "Accountability Update." December 4, 1989.

Nohe, Timothy (UMBC), Richard Y. Zhao, (UMB), Nicholas Eugene, (Coppin), Timothy Sullivan, (Towson), and Ordeana R. Neal (UB), to Orlan M. Johnson, Regents President, November 30, 2011.

Pear, Phillip to William P. Chaffinch, MCHE, Chairman, report transmission letter. November 2, 1974.

Pittenger, Arthur O. memo to Department Chairs and Program Directors, "Accountability." July 11, 1989.

Rous, Philip to UMBC Community, "Warm Support for the Hrabowski Fund for Innovation." October 23, 2012. Giving to UMBC, http://umbcgiving.wordpress.com/2012/10/23/warm-support-for-hrabowski-fund-for-innovation/.

Shriver, Sargent remarks at a memorial for Adam Yarmolinsky, May 4, 2000, UMBC Albin O. Kuhn Library Gallery.

Sinnigen, Jack, Coordinator of Graduate Studies, UMBC Modern Languages and Literature to Stephen Max, Acting Vice President for Graduate Studies and Research. "Change in Consortium Agreement," November 11, 1990.

Smith, Hoke L., Towson State University President, memorandum to William Donald Schaefer, Baltimore City Mayor, September 24, 1981.

Sparks, David S., Vice President for Graduate Studies and Research, University of Maryland to Sheldon H. Knorr, Commissioner, SBHE, February 8, 1985.

Storch, Rudy, emeritus professor, e-mail to Freeman Hrabowski, November 14, 2011.

Thomas, Valerie, "Temporary Salary Reduction Plan," Memo, June 22, 2010.

Toll, John, S., President of UMS and John Dorsey, Chancellor of UMBC, July 17, 1982, UMBC Archives (UARC 1999–03).

Toll, John S to UMBC Faculty Committee on Statewide Reorganization, October 8, 1987, UMBC Archives.

Tschernisch, Sergei P., Theatre Chair memorandum to Richard Neville, Dean of Arts and Sciences, "Space Needs for the Theatre Department (Old Student Center-Bookstore)" July 30, 1981. UMBC Archives, UARC 1999–03.

Turner, H. Mebane, University of Baltimore President, memorandum to William Donald Schaefer, Baltimore City Mayor, September 11, 1981. UMBC Archives (UARC 1999–03).

UMBC Senate Committee on Statewide Reorganization, memorandum to the UMBC Faculty Senate and Departmental Chairs. February 29, 1988.

Wasserman, Adam memo to Baltimore County Council, February 11, 1995. See also similar letters from Coppin President Calvin W. Burnett, September 16, 1981, Maryland Institute College of Art President Fred Lazarus, IV, September 16, 1981 and Morgan State University President Andrew Billingsley, October 19, 1981.

Yarmolinsky, Adam University of Maryland, Baltimore County Campus Plan Summary, February 2, 1988.

Press Releases

GP Strategies Corporation. "GP Strategies Completes RWD Technologies Acquisition." April 18, 2011.

Maryland Department of Health and Human Services. "Approximately 1 in 30 Maryland Adults Have a Gambling Problem: Baseline Study Will Help with Design of Prevention and Treatment Services." June 13, 2011.

Thomas Moore, Director of Arts Management. "UMBC Announces Nation's First Post-Baccalaureate Certificate Program in Music Entrepreneurship." July 2, 2012.

Morgan State University. "Morgan State Receives Major NASA Grant to Study Earth Sciences." April 5, 2010.

Northrop Grumman. "Northrop Grumman and UMBC Cite Progress After Cyber 'Cync' Program's First Year." August 1, 2012.

TIAA-CREF. "TIAA-CREF Honors Freeman Hrabowski with 2011 Theodore M. Hesburgh Award for Leadership Excellence." March 7, 2011.

UMBC. "Aether Systems and UMBC Form Computing Partnership." May 10, 2000.

UMBC. "Assured Information Security, Inc. to Open New Office at UMBC." April, 2012.

UMBC. "President Obama Appoints UMBC President as Chair of National Education Commission." July 26, 2012

USM. "USM Regents Approve University of Maryland: MPowering the State: Bold Collaboration for Leveraging UMB and UMCP Resources." March 1, 2012.

White House, "President Obama Signs New Initiative to Improve Educational Outcomes for African Americans." July 26, 2012.

Interviews

(All interviews where transcripts or formal notes were taken notes can be found in Special Collections, Albin O. Kuhn Library.)

Evelyn Barker, interview by Joseph Tatarewicz, October 7, 2002.

Mark Behm, interview by Joseph Tatarewicz, April 23, 2013.

Mike Bowler, interview by author, October 27, 2010.

Bill Brown, interview by Nimit Bhatt, December 14, 2010.

Charlie Brown, interview by author, November 30, 2009.

Robert Burchard, interview by Joseph Tatarewicz, May 6, 2003.

Schlomo Carmi, interview by Joseph Tatarewicz, April 23, 2013.

Guy Chisholm, interview by Edward Orser, 1993.

George Colcott, interview by author, May 5, 2011.

Tony Deering, interview by author, August 18, 2011.

Bob Dietrich, interview by Joseph Tatarewicz, for the 40th Anniversary of UMBC.

John Dorsey, interview by Joseph Tatarewicz, no date listed.

Jonathan Finkelstein, interview by Joseph Tatarewicz, April 16, 2013.

Lisa Gambino, Coordinator of Student-Athlete Affairs, interview by Bridget Flynn, October 8, 2010.

Betty Glascoe, interview by Joseph Tatarewicz, no date.

Carol Hess, interview by Joseph Tatarewicz, April 11, 2003.

Carol Hess-Vait, interview by author, May 18, 2011.

Ray Hoff, interview by author, April 9, 2013.

Freeman Hrabowski, interview by Byron Pitts on *Sixty Minutes*, CBS, November 13, 2011.

Ralph T. Jackson, Principal Architect, Shepley Bulfinch, interview by Aviva Karpe, March 15, 2011.

John Jeffries, interview by Joseph Tatarewicz, July 18, 2006.
John Jeffries, interview by Joseph Tatarewicz, August 4, 2006.
John Jeffries, interview by Joseph Tatarewicz, May 3, 2013.
Arthur Johnson, interview by Joseph Tatarewicz, April 16, 2013.
Arthur Johnson, interview by the author, April 25, 2013.
Joan Korenman, interview by Joseph Tatarewicz, November 16, 2006.
Albin O. Kuhn, interview by Edward Orser, February 4, 1994.
Albin O. Kuhn, interview by Larry Wilt, January 4, 2001.
Albin O. Kuhn, interview by Joseph Tatarewicz, August 14, 2001.
Albin O. Kuhn and Homer Schamp, interview by Larry Wilt, January 4, 2006.
Albin O. Kuhn and Homer Schamp, interview by Larry Wilt, February 1, 2006.
Julie Kuhn, interview by author, February 14, 2013.
Donald Langenberg, interview by author, July 4, 2009.
Larry Lasher, interview by Joseph Tatarewicz, March 21, 2003.
Marvin Mandel, interview by Joseph Tatarewicz, no date.
John Martello, interview by Bridget Flynn, October 20, 2010.
Sam McCready, interview by author, July 19, 2011.
Xerxes Metha, interview by Nimit Bhatt, December 15, 2010.
James Milani, Director of Administrative Affairs, COEIT, interview by author, April 2, 2013.
Edward Orser, interview by Joseph Tatarewicz, September 26, 2006.
Fred Pincus, interview by Surena Ehrahimi, January 26th, 2010.
Howard R. Rawlings, interview by Joseph Tatarewicz, October 28, 2002.
Richard Roberts, interview by Joseph Tatarewicz, August 14, 2001.
William Rothstein, interview by Joseph Tatarewicz, no date.
William Rothstein, interview by author, November 9, 2001.
Jack Seuss, interview by Joseph Tatarewicz, May 7, 2013.
Homer Schamp, interview by Ed Orser, no date.
Homer Schamp, interview by Joseph Tatarewicz, August 1, 2001.
Bob Somers, UMBC Book Store Director, interview by author, June 6, 2013.
Johnny C. Taylor, Jr. and R. L'Heureux Lewis, interview by John Hockenberry, *The Take Away*, August 26, 2011.
UMBC Founders II Group Interview (Albin Kuhn, William Rothstein, Homer Schamp) by Barry Lanman and John Willard, November 23, 2005.
David Yager, interview by author, June 20, 2012.
Childs Walker, *Baltimore Sun* reporter, interview by author, December 15, 2011.
Elizabeth Walton, interview by author, May 3, 2011.
Dick Watts, interview by author, August 3, 2011.
Larry Wilt, interview by Aviva Karpe, March 3, 2011.
Kathy Zerrlaut, interview by author, January 20, 2010.

Presentations at Meetings or Conferences

Arnold, Joe. "A Signature Building—the Heart and Soul of the Campus." Tower Dedication December 12, 1994 (Founder's Binder).
Hrabowski, III, Freeman. 2011 Legislative Testimony. March, 2011. Office of the President, http://president.umbc.edu/selected-speeches/.
Hrabowski, III, Freeman. "State of the University Address." September 5, 2003. Office of the President, http://president.umbc.edu/selected-speeches.

Hrabowski, III, Freeman. "State of the University Address." August 19, 2010 Office of the President, http://president.umbc.edu/selected-speeches/.

Hrabowski, III Freeman. "The Value of Community." Installation Address, September 24, 1993, Office of the President, http://president.umbc.edu/selected-speeches/.

Kuhn, Albin O., Chancellor of the Baltimore Campuses, statement, August 1, 1969.

La Noue, George R. and Van Orden, Alexia. "Dual Sovereignties: The Four Decade Struggle between the U.S. Office of Civil Rights and the State of Maryland over the Desegregation of Higher Education." Presented at the Policy History Conference, Richmond, VA, June 2012.

Lee, Calvin B. T. Presentation to the Commission on the Structure and Governance of Higher Education. December 24, 1974 (UMBC archives).

Lee, Calvin B. T. Transcript of remarks to the UMBC Senate. March 16, 1976, Box 6, Folder 25, University Senate records, Albin O. Kuhn Library Special Collections, University of Maryland, Baltimore County.

UMBC Faculty Senate minutes, September 15, 1987, Box 13, Folder 15, University Senate records, Collection 52, Albin O. Kuhn Library Special Collections, University of Maryland, Baltimore County.

UMBC, Faculty Senate minutes, September 10, 2002, Box 21, Folder 2, University Senate records, Collection 52, Albin O. Kuhn Library Special Collections, University of Maryland, Baltimore County.

Websites

Albin O. Kuhn Library. "Photography, Slides and Digital Images," Albin O. Kuhn Library, University of Maryland, Baltimore County (accessed May 13, 2013), http://aok.lib.umbc.edu/specoll/photog.php.

"Popular Culture Collections." Albin O. Kuhn Library, University of Maryland, Baltimore County, accessed May 13, 2013, http://aok.lib.umbc.edu/specoll/popcul.php.

"UMBC at 40 Timeline," Albin O. Kuhn Library, University of Maryland, Baltimore County (accessed May 13, 2013), http://lib.guides.umbc.edu/umbctimeline.

America East Conference. "AE On Campus, Season 6, Episode 1-Freeman Hrabowski." YouTube. http://www.youtube.com/watch?v=jdd-TwmtKFA (accessed February 14, 2013).

Arlington Independent Media. "Rosebud Film and Video Festival." http://www.arlingtonmedia.org/rosebud (accessed May 14, 2013).

Ashburn, Elyse. "Carnegie Corporation Honors UMBC President Freeman Hrabowski with 2011 Academic Leadership Award." UMBC News, November 3, 2011. http://www.umbc.edu/blogs/umbcnews/2011/11/carnegie_corporation_honors_um.html (accessed May 13, 2013).

"Baltimore Manual Labor school for Indigent Boys (Farm School) 1839–1922." History of the Arbutus Area, Baltimore County Public Library. http://www.bcpl.info/community/history-arbutus-farm-school (accessed August 12, 2013).

"Best Places to Live in America." *Money Magazine.* July 2010, http://money.cnn.com/magazines/moneymag/bplive/2010/ (accessed Oct. 15, 2012).

Bond, Julian. "Explorations in Black Leadership." Institute for Public Policy, University of Virginia. http://www.virginia.edu/publichistory/bl/index.php?uid=44 (accessed May 13, 2013).

bwtech@UMBC: Research and Technology Park. "Maryland Clean Energy Technology Incubator (CETI)." www.bwtechumbc.com//programs/ceti.html (accessed November 25, 2013).

Campus Compact. "Who We Are." http://www.compact.org/about/history-mission-vision/ (accessed May 13, 2013).

Choice Program. "The Choice Program: Empowering Youth and Families Choosing to Make a Difference." www.choiceprograms.net (accessed December 12, 2010).

Cobb, Terry. "UMBC Department of Theatre Production History: 1960s and 1970s." Cobb, Terry. "UMBC Department of Theatre Production History: 1960s and 1970s," http://userpages.umbc.edu/~cobb/p/1970s.htm (accessed July 15, 2014).

"College and University Endowments," chronicle.com, April 10, 2013.

http://userpages.umbc.edu/~cobb/p/1970s.htm (accessed May 13, 2013).

Finin, Tim. "Aether Systems, once Baltimore's dot.om favorite, leaving the city." UMBC ebiquity. http://ebiquity.umbc.edu/blogger/2006/06/08/615/ (accessed May 13, 2013).

Franklin, Benjamin. "Proposals relating to the education of youth in Pensilvania." University of Pennsylvania University Archives and Records Center. http://www.archives.upenn.edu/primdocs/1749proposals.html (accessed May 15, 2013).

Glasscock, Kim. "UI-Chicago panelists give advice on merger pitfalls." University of Colorado, April 1, 2004. https://www.cu.edu/sg/messages/3482.html (accessed April 30, 2013).

Hoffman, David. "Real People Profiles: Michele K. Wolff." Co-Create UMBC (blog), March 25, 2010. http://cocreateumbc.blogspot.com/2010/03/real-people-profiles-michele-wolff.html (accessed February 18, 2013).

Levy, Steve. "UMBC Sports Team Media Guides." http://www.umbcretrievers.com/ (accessed May 13, 2013).

Maryland Higher Education Commission. "Maryland's Report and the Partnership Agreement between the State of Maryland and the U.S. Department of Education, Office for Civil Rights (OCR)." October, 1999. http://mhec.maryland.gov/highered/ocrplan/index.asp (accessed on May 13, 2013).

Maryland Morning. "To Merge or Not to Merge." June 1, 2011. http://mdmorn.wordpress.com/2011/06/01/61111/ (accessed December 9, 2013.)

Mason Dixon Athletic Conference. "The Mason Dixon Track and Field/Cross Country Conference." http://www.themasondixonconference.com (accessed February 14, 2013).

Sargent Shriver Peace Institute. "American Idealist: the Story of Sargent Shriver." americanidealistmovie.com (accessed May 13, 2013).

Sixty Minutes Report. "Changing Lives Through Music." July 16, 2008. http:www.cbs.news.com/2012-18560-162-4009335html?tag.

Spring Grove Hospital. "A History of Spring Grove." www.springgrove.com/history.html (accessed May 13, 2013).

UMBC. "Jari Villanueva." http://www.umbc.edu/pepband/index.php/page/jari (accessed May 13, 2013).

UMBC. "UMBC Department of Theatre Celebrates Seventh Trip to the Kennedy Center." www.umbc.edu/lasmeninas (accessed May 13, 2013).

UMBC. "UMBC Mama's Boys." www.umbcmamasboys.org (accessed May 13, 2013).

UMBC. "UMBC Mission Statement." http://www.umbc.edu/provost/planning/Mission_Statement_Dec2000.htm (accessed May 13, 2013).

UMBC Center for Art, Design and Visual Culture. "About CADVC." http://www.umbc.edu/cadvc/about/ (accessed August 25, 2012).

UMBC Center for Art, Design and Visual Culture. "CADVC's K-12 Teacher/Student Resources." http://www.umbc.edu/cadvc/education/resources.php (accessed August 25, 2012).

UMBC Center for Art, Design and Visual Culture. "For All the World to See." http://www.umbc.edu/cadvc/foralltheworld/index.php (accessed August 28, 2012).
UMBC Imaging Research Center. "About." http://www.irc.umbc.edu/about/ (accessed August 25, 2012).
UMBC Imaging Research Center. "Virtual Tour: The Cone Sisters Apartment." http://www.irc.umbc.edu/2005/10/01/cone-sisters/ (accessed May 13, 2013).
UMBC Office of Alumni Relations. "UMBC by the Numbers: Alumni & Giving." Alumni.umbc.edu/s/1325/images/editor_documents/boardonlinetoolkit/alumni_flyer.pdf (accessed May 15, 2013).
UMBC Office of Student Life. "About the UMBC Chapter of Golden Key." http://www.umbc.edu/studentlife/orgs/gknhs/info.html (accessed December 4, 2010).
UMBC Interdisciplinary Studies. "Find your place." http://www.umbc.edu/inds/findyourplace/history.html.
UMBC Shriver Center. "Facts." The Shriver Center at UMBC. http://www.shrivercenter.org/about/facts/ (accessed May 13, 2013).
UMBC Shriver Center. "Shriver Center Mission Statement." The Shriver Center at UMBC. http://shrivercenter.umbc.edu/about/ (accessed September 17, 2012).
UMBC Shriver Center. "Results." The Shriver Center at UMBC. http://www.shrivercenter.org/about/results/ (accessed December 4, 2010).
UMBC Visual Arts Website. "Undergraduate Program." http://art.umbc.edu/undergraduate/index.php (accessed August 25, 2012).
USM Board of Regents. "Bylaws, SectionVIII-2.01: Policy on Tuition." http://www.usmd.edu/regents/bylaws/SectionVIII/VIII201.html (accessed May 13, 2013).
Yale University Investments Office. "The Yale Endowment 2009." http://investments.yale.edu/images/documents/Yale_Endowment_09.pdf (accessed May 13, 2013).

Index